LOVE AND LIBERATION

LOVE AND LIBERATION

Autobiographical Writings of the Tibetan Buddhist Visionary SERA KHANDRO

SARAH H. JACOBY

COLUMBIA UNIVERSITY PRESS
NEW YORK

A special thanks to the Shelley & Donald Rubin Foundation
for crucial financial support for the publication of this book.

Columbia University Press
Publishers Since 1893
New York Chichester, West Sussex
cup.columbia.edu

Paperback edition, 2016

Library of Congress Cataloging-in-Publication Data

Jacoby, Sarah, author.
Love and liberation : the autobiographical writings of the Tibetan Buddhist visionary Sera Khandro / Sarah H. Jacoby.
pages cm
Includes bibliographical references and index.
ISBN 978-0-231-14768-2 (cloth : alk. paper)—ISBN 978-0-231-14769-9 (pbk. : alk. paper)—ISBN 978-0-231-51953-3 (electronic)
1. Bde-ba'i-rdo-rje, 1892–1940. 2. Buddhist women—China—Amdo (Region)—Biography. 3. Women religious leaders—China—Amdo (Region)—Biography. I. Title.
BQ942.D427J33 2014
294.3′923092—dc23
[B]
2013043777

Columbia University Press books are printed on permanent and durable acid-free paper.
Printed in the United States of America

Cover design: Jordan Wannemacher
Cover image: Sera Khandro scroll painting from the region of Getsé Tralek Monastery in eastern Tibet; photograph of painting courtesy of Tralek Khenpo Tendzin Özer

This book is dedicated to the lineage of Sera Khandro Künzang Dekyong Chönyi Wangmo, and to all the *ḍākinīs* of Tibet whose voices we can no longer hear.

CONTENTS

List of Illustrations ix
Preface and Acknowledgments xi
Technical Note on Tibetan and Sanskrit Words xix
Abbreviations xxi
Chronology xxiii
Maps xxvi

INTRODUCTION 1

1. THE LIFE AND TIMES OF SERA KHANDRO 23

2. A GUEST IN THE SACRED LAND OF GOLOK 76

3. *ḌĀKINĪ* DIALOGUES 131

4. SACRED SEXUALITY 188

5. LOVE BETWEEN METHOD AND INSIGHT 249

EPILOGUE: LOVE AFTER DEATH 319

Spelling of Key Tibetan Names and Terms 325
Notes 337
Bibliography 379
Index 395

ILLUSTRATIONS

Map 1	Sera Khandro's journey from Lhasa to Golok in 1907	xxvi
Map 2	Central sites of Sera Khandro's life in Golok and Serta	xxvii
Fig. 1.1	Lhasa street scene	26
Fig. 1.2	Contemporary nomad tent made of yak hair in Golok	41
Fig. 1.3	Kelzang Monastery in Dartsang, Serta	49
Fig. 1.4	Benak Monastery in Pema County, Golok	53
Fig. 1.5	Tashi Gomang Monastery in Pema, Golok	57
Fig. 1.6	Sera Tekchen Chönkhor Ling Monastery in Serta	67
Fig. 2.1	Yeshé Tsogyel	88
Fig. 2.2	Padmasambhava's Copper-Colored Mountain Buddhafield	93
Fig. 2.3	Drongri Mukpo, resident land deity of Drong Mountain in Serta	104
Fig. 2.4	Anyé Machen Mountain	105
Fig. 2.5	Drongri or "Wild Yak Mountain" in Serta	113
Fig. 2.6	Annual Washül Serta Drongri Mukpo propitiation	118
Fig. 3.1	Vajrayoginī	134
Fig. 3.2	Sera Khandro statue from Tralek Monastery, Kandzé	136
Fig. 5.1	Hayagrīva and Vajravārāhī in union	250
Fig. 5.2	Vajrasattva *yab yum*, with Samantabhadra and Samantabhadrī *yab yum*	251
Fig. 6.1	Namtrül Jikmé Püntsok and Tāré Lhamo	320
Fig. 6.2	Khandro Rinpoché and Choktrül Rangrik Dorjé	322

PREFACE AND ACKNOWLEDGMENTS

THIS IS A BOOK about relationships—between people and the land they inhabit, between religious seekers and the divine presences with whom they interact, between women and men dedicated to spiritual liberation, and between lover and beloved. The main protagonist in the stories and conversations that fill this book is the Tibetan female visionary Sera Khandro Künzang Dekyong Chönyi Wangmo (1892–1940). She would have described these relationships using the language of auspicious connections (*rten 'brel*), the matrix of conditions including specific times, places, and persons that must constellate in order for an individual cog in the larger wheel of life to accomplish her purpose.

Auspicious connections extend through space and time beyond the meaningful synergies bound within Sera Khandro's texts, touching us here and now. In particular, specific auspicious connections have made this book possible; without them I could never have written it. The catalyst for this project came during my undergraduate years on a Tibetan Studies junior semester abroad program administered through the School for International Training. In Nepal while conducting fieldwork about Nyingma Buddhist laywomen, I had the good fortune to meet Semo Saraswati, who introduced me to her father, Jadrel Sangyé Dorjé Rinpoché

(b. 1913), the seniormost living lineage master within the Nyingma school of Tibetan Buddhism and also a direct disciple of Sera Khandro. Meeting Jadrel Rinpoché and his daughter would change the course of my life, but at the time, I could barely figure out how to offer him a ceremonial scarf (*kha btags*) properly, let alone understand his deeply resonant, Kham dialect-inflected Tibetan speech well enough to inquire about his extraordinary female guru.

After graduating from Yale College, I remained fascinated with Tibetan civilization, and dedicated myself to studying Tibetan language, religion, and culture both in Asia and in graduate school at the University of Virginia's Department of Religious Studies. It took me five years of returning annually to visit Jadrel Rinpoché to gain the courage and the linguistic proficiency to ask him for permission to read his copy of Sera Khandro's autobiography, which was unavailable elsewhere. During our conversations, Jadrel Rinpoché described Sera Khandro with the utmost reverence, telling me how she set the course of his future religious training when he first met her at the age of fourteen (fifteen in Tibetan years) in 1927. At this meeting Sera Khandro prophesied that his root lama would be Khenpo Ngawang Pelzang (Khenpo Ngakchung, 1879–1941) from Katok Monastery, prompting him to go straight there to study with him.

Receiving Jadrel Rinpoché's permission and a copy of his manuscript set this project in motion, but the help of many other teachers and friends have made it possible to complete. In particular, Lama Tsondru Sangpo of Rangbul, India, aided me from the beginning, as did my friend Heidi Nevin, who was by my side in spirit and also sometimes in person through this story. Learning how to read Sera Khandro's auto/biographical works, consisting of more than six hundred folios of cursive Tibetan handwriting filled with abbreviations and Golok colloquialisms from nearly a century ago, many unfindable in any dictionary, proved to be a major challenge. It was only through the kindness of Khenpo Sangyé from Gyalrong (Khenpo Tupten Lodrö Tayé), who painstakingly read both Sera Khandro's autobiography and later her biography of Drimé Özer with me over the course of several years and endless hours, that I understood anything of her writing. Khenpo Sangyé's insights into Tibetan language, idiom, and religion opened up a new world of thought for me. I will always be grateful for this enrichment, as well as for the congeniality and hospitality of all in the Gyalrong House in Boudhanath, Nepal, the site of our Sera Khandro reading marathons.

Auspicious connections sometimes operate in subtle forms and other times in dramatic ones. In the early days of 2002 I was staying at Jadrel Rinpoché's monastery complex in Salbari, India, trying to figure out when and how to ask permission not just to read, but to translate and publish Sera Khandro's autobiography (this study is the first part of the project; the full translation of her long autobiography will be the second). Jadrel Rinpoché is famous for his discretion in granting access to his precious manuscripts and teachings; I had good reason to fear making this request. In doubt, I phoned Lama Tsondru Sangpo in Rangbul, who urged me that I must go ahead and ask Jadrel Rinpoché everything that very day without fail. Later that afternoon, I found the right chance to speak with Rinpoché privately and received his blessing to accomplish these endeavors. The very next day, circumstances changed and access to private audiences with Jadrel Rinpoché was severely restricted, as it has remained to this day. Had I not followed Lama Tsondru-la's advice, I might never have had the chance again.

Another dramatic auspicious connection electrified the possibilities for my research on Sera Khandro, this one beginning in the U.S. graduate school context and ending in eastern Tibet. My main dissertation adviser, David Germano, invited Alak Zenkar Rinpoché Tupten Nyima of Dartsedo, Tibet, to a symposium at the University of Virginia in the spring of 2004. David requested Zenkar Rinpoché to write me a letter of introduction for my upcoming research trip to eastern Tibet, where I planned to follow in Sera Khandro's footsteps through the regions of Serta and Golok in which she lived. Several days of flights and dusty bus rides later, I ended up in the town of Serta knowing no one, armed only with my letter of introduction from Zenkar Rinpoché to a man he had identified only by first name, Khedrup. What to do? How to find the mystery man? In Sera Khandro's day the treeless, rolling alpine grasslands dotted with yak herds and black nomads' tents in the Washül Serta and Golok territories were infused with religious masters, but they were also dangerous places to travel without the proper local alliances. A century later, I found some of the same to be true as a foreign woman often traveling alone. Luckily Serta is small, and word gets out fast when an American is looking around an eastern Tibetan town for someone. Zenkar Rinpoché's letter opened the door to Khedrup and Kyachung's hospitality and to many in the Serta community for me, without which my research would have been much more difficult.

Khedrup brought me to his birthplace in rural Serta called Dartsang, where Sera Khandro first arrived from Lhasa with her guru, Drimé Özer, whose descendants still live there today. He introduced both me and my colleague Holly Gayley, with whom I traveled briefly, to a contemporary Treasure revealer from Nyenlung, Serta, named Namtrül Jikmé Püntsok (1944–2011), whose late consort, Tāré Lhamo (1938–2002), was renowned as Sera Khandro's incarnation. Unbeknownst to us, the day we arrived at Nyenlung was Ḍākinī Day, the twenty-fifth of the Tibetan month, which Namtrül Rinpoché took as an auspicious sign that he should give both of us copies of his revelations and invite us to join him and his community on a pilgrimage they had scheduled to begin the very next day. On pilgrimage with Namtrül Rinpoché, we visited many sacred sites associated with Sera Khandro in Golok, including mountains from which she revealed Treasures (Solung Drakar, Drakar Dreldzong, and Chakri Ömbar) and monasteries affiliated with her, including Tashi Gomang and Benak Monastery, all located in what is today Pema County, Golok.

En route we met Namtrül Rinpoché's cousin Tulku Thondup, who was and has continued to be a wellspring of information and translation expertise for me. Though any remaining mistakes in my translations are my fault alone, they are considerably fewer thanks to Tulku Thondup's unfailingly generous editorial advice. Another lama whom I met with Namtrül Rinpoché was Gelek Pema Namgyel Rinpoché of Pema County, Golok, whose deep knowledge of the Benak Monastery area where Sera Khandro lived for many years has enriched this book. On later trips to Golok, Lama Gelek not only found the time to answer my many questions and take me to Nyenpo Yutsé Mountain, among other places, but also gave me a rare copy of the autobiography of one of Sera Khandro's teachers, Gara Terchen Pema Dündül Wangchuk Lingpa. Integral to many of these trips was my friend Britt-Marie Alm, whose fascination with asking people in Golok about their mountain deities changed my perception of Tibetan religion. I will never forget our "short" circumambulation of Drong Mountain in Serta, where we observed the annual Washül Serta propitiation rites, arranged, like so much else, by Khedrup and his family.

These are only a few of the auspicious connections with people in Tibet and its diaspora that have fortified this study over several years of research funded in part by a year-long Foreign Language and Area Studies Grant in Lhasa and another year-long Fulbright-Hays Doctoral Dissertation Research Grant in Golok and Nepal. Other Tibetan experts whose help has been invaluable include Kyapjé Trülku Sonam Chömpel of Jomda, Lama Dorjé of Chamdo, Khenchen Tashi of Lhagang, Khamtrül Rinpoché of Lhasa, Tsültrim Dargyé of Serta, Pema Ösel Tayé of Serta, Tsedrup Gön of Serta, Lama Gönpa Kyap of Dartsang, Khenpo Tendzin Özer of Tralek Monastery, Khandro Rinpoché of Darlak, Lama Tharchin Rinpoché of California, Pema Bhum of New York, and many others.

Auspicious connections don't just make things happen in faraway Himalayan locales; under other names such as strategic relationships, conducive circumstances, and good timing, they make things happen in the U.S. university context as well. All of these factored favorably into the initial version of this study, which was my doctoral dissertation, funded by a Charlotte W. Newcombe Doctoral Dissertation Writing Fellowship. The present version has been greatly augmented by the feedback from my dissertation committee at the University of Virginia, including David Germano, Karen Lang, Kurtis Schaeffer, and Nicolas Sihlé. Special thanks to Janet Gyatso for taking the time to participate in my defense as an external committee member from Harvard University. Her ongoing encouragement and constructive criticism have made this a much better book.

After graduate school, my sojourn as a postdoctoral fellow at Columbia University's Society of Fellows in the Humanities was important for the present shape of this project. Productive and inspiring conversations with fellows and faculty affiliated with the Heyman Center have informed my work in positive ways. Columbia's resident titans of Tibetan Studies, especially Robert Thurman, Gray Tuttle, Robert Barnett, and Lauran Hartley, were excellent colleagues. I am grateful to both Gray and Robbie for allowing me to ply various drafts of these chapters upon them, which has led to considerable improvements. Also central to my years in New York was proximity to the Tibetan Buddhist Resource Center and its founder, the late Gene Smith, whose brilliance shed light on this project as on so many others' studies of Tibetan texts.

Most recently this book project has found fertile ground at Northwestern University, fostered by congenial colleagues in the Department of Religious Studies as well as a year-long research leave funded by an American Council of Learned Societies Fellowship. My focus on Sera Khandro's relationships with other members of her communities and spiritual presences in the Tibetan earth and sky has been influenced by my colleague Robert Orsi's approach to thinking about relationships in religion developed in his book *Between Heaven and Earth: The Religious Worlds People Make and the Scholars Who Study Them* (Princeton University Press, 2005). The workshop organized in 2010 by my colleague Christine Helmer titled "Relationships in Religion" inspired me to consider this theme further. My participation in the five-year-long biannual American Academy of Religion seminar on "Tibetan Religion and the Literary," organized by Andrew Quintman and Kurtis Schaeffer, has also been valuable to my process of thinking through Tibetan literature. At Northwestern, special thanks to Robert Linrothe, Barbara Newman, Susan Phillips, the members of the East Asian Research Society, and my fellow Religious Studies faculty for reading various parts of the manuscript. Hubert Decleer, Wendy Doniger, Barbara Rosenwein, and Paola Zamperini have also graciously provided feedback at various stages of the writing process. Many thanks to my editor, Anne Routon, for her patience and persistence in ushering this book into print, to Tsering Wangyal Shawa for his cartographic skills, to Hildegard Diemberger and Anne Klein for their helpful reviews, and to Leslie Kriesel for her attention to detail in copyediting. Integral to the publication process were generous subventions from The Shelley & Donald Rubin Foundation and The Graduate School at Northwestern's University Research Grants Committee. Additionally, many friends have supported this endeavor, including Lynna Dhanani, Gyalrong Lama Jikmé Dorjé, Gyalrong Tsultrim Yarmpel, Christina Monson, the Nevin family, Pam Novak, Jann Ronis, Carol Schlenger, and many others.

I would never have had the chance to even begin this journey without the steady backing of my parents, George and Lee Jacoby, nor would I have been able to continue it without my husband and partner in all things, Antonio Terrone, who has sustained me throughout the process of writing this book in every way. May our daughter, Isabella, not hold it against me for having spent so many hours hard at work on this project instead of playing with her. And may our son, Adrian, who so considerately waited to begin the process of being born until an hour after I sent this book to press, one day grow to appreciate its contents.

Auspicious connections bring people and resources together to make things happen. They tie Himalayan lands with American academic centers, generations past with those currently living. Religious knowledge was transmitted orally in Tibet, through not dead letters on a page but the living breath of lineage masters speaking directly to their disciples. To learn a text meant first receiving the *lung*, or reading transmission, from a master who herself had received it from her master. In this way, the meaning of the words lives on in an unbroken chain of connection back to their author or divine inspiration. The echoes of dialogues Sera Khandro fixed in the pages of her prolific auto/biographical writings still resonate today, however faintly, animated through those who maintain her lineage. This book is an endeavor to listen to those words and to transpose them with care into our contemporary conversations.

Sarah Jacoby
Evanston, Illinois

TECHNICAL NOTE ON TIBETAN AND SANSKRIT WORDS

FOR EASE OF READING, I have phoneticized all Tibetan words that appear in the main body of this book largely in accordance with the Simplified Phonetic Transcription of Standard Tibetan devised by David Germano and Nicolas Tournadre of the Tibetan and Himalayan Library (see http://www.thlib.org/reference/transliteration/#!essay=/thl/phonetics/s/b1 for more information). Periodically I write Tibetan words that appear in parentheses in the main body of the book according to the standard Wylie transliteration of Tibetan, which is largely unpronounceable in English but conveys the exact spelling of the Tibetan. In cases in which I include both Sanskrit and Tibetan words in parentheses, I always write the Sanskrit first followed by the Tibetan, for example, (Skt. *samaya*, Tib. *dam tshig*). Each time I quote Sera Khandro referring to a Tibetan text by its proper name for the first time, I phoneticize the Tibetan text title and follow it with a comma and my English translation of that title, for example, *Khandro Nyingtik, Heart Essence of the Ḍākinīs*. For those who are interested in the exact spellings of Tibetan names, places, and key terms that I have phoneticized, please see the section "Spelling of Key Tibetan Names and Terms" toward the end of the book.

ABBREVIATIONS

WORKS WRITTEN BY SERA KHANDRO

DDNT Bde ba'i rdo rje. *Dbus mo bde ba'i rdo rje'i rnam par thar pa nges 'byung 'dren pa'i shing rta skal ldan dad pa'i mchod sdong* (*The Biography of the Central Tibetan Woman Dewé Dorjé: A Chariot Leading to Renunciation and a Reliquary of Faith for Fortunate Ones*). Unpublished manuscript, ca. 1934.

DDP Dbus bza' mkha' 'gro. "Rnam thar nges 'byung 'dren pa'i shing rta skal ldan dad pa'i mchod sdong (The Biography: A Chariot Leading to Renunciation and a Reliquary of Faith for Fortunate Ones)." In *Dbus bza' mkha' 'gro'i gsung 'bum*. Chengdu: Si khron mi rigs dpe skrun khang, 2009, vol. 1.

SLNT Mkha' 'gro bde skyong dbang mo. *Skyabs rje thams cad mkhyen pa grub pa'i dbang phyug zab gter rgya mtsho'i mnga' bdag rin po che pad+ma 'gro 'dul gsang sngags gling pa'i rnam par thar pa snying gi mun sel dad pa'i shing rta ra tna'i chun 'phyang ut+pala'i 'phreng ba* (*The Biography of the Omniscient Refuge Master, Lord of Accomplished Ones, the Precious Sovereign of the Ocean of Profound Treasures Pema Drondül Sangngak Lingpa: A Chariot for the Faithful That Dispels the Heart's*

Darkness, a Garland of Blue Lotuses and Cascading Jewels). Dalhousie: Damchoe Sangpo, 1981.

KSL Dbus bza' mkha' 'gro. "Ku su lu'i nyams byung gi gnas tshul mdor bsdus rdo rje'i spun gyis dris lan mos pa'i lam bzang (The Excellent Path of Devotion: The Short Story of a Mendicant's Experiences in Response to Questions from My Vajra Kin)." In *Dbus bza' mkha' 'gro'i gsung 'bum*. Chengdu: Si khron mi rigs dpe skrun khang, 2009, vol. 5.

OTHER WORKS

DLNT Khrag 'thung bdud 'joms gling pa. "Chos nyid sgyu mar rol pa'i snang lam gsang ba nyams byung gi rtogs brjod gsal ba'i me long (A Clear Mirror: The Biography of My Secret Visionary Experiences of the Illusory Display of Reality)." In A bu dkar lo, ed., *Khrag 'thung bdud 'joms gling pa'i rnam thar*. Xining: Zi ling mi rigs par khang, 2002.

GTNT Mgar gter chen pad+ma bdud 'dul dbang phyug gling pa. "Rnal 'byor bdag gis sa lam bsgrod pa'i rang bzhin gyi rtogs brjod zol zog med pa'i drang gtam brjod pa (An Account of How This Yogi Traversed the Grounds and Paths Spoken Truthfully Without Deception)." In *Mgar gter chen pad ma bdud 'dul dbang phyug gling pa'i rang rnam*. Chengdu: Si khron zhing chen khron lin par 'debs bzo grwa, 2005.

YSNT Stag sham nus ldan rdo rje. *Bod kyi jo mo ye shes mtsho rgyal gyi mdzad tshul rnam par thar pa gab pa mngon byung rgyud mangs dri za'i glu phreng* (*The Biography of the Activities of the Tibetan Lady Yeshé Tsogyel: A Garland of Gandharvas' Lute Songs That Reveals What Is Hidden*). Kalimpong: Zang mdog dpal ri Monastery, 1972.

CHRONOLOGY OF MAJOR EVENTS IN SERA KHANDRO'S LIFE

1892	Sera Khandro is born in Lhasa on the first day of the Tibetan water dragon year.
1902–3 (age 10–11)	Sera Khandro's father arranges a politically advantageous marriage for her.
1903 (age 11)	She attempts suicide by drinking a mixture of opium and alcohol, in despair over her betrothal.
1904 (age 12)	Her mother dies and her father remarries; she has a prophetic dream in which Vajravārāhī gives her prophetic guides (*kha byang*) and empowers her to reveal two Treasure cycles that will come to her over the course of her lifetime.
1906 (age 14)	Drimé Özer and his religious encampment members arrive on pilgrimage at her brother's house, seeking a place to set up camp.
1907 (age 15)	She escapes from her brother's house in Lhasa to follow Drimé Özer and his entourage back to eastern Tibet.
1907–8 (age 15–16)	After arriving in Dartsang, Serta, she works as a maidservant for a nearby Golok nomadic family in order to afford the winter religious teachings at Dartsang.
1910 (age 18)	Gara Terchen Pema Dündül Wangchuk Lingpa of Benak Monastery in Golok summons her to dispel obstacles to his longevity,

	but because his consort, Yakshülza, prevented her earlier arrival, he dies.
1911 (age 19)	She returns to Benak Monastery on account of a prophecy.
1912 (age 20)	Sera Khandro settles with Gara Terchen's son, named Gara Gyelsé Pema Namgyel.
1913 (age 21)	Sera Khandro gives birth to her first child, a daughter named Yangchen Drönma; Gyelsé disapproves of her Treasure revelations, leading her to try to keep them secret.
1915 (age 23)	Gochen Trülku Jikdrel Chökyi Lodrö (a.k.a. Gotrül Rinpoché) of Pelyül Dartang Monastery in Golok recognizes Sera Khandro as a *khandroma* (Skt. *ḍākinī*); Gyelsé and Drimé Özer discuss the idea of exchanging Sera Khandro and decide that she will eventually become one of Drimé Özer's consorts.
1918 (age 26)	Amid increasing tensions at Benak, Sera Khandro gives birth to a stillborn son and then moves with her faction of the community to Yeru religious encampment, the residence of Gyelsé's brother Jikmé Könchok.
1919 (age 27)	She gives birth to Rindzin Gyurmé Dorjé, whom she describes as the "consciousness" (*rnam shes*) of Gotrül Rinpoché.
1921 (age 29)	Repeated invasions by the Ma family warlords from Qinghai cause unrest in Golok and lead both Gyelsé and Drimé Özer to move their encampments. Meanwhile Sera Khandro becomes increasingly ill with an arthritic condition. As she nears death, Gyelsé sends her to live with Drimé Özer. After intensive practice in union with him, she attains spiritual liberation.
1923 (age 31)	Andzom Drondül Pawo Dorjé summons her to visit him at Andzom Chögar; the two Treasure revealers exchange religious teachings and nurture auspicious connections.
1924 (age 32)	Gyelsé presses a lawsuit in Golok courts for custody of Sera Khandro's son Rindzin Gyurmé Dorjé, but a plague sweeps through Dartsang and the boy passes away at age five, followed three days later by Drimé Özer at age forty-three. Sera Khandro accepts Sotrül Natsok Rangdröl Rinpoché's invitation to move with him to Sera Monastery in Serta.
1925 (age 33)	Sera Khandro begins to teach the Dharma widely throughout eastern Tibet, including primarily her Treasure teachings and those of Düjom Lingpa and Drimé Özer, as well as other Great

	Perfection teachings such as those of Longchenpa; she writes Drimé Özer's biography.
1926 (age 34)	She teaches Düjom Lingpa's *Refining One's Perception* at Sera Monastery, among other teachings, and commences writing her long autobiography.
1927 (age 35)	She teaches Drimé Özer's eighteen volumes of Treasures to a group of prominent *trülku*s.
1929 (age 37)	She begins compiling the complete works of Düjom Lingpa and finishes her short verse autobiography.
1932 (age 40)	Sera Khandro gives teachings from her Treasures to the King of Lingkar and his royal family.
1933 (age 41)	Sera Khandro finishes compiling forty-four volumes of Treasure scriptures, including twenty-two of Düjom Lingpa's, eighteen of Drimé Özer's, and four of her own.
1934 (age 42)	Sera Khandro completes writing her long autobiography.
1939 (age 47)	Zhapdrung Tsewang Drakpa invites Sera Khandro to Riwoché in Kham, where she gives teachings on Düjom Lingpa, Drimé Özer, and her own Treasures.
1940 (age 48)	Sera Khandro passes away at the estate of Zhapdrung Tsewang Drakpa in Riwoché.

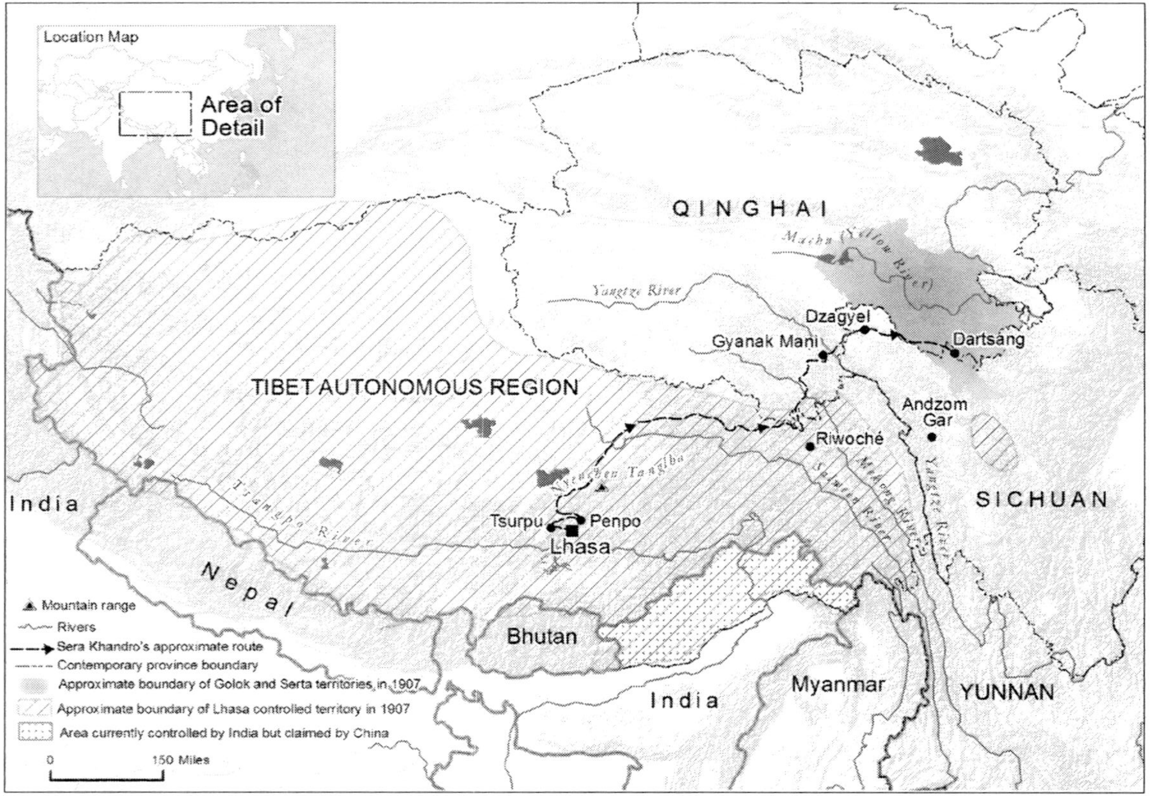

MAP 1 Sera Khandro's journey from Lhasa to Golok in 1907

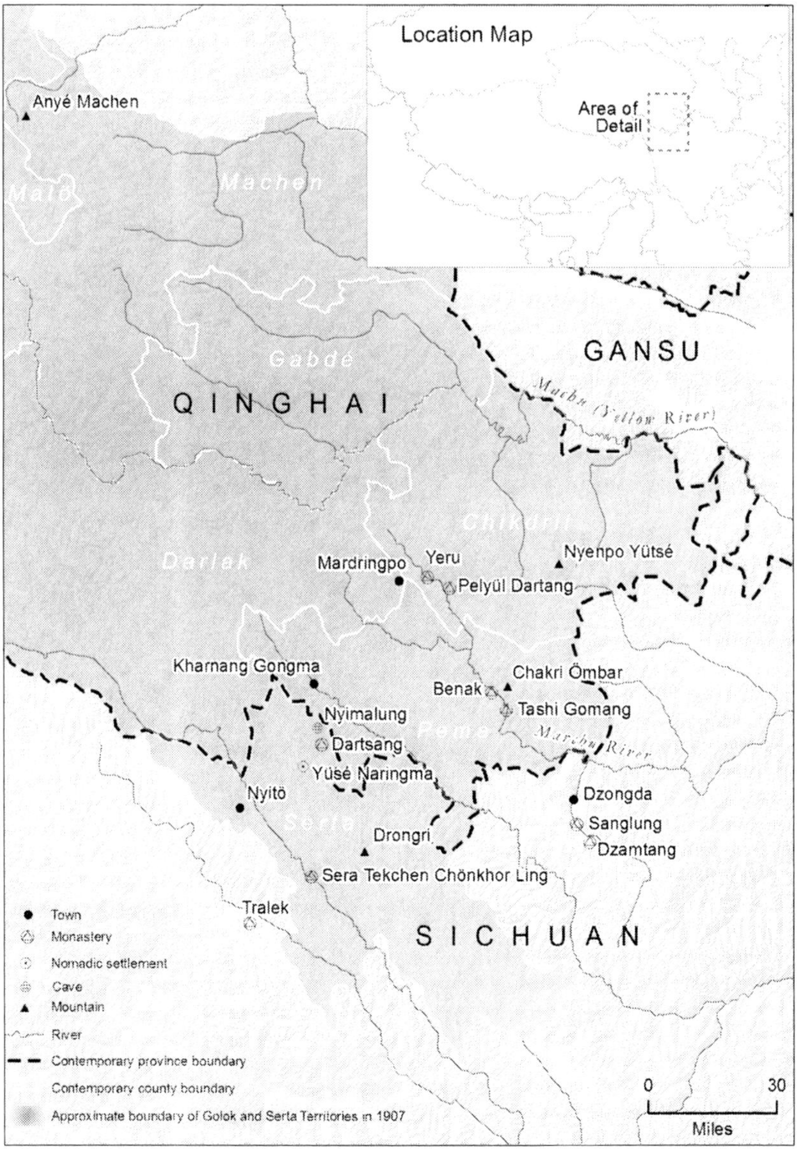

MAP 2 Central sites of Sera Khandro's life in Golok and Serta

LOVE AND LIBERATION

INTRODUCTION

THE ROLES OF WOMEN and sexuality within Tantric Buddhist communities are topics of fascination for many, despite the scarcity of reliable sources. Tibetan doctrinal, liturgical, and biographical works are pervaded by references to female celestial figures known as *ḍākinīs* (Tib. *mkha' 'gro ma*), literally "female sky-goers," but the lives, experiences, and perspectives of historical Buddhist women who attained religious mastery in India, across the Himalayas, and in Tibet remain by and large elusive. The vast majority of Tantric scriptures were written by men and represent meditation practices from the perspective of the male subject. The dearth of Tantric Buddhist texts written by women has led to conclusions about their religious roles that are based as much on ideology as on data.[1] These studies often present Tantric practices involving sexuality in polarized form, as either gynocentric celebrations of female spirituality or misogynist objectifications of women for men's gratification. Only rarely do we catch sight or sound of the historical women who were important participants in Tibetan religious communities.[2]

One important and heretofore overlooked source that belies such interpretations is the writing of the Tibetan visionary Sera Khandro (1892–1940), whose full name was Künzang Dekyong Chönyi Wangmo or Dewé

Dorjé. Sera Khandro was perhaps the most prolific female author in Tibetan history prior to the momentous changes brought about by Tibet's incorporation into the People's Republic of China in the 1950s, yet until now her works have received no scholarly attention. They include more than four volumes of her collected revelations; a biography of her guru and Tantric partner, Drimé Özer (1881–1924); her own autobiography; and a commentary on the meditation manual titled *Refining One's Perception*, written by Drimé Özer's father, the famous visionary Traktung Düjom Lingpa (1835–1904).[3] She was one of only a handful of women in Tibetan history to write an autobiography, and a very long one at that, totaling more than 400 folios in Tibetan script.[4] Out of this small cohort of female autobiographers who wrote in Tibetan, Sera Khandro was one of the few who was not a nun. Instead of renouncing the world in the external form of joining a nunnery, she rejected the householder life her parents had arranged for her, escaping Lhasa to devote herself to Drimé Özer, who would become her most important guru and consort. Sera Khandro and Drimé Özer, like his father Düjom Lingpa before him, became renowned throughout eastern Tibet for being Treasure revealers (*gter ston*), religious specialists who discovered Buddhist scriptures and artifacts in Tibet's earth and in their minds through visions. Treasure revealers' devotees trace these revelations back to Buddhist luminaries from Tibet's golden age of imperial power, from the seventh through ninth centuries, most notably to Padmasambhava, the Indian Buddhist master celebrated for converting Tibet to Buddhism. Integral to his religious activities was his Tibetan consort, Yeshé Tsogyel, with whom Sera Khandro came to closely identify through her visionary experiences as a Treasure revealer.

This book is the first study of the life and works of Sera Khandro, and more generally the first monographic study of a nonmonastic Tibetan woman's autobiography. It is an exploration of Sera Khandro's life and social world as she recorded it, focusing on her 400-plus-folio autobiography and the 248-folio biography she wrote of Drimé Özer. The following questions form the heart of this project: How and why did Sera Khandro accomplish what few other women in Tibetan history did, becoming the author of her own life story? What narrative strategies and literary models did she use to convey her autobiographical self? What can her auto/biographical writings tell us about the social and religious world in which she lived? In particular, how does Sera Khandro portray the consort relationships in her religious communities, most centrally her *yab yum* (male-female) partnership with Drimé Özer? The following chapters will explore these questions by listening to selections from the many dialogues Sera Khandro narrates in her auto/biographical writings, with both human and superhuman interlocutors. Sounding loudly in this cacophony of conversation are the progenitors of the Treasure tradition, Padmasambhava and Yeshé Tsogyel, who beckon Sera Khandro into their buddhafields regularly in her visionary experiences to console and empower her. Joining them are the voices of celestial *ḍākinīs*, whose unfailing encouragement and unerring prophecies drown out all doubters, and terrestrial Tibetan land deities (*gzhi bdag*), who lend her powerful local credentials to discover Treasures from Golok's most sacred mountains. Also resounding are the voices of Sera Khandro's lamas and religious community members, who had no shortage of counsel and at times critique for her. Through Sera Khandro's renditions of her relationships with these spirits, saints, and fellow students of Tibetan Buddhism, we may begin to perceive the contours of life as a Tantric consort and a female visionary in early twentieth-century eastern Tibet.

SERA KHANDRO'S JOURNEY FROM SUFFERING TO SANCTITY

Sera Khandro's autobiography is the story of her transformation from a central Tibetan noble girl to a beggar in Golok and then a *ḍākinī* incarnation of Yeshé Tsogyel famed for her skill as a Treasure revealer. Hers is not a cool tale of an individual seeker detaching from the miseries of the world, but is colored by intense relationships with others that both complicated and created the conditions for her spiritual liberation. If we isolate the narrative arc of Sera Khandro's life story for a moment from the larger chorus of conversations through which she conveys it, we find the following trajectory: Sera Khandro was born in 1892 to a mother from Tibetan nobility and a father who was a Mongolian official. She writes of growing up on a lavish estate in Lhasa, the capital city of Tibet, near its most sacred Jokhang Temple. Her parents treated her affectionately, but tensions arose between her and them because, in her words, "they were political leaders who wanted power," whereas from her earliest years she yearned to live a life dedicated to religion.[5] Extraordinary visions and miraculous events such as healing victims of one of Lhasa's many smallpox epidemics and pulling a ritual dagger partway out of a rock confirmed her religious predilections, even as her parents prepared her for a high-profile secular life. The conflict between Sera Khandro's and her father's conceptions of her future reached an apex when he began making preparations for her marriage to the son of a Chinese district official, inspiring her to attempt suicide rather than agree to the engagement. When she was twelve, her beloved mother died and her father remarried.[6] These events confirmed her decision at age fourteen to "abandon my homeland as if it were a land of demons."[7] Her chance to escape the confines of her Lhasa life came when a group of traveling religious pilgrims from Golok, headed by Drimé Özer, sought shelter at her brother's residence. Instantly she felt great devotion for Drimé Özer, and she secretly followed his entourage out of the city, vowing to spend the rest of her life practicing the Great Perfection (*rdzogs chen*), the pinnacle contemplative teaching of the Nyingma school of Tibetan Buddhism.

Sera Khandro left Lhasa with strong resolve, but the land of Golok to which she traveled proved to be a harsh environment. Sandwiched between Kham and Amdo in an area that today straddles the border between the People's Republic of China's western provinces of Qinghai and Sichuan, Golok is known for its many illustrious Tibetan Buddhist masters as well as its history of aggression and banditry. With an average altitude of 13,000 feet and below-freezing temperatures most of the year, the majority of Golok's rolling grasslands and snow peaks are hostile to any livelihood other than nomadic pastoralism. During Sera Khandro's time there from 1907 to 1940, Golok's severe climate and remote location at the headwaters of the Yellow River (Rma chu) helped its people maintain their status as a polity largely independent from both the Dalai Lama's Tibetan government to the west and the Chinese government (first the Qing dynasty, and after 1911 the Republican government) to the east.

When Sera Khandro left Lhasa in 1907, she left her urban upper-class estate-dwelling life for a future finding shelter among nomads living in yak-hair tents. She traded her fine brocade clothing and diverse diet for coarse leather attire and beggar's food—mostly poor-quality roasted barley flour, *dri* yogurt, wild sweet potatoes, and butter, when she could find these. Her privileged life retreated into the distance as Drimé Özer's group of pilgrims journeyed on foot for several months eastward toward Golok. Instead, Sera Khandro found herself shunned as an outsider. Not only was she illiterate in Tibetan and therefore unable to participate in the community's scriptural recitations, but also her refined Lhasa Tibetan and the Goloks' guttural Tibetan dialect were mutually unintelligible. Her lodestar throughout this difficult period was Drimé Özer, with whom she became increasingly close. They became so close that when the weary pilgrims finally reached home in the Dartsang region of the Washül Serta territory, just south of Golok proper (see maps 1 and 2), members of Drimé Özer's community partial to his consort, Akyongza, refused to allow her to rent a room in his residence, instead sending her off to work as a maid-servant for a local Golok nomad family. This was the first incident of a lifelong pattern of contention between Sera Khandro and other female consorts of important male Treasure revealers with whom she associated.

Her two-year stint as a servant was interrupted by a summons from a Golok Treasure revealer named Gara Terchen Pema Dündül Wangchuk Lingpa (1857–1910), who invited Sera Khandro to his residence at Benak Monastery in what is now Pema County, Golok, because he had received prophecies that she could aid his deteriorating health. Sera Khandro's chance to apply her curative powers to Gara Terchen was thwarted by his acerbic consort, Yakza, who threatened open hostility should she approach. Even so, in time she not only went to Benak but also settled there with the man who would become her "life partner" (*tshe grogs*), Gara Terchen's eldest son, Gyelsé Pema Namgyel (1882/3–?). The following decade of her life at Benak was turbulent: Sera Khandro describes their relationship as an antagonistic one in which Gyelsé disapproved of her increasingly prolific Treasure revelation activities, eventually taking up with another woman from Golok named Seldrön while still living with Sera Khandro. Meanwhile she gave birth to three children, only one of whom lived to adulthood, her firstborn daughter, Yangchen Drönma (1913–?). The anger and pain from this phase of life at Benak reverberate through her hundreds of pages of auto/biographical reflections. Nevertheless, even though "negative circumstances swirled around me like the wind,"[8] they did not hinder her many Treasure discoveries during this period.

Throughout her life at Benak with Gyelsé, Sera Khandro yearned intensively to be near Drimé Özer. On four occasions during this decade, the predestined *yab yum* partners Drimé Özer and Sera Khandro met, nurturing each other's proclivities as Treasure revealers and healing each other's illnesses. Finally, in 1921, their forced separation ended when the twenty-nine-year-old Sera Khandro became so ill with an arthritic condition that Gyelsé feared she would soon die. Rather than have her blood on his hands, he sent her back to Drimé Özer, who even Gyelsé agreed was her prophesied consort. Drimé Özer nursed her back to health, and the *yab yum* partners performed meditation retreats together that resulted in their spiritual liberation. As joyous as their reunion was, it was also short lived. In 1924 an epidemic overtook Dartsang, sickening everyone and causing the death of both Sera Khandro's five-year-old son, Rindzin Gyurmé Dorjé, and Drimé Özer himself within a matter of days. Before the embers of Drimé Özer's funeral pyre had cooled, the factions within his household who didn't like Sera Khandro, namely those affiliated with his other consort, Akyongza, expelled the deeply grieving Sera Khandro and her eleven-year-old daughter from their community. Sera Khandro was "left behind without a protector" and "without a partner or a home."[9]

The one who stood up for her at this critical moment was Sotrül Natsok Rangdröl Rinpoché (1869–1935). He was a close disciple of Drimé Özer as well as an important and powerful incarnate lama from Sera Tekchen Chönkhor Ling Monastery in Serta, now part of Kandzé Tibetan Autonomous Prefecture in Sichuan (see map 2). Sera Khandro, meaning the *Ḍākinī* of Sera, came to be known as such because Sotrül Rinpoché housed her at Sera Monastery for several years. Her time at Sera was sorrowful but prolific. Grieving for Drimé Özer took on a textual tone only months after his death, when she began writing his biography; the next year, she commenced writing her own autobiography. In the midst of this auto/biographical writing, she continued to reveal Treasures. She also began teaching widely throughout eastern Tibet, primarily the Treasure revelations of Düjom Lingpa and Drimé Özer as well as her own. Late in her life, Sera Khandro's prominence as a Treasure revealer and as an important holder of the Düjom lineage burgeoned. Many Nyingma retreat centers and monasteries throughout Golok and Kham invited her to give teachings. She also taught disciples from the Jonang, Kagyü, and Bön lineages. She died in 1940 at the age of forty-eight at Riwoché, while residing at the estate of her disciple, the Riwoché Zhapdrung Tsewang Drakpa.

SOURCES

The main sources for this study are Sera Khandro's long autobiography and the biography she wrote of Drimé Özer. Completed in 1925, one year after his death, this 248-folio work is titled *The Biography of the Omniscient Refuge Master, Lord of Accomplished Ones, the Precious Sovereign of the Ocean of Profound Treasures Pema Drondül Sangngak Lingpa: A Chariot for the Faithful That Dispels the Heart's Darkness, a Garland of Blue Lotuses and Cascading Jewels.*[10] I have seen only one version of it, a reproduction of a cursive (*yig nag*) handwritten original housed in the Library of Tibetan Works and Archives in Dharamsala, India. Similar in form to the autobiography she later wrote, about half of Drimé Özer's biography recounts his visions of Padmasambhava and other illustrious Indian and Tibetan spiritual masters; the other half covers this-world events and is written in Golok-dialect infused Tibetan, with an emphasis on his dialogic encounters with a wide range of interlocutors. Sera Khandro did not take credit for composing Drimé Özer's biography, attributing it instead to *ḍākinīs*' prophecies. In the text's colophon she explains that without the *ḍākinīs*' inspiration, even though Drimé Özer himself had appeared before her and conferred his blessings, she couldn't compose his biography:

> Because I had lived with the lama for a short time and before that the place I lived was far away, I didn't know the details of the Master's good deeds. Not only that, since someone like me has a narrow mentality like that of a lowly stupid animal, I wondered how I could possibly know how to express even a bit of the Lama's good qualities and deeds, so I let it go.[11]

It is a fortunate turn of history that she overcame her authorial misgivings, because Sera Khandro's biography of Drimé Özer appears to be the only source of information about his life: the majority of his extensive volumes of revelations seem not to have survived the Cultural Revolution.

The following year, 1926, while still residing at Sera Monastery, the 34-year-old Sera Khandro commenced her own long autobiography, titled *The Biography of the Central Tibetan Woman Dewé Dorjé: A Chariot Leading to Renunciation and a Reliquary of Faith for Fortunate Ones.*[12] Until more than half a century after her death, Sera Khandro's autobiography remained unpublished in Tibetan and circulated only in handwritten manuscript form among her disciples and their descendants in the eastern Tibetan regions of Serta, Kandzé, and Riwoché as well as in the Tibetan diaspora, primarily among the disciples of Düjom Jikdrel Yeshé Dorjé Rinpoché (1904–1987) and Jadrel Sangyé Dorjé Rinpoché. I have collected two manuscript versions of this work, one 407-folio version given to me by

Jadrel Rinpoché (cited above) and one 526-folio version from a private library in Serta County, Kandzé Tibetan Autonomous Prefecture. The rarity of Sera Khandro's autobiography changed for the first time in 2009 through the efforts of the Golok Regional Government Office of Historical Manuscripts under the main editorship of Ju Kelzang, who published a version of her collected works including her long autobiography.[13] In their preface, Ju Kelzang et al. laud Sera Khandro as "the second Machik [Lapdrön] of Tibet" and explain that "although there were many [Sera Khandro] religious teachings, after they fell prey to a time of disturbance, only a few remain, and copies of those manuscripts are extremely rare."[14] One of the features of Sera Khandro's biographical writing that Ju Kelzang and company praise is its clear and flowing style. They note that "Because [her writing] is strongly influenced by the way the common people of the region [of eastern Tibet] naturally speak, it gives the feeling of a pleasant, intimate, and straightforward composition. The writing style doesn't move into self-aggrandizement, giving it a truthful feeling and a believable quality."[15]

If writing Drimé Özer's biography inaugurated Sera Khandro's penchant for biographical writing, it did so with verve, as her autobiography is nearly double his biography in length. Additionally, unlike with his biography, she claims authorship of hers in her own name for the purpose of "inspiring those fortunate ones entrusted with her teachings and those who will become disciples."[16] The autobiography concludes with a double colophon, indicating that she wrote the work in two phases: the first, recounting her life from birth through age thirty-four, completed in 1927 and the second, narrating her life from age thirty-five through forty-two, completed circa 1934. In the first colophon, she writes in prose,

> The lowest of all the great Treasure revealer lama's retinue, the one who was merely his consort (*gzungs ma*) and who has the degenerate age Treasure name Dechen Dewé Dorjé, or the nonsensical wild woman who has destroyed illusion named Künzang Dekyong Chönyi Wangmo, began this account in which my faults and good qualities are mixed during an auspicious month when I was thirty-four. I finished it when I was thirty-five, on the first day of the eleventh month in the female fire hare year (1927) at the secluded mountain hermitage of Sera Monastery, the supreme place where the natural *ḍākinīs* gather. My disciple of pure commitment Tsültrim Dorjé acted as the scribe.

In all the directions in which this Dharma spreads, may fortunate occurrences spontaneously arise such as long life, health, and the expansion of the Dharma. May it be auspicious![17]

In the second colophon, written in verse, Sera Khandro concludes the work with the following words,

Because [my disciples] exhorted me over and over [to write this],
my heart could not bear it, and this perpetual liar,
this guide of degenerate age beings with a degenerate age Treasure name
who is an object of pity as one who behaves as a householder,
this ordinary one who yearned for the isolated hermitage of a homeless one,
the lowest of all, Dewé Dorjé,
wrote a partial account of my deeds and activities
from age thirty-five to forty-two.

By the power of this, may the obstacles of those great beings who are doctrine holders be dispelled!
May the lives of those who adhere to the teachings be prolonged and may benefactors' power increase!
May sentient beings be joyfully happy and always practice the Dharma!
May the fruit of benefiting oneself and others ripen like that of a wish-fulfilling tree!
May good deeds and enlightened activity proliferate and be auspicious!

I wrote this myself.
May virtue prevail! May virtue prevail! May virtue and excellence prevail! *Sarva Mangalaṃ*![18]

TIBETAN STORIES OF THE INTERDEPENDENT SELF

Sera Khandro's life narrative fits into the Tibetan literary genre of spiritual biography or *namtar* (*rnam thar*), literally meaning "full liberation." *Namtar*s relate the story of an individual's chronological trajectory from suffering to spiritual awakening. Those written prior to Tibet's incorporation into the People's Republic of China in 1951 were almost always religious in nature, as can be ascertained by the genre's name, although political achievements and aesthetic aims also appeared to varying degrees. *Namtar* can be translated more precisely as "spiritual biography" than just "biography," given its teleological focus on the path to religious liberation. It could also be termed hagiography or "holy writing," a designation most often used in relation to the lives of Christian saints. Both Buddhist and Christian spiritual biographies focus on their protagonists' accomplishment of miracles and visionary encounters with the divine, and both emphasize reverence over realism in their depictions of their saintly subjects. Also like Christian hagiography, Tibetan *namtar*s served pivotal social functions, including edifying the faithful and promoting religious figures' cults. Nevertheless, *namtar* has a distinctly Buddhist genesis deriving partly from Indic Buddhist genres such as *jātaka* stories (Tib. *skyes rabs*), which are tales of the Buddha's former lifetimes. *Jātaka* was itself a subcategory of *avadāna*, one of twelve Buddhist scriptural categories consisting of moral stories presenting events in a person's current life as consequences of their acts in previous lives. The Tibetan translation of *avadāna* is *tokjö* (*rtogs brjod*), or "expression of realization." In practice, Tibetan *namtar* and *tokjö* overlap in meaning; Sera Khandro and others in her religious milieu used both terms to refer to their biographical writings.

Beyond their Indic Buddhist roots, *namtar*s demonstrate distinctively Tibetan attributes. One is the prevalence of autobiography, or *rangnam* (*rang rnam*), which, translated literally, means "one's own full [liberation]." There are hundreds of extant Tibetan autobiographies dating from the twelfth century forward, in contrast to the relative absence of autobiographical writing in classical India and China. Reasons for Tibet's extensive tradition include the Tibetan penchant for genealogical writing and the dominance of Buddhism over older forms of cultural identification, which led to a competitive religious climate in which individual religious masters established themselves partly via recording their personal accomplishments in autobiographies.[19] For all its distinctiveness in comparison to genres used by Tibet's neighbors, Tibetan *rangnam* shares a great deal with *namtar* in terms of form, content, and purpose. Tibetan writers such as Sera Khandro titled both their biographical and autobiographical writings "*namtar*." Disciples often drew on autobiographical materials when formulating biographies of their masters, and masters often dictated their autobiographies to scribes.[20]

Despite these points of overlap, *rangnam* is self-referential in a way that *namtar* is not, thus making "spiritual autobiography" an appropriate translation of the genre. *Rangnam* accords with recent definitions of autobiography such as that of Sidonie Smith and Julia Watson, who define it as "a historically situated practice of self-representation" in which "narrators selectively engage their lived experience through personal storytelling."[21] Smith and Watson distinguish between "autobiography," which they associate with the Enlightenment celebration of individual autonomy, and the more general term "life narrative," by which they refer to various types of self-referential writing. In this study, I use "life narrative" and "auto/biographical writing" interchangeably to refer to Sera Khandro's twofold biographical writing projects, including the biography she wrote of Drimé Özer and her own autobiography. By calling Sera Khandro's *namtar* her spiritual autobiography, or autobiography for short, I don't mean to imply that the self she narrates is an autonomous individual relating the story of her personality, for the opposite is the case. Sera Khandro's autobiography emphasizes the profound relationality of the self, its interconnectedness with others.

That the subject of Sera Khandro's autobiography is a self profoundly interconnected to others in her spiritual and social world should come as no surprise, given her religious career as a Tibetan Buddhist Treasure revealer. The process of revealing a Treasure, be it a scripture, religious artifact buried in the Tibetan earth, or a vision appearing in the revealer's mind, involves a complex network of conditions called "auspicious connections" or *tendrel* (*rten 'brel*). Five specific auspicious connections are required to successfully discover Treasures, including 1) being the right Treasure revealer prophesied to reveal a given Treasure; 2) being at the proper place; 3) at the proper time; and being accompanied by 4) a "doctrine holder" (i.e., a disciple whom the revealer will entrust with preserving and passing on a given teaching) and 5) the proper consort (to aid in the discovery and decoding of the Treasure). Treasure revealers' autobiographies are replete with not only prophecies decreeing what, where, when, and with whom they should make their discoveries but also introspective reflections on their identities as revealers and on whether, how, and why these auspicious connections did or did not come together. Though prophesied, a revelation was never a foregone conclusion until the network of interconnections converged; Treasure revealers were thus embedded in a web of relationships without which they could not accomplish their calling. Sera Khandro's autobiography is typical of Treasure revealers' writings with its focus on gathering together auspicious connections, heeding prophecies, and recounting visionary interactions with bodhisattvas, *ḍākinīs*, and other divine presences. Yet it stands out from others in that the Treasure revealer was female and the requisite consorts were male, which led to considerable challenges gathering auspicious connections. This book will consider the constellation of differences this change of subject makes for Tibetan autobiographical self-presentation.

AUTOBIOGRAPHY, WOMEN, RELATIONAL SELFHOOD, AND TIBET

The variety of voices that populate Sera Khandro's life narrative not only exemplify the Buddhist doctrine of interdependence but also resonate with developments in autobiographical criticism that assert the centrality of others in narrating the self. Starting with studies of women's autobiography, theorists have critiqued the idea of a unified autobiographical subject such as that of Philippe Lejeune's "autobiographical pact" asserting the identity of author, protagonist, and narrator.[22] Lejeune was hardly alone in defining autobiography in conjunction with the European "Enlightenment celebration of individual autonomy," as Sidonie Smith expressed it. In 1956, pioneering autobiography theorist Georges Gusdorf professed autobiography to be "peculiar to Western man."[23] As a product of the Copernican Revolution and the resulting "conscious awareness of the singularity of each individual life," he claimed autobiography is impossible among those who believe in "the transmigration of souls."[24] Similarly, Karl Weintraub, among others, associated autobiography with the rise of the individual, which he understood as those who "perceive themselves as unique personalities," as opposed to those who do not differentiate themselves from their social environment.[25] Perhaps unsurprisingly, the vast majority of the autobiographers these early theorists listed in their canons were white, land-owning European or American men, for their domain of public life enabled achievements considered worthy of autobiographical accolade.

Beginning in the 1980s, theorists of women's autobiography reenvisioned the autonomy of the autobiographical subject, effecting what Paul John Eakin has stated is "the single most important achievement of autobiography studies in the last decade [the 1990s]."[26] Early theorists of women's autobiography such as Mary Mason and Estelle Jelinek argued that the subject was constituted by relationships with others rather than separation from them. In 1980 Mason and Jelinek published works theorizing the differences between women's and men's autobiography by focusing on female autobiographical subjects who had previously been left out of the literary canon.[27] These pioneering studies ignited an explosion of scholarship on women's autobiography that has since refined earlier essentialist distinctions between men's and women's autobiography as well as incorporated autobiographies from diverse ethnicities, nationalities, sexualities, genders, and social classes into the canon.[28] One effect of this attention to selfhood as relational, emerging out of interconnections with others, is that this insight is no longer confined to women's autobiography.[29] Nevertheless, studies on this topic remain committed to probing the relationality of the self, or the ways relationships with others formulate selfhood, as well as the plurality of voices that tell the story of a woman's life.[30]

Through studying Sera Khandro's auto/biographical writings, this book aims to expand the study of life writing to encompass an alternative register of relational selfhood in a woman's autobiography, one that incorporated her human communities as well as her physical environment and other dimensions of spiritual presences into her self narrative. In crafting such an autobiographical subject, Sera Khandro struggled not to overcome Euro-American biases towards a singular male subjectivity but to enter the canon of Tibetan *namtar* that was almost the exclusive preserve of religious men. But this very exclusivity poses a major challenge: given the paucity of female-authored Tibetan autobiographies prior to the 1950s, to make claims about Tibetan women's writing as opposed to men's is to assume more than we know about Tibetan women as authors. Monasteries were the central source of education outside of the upper classes of society prior to Tibet's incorporation into the PRC, and the literacy rate among women, both monastic and lay, was low compared to that of men. Religious virtuosity was the main theme of Tibetan *namtar*, which privileged learned religious men and hindered both women and laymen from recording their life story.[31] The collection of *namtar*s whose subjects are historical Tibetan women comprises less than 1 percent of extant Tibetan *namtar*s, which number in the thousands.[32] One of the most famous female Tibetan religious virtuosos is Machik Lapdrön (eleventh–twelfth centuries), who is renowned for founding the practice of "Severance" (*gcod*), in which one mentally offers one's body as food in order to annihilate self-cherishing.[33] Life stories of Tibetan women have also appeared in other genres of Tibetan literature related to *namtar*, most notably Tibetan opera (*lha mo*), such as the life story of Nangsa Obum, and accounts of "returning from the dead," or *delok* (*'das log*). In these stories, the protagonist dies, travels to the hell realms, witnesses the extreme suffering of people who have accumulated bad karma, and returns to counsel the living on the benefits of good deeds. *Delok* accounts are unique among Tibetan literary forms in that the protagonists in roughly 50 percent of the extant manuscripts are female. *Delok* literature is therefore an important source for Tibetan women's life stories, although they differ from *namtar*s in that they focus on episodes of their protagonists' travel to the realm of the dead and not their full life from birth to death.[34]

Given the rarity of female-authored Tibetan-language autobiographies prior to the 1950s, not to mention women's authorship of any other type of Tibetan texts, it is neither possible nor productive to generalize about Tibetan women's writing styles. Nevertheless, this book suggests that we can perform a micro-study of gender and life narrative among the particular communities in which Sera Khandro lived that can inform our understanding of a range of topics, including the positions of women as nuns and consorts, tensions between celibate and noncelibate interpretations of ideal Vajrayāna conduct, and public opinion on these sensitive matters. To explain how we can best explore such issues through Sera Khandro's writings, I first step back to consider how a literary form such as Tibetan spiritual biography can (and cannot) be a resource for social history.

APPROACHING LIFE THROUGH LITERATURE

A study of Sera Khandro's auto/biographical writings as a "window into the world" of particular early twentieth-century religious communities in the Golok region of eastern Tibet confronts the familiar challenge of parsing the relationship of literature to life. To what degree can we read life narratives as accurate reflections of historical realities? To what degree are they stylized products of narrative form? On the one hand, literary critics such as Hayden White argue that the messiness of lived experience is incommensurable with the sequential beginnings, middles, and ends that comprise narrative representations of it. He claims that "the notion that sequences of real events possess the formal attributes of the stories we tell about imaginary events could only have its origin in wishes, daydreams, reveries."[35] The problem with narrative as a reflection of historical reality for White is that it hides moralizing judgments in the name of objectivity because life in the world never really has the closure that narrative sequence affords it. Louis Mink concurs, positing that "Stories are not lived but told. Life has no beginnings, middles, or ends; there are meetings, but the start of an affair belongs to the story we tell ourselves later, and there are partings, but final partings only in the story."[36] According to this logic, a life narrative like that of Sera Khandro is so replete with literary devices and formulaic elements that it affords little, if any access to the historical figure Sera Khandro.[37]

But must we draw such a rigid distinction between literature and life in the realm of autobiography, in which one ostensibly refers to the other in some manner? Are not the few auto/biographies written by and about Tibetan women among our best sources to shed light on their lives? This study argues that Sera Khandro's auto/biographical writings are indeed vital sources for understanding more about her and her social world, even though ultimately they do not disclose her real self but rather stories about it.[38] This last caveat is hardly a deterrent, given that Buddhists and critical theorists would agree that a "real self" is an unfindable abstraction. There can be no sharp dividing line between life and the stories we tell about it because experience is "always already an interpretation," to quote Joan Scott's seminal essay.[39] In Jerome Bruner's words, "a life as led is inseparable from a life as told—or more bluntly, a life is not 'how it was' but how it is interpreted and reinterpreted, told and retold."[40] Put strongly by Oliver Sacks, this narrative identity thesis, as it is sometimes called, is the idea that "each of us constructs and lives a 'narrative,' and that this narrative *is* us, our identities."[41] If so, Bruner concludes, "narrative, rather than referring to 'reality,' may in fact create or constitute it."[42] But people do not have a limitless number of narratives by which to story their lives. The stories people tell about themselves reflect the stories they have heard in the past and the contingencies of their present location. Autobiography is thus always historically situated, grounded in a matrix of meaning that cannot be isolated from its larger cultural domain. Culture constrains an individual's ability to invent and reinvent herself, but it also provides a repertoire, to use Ann Swidler's term, or "a set of skills, which one can learn more or less thoroughly, enact with more or less grace and conviction."[43] Auto/biographers like Sera Khandro did not construct a life narrative *ex nihilo*, nor did they simply apply available narrative scripts to formulate their life stories. They creatively engaged, adapted, and resisted elements of their cultural repertoire. Sera Khandro's life writing is therefore both a product of her place and time and a unique literary production.

That literature and life cannot be so easily separated does not mean that Sera Khandro's auto/biographical writings can serve as a clear window into "what happened" in early twentieth-century eastern Tibet; there is no Archimedean access point into a historical moment or a person's life. Nor is there a simple way to separate fact from fiction in Tibetan auto/biographical texts, something that early Tibetan Studies scholars lamented. For example, A. I. Vostrikov found much of historical value in Tibetan biographies, but he also cautioned that "some are full of legends and are interesting not from the historical but only or almost only from the folkloristic and literary standpoint."[44] Giuseppe Tucci noted that Tibetan biographies "set out to edify the faithful, not to portray the historical background or supply a precise biography based on verified facts. Their historical value is rare and indirect."[45] Even in the case of autobiography, where we may be closer to reliable real-life testimony than pure literary invention, it is not possible to separate fact from fiction because, for one thing, all that an author writes can in some sense be read as a reflection of him- or herself.[46] With this in mind, I suggest that Sera Khandro's auto/biographical writings can tell us a great deal about her social and religious world precisely because they are *not* a clear window into life in early twentieth-century Tibet, or into the mind of a Tibetan female religious exemplar. Life narratives including autobiography, hagiography, and other forms of written and oral life stories are always situational and perspectival; they don't erupt from author's pens or mouths without specific reasons, motivations and agendas for producing them. As Jaber Gubrium and James Holstein attest, "Stories are assembled and told to someone, somewhere, at some time, for different purposes, and with a variety of consequences."[47] Life narratives are therefore tied to social life not only if we accept the theory that experience is inseparable from narratives about it but also because authors produce life narratives in and for others in specific social worlds. This has led scholars of hagiography such as Patrick Geary to assert that "a primary aspect of this literature [hagiography] is that it is, in part, consciously propaganda."[48] Similarly, Robert Campany argues that "Each hagiographic narrative is an artifact of an attempt to persuade an audience."[49] We can therefore gather something of the agenda not only of the writer but also of the community for which she wrote through close examination of the formal elements of a given work, the context in and for which it was written, and a comparison of it with other works from its milieu. This book attempts to do just this through examining key narrative features of Sera Khandro's autobiography, paying attention to evidence both internal and external to her writings about her social world. With regard to the external evidence, major points of comparison are the autobiographies of Traktung Düjom Lingpa, the father of Sera Khandro's guru and consort Drimé Özer; and Gara Terchen Pema Dündül Wangchuk Lingpa, the father of her "life partner" Gara Gyelsé. Given that both of these works very likely provided spiritual and literary inspiration for Sera Khandro, they are well suited to setting the distinctive features of her autobiography into relief.

HEARING RESONANCES OF A SOCIAL WORLD THROUGH CONVERSATIONS

The primary feature of Sera Khandro's writing that this book explores is the many conversations she narrates between herself and a host of interlocutors, including bodhisattvas, *ḍākinīs*, local deities, demonic forces, animals, religious teachers, family, and religious community members. Through listening to selections from the several hundred pages of direct-speech dialogues through which she tells her life story, we can learn a great deal about the values of the audience about and for whom she wrote. We need not attempt to extract this-world biodata from the larger mélange of dreams, visions, songs, and stories contained in her works. Rather than dividing real from unreal according to a metaphysics foreign to Sera Khandro's writing, this book understands her social world to include not only others in her human communities but also supermundane forces, including enlightened Buddhist figures and powerful Tibetan deities and demons integral to her ability to reveal Treasures in specific places in the Tibetan environment, such as sacred mountains and lakes. The self that is the subject of Sera Khandro's autobiography emerges through dialogue with these voices, as one point in a web of interconnected relationships that encompass multiple lifetimes and stretch into Tibet's earth and sky via the land deities and celestial *ḍākinī*s who animate them. Amid this symphony of voices, *ḍākinī*s' prophetic words sound especially strongly, offering Sera Khandro encouragement and inspiration to awaken to her true identity as an incarnation of the *ḍākinī* par excellence, Yeshé Tsogyel.

Given that some of the other voices in her life narrative—those of her religious community members and students—read her manuscripts, carefully preserved them, and passed them down to their children and grandchildren, we can reasonably conclude that they found value and verisimilitude in Sera Khandro's account of their world. By verisimilitude, I am not suggesting that others' speech in Sera Khandro's auto/biographical writings is necessarily a direct simulation of what occurred. Rather, Sera Khandro's life writing is a stylized version of the lives and voices she represents. In his analysis of narrative, Roland Barthes stated that "Art does not acknowledge the existence of noise," drawing the distinction between narrative as a system in which every element is deliberate and meaningful and life, which is chaotic and unstructured.[50] Autobiography, like other forms of literature, is a rendition of a life filtered through authorial interpretation, a story from which elements deemed random, inconsequential, or unworthy have already been culled. This structured and selective nature of the dialogues in Sera Khandro's auto/biographical writings heightens their ability to convey the tensions, activities, sentiments, concerns, and attitudes that shaped her narrative self and were important to those for and about whom she wrote. If utterances of all kinds, in Mikhail Bakhtin's view, are "oriented toward the listener and his answer," then actual dialogue in autobiography concretizes this situation by including the responses of others.[51] Moreover, if life narrative is propagandistic literature in the sense that its authors intended to persuade readers of something, dialogue is an especially good place to think about the stakes of Sera Khandro's auto/biographical writing projects because we get to hear her version of both sides of the conversations. We may never know if those interlocutors whose voices Sera Khandro ventriloquizes would have agreed with her renditions of their words, but the presence of their interactions in her writing is proof that the import of the conversations was not "noise" but had significance for Sera Khandro and others in her milieu.

In writing a Tibetan autobiography filled with dialogue, Sera Khandro was not unique. Direct-speech dialogues with a variety of others, such as visionary bodhisattvas, *ḍākinīs*, land deities, religious teachers, disciples, and family relations, are regular features of Tibetan *namtar*. Some of the most celebrated *namtars* in Tibetan literature—*The Life of Milarepa* and *The Life of Shabkar*, to name just a few—are filled with conversations, songs, and prophecies written as direct speech. What this book pays close attention to are the flashpoints of tension and topics that repeatedly elicit strong sentiment in Sera Khandro's conversations. Among these are questions about the status of the female body—is it inferior and lowly or a superior vessel in which to benefit beings? Others are dilemmas Sera Khandro faced about the proper circumstances for engaging in consort practices—are they justified if they will prolong the life of a celibate monastic? Or if the female consort of a noncelibate religious man threatens hostility? And who decides what Sera Khandro should do in these situations—her "life partner," Gyelsé; her root guru, Drimé Özer; the *ḍākinīs* who often drop in with their own strong views; or herself? To whom does Sera Khandro owe allegiance—the three Buddhist Jewels (Buddha, Dharma, and Saṅgha) alone or also the earthbound Tibetan land deities (*gzhi bdag*) on whose territory she reveals her Treasures? And finally, what type of attraction drove Sera Khandro toward Drimé Özer—was it lust or love, a connection based on desire or prophecy? Resounding through talk about these topics are strong feelings of love, grief, joy, jealousy, fear, and suspicion that invite us to reconsider what it meant to embody the Buddhist ideals of nonattachment, impermanence, and liberation.

OVERVIEW OF THE CHAPTERS

In order to begin our conversation about Sera Khandro, the book's first chapter, "The Life and Times of Sera Khandro," is a narrative retelling of the plot of Sera Khandro's life story as she recorded it in her autobiography. Interspersed throughout, I provide contextual information about the towns, monasteries, and people she mentions as well as relevant historical background drawn from Tibetan local histories of the Golok region and European travelogues. After this introduction to the contours of her life, the following four chapters focus on Sera Khandro's conversations with interlocutors who shaped key elements of her self narrative, including Tibetan land deities (highlighted in chapter 2), *ḍākinīs* (chapter 3), consorts (chapter 4), and her "*yab*," Drimé Özer (chapter 5).

The second chapter, "A Guest in the Sacred Land of Golok," draws its title from an expression Sera Khandro repeatedly used to describe the relationship she maintained between herself as a guest in sacred lands and the land deities (*gzhi bdag*), literally "masters of the territory," who controlled them. She termed this bond the "sacred land [deity] and guest commitment vow" (*gnas mgron gyi dam tshig*). This chapter explores the significance of this commitment to local terrestrial forces as well as her relationship to the transregional Tibetan progenitors of the Treasure tradition. Each of the three parts focuses on a specific type of relationality that formed the core of Sera Khandro's identity as a Treasure revealer in Golok. First, a look at the frame narrative through which Sera Khandro opens the story of her life demonstrates the intersubjectivity between Sera Khandro and her predecessor, the Ḍākinī Yeshé Tsogyel. Second, the chapter explores relationality in terms of the auspicious connections (*rten 'brel*) integral to the process of revealing Treasures. Third, the chapter demonstrates the ways Sera Khandro's situation in Golok's Treasure tradition connected her closely to local networks of authority embedded in the region's sacred mountains that were both the sites of many of her Treasure revelations and the sources of political authority in Golok. Through examining these various dimensions of Sera Khandro's relational self, we see how she participated in a larger reciprocal exchange between the environment and its inhabitants that had ramifications for everyday life on the grasslands as well as esoteric religious affairs.

Sera Khandro began her autobiography by charting her genealogy as an emanation of Yeshé Tsogyel, but the bulk of the conversations comprised by the story of her present incarnation indicate that she and her audience needed extensive convincing of this. The book's third chapter, "*Ḍākinī* Dialogues," listens to the many instances in which Sera Khandro laments her "inferior female body" (*skye lus dman pa*). In addition to being symptomatic of her social milieu, I suggest that Sera Khandro's repeated lamentations about her lowly female form provided occasions for other voices in her narrative, especially *ḍākinīs* and her male religious teachers, to laud her accomplishments. We can therefore think of this narrative strategy, in which she asserts her superior status through the words of others only to then deny their praise, as a type of autobiographical ventriloquy. A comparison of Sera Khandro's *ḍākinī* dialogues with other female-authored Tibetan autobiographies and with male Treasure revealers' autobiographies from her religious communities suggests that *ḍākinī*s had even more work to do encouraging Sera Khandro than with these other religious specialists. But as outspoken as the *ḍākinī*s were, their input seems to have set the stage for Sera Khandro's own first-person authorial voice to sound forth increasingly strongly in each of her successive auto/biographical writings.

The fourth chapter, "Sacred Sexuality," examines the purposes of sexuality in Tibetan Buddhist practice and its relationship to celibacy as Sera Khandro represented it. Reversing the volumes of Tantric literature in which female consorts appear only as unnamed appendages of male religious aspirants, Sera Khandro makes clear that all three of the main uses of religiously sanctioned sexuality that emerge in her writing, including what I term soteriological, hermeneutical, and pragmatic purposes, apply to both female and male meditators. Through the many conversations Sera Khandro records that concern with whom, when, and why to engage in religious practices involving sexuality, two at times divergent moral compasses recur: doctrinal precedence and public opinion. This chapter traces the tensions between these as well as between the virtues of celibacy and the expedient means of sexuality, focusing on the particularly sensitive question Sera Khandro faced repeatedly: what to do when those soliciting her services as a Tantric consort were monks? In the course of Sera Khandro's conversations with *ḍākinī*s and male lamas, what emerges are sound bites from a complex social climate that resist simple classification as entirely misogynist or gynocentric.

The truism that Tantra involves sex, literal or imagined, has not extended among its scholarly interpreters to suggest that it involves any sort of love between partners. The fifth and final chapter, "Love Between Method and Insight," seeks to make a case that Sera Khandro's rendition of the sacred commitment between *yab* and *yum* was more than a utilitarian modeling of Vajrayāna theology in which buddhahood is expressed as the union of the method or skillful means of compassion, gendered male, and the insight realizing emptiness, gendered female. Rather, this chapter demonstrates that Sera Khandro's 600-plus folios of auto/biographical writings were suffused with sentimental renditions of longing for, loving, and eventually losing Drimé Özer. The first part of the chapter explores the languages of love salient for Sera Khandro, endeavoring to situate her rendition of her mutually loving relationship with Drimé Özer in its "emotional community," to invoke historian of sentiment Barbara Rosenwein's term for the systems of feeling relevant to a given literary, social, and historical context.[52] The second part spotlights Sera Khandro's terms of endearment for describing her relationship with Drimé Özer as a mutual and complementary partnership. She uses a special locution only for her sacred relationship with Drimé Özer—the two are bound by male and female partners' commitment vows (*yab yum dam tshig*). One of the consequences, if not also the intentions, of this two-halves-of-a-whole depiction of herself and Drimé Özer is that in mirroring the Tantric vision of complete buddhahood as the union of gendered principles, Sera Khandro effectively carved a place for herself and her life story in the male-dominated ecclesiastic world of early twentieth-century eastern Tibet.

1

THE LIFE AND TIMES OF SERA KHANDRO

I, this inferior woman, will tell you a bit about my circumstances—
from the time I was seven, *ḍākinīs* took care of me;
they reassured me in reality, in visions, and in dreams.
From the time I was eleven, the Master Accomplished Awareness Holder
Saraha took care of me and bestowed ripening [empowerments] and liberating [instructions] upon me.
When I reached the age of twelve, I obtained the genuine prophetic guide of the *Ḍākinīs*' Oral Transmission Profound Treasure.
From the time I was thirteen, I exerted myself only in benefiting others.
At fourteen, in accordance with the *ḍākinī*'s command, I came eastward
to the land of eastern Tibet, which is like the demons' island.[1]
Not dying, while living I experienced the suffering of hell.[2]

The hell on earth Sera Khandro spoke of in a visionary interaction with the paramount female saint of Tibet, Yeshé Tsogyel, began amid the nobility of late nineteenth-century Lhasa and continued among the nomads in the grasslands of Golok in eastern Tibet. Lhasa during Sera Khandro's childhood was the cosmopolitan center of Tibetan political and cultural life on the edge of the Qing dynasty. This urban context could hardly have been more different than the vast pasturelands and snow peaks of Golok and Serta that later became her home. Located at the crossroads of the eastern Tibetan regions of Amdo and Kham that today form the western parts of Sichuan and Qinghai provinces, the majority of the Golok and Serta territories were independent confederations controlled neither by the Dalai Lama's Tibetan government nor by the Chinese authorities during Sera Khandro's time there from 1907 to 1940. The narrative Sera Khandro weaves over hundreds of manuscript pages provides a rare account of life in a wealthy noble family in Lhasa in the early twentieth century, then escape and entry into the closed ranks of religious hierarchy in Serta and Golok, and finally renown throughout the eastern Tibetan highlands as a Treasure revealer (*gter ston*) and a *ḍākinī* incarnation of Yeshé Tsogyel. The present chapter concentrates on her description of everyday life in this world from 1892 to 1940 in its historical context. Reserved for further analysis in later chapters are questions about style, voice, topos, and literary influences within Sera Khandro's auto/biographical writings. Here the focus is on the narrative sequence of events in Sera Khandro's life as she portrayed it, replete with a magical realist-like flavor in which the ordinary and extraordinary overlap.

In the late 1920s, while Sera Khandro was writing the long autobiography examined in this book, she also wrote a condensed autobiography in verse summarizing the main contours of her life.[3] In this short version, she divided her life into five different phases: 1) her religious aspirations and obstacles during her childhood in Lhasa from birth through age twelve; 2) the difficulties of her departure from Lhasa and entry into Golok from age thirteen through seventeen; 3) her life as Gyelsé's spouse at Benak Monastery in Golok from age eighteen through twenty-seven; 4) her reunion with her root lama, Drimé Özer, from age twenty-eight through thirty-one; and 5) her life afterward based at Sera Monastery in Serta, from age thirty-two on. This chapter follows the general structure of Sera Khandro's delineation of these phases of her life. It concludes with a summary of the eyewitness account of her last years and her death written by her close attendant and scribe, Tsültrim Dorjé, as well as a later rendition of her last years written by her disciple Jadrel Sangyé Dorjé Rinpoché.

LHASA AT THE TURN OF THE TWENTIETH CENTURY

The Lhasa into which Sera Khandro was born in 1892 was a vibrant religious, political, and commercial center within Asia. In the words of L. Austine Waddell, a British explorer who toured the city as a member of Sir Francis Younghusband's infamous 1904 invasion of Tibet, Lhasa was "the pivot of the world of High Asia," a Mecca of religious devotion as well as international trade.[4] At this time central Tibet was part of the Manchu-controlled Qing dynasty (1644–1911), although Qing sovereignty in Tibet was in decline. While the Qing government was focused on affairs farther east, such as the Sino-Japanese War of 1894–95 and the Boxer Rebellion of 1898–1901, the Thirteenth Dalai Lama, Gyelwa Tupten Gyatso (1876–1933), assumed power in 1895.

Sera Khandro never mentions encountering any Caucasians in her autobiography, nor does she allude to the British invasion of Tibet that forcibly entered Lhasa in 1904. But several of the soldiers, journalists, explorers, and spies who found their way there at the turn of the twentieth century left detailed field notes about what they discovered about the Lhasa in which Sera Khandro grew up. In the words of the Indian national and British spy Sarat Chandra Das, who journeyed to Lhasa in 1881–82:

> It was a superb site, the likes of which I have never seen. On our left was the Potala with its lofty buildings and gilt roofs; before us surrounded by a green meadow, lay the town with its tower-like, whitewashed houses and Chinese buildings with roofs of blue glazed tiles.[5]

The Buriat Russian explorer G. Tsybikoff, who visited Lhasa in 1900, remarked that "the gilt roofs of the two principal temples glisten in the sun and the white walls of the many storied buildings shine among the green tops of the trees."[6] Tsybikoff reported that the city was surrounded by orchards and trees, which a few years later the British journalist Edmund Candler, who also accompanied the Younghusband expedition, described as "willow groves intersected by clear-running streams, walled-in parks with palaces and fish-ponds, marshes where the wild-duck flaunt their security, and ripe barley-fields stretching away to the hills."[7] Inside Lhasa's green circumference, Waddell recorded that

> The compact town is barely half a mile square. Its streets are rather narrow and neither drained, nor paved, nor metalled, but the main ones are laid out on a fairly good plan. The houses are substantially built of stone walls two to three storeys high, with flat roofs (none sloping) and carefully white-washed, the beams of the eaves being often elaborately picked out in red, brown and blue.[8]

The multistoried whitewashed houses of Lhasa were built to last, with solid walls punctuated by windows without glass panes, hung with cotton curtains or protected from the winter chill with oiled Tibetan paper.[9] Mitigating their fortresslike quality were occasional birdcages hanging from windows that sheltered singing birds, larks, and doves as well as rows of flowerpots brightening the windowsills and bordering the entrance walls.[10] These houses lined wide, unpaved roads and narrow lanes interspersed with tall poles strung with prayer flags and numerous incense kilns.

At the turn of the twentieth century, Lhasa's streets saw no wheeled traffic whatsoever, but there was a steady stream of Tibetan townspeople, pilgrims, and traders from far afield as well as numbers of Mongolian, Manchu, Chinese, and central and South Asian city residents.[11] Lhasa's

FIG. 1.1 Lhasa street scene, photograph taken by F. M. Bailey on the Younghusband Mission to Tibet, 1903–4

permanent lay population consisted of about 10,000 residents, the majority of whom were women, with a monastic population of about 20,000 men who lived in the three largest monasteries outside the city: Ganden, Drepung, and Sera. Out of the Lhasa population, in 1904 the Nepalese Consul in Lhasa estimated that 7,000 were Tibetans; 2,000 were Chinese and half Chinese-Tibetan traders, military, and police; 800 were Nepalese merchants and artisans; 200 were Muslim traders from Ladakh and western China; 50 were traders from Mongolia, and 50 were traders from Bhutan.[12] Many visitors were drawn to Lhasa for its position as Tibet's political and religious center as well as its brisk markets. Tibetan, Chinese, Nepalese, Kashmiri, and Bhutanese shops lined the streets, encircling the main market area in the great square before the seventh-century Jokhang Temple. Waddell describes the articles on display in street stalls outside the shops in 1904 as "chiefly native eatables, trinkets, drugs, books, clothes, and broadcloth."[13] Perhaps among those books for sale were both Tibetan-language works and Chinese-language literature that circulated throughout the Qing dynasty, though foreign accounts do not specify. The many Chinese shops sold primarily bricks of tea, Tibetans' beverage of choice, as well as silk and cotton fabrics, wooden furniture, and ceramics. Nepalese merchants' stock included cloth, drugs, brass bowls, and lamps, while Kashmiris sold spices and dried fruits including persimmons, cooking peaches, crabapples, mulberries, gooseberries, and red currants.[14] Various specialty items of British design imported from India by Bhutanese, Nepalese, Kashmiri, and Chinese merchants were also becoming fashionable in Lhasa at the turn of the century, including mirrors, beads, jars, matches, penknives, cloth, enameled vessels, teapots, plates, and cups.[15] Waddell even found two quart bottles of English Bulldog stout at six shillings a bottle and was told that wealthy Tibetans enjoyed it as a liqueur.[16] In return for all these foreign delicacies, Tibetans sold and exported animal furs of many varieties, yak tails, sheep's wool, borax, salt, silver, gold, yaks, horses, and mules. Though not sold in the Lhasa markets because of their sacred status, Buddhist ritual implements, statues, and scriptures were exported to Mongolia.[17] Much of this trade took place by barter, bricks of tea being a convenient form of currency, but Lhasa's international flavor came through in the plethora of monies in use in the early 1900s, including coins minted by the Tibetan government in Lhasa, Indian rupees, Russian rubles, and Chinese coins and silver ingots.[18]

LHASA BIRTH AND CHILDHOOD

This dynamic multicultural context of early twentieth-century Lhasa emerges through Sera Khandro's description of her birth and its aftermath:

> First, regarding how I was born, north of Bodhgaya, India, is the seat of the supremely noble incarnation of Avalokiteśvara, the Dharma King Songtsen Gampo. In this eastern part of Tibet, the Land of Snow, west of the Rasatrül Temple [the Jokhang Temple], there is a place called Lumotil (*klu mo mthil*), whose earth guardian is Dorjé Yudrönma. Near the location of various amazing statues, including the main statue of the land, the Jowo Śākyamuni, there was an estate more sublime than all the others named Gyaragashar (*rgya ra ga shar*). Inside lived Prince (*lha sras*) Jampa Gönpo, a ruler endowed with power, wealth, and stability who belonged to a royal Mongolian lineage named "pure divine lineage" (*dkar po lha yi rigs*). Renowned as an incarnation of Rongtsa,[19] he was empowered in mind Treasures and manifested marks of accomplishment and so forth without difficulty. He lived as a householder in accordance with the following prophecy from the Nechung Dharma Protector:
>
> > Dress as a *ngakpa*.[20] Since the Lady of the Nup clan named Tsering Chöndzom is from a *ḍākinī* lineage, if you marry her *siddhas* and *yoginīs* will be born in your household again and again.
>
> Since all his neighbors and relatives told him to do this, he married Tsering Chöndzom and adhered to the tradition of his forefathers.
>
> I took birth in a family of "royal divine lineage" (*mi dbang lha yi rigs*) that was respected and venerated by all people, high and low. On the first day of the first month of the water dragon year [1892], my mother gave birth to me without pain. The baby was unlike others, born in an egg.[21] Not daring to touch me, Mother told my father the story.
>
> When she did, Father said, "An excellent sign."
>
> As he opened the egg with a feathered arrow ornamented with five colors of silk, rainbow light gathered, vultures danced above the house, a pleasant aroma pervaded the area, and more. Since the sound of a conch trumpet filled the house, both Mother and Father said, "We thought this baby was an incarnation, but she isn't. Why does this girl have these special signs?"

All the neighbors said, "An amazing incarnation was born in the leader's family!"

Then they called a Brahmin, and after he washed the baby's body with perfumed water and looked at her marks, he said, "It is appropriate for her to be an awareness woman[22] who is an accomplished one adhering to Secret Mantra. Living as a householder will be extremely bad for her. But she is also not to be a shaven-headed nun. Her hair shows signs of being blessed."

My father, mother, and relatives announced that on my body there were letters and that my hair showed signs of being blessed by *ḍākinī*s and in particular, that "*baṃ*," "*ha*," "*ri*," "*ni*," and "*sa*" were written on my five *cakra*s. Everyone rejoiced and held a grand celebration feast for my birth.

Then, saying that I needed to be given a name, the Chinese group (*rgya sde rnams*) said, "She should be given our year as her birth year. Since there were two 30th days, she was born in the hare year [1891]."

The Tibetan faction (*bod shog pa rnams*) said, "Since she was born on the first day of the Tibetan year, she was born in the dragon year [1892]."

Since the Chinese and Tibetans were not in agreement about giving me a name, they asked Taklung Mahā Rinpoché to proclaim my name. He gave me the name Kelzang Drönma.

The Brahmin said, "You all, the Chinese group and the Tibetan group, don't quarrel with each other! Since this girl with unusual marks is amazing, it seems she won't be our female leader. We must use the name that Mahā Rinpoché gave her." But everyone was displeased.

Mother said, "In the past, even though in our family we had many sons and daughters, the two [Chinese and Tibetan] groups have never had the custom of quarreling. Now, since the two groups' leaders are agitated over this girl, I should give her to someone else."

The minister Tsering Tashi offered the female leader a "good day" offering scarf and said the following:

> Madam, although previously incarnations have come to our family, we have never had a princess like this who is unstained by any faults and possesses merit and good qualities. Everyone thinks that she will certainly become someone who maintains the white silk knot of religious law.[23] Besides, why does she have to go on account of the two groups' agitation? Please don't give her to her father's land.

After he said this, everyone's enmity dissipated and the land became happy and abundantly fortunate. Everyone called me by the nickname Künga Wangmo.[24]

Many aspects of Sera Khandro's description of her birth follow paradigmatic elements of Tibetan biographical writing, including the stylized description of her birthplace, which situates it in reference to Indian Buddhist landmarks such as Bodhgaya and important Tibetan imperial figures such as the seventh-century Tibetan King Songtsen Gampo. Also paradigmatic is her description of the miraculous signs that accompanied her birth: rainbows, vultures circling the house, a pleasant aroma, the sound of a conch shell trumpet, and the discovery of marks indicating that she was a *ḍākinī*. Indeed, we may trace some familiar-sounding aspects of her birth account to the quintessential Buddhist biography, that of the Buddha himself. Both were born from royal parents into a wealthy palace life, only to later renounce it in favor of seeking spiritual liberation. Just as the Buddha's birth was marked by miraculous signs interpreted by Brahmin specialists to mean that he was destined for either worldly power or spiritual greatness, so too in Sera Khandro's narrative a Brahmin foretells her future spiritual prowess while her father aspires for her to become a political leader. In spite of these references to the Buddha's life, the inferiority of being female also comes through; even after her parents witness the telltale miraculous signs indicative of giving birth to an incarnate lama, they can only conclude, "We thought this baby was an incarnation, but she isn't."

In addition to these elements of Sera Khandro's birth account that are characteristic of Tibetan Buddhist biography, some distinctive details stand out as well. Who was Sera Khandro's Mongolian father named Jampa Gönpo? What Chinese and Tibetan factions were there in early twentieth-century Lhasa? What does it mean to be predestined to be a noncelibate Tantric master blessed by *ḍākinīs*? Mongols have been heavily involved in Tibetan internal affairs since the Yuan dynasty (1271–1368). At the close of the Ming dynasty (1368–1644), Tibetan Geluk hierarchs sought the political and military backing of the Khoshot tribe of Mongols headed by Gushri Khan (1582–1655) in order to unify their rule over Tibet and wrest control from their rivals, the Tsang kings affiliated with the Kagyü school of Tibetan Buddhism. Some of Gushri Khan's descendants settled in central Tibet and in Amdo. Later, in the eighteenth century, a rival Mongolian faction, the Zunghars, destabilized the power of Gushri Khan's descendants in central Tibet, but were themselves defeated by Manchu and Tibetan military forces. From the late eighteenth century until the fall of the Qing dynasty in 1911, Manchu authorities endorsed the rule of Tibet by the Dalai Lamas or their regents in conjunction with two Qing imperial representatives in Lhasa, called Ambans. The Ambans' actual power varied widely during the two-plus centuries of Qing "suzerainty" (as the British later termed it) over Tibet. In Waddell's eyewitness account of Younghusband's 1904 invasion of Tibet, he reported that "The Amban had very little power over the Tibetans, and latterly had been almost a prisoner and unable to venture out for weeks until our force arrived."[25] Even so, during this period Lhasa maintained vestiges of its connections with present and previous imperial dynasties, most visible in its Mongol, Manchu, and Han Chinese minority populations.

Could Sera Khandro's father, Jampa Gönpo, whom she describes as a descendant of a royal Mongolian lineage, have been descended from the Khoshot Mongols who made central Tibet their home? In 1900, when Tsybikoff made the three-month journey from Kumbum in Amdo to Lhasa, he reported that the Dam Valley he passed before entering Lhasa was inhabited by the Mongol descendants of Gushri Khan, who had settled in Tibet in the middle of the seventeenth century and were subjects of the Manchu Amban. He described them as "at present practically assimilated with the Tibetans," with all but a few Mongol words having disappeared from their language.[26] Alternatively, could Jampa Gönpo have immigrated to central Tibet more recently from the eastern Tibetan region of Amdo, home to large populations of Mongols? Sera Khandro gives us few clues. She describes her father as a devout Nyingma Buddhist practitioner of the Heart Essence (*snying thig*) lineage as well as a wealthy and powerful member of Mongolian nobility. The strongest indication she gives is her mention that he was a descendant of Chögyel Ngakyi Wangpo (1736–1807), who was himself a descendant of Gushri Khan in addition to being the famous Nyingma root guru of Shabkar Tsokdruk Rangdröl (1781–1851).[27]

Sera Khandro also repeatedly describes her father as a "Chinese leader" (*rgya dpon*) and their family as a Chinese leader's family (*rgya dpon sang*). It is possible that "Chinese" (*rgya*) was a generic term she used to refer to non-Tibetans, including Mongols, Han Chinese, and Manchus who held positions within the Qing court in Lhasa, which was centered at the Amban's residence. Given that most Ambans and their assistants in Lhasa came from Manchu and Mongolian noble families, Sera Khandro's description of her father as both "Mongolian" (*sog po*) and someone who held "Chinese" (*rgya*) political office could make sense in reference to the Amban and his officers in Lhasa.[28] During her childhood there was a Chinese quarter southwest of the Jokhang Temple where the Amban's residence was situated; Chinese men stationed at the nearby garrison lived there with their Tibetan wives and children. Waddell describes his approach to this neighborhood:

> As we turned right toward the Amban's quarters, past a Chinese theatre and restaurants, the houses were nearly all one-storeyed, as in the Flowery Land, with neat turf-walls in front enclosing little flower-gardens with pots of blooming asters, marigolds, stocks and hollyhocks, and nasturtiums within and on the window-sills.[29]

Though Sera Khandro's family estate, Gyaragashar, was several stories high, given that its first syllable, "Gya" (*rgya*), can mean "Chinese," Sera Khandro's family could have been among these half-Chinese, half-Tibetan families who lived in the Chinese quarter of Lhasa. That Gyaragashar does not appear on maps of early twentieth-century Lhasa could also indicate its location in the Chinese quarter, as the neighborhood vanished only a few years after Sera Khandro left Lhasa, when the Thirteenth Dalai Lama ousted the Ambans and the Chinese army from Tibet in 1912 after the fall of the Qing dynasty. Early twentieth-century maps of Lhasa do show another estate near the Chinese quarter southwest of the Jokhang Temple with a similar name, Rakhashar, which belonged to the Tibetan noble family Dokhar, but there is limited evidence linking Sera Khandro to this family.[30]

Despite the uncertainties regarding Sera Khandro's ancestry, we can ascertain that hers was a wealthy family with multiethnic roots whose members could both coexist peacefully and clash, just like the wider populace of the city of Lhasa. Tensions emerged between "Chinese" and Tibetan factions of Sera Khandro's family not only about the tabulation of her birth date but also regarding how she should be educated. Sera Khandro writes that when she was seven, her father determined that she would study literary Chinese before beginning Tibetan, despite her mother's wishes for her to study Tibetan. While literacy in Tibetan was unusual among rural Tibetan women, girls in Lhasa and particularly those from the Tibetan nobility had access to private Tibetan schooling.[31] Literacy in Chinese among Lhasa girls was more rare, although there are other examples. The part-Chinese, part-Tibetan secretary to the Amban named Canzhi Zhen, born in 1893, one year after Sera Khandro, wrote an autobiography in which he recounts growing up in the Chinese quarter of Lhasa and becoming a clerk in the Sino-Tibetan Translation Department of the Amban's office. While he attended a Chinese school for boys, his sisters were taught Chinese at home by a private tutor.[32] Sera Khandro writes of studying Chinese characters with a clerk who was expert in both spoken and written Chinese. Though she notes that she excelled at her Chinese studies and surpassed the other girls with whom she was sent to class, she despaired at this education, thinking it was leading her only toward further worldly ensnarement.

Sera Khandro's account of her childhood is suffused with references to her religious aspirations despite her father's continual efforts to steer her in the direction of worldly political power, just as the Buddha's father attempted with Siddhārtha. She recounts that when she was an infant, she caught hold of a sun ray and told her mother,

> I go, I go to the Lotus light.
> I go to the presence of Mother Tsogyel,
> who has uncontaminated mother's milk.
> I have no need for contaminated food.[33]

For seven days after this she was unconscious as if she had died, but after her parents performed extensive rituals for her, she awoke free from illness. A few years later, she remembered details about her previous incarnation in Khotan as Jangchup Chödrön, daughter of Agyaya and Salé. She recalls reciting Tārā and Avalokiteśvara mantras with intensive devotion even though other children playing nearby made fun of her. Though her religious conviction did not catch on with them, she managed to convince her parents of her sincerity, inspiring them to take her when she was seven years old for an audience with Changdrong Druptop Rinpoché. She describes this religious figure as an incarnation of the famous Tibetan Buddhist master and iron bridge builder Tangtong Gyelpo (1361–1485) as well as the head lama of the group of eighteen Chinese officials (*rgya shog dpon khag*). Their conversation hinged on the question of whether she should become a worldly political leader or a religious renunciate:

The lama said,

> This girl is an authentic incarnation of Sakya Tamdrin Wangmo. Hence, it is not appropriate for her to be either a householder or a nun. When it is time, her *ḍākinī* heritage will awaken, so until then do whatever you want.

Mother replied,

> Sir, it is difficult to compel this girl to be a leader with great affection for her subjects. If she were allowed to be a nun, she has a strong aspiration to live in a secluded hermitage.

The lama said,

> Since this girl is a fortunate one, I am not sure if she will govern your subjects. Now, for some years, do what you like and this will become clear.[34]

The lama then gave her blessings and conferred the refuge ceremony upon her. Shortly after this meeting, Sera Khandro went to visit a Tārā statue in the Jokhang Temple. Perceiving that the statue blessed her, she prayed single-pointedly to Tārā and spontaneously knew the prayer called "The Twenty-one [Tārās] Supplication."[35]

Later in her seventh year Sera Khandro revealed her very first Treasure (*gter*), which links her to a long tradition of Buddhist revelation that Tibetans trace back to the Tibetan imperial period from the seventh to ninth centuries. In brief, adherents of this system of revelation believe that the eighth-century Indian Tantric master Padmasambhava and some other masters associated with him hid teachings in the Tibetan earth and sky for the benefit of future generations. These teachings were to be revealed at the proper times by incarnations of Padmasambhava's original twenty-five disciples, one of whom was his Tibetan consort, Yeshé Tsogyel. Treasures can be material objects (*sa gter*, earth Treasures) such as scriptures and religious artifacts that Treasure revealers discover in the ground, or they can be visionary revelations (*dgongs gter*, mind Treasures) that appear in the mind of the appropriate Treasure revealer, who then records them. Sera Khandro writes that her first Treasure revelation experience occurred in 1899, when she accompanied her father and six other political leaders to the mountainside cave hermitages of Drak Yerpa, not far from Lhasa. There they performed a feast offering in front of a Padmasambhava statue in the Dawa Cave. The next morning when she was near a hill called Lharigo, Sera Khandro pulled a ritual dagger made of precious substances partway out of a large boulder. Just as she was doing this, other children arrived and teased her, causing her to feel doubt and leave the dagger still partly embedded in the rock. After she reported this to her father, he ordered her to return to the caves of Drak Yerpa to retrieve more Treasures. Sera Khandro impressed him with her revelatory skill, but both he and her mother commanded her to keep her abilities secret.

While the family was at Drak Yerpa, Sera Khandro experienced another vision that was to have a significant influence on her life. When the adults were eating a meal at a place called Otang, she and the other children went off to collect firewood. A magnificent white man with a ruddy complexion, mounted on a horse, appeared before her and introduced himself as her father. This apparitional man was none other than Nyenchen Tanglha, the most important mountain deity of central Tibet, who inhabited a range north of Lhasa and was famously bound by Padmasambhava himself to protect the Buddhist teachings.[36] Though Sera Khandro initially protested his allegation of paternity and insisted that she was from the Chinese leader's family, in time she came to believe that Nyenchen Tanglha was her real father, thus further validating her religious aspirations and helping her to relinquish her feeling of obligation to follow in the footsteps of the Chinese leader Jampa Gönpo.

As Sera Khandro grew older, the *ḍākinī* heritage intuited by Changdrong Druptop Rinpoché emerged more strongly. She writes that at the age of eight she went on pilgrimage with her parents to Önpu Taktsang, a sacred site linked to the activities of Padmasambhava and Yeshé Tsogyel. She recalled events that had transpired there in a past life, but when she spoke of this, her mother reprimanded her for disclosing her clairvoyance. When their pilgrimage brought them to Tashi Lhünpo, the large Geluk monastery home to the Penchen Lama incarnation line founded in the fifteenth century, a Sakya *ngakpa* recognized Sera Khandro's *ḍākinī* marks, such as the white hairs growing on the crown of her head. All the while during her waking and dreaming life, visions of *ḍākinī*s and buddhafields proliferated. Even Sera Khandro's father further ignited her religious devotion during this phase by being the first person to tell her about the Great Perfection (*rdzogs chen*) teachings. Sera Khandro writes that

> Just by hearing the name of that Dharma, faith arose in me, tears flooded my eyes, the hair on my body stood on end, and I vowed that until I reached

the point of death, I had to see if I could accomplish this Dharma called the Great Perfection.[37]

Despite her parents' partial acceptance of her religious yearnings, tension ran high between family expectations that she would assume a role of political leadership and her own ambition to dedicate herself to religion. While the ten-year-old Sera Khandro was experiencing many inspiring visions in which various *ḍākinīs* bestowed religious teachings upon her, the course of her future abruptly shifted when her father began arranging her marriage. She writes,

> When I was wondering, "Can I be alone and accomplish the genuine Dharma?" Tibetan cabinet ministers who were representatives of the Dalai Lama, such as those from the honorable Shartra house, Doring house, and Zurkhang house, coveted me as a bride and gave my father many gifts, demanding that he must give me to them. Because they were from the Tibetan faction, my father did not give me to them and returned all of their gifts. There was a chairman (*dpon kru'u*) of the Chinese faction from the western region called Kyilung Drongchen[38] named Daloyi[39] whose attire was Chinese and who belonged to the religious sect Heart Essence (*snying thig*), just like us. Since he was a wealthy man with only one son, even though that son said he would not govern subjects and wanted to take ordination, his parents did not give their permission.
>
> They told him, "You must become a householder and marry a girl who truly pleases you."
>
> He replied, "If henceforth I must be a householder, I will only be a householder if I marry the youngest of the three daughters of the Gyaragashar house named Künga Wangmo. Otherwise, since a king only speaks once, I will not become a householder."
>
> They said, "All right, we'll do what you say," and they sent my father a request.
>
> All the ministers and subjects discussed this, saying, "Since they are rulers of [administrative units comprised of] ten thousand families (*khri sde*), it is acceptable if they take control over both.[40] The young leader is very intelligent regarding both worldly and religious affairs."
>
> The Westerners [from Kyidrong] also said, "We'll do it like this," and everyone having agreed, they returned home joyously.[41]

One person who was decidedly not joyous about this arrangement was Sera Khandro. Not only was her future looking miserable, but also around the turn of the twentieth century a smallpox epidemic raged through Lhasa. Tsybikoff mentions that in 1900 more than 10 percent of the Lhasa population and that of the neighboring monasteries died of smallpox.[42] Waddell reports that in 1904 he discussed the great smallpox epidemic of 1900 with physicians at the Chakpori Medical School in Lhasa; they told him that even the Thirteenth Dalai Lama had nearly died from the disease, which left characteristic pockmarks on his face.[43] Sera Khandro writes that on account of receiving some instructions in her visions, she was able to cure people sick with smallpox by reciting mantras, blowing on them, and giving them blessed water. Even her father was impressed by her healing powers:

> One day Father asked, "People are saying that you are giving blessed water to smallpox victims. Who taught you to do this? Tell me honestly and I will allow you to become a nun."
>
> Since he was my father, it wasn't acceptable to lie, but I wondered if I could tell him the truth. Unable to bear him asking me again, I replied, "Father, sir, since I don't know anything but Chinese characters and I have never trained in mantra, I recited whatever I remembered and blew on water. I gave it to the sick people and they were cured."
>
> Father said, "You speak and I will write."
>
> I answered, "All right," and without hiding or keeping anything secret, I told him the actual mantras and everything that I knew.
>
> He said, "This is amazing! From among the *One Hundred Treasure Revealers* that have come before, like the one named Jipa Treasure revealer[44] who benefited beings only by [revealing] a collection of mantras and was called 'one who takes out Treasures,' you are one who reveals mantra Treasures!"[45]

Although her father's faith in her spiritual insight was deepening, it was put to the test during her eleventh year. A minister named Sonam Tendar arrived from the Kyidrong leader's household to whom she was betrothed bearing many precious gifts, including silver and gold. Sera Khandro's father recanted his agreement to give her to them, saying that it seemed as if she was not meant to be a laywoman, but the minister demanded that he keep his previous word. Just as Yeshé Tsogyel's suitors threatened violence if she did not marry them, the Kyidrong minister threatened war if Sera Khandro's father did not keep his promise. After consulting with his ministers, Jampa Gönpo acquiesced and accepted all the gifts, thus sealing Sera Khandro's fate. Feeling that her father did not care about her and knowing that she could not escape marriage without causing people to be killed, Sera Khandro decided to commit suicide by drinking a mixture of opium and alcohol. Before the toxic blend took effect, her father realized what she had done and poured an entire bowl of seed oil into her mouth via a straw, causing her to regurgitate the poison. Shortly after this, she had another near-death experience of a different sort, akin to the stories told by *delok*, or those who "return from the dead" to warn the living about the terrible consequences that await those who commit misdeeds. Sera Khandro told her parents about her *delok* experience, in which she wandered through the lower realms and saw the suffering taking place there. She brought tears to their eyes and inspired her father to write down everything she reported.

During this turbulent period of her life between girlhood and womanhood, Sera Khandro experienced many extraordinary visions. One such vision occurred in 1903 when she and her family were visiting Drepung Monastery to watch a Tibetan opera near Drepung's Takrong residence hall, where her older brother Geshé Lodrö lived as a monk. That night, she had an elaborate dream vision in which Vajrayoginī transformed into the Indian *siddha* Saraha and gave her empowerments and profound teachings on channel and wind (*rtsa rlung*) practices and on perfection stage (*rdzogs rim*) meditation. She notes that even though she practiced the teachings Saraha taught her, she became ill due to her father's lack of concern for her. Her father responded to her duress by delaying her wedding date until she was fifteen. Yet her sickness remained until she had another dream vision, in which the Tibetan master Tāranātha (1575–1634) gave her an even more detailed teaching on channel and wind practices.

In 1904, when Sera Khandro was twelve, her beloved mother passed away. Just as she was seared by grief and mired in depression, a life-changing vision came to her: Vajravārāhī appeared and empowered her in the two cycles of Treasure teachings that she would spend her life revealing, *The Secret Treasury of Reality Ḍākinīs* and *The Ḍākinīs' Heart Essence.*[46] This was the clearest indication the young Sera Khandro had received that her life would be spent not fulfilling her family's secular wishes but rather devoting herself to her spiritual purpose of revealing Treasures.

This destiny was further confirmed when, at thirteen, she visited Changdrong Druptop Rinpoché again, who secretly advised her:

> The meaning of the *ḍākinī* prophecy indicating that you need to go to the sun's eastern direction is that on account of the karmic residue from your former aspirations, your disciples reside in eastern Tibet. Since the time has come to go there, not listening to what your relatives, countrymen, and so forth say, think about this: if you accomplish the *ḍākinī*'s command, there will be excellent benefit for this life and the next.[47]

The lama's advice and the *ḍākinī* visions motivated Sera Khandro to take decisive action about the course of her future. Only one year after her mother died, her father remarried. She took this as an opportunity to ask him for permission to stay at the home of her brother Pünsumtsok Chömpel. Her secret reason for this move was that her brother's house had only three stories, as opposed to her father's four-story home—it would be an easier place from which to escape.

The next chapter of her life began when, at the age of fourteen, she spied some pilgrims from eastern Tibet arriving at her brother's house to request temporary shelter. Watching from an upper-floor window along with her sister-in-law Drönkar, Sera Khandro surveyed the guests. As soon as she saw a long-haired lama whom she later came to know was Drimé Özer, she felt a thrill and realized he was an incarnation of the famous Nyingma polymath Longchen Rapjampa (1308–1363). Tears welled up in her eyes, the hair on her body stood on end, and she prayed, "Have compassion on me—in all my lifetimes may I never separate from you."[48] Drönkar doubted the sincerity of Sera Khandro's emotional outburst, teasing her by saying that her "religious devotion" toward this lama was really lustful infatuation. Nevertheless, Druptop Rinpoché confirmed that her opportunity to escape and dedicate herself to the religious life had indeed arrived. In one month, the New Year celebration of 1907 would usher in her fifteenth year and with it her impending marriage, so she prepared to depart. As if her father could sense her plans, Jampa Gönpo experienced dreams and premonitions that he would not see his young daughter again. Knowing this to be true, Sera Khandro returned to his estate for a final visit, during which he lamented that they were soon to part and treated her affectionately, giving her sweets, dates, grapes, and peaches.

The signs that she was meant to follow Drimé Özer and his entourage from Golok only intensified until the moment for her to escape from her brother's house arrived. Reminiscent of the Buddha's palace departure while his entertainers slept in a drunken stupor, Sera Khandro narrates that she orchestrated the conditions for her departure by secretly buying beer for her two maidservants and sending them drunk off to bed in the hallway outside her door. She then removed all her head ornaments and donned a new servant's cloak over her brocade dress. Taking nothing with her save her father's gifts of sweets and fruits stashed in her pocket, she broke the window in her room and slowly began to climb down the wall from the third story. By reciting, "Venerable Tārā, think of me!" and holding her breath, she was able to scale the wall and exit the estate compound without drawing the attention of the guard stationed at the main gate. She writes that demons of all sorts terrified her on the road, but when she recalled their illusory nature, they disappeared and she was able to make haste "as fast as a wild horse."[49] By the following morning, she had caught up with Drimé Özer's group in the upper regions of Tölung Valley near Tsurpu Monastery (see map 1).

GREATER GOLOK IN THE EARLY TWENTIETH CENTURY

When Sera Khandro left her family behind in Lhasa, she also left behind the people, wealth, food, clothing, and lifestyle she had known and struggled to make her way in a society radically different from her own. The few snacks she carried and the refined Lhasa clothing she wore quickly proved insufficient for the rigors of life as a religious pilgrim. Not finding any food or drink for many days, she drank river water. Soon she came upon a large plain where she caught her very first glimpse of a nomad's tent made of black woven yak wool, which would have resembled figure 1.2 below (of course without the solar panel and motorcycle). Mistaking the tent for a wild yak, she didn't dare approach it until evening, when she saw the nomads returning to the tent driving their horses, yak, and sheep. She begged them for food, but because she didn't have a bag in which to put the *tsampa* (roasted barley flour) they gave her, she put it in her shoe. They laughed at her, calling her a "crazy woman." Only an old woman from the tent understood that she was just a new beggar. Giving

FIG. 1.2 Contemporary nomad tent made of yak hair in Golok

PHOTOGRAPH BY SARAH JACOBY, 2005

her a proper food bag, she spoke these prophetic words: "Hey! Beautiful girl, you may be able to get free from the mouths of dogs, but with that figure it will be difficult for you to free yourself from being underneath men."[50] Despite their charity, Sera Khandro could not stomach the poor-quality *tsampa* they had given her. After a while she was able to beg for a kettle from an old woman from Penpo. But then she had to ask for instructions on how to use it. The old woman told her, "Put the clay pot on three rocks, pour water in, put some tea in, light a fire, and the tea will boil."[51] She tried to follow her advice, but because she had only ever smelled the aroma of sandalwood incense, the wood fire smoke stung her eyes so badly she felt she was going blind. Her nights were tormented by the wind chill, and as a result of overexposure, painful bloody sores erupted all over her body, which then itched intensely as they healed.

It is not surprising that Sera Khandro faced difficulties adjusting to her new life, given that the hardy pilgrims with whom she found herself came from a land distant from Lhasa in many senses (see map 1 for a depiction of her journey from Lhasa to Golok and map 2 for the location of Golok and Serta). Golok lies more than 600 miles northeast of Lhasa, and in the best of circumstances was an arduous multimonth journey on horse or foot. Golok is today known as the Golok Tibetan Autonomous Prefecture and is situated in the southeastern region of Qinghai Province, just north of Sichuan Province. Covering about 30,000 square miles, it is about the size of the Czech Republic, although in earlier periods it totaled about 40,000 square miles, closer to the size of Iceland.[52] Prior to its incorporation into the People's Republic of China in 1954, Golok was not a monolithic polity but rather a confederation containing three main parts (*mgo log khag gsum*), Akyong Bum, Wangchen Bum, and Pema Bum, each of which contained many subdivisions.[53] Just south of tripartite Golok was Serta, a confederation ruled by the Washül family, to which Drimé Özer and his group of traveling pilgrims belonged. Today Serta is a county in the Kandzé Tibetan Autonomous Prefecture that comprises the northwest tip of Sichuan Province. Serta and Golok were distinct regions run by different leadership, but I refer to both as part of a greater Golok cultural region because of the linguistic, genealogical, religious, and cultural ties between the two; Sera Khandro traveled without mention of any political hindrances back and forth from Washül Serta-controlled territory to Golok.[54] It is no wonder that she suffered from overexposure during her journey eastward, since the altitude in the greater Golok region averages above 13,000 feet and the low temperatures reach well below zero degrees Fahrenheit. This harsh and tumultuous climate, where sun and rainbows regularly give way to golf-ball size hailstorms within minutes, consists primarily of rolling grasslands punctuated by high ridges and snow-covered mountains, the most famous of which is Anyé Machen, with an altitude of over 20,000 feet. These alpine grasslands were by and large inhospitable to agriculture aside from about 22 square miles in southwestern Golok and a similar segment of lower Serta where farmers grew wheat, barley, peas, mustard, turnips, and radishes.[55] Elsewhere animal husbandry was the main livelihood. Herders of yaks, horses, and sheep lived as nomads in tents much like the first one Sera Khandro encountered, so they could migrate seasonally to the appropriate pasturelands, higher grasslands in the summer and lower, more sheltered areas in the winter.

In addition to the topographic distance that separated the urban, upper-class, estate-dwelling Sera Khandro from Drimé Özer's group of rugged nomadic renunciants were vast cultural differences. Although they all spoke Tibetan, Sera Khandro's Lhasa dialect and the Goloks' strong nomadic dialect were at least initially mutually unintelligible. Sera Khandro records that when she caught up with Drimé Özer's group at Tsurpu,

> Everybody spoke, but I didn't understand what they said. Even though I spoke to them, they didn't understand me. I thought, "Their bodies are human but they wear leather for clothes and when they speak, they seem like savage barbarians. It will be difficult for that which is called 'the Great Perfection' to flourish in their land."[56]

Sera Khandro was hardly the first to call the people from Golok barbaric. Nearly all outsiders who crossed their path reported some version of this sentiment. In the words of the Austrian botanist Joseph Rock (1884–1962), who visited Golok in 1926:

> They [Golok people] acknowledge no one's authority except that of their chiefs. . . . They enjoy attacking anyone, especially foreigners who penetrate their mountain fastness. . . . Their life is spent on horseback, always ready for battle and even among themselves they squabble to the point of combat.
>
> They are a marauding fraternity, going often six hundred strong on robbing expeditions, making the caravan roads west of the Am-nye Machhen unsafe. . . . They bring terror to the hearts of all their neighbors and travelers.[57]

Golok also elicited tales of violence and banditry from their most powerful neighbors. In the early twentieth century, these included the Thirteenth Dalai Lama's Tibetan government to the west and the Ma family of Chinese Muslim warlords to the east, rulers of much of the area that became Qinghai Province in 1929. Tibetans and Chinese Muslims purportedly claimed:

> The Golok make nothing of robbery and murder, although they constantly pray to the Three Holy Ones. . . . The Golok are all robbers. Their chief weapon used to be the long Golok lance, "Golok dung-ring," which was six feet in length, its shaft bound round with wire to turn the edge of a sword, and decked with a piece of red cloth near the blade; but nowadays [the 1920s] they have plenty of Russian rifles.[58]

More recently, one of Golok's Tibetan neighbors reported:

> The region [of Golok] was inhabited by some of the most aggressive and least accessible people in pre-modern Tibet. . . . "Golok" (Tibetan *mgo log*) means something like "turncoat" or "rebel." Golok functioned as something of a haven for miscreants, malcontents, refugees and even perhaps criminals.[59]

The people of Golok also promoted an image of themselves as dangerous and independent warriors.[60] They presented themselves as people who had managed to maintain their political autonomy for centuries, resisting inclusion in the Dalai Lama's Tibetan government in Lhasa or in China, under Qing dynasty rule until 1911 or the Republic of China. In 1908 the Russian explorer P. K. Kozloff quoted a person from Golok saying,

> "You cannot compare us N'goloks with other people. You"—to whatever Tibetan they may be addressing—"obey the laws of strangers, the laws of the Dalai Lama, of China, and of any of your petty chiefs. . . . We N'goloks, on the other hand, have from time immemorial obeyed none but our own laws, none but our own convictions. . . . This is why we have ever been free as now, and are the slaves of none—neither of Bogdokhan, nor of the Dalai-Lama. Our tribe is the most respected and mighty in Tibet, and we rightly look down with contempt on both Chinaman and Tibetan."[61]

More recent local histories from greater Golok echo this sentiment, showing pride in their independence and military prowess prior to their incorporation into the PRC. In the *Annals of Golok History* written in the 1990s, Döndrup Wangyel and Nordé state:

> The most important [feature of our history] is that for the duration of the 600-odd years between the Golok people's arrival in this land until the new country was founded [the PRC], we have been different from other races and all other communities within our own race from Amdo, central Tibet, and Kham in that no matter which of the three—China, Mongolia, or Tibet—held power at a given time, they were not really able to subjugate and control us.[62]

A local history of the Serta region written in the 1980s, based on earlier sources, expresses a similar claim:

> The leader of the Washül confederation said, "My Washül Serta has never had to pay a tribute of gold to golden-headed ones and never had to pay a tribute of tea to the black Chinese people.[63] We have maintained control over each and every gold coin of ours." . . . Even though Washül Serta is located between Tibet, Sichuan, and Qinghai, it was never controlled by central Tibet, never controlled by Ma Bufang's Qinghai, nor was it ever controlled by the regions of Kham such as Drakgo, Kandzé, and Nyarong. . . . Sertar never came under the control of China or central Tibet because [its people] rioted and rebelled in every way.[64]

Though claims like this boast a hyperbolic flair, they are not without truth. Given the Goloks' penchant for banditry and marauding, their territory was notoriously difficult for outsiders to approach, let alone conquer, which often made travel on the nearby caravan route from Xining to Jyekundo dangerous. *The Annals of Golok History* understands the Goloks' military success to derive in part from their nomadic lifestyle; they were permanently on the move, traveling with their livestock instead of maintaining stable residences in need of defense. Geography and climate were also in their favor. Winter brought snows that completely obstructed routes into their terrain, and by autumn their very fast horses were strengthened by nutritious summer grasses. Invaders' horses could not successfully pursue because they were exhausted after their long march into Golok. Even if some Golok subdivisions could be subjugated during the spring and summer, since they were a race of "savages" (*dmu rgod*), according to the *Annals*, there would be no common language with which to communicate with them.[65] As the Tibetan anthropologist Gelek notes, Chinese sources also referred to people from Serta as "wild barbarians" (Chin. *ye fan*) and their land as "the region beyond the boundaries" (Chin. *hua wai zhi yu*).[66] Similarly, the etymology of the term Sera Khandro chose in the passage quoted above to refer to people from Serta (*mtha' 'khob pa kla klo*), which I translated as "savage barbarian," refers to their status as "uncivilized" (*kla klo*) and as "people from the border region" (*mtha' 'khob pa*). We can deduce from these choices of terms used by Sera Khandro and others from their most powerful neighboring regions that large parts of greater Golok did successfully maintain their status as areas "beyond the borders" of central Tibet and China. Golok was never a monolithic political entity—eyewitness accounts demonstrate that at least a few subdivisions did choose to submit to the Dalai Lama's Tibetan government, and more still were forced to submit at different times to the Mongols, Manchu Qing, and later Chinese Muslim Ma warlords.[67] Nevertheless, it is fair to call greater Golok in the early twentieth century a region inhabited by independent confederations. These groups fought hard both within and outside their ranks to maintain their autonomy, and they succeeded until the Communist Party established the People's Republic of China government on the Golok grasslands on January 1, 1954.[68] Although Sera Khandro did not live to see it, harbingers of this seismic shift reached her as early as 1936, when her religious communities had to flee repeatedly to avoid confrontations with the Communist "red army" that marched through Pema and Chiktril counties.

HARD ENTRY INTO GOLOK

Given the levels of violence, defiance, and autonomy embedded in the history of Golok, one might expect that a lone outsider from central Tibet would not have received a warm welcome. Indeed, despite the religious affinity Sera Khandro shared with Drimé Özer's cohort of traveling pilgrims, they initially reacted to her presence with a combination of surprise, disdain, concern, and pity. The first one to spot her was a nun named Jikdrön, who said, "You, crazy girl, why did you come after us? Without food or clothes, won't you die of starvation and the cold wind?"[69] But this did not dissuade Sera Khandro. When the fifteen-year-old finally appeared in front of the entire group of pilgrims in 1907, right away two of its members named Jiksam and Penchen, from the Tashül subdivision of the Washül Serta region in which Drimé Özer and his group belonged, protested, telling her that she was not allowed to join them. They threatened her, saying, "Shouldn't I make you a shooting target?"[70] Although she assured them that she would not cause any harm, they wouldn't listen and insulted her. Even the man named Drongwasang who was translating the conversation between Jiksam and Penchen's Golok Tibetan and Sera Khandro's Lhasa Tibetan discouraged her. After a while, Sera Khandro became angry and retorted, "Both the Tashül men Penchen and Jiksam can make me a shooting target until I am a corpse, but I have decided that I will not return to my homeland."[71] At that, Drimé Özer himself joined the fray, telling Sera Khandro,

> Now go back to your homeland. Your family won't punish you because I'll send a letter with Ömbar. Since we are connected by commitment vows (*dam tshig*), it will be okay. With that, he gave me a scarf, sacred substances, and a protection cord.

I said,

> Very well, how could I dare to go against Rinpoché's command? My motive [for coming here] was that I wondered if I could accomplish the authentic holy Dharma. For this, I am casting my own land behind me and focusing my aspirations on another land. Not thinking of my father, brother, or all of our wealth, I entrust myself to you as my lama and to the Three Jewels and am traveling to unknown places. If this is not necessary and if it is possible to live as a householder and attain the stage of a non-returner,[72] then you don't need to escort me. I can return home alone.

I sent the scarf back to him, tied the protection cord around my neck, and lay on the ground. The Master [Drimé Özer] responded,

> The reason I told you to go back is that our central Tibetan friends will say, "It seems you brought this central Tibetan girl with you. What's the use of letting her freeze and starve to death?" and they will not allow you to stay with me. That is why I told you to go. That said, how can one both live as a householder and accomplish the authentic Dharma? Therefore, do what you want to do.[73]

By getting Drimé Özer to admit that householder life in Lhasa could not lead her to buddhahood, Sera Khandro skillfully persuaded him to permit her to join his religious community, for he could not fault her for seeking the authentic Dharma. After that a few members of the group looked after her, pouring her hot tea and lending her some clothes, but most avoided her. Sera Khandro records that "Although there were more than thirty groups [of people among the pilgrims], they were suspicious of me as if I were a leper, saying that it was unacceptable for me to meet even one of them."[74]

As they progressed toward eastern Tibet, the Goloks' predictions that Sera Khandro would freeze and starve nearly came true during the fourth and fifth Tibetan month of 1907, when they failed to find nomads from whom to beg for food as they traveled eastward on the northern route. Without his disciples seeing him do it, Drimé Özer gave Sera Khandro medicine for her wounds and some food and drink. He had to be secretive because his disciples were talking about how his consort, Akyongza, would be displeased by the presence of Sera Khandro, or as they called her, Ümo, "the girl from central Tibet." Her auto/biographical writings give little information about Akyongza. That said, the consort's name, which literally means "the lady from Akyong," suggests that she was from a powerful family in Akyong Bum, one of the three major parts of Golok. Sera Khandro's writings make it clear that Akyongza's opinion was important for many affiliated with Drimé Özer. Although she hesitated to stay near him on account of this, nevertheless signs appeared on their journey that not only were the two meant to be disciple and guru but also she would become his consort.

Meanwhile her own identity as a Treasure revealer began to emerge, a role Sera Khandro attributed to no other woman she knew in either Lhasa or greater Golok. When the pilgrims finally reached the town of Jyekundo, they spent a few days at the Gyanak Maṇi, or "Chinese Maṇi," which was (and remains today) a huge collection of prayer-inscribed stones (see map 1). There they circumambulated, prostrated, and made offerings of turquoise and coral to the stone carvers before setting off again to beg for provisions. Sera Khandro records that before they left a man approached her, saying, "You are a miraculous emanation of a sky-coursing woman (*mkha' spyod ma*). I had a greatly amazing dream [about you]."[75] He offered her supplies for her journey and agreed to write down a few scriptures that had come to her as visionary revelations. He was delighted to receive her teachings and escorted her on horseback for three days. Despite these early glimpses of the recognition she would later receive for her visionary expertise and her status as a *khandroma* (Skt. *ḍākinī*), she was still far from being accepted by Drimé Özer's community. At length the group arrived at Dzagyel Monastery (see map 1) in the nomadic grassland area of Sershül, just west of Serta, for the enthronement ceremony of Drimé Özer's brother Namkha Jikmé, who had been recognized as the incarnation of Patrül Orgyen Jikmé Chökyi Wangpo (1808–1887).[76] While the entire group was fed and feted for many days, Sera Khandro and another "beggar woman" named Chödrön were excluded from the festivities.

After more than eight months journeying across Tibet, the pilgrims finally arrived near Drimé Özer's residence in Dartsang, then a part of the grasslands belonging to the Tashül subdivision of the Washül Serta confederation. Today Dartsang is located in Serta County, Sichuan, forty-two miles north of the Serta county seat and less than six miles away from the Sichuan-Qinghai border, the other side of which is Pema County, Golok Tibetan Autonomous Prefecture. The main monastery in Dartsang,

FIG. 1.3 Kelzang Monastery in Dartsang, Serta

PHOTOGRAPH BY SARAH JACOBY, 2004

called Kelzang, was founded by Yungshül Sungchok Dorjé in 1871 as a branch monastery of Taktsé Monastery (est. 1769), also in Serta. Taktsé in turn is a branch of Katok Monastery (est. 1159), a large and centrally important Nyingma monastery in Kham. Local histories of Dartsang record that Drimé Özer's family became connected to Kelzang Monastery when Yungshül Sungchok Dorjé and Tashül Tsedrupkyap invited Drimé Özer's father, Düjom Lingpa, to be the abbot. In his autobiography, Düjom Lingpa records assuming this position when he was fifty-five, in approximately 1890.[77] During the last decade of the nineteenth century until his death, Düjom Lingpa galvanized Kelzang into a flourishing religious institution by building a new temple to house the complete Buddhist scriptures (the Kangyur and Tengyur) and by giving expansive teachings on his more than twenty volumes of Treasure revelation scriptures. His fame spread not only among the monastery's parishioners (*lha sde*) in the upper Tashül region but also across the three parts of Golok.[78] Düjom Lingpa's renown stretched forward into our own time via his reincarnation, Düjom Jikdrel Yeshé Dorjé (1904–1987), whose religious centers and disciples ring the globe.

Düjom Lingpa had passed away only a few years before Sera Khandro arrived in Dartsang. But there she encountered several of his eight sons, who had been recognized as important reincarnations and were propagating their father's lineage as well as producing their own revelations. Prominent among them was Düjom Lingpa's oldest son, who became the third Dodrup Rinpoché Jikmé Tenpé Nyima (1865–1926) of Dodrupchen Monastery in Golok. Drimé Özer, who was about sixteen years his junior, spent part of his childhood studying at Dodrupchen under the tutelage of his elder brother before returning to Dartsang to be closer to their father. At Dartsang she also met Drimé Özer's younger brothers Lhachen Topgyel (n.d.) and Dorjé Drandül (a.k.a. Sangdak Mingyur Dorjé, 1891–1959). The latter established his own community in Dartsang in the early twentieth century called Lungshar Gar, which along with Kelzang Monastery is still active today.

Sera Khandro's delight at finally reaching her destination soon gave way to sadness as relatives of all her fellow pilgrims came to welcome them, including Drimé Özer's family. As each traveler filed off home, Sera Khandro found herself with no welcome and nowhere to go. This was the first of many such experiences in her life in eastern Tibet, where she was homeless in the literal sense of the word, although she never renounced householder life in the sense of taking monastic vows. As she wondered where to stay, a man named Akhu Darlo came and offered her a room to rent in the lower part of the lamas' residence (*bla brang*) where Drimé Özer and his family lived. Her stay there proved short because the caretaker of the residence was partial to Drimé Özer's consort, Akyongza, and demanded that Sera Khandro leave.

Sera Khandro was saved by another of Drimé Özer's close disciples named Ömbar. He mediated the situation by suggesting that she work as a maidservant in a nearby nomadic household in exchange for provisions to tide her over during the upcoming winter's religious teachings. Convinced that Akyongza would berate her if she stayed at Drimé Özer's residence, she agreed to this plan. Sera Khandro writes that once she arrived, "Since it was a Golok household, at first I didn't understand their language and because I didn't know how to do the work properly, I experienced great hardship."[79] Only gradually did she become familiar with their way of speaking and with the work involved in maintaining a nomadic household. After a little over a month, it became time to request the winter teachings. Sera Khandro set out with a nun named Tsüldrön, but because Akyongza was present at Drimé Özer's residence, she didn't dare approach. Instead she sent a message via Ömbar asking what religious teachings she should request. Drimé Özer responded with the following advice:

> First, since the source of all Dharma is the preliminary practices, request these teachings and thoroughly complete the five [sets of] 100,000 and so forth.[80] Then, gradually you will receive teachings on *Refining One's Perception* (*snang sbyang*) and Direct Transcendence (*thod rgal*).[81]

That year Sera Khandro took his instructions to heart. From Akyap Trülku, she received teachings on channel and wind practices (*rtsa rlung*). Drimé Özer himself gave her instructions on Düjom Lingpa's *Refining One's Perception* (*snang sbyang*)[82] as well as on Direct Transcendence (*thod rgal*) and Severance (*gcod*). Sera Khandro would later write her own commentary on *Refining One's Perception*, which she presented as a transcription of the teaching Drimé Özer had given her, with her own clarifications.[83] She also received teachings from Drimé Özer's younger brother Lhachen Topgyel on preliminary practices, which she memorized in full. During those first winter teachings, each morning and afternoon she attended a teaching session with Lhachen Topgyel. At night she slept only a few hours. At all other times, she continually prostrated, persevering through snow and icy wind to complete some 6,000 prostrations per day. By the seventeenth day, she had completed the required 100,000 prostrations. Others who requested preliminary practices along with Sera Khandro, including Tashül Penchen, teased her constantly about her dedication:

> While I was prostrating, they said, "The central Tibetan girl doesn't know the difference between heat and cold—she is like a yak!" They gathered grass from inside their shoes[84] and rotten grass from the side of the monastery and said, "Let's see if it will stick on her back!" Some people pressed it down on the top of my head with the sole of their shoe. Some put it in front of me and said, "Put this in your mouth!" Also some people said that I had no sense of clean or dirty like a dog. Picking up human and dog excrement with a spoon, they put it in front of me and on my head and so forth.[85]

Even the more seasoned Dharma practitioners who witnessed this laughed and allowed the teasing to continue. Sera Khandro was determined not to retaliate. Instead she reminded herself not to mix prostrations with anger and to think of her tormenters as "Dharma siblings," or disciples who have requested teachings from the same lama. Eventually a nun named Yeshé Drön chastised those who were teasing her, threatening to report them to Drimé Özer. Subsequently, the novices moved on to learn how to practice "transference of consciousness" (*'pho ba*), a technique of ejecting the consciousness of oneself or another person who has just died out of the top of the head in order to propel her toward liberation or a positive rebirth. As the winter teachings came to an end, all the disciples gathered in the assembly hall at the lama's residence for a feast offering ritual. Sera Khandro attended as well, but she sat at the end of the row of practitioners and recited prayers instead of the feast offering liturgy because unlike the others, she did not know how to read. When the disciplinarian—the monk who oversees the behavior of the disciples—saw her sitting there, he ordered her to leave despite her dedication to practicing the teachings she had received. "You are a beggar woman," she recalled him saying. "Get out—you cannot stay in the assembly hall."[86] Sera Khandro describes falling into a depression at this point. But just then the powerful *ḍākinī* and Tantric meditation deity Vajravārāhī, who had bestowed Treasure teachings upon Sera Khandro when she was twelve, reappeared in a vision. Vajravārāhī encouraged her, promising that despite the difficulties that had befallen her since leaving Lhasa, in the end she would achieve her life's purpose of revealing Treasures and accomplishing the Buddhist teachings.

Sera Khandro feared the following winter's chill, worrying that her clothes would not be warm enough. She returned to work at the same Golok household in her sixteenth year, hoping that she could earn a fur coat as payment. This time she excelled at the housework and livestock herding, so much so that her employers asked her to marry one of their sons. As this ran counter to Sera Khandro's plans to dedicate her life to religious practice, she sought a way to extricate herself. She heard that a lama named Dza Mura Trülku would be giving teachings at an encampment in the Kharnang Gongma area of Golok and decided to go there (see map 2). Kharnang was one of the eight principalities (*dpon khag*) of Pema Bum, one of the three main parts of Golok, today located in Pema County, Qinghai. When the teachings were over, she returned to her employers' household, but she was unhappy there and soon bade them farewell. They did not forget their promise: in return for her work, they gave her a fur coat, but one of only middling quality.

FIG. 1.4 Benak Monastery in Pema County, Golok

PHOTOGRAPH BY SARAH JACOBY, 2004

LIFE AT BENAK MONASTERY

At this moment of flux in Sera Khandro's life, her future was transformed by a letter: a prominent Treasure revealer named Gara Terchen Pema Dündül Wangchuk Lingpa (1857–1910) sent a letter to a lama named Tongpön Mönlam Gyatso[87] indicating that she was Gara Terchen's prophesied consort and requesting her presence. Sera Khandro records that she had received similar prophecies indicating that Gara Terchen would be important in her life. She wanted to go see him at his monastery named Benak (alt. Benyak, Penak), on the banks of the Mar River, today a few miles outside Selitang in Pema County. Benak lies within the more temperate, lower-altitude region of Golok that is rich with arable land, although the monastery was still quite high at 11,922 feet. Pema has a long history; 45 sites dating to the Bronze Age are located in the county, and farming has been established there for at least 900 years.[88] Pema is also home to Golok's oldest monasteries, although Benak was much more recent—it was established in 1824 by Pema Drondül Dorjé, and Gara Terchen was the fourth abbot.[89] Its religious affiliation was Nyingma, with a specific connection to Pelyül Monastery (est. 1665), a leading religious center in the Degé region of Kham.

Sera Khandro wanted to respond to Gara Terchen's summons right away, but obstacles and ill omens prevented her. Central among these hindrances was Gara Terchen's consort (*yum*), Yakshülza—whose name indicates that she was a "lady from Yakshül," which was a subdivision of the Washül Serta confederation. Yakshülza (or Yakza for short) sent Sera Khandro several increasingly wrathful warnings not to come anywhere near her or the ailing Gara Terchen. He had requested Sera Khandro's presence because he intuited that she was a *khandroma* with the power to cure his illness and prolong his life. Yakza, however, had no interest in hosting the young and attractive girl. Messages went back and forth between Sera Khandro, Gara Terchen, his consort, and various intermediaries trying to settle the disagreement. Finally in 1910, when Sera Khandro was eighteen, she set out for Benak Monastery in response to another urgent call from Gara Terchen, traveling with an old woman named Chökyi. The two perceived various foreboding signs on the road. They finally arrived at Benak only to be prevented by Yakza from visiting Gara Terchen, who by that time was on his deathbed. At the very last moment, Yakza relented. But it was too late—Gara Terchen passed away in front of Sera Khandro.

Gara Terchen's death, however, did not bring an end to the connection between them. Sera Khandro recounts that Gara Terchen appeared to her in a vision and empowered her to practice and disseminate his cycles of revelations. This visionary encounter transformed her status among some of his close disciples. Even the way people spoke to her changed overnight: "from that time forward, everyone near and far forgot my name and called me '*khandroma*.'"[90] Shortly after this she attended a ritual in Kharnang performed by a lama named Khangdong Wönpo Gönwang. Once the ceremony was over, the lama delivered the following prophecy to Sera Khandro, reiterating her special status as a *ḍākinī* with the additional directive that she should go live with the son of Gara Terchen named Gara Gyelsé:[91]

> You are a pillar—you are extraordinary. Whichever outer, inner, and secret characteristics I examine, you are certainly of *ḍākinī* heritage. In particular, you are an authentic emanation of the Tibetan Lady Yeshé Tsogyel. Now, go to Benyak and live temporarily with Gara Gyelsé. If you do not help take

care of the Great Treasure Revealer Longyang's [i.e., Gara Terchen's] Treasure teachings, the lama's teachings will completely disappear—the religious texts will get put into a clay statue house and thieves will buy and sell all the Treasure substances as talismans.[92]

At first Sera Khandro was not enthusiastic about this new arrangement: "Although I didn't want to go," she wrote, "I could not find a way to go against the orders of a lama from whom I had received an empowerment, so I promised to go there."[93] But still she did not rush to carry out his command. Only when a member of the Gara family came to see her and urged her to return with him did she venture forth. Even then, Sera Khandro explains that she did it only to comply with Khangdong Gönwang's command.

She had just turned nineteen when she returned to Benak. Initially, her prospects appeared bright. Everyone said that a *ḍākinī* had arrived and asked her to perform divinations and give prophecies. People gave her butter, cheese, barley, sheepskins, and other gifts; suddenly she was no longer deprived of food or clothes. She was able to cure the sick by giving them medicinal pills, and once they had been healed, those patients in turn became her sponsors. But she also had her detractors, and leading them all was Yakza. To Yakza and her friends, Sera Khandro was not a *ḍākinī* but a demoness whom Drimé Özer had expelled from his religious community. Yakza rejected the idea that Gara Terchen had received prophecies about Sera Khandro. She doubted her claim to be illiterate, insinuating that she had made up the revelations that she said she received through visions and in meditation.[94] Her ability to cure the sick, they suggested, was a form of magic stemming from her knowledge of various occult mantras.

Gyelsé was not among her detractors when Sera Khandro first arrived. He welcomed her into his circle, bringing her along with him on a pilgrimage to Anyé Machen, where she had visionary encounters with some of the region's most important mountain deities. But life with Gyelsé quickly proved difficult. She asked him to give her Great Perfection teachings, but he belittled her understanding, claiming that she was someone who knew nothing about the nature of mind and had only completed the preliminary practices according to Patrül Rinpoché's *Künzang Lamé Zhelung, The Words of My Perfect Teacher*. When she asked for clarifications about a verse spoken by the great eighteenth-century Treasure revealer Rindzin

Jikmé Lingpa, instead of explaining it, Gyelsé replied that she knew nothing about Jikmé Lingpa's realization. This remark seems to have been a turning point: afterward, although Sera Khandro lived with Gyelsé for another eight years, she never dared to ask him for a word of instruction.[95]

Because of Yakza's wrath, from the start life at Benak Monastery was filled with tension for Sera Khandro, and it only worsened with time. When the moment came for Gara Terchen's 's two sons and Yakza to divide the Treasure scriptures and objects that he had left behind, they squabbled about who should get what. After arguing with his family over his inheritance, Gyelsé came alone to the retreat house above the monastery where Sera Khandro was staying and stated that he needed to live there with her. She sensed that the time had come to actualize Khangdong Gönwang's prophecy. In 1912, when she was twenty years old, Sera Khandro gave him the following ultimatum:

> If I am allowed to take care of the precious lama's Treasure teachings and Treasure substances, you may live with me. If I am not allowed to do this, then you cannot live with me. Like the proverb "Being near a dog is being near a wound," [living with me without the Treasure teachings] will lead to unnecessary activity.[96]

Gyelsé protested, pointing out that all the religious objects and texts were in his family's residence, where Sera Khandro's nemesis, Yakza, lived. Sera Khandro insisted, urging him to find a way to remove them one by one. At last Gyelsé managed to make off with his father's entire collection of scriptures and sacred objects. Sera Khandro then settled down with Gyelsé, whom she describes as her "life partner" (*tshe grogs*) or spouse, although she does not write of any particular marriage ceremony.

Yakza and her cohort protested when they realized that Gyelsé and Sera Khandro had taken all of Gara Terchen's Treasure teachings and substances, but the deed was done. Antagonism between Yakza and Sera Khandro grew; and now Yakza and her friends set out to expel her from the community. Sera Khandro responded by visualizing her enemies and beseeching the Dharma protectors to punish them, not unlike the sorcery found in the *Life of Milarepa*. But when undesirable things began happening to her detractors, like Milarepa she regretted her misdeed. She vowed at the risk of her life not to harm anyone again, and burned the incantation texts she had used.

FIG. 1.5 Tashi Gomang Monastery in Pema, Golok

PHOTOGRAPH BY SARAH JACOBY, 2004

In 1913 Sera Khandro traveled south from Benak about fifteen miles along the Mar River to circumambulate Tashi Gomang Monastery. Founded in 1816, Tashi Gomang was another Nyingma Pelyül branch monastery, like Benak. While there, the twenty-one-year-old Sera Khandro discovered two chests, out of which she revealed two scriptures from her Treasure cycle called *The Secret Treasury of Reality Ḍākinīs.* When she showed them to Gyelsé, he doubted that they were real. Gyelsé disapproved of several other revelations Sera Khandro produced over the next few years, causing further strain in their relationship.

Amid these tensions, Sera Khandro realized that she was pregnant. Based on her prophetic dreams, she suspected that her child was an incarnation of Gyelsé's father, Gara Terchen. She had also received prophecies indicating that her child would be harmed unless they traveled away from their home. Gyelsé dismissed her warnings and as a result,

> That year [1913] in the first month of fall when it became time to see the face of my child, I went to collect firewood near a man named Chölhün, who Gara Terchen previously said was one who adhered to demonic scriptures. Because he called out in a fierce voice and performed curses and so forth, the sex of my child was reversed and he became a girl. At that time Gyelsé felt great regret. Saying, "If this girl dies I'll be happy," he treated her really badly. Although I wasn't pleased with this, I didn't say anything.[97]

That Sera Khandro attributed the birth of a daughter to demonic intervention serves as a good indication of the prevailing opinion within her milieu regarding girls. After the child's inauspicious transformation from boy to girl, there was no more discussion of her being Gara Terchen's incarnation. Nevertheless, when Sera Khandro brought her baby to one of Gara Terchen's disciples to request a name, he announced that the infant had great merit and named her Yangchen Drönma, although Sera Khandro more commonly called her Chöying Drönma. Sera Khandro too felt that her daughter was special despite being female, noting that "Gradually as she grew up, she had many extraordinary outer, inner, and secret characteristics, but I didn't call attention to them."[98]

Gyelsé may not have encouraged Sera Khandro to reveal Treasures, but others took notice of her extraordinary religious capacities, in particular a lama named Gochen Trülku Jikdrel Chökyi Lodrö (c. 1876–1919) from Pelyül Dartang Monastery in Golok, whom Sera Khandro called Gotrül Rinpoché. In 1915 Gotrül Rinpoché recognized the twenty-three-year-old Sera Khandro as a *khandroma* and a Treasure revealer and commanded her to send some of her revelations to him in order to dispel obstacles to his longevity. Over the next several years, her connection with Gotrül Rinpoché became a ray of light in her dark days living with Gyelsé at Benak.

That same year, Gyelsé received an invitation from a lama named Hor Öchung to attend a consecration ceremony for a large prayer wheel that he had built at his religious encampment in Mardringpo (see map 2). Drimé Özer also came to the consecration and gave teachings from his father's *Tersar* or "New Treasure" teachings. During the ceremony, Sera Khandro perceived that a *ḍākinī* named Dorjé Yudrönma appeared before her and gave her a crystal Treasure chest, which she tried to conceal from the others. Drimé Özer saw the chest and demanded Sera Khandro give it to him, thereby creating an auspicious connection (*rten 'brel*) between them. After the rituals were completed, Drimé Özer and Gyelsé exchanged pleasantries and agreed to meet again shortly. When they did, they had a serious conversation that set the course for her future. Drimé Özer urged Gyelsé not to treat Sera Khandro like a servant and instead to buy her jewelry and nice clothes befitting her status as his consort (*thabs grogs*). Gyelsé replied,

> She only has a relationship with me on account of my father's former aspirations; she is not one who is prophesied for me. Perhaps she is your prophesied consort? She constantly prays to you and your father and concentrates her mind single-pointedly on you both. In particular, when she hears your name, with tears flowing uncontrollably from her eyes and the hair on her body standing on end, she prays in a loud voice and sings hymns of sadness. At least, if you do a retreat with her, perhaps obstacles pertaining to those close to you and to your longevity will be dispelled. I offer you this *ḍākinī* of mine—aside from you, she has no guardian.[99] She has a gentle disposition, a lucid intellect, and she doesn't associate with other men.[100]

Just like that, in 1915 Sera Khandro was exchanged between the two men without ever being consulted. Signs, omens, prophecies, and advice from her lamas all pointed toward the fact that life with Gyelsé was not right for Sera Khandro. Nevertheless, she resisted his unceremonious decision to give her away for as long as possible, withstanding their contentious relationship for four more years. During that time she made trips with her daughter to sacred places, including the sacred Golok mountains Anyé Machen and Nyenpo Yutsé, where she revealed Treasures. Her life with Gyelsé, however, had reached a crisis. In 1918, when she was twenty-six years old, she returned from a visit with Gotrül Rinpoché to find that

Gyelsé's residence had split into two factions and that he wanted Sera Khandro and those close to her to leave. Sera Khandro does not specify the catalyst for the factionalization of the community, but part of it was probably the growing rift between her and Gyelsé.

Sera Khandro writes that on account of this turbulence surrounding her, the child she was carrying at the time, whom she believed to be an incarnation of Gyarong Ternyön, passed away in utero. Realizing that she was about to give birth to a stillborn child, she entrusted her young daughter to her disciple Tupzang and asked him to attend to Gyelsé's needs for the day. Meanwhile, she labored in excruciating pain by herself. Finally, after intense agony and many prayers to Guru Rinpoché, she gave birth to a beautiful boy who almost looked alive. When she told Tupzang and Gyelsé that her child had died, they felt great regret and sorrowfully performed purification rituals. Others, including Gotrül Rinpoché and several of Gyelsé's disciples, sent offerings and consoled Sera Khandro for her loss.

At the same time, the faction of Gyelsé's community who hated her, chief among them Yakza, rejoiced in the face of her misery, saying,

> The central Tibetan girl's merit is exhausted and her son died. Still, what misery doesn't she give to the Golok Lady and Gyelsé? All that she says about her son dying in her abdomen and giving birth to the corpse in the breech position is certainly lies. Whenever a calf dies in a *dri*'s [female yak's] abdomen everyone can see that both mother and baby die. Her son was not a corpse in his mother's abdomen; he didn't die [in utero]. Because she didn't die, there is absolutely no way she could have gotten the baby's corpse out.[101]

Yakza and her sympathizers essentially accused Sera Khandro of infanticide because they could not believe she could have delivered a stillborn child without dying herself. From the passage above, we can also see another problem that had arisen for Sera Khandro at Benak: Gyelsé had taken on another woman, referred to as the "Golok Lady" (*mgo log bza'*) but elsewhere named Seldrön.

Meanwhile, everyone in Gyelsé's community was quarreling. Sera Khandro writes that she tried to help reconcile the disputing factions, but her efforts failed. A few months later, Sera Khandro and her group, including her daughter and her close disciple, the monk Tupzang, moved to the religious encampment of Gyelsé's brother Jikmé Könchok called Yeru (see map 2). Jikmé Könchok supported Sera Khandro's entourage and Gotrül Rinpoché provided pack horses and yak-hair tents, enabling Sera Khandro and her companions to establish themselves. They moved frequently: at one point that year they went to see Drimé Özer at his place called Naidro Dorjé Dzong in Serta. At another they went, along with Gyelsé, to see Gotrül Rinpoché at his place near Nyenpo Yutsé in Golok.

At the end of her twenty-sixth year in the winter of 1918–19, Sera Khandro had an extraordinary experience during a feast offering she attended along with her daughter, Tupzang, some other monks, Gyelsé, and his brother. She perceived a tiger-skin clad hero (*dpa' bo*) adorned with bone ornaments, his hair in a topknot, transform into the letter *haṃ* and disappear into the crown of her head. With this, her body became "uncomfortable as if she had conceived a child."[102] Although Sera Khandro describes this miraculous fetus as fatherless, she also indicates that Gotrül Rinpoché suggested that the child was his incarnation shortly before he died in the second month of 1919 of a contagious disease that swept through Pelyül Dartang Monastery. Although this is not the same as claiming paternity, it is an articulation of a type of genealogical relationship between the two beings.

As Sera Khandro's pregnancy progressed, letters arrived from Drimé Özer requesting her presence in order to dispel hindrances to the life force of his nephew, Rindzin Künzang Nyima (1904–1958). Also known as Nüden Dorjé, Künzang Nyima was the reincarnation of Drimé Özer's older brother Khyentrül. He was only a boy of about fourteen at this time, but he would later inherit the mantle of Düjom Lingpa's lineage and become a very important Treasure revealer in his own right, producing more than twenty volumes of revelations. Sera Khandro relished the chance to revitalize her connection with Drimé Özer and exchange Treasure teachings with him. At the same time she despaired at Gyelsé's treatment of her, which she summed up to her friends with the following words:

> I told them everything about how Gyelsé gave me away to the Treasure revealer's [Drimé Özer's] household during the male hare year [1915], how since I had no paternal relatives to back me up he married Seldrön and gave me domestic troubles, and how Gyelsé separated out his wealth and forbade me and my child to use any of his possessions.[103]

Not having "paternal relatives to back me up" (*rgyab pha ming med pa*) referred to the fact that Sera Khandro had no male relatives anywhere near Golok who could hold Gyelsé accountable for his mistreatment of her. Although she embodied the Buddhist ideal of wandering in unknown lands as a religious pilgrim, in the terms of secular Golok society she ranked low. The missionary and later anthropologist Robert Ekvall, who spent extended periods in the 1920s and '30s living with nomads in northeastern Tibet, observed, "The value of a stranger's life is the lowest in the community."[104] One reason was that a stranger or wanderer far from home lacked kin who could threaten retribution if he or she were injured or killed.

In spite of these disadvantages, in 1919 the twenty-seven-year-old Sera Khandro gave birth to a healthy son amid many miraculous signs. Gyelsé initially treated the infant attentively, safeguarding his health by forbidding outsiders to see the baby for many months. Even so, the child sickened, and after a year of increasingly severe illness, everyone in Gyelsé's community agreed that Sera Khandro needed to heed prophecies they had received indicating that only Drimé Özer would be able to perform healing rituals to cure the boy. For this reason, Sera Khandro returned to see Drimé Özer again at a place called Naringma when she was twenty-eight, accompanied by her two children and Tupzang. As prophesied, Drimé Özer cured Sera Khandro's infant son by performing healing rituals and gave him the name Rindzin Gyurmé Dorjé.

Sera Khandro herself also suffered from illness, a worsening arthritic condition (*'bam*) that caused her legs to swell and made it difficult for her to walk. Additionally, political turmoil erupted around her in 1921. The "northern Chinese" (*byang rgya*), as Sera Khandro called the troops commanded by the Ma family warlords based in what later became the eastern parts of Qinghai Province, were attacking greater Golok in an attempt to incorporate these territories into their jurisdiction. They fought the Goloks near Benak Monastery as well as near Dartsang in the northern reaches of Washül Serta. One positive repercussion of this external threat was that it propelled the two factions of Gyelsé's household to reconcile and to agree that Gyelsé needed to establish another seat elsewhere, away from the fighting.

While all this was going on, Gyelsé's brother Jikmé Könchok and Tupzang convinced Gyelsé to allow Sera Khandro to heed prophecies she had received indicating that she needed to go to Drong Mountain, where she revealed Treasures and had another chance to visit Drimé Özer, who was staying nearby. When she returned to the Gara family's newly reunited encampment circle (*mgar skor*), she intuited based on a *ḍākinī* prophecy that they should move to the vicinity of a sacred mountain called Dzongné. Gyelsé disregarded Sera Khandro's request, thinking it was a ploy to separate him from Seldrön, to whom he seems to have become very attached.

The consequences for ignoring the *ḍākinīs*' command were severe. Sera Khandro records that one day in 1921 when she was herding livestock she passed through a densely forested area wet with dew. From this moisture and the snow and rain that pelted down on her, she was soaked through. The next day, she discovered that the arthritis in her legs had left her completely unable to walk. Even then she kept herself busy sewing while in bed, with Tupzang and Jikmé Könchok tending her. Gyelsé scoffed at Sera Khandro's illness, thinking she was faking it, instead of performing the healing rituals necessary to cure her. Meanwhile, two messengers from Drimé Özer's community arrived with a Hayagrīva and Vajravārāhī liturgy handwritten by Drimé Özer as well as a letter he wrote foretelling his imminent death. With this additional blow, Sera Khandro's devastation deepened and she felt herself also nearing death. Finally others in the community, including Gyelsé, realized the severity of her illness and called for a doctor, who diagnosed her arthritic condition. Fearing that her death was imminent, Gyelsé sent her to live with Drimé Özer permanently, as they had agreed six years earlier.

REUNION WITH DRIMÉ ÖZER IN DARTSANG

When the twenty-nine-year-old Sera Khandro arrived in the fall of 1921 at Nyimalung, where Drimé Özer was staying at the time, she could hardly speak. Drimé Özer performed healing rituals for her, and gradually her condition improved. He insisted that she stop eating the vegetarian diet she had previously maintained and instead fed her blessed meat in order to restore her physical energies. Sera Khandro's reunion with Drimé Özer catalyzed the narrative and religious climax of her autobiography, when she regained her physical health and attained spiritual liberation. Sera Khandro records her awakening as a moment not of individual transcendence, but rather of union with her guru as male and female partners (*yab yum*). This symbolized the unification of the two essential qualities of enlightened mind according to Mahāyāna Buddhism, the method or skillful means (Skt. *upāya*, Tib. *thabs*) of compassion and the insight (Skt. *prajñā*, Tib. *shes rab*) of realizing emptiness (a duo that will be the focus of chapter 5). The effects of this realization reverberated from the Tantric couple through their community of disciples. In particular, Sera Khandro records that both her and Drimé Özer's physical ailments disappeared, both were able to decode the symbols they discovered as Treasure with extreme speed, and Drimé Özer's retinue of disciples expanded "like a constellation of stars."[105] Sera Khandro's thirtieth year, following this dramatic experience, was filled with intensive practice retreats. Drimé Özer gave many teachings, including private teachings just for Sera Khandro, such as a clarification of Düjom Lingpa's *Refining One's Perception*, and public teachings, such as one on his Treasure teachings to a crowd of more than three hundred disciples. During this fruitful time, an abundance of revelations came to both Sera Khandro and Drimé Özer. Sera Khandro wrote them down assiduously, including a recipe for blessed medicine that came from a vision of Hayagrīva and Vajravārāhī.

By the time Sera Khandro was thirty-one in 1923, her acclaim as a Treasure revealer and as a Tantric consort endowed with the ability to cure illness, lengthen lifespan, and dispel obstacles had spread beyond Golok and Serta. It reached Andzom Drondül Pawo Dorjé (1842–1924), who sent a letter to Drimé Özer summoning Sera Khandro to his seat at Andzom Chögar in the Pelyül region of Kham. Her meeting with the accomplished eighty-one-year-old Andzom Rinpoché served as an auspicious connection (*rten 'brel*) that inspired further revelations, improved both of their health, and fostered a warm connection between Sera Khandro and Andzom Rinpoché's family, whom she returned to visit in later years. After she rejoined Drimé Özer at Dartsang, he recognized Sera Khandro's important position as his lineage heir, telling her, "You need to maintain and uphold the two profound Treasures [his and his father's]. I am old, and since my community of disciples is large, it is difficult for me to fulfill all their wishes."[106]

Although this period, when Sera Khandro and Drimé Özer had finally managed to live together after more than a decade of obstacles, was a time of religious efflorescence for both of them, it was not without challenges. In 1924, when Sera Khandro was thirty-two, contention with Gyelsé flared up again. A delegation from the Yeru encampment where Sera Khandro had previously lived with Gyelsé's family arrived to settle a lawsuit that Gyelsé had initiated against her. Not unlike divorce proceedings in contemporary courts, the controversy centered on the issue of child custody, or more specifically custody of their son, Gyurmé Dorjé; it seems to have been presumed that their daughter, Yangchen Drönma, would stay with her mother. Initially Gyelsé's relatives tried to settle the dispute by encouraging Sera Khandro to move back to Yeru with them, but Gyelsé rejected this solution, insisting that they needed to adjudicate the lawsuit formally in both the "religious court" (*chos sgo*) of Pelyül, meaning Pelyül Dartang Monastery, as well as the "legal court" (*khrim sgo*) of Akyong Khangen, which was the largest and most powerful division of the Akyong Bum part of Golok. After the case was presented to the courts, Sera Khandro records that she was found to be without fault from both religious and secular perspectives. Nevertheless, the judgment ruled that she would be paid twelve *dotsé*[107] of silver and "even though my young son was not Gara's, for a while he would be considered his."[108] Despite her perception that this judgment was unfair and her attempt to refuse it, Drimé Özer insisted she accept it. His close disciple Sotrül Natsok Rangdröl and others promised to support Sera Khandro with whatever provisions, horses, and livestock she needed, and with that the lawsuit was settled. Even so, trouble was brewing. *Ḍākinī* prophecies indicated to Sera Khandro that if she didn't find a way for Gyurmé Dorjé to be enthroned as an incarnate lama at a monastery according to his karmic destiny, he would not live long. Although Sera Khandro stated that the boy was the reincarnation of the Pelyül Dartang Monastery lama Gotrül Jikdrel Chökyi Lodrö, for an unspecified reason it was not convenient for him to be enthroned there. Instead, Sera Khandro and Drimé Özer tried to arrange his enthronement as a *trülku* at another monastery, affiliated with the Washül Rokza family, but this too failed.

While these negotiations were under way, Akyongza's wrath toward Sera Khandro continued unabated, as it had from the moment of her arrival in Dartsang as a teenager. No matter what Drimé Özer or anyone else said, Akyongza pronounced, "It is unacceptable for the central Tibetan woman and her children to maintain a position in the Treasure revealer's residence. She is not allowed to contaminate us with even a single unnecessary word about needing to live with the Master."[109]

Those close to Drimé Özer warned that this hostility was surely a sign of great obstacles in store for him and Sera Khandro. On top of that, Drimé Özer received a prophecy from his late father indicating that he and Sera Khandro should move somewhere else to avoid obstacles resulting from this household tension. At the time he was busy building a new temple at Dartsang and gathering the resources to publish his father's entire twenty-plus volume corpus of revelations. This unfinished work and the objections of Drimé Özer's siblings to their departure plan led them to ignore Düjom Lingpa's prophetic advice.

Sure enough, a plague struck the Dartsang area in 1924. Everyone—Drimé Özer, Sera Khandro, her young son Rindzin Gyurmé Dorjé, and all their disciples—was on the verge of death. Five-year-old Gyurmé Dorjé succumbed to the disease and died. Three days later, the forty-three-year-old Drimé Özer passed away. Sera Khandro "was left without a protector or guardian, oppressed with great suffering like that of a blind person abandoned in the middle of a plain, but there was nothing to be done."[110] She wrote extensively of the devastation she experienced during this phase of her life in her auto/biographical writings as well as in the cycles of prophecies, hymns, and advice that are included in her Treasure scriptures. Even before Drimé Özer's funeral proceedings had finished, Akyongza and her cohorts unceremoniously expelled Sera Khandro and her daughter from his household. A few of his close disciples who had known Sera Khandro well demanded she be allowed to stay for the memorial services, but other than that, no one acknowledged her position as someone Drimé Özer had earlier appointed as responsible for maintaining and upholding his and his father's Treasure teachings.

LIFE AS THE *ḌĀKINĪ* OF SERA MONASTERY

The person who offered Sera Khandro refuge during this extremely difficult time was Drimé Özer's close disciple Sotrül Natsok Rangdröl Rinpoché (1869–1935), who she explains was honoring a request Drimé Özer had made prior to his death. Sotrül Rinpoché was a member of the ruling Washül Serta family as well as an incarnate lama (*trülku*) at Sera (Tekchen Chönkhor Ling) Monastery in the western part of Washül Serta (see map 2). Founded in 1736, Sera Monastery was named for the Sera Valley in Serta, where it was originally situated. In 1868, during the period that Sotrül Rinpoché was abbot, he moved the monastery to its current location in the Nyi Valley in Serta and initiated its transformation from a Pelyül Nyingma institution to a nonsectarian monastery in which the resident monks performed Nyingma liturgies and also studied the Geluk

FIG. 1.6 Sera Tekchen Chönkhor Ling Monastery in Serta

PHOTOGRAPH BY SARAH JACOBY, 2005

textbooks of Jamyang Zhepa. With the patronage of the Washül Serta leader, Sotrül Rinpoché lavishly rebuilt Sera in its new location, with a temple, many statues, and a practice center dedicated to the "New Treasure" teachings of Düjom Lingpa.[111] Likewise, Sotrül Rinpoché's ardent moral and material support for Sera Khandro encouraged the widespread teaching and prolific writing that defined her years at his monastery.

With the help of some of Drimé Özer's close disciples, including his nephew Künzang Nyima and Drimé Namdak, thirty-two-year-old Sera Khandro, her daughter, and her lifelong attendant, Tupzang, arrived at Sera Monastery in 1924. She lived there on and off for many years, referring to it as "her home" (*rang yul*) and eventually earning the nickname "the *Ḍākinī* of Sera" or "Sera Khandro" that was used by some of her disciples and exported with them into exile in the 1960s. Though her grief at losing Drimé Özer as well as her young son did not abate, the tone of her autobiographical writing becomes more confident from this point forward. Whereas the first three quarters of her narrative recount the difficult circumstances of her earthly life followed by encouraging visions of *ḍākinī*s and buddhafields, from her arrival at Sera, visions emerge more often in the context of empowerment rituals, teachings, and feast offerings. Her account of her later years foregrounds the *trülku*s and lamas she taught, the teachings she gave, the monasteries and retreat centers throughout eastern Tibet that she visited, and the voluminous number of texts she wrote and edited.

Among the many teaching tours she made after Drimé Özer's death was a trip to Sanglung Monastery (see map 2) when she was thirty-three years old in 1925 (and again in 1927 and 1930). Situated in a small valley called Dzika between the Do and Mar valleys of Golok, near Namda Township, Sanglung was a branch monastery of Dodrupchen Monastery (or Tsangchen, as Sera Khandro called it).[112] At Sanglung, Sera Khandro taught large crowds of lamas and monks Longchenpa's *Nyingtik Yabzhi, Heart Essence in Four Parts*, a commentary on Düjom Lingpa's *Refining One's Perception*, teachings from her own Treasure volumes, and other Great Perfection texts. While there she inspired a crowd of about one thousand laywomen to complete more than seven billion "*Oṃ maṇi padmé hūṃ*" mantras dedicated to the bodhisattva of compassion, Avalokiteśvara. In 1926 she again gave a detailed oral commentary on *Refining One's Perception* to monastics, this time at Sera Monastery. She repeatedly gave empowerments (*dbang*), reading transmissions (*lung*), and explanations (*khrid*) of Düjom Lingpa and Drimé Özer's Treasure teachings as well as her own at Sera, Sanglung, and other places throughout eastern Tibet, including Trakor Monastery, Yaktsé, Kyala, Dzongda, Andzom Gar, Tsang Gar in Damé, the Vairotsana Cave named Khandro Yangdzong in Dzakhok that was the residence of her disciple Sherap Özer,[113] and Riwoché.

She taught many of the most prominent local *trülkus* of her generation. When she was thirty-five in 1927, Asé Khenpo Norbu Wangyel insisted she teach the eighteen volumes of Drimé Özer's Treasures to a group including Drimé Özer's disciple Akyap Lama Karma Döndrup; the lama from Hashül named Chödrak; Sherap Özer; the incarnation of the Sera Monastery throne holder, Jikga, named Rindzin Chönyi Döntok; Drimé Özer's nephew Rindzin Künzang Nyima, and others.[114] Lists such as this of important religious personages who requested teachings from Sera Khandro demonstrate that toward the end of her life she had transformed from the outcast consort left out of Drimé Özer's funeral proceedings to a renowned lineage holder of Düjom Lingpa and Drimé Özer's teachings as well as a widely celebrated revealer of her own Treasures.

She was also recognized by practitioners of the Jonang, Pelyül, and Kagyü lineages, who, according to Sera Khandro's words, appreciated her teachings "without bias."[115] She specifically mentions being invited to teach Jonang practitioners at Dzamtang Monastery in present-day Ngawa Prefecture in Sichuan Province, where she gave teachings from her Treasure cycles to the abbot and some of the monks. She even went on pilgrimage to a Bön monastery called Tengchen, where she gave teachings and blessings to all present. She taught a diverse array of elite religious specialists but also gave ordinary laymen, laywomen, and elders teachings appropriate for them, such as reciting *maṇi* mantras, liberating the lives of animals (*tshe thar*), and fasting (*smyung gnas*).

Important secular leaders requested teachings from Sera Khandro, such as the leader of the Kharnang principality of Pema Bum, Drogön, who requested teachings from the three Treasures (those of Düjom Lingpa, Drimé Özer, and her own). In 1932 the King of Lingkar summoned Sera Khandro to confer a long life empowerment and her own Treasure teaching titled *Pakmo Zapdrup, Profound Vajravārāhī Liturgy*, on his entire royal family.[116] They became her benefactors and provided the financial resources for her to publish her liturgical recitations for the tenth day (Guru Rinpoché day) and twenty-fifth day (Ḍākinī day) of the Tibetan month as well as her commentaries on the Great Perfection practices of Breakthrough (*khregs chod*) and Direct Transcendence (*thod rgal*). Additionally, Sera Khandro mentions that on her way back to Sera Monastery from her second visit to the Andzom encampment, the leader of the Dzongda region named Sogyé was on his deathbed and requested her presence to perform *powa*, the transference-of-consciousness ritual performed at death.

During this period after Drimé Özer's death from 1925 through 1934, Sera Khandro also wrote and edited manuscripts with prolixity. Inspired by *ḍākinīs*' prophecies, in 1925 she commenced writing Drimé Özer's biography and completed it eight months later. The following year she began her long autobiography. A few years later, in 1929, when she was thirty-eight years old, Sera Khandro began her largest textual project yet: she promised Sotrül Rinpoché that she would collect, edit, and transcribe Düjom Lingpa's entire corpus of teachings. This was a massive commitment not only given the quantity of texts to be edited and copied, which totaled more than 20 volumes, but also because many of the original manuscripts were housed at Dartsang, or as she called it, "the place of my enemies"[117]—Akyongza and her associates—from which she had been expelled upon Drimé Özer's death only five years earlier. With this in mind, many at Sera Monastery doubted the feasibility of her mission, warning her that Düjom Lingpa's descendants would scorn her should she return.

Despite this, Sera Khandro resolved that she would go and try to borrow the manuscripts. First she gathered her own resources and her disciples' offerings, amassing more than 300 *tam*[118] to cover the costs of writing the texts. When she, her daughter, and her two monk attendants, Tupzang and Tsültrim Dorjé, finally arrived at Karlung Hermitage near Dartsang, "all of [Drimé Özer's] disciples rejoiced as if seeing someone raised from the dead."[119] Drimé Özer's younger brother, Trülku Dorjé Drandül, responded to Sera Khandro positively and allowed her to borrow whichever manuscripts she needed. For more than one month, she and her group stayed there, editing and proofreading the copies they made of Düjom Lingpa's manuscripts in great detail. After finishing this, Sera Khandro concluded her time at Dartsang by offering everyone teachings on the biography of Drimé Özer she had recently completed as well as other teachings they requested.

When Sera Khandro and company returned to Sera, Sotrül Rinpoché was delighted by their success in Dartsang and requested that she give Düjom Lingpa's complete teachings to everyone at the monastery in the early fall of 1929. She records that among the crowd of lamas and monks at these teachings were her disciples Sherap Özer, the Jikga Trülku Chönyi Döntok of Sera Monastery, and Drimé Özer's nephew Künzang Nyima. With her scribes, Tsültrim Dorjé and Lhaten, Sera Khandro completed compiling, copying, and editing the Treasure revelation volumes of Düjom Lingpa, Drimé Özer, and herself in 1933, when she was forty-one years old; the volumes totaled forty-four, with twenty-two of them Düjom Lingpa's revelations, eighteen Drimé Özer's revelations, and four her own. The following year, 1934, Sera Khandro completed writing her long autobiography, upon which this chapter's narrative is based. It was not her last work; she continued revealing Treasures, recording prophecies, and writing down hymns and advice she gave to her disciples throughout her life.

THE FINAL YEARS

Sera Khandro's autobiographical account concludes five years before her death in 1940, at the age of forty-eight, but two other sources document her final years. The earliest is a twelve-folio manuscript handwritten in 1948 by her close disciple and scribe, Tsültrim Dorjé, titled *Posthumous Biography of Khandro Rinpoché Dewé Dorjé Who Arose as a Manifestation of the Mother of the Buddhas Yeshé Tsogyel.*[120] Sera Khandro's disciple Jadrel Sangyé Dorjé Rinpoché drew from Tsültrim Dorjé's text as a foundation for the twenty-folio work he wrote in 1976 titled *Turquoise Inlay: A Short Supplement to the End of the Great Biography of the Central Tibetan Ḍākinī Dewé Dorjé.*[121]

From these two sources we learn that in 1935, when the forty-three-year-old Sera Khandro was giving teachings at Sera Monastery from both Düjom Lingpa and Drimé Özer's Treasure volumes, her staunch supporter Sotrül Natsok Rangdröl Rinpoché passed away. Sera Khandro too perceived signs that her existence in this world would soon dissipate. In order to dispel the obstacles that had arisen to her life that year, Chaktsa Trülku Pema Trinlé Gyatso, who was the fourth incarnation of Ngedön Wangpo from Katok Monastery, offered Sera Khandro many sacred substances.[122] Another positive occurrence that amended all of the damage caused by her missed opportunities to reveal Treasures was a visit to Düjom Lingpa's Kelzang Monastery in Dartsang, where Lama Tsechok conferred empowerments and reading transmissions from the Treasure revelations of Lerap Lingpa (1856–1926).[123] While she was there, Drimé Özer's younger brother Dorjé Drandül summoned her and trained her on how to recite the melody of some Treasure liturgies revealed by his father. This was also a beneficial meeting for her personally; Tsültrim Dorjé explains that by "the auspicious connections of relying on the quick path of method and insight," Sera Khandro was cured of her illness and was able to decode some symbolic text that had come to her as a revelation.[124] Jadrel Rinpoché's text clarifies that these positive outcomes arose through Sera Khandro acting as Dorjé Drandül's "secret consort."[125]

In 1936, when Sera Khandro was forty-four, her disciple Sherap Özer invited her to his residence in Dzakhok at the Khandro Yangdzong Cave. She gave many teachings to the disciples gathered there, including monks, nuns, and laypeople. That year Tsültrim Dorjé records that in order to avoid battles with the Chinese, or as Jadrel Rinpoché refers to them, "the Communist Chinese barbarians (*rgya dmar kla klo*)," their religious encampment had to move repeatedly to Dzakhok, Dayül, and Nyitö. Despite all the fighting, Jadrel Rinpoché writes that, "Thanks to the power of the Venerable Lady's compassion, not even a bit of harm came to all the people and livestock."[126] After the Chinese retreated from the area, Sera Khandro revealed some Treasures at the sacred mountain called Ado in Nyitö. Her group resettled in Getsé Datö in a place called Drokchen Khobü

Valley, where she taught preliminary practices from Düjom Lingpa's "New Treasure" teachings as well as his Great Perfection teachings. After this, she and her disciples conducted a one-hundred-day retreat.

When Sera Khandro was forty-five years old, in 1937, the monastic disciples of Gar Lama Gelek Gyatso, himself a disciple of Düjom Lingpa and Drimé Özer, invited her to give teachings at his hermitage, Tsang Gar. That year, she also returned to Tralek Monastery in the Getsé region to enjoy the Guru Rinpoché festival on the tenth day of the sixth Tibetan month. After this, she went to give further teachings at the Khandro Yangdzong Vairotsana Cave in Dzatö again before returning to Tsang Gar, where Chaktrül Rinpoché came to request particular teachings from Sera Khandro's Treasure scriptures. She gave the assembly of disciples gathered there instructions from her Treasures on preliminary practices, *Refining One's Perception*, and Direct Transcendence. Everyone then performed a one-hundred-day retreat followed by an expansive feast offering. Tsültrim Dorjé mentions that a lama from Nyarong named Tsültrim Norbu arrived and requested the complete empowerments (*dbang*) and reading transmissions (*lung*) from Sera Khandro's teachings. He later copied her entire manuscript collection and taught their contents, which totaled six volumes, according to Jadrel Rinpoché.

In 1938, at age forty-six, Sera Khandro taught the three Treasure teachings from Düjom Lingpa, Drimé Özer, and herself to Drimé Özer's reincarnation and his entourage of lamas and monastics. On her way to the hot springs in Dzakhok, she stopped by the Gyerza Hermitage affiliated with the Bön monastery named Tengchen and asked to see the relics of hair and nails left by the important Bön teacher named Shardzapa Tashi Gyatso, who had taken the rainbow body.[127] After she fulfilled all the wishes of the many monastics and laypeople gathered there by giving blessings and teachings, she returned to Tsang Gar. She gave teachings and collected alms among the locals in the upper Getsé region nearby. To her own disciples she gave much religious advice and spoke about the biographies of past masters. Jadrel Rinpoché adds that at night, when she gave a reading transmission of the *Katang Sheldrakma, Crystal Cave Chronicles,*[128] everyone saw that her body had no shadow in the light of the butter lamps. That winter, together with all her disciples, she did another one-hundred-day retreat.

In the fourth Tibetan month of 1939, when she was forty-seven years old, Zhapdrung Tsewang Drakpa (1882–1962) from Riwoché, Kham, sent messengers with a letter inviting Sera Khandro for a visit (see map 1).[129] En route, her entourage, including her disciple Sherap Özer and his students, went to the Lingkar King's palace, where Sera Khandro gave empowerments from Düjom Lingpa's and Drimé Özer's teachings. After this, they stopped at a sacred place connected to Vajravārāhī in Marong not far from Degé in Kham, where Sera Khandro held a feast offering and revealed a Treasure from Drugu Tingkar Cliff, where Jadrel Rinpoché notes that Jamgön Kongtrül (1813–1899) had revealed Treasures. Finally, after seven months of traveling, they arrived at the palace of the Riwoché Zhapdrung. While she was giving teachings on the three Treasures—Düjom's, his son's, and her own—signs that her death was nearing appeared. Tsültrim Dorjé recounts,

> During the time she was preparing to give an empowerment, Lama Sherap Özer and I were on the outside of a curtain when Khandro Rinpoché said to us,
>
> > The space between this life and the next is not distant, no greater than that between the outside and the inside of this curtain between us.
>
> Also on one occasion she said,
>
> > We have protected and maintained the father and son Lama's teachings well. Now, I don't know how much life we have left.
>
> It seemed that she would not live long.[130]

When Sera Khandro turned forty-eight, in 1940, she secretly went off with only a few others to visit a meditation cave in the Pom region of Kham called Orgyen Dzong. There in the rock cave called Māratika, Sera Khandro discovered several Treasures. After she did a retreat in the cave for a few days, Tsültrim Dorjé, along with a few other disciples, observed her reveal several "public Treasures" (*khrom gter*), which are Treasures meant to be discovered in front of others, from a rock crevasse. She then taught a selection of her Treasure scriptures to the Riwoché Zhapdrung and Jedrung incarnate lamas. In the second Tibetan month of 1940 she went to Samdo Tashikyil, where she gave expansive teachings on the three Treasures to Nyaktrül Guru Özer, his son, and their community. People there said, "At that time, from between her eyebrows, a bright light radiating the assembly of [one hundred] peaceful and wrathful deities sequentially appeared and then faded away."[131] In the beginning of the fourth Tibetan month, Sera Khandro became ill again. Despite the rituals and prayers her disciples performed, her condition did not improve. In the beginning of the fifth month, she asked to be taken to Riwoché, where she stayed at the Zhapdrung's estate. Tsültrim Dorjé writes,

> On the twentieth of the fifth month around noon, she forcefully cried out the sound "*Hik*" and then went to the buddhafield. As soon as she passed away, although we heard the sound of her voice, we didn't understand the meaning.[132]

He also records that

> Rainbow clouds gathered, a sound roared, and so forth. After a few days of making offerings to the body, on the twenty-fifth day, in a very nice place on the right side of the mountain behind Riwoché, we offered the body to the fire. When it was burning, many amazing signs emerged from the relics, such as one eye flying into the southern direction of the sky.[133]

Jadrel Rinpoché adds that when they brought her out to the cremation site, "Her body had dissolved into light and all that remained was about the size of a seven-year-old child."[134] He describes the reliquary that Sera Khandro's daughter and Tsültrim Dorjé made for her relics—it was about as long as an arrow, made of silver with gold and various jewels inlaid in patterns. Inside they put the *ḍākinī*'s bone relics, her hair, her rosary, her Treasure volumes, a Śākyamuni statue, and blessed items including stone chests and yellow scrolls that Sera Khandro had revealed as Treasures.

Sera Khandro's story of spiritual liberation is a journey from suffering to sanctity paradigmatic of the Tibetan biographical genre of *namtar*. At the same time, it stands out for its detailed descriptions of her sentiments and interpersonal relationships with women and men from her religious communities as well as with visionary *ḍākinī*s, land deities, bodhisattvas, and buddhas whom she encountered regularly. Her conversations with these characters evoke a world both distant and proximate, replete with uncanny divine interventions as well as mundane challenges including domestic quarrels, child care issues, and even a lawsuit over child custody. The voices who speak with Sera Khandro are not just bit players in a monological story in which she stars, but integral parts of her subjectivity. Fortified with this overview of the trajectory of Sera Khandro's life narrative, we turn now to listen first to talk about the *raison d'être* of her auto/biographical works, her process of revealing Treasures.

2

A GUEST IN THE SACRED LAND OF GOLOK

From the Treasure prophecy of the Omniscient Refuge Lord Pema Lendreltsel:

> The speech emanation of Tsogyel is the key to profound Treasures.
> Of a Brahmin lineage, she is empowered in the profound Treasures
> of Padmasambhava.
> She is an authentic wisdom *ḍākinī* named Sukha.[1]
> After you meet her by the power of your aspirations,
> the auspicious connections will come together excellently
> to open the door of the secret Treasure, the tightly hidden profound
> essence of
> the cycles of mother and child clear light together with their key.
> May this bring vast benefit to many types of beings![2]

What did it mean for Sukha, or Sera Khandro Dewé Dorjé, to be a *ḍākinī* emanation of Yeshé Tsogyel empowered in the profound Treasures of Padmasambhava? What were these Treasures, and how could she open the door of their hidden essence? What did auspicious connections (*rten 'brel*) have to do with the process of revelation, and what types of vast benefit were these Treasures meant to provide? The prophecy above that Sera Khandro attributes to Pema Lendreltsel, an epithet of her guru Drimé Özer, is one of seven that introduces her autobiography. It announces the central topic of Sera Khandro's auto/biographical works—the process of revealing Treasures (*gter ma*). Revelation is the main subject of the nearly one hundred visions that comprise about half of her long autobiography; the other half documents her experiences in this world. Dozens of these visions inspired Sera Khandro to write down what appeared to her as mind Treasures (*dgongs gter*), which consist of Tantric liturgies, explanations of Buddhist doctrine, religious histories, spiritual biographies, prophecies, and more. Her visions also led her to discover earth Treasures (*sa gter*) including scriptures, chests, statues, precious pills, ritual implements, and other sacred objects from powerful places in the Tibetan landscape, especially mountains and lakes.

This chapter examines Sera Khandro's range of relationships with divine presences who were integral to her career as a Treasure revealer. Focusing on her interactions with these figures draws on autobiographical theorists' notion of "relational selfhood," referring to the interconnectivity of autobiographical subjects with others in their social worlds.[3] In the context of Tibetan Treasure revealers' spiritual biographies, relational selfhood takes on an extended significance: relationships with buddhas and bodhisattvas, who inhabit pure realms known as buddhafields, as well as land deities and *ḍākinīs*, who animate Tibet's earth and sky, form an inseparable part of the subjectivity of the biography's protagonist. Relationality, not just of selves but of all phenomena, is a central feature of the Tibetan Treasure tradition. A term that overlaps in meaning with "relationality" in Tibetan is *tendrel* (Skt. *pratītya-samutpāda*, Tib. *rten 'brel*). Beyond the context of Treasure revelation, *tendrel* is often translated as "dependent arising." Dependent arising describes the way people and phenomena in the world exist according to Buddhist philosophy: dependent on causes and conditions, subject to change, and impermanent. The *Saṃyutta-nikāya* includes passages that describe this concisely, such as: "When this exists, that comes to be; with the arising of this, that arises. When this does not exist, that does not come to be; with the cessation of this, that ceases."[4] Dependent arising thus characterizes the fundamental interdependence of all beings and phenomena, within which the relationality of the self with other beings and environmental factors is one subset. In the Treasure Tradition, *tendrel* refers not only to the interdependent nature of existence in the Buddhist philosophical sense but also to the concrete circumstances, good signs, omens, and interpersonal connections that must come together for a Treasure revealer to successfully reveal scripture or sacred artifacts. In this specialized context, *tendrel* is therefore better translated as "auspicious connection" or "favorable circumstance." Like the self can exist only in relation to others with and against whom a person defines it, successful Treasure revelation can only occur through the alignment of a constellation of conditions including geographic, temporal, and social factors.

This chapter delineates three dimensions of Sera Khandro's relational selfhood that are all intricately tied to the Tibetan Treasure tradition. The first is her strong alignment with its progenitors, most centrally Padmasambhava and his *ḍākinī* consort, Yeshé Tsogyel. More than any other transregional Tibetan "saint," Yeshé Tsogyel was an important model and object of devotion for Sera Khandro, which we will see right away in the opening frame narrative of her autobiography. Second, the chapter explores relationality in the specific sense of the auspicious connections necessary for revelation, observing both the set of conditions required for Sera Khandro to accomplish her religious mission as well as the consequences of those conditions failing to coalesce. Third, the chapter examines Sera Khandro's relational selfhood vis-à-vis the many local deities inhabiting sacred mountains with whom she interacted regularly to reveal her Treasures. The great importance of these autochthonous Tibetan deities in her life narrative suggests that the ongoing vitality of the Treasure tradition in early twentieth-century Golok had as much to do with its close connections to local networks of authority upheld by the region's sacred mountains as it did with connections to transregional Tibetan personages such as Padmasambhava and Yeshé Tsogyel.

Before exploring these three dimensions of relationality, two classes of beings require introduction: *ḍākinī*s and land deities. Since *ḍākinī*s take center stage in the following chapter, here we focus only on their relationship to the Tibetan Treasure tradition. *Ḍākinī*s are classes of female divinities associated with the sky as beings who fly, an etymology derived from the Sanskrit root *dī* and prominent in the Tibetan translation, which is *khandroma* (*mkha' 'gro ma*), literally "sky-going woman." With a history in South Asia long pre-dating Tibet's conversion to Buddhism, *ḍākinī*s flourished in Tibet in the forms of enlightened buddhas such as Vajravārāhī, bodhisattvas such as Tārā, and human women who attained buddhahood, such as Yeshé Tsogyel.[5] Yeshé Tsogyel has a special significance in the context of the Treasure tradition as Padmasambhava's Tibetan consort who helped him write down and conceal his Buddhist teachings for future disciples until the appropriate time for their discovery. Like Yeshé Tsogyel, *ḍākinīs* inscribe, protect, and help Treasure revealers decode the symbolic scripts in which they conceal Treasures.[6] Additionally, in Treasure revealers' autobiographies, a prominent function *ḍākinīs* perform is prophecy—they foretell Treasures to be found, people to associate with and avoid, and dangers to be averted. Their elusive missives direct Sera Khandro's actions and demand her obeisance as well as require her constant introspection, for their symbolic words leave much open to interpretation.

Tibetan territories are pervaded with powerful forces that control specific localities, most often mountains, lakes, and boulders. These presences that I call by the general term "land deities" include most prominently "local deities" (*yul lha*), "masters of the territory" (*gzhi bdag*), and "masters of the ground" (*sa bdag*). In some cases pre-dating the arrival of Buddhism in Tibet, land deities' genesis is inextricably tied to Tibetan regional understandings of place, politics, and identity.[7] In the nomadic grasslands of greater Golok, where Sera Khandro spent the majority of her life, each valley and community had (and still has) their own local land deities whom they propitiate regularly in order to prevent calamities such as livestock casualties, weather disruptions, sickness, and warfare. The most powerful land deities inhabited Golok's sacred mountains, such as Anyé Machen, Nyenpo Yutsé, and Drong Mountain, to name only a few of the most prominent. Padmasambhava and his cohort pressed some among these originally non-Buddhist alpine forces into service as Treasure protectors, or beings who guard sacred Treasures until the appropriate prophesied Treasure revealer appears to retrieve them at the proper time. Treasure revealers such as Sera Khandro interacted closely with Tibet's territorial spirits as Tantric masters who had inherited Padmasambhava's power to subjugate them, to retrieve Treasures safeguarded by them, and to nourish them through ritual exchanges of sacred substances. These interactions influenced political and social dynamics in this world as well as beyond it, because the people of greater Golok perceived the land deities associated with certain important mountains to be the biological ancestors of their regional political leaders. Treasure revealers played essential roles as mediators between these spiritual "masters of the territory," the political leaders whose right to rule derived from them, and the local population of greater Golok. In some cases, Sera Khandro used a specific locution to describe her special bond with the land deities who protected her Treasures, literally "the commitment vow between sacred land and guest" (*gnas mgron gyi dam tshig*), referring to the sacred relationship between the land deities inhabiting sacred sites and herself as the guest who ventured onto their terrain. Concentrating on her exchanges with powerful presences at Anyé Machen and Drong Mountain, this chapter will explore the significance of this relationship between guest and spiritually inhabited land for both the arcane domain of revelation and everyday survival on Golok's grasslands. And in the process, pragmatic purposes of revelation and spiritual dimensions of survival will also emerge.

PART I: THE FRAME NARRATIVE

After a few folios of opening prayers, Sera Khandro begins the story of her life by catapulting her readers into an expansive cosmic vision of the Tantric Buddhist universe comprised of countless buddhafields populated by myriads of buddhas, bodhisattvas, and *ḍākinīs* who emanate into and out of each other. Central to this luminous display is Padmasambhava, whom Sera Khandro calls Pema Tötrengtsel or "Lotus with the Power of a Skull Garland" in her opening frame narrative, translated below. But just as important are the many *ḍākinīs* he invokes. In particular, Yeshé Tsogyel plays a critical role in this phantasmagoric drama:

> The essence of the buddhas of the three times,[8] who is the one known as the Great Awareness Holder Pema Tötrengtsel, was born untainted by the womb in a faultless lotus bud. Pema Tötrengtsel's good deeds and enlightened activity exceeded that of the leader of the two-footed ones, the Victorious King of the Sages [Śākyamuni Buddha]. As the one who possessed the enlightened activities of all the buddhas of the three times in one, he thought,
>
> > Now, through relying on skillful means I need to spread the difficult-to-spread Secret Mantra Vajrayāna teachings here in Tibet. Hence, the time has come for me to display an emanation of Vajravārāhī, mother of the ultimate sphere.

The guru himself departed from the Unsurpassed Realm.[9] For seven years he wandered in one hundred Emanation Body buddhafields. He then gathered together all of the wisdom *ḍākinīs* of the Three Bodies,[10] including Vajrayoginī, the sky-coursing *ḍākinīs* of the three realms such as Noble Tārā, and the four classes of sacred place *ḍākinīs* such as Sarasvatī. He pleased them with the taste of stainless bliss, and they abided in the realization of the great primordial wisdom of bliss and emptiness.

Pema Tötrengtsel invoked the mind of Vajravārāhī. For the sake of taming the red-faced Tibetan people, she emanated six manifestations, including body, speech, mind, good qualities, enlightened activity, and suchness, and she acted as the Guru's consort.

The Goddess Sarasvatī herself, whose identity is these manifestations condensed into one, arose in the center of the *maṇḍala* and spoke to the *ḍākinīs*:

> The time has come for me to tame those who harm the Buddhist teachings, those who are difficult to tame in the world, including the demonic Tibetan people, [beings in] the southwestern island of demons, and the group of Bön heretics, to preserve the difficult-to-spread Secret Mantra Vajrayāna teachings for a long time, to be the Guru's consort, and to collect his teachings.

She emanated beings not other than herself such as Kalasiddhi in Nepal, the woman from Mön[11] named Tashi Chidren, and Shelkar Dorjetso in the region of central Tibet. Sarasvatī also arose in the form of the Great Bliss Yeshé Tsogyel, who acted as the collector of the Secret Mantra teachings and whose enlightened activity equaled that of the Guru. Her good deeds and enlightened activity were unrivaled in the three regions.[12]

Finally, Yeshé Tsogyel had the intention to demonstrate impermanence for the sake of disciples who grasped onto permanence by gathering her body into the ultimate sphere and departing for the Unsurpassed Realm. She gave instructions and advice as individually appropriate for the Nepali citizen Kalasiddhi and the woman from Mön named Tashi Chidren and so forth, as well as for the king, his subjects, the translators, and the scholars. In particular, she spoke the following to both Siddhi and Chidren:

Illusory primordial wisdom emanations of the Tibetan woman
  Tsogyel,
Appearing from the ultimate sphere, you arise as an ornament of
  the ultimate sphere.

From the dynamism of spontaneous presence, you two sisters
manifest.
Revel in the expanse of the ultimate sphere of reality in which
awareness and emptiness are equal.

As soon as she said this, Tashi Chidren transformed into an eight-petaled blue lotus flower with a "*hūṃ*" in the middle and eight "*phaṭ*" [letters] on the surrounding petals and disappeared into the right side of Yeshé Tsogyel's heart center. Kalasiddhi transformed into a red lotus with a "*hrī*" in the middle of its sixteen petals, decorated with the sixteen "*a li*" [Sanskrit vowels], and dissolved into the left side of Yeshé Tsogyel's heart center.

Then the Lady of Shelkar, Shiwa Dorjetso, arranged a golden *maṇḍala* heaped with turquoise and offered it together with her body and wealth. She said to the Lady,

Alas, *ḍākinī* of Tibet,
Master on whom we depend,
if you depart for the invisible ultimate sphere,
don't stop having compassion for us.
Please take care of us and guide us to the Glorious Lotus Light.

Having requested this, she was choked with tears and fainted.
Again, the Lady [Yeshé Tsogyel] blessed and resuscitated her.
Tsogyel said,

How wonderful, listen Lady of Shelkar,
wisdom *ḍākinī* Dorjetso—
because disciples still remain,
I cannot guide you to the Lotus Light.

In the secret *ḍākinī* cave in Sheldrak,
indivisible from the fully ordained monk Namkhai Nyingpo,
join method and insight.

Meditating on channels and winds is the method to bring
your corporeal body of flesh and blood to course in the sky.
If you are able to mix the wind and mind as one,
your activities as an accomplished master will be without reversal.

In all times and situations,
not losing our association for an instant,
pray to me.
Meditate on being inseparable from me in your heart center.

Having seen my face during the six times,[13]
you will certainly bring inexpressible benefit to sentient beings
such as the 1 billion, 10 million disciples dispersed in the
demonic land of the border continent.

Then, after passing through three lifetimes,
you will manifest in the land of the Glorious Mountain of Lotus
  Light
as the one called Dorjé Dechen Pematso.
Inseparable from the Guru, you will gloriously enjoy great bliss.

At that time, you will manifest as thirteen emanations and
benefit beings by means of profound Treasures.
After thirteen thousand human years,
in the greatly secret charnel ground of the Unsurpassed Realm,
not separate from Vajravārāhī's vast mind
you will become an actual buddha.

Having said this, Yeshé Tsogyel opened the *maṇḍala* of Vajravārāhī and conferred the outer, inner, and secret empowerments in the royal manner of anointment. After entrusting Shiwa Dorjetso with a Treasure, she made aspiration prayers.[14]

Sera Khandro's choice to begin her life story with an expansive account of her genealogical relationship to the progenitors of the Treasure tradition follows a familiar paradigm in Buddhist biographical writing. Biographies of Tibetan Buddhist masters in general do not begin with an account of their protagonists' birth and upbringing, but rather reflect the Buddhist understanding of life as a cycle of rebirth, a story without a beginning but with a potential end, however distant, in buddhahood. In keeping with this, they usually commence with a series of past incarnations of which the present lifetime is the karmic consequence. Elaborating past lives has a special importance in biographies of Treasure revealers because one of their primary marks of authenticity is being identified as an incarnation of one of Padmasambhava's original disciples, usually enumerated in a list of twenty-five figures called "the king and his subjects" (*rje 'bangs*), which Sera Khandro mentions above. These refer to Tibet's King Tri Songdetsen (ruled 742–c. 797) and twenty-four notable Buddhist masters who ranked among his Tibetan subjects. Among these, only one was female, Yeshé Tsogyel.

Moreover, throughout the labyrinthine transmutations and emanations of one *ḍākinī* into another in Sera Khandro's opening frame narrative, one message is clear: she presents herself from the beginning of her autobiography as an incarnation of the *ḍākinī* from Shelkar in central Tibet named Shiwa Dorjetso, who was herself an emanation of Yeshé Tsogyel. This connection is particularly apt given that a distinctive feature of Sera Khandro's identity in Golok was her birthplace—to this day people in Golok refer to Sera Khandro by the name Üza Khandro, "the *Ḍākinī* Lady from central Tibet." In the narrative above, Yeshé Tsogyel reabsorbed Kalasiddhi and Tashi Chidren, who were both "not other than herself," but left Shiwa Dorjetso behind because her "disciples still remain." Sera Khandro thus sets the stage for a story about how this forlorn emanation of Yeshé Tsogyel accomplished the remainder of her duty of teaching the Buddhist Dharma to sentient beings in preparation for her future buddhahood.

On the one hand, Padmasambhava's conversion of Tibet to Buddhism by journeying through buddhafield after buddhafield, corralling and cavorting with enlightened Buddhist *ḍākinīs*, is a natural beginning point for Sera Khandro's life story, for what more ideal way to begin a Treasure revealer's autobiography than with the enlightened activities of Padmasambhava and Yeshé Tsogyel? Others in Sera Khandro's religious lineage also heralded their foundational status in the Treasure tradition. For example, in the words of Düjom Jikdrel Yeshé Dorjé, the reincarnation of Düjom Lingpa:

> It was his [Padmasambhava's] particularly great enlightened activity to conceal uncountable treasure troves containing doctrines, wealth, medicines, astrological calculations, images, sacramental substances and so forth in the lands of India, Nepal, and Tibet, with the intention of providing a harvest for future disciples and for the teaching. Above all, skillfully

> teaching each according to his needs here in Tibet, Guru Rinpoche taught approaches to the doctrine in general, and, in particular, an infinite mass of Tantras, transmissions, esoteric instructions and rites associated with the three classes of yoga [Mahāyoga, Anuyoga, and Atiyoga]. All of those transmitted precepts were compiled by the mistress of secrets, the queen of the expanse, Yeshe Tshogyel, who retained them in her infallible memory. She arranged them on five kinds of yellow scroll [symbolizing the five families] in the symbolic script of the ḍākinīs and, inserting them in various treasure chests, sealed them to be indestructible.[15]

Yeshé Tsogyel plays a crucial part in Düjom Rinpoché's sacred history as the one "who retained them [Treasures] in her infallible memory," wrote them down, and hid them in sealed chests. Sera Khandro alludes to such associations with remembering, writing, and hiding the Treasures in her opening narrative when she describes Yeshé Tsogyel as the one "who acted as the collector of the Secret Mantra teachings." She reserves no amount of praise for both male and female consorts—Padmasambhava's good deeds and enlightened activity exceeded those of even Śākyamuni Buddha, and Yeshé Tsogyel's "enlightened activity equaled that of the Guru [Padmasambhava]" and was "unrivaled." Thus, in her opening words, Sera Khandro put forth a model of Padmasambhava and Yeshé Tsogyel as joint progenitors of the Treasure tradition that emphasized their exalted status as equal partners in a grand project of Buddhist conversion.

On the other hand, Sera Khandro's opening frame narrative bears distinctive elements. By the time she commenced her autobiography with these lines, she was already well versed in the art of reading and writing Tibetan spiritual biographies. One of the first and most important of these was the autobiography of Düjom Lingpa. Though he had passed away in 1904, a few years before Sera Khandro arrived in Golok, she became acquainted with his life story when she was a teenager en route to Golok with his son Drimé Özer. She writes that while journeying eastward, "I prostrated to the Master and circumambulated him from afar while the he was teaching his other disciples the story of Lama Rinpoché's [Düjom Lingpa's] biography. When I heard it, extraordinary faith and devotion arose in me toward father and son."[16] Later on as well Sera Khandro had occasion to become very familiar with Düjom Lingpa's autobiography—she mentions receiving further teachings from Drimé Özer about his father's life as well as compiling, editing, and copying Düjom Lingpa's complete works, totaling more than twenty volumes. Unlike Sera Khandro's elaborate opening passage describing her relationship to the enlightened activities of Padmasambhava and his *ḍākinī* entourage, Düjom Lingpa's autobiography, *A Clear Mirror: The Biography of My Secret Visionary Experiences of the Illusory Display of Reality*, opens simply with the following sentence: "To begin with, if I don't explain anything about my family genealogy, I would commit the fault of not knowing anything about one's paternal ancestry like a monkey in the forest. Hence, I will explain a bit about this."[17] After giving an account of the ancestry of his present lifetime, he lists his previous incarnations, from Buddha Vajradhāra up to his previous incarnation, Dorjé Rolpa Tsel. But even in the final events of his last lifetime, the central protagonist in his story is Rolpa Tsel, not the enlightened progenitors of the Treasure tradition. Hence, in Düjom Lingpa's autobiography, biological genealogy is the first descriptor of identity, prior to incarnation status or spiritual lineage.

Sera Khandro was also likely familiar with the autobiography of Gara Terchen Pema Dündül Wangchuk Lingpa, her "life partner" Gyelsé's father. Though she does not mention Gara Terchen's autobiography specifically, it could have numbered among his works that Sera Khandro demanded Gyelsé collect in their retreat house above Benak Monastery as a precondition for their partnership. Unlike Düjom Lingpa's widely popular writings, now available in multiple published editions, Gara Terchen's writings are rare and remain largely unpublished. One exception is the first half of his autobiography, recounting his life until the age of thirty, titled *An Account of How This Yogi Traversed the Grounds and Paths Spoken Truthfully Without Deception*.[18] After opening prayers, Gara Terchen commences with a few self-deprecating sentences about himself as an old mantrin to whom attributing spiritual accomplishments would be like an "old watch dog being called a lion."[19] He then lists two reasons he wrote his autobiography: Padmasambhava blessed him and endowed him with a share of Dharma Treasures, and the auspicious connections predicted in prophecies from Padmasambhava and the *ḍākinīs* had come to pass, so his disciples had urged him intensively to write his life story. Though these reasons invoke the Treasure tradition, Gara Terchen's autobiography does not include an opening frame narrative like that of Sera Khandro, but rather launches directly into prophecies foretelling his present rebirth, descriptions of a few of his former incarnations, and an account of his ancestry and the reason his family name is "Gara," or "blacksmith."[20] Hence, similar to Düjom Lingpa's autobiography, Gara Terchen's autobiographical beginning point was the biological genealogy of his present lifetime as much as it was the "spiritual genealogy" that associated him with Padmasambhava. In Gara Terchen's case, the latter did not even include Yeshé Tsogyel, let alone laud her as Padmasambhava's equal.

Sera Khandro heeded these immediate literary precedents when she began writing Drimé Özer's biography in 1925. She omitted an extensive frame narrative linking Drimé Özer to Padmasambhava and Yeshé Tsogyel's Treasure-hiding activities. After opening prayers, Sera Khandro included several prophecies predicting Drimé Özer's birth and then a copious list of twenty of his former incarnations, including illustrious figures such as the Buddha's cousin Ānanda, the Indian translator Vimalamitra, and Pema Lingpa from Bhutan. After this, Sera Khandro introduced his parents as Traktung Düjom Dorjé (Düjom Lingpa) and Keza Sangyé Tso, launching from there into the story of his birth and childhood.[21]

Sera Khandro did not model the opening frame of her life story directly on those male Treasure revealers' biographies that she knew best, but found another inspiration in the biography of Yeshé Tsogyel. Not only was she a model for Sera Khandro in the religious sense of being the source of her emanation, but her biography also appears to be a model in a literary sense. Intertextuality between the two *ḍākinīs*' life stories emerges in terms of both plot similarities and the wording of several key passages. In particular, parts of Sera Khandro's writing closely adhere to a version of Yeshé Tsogyel's life produced by Taksham Nüden Dorjé in the seventeenth century as a Treasure revelation. Taksham Nüden Dorjé's account follows this general outline: amid miraculous signs, Yeshé Tsogyel was born to Kharchen Pelkyi Wangchük and Getso from the Tibetan clan of Nup. Because of her unusual beauty, suitors came from all directions to ask for her hand in marriage. In particular, two local lords vied for her, each attempting to seize Tsogyel and drag her away with them. Finally, the Lord of Kharchu won, but that evening when all in his entourage had become drunk and fallen asleep, Tsogyel escaped. Though she managed to stay alone in the wilderness for a period of time, ultimately the other local lord, Surkharpa, discovered her. Each of the lords threatened war on the other until the King of Tibet, Tri Songdetsen, stepped in and claimed Tsogyel for his own wife. Tsogyel married the king and became his steward of religion. The king was a pious Buddhist and a disciple of

FIG. 2.1 A close-up of Yeshé Tsogyel

RUBIN MUSEUM OF ART, NEW YORK, F1997.12.1

Padmasambhava; as a devotional offering to his guru, he gave Tsogyel to Padmasambhava in order for them to practice Vajrayāna teachings together. From this time forward Yeshé Tsogyel devoted herself to Padmasambhava, gradually training in many cycles of teachings such as those dedicated to Hayagrīva and Vajravārāhī, Vajrakīlaya, and many others. Padmasambhava gave her the first three of the four Tantric Buddhist empowerments, but before giving her the fourth, he commanded Yeshé Tsogyel to go to India to purchase a young male servant named Atsara Salé to be her consort for the benefit of her religious development. When the king's non-Buddhist ministers discovered that he had offered his wife to Padmasambhava, they were outraged and plotted revenge against the king, thus igniting tensions between proponents of Tibet's pre-Buddhist religion, Bön, and Buddhists, resulting in a great debate in which the Buddhists emerged victorious. Meanwhile, Yeshé Tsogyel practiced austerities in retreat, overcoming great obstacles, from robbers and solicitors to demonic attacks. After this, both she and Padmasambhava practiced intensively, each engaging with different consorts as appropriate to accomplish particular teachings. Finally, Padmasambhava's time in Tibet drew to a close and he beamed off toward the southwest, to his Glorious Copper-Colored Mountain Buddhafield, but not without a long exchange of emotional laments and reassurances with Yeshé Tsogyel. Yeshé Tsogyel then performed acts of great compassion in the world and hid Treasures throughout the land of Tibet. When it came time for her to pass away, her disciples beseeched her to stay with tear-filled lamentations. Reassuring them that she would always be available to those who prayed to her, she transformed into light and disappeared in the southwestern direction.[22]

Like Yeshé Tsogyel, Sera Khandro writes that her mother descended from the powerful Tibetan Nup clan and her father was a local ruler. Both Yeshé Tsogyel and Sera Khandro were beautiful girls who attracted many suitors, but their fathers made politically advantageous marriage agreements against their will. Both felt extreme repulsion toward secular marriage and resisted unwanted male attention throughout their lives. Although they sought to lead independent religious lives, neither chose to become a celibate nun. Instead, they engaged in multiple consort relationships for the benefit of male and female partners' spiritual insight. Even though theirs were not monogamous relationships, both *ḍākinīs* formed especially close bonds with their male spiritual gurus.

More than narrative similarities, the two *ḍākinīs*' biographies share the same wording in key passages. For example, their first sentences are nearly verbatim:

> Padma Thödrengtsel, master of mantra, whose nature is that of all the Buddhas, past, present, and to come, is indeed a mighty siddha, born within a lotus blossom, undefiled by human birth. Surpassing even Shakyamuni, he accomplishes the enlightened activity of the Buddhas of the three times.[23]
>
> (Yeshé Tsogyel)

> The essence of the Buddhas of the three times, the one known as the Great Awareness Holder Pema Tötrengtsel, was born untainted by the womb in a faultless lotus bud. Pema Tötrengtsel's good deeds and enlightened activity

exceeded that of the leader of the two-footed ones, the King of the Victorious Sages [Śākyamuni Buddha].[24] (Sera Khandro)

The opening passages of both *ḍākinīs*' biographies describe Padmasambhava's method of propagating Buddhism in Tibet with the following:

But the truth was that the Guru was ranging through hundreds of Nirmankaya Buddhafields, remaining there for seven years in human reckoning. He summoned to him Vajrayogini, goddess Sarasvati, Wrathful-Frowning Tara, the dakinis of the four classes and those of the sacred lands and places, and elsewhere—all without exception. He took his pleasure with each and every one.[25] (Yeshé Tsogyel)

The guru himself departed from the Unsurpassed Realm. For seven years he wandered in one hundred Emanation Body buddhafields. He then gathered together all of the wisdom *ḍākinīs* of the Three Bodies, including Vajrayoginī, the sky-coursing *ḍākinīs* of the three realms such as Noble Tārā, and the four classes of sacred place *ḍākinīs* such as Sarasvatī. He pleased them with the taste of stainless bliss, and they all abided in the realization of the great primordial wisdom of bliss and emptiness.[26]
(Sera Khandro)

The two *ḍākinīs*' life stories again interconnect when they describe Yeshé Tsogyel's departure toward Padmasambhava's Glorious Copper-Colored Mountain Buddhafield:

Then, with her right hand, Tsogyel touched Trashi Chidren, the girl from Mön. She was transformed into a blue utpala lotus with eight petals marked with the syllables *Hung* and *Phat*, and dissolved into the right side of the Lady's heart. Then with her left hand, Tsogyel touched Kalasiddhi of Nepal, who changed into a red lotus of sixteen petals marked with the sixteen vowels and *Hri* and dissolved into the left side of her heart.[27]
(Yeshé Tsogyel)

As soon as she said this, Tashi Chidren transformed into an eight-petaled blue lotus flower with a "*hūṃ*" in the middle and eight "*phaṭ*" [letters] on the surrounding petals and disappeared into the right side of Yeshé Tsogyel's heart center. Kalasiddhi transformed into a red lotus with a "*hrī*" in the middle of its sixteen petals decorated with the sixteen "*a li*" [Sanskrit vowels] and dissolved into the left side of Yeshé Tsogyel's heart center.[28]

(Sera Khandro)

These resonances of Yeshé Tsogyel's biography in Sera Khandro's autobiography are not instances of plagiarism; borrowing without attribution was commonplace in Tibetan literature. Ingenuity was not necessarily the hallmark of literary prowess in Tibet, especially in the context of the Treasure tradition in which those who wrote revelations explicitly denied authoring *ex novo* the texts they produced. Examining only these very first pages of Sera Khandro's autobiography demonstrates that we are reading a type of self narrative far from the "process of singularization" autobiography theorist John Sturrock imagined, in which "the autobiographer traces the purposeful, seemingly anticipated course of his own separation out from others."[29] Here the opposite is the case: Sera Khandro made her life meaningful through establishing relationships with others, especially Yeshé Tsogyel, whose identity permeated her own on many levels.

Other Treasure revealers close to Sera Khandro, such as Düjom Lingpa and Gara Terchen, also formulated their life narratives in relation to central figures from the Treasure tradition, but they did not foreground their genealogical connection to Padmasambhava or Yeshé Tsogyel to the extent that Sera Khandro did. Reasons for her stronger emphasis on her connection to Yeshé Tsogyel include more than their shared female gender, though this no doubt lent the association credence. Unlike Düjom Lingpa, Drimé Özer, or Gara Terchen, Sera Khandro lacked Golok roots and claimed only distant links to the Treasure tradition. As Düjom Lingpa said, not knowing one's paternal ancestry is like being a monkey in the forest. Sera Khandro knew hers, but her repeated laments about not having "paternal relatives to back me up" in the Golok headlands in which she made her lifelong home suggest the disadvantage of not having a recognizable local genealogical ancestry. Treasure revealers in Golok were incarnations of Padmasambhava's original twenty-five disciples, but they were often also sons or nephews of other Golok Treasure revealers and religious specialists. Sera Khandro may not have had an obvious biological pedigree from her present lifetime to reinforce her identity as a Treasure revealer, but the opening passages of her autobiography make an even stronger claim: she was none other than Yeshé Tsogyel incarnate.

PART II: THE INTERDEPENDENT PROCESS OF REVELATION

That Treasure revealers' credibility was based on both transcendent enlightened and locally salient sources of authority mirrors the multistage process of revelation, which depended on receiving Treasure teachings directly from Padmasambhava and other imperial Tibetan personages as well as on synchronizing local conditions into favorable circumstances for revelation. Padmasambhava and Yeshé Tsogyel commanded Sera Khandro to be a Treasure revealer and *ḍākinī*s' prophecies emphasized this, but accomplishing her mission was never a foregone conclusion. Instead, Sera Khandro's ability to reveal Treasures depended upon her attunement with an array of human and nonhuman elements in her environment.

Unlike other forms of Buddhist lineage transmission that are "long" in that they trace from student to teacher directly back to Śākyamuni Buddha, the Treasure tradition is "short" because it is a direct lineage from the buddhas via Padmasambhava (or another of his associates such as King Songtsen Gampo, Vimalamitra, or Vairotsana) to a human recipient. Most prominent in the Nyingma school of Tibetan Buddhism, the Treasure tradition includes three unique stages of transmission between Padmasambhava and those appointed to reveal the Treasures he hid.[30] The first is called the prophetic authorization (*bka' babs lung bstan*), in which Padmasambhava gave a prophecy to the future Treasure revealer indicating the specific time and place to disclose his teaching. Such prophecies foretelling details of future revelations pervade Sera Khandro's auto/biographical writings. The second unique stage of Treasure transmission is the aspirational empowerment (*smon lam dbang bskur*), also called the mind-mandate transmission (*gtad rgya*), in which Padmasambhava concealed the Treasure teaching in the Treasure revealer's mind through the power of his aspirations. The last stage is the entrustment to the *ḍākinī*s (*mkha' 'gro gtad rgya*). After Padmasambhava concealed Treasures in the earth or sky, he entrusted the *ḍākinī*s and Treasure protectors, often land deities, with the task of guarding them until the prophesied Treasure revealer arrived at the appropriate time.[31]

In many of the nearly one hundred visions Sera Khandro included in her autobiography, she describes elaborate encounters with Padmasambhava and Yeshé Tsogyel in which they bestowed mind-mandate

FIG. 2.2 Padmasambhava's
Copper-Colored Mountain Buddhafield

RUBIN MUSEUM OF ART, NEW YORK, C2002.30.7

transmission upon her. One such encounter is the longest and most detailed visionary experience in the autobiography, comprising more than sixteen folios. Sera Khandro writes that when she was thirty-four, in 1926, she traveled to Padmasambhava's Glorious Copper-Colored Mountain Buddhafield along with Drimé Özer and two *ḍākinī* emissaries. This is part of her account of what she saw there:

> Regarding the layout of the Glorious Mountain palace, the expansive and vast ground was made of various precious substances. If you pressed down on it, it was soft and bounced back up when you lifted [your feet]. In the four directions an aromatic mist wafted from the medicinal herb-covered mountains. All around were springs and bathing pools filled with water endowed with the eight qualities[32] and completely adorned with multicolored lotuses, water lilies, and so forth. Golden sand and a turquoise meadow pervaded everywhere. A dense, unbroken expanse of wish-fulfilling trees surrounded that. Garlands, hanging tassels of silk and jewels, and the divine raiment "*banyatsali*" ornamented the leaves. Many types of birds with melodious voices who were incarnations of buddhas and bodhisattvas sang the holy Dharma unceasingly while they circled a lake with the eight qualities and perched on the wish-fulfilling trees.[33]

In the middle of this enchanted land rose a fabulous mansion in which Sera Khandro beheld Padmasambhava and his entourage; she records that "when I saw the Guru, the king and subjects, and their groups of disciples, the hair on my body stood on end and tears flowed from my eyes."[34] She offered a supplication prayer to the assembly and then bemoaned her incapacity to carry out the command from the "Guru Couple" (Padmasambhava and Yeshé Tsogyel) to reveal Treasures. In response, Yeshé Tsogyel, Shiwa Dorjetso, and Sera Khandro engaged in an extended conversation about Sera Khandro's abilities as a Treasure revealer in which the others assuaged her concerns before Yeshé Tsogyel conferred the mind-mandate transmission upon her:

> The Queen [Yeshé Tsogyel] replied,
>
> > Noble Lady, still your enlightened activities are not complete.
> > Not weakening the armor of your aspiration to benefit others,

act in accordance with the *ḍākinī* prophecies and
we will help you.
In particular, the enlightened activities of a Treasure revealer depend on consorts and doctrine holders,
so it is important that you behave in a manner that does not allow auspicious connections to disperse.

I responded,

If I, this inferior woman (*lus dman*), am capable of fulfilling the aspirations of the Guru Couple with the actions of my body, speech, and mind, and if I can be a small help to sentient beings, thereby achieving a modicum of benefit for myself and others, even if I have to go back [to the world] temporarily, how can I bear the suffering? You all know what is necessary. For me, even though there is no difference in the amount of suffering between going to the Hell of Incessant Torment and to the human world, I think that not returning would contradict my bodhisattva training. Understanding this, even if I have to return many times only to help one being, it seems that there is nothing to be done but see if I can endure it.

Dorjetso said,

Noble Lady, when you are capable of benefiting one being like that, you are fulfilling the aspirations of the Guru Couple. When you write down one chapter of profound holy Dharma, even if it doesn't bring about any type of benefit for beings, you are fulfilling the aspirations of the Guru Couple. When you exert yourself only in benefiting beings without [any difference between] public and private holy vows, even though beings on the wrong path criticize you, you are fulfilling the aspirations of the Guru Couple. This is to say that until beings' karma is exhausted, the enlightened activity of the Guru's compassion is not exhausted. Until beings' karma is exhausted, his compassionate enlightened activity manifests as a great, eternally pervading, spontaneous presence in whatever form is necessary to tame beings and dredge the depths of *saṃsāra*. Hence, like him, you must don the armor of the completely pure intention to benefit the teachings and beings. In the future when the time comes, you will be reborn in this buddhafield, together with the beings that are connected to you. It is certain that you will become one with me.

Everyone gathered there performed a vast feast offering. In particular, [Padmasambhava] opened the *maṇḍala* of the *Kadü Chökyi Gyatso, Ocean of the Compendium of Dharma Teachings*, and gave ripening [empowerments] and liberating [instructions] to each of the king and subjects. Having done this, he collected the teachings and sealed the entire library in a miraculous box. He gave it to his disciples as their paternal inheritance and performed aspirations.

In particular, the Wish-fulfilling Jewel [Drimé Özer] acted as my hero for the means of accomplishment section[35] and placed me [on the path of] ripening and liberation.[36] Yeshé Tsogyel looked after me with great love. She gave me the golden pages of the fifty-eight-section Dharma cycle *Yangsang Khandrö Tuktik, Extremely Secret Ḍākinī's Heart Essence*, in the manner of oral transmission, and then conferred a symbolic empowerment upon me. She gave me a secret name, Khandro Gyepé Dorjé, and performed the mind-mandate aspiration prayers.[37]

Sera Khandro emphasized the strong connection among herself, Dorjetso, and the Guru Couple Padmasambhava and Yeshé Tsogyel through such visions, but this alone did not guarantee the success of her revelation efforts. Instead, the constellation of circumstances called auspicious connections or *tendrel* determined their outcome. Specifically, the auspicious connections necessary for Treasure revelation are fivefold: 1) being the right person to reveal a given Treasure; 2) arriving at the right place; 3) arriving at the right time; and being accompanied by the right people, including 4) the prophesied doctrine holder (*chos bdag*), the heir who will transmit the revealed teaching, and 5) the right consort (*thabs grogs*), who helps the Treasure revealer find and decode his or her discovery. In the aforementioned vision, once Yeshé Tsogyel empowered Sera Khandro and conferred the mind-mandate transmission upon her, all twenty-four of Padmasambhava's other close disciples offered her pithy advice in eloquent verses about how to realize the natural state of liberation. After this,

Then, the *ḍākinīs* from before escorted me out of the palace. Yeshé Tsogyel said,

Noblewoman, in order for you to tame beings of the degenerate age, you are the emanation of the enlightened activity of seven *ḍākinīs*. You have

> been sent out in the form of an insight woman (*shes rab mi mo*), so secretly take care of beings, and after sixty years I will invite you back here. If you don't follow this crucial point, it will become difficult to maintain the two Treasure teachings in accordance with the *ḍākinīs*' miraculous symbols. Abandon the hustle and bustle of doing many things. If you become attached to this illusory world, don't prepare to stay very long. If you meet someone born in the tiger, monkey, bull, or sheep year, your temporary hindrances will be dispelled. Because everything—disciples, longevity, and Dharma—depends on consorts and doctrine holders, it is imperative that you are careful regarding the crucial point of auspicious connections.

Saying this, she treated me lovingly and went back into the palace.[38]

The *ḍākinī* prophecies that permeate Sera Khandro's autobiography promised that she had the potential to accomplish her religious purpose of revealing Treasures, but they also warned her of constant dangers that threatened the fleeting connections required for revelation. For example, when she was twenty-five,

> At that time, the auspicious connections for many Treasures went away. In particular, I left behind the profound Treasures from Drakar Dreldzong called *Khandro Gongpa Düpé Chöter, Embodiment of the Ḍākinīs' Realization Dharma Treasures.* The Treasure protector actually came and all the people gathered there saw the auspicious connections go away on account of other conditions. But because of the great power of my inferior merit regarding place and time, it was as if I had no way to stop the auspicious connections from going away.[39]

Treasure protectors were bound by Padmasambhava under oath to guard Buddhism, but they could be irritated into taking great offense if Sera Khandro did not pay attention to the prophesied auspicious connections. Revealing Treasures at the right time and place was not just a privilege, it was also an obligation. Failure to gather together auspicious connections resulted in many types of disturbances. For example, in 1925, when the thirty-three-year-old Sera Khandro had just finished giving empowerments at the branch of Dodrupchen Monastery called Sanglung Monastery,

> At that time because I had some Treasures to take out near the seat of the Treasure revealer from before named Sangngak Lingpa, I went there with my group. An old woman said, "I heard that you, the central Tibetan woman, passed away last year. You didn't die?"
>
> All the monks became fiercely angry. Although I told her, "I didn't die; I came here," she didn't believe me and said this again and again. Hence, I thought that it was certain that now my Treasures would go away. Despite this, since I had a prophecy about what I was to do regarding the final [parts] of Akyé Sangngak Lingpa's Treasures, I wondered if I would have a way to do it. When I was doing preparations, the auspicious connections went away, causing the Treasure protectors to become offended. Suddenly undesirable things happened to us.
>
> I invoked the beneficial activity of the land protector (*yul skyong*) Lharek Nyentsé, who ensured that the cliff demon (*brag btsan*) remained bound under oath. I gave everyone gathered there, high and low, whatever advice they desired. After I taught detailed pith instructional teachings, everyone's faith and devotion were nurtured.[40]

Inauspicious comments such as the old woman's insistence that Sera Khandro had died the year before could taint otherwise favorable circumstances. In this case, invoking the land deity Lharek Nyentsé helped her to quell hindrances and restore auspicious connections. However, land deities were not always so compliant. When she was thirty-eight, in 1930, after giving religious teachings to her disciples at Kardon Hermitage,

> At that time, although the protectresses of that place clearly taught me the meaning of the symbols in the Treasure's prophetic registry, the auspicious connection of the right time did not occur, so the Treasure went away. During that year, even though enemies and demons caused a few undesirable hostilities and attacks, I thought it was [Treasure protectresses'] offense caused by auspicious connections not coming together. With whatever power I could muster, I forced the Treasure protectors to promise that they would quickly fulfill what they were asked to do, and their offense dissipated.[41]

The negativity caused by not making the most of auspicious connections manifested at times in the form of physical sickness, such as when the forty-year-old Sera Khandro was en route to Andzom Drukpa's religious encampment: "At that time, although there was a bit of Treasure, I let it go. Because of this, the Dharma protector became offended, and my disciple, Rikzang, suddenly fell ill. We then stayed in the Remda Valley for a few days."[42] Environmental disturbances could also result from Treasure protectors' outrage when Sera Khandro did not manage to bring auspicious connections together. After her visit to Andzom's encampment,

> Then, during that year on the 25th of the 8th month, when my group was on the road returning home, I received a bit of a prophecy foretelling the arrival of Treasures of the three Treasure protector siblings of Dungra Drakar. Because I neglected it, fierce hail fell on us, and it was difficult to bear the frightful thunder and lightning. Having prayed to my Lama and abided without separating from the dimension of equanimity, we didn't experience great harm.[43]

More than a philosophical illustration of the Buddhist truth of interdependence, the worldview invoked by the Treasure tradition brought weather conditions, social interactions, and physical health into its network of relationality. These conditions both affected and were affected by Treasure revealers and the texts and ritual objects they discovered with the help of Treasure protectors.

So far we have seen that Padmasambhava and Yeshé Tsogyel dominate Sera Khandro's religious devotion and prefigure the story of her life from the very first pages of her autobiography. Visionary experiences of receiving empowerment directly from them in Treasure teachings form pivotal episodes in her self-narrative, proving her authenticity as a Treasure revealer and emphasizing the divine providence of the scriptures she wrote. Even so, the bulk of Sera Khandro's biographical writings narrate the difficulties she experienced attempting to reveal Treasures. Prophetic voices exalted her enlightened potential at the same time as they warned of the malevolent forces threatening to disturb the delicate balance of auspicious connections. Crucially important in this web of relationships necessary for successful revelation were the intermediaries between Padmasambhava and Yeshé Tsogyel and the person they designated as revealer, such as the Treasure protectors who figure prominently in the passages above. These were most often the powerful Tibetan spirits whose identity as "masters of the territory" (*gzhi bdag*) signaled their status in networks of local authority that bridged the esoteric domain of protecting Treasures with everyday social and political interests. The multidimensional stakes of maintaining auspicious connections with these spirits of the land is the topic we turn to next.

PART III: GROUNDING TREASURE REVELATION IN GOLOK

According to many of its scholarly interpreters, the Tibetan Treasure tradition developed as a response to intersectarian Buddhist competition brought about by the importation of new Tantric scriptures after the fall of the Tibetan royal dynasty in the ninth century and the ensuing period of political fragmentation.[44] Around the same time as the "new" schools of Tibetan Buddhism, such as the Kagyü and Sakya, formed in the eleventh century, the Buddhism claiming imperial Tibetan roots came to be known as the "old" or Nyingma school, and the first Treasure revealers, such as Sangyé Lama, appeared. Nearly a millennium later, Sera Khandro's writings suggest that the Treasure tradition's vitality in her era had more to do with powerful associations with indigenous Tibetan conceptions of sacred geography and regional political organization than with intersectarian competition. These associations are clearest in Sera Khandro's interactions with the Tibetan deities who were incorporated into the tradition as Treasure protectors. The majority hailed from a larger category of "land deities," including a spectrum of forces such as "local deities" (*yul lha*), "local protectors" (*yul skyong*), "masters of the territory" (*gzhi bdag*), "masters of the ground" (*sa bdag*), local spirits associated with mountains called *nyen* (*gnyan*) and *tsen* (*btsan*), nature spirits called *nöjin* (*gnod sbyin*), "war gods" (*dgra lha*), serpentine spirits associated with water called *lu* (*klu*), and demonic forces called *men* (*sman*). Land deities are "worldly deities" (*'jig rten pa'i lha*) who are not enlightened buddhas or bodhisattvas and therefore lack the capacity to aid devotees in realizing liberation or gaining a better rebirth. Their domain of influence is this world, and they specialize in rewarding those who propitiate them properly with good health, good harvests, prosperity, progeny, and military power. Failure to propitiate local land deities could have disastrous consequences, for they could harm as well as help inhabitants of their territories. Land deities are divided into two main classifications: benevolent (*dkar phyogs*), especially those that Padmasambhava and his disciples converted to Buddhism and bound under oath to foreswear harming beings; and malevolent (*nag phyogs*), untamed by Buddhism's civilizing influence and potentially dangerous. Like other Treasure revealers' biographies, Sera Khandro's life story presents this dual nature of land deities as presences whom she subjugated and controlled but also depended upon. At times, they were no more than demonic influences awaiting her exorcism, such as the following encounter when she was twenty-five and traveling on pilgrimage with Gyelsé's entourage to Anyé Machen Mountain:

> Then, that month on the nineteenth we set off on the road and arrived at the uppermost part of the Mar Valley called Tagé Sumdo. The horse I was riding, named Kyangö, suddenly got sick and I wondered what had happened. The owner of that land was a cliff demoness (*sman*) and [I intuited that] this was her miraculous display, so I loosened my belt and lay down on the road right where I was.
>
> Gyelsé said, "Khandro, if your horse is dying, what's the use of lying down? Let's get back on the road and go as far as we can."
>
> "I need to sleep a bit," I replied, so Gyelsé got angry and left.
>
> My other companions and even Tupzang said, "Now let's go," but I didn't listen to them.
>
> Lhapel said, "Well, it seems as if this horse is tired. I will go slowly and come later. You all go first and stay at a place where there is grass and water."
>
> I added, "You all go first, let's do it this way. We two—the horse and I—will arrive later. If the horse dies, I will recite whatever Dharma I know, and if he lives, we will come together." Then I fell asleep.
>
> After some time, I heard what sounded like a woman's voice call out to me. I thought that it didn't make sense for there to be a human voice in this desolate red valley, so I disregarded it. The cliff demoness actually appeared, but it seemed as if she dared not approach me. By generating the divine pride of Tröma [a wrathful female deity], I vanquished her and bound her by oath, thereby dispelling the negative circumstances. With that, my stallion's illness was cured.[45]

Sera Khandro prevailed over this noxious spirit, but negotiating with local land deities was not always so straightforward. As worldly deities, land deities were not part of the Three Jewels (Buddha, Dharma, Saṅgha) revered by Buddhists as the sources of refuge. Nevertheless, their support was crucial for successful revelation. This ambivalent status emerges in Sera Khandro's portrayal of her relationship with these earthbound powers:

> Then, that month on the fourteenth day [in 1927] my attendant Śīla Vajra [Tsültrim Dorjé], my daughter, Chöying Drönma, and I went together with two people who came to invite us to Dzirong Sanglung Monastery. When we were staying there, a white man on a white horse saying he was the land protector Lharik Nyentsé[46] came and said: "You should make offerings to us and we will do whatever you desire." Having said this, he disappeared.
>
> I thought that from the time I was nine years old until now, I had set my mind on the Three Jewels. Aside from praying to them, it seemed that I had no custom of taking refuge and making offerings to land protectors and land deities and so forth. Despite this, because he was my Treasure protector, thinking of our sacred relationship as land [deity] and guest (*gnas mgron gyi dam tshig*), I visualized him. When I made some offerings to him, I got whatever provisions I needed.[47]

Even if land deities were not part of the Three Jewels, they were still the owners of the territory that Sera Khandro treaded upon. They too required respect and recognition through ritual propitiation, for Treasure revealers like her were guests on their sacred ground.

The ambivalent status of land deities is reflected in the Treasure tradition, whose alpine revelation sites in Golok were locations in which Buddhist and indigenous Tibetan conceptions of spiritual power converged. According to Samten Karmay, mountains in Tibet can be sacred in two distinctive ways: as Buddhist holy mountains (*gnas ri*) or as residences of local Tibetan territorial deities, many of which pre-date the arrival of Buddhism.[48] Buddhist holy mountains are pilgrimage destinations for devotees from all regions of Tibet, who come to circumambulate them because of their associations with Buddhist deities, significant historical events, religious masters, and ritual objects. In contrast, what Samten Karmay has termed "the Tibetan mountain cult" venerates mountains as residences of local Tibetan territorial deities for aid in mundane pursuits. Mountain cult worshippers are exclusively male residents of the region, who make annual trips to their local deity's mountainside cairn to offer incense, ritual arrows, prayer flags, and wind horses.[49] Tibetan mountain cult deities are depicted most often as warriors mounted on horses (see fig. 2.3), whereas Buddhist sacred mountains are rarely represented iconographically.[50] Karmay notes that a few mountains connected to the Treasure tradition, such as Mount Murdo in Gyalrong and Anyé Machen in Golok, demonstrate characteristics of both Buddhist holy mountains and sites associated with the Tibetan mountain cult; Sera Khandro's writings suggest a greater intersection between the two at the mountains from which she revealed Treasures. Examples include smaller, more locally important sacred mountains in greater Golok such as Tashi Gomang, Drakar Dreldzong, Solung Drakar, and Chakri Ömbar, as well as major mountains including Anyé Machen, Nyenpo Yutsé, and Drong Mountain.

In many parts of the Tibetan plateau, communities understood their local sacred mountains to be the ancestors of their regional leaders, thus connecting systems of political power and social organization with the spiritual power embodied in the mountains. One way that Treasure revealers fit into this equation was as mediators between the land deities cum sacred ancestors and the political leaders of the region, whose hegemony was tied to receiving the favor of their ancestral mountain deities. Treasure revealers assured this by balancing the interests of the spiritually inhabited land and its human residents via their revelations. Through gathering their auspicious connections, Treasure revealers like Sera Khandro participated in an economy of relationships aimed at maintaining equilibrium among the mandates they received from enlightened imperial Tibetan figures, celestial and earthly demons and divinities, and their patrons, including ordinary laity as well as local leaders in eastern Tibet. Treasure revealers calibrated this equilibrium through the exchange of precious substances into and out of the earth at key locations. Most scholarship on the Treasure tradition has focused on the scriptures and artifacts that revealers claim to have withdrawn from the Tibetan earth and sky, but Treasure revealers also often inserted sacred substances back into the earth and water called "Treasure substitutes" (*gter tshab*) or "Treasure vases" (*gter 'bum*) filled with precious materials.[51] Given that the term "Treasure" (*gter*), or more commonly "Treasure substance" (*gter kha*), is also the Tibetan word for mineral, it has an etymological link with natural resources more generally. Although thoroughly imbricated in Tibetan Buddhism, the reciprocal exchange between

FIG. 2.3 Drongri Mukpo, resident land deity of Drong Mountain in Serta

PHOTOGRAPH BY BRITT-MARIE ALM, 2005

discovering a Treasure and offering a substitute for it resonates more with the system of exchange between pilgrim and divinity associated with Tibet's non-Buddhist mountain cult than with Buddhist forms of veneration in which the pilgrim beseeches the divinity for religious and worldly gains.[52]

FIG. 2.4 Anyé Machen Mountain

PHOTOGRAPH BY SARAH JACOBY, 2005

GOLOK AND ITS GRANDFATHER, ANYÉ MACHEN MOUNTAIN

The most powerful of the motley group of land deities were those inhabiting sacred mountains (variously called *yul lha*, *gzhi bdag*, *gnyan*, and *dgra lha*), who ruled over the "masters of the ground" (*sa bdag*) in their territories.[53] The fulcrum of greater Golok was Anyé Machen Mountain, whose name translates as "Grandfather of the Great Ma [Valley]." Located in the northern reaches of Golok territory in Machen County, Anyé Machen towers at over 20,000 feet (see map 2). It is the abode of the "master of the territory," Machen Pomra, and his retinue and family, whose kinship network formed systems of genealogical relationships with other sacred mountains in the region that mapped the political territory of the inhabitants of these mountains' respective jurisdictions. Goloks trace their history to a series of human-sacred mountain interrelationships that gave rise to their social structure. According to the *Annals of Golok History*, a fourteenth-century Tantric householder priest named Dri Lha Gyelbum settled in a valley called "Gukho" in the Pelyül region of Kham, eastern

Tibet. Dri Lha Gyelbum married one of the five daughters of the mountain god Nyenpo Yutsé. Their son Ambum Gyel married a princess from the kingdom of Ling. Because Ambum Gyel did not get along with the king of Ling, he needed to find another place to live. Heeding divinations and a dream in which Machen Pomra beckoned him to his territory, Ambum Gyel brought fifty households there at the end of the fourteenth century. The *Annals* records that locals referred to them as the Gulokpa ('Gu log pa), or those who departed from the Gu valley. Dri Lha Gyelbum built several Bön temples as well as an offering temple to Machen Pomra at Anyé Machen. Reinforced by the mountain god's support, Dri Lha Gyelbum and Ambum emerged victorious from battles with the local inhabitants (the Gnyan rtse, Mkhar re, and Ba le) of the area (the Rdo and Smra valleys of Golok). Ambum and the Ling princess had three sons, the youngest of whom, Bumyak, inherited his father's jurisdiction. Nyenpo Yutsé then challenged Ambum to perform a series of feats. As a final test, Nyenpo Yutsé sent his youngest daughter in the form of a slithering snake and promised that she would marry his son if they could touch her with a silk arrow.[54] When they did this, she transformed into a human woman, and two years later the couple produced a son named Chaktar (b. 1443). From Chaktar's lay children and the territories they controlled, the three parts of Golok (*Mgo log khag gsum*), Akyong Bum, Wangchen Bum, and Pema Bum, formed.[55] The *Annals of Golok History* records that when the People's Republic of China "liberated" Golok during the 1950s, the three parts included 52 different encampment groups (*tsho ba*) comprising more than 200 different smaller divisions (*shog chung*) consisting of 13,199 households in which there were 59,395 people.[56] Encampment groups ranged in size from about 20 to 400 households that were not necessarily biologically related but shared a common grazing territory and were obligated to defend its reaches from encroaching neighbors as well as foreign attacks.[57] Each part of Golok and the encampment groups within had their own leaders who propitiated both general and regionally specific land deities in order to ensure favorable conditions. Wangchen Bum and Pema Bum always propitiated Yungdrung Chaktsé, whereas Akyong Bum propitiated Nyenpo Yutsé. All three, however, made offerings to Anyé Machen.[58]

Another of Chaktar's sons, Sonam Khyap, became a monk at Katok Monastery and returned to Golok to found the first Buddhist monastery, Drakargo, in ca. 1493. The Nyingma Buddhist lineage of Katok proliferated in Golok from that time forward, as did Pelyül and Dzokchen branch monasteries to lesser degrees. In 1632 a Kagyü monastery was founded, and in 1716 Drakargo became a Jonang monastery. Only in 1842 was the first Geluk monastery founded. The *Annals* lists a total of fifty-four monasteries in Golok extant in the 1950s, not including Washül Serta territory.[59] In Sera Khandro's day, many of these were not sedentary institutions with large assembly halls. In the nomadic regions, pastoralists traveled with their herds according to seasonal grazing patterns. Likewise, the *Annals* explains, "Most of the monasteries in the nomadic regions had to be mobile in accordance with the livelihoods of their patrons, hence there was no choice but for them to be 'black [tent] encampments' (*nag sgar*) or 'tent monasteries' (*sbra dgon*)."[60] Also called "religious encampments" (*chos sgar*) or simply "encampments" (*sgar*) in Sera Khandro's writings, these were communities centered around living charismatic Treasure revealers and their disciples, including both monastic and nonmonastic religious devotees, mostly from the same or contiguous encampment groups, who traveled together and lived in tents. Both Drimé Özer and Gara Gyelsé's religious communities were religious encampments, although there was considerable overlap between them and the monasteries (*dgon pa*) led by their fathers (Kelzang and Benak, respectively), which were fixed locations established generations earlier and inhabited by monastics from the region.

Whether they were mobile encampments or fixed monasteries, Golok's religious communities were primarily Nyingma with a strong non-Buddhist legacy. Of the fifty-four monasteries in the three parts of Golok, thirty-six were Nyingma, eight Jonang, seven Geluk, one nonsectarian, one Kagyü, and two Bön.[61] Even though only two Bön monasteries survived until the 1950s, the ruins of many others remained. As the *Annals* reports, at the time of Dri Lha Gyelbum in the fourteenth century,

> Not only did even the name "Buddhist Monastery" not exist in this region [Golok], but in this place known [then] as the three Nyen, Khar, and Ba,[62] everyone made offerings only to local deities (*yul lha*) and land deities (*gzhi bdag*) such as Nyenpo Yutsé and so forth. The tradition of having faith in the Buddhist religion had not been established.[63]

It was not until five generations later, in the fifteenth century, that Sonam Khyap established Golok's first Buddhist monastery. As a result, many mythological tales remain about divinities (*lha*), serpentine water spirits (*klu*), and mountain gods (*gnyan*) who were connected to the hegemony of the Golok rulers. The *Annals* claims that, "One may say that there isn't another region in which traditions pertaining to the ancient Tibetan system of political governance involving Bön, narrations (*sgrung*), and symbolic languages (*lde'u*) are more visible than in Golok."[64]

Given this confluence of Buddhism with the region's network of politically and spiritually significant sacred mountains, we may now better understand why territorial powers such as Anyé Machen have such prominent voices in Sera Khandro's autobiography. For example, early in her relationship with Gara Gyelsé, before they settled together at Benak, the nineteen-year-old Sera Khandro joined him on her first pilgrimage to Anyé Machen:

> That year [1911], Gara Gyelsé and several of his entourage were preparing to go to [Anyé] Machen. The nun Samkar Drön and I joined the group and went to Machen. When we arrived at uppermost Tachok,[65] Machen's minister named Drandül Wangchuk came to welcome me, riding an actual horse made of cloud. We went into his palace, where there was a sumptuous spread of food and drink. As if meeting someone they had known before, he and his queen, children, entourage, and servants were greatly delighted. The gatekeeper war god named "One with a Conch Top Knot" said the following:
>
>> Great female bodhisattva, thank you so much for coming to our sacred land. Stay here for a few days. For the sacred land, we need you to perform a cleansing ritual and [to bury] a vase of prosperity as a means of restoring the earth's vitality. For us, we need you to teach the Dharma expansively.
>
> I fulfilled all their desires, and our sacred relationship as land [deity] and guest became unified.[66] I said,
>
>> I need to find a way to retrieve my *Zap Ter Tsogyel, Tsogyel Profound Treasure*, and *Pakmö Druptap, Vajravārāhī Liturgy*, which have been entrusted to the Seven Sovereign Ladies.
>
> In an instant, the war god "One with a Conch Top Knot" departed like a lightning flash to the sacred land of Magyel's western gatekeepers, The Seven Sovereign Ladies. From them, he retrieved Tsogyel's profound pages together with a statue and "soul stones" of the *ḍākinī* and gave them to me. He said,

Because the auspicious connections of a doctrine holder and consort have not yet gathered together, the Seven Sovereign Ladies said that the time has not arrived for the profound pages of Vajravārāhī. Hence, I did not retrieve that Treasure chest.

Then I did whatever they needed me to do. When I prepared to return home, the Queen Drakgyelma said,

Now that our sacred relationship [as land deity and guest] is unified, if you come here to Magyel three times, your longevity and enlightened activities will be without comparison. If you don't do this, at times you run the risk of experiencing undesirable things. In particular, since there will be an extremely serious obstacle to your longevity, it is important to be careful.

Then, as before, I rode the cloud horse through the sky and returned home while my travel companions were boiling some lunch. Among them a monk disciple of Gara Terchen named Ngakpa Lhakpa asked, "Where did you go? This morning when the sun rose you left. What is the meaning of your returning here when the sun is moving into afternoon?"

I replied, "I went into a cave and fell asleep there, so I couldn't catch up with you all." They believed this was the truth.[67]

Sera Khandro's authority to reveal Treasures came from the geographic and genealogical summit of Golok, the "grandfather," or Anyé, of the region. Her interlocutors were none other than the main land deity Machen Pomra's minister (sometimes described as his younger brother) Drandül Wangchuk, whose name means "Powerful One Who Conquers Enemies," and Machen Pomra's female consort, Queen Drakgyelma, whose name means "Illustrious Victorious Lady."[68] Nevertheless, Sera Khandro's humble denial of her miraculous adventure alludes to the fact that others in her religious community would need further proof of her extraordinary encounters with the reigning terrestrial powers.

Later, when Sera Khandro was twenty-five years old in 1917, she returned to Anyé Machen for another pilgrimage with Gyelsé and company and had another miraculous experience:

Our religious encampment was staying in front of the Tachok mountain pass. When evening came, based on a prophetic indication we requested from the Seven Sovereign Ladies who were gatekeepers of Magyel [Anyé

Machen Mountain], I went to the residence of the Seven Sovereign Ladies near the snow mountain together with the nun Chötreng; Kachö Drön; Dechen Drönma; my daughter, Chöying Drönma; and Garter Rinpoché's son, the monk Jikmé Könchok, who served as the commitment vow substance.[69] En route, the entire sky was filled with rainbow clouds in myriad shapes including those standing upright, in curved lines, crescents, and lotuses.

They said, "This is extremely amazing! It seems that we will receive a blessing substance!"

I didn't say anything. Then, when we reached the Treasure entrance, on top of the rainbow clouds appeared many beings with bodies like offering goddesses who seemed to be holding offering substances in their hands. They gathered just below the Treasure site, standing on its right and left sides. My companions were amazed and offered prostrations and prayers to them.

At that time, from between the dark clouds something like sunlight illuminated our path on the long road, particularly the Treasure entrance. I said to them, "You all go and circumambulate this cliff. Because my daughter is young and my leg is bad, it seems that I can't circumambulate, so we will stay here and wait for you."

After they went to circumambulate, I made a gesture with a *vajra* wrapped with the hair of Vimala Raśmi,[70] who was my secret consort [necessary to open] the Treasure entrance. As soon as I did that, the crescent-shaped Treasure entrance opened and I took out a precious leather chest sealed with a vajra containing the *Dorjé Pakmo Zabdrup, Profound Vajravārāhī Liturgy*; a marble statue of Sarasvatī about the size of the measure of a *ḍākinī*'s thumb to index finger; a secret explanation of the *Yabzhi*[71] [written on] a Treasure page about the size of the thumb to index finger [made from] the skin of Rudra's heart; a turquoise chest; a semiprecious stone[72] chest; three woven chests; other sacred medicine; and saffron pills, which liberate through taste. Then I offered a Treasure substitute. Because I didn't have an actual consort or doctrine holder, I left behind the auspicious connections of the mind-support and enlightened activity chests for later. At that time, a fragrant aroma permeated the valley, miraculous water sprang forth from the Treasure site, the earth quaked, a sound emerged, and so forth.

When all this happened, my companions wondered what it was and came back quickly, saying, "It is certain that you have taken out a Treasure. You need to show it to us."

I replied, "This is my daughter that I have taken out as a Treasure—now I wonder if I can take out a son?"

When I said this, Chötreng said, "Your daughter has already seen the Treasure. We need to see this Treasure from which a fragrant aroma wafts!" and she repeated this again and again.

Thinking of my commitment vows to the *ḍākinīs*, I didn't dare tell an outright lie. I said, "After you prostrate to the goddesses amid the clouds, offer prostrations to me and to this site. Since I have extracted miraculous water in the manner of a Treasure, everyone taste it—it is the accomplishment substance of this place."

They said, "It is amazing that you suddenly extracted a self-emergent spring from a dry cliff like this!" When everybody tasted the ambrosia, they said it had an unusual potent flavor and a fragrant aroma.

Then the amount of miraculous water diminished a bit, while all the rainbow clouds that appeared before dissolved into the sky. When all the mountains and valleys became dark, they said, "Now how will we make the difficult return home?"

I replied, "If one can traverse even the intermediate state toward one's next life by praying to the Lama and the Three Jewels, we certainly can make it home tonight! But I wonder what Trülku Gyelsé will say?"

Chötreng said, "Since Gyelsé can say whatever he wants, let him say it. It seems that our role is to listen, so how can we not do that? In short, our purpose at this time is a good one. Now I will go home first, and even if he scolds me and slaps me, I'm not afraid."

Then, when we were looking to see if we could find the way home, since the road was obstructed by rocks, snow, and boulders, it was difficult to follow. I prayed to the Lama and Three Jewels and as a result, a flame about the size of a thumb went in front of us and illuminated our path. After this, we were able to travel on the road without trouble. They said it was incredible, and their minds were satisfied.[73]

As Sera Khandro and her entourage proceeded on their pilgrimage around Anyé Machen, at a place called Mowatowa they discovered a Mañjuśrī cave in which Gotrül Rinpoché had prophesied that Gyelsé should do a retreat, but he chose to ignore the advice.[74] Following this dissipation of auspicious connections, which Sera Khandro felt were important for Gyelsé to cultivate,

Then we arrived at Drandül Wangchuk's holy site. While everyone was offering incense and throwing wind horses and so forth, a beautiful and attractive woman who said she was Queen Drakgyelma arrived before me riding a peacock. She wore a flowing gown made of blue-patterned silk and was adorned with many jewels. I spoke:

Beautiful-faced, attractive, Powerful One,
sole wife of the ground-attaining bodhisattva,[75]
great protectress of the Buddhist teachings, Drakgyelma,
Mother who grants the prosperity elixir accomplishment substance,
Queen Sky Lady, Mother of all,
I rely on you, Great Mother.
May you quickly accomplish all of your boundless activities.

She replied,

One sister of the heroes,
secret consort of the awareness holders,
we rely upon you, protector of all beings.
Bring the commitment vows of land [deity] and guest together as one.

She gave me a crystal vase about one inch wide filled with blue-black pills the size of mustard seeds, saying:

> During the lifetime of Magyel's divine son Dünkyong, he gathered all of the Good Fortune Treasure elixir of this world and hid it as a Treasure in Magyel's Treasury, the Maroon Royal Palace. At that time, he gathered the Treasure substances of the one hundred Great Treasure revealers, including the five types of yellow scrolls, five types of pills, five types of Dharma medicine, five types of longevity elixir, five types of prosperity elixir, and a variety of other types of Treasure substances and blended these together as an elixir. I offer this to you. If you hide this in the realm of the four elements [earth, water, fire, and air], by the power of these types [of Treasure substances], it is certain that many sentient beings' rounds through the lower realms of *saṃsāra* will stop.

After uttering these words, she disappeared.[76]

Beyond being Yeshé Tsogyel's emissary, Sera Khandro had local support from the highest places. The Queen of Anyé Machen, Drakgyelma, anointed her and entrusted her with Treasure substances so powerful they would relieve human suffering in the world. Even so, they would only become effective if Sera Khandro nourished the region by hiding them there. In this instance as above, Treasure revelation was about not only extracting precious items from the mountain but also interacting with it in a reciprocal exchange, which Sera Khandro did by offering substitutes for the Treasures she removed. As a sign of her approval, Drakgyelma beseeched Sera Khandro to strengthen their bond as land deity and guest.

THE HEAD OF WASHÜL SERTA, DRONG MOUNTAIN

When Sera Khandro first arrived in the greater Golok region as a fifteen-year-old runaway, she entered the domain of Drongri or "Wild Yak Mountain," the anthropomorphic head of the Washül Serta territory. Today

FIG. 2.5 Drongri or "Wild Yak Mountain" in Serta

PHOTOGRAPH BY SARAH JACOBY, 2005

this region is roughly analogous to Serta County in Kandzé Tibetan Autonomous Prefecture, Sichuan. According to local histories, the presiding force at Drong Mountain, named Drongri Mukpo or "Maroon Wild Yak Mountain," was a land deity (*gzhi bdag*), a war god (*dgra lha*), and a Buddhist bodhisattva in addition to being the biological ancestor of the ruling Washül family. These histories trace the Washül hegemony over Serta to 1606, when auspicious circumstances at Drong Mountain indicated that Śākya Tar of the Washül lineage should lead.[77] Five generations later, the Washül man named Wangchen who inherited the leadership did not have a son. He received prophecies that if he made incense offerings to Drong Mountain, the mountain's "soul son" (*bla bu*) would incarnate in the womb of his wife. The following year, his wife gave birth to this "soul son" named Lhasé Sonam Dorjé. He had four sons, one of whom, Lhasé Sonam Norbu, built the Gogentang Stūpa in 1913, a landmark still standing next to the town of Serta.[78] Another of the sons of the "soul son" was Sotrül Natsok Rangdröl, incarnate lama at Sera Tekchen Chönkor Ling Monastery in upper Serta, who sheltered Sera Khandro after Drimé Özer's death and fostered her religious teaching career. In Serta I met the descendant of another of these four sons, who is the current Washül Serta leader and described himself to me as "the great-grandson of Drong Mountain."[79] Despite his dramatically altered political stature resulting from Serta's incorporation into the PRC in the 1950s, he remains a highly respected figure in the region.

In Sera Khandro's day, Serta was politically distinct from the three parts of Golok but shared with them linguistic, genealogical, religious, and cultural ties. Like Golok, Serta was a confederation of smaller encampment groups and subdivisions including primarily communities of nomadic herdsmen but also sedentary farmers. The Washül Serta confederation envisioned itself as a white tent, with the Washül family lineage as the tent roof or central axis. Surrounding this were four long ropes holding up the tent, comprising four different collections of smaller groups not biologically related to the Washüls but part of the larger community.[80] Düjom Lingpa's monastic seat, Kelzang Monastery in Dartsang, was affiliated with one of the four "long ropes" of Serta society called "the four subsidiary encampments" (*bu chung tsho bzhi*) and the Tashül subdivision within it. In 1950 Washül Serta included 89 different encampment group leaders (*tsho dpon*), beneath whom were more than 600 "leaders of 10 [households]" (*bcu dpon*), who despite their name controlled between 20 and 40 households each. In 1950 more than 30,000 people, more than 16,900 households, lived in Serta.[81] Serta was a Nyingma stronghold, as was Golok; in 1950 there were 42 monasteries, all of which were Nyingma, including mostly Pelyül but also Katok and Dzokchen lineages.[82]

Drong Mountain's significance for Serta society is well attested in Sera Khandro's biographical writings, as in the writings of other Treasure revealers from the region.[83] In Drimé Özer's biography, Sera Khandro depicts the mountain's multilayered identity:

> That night in his [Drimé Özer's] dream, two attractive women wearing white silk clothing and adorned with assorted precious jewels approached the Master riding a doe and a peacock. They asked him, "Are you well?"
>
> He replied, "I'm well. Who are you two?"
>
> "We are Drong Mountain's two wives," they responded. "Do you want to go inside the sacred land?
>
> "If you two will help me, let's go," said the Master, and he went with the two *ḍākinīs*. At the place called Dünlung Barma they arrived at a door and a staircase made of conch shell. The Master asked his two companions, "Which sacred land is this?"
>
> The two *ḍākinīs* replied, "This is the sacred land [of] the lay disciple Drongri Mukpo."
>
> When they went inside, they saw a three-story celestial palace. In the lower courtyard was the one named Sechok Norbu Ömbar wearing a golden helmet and golden armor and holding a whip and a jewel. A retinue of fifty-eight warriors surrounded him. Many offering goddesses held various foods preferred by each of them and treated them like guests.
>
> In the middle story, a man with red-maroon eyes and a fierce expression wearing a loose-fitting blue silk cloak, named Drongri Mukpo, sat on a bejeweled throne in the posture of royal ease. Surrounding him were many protector deity troops.
>
> The Master said to his two companions, "Now, let's go to the upper story."
>
> "In the upper story, since there are many things to see, go up there. You may go anywhere," said the *ḍākinīs*.
>
> The Master responded, "What is there to see?"
>
> The *ḍākinīs* replied, "This is the region of the sacred mountain of Avalokiteśvara called the Potala. That maroonish figure over there is an

incarnation of Avalokiteśvara named Protector Lion. If you look from the outside, he is the lay disciple lama and leader Drongri, the meritorious war god (*dgra lha*) and powerful land deity (*gzhi bdag*). If you look from the inside, he is the Glorious Protector Lion, the general guardian of the Buddha's teachings. He is the great enemy of barbarians and negative beings with broken commitment vows who harm the Buddhist teachings and a divine protector for those with [pure] commitment vows. If you make offerings to him, he will help you. If you exhort him, he is greatly powerful and possesses the strength to shake the three-thousandfold universe."

The Master inquired, "Who is the sovereign of the lower floor named Sechok Norbu Ömbar?"

The *ḍākinīs* explained, "The incarnation of Avalokiteśvara's son Norbudzin is Norbu Ömbartsel."

One *ḍākinī* added, "He is the father of the Washül leader."

"He is his younger brother," the other stated, and their words didn't agree.

The Master asked, "If Drongri is an emanation of Avalokiteśvara, how can you two who say you are his wives be both his incarnations and the sources from which he incarnates?"

"If you want to see from whom we emanate," said the *ḍākinīs*, "it is like this." They transformed into a light green "*taṃ*" letter, and disappeared into his heart. At the same time as the Master perceived this, he awoke from sleep.[84]

Strong non-Buddhist elements appear in this portrayal of Drong Mountain, such as the doe and peacock mounts, the whip and jewel accouterments, the lay status of Drongri Mukpo, as well as his identity as a war god, a land deity, and the biological ancestor of the human leader of the Washül Serta confederation. Overlaid onto these local features is his transregional Buddhist identity as an emanation of Avalokiteśvara, the bodhisattva of compassion.

In Düjom Lingpa's autobiography as well there is a connection between Drong Mountain and Avalokiteśvara, similar to Sera Khandro's description written a quarter of a century later. When Düjom Lingpa was sixty-two, in 1897, he dreamed that a supernatural girl brought him to Drong Mountain, where he beheld a five-story palace. In the penultimate story, a dazzling bejeweled blue-green woman said:

> I am the queen of the greatly powerful land deity, protector of beings, the Glorious Protector God of the Cliff, who is none other than the Supremely Noble Sovereign of Compassion [Avalokiteśvara]. I am Yu Chama, daughter of the Eastern Nyenpo Yutsé, emanation of Venerable Tro Nyerma.[85]

Here we see another image of the wife of Drong Mountain, this one modeled on an exogamous marriage between the mountain god Nyenpo Yutsé, the main mountain god of the Akyong Bum part of Golok, and Drong Mountain. This Golok-tailored version of Avalokiteśvara doesn't look like a Buddhist bodhisattva, but like a local land deity: when Düjom Lingpa ascends to the top floor of the palace, he encounters the sovereign mountain deity of Serta, Drongri Mukpo, who was "a maroon (*mukpo*) man wearing a white silk turban and clothed in a red and blue garment, seated in a dignified manner on a bejeweled golden throne with silk brocade cushions stacked up high."[86]

Multilayered iconographic depictions of Drong Mountain such as these provide traces of a gradual assimilation process in which local deities were incorporated into the Buddhist fold. This process of Buddhicization appears still under way at Drong Mountain, whose Buddhist surface exposes underlayers of war god and land deity, replete with old correspondences between sacred mountains and human rulers. Rather than routing out these non-Buddhist systems of power, the Treasure tradition tapped directly into them. As the Third Dodrupchen (1865–1926) explained in his *Wonder Ocean: An Explanation of the Dharma Treasure Tradition*,

> One of the purposes in making these spirits the Terma protectors comes from the fact that the evil forces that cause obstructions to Dharma practitioners are the retinues of those chiefs among their spirit classes [*gyelpo*, *tsen*, *theurang*], so that by appointing their chiefs as the protectors, their subjects won't be able to transgress the orders.[87]

By making the dominant sources of temporal power such as Anyé Machen and Drongri Mukpo into protectors of the Treasure tradition, Buddhism did not have to vie with these indigenous Tibetan sovereigns, for they had already joined its forces.

Drong Mountain's dual nature as a local nexus of power and a Buddhist sacred mountain also manifests in ritual activities. Drong Mountain is the

FIG. 2.6 Annual Washül Serta Drongri Mukpo propitiation

PHOTOGRAPH BY SARAH JACOBY, 2005

site of the Washül Serta encampment group's annual local deity propitiation. Only men from Washül are allowed to make offerings at their rock cairn on the Drong mountainside, where they meet every year in early summer. The cairn is shot through with ritual arrows, which men plant there to place themselves under the mountain deity's protection.[88] After a Washül Serta-born Buddhist lama circumambulates the cairn, followed closely by the Washül Serta leader, the ritual begins. Smoke billows from the large quantities of aromatic herbs Washül laymen burn as incense, small sheets of paper printed with good luck prayers called wind horses fly about, and the shrill screams of men shouting to the mountain deity echo through the valley as the men thunderously circumambulate the cairn on horseback (and these days also on motorcycle). The Drong Mountain annual propitiation is a multiday affair, with everyone camped out by the mountain in white tents. After the offering ritual, a local lama preaches a Buddhist sermon to the men, and then the fun begins: bareback horse racing and feasting.[89] Buddhist lamas of the Washül bloodline participate, but the ritual's focus is largely non-Buddhist—the primary actors are laymen, and their goals are this-world power, prosperity, and progeny—not Buddhist liberation or ensuring a good rebirth.

Drong Mountain is also a Buddhist holy mountain that appeals to Buddhist pilgrims more generally, primarily from the greater Golok region but not exclusively of Washül ancestry. They include men, women, monastics, and laity who come to walk around the base of the mountain on a circumambulation path that takes several hours to complete. They do not necessarily seek protection from the mountain's local deity, but rather strive to gain merit for the benefit of this life and the next by honoring Drong Mountain as a sacred abode of Avalokiteśvara.

Sera Khandro fit into this latter category of Buddhist devotee who came to circumambulate Drong Mountain. Perhaps because she was foreign to the Washül territory (and also because she was female?), she did not envision Drongri Mukpo in the same way as the locally born Drimé Özer and Düjom Lingpa did. Nevertheless, the site held special power for her as well. When the twenty-nine-year-old Sera Khandro was becoming increasingly ill, two of her supporters among Gyelsé's community sought a prophecy from Drimé Özer, who responded: "Until the twenty-fifth, it is very important that you circumambulate Drong Mountain and do as many Vajrayoginī fire offerings as you can, and that you perform as many feast and ablution rituals as possible."[90] In compliance with this prophecy, Sera Khandro reports in her autobiography that

> The three of us mother and children, both Tupzang and his relative, and some other Drong Mountain circumambulators set off on the road on the twentieth. On the twenty-fifth, as we approached Drong Mountain, my perception was not the same as before, and at times I saw the Glorious Mountain[91] and at other times it seemed to disappear. In the middle of the sky, a house made of five-colored rainbow light blazed forth. Additionally, rainbow clouds and something like many vital nuclei made of rainbow light seemed to pervade the entire sky. All this coalesced in our direction as if blown by the wind. Initially, Tupzang and all the others were amazed, saying, "It's as if the sacred site is welcoming us."
>
> Then we were confused about where to go and from which direction we had come. "What seems to be causing these things?" they asked.
>
> I replied, "I don't know why rainbows commonly shine in the summer sky!"
>
> Then they departed to circumambulate Drong Mountain. When my two children and I were in our tent, someone appearing in the form of a monk and saying he was a nature spirit (*gnod sbyin*) arrived.

I demanded, "Who are you? You may not come toward me. Now the monks will speak badly of you. Since I am an invalid, I am refraining from going [to circumambulate]."

He replied, "You don't know that I am not like other guests?"

"I am ill to the point of being on the verge of death, so I am not inclined to figure out who you are," I said. Pulling the covers over my head, I slept.

"I am a messenger of your consort Lendreltsel. You are not allowed to die." As he said this, I perceived that a "*kṣa*" letter disappeared into my secret center.[92] The previous vision became clouded, and everything transformed into red light. At the same time as the red light disappeared into the heat at my navel, I gained the ability to differentiate everything in my perception and I began to recover from my illness.

Then on the left side of Dünlung Gongma, from the slope of the mountain cliff that looks like a lion jumping into the sky, I removed the profound pages of *Tsedrup Nyinda Khajor, The Union of the Sun and Moon Longevity Liturgy,* which was in an eight-cornered agate chest, and profound pages of *Tamdrin Letsok Düpung Tsarchö, Hayagrīva's Activities Liturgy [Called] Vanquishing the Hordes of Demons,* which was in an amulet box made of meteorite; and I also revealed several other Treasures as secret Treasures that I recollected from my former lifetimes. The Treasure protectors gave me each of them. I reconcealed some of these as Treasures and I gave some to the doctrine holders with the intention of having them clearly write down and propagate them. Then those who had circumambulated Drong Mountain returned to where I was.[93]

Sera Khandro's exchanges with supermundane forces at Drong Mountain both cured her temporarily of her increasingly serious arthritic condition and energized her with the capacity to reveal spiritual Treasures from its mountainside. She returned their generosity by putting some of the precious objects back in the mountain, and the signs of success manifested in her ability to transmit the new teachings.

PRACTICAL PURPOSES OF TREASURE REVELATION IN GOLOK

The exchanges of precious materials into and out of the earth during the process of Treasure revelation were significant not only for Buddhist soteriological aims but also for a range of environmental, social, and political interests. These benefits are well attested in the Third Dodrupchen's *Wonder Ocean*:

> Also, until the end of the age comes, because of ceaseless efforts of those such as the Tertons [Treasure revealers], Termas [Treasures], both of teachings and materials, detailed and appropriate prophecies will appear in time to protect Tibet from foreign invasions, internal fighting, disease, famine, and so on.[94]

Sera Khandro's writings exemplify Dodrupchen's description, for they describe revelation as a means to avert temporal dangers such as land disputes, banditry, livestock disease, and war at least as much as a means to reach spiritual liberation. In Drimé Özer's biography, Sera Khandro reports the following sequence of events that occurred at Drong Mountain when he was forty years old:

> Relying on the symbolic indications and prophecies of a *ḍākinī* saying she was Künkhyap Wangmo, who had come to him that night in his dream, the Master wrote down the profound Treasure *Guru Tapak, Guru Hayagrīva and Vajravārāhī*, from Kham Sengé Namchong. At that time, based on an earlier prophecy from Drong Mountain, he put Treasure vases in Drong Mountain to fulfill the desires of the Washül leader. He recited the *Lhachen kyi Drupa, The Great Deity Liturgy*, performed [the ritual] thoroughly, and took out some Treasures.
>
> At that time in front of Drong Mountain there was a retreatant lama who was known as the nephew of the head of the land. He told the Master, "It is certain that you are an emanation of Künkhyen [Longchen Rapjampa] because I had a good dream about this," and more. Having requested prayers from the Master to establish a Dharma connection with him, he offered material goods as an auspicious connection.
>
> Then, the Master gradually went to his seat [in Dartsang]. As his representative, Sotrül Rinpoché had gone out to tame disciples.[95] When he came back he gave all the gathered offerings to the [lama's] residence.
>
> At that time the Washül leader settled a land dispute. Everybody reached an agreement and the animosity was pacified.[96]

This passage demonstrates one way Drimé Özer mediated between the Washül Serta leader and the source of his hegemony, Drong Mountain. The currency of exchange with which he propitiated the mountain on the Washül leader's behalf was Treasure vases filled with precious substances. The offering of blessed substances nourished both the land and the Washül leader's ability to control it, ensuring his capacity to settle a land dispute between factions of his community. Such disputes, mostly concerning pastureland usage rights, were common among eastern Tibetan nomadic communities. Sera Khandro even mentions that a land dispute temporarily divided Gyelsé's religious community, forcing one faction to relocate. When one encampment group (*tsho ba*) encroached upon another's territory or stole herds, fighting to the point of death was not unheard of; if it was not properly arbitrated, multigenerational blood feuds could ensue. In these cases, the leaders of the encampment groups would gather to settle the conflict and to offer a price for any loss of life in order to stop the fighting.[97] The man who would have been the current Washül Serta leader had it not been incorporated into the PRC told me, "My role in the old society would have been to resolve disputes among the public. They would have listened and obeyed my word."[98] In addition, Treasure revealers and other religious authorities often acted as the mediators between disputing factions because the laity's faith in them allowed the lamas to achieve widespread consensus between different encampment groups. Sera Khandro mentions Drimé Özer and Sotrül Rinpoché of Sera Monastery solving land disputes, as did many other lamas from Serta, including Düjom Lingpa before them and more recently, Khenpo Jikmé Püntsok of Larung Gar.[99]

Treasure revealers' ability to balance the land and its inhabitants through inserting and removing sacred substances at key power places also helped to reduce the ever-present danger of banditry on the Golok roads. Bandits plagued outsiders who dared to trespass in Golok territory, but they also posed dangers to local religious figures traveling outside their immediate home areas. The famous nineteenth-century Nyingma lama from Amdo, Shabkar Tsokdruk Rangdröl, writes of being repeatedly attacked by bandits in Golok, and troubles caused by bandits also appear in Düjom Lingpa's autobiography.[100] Sera Khandro's biography of Drimé Özer mentions that when the twenty-four-year-old lama was en route westward from Golok to Chamdo with his religious encampment,

> Then, gradually when some days had passed, although the mother *ḍākinīs* had given him teachings as Treasure symbols, on account of other things he

had let them go. As a result, the Treasure protectors became offended and bandits and other undesirable occurrences affected both the encampment bases of the Treasure revealer [Drimé Özer] and the doctrine holder [Sotrül Rinpoché]. The Master incited the actions of the protectresses of profound Treasure according to an earlier *ḍākinī* prophecy. The signs of their manifest activity occurred and all the harm was pacified.[101]

Also imbricated in the Treasure tradition's web of auspicious connections was another peril of nomadic life, livestock disease, as we hear in Drimé Özer's biography:

> At that time [when Drimé Özer was thirty-nine] a woman saying she was Sengcham Trukmo came from out of a cloud and gave him a yellow scroll. The mind-mandate for it having awakened, he wrote down the outer liturgy *Gesar Norbu Drandül kyi Drupa, The Liturgy of Gesar the Jewel Who Tames Enemies*, and the inner liturgy Dharma cycle *Orgyen Norlha, The Wealth Deities of Orgyen*. In the lama's residence, the *hon* sickness struck the livestock and they sickened. He recited Gesar's prosperity liturgy and they revived.[102]

Beyond its connections with the Tibetan mountain cult, the Treasure tradition was linked to other non-Buddhist Tibetan traditions such as the important Tibetan epic *Gesar of Ling*: Sengcham Trukmo was none other than Gesar's wife. What some claim to be the longest epic tradition in the world, *Gesar* is immensely popular in Golok and seems to have originated in the Anyé Machen region.[103]

Gesar was a victorious and powerful Tibetan warrior, and his appearance as a source of a Treasure liturgy demonstrates the tradition's capacity to repel yet another persistent bane of life in early twentieth-century Golok: warfare. In religious literature from greater Golok, Treasure revelation often appears as an antidote to bloodshed, alluding to a record of recurrent violence that local histories of the region confirm. The Goloks fought repeated battles with their powerful neighbors to the north and east, the Mongols, Manchus, and Han Chinese. During the Qing dynastic period (1644–1911), Emperor Yongzheng (r. 1723–1735) violently suppressed the northern regions of eastern Tibet, eventually securing all of Tibet as a dependency of the Qing dynasty. In Golok, the Qing-backed troops destroyed more than forty Golok encampment groups and temporarily forced the entirety of the three parts of Golok under its empire, with the obligation to pay tribute to the nearest military garrison, called Tranglayun, in Songpan, now part of Ngawa Tibetan and Qiang Autonomous Prefecture in Sichuan Province. In return, the Qing emperor distributed official ranks and titles to some Golok leaders until at least the early nineteenth century.[104] But by this time Qing control over the greater Golok region had diminished; the *General History of Sichuan* composed in 1814 mentions that the three parts of Golok no longer paid tribute to the Qing military garrison.[105]

According to their own histories, one source of the military power that helped Golok and Serta maintain autonomy despite repeated incursions on their territories was propitiating the regions' sacred mountains, in particular Anyé Machen in Golok and Drong Mountain in Serta. Treasure revealers and their discoveries were instrumental in this project, according to several biographies from Sera Khandro's milieu. For example, Drong Mountain appears in Düjom Lingpa's autobiography as a source of Treasures that could repel military invasion. In a vision Düjom Lingpa writes he had in 1897, his first question to Drong Mountain's resident land deity, Drongri Mukpo, inspired the following dialogue between the two:

> "Now it seems it will be difficult to prevent a rain of blood [caused by] fighting with outsiders? What will transpire here in Serta?"
>
> "My son upholds justice," Drongri Mukpo replied, "so the land will not be greatly devastated."
>
> "Will there be a great fight?"
>
> "I don't have to tell you; it's easy to understand [that there will be]."[106]

Drongri Mukpo assuaged Düjom Lingpa's concern by asserting the authority of his "son," meaning the Washül Serta leader, who could have been the mountain's "soul son," Lhasé Sonam Dorjé (r. mid-1800s), or his son. Drongri Mukpo then acted as a Treasure protector by bestowing a stone chest upon Düjom Lingpa as a Treasure and advising him to return home without delay or his path would be obstructed by an invading army, which Düjom Lingpa later envisioned as "many Chinese people who would fill the land."[107]

Düjom Lingpa's vision was realized during Sera Khandro's lifetime as the army of the Ma warlords, whom she called "the northern Chinese" (*byang rgya*). After the fall of the Qing dynasty in 1911 and during the subsequent Republican era (1912–1949), Golok was nominally a part of the northwest provinces claimed by China. However, Golok was never effectively controlled by Republican China, which was absorbed in a succession of internal power struggles. In this power vacuum, the Chinese Muslim Ma family warlords took over a broad swath of China's northwestern territories, including Qinghai, Gansu, and Ningxia. Ma Qi controlled the Qinghai region, which became a Chinese province under his governorship in 1929. But Ma family control of Qinghai was based in its capital, Xining, and stretched only to the eastern section of the province, which was farmed by Chinese agriculturalists. Although their soldiers were stationed in Jyekundo, a Tibetan region west of Golok, by and large the Ma warlords did not control the large western regions of Qinghai inhabited by Tibetan and Mongolian pastoralists.[108] Ma Qi and later Ma Lin and Ma Bufang sought to subdue the Golok encampment groups because their land intersected the important route between Xining and Jyekundo that was used for trade and sending supplies to Jyekundo. The Goloks made this route extremely dangerous by engaging in widespread raiding and plundering travelers' caravans, earning a reputation for violence throughout Tibet and western China. In return, Ma Qi, Ma Lin, and Ma Bufang successively launched a series of ruthless attacks in Golok. In 1917 Ma Qi inspired the Goloks' ire when he sent two hundred men to mine for gold in the vicinity of Anyé Machen Mountain and to plunder the nearby Golok encampments. The Golok leader of the Akyong Gongma subdivision retaliated, killing many of Ma Qi's men and stealing five hundred of their pack animals. Thirty years of battles between Ma forces and the Goloks followed, the most severe of which were 1917, 1920, 1921, 1927, 1933, 1935–1938, and 1940–1941.[109] Ma troops killed many thousands of monastics and laypeople from Golok, burned entire communities' tents, stole tens of thousands of livestock, and killed many Golok leaders. The Goloks resisted the warlords' attacks whenever possible, killing large numbers of soldiers.

Aiding in these resistance efforts were the ritual interventions of Golok's religious specialists. For example, the biographies of Sotrül Natsok Rangdröl of Sera Monastery claim that when Ma Bufang's powerful army reached the borders of Serta and prepared to invade, Sotrül Rinpoché went to Drong Mountain and performed a Vajrakīlaya rite of expulsion, causing Ma Bufang and his army to abandon their plan to attack.[110] Sera Khandro too refers to several of the battles listed above. In particular, in 1920 and 1921 Ma's encroaching armies forced both Drimé Özer's and Gyelsé's religious encampments to move. In Drimé Özer's biography, Sera Khandro records that when he was forty, in 1921, people warned him of the impending danger of Chinese attack:

> At that time, Akyong said, "The terror of the Chinese (*rgya*) has arrived and they are fighting. We need to move the encampment base to another area." Although the local people, his close entourage, and the inhabitants of the lama's residence repeatedly said this, the Master himself disregarded their words.[111]

Later that year, when they were in Serta near Drong Mountain, Drimé Özer's community again worried about the agitation caused by the Chinese attacks even though their lama remained unperturbed:

> Then when everybody said that there was fighting and that he needed to move the encampment base, the Master said, "It seems that there is no problem, but since people are concerned, it is okay if we move the encampment."
>
> In accordance with a *ḍākinī* prophecy, they went together with their encampment base to the [Treasure] concealment site under the power of the western gatekeeper of Golden Drong Mountain named Nyenchen Yusé. There new Treasures came to both *yab* and *yum* [Drimé Özer and Sera Khandro] and they performed empowerments, reading transmissions and so forth.[112]

These revelation activities under the protection of Drong Mountain and its gatekeeper mountain, Nyenchen Yusé, seem to have quelled the threat. Gyelsé's religious encampment in Benak also faced attack by the Ma army in 1921:

> That year the northern Chinese became more powerful and attacked. When everyone said that we should move to another area, Bön Rindzin from Benak and Gara Terchen's disciple, a renunciate from Benshül named Lama Ngawang Demchok, had a discussion. They found a way to resolve the land

> dispute between the two factions of the lama's residence and decided that Gyelsé needed to establish a seat. Everybody from both sides reached an amicable agreement about this. At that time, because we, mother and child, received unfavorable prophecies and divinations, we didn't go to the seat but set up camp in a place called Chi Wangchentang.[113]

Ironically, outside attack seems to have catalyzed reconciliation within Gyelsé's community as well as required them to relocate to safer ground.

Sera Khandro and others believed that revelations had the power to repel warfare, but the future predicted by Treasure revealers was often less optimistic. Sera Khandro recounts the following prophecy given by Düjom Lingpa to Drimé Özer when he was eighteen, in 1899:

> The lama said, "On account of the great wrong views and weak merit of sentient beings of this place and time, on account of the many wars, contagious diseases, famines, and so forth of this time period, and in particular because when the old lady[114] and I die it is certain that the terror of the Chinese Mongols (*rgya hor*) from the borderlands will come near, it is unclear what will happen in these changing times. When this occurs, people's mind streams will be possessed by demons and they will be the ruin of themselves and others. The power of the barbaric people of the borderlands will spread. Much of the lives, deeds, and beneficial actions of people who adhere to the [Buddhist] teachings will be affected by negative circumstances, and it will be difficult to do anything about it. Because of this, since you are a person who nurtures the teachings and sentient beings, you need to be careful regarding demonic power in these changing times and places. When I am here, negative forces will not harm you. Later I will help. If you do everything, good and bad, according to the mother deity and *ḍākinīs*' prophecy, great benefit for yourself and others will arise.[115]

Treasure revealers such as Sera Khandro and Drimé Özer incorporated the growing problem of Chinese agitation into their Buddhist understanding of the contemporary age as a degenerate era in which the Buddha's teachings were in decline. Put into this apocalyptic perspective, the threat of the Chinese was something that could be deterred through adherence to the *ḍākinī* prophecies that constantly interpenetrated their lives. For example, the *ḍākinī*s Künsel and Shiwa Dorjetso prophesied in unison to Drimé Özer in his biography:

> Earlier in Samyé in the presence of Guru Padmasambhava
> we gathered together as an auspicious connection.
> Because of my vast aspirations and prayers,
> up until now I have manifested as your consort.
>
> Completely dispel the troubles between China and Tibet.
> Accomplish the aspirations of Padmasambhava and Tsogyel!
>
> The illusory emanation of the mother of the ultimate sphere,
> Tsogyel,
> the woman who is a light ray from my heart,
> will arise as the consort for the entrance to the three Treasures.
>
> By the profound power of the enlightened activities of the mother
> *ḍākinī*s,
> if you inseparably unite method and insight,
> you will repel the expansion of the demonic barbarians for one
> hundred years.[116]

"The woman who is a light ray from my heart" was none other than Sera Khandro, who received prophecies indicating that she and Drimé Özer had a vital role to play in preventing agitation and promoting peace in Golok. Her authority to provide this salvation came both from sources tied to the Tibetan earth and from those who had transcended it. Just as the Treasure tradition often overlaid Buddhist sanctity on sites already significant in Golok's mountain cult, so too Sera Khandro's identity bridged these dimensions. More than "the illusory emanation of the mother of the ultimate sphere Tsogyel," she was also a guest welcomed to the Golok land by Queen Drakgyelma of Anyé Machen Mountain. And even without paternal relatives nearby, Sera Khandro asserted another kind of paternal authorization to be a Treasure revealer; like Golok's leaders were descendants of their region's sacred mountains, Sera Khandro claimed that her true father was Nyenchen Tanglha, the most powerful mountain god of central Tibet.

Sera Khandro's autobiography presents a self narrative defined in relation to powerful others beyond the scope of her human social networks, including denizens of subterranean, earthly, and celestial domains. Her selfhood is constituted in conversation with these forces, who vitalized both the earth and its inhabitants through exchanges of words and precious objects. A close read of the plethora of visionary experiences Sera Khandro interspersed throughout her biographical writings demonstrates that her inspirations were as local as they were transregional, as tied to Golok society and landscape as more universally Buddhist, and as implicated in sociopolitical dynamics as in spiritual liberation. If Sera Khandro was an emanation of Yeshé Tsogyel, Anyé Machen and Drong Mountains' endorsement also held great value in Golok. If being a Treasure revealer was preordained by Padmasambhava and the *ḍākinīs*' prophecies, successfully living up to their commands was contingent on maintaining conducive relationships with people and places in her present situation. And if the purpose of Treasure revelation was to transform *saṃsāra*'s ocean of suffering beings into buddhas inseparable from Padmasambhava and his entourage, it was also to protect people from the menaces of everyday life on the Golok grasslands.

Sera Khandro made meaning of her life through the dynamism of her connection to the progenitors of the Treasure tradition as well as careful attunement to temporal, geographic, and interpersonal conditions. In these respects, her biographical writings share much with those of other Treasure revealers. However, one distinguishing feature is the degree to which she emphasized her connection to Yeshé Tsogyel, through her opening frame narrative and the elaborate visions that pervade her autobiography. More than a repetition of a familiar Tibetan Buddhist narrative, the ways Sera Khandro embedded her life story within that of Yeshé Tsogyel can be considered a creative application of her cultural repertoire through which she articulated both her sense of self and her story about it. If it is true, as Ann Swidler suggests, that people use elements of their cultural repertoire more in moments when their lives are unsettled, in flux, and in need of guidance, perhaps we can understand Sera Khandro's choice to emphasize her alignment with Yeshé Tsogyel as a sign that her identity as a Treasure revealer was in doubt and needed more spelling out than did the positions of other male religious hierarchs in her communities.[117] Indeed, the way Sera Khandro narrates the story of her apotheosis into being recognized as "the speech emanation of Tsogyel," the subject to which we now turn, demonstrates that embodying this identity turned out to be more of a challenge than the many prophecies *ḍākinī*s bestowed upon her had foretold.

3

ḌĀKINĪ DIALOGUES

This inferior female body (*skye lus dman pa*) cannot get free from the mouth of my husband;
when I wander about this country, it can't get free from the mouths of dogs.
Whatever I do doesn't appeal to people.
When things like these occur, I feel I should abandon this body.

Even though there is no difference between men's and women's altruistic intention to become enlightened,
in the perspective of disciples, my body is inferior.
I think that if I were to transform into a [male] hero with a supreme body,
I would certainly accomplish great benefit for all beings who have been my mother.

Without this, how will this body
have a way to accomplish great benefit for the teachings and sentient beings?
Lady, give me advice.[1]

The passages from Sera Khandro's auto/biographical writings examined in chapter 2 presented her status as Yeshé Tsogyel's emanation as a *fait accompli*, predetermined by her aspirations and actions in former lifetimes. However, when the twenty-four-year-old Sera Khandro bemoaned her "inferior female body" to the *ḍākinī* who appeared in her vision, her words suggest that actualizing Padmasambhava and Yeshé Tsogyel's command to reveal Treasures was easier said than done: both she and others for and about whom she wrote seem to have needed extensive convincing of her spiritual potential. That Sera Khandro's autobiography is filled with a litany of self-deprecating comments demonstrates her humility in a manner characteristic of Tibetan autobiographical writing.[2] But these pervasive expressions of her fears and failings also occasion responses from many other human and superhuman figures who defend and encourage her. Interlocutors who sound most strongly in these dialectics about her true identity are *ḍākinī*s and male religious hierarchs from eastern Tibet. Through quoting their positive words, Sera Khandro conveys her extraordinary status while making very few claims about herself in her own voice. We can think of this narrative strategy as a type of autobiographical ventriloquy in which Sera Khandro asserts her identity as a *ḍākinī* and a Treasure revealer through others' voices at the same time as she denies their praise.

The aim of this chapter is to listen to a cross-section of conversations including sound bites about life as a woman who endeavored to enter the ranks of a predominantly male religious calling, and to consider these conversations in comparison to other relevant works. We will hear about the complex relationships with specific earthly and celestial beings that shaped Sera Khandro's self and social world, making it possible for her to become a *ḍākinī* and a Treasure revealer. Key figures featured in part I include her parents, her "life partner" Gara Gyelsé and his family at Benak Monastery, and her teacher and friend Gochen Trülku Jikdrel Chökyi Lodrö from Pelyül Dartang Monastery in Golok. *Ḍākinī*s' dialogues with Sera Khandro inflect her relationships with all of these figures, insisting on their version of her future. Though Sera Khandro was the author of all sides of the conversations that populate her autobiography, the tensions, insecurities, ambitions, and inspirations that vitalized these interactions reflect not only her internal self-perception but also elements of the values and concerns salient for others in her communities. In particular, the conversations presented in this first part of the chapter highlight the difficulty of assuming religious authority as a nonmonastic Tibetan woman in early twentieth-century Tibet and the delicacy with which she made such claims.

One of the most startling elements of Sera Khandro's side of these conversations is the emphasis she places on her "inferior female body." Translated literally, in her autobiography she describes herself as one with an "inferior birth body" (*skye lus dman*) twenty-nine times, as an "inferior birth" (*skye dman*) twelve times, and as one with an "inferior body" (*lus dman*) fourteen times, totaling fifty-five mentions, all in conversations with *ḍākinīs* and male lamas. In Drimé Özer's biography she describes herself once as an "inferior birth" and twice as one with an "inferior body." I translate these instances of self-deprecation as marking her birth inferior on account of her femaleness based on context, and because these terms are all variants of the common colloquial Tibetan word for woman, *kyemen* (*skye dman*), or literally "inferior birth."[3] That Sera Khandro regarded *kyemen* and its variants as derogatory is underlined by the fact that she only used it to refer to herself, never for the hosts of *ḍākinīs* with whom she interacted, to whom she refers using the more neutral word for woman, *bumé* (*bud med*).[4]

If Sera Khandro's focus on the lowly nature of her female body was a rhetorical device that occasioned other powerful figures' praise, it was also a reality. Tibetan culture has often been heralded for its gender egalitarianism, especially in comparison to its Chinese and Indian neighbors, by both Tibetan and non-Tibetan writers.[5] However, when it came to Tibetan Buddhism, "low birth" was an especially fitting appellation for women given that Tibetans imported misogynist attitudes toward women and nuns inscribed in Indian Buddhist scriptures into their own conceptions of gender categories.[6] For example, Tibetans considered nuns to be a lesser "field of merit" than monks, meaning that donating to nuns earned lay patrons less merit than donating to monks. Gender hierarchies like this both resulted from and reinforced significant economic and educational disparities, leaving nuns with less funding, fewer educational opportunities, and lower literacy rates than their male monastic peers.[7] This in turn further bolstered the stereotype that nuns were inferior to monks, as did the gossip and jokes that circulated in many Tibetan cultural areas about nuns' alleged sexual infractions.[8] Laywomen came up short in the Buddhist gender hierarchy as well, although some among them were valued for their patronage of Buddhist institutions. Even so, as those who

FIG. 3.1 Vajrayoginī

RUBIN MUSEUM OF ART, NEW YORK, F1997.19.2

lured men into the obligations of householder life and perpetuated the cycle of rebirth that is *saṃsāra* through what many Buddhist sources describe as the bloody and polluting process of giving birth, laywomen occupied the lowest status in the fourfold Buddhist community made up of monks, nuns, laymen, and laywomen.[9] In contrast, some Mahāyāna and later Indian Tantric scriptures that Tibetans imported turned that status on its head, honoring women as goddesses worthy of worship and praising their wombs as the source of all buddhas.[10] Nevertheless, Sera Khandro's writings suggest that in Tibet, even though this Tantric reversal of women's misfortune may have gained some traction in theory, in practice it required further emphasis.

The lion's share of this emphasis in Sera Khandro's autobiographical works comes through the voices of the many *ḍākinīs* who pervade her visionary experiences. *Ḍākinīs* have a very long history in South Asia preceding their entry into Tibet. Along with other classes of female divinities who were later incorporated into Vedic religion, *ḍākinīs* may have descended from indigenous goddess cults whose earliest evidence has been found in the Indus Valley civilizations dating from two millennia B.C.E.[11] They appear in Pāṇini's famous Sanskrit grammar, probably composed in the late fourth century B.C.E. After the fall of the Gupta Empire they reemerged as dangerous bearers of pestilence and as human-flesh-eating female spirits associated with cremation grounds. During the sixth and seventh centuries, Indian Tantric traditions incorporated *ḍākinīs* as carnivorous flying female deities serving forms of Śiva and other deities.[12] *Ḍākinīs* traveled along with Indian Buddhism over the Himalayas to Tibet, where they took on the name *khandroma*, though Tibetan transliterations of the Sanskrit word *ḍākinī* or diminutives such as *ḍākkī* also abound in Tibetan texts. Literally translated as "sky-going woman," *khandroma* encompass a wide range of forms in Tibet.[13] Some of these bear distinctive resemblances to their earlier Indian sisters' predatory malevolence, such as the "flesh-eating *khandroma*" (*sha za mkha' 'gro*) that Tibetan Buddhist practitioners invite to various types of ritual feasts. Among their many classifications in Tibetan Buddhism, *khandroma* can be worldly (*'jig rten*), still enmeshed in *saṃsāra* and thus of questionable virtue, or they can be wisdom *ḍākinīs* (*ye shes pa'i mkha' 'gro ma*), who are fully enlightened buddhas and bodhisattvas, such as the Vajrayoginī image above. *Khandroma* permeate the boundary between divine and human; as celestial goddess figures, they appear in Tibetan temple iconography and scriptures in myriad guises—naked dancing sprites adorned in bone ornaments, radiantly beautiful maidens in bejeweled raiment, or terrifically ugly wrinkled hags—all of whom manifest to aid Tibetan Buddhist practitioners in transcending delusion. As human figures, *khandroma* are often, though not always, "spiritual wives" or consorts of prominent male Tibetan

FIG. 3.2 Sera Khandro statue from Tralek Monastery, Kandzé

PHOTOGRAPH BY SARAH JACOBY, 2007

lamas, although they can also be religious masters in their own right, as Sera Khandro was herself.

Khandroma form parts of the Vajrayāna Buddhist trinity of the three roots, including the guru, tutelary deity, and protector, which are the inner aspects of the Buddhist Three Jewels (Buddha, Dharma, and Saṅgha).

Within this trinity *khandroma* can be protectors, but also often tutelary deities and sometimes gurus. As we have seen in the previous chapter, *ḍākinīs* perform important functions within the Treasure tradition as female forces who encode and protect Treasures and aid Treasure revealers in deciphering them. They appear to Sera Khandro most often as messengers from the buddhafields with pithy prophecies foretelling the auspicious circumstances she must gather to reveal her Treasures. *Ḍākinīs* also appear regularly in Tibetan biographies, offering enlightened insight to the protagonist and pushing him (occasionally her) beyond superficial study toward true understanding, such as the old woman who famously exposed Nāropa's scholarly hubris and catalyzed his true realization. In religious biographies, *khandroma* are often messengers (*pho nya*) who usher the protagonist from the realm of this world to the buddhafields, both within his or her visionary experiences and at the moment of death. In their most abstract meaning, *ḍākinīs* are not women at all, but rather symbols of insight (Skt. *prajñā*, Tib. *shes rab*). "Insight" in this context refers to the realization of emptiness (Skt. *śūnyatā*, Tib. *stong nyid*), that people and phenomena are empty of permanent and separate existence. In contemplative terms, the *ḍākinī* is the "unborn primordial wisdom dimension" of mind.[14] As such, she is not only a class of female Buddhist divinity with whom extraordinary women such as Sera Khandro had a special relationship but also an internal nondual awareness realizable by all devotees through meditative encounter.

Ḍākinīs' ubiquity in Tibetan religion stands in stark contrast to the relative scarcity of human women in Tibetan historical records and Buddhist hagiographical literature. This has prompted some European and American scholars influenced by Jungian analysis to conclude that "The feminine sky-dancers or *ḍākinīs* are a powerful representation of the repressed feminine aspects of the male psyche."[15] Sera Khandro's auto/biographical writing does little to support this view, as her works are drenched in edifying *ḍākinī* encounters beyond any significance *ḍākinīs* may have for men.[16] *Ḍākinīs* appear frequently in male Treasure revealers' autobiographies from Sera Khandro's religious communities, such as those of Düjom Lingpa and Gara Terchen Pema Dündül Wangchuk Lingpa, examined in part II of this chapter. But in comparison to these works, *ḍākinīs* hold a distinctive significance for Sera Khandro. More than her male colleagues, she engages in extended dialogues with *ḍākinīs* in which they lavish encouragement upon her, refuting her every complaint about being inferior on account of her sex. *Ḍākinīs* cheer her on with the most fervor just at the lowest moments in her life—when her father insists on her marriage, when her partner Gyelsé chastises her, and when she feels powerless to gather together the necessary auspicious connections to reveal her Treasures. As in other Treasure revealers' biographies, *ḍākinīs*' prophecies are not always easy to understand, but their support for Sera Khandro is unequivocal.

For Treasure revealers such as Jikmé Lingpa (1730–1798), one of the effects of *ḍākinīs*' elusive talk was to emphasize the empty and unformulatable nature of selfhood.[17] However, in Sera Khandro's autobiography, *ḍākinīs*' words destabilize only her low opinion of herself, focusing instead on boosting her self-confidence and countering her numerous critics. Perhaps *ḍākinīs*' supportive words were especially necessary for female Tibetan Buddhist religious specialists such as Sera Khandro, who mentions knowing of only one other female Tibetan religious master teaching in her era.[18] But if we can correlate the way Sera Khandro wrote of her many dialogical encounters with *ḍākinīs* to her status as a female Tibetan Buddhist master, part III of this chapter demonstrates the diverse ways *ḍākinīs* figure in Himalayan women's autobiographies through comparing Sera Khandro's writing with that of Jetsün Ani Lochen Rinpoché (1865–1951) and Orgyen Chökyi (1675–1729). The passages we will examine suggest that even more than for these two women or for Düjom Lingpa and Gara Terchen, *ḍākinīs* not only provided Sera Khandro with encouragement in a hostile world but also played a major role in creating the conditions that enabled her to become the author of the story of her life.

PART I: SERA KHANDRO'S INTERACTIONS WITH *ḌĀKINĪS* AND LAMAS

Ḍākinīs Respond to Parental Pressure with Prophetic Guides

The very first face-to-face encounter with a *ḍākinī* that Sera Khandro reports in her autobiography occurred after her father ordered his seven-year-old daughter to study Chinese instead of Tibetan. Despairing that her Chinese education was preparing her for nonreligious work, Sera

Khandro threw her schoolbooks into the river and contemplated casting herself in after them, praying:

> Alas, I pray to Padmasambhava from Oḍḍiyāna, all refuges condensed into one,
> to Mother Tsogyel, and to the Venerable Noble Lady Tārā—
> look upon me with compassion!
>
> This inferior female body (*skye dman*) of mine is the foundation of *saṃsāra*.
> After I throw away this contaminated, unclean, negative body,
> bless me with attaining a body replete with the freedoms and advantages.
> As soon as I am born, having met with the Dharma,
> may I have the freedom to practice properly.
>
> Before my body touched the water to meet its end, suddenly a terrifying woman (*bud med*) with an ugly physique arrived. "You who are about to put an end to yourself in the water, I need to kill you," she said as she grabbed a sword and came toward me.[19]

From that day forward, Sera Khandro writes, the terrifying woman followed her everywhere. Soon after this, she describes going with her mother to Önpu Taktsang in Lhokha, a site south of Lhasa famous for being the location where Yeshé Tsogyel received Vajrakīlaya empowerments from Padmasambhava:

> Then, when I was eight years old, my parents and I went to do the medium-length circumambulation route around Üri (Central Mountain). When we arrived at the Önpu Taktsang[20] Hermitage, I remembered my former karmic connection [to the place] and said the following to my mother:
>
> > It seems as if I lived here in a previous life. I remember my earlier activities and my share of texts that are here.
>
> Mother admonished,
>
> > Don't speak like that. From the time of our forefathers such as the Dharma King Ngaki Wangpo[21] until now, there have been many accomplished

masters. Since it is impossible for a woman (bud med) to retrieve scriptural Treasures, shut up, or the king will quickly reprimand you.

That night in my dream a *ḍākinī* arrived, wearing bone ornaments and a silk dress decorated with various jewels. She gave me a skull cup full of beer and said, "Noble woman, drink this. It is your share of the *ḍākinīs*' feast."

I replied, "If I don't join the assembly at the *ḍākinīs*' feast, what good is just this share?"

The *ḍākinī* responded, "Train your vajra body in yogic exercises. Because you are a miraculous emanation of the *ḍākinīs*' energetic mind, you will meet them soon," and then she disappeared.[22]

Ḍākinīs' interventions in the course of her childhood reached a crux when the twelve-year-old Sera Khandro was grieving her mother's recent death and her father had just finalized plans to marry her off to the "Chinese political leader" from Kyidrong. Amid these traumas, *ḍākinīs* unveiled the central mission of Sera Khandro's life:

One day in my dream, in an attractive land with green pastures and a forest replete with flowers, there were many birds and animals frolicking contentedly. In the middle of this, many different women (*bud med*) had gathered. Wondering if my mother was over there in that assembly of women, I went toward them.

When I thought that Mother wasn't there and that I didn't recognize any of them, from among them the nun who had given me advice about death in my previous dream and the girl who had accompanied me to visit Sarahapa both came to me.

They said, "Are you tired? It is amazing that you have come here now."

"How are you both? It is amazing that we are meeting," I replied and prostrated.

They said, "Because we are of the same birth, it is not appropriate to prostrate. Prostrate to the Principal Lady of the *maṇḍala*—the time has come for you to take your accomplishment wealth."

I asked again, "How is it that we are of the same birth line?"

They said, "This nun is Künga Buma. We are said to be Sukhasiddhi and Dīpam Tāré." Saying this, they disappeared without a trace.

In accordance with their words, I prostrated to the Principal Lady. She arose from her seat and cut open her navel with a curved knife without any bleeding.

Extremely terrified, I couldn't bear to watch with my eyes. I yelled, "Mother!" and prepared to return home.

The women said, "Don't say this. Open your eyes and look—there is no harm done. The time has come for you to meet the great self-emergent perfected *maṇḍala*."

I opened my eyes and when I slowly looked, all the women had transformed and were garbed entirely as *ḍākinīs*. The Principal Lady also had transformed into the form of Vajravārāhī. She conferred the empowerment of the *Lükyil Kyeché kyi Lhatsok, Assembly of Sense-Base Deities of the Body Maṇḍala*, and gave me an introduction [to them]. She conferred a symbolic empowerment of the *Chönyi Khandro Sangdzö, The Secret Treasury of Reality Ḍākinīs*, and the *Khandro Tuktik, The Ḍākinīs' Heart Essence*. She bestowed upon me the guide (*kha byang*) and prophetic guide (*lung byang*), including the time to reveal these two religious teachings, the place to spread them, the beings who would be the Dharma holders, the place where the disciples would be, the way auspicious connections would appear, and the consorts (*thabs kyi grogs*). She said,

> Since the time has come for you to benefit sentient beings with these Dharma teachings, keep the meaning of these guides in your mind and don't forget it. Because you are my messenger, benefit to the teachings and to sentient beings will certainly arise.

The Principal Lady and her retinue resided in space, upraised about a foot[23] above the earth, with bodies of light.

I replied to the Ḍākinī Sukhasiddhi,

> You are extremely kind to bestow empowerment and instruction upon me. Because I am one with an inferior female body (*skye lus dman pa*), it is difficult to accomplish the Dharma and [benefit] beings. However I can do this, how great! Why do I have the karmic connection to be empowered in these two profound Treasures?

The *ḍākinī* answered,

> "Noble woman, you are not one with an inferior female body (*lus dman pa*). Before, in response to Tsogyel's inquiry, Guru [Padmasambhava] proclaimed:

Generate the aspiration to attain a supreme body that is
the supreme bodyless body of a female bodhisattva,
the joy-generating consort (*yum*) of the ones gone to bliss (Skt. *sugata*) who has perfected the great accumulations [of merit and wisdom] from the beginning,
the great Vajra Queen of the ultimate sphere of emptiness and insight.

The enlightened activities of the buddhas of the three times, a dance of the moon reflecting in water,
arise in physical form in response to disciples' devotion.
Their source, the lotus mouth of the Vajra Queen,
is the foundation of the Buddha's teaching, like a ripening bud.
This female body (*bud med lus*) is not inferior; this body is good.
Tsogyel, you must generate the pure aspiration prayers
never to part with this [female] body.

Because [the Guru] spoke like this, your body is not inferior.[24]

Sera Khandro's account of Vajravārāhī's gift of spiritual empowerment in the form of prophetic guides (*kha byang*) marks a critical stage in a Treasure revealer's life. Alternately translated as "certificate," "inventory," or "prophetic guide," these prophecies foretell when and where a Treasure revealer will reveal Treasures, with whom she must associate, whether the discovery should be secret or public, what offerings should be made, how to appease the Treasure protectors, what types of religious objects should be offered in return for the Treasures as "substitutes," and how to close the opening in the earth after a Treasure discovery.[25] In Sera Khandro's case, the prophetic guides Vajravārāhī bestowed outlined information about the two major Treasure cycles called *The Secret Treasury of Reality Ḍākinīs* and *The Ḍākinīs' Heart Essence* that she would reveal piece by piece over the course of her lifetime. Each of these Treasure cycles contained hundreds of smaller texts, including Tantric liturgies, empowerments, explanations of contemplative practices, biographical writings, prophecies, and advice, totaling more than two thousand pages of written material.

Sera Khandro's response to Vajravārāhī's precious gift was to lament her inferior female body, even though this would hardly seem to be an obstacle in the company of the enlightened women she envisioned. By calling attention to her femaleness, Sera Khandro highlighted a potentially problematic aspect of her claim to be a Treasure revealer, as if to pre-empt potential critics who might cast doubt on this basis. In this instance as in many others, the *ḍākinī*s' responses countered Sera Khandro's (and some of her readers'?) concerns by calling upon the precedent of Yeshé Tsogyel's hagiography. If Padmasambhava reassured Yeshé Tsogyel that her female bodhisattva body was the supreme maternal source of all the buddhas and Sera Khandro was her emanation, then she too could not possibly have an inferior body.

Problems and Possibilities with the Gara Family at Benak

*Ḍākinī*s' reassurance was never more necessary than during Sera Khandro's turbulent life with the Gara family at Benak Monastery on the bank of the Mar River in Pema County, Golok. Sera Khandro writes that when she was sixteen in 1908, Gara Terchen summoned her to Benak, but it wasn't possible for her to visit the then fifty-one-year-old Treasure revealer because

> At that time since Yakshülza was Gara Tertön's consort (*yum*), she sent me a message saying, "There is no reason for you to come near us. If you come, I will cause you verbal and physical injuries—people will talk about how such and such has happened to the woman from central Tibet."[26]

Despairing that Yakza's antics had caused the auspicious connection between Gara Terchen and herself to dissipate, a few months later, when she was seventeen, she experienced the following visionary interaction with Yeshé Tsogyel:

> Mother Tsogyel smiled and said the following:
>
> Noble woman, how is benefiting beings going?
> Have you had great difficulties in the world?
> Have you not grasped onto the illusory place in which you live as real?
>
> When she said this, thinking of the suffering I felt coming from my land and the suffering I had experienced since arriving in eastern Tibet, I bowed before the feet of the Lady and offered these words:

Alas! Lady endowed with eyes of the treasury of primordial wisdom—
I, this inferior woman (*lus dman*), will tell you a bit about my circumstances:
from the time I was seven, *ḍākinīs* took care of me;
they reassured me in reality, in visions, and in dreams.
From the time I was eleven, the Master Accomplished Awareness Holder
Saraha took care of me and bestowed ripening [empowerments] and liberating [instructions] upon me.
When I reached the age of twelve, I obtained the genuine prophetic guide of the *Ḍākinīs*' Oral Transmission Profound Treasure.
From the time I was thirteen, I exerted myself only in benefiting others.
At fourteen, in accordance with the *ḍākinī*'s command, I came eastward
to the land of eastern Tibet, which is like the demons' island.
Not dying, while living I experienced the suffering of hell.

Although it was possible that in time karmic connections and former aspirations would come together,
suddenly, on account of *sapta* demons,[27] they went away again and again.
Someone like me in a demonic land without virtue
can forget about benefiting beings—on account of obscurations from deteriorated [vows],
it is difficult to maintain the pure morality to benefit myself.

The beings who were consorts and doctrine holders of my profound Treasures
were influenced by other circumstances to put on the pretense of adhering to monastic regulations,
and therefore saw me, this inferior woman (*skye dman*), as something to abandon.
I did not benefit myself and others; I did not accomplish the *ḍākinī*'s orders.
Because one cannot see or hear of someone with karma as bad as mine,
now I won't go to the realm of the world.

Saying this, I cried. The *ḍākinī* [Yeshé Tsogyel] said,

Listen one with fortunate karmic connections—
don't be saddened by this illusory land.
Adhere to the stronghold of changeless awareness.
Happiness and suffering are like a dream city.
Don't weaken your capacity to incorporate awareness and emptiness on the path.
This hollow illusory body
must rely on a consort (*phyag rgya*) to enhance bliss and emptiness.
By the power of Padmasambhava's prayers,
gradually you will meet consorts and Dharma holders.

When karma, prayers, and [the proper] time come together,
you will tame the five fields of disciples with skillful means.
You will summon the noble hero who is your consort
with the iron hook that grasps the heart of the pith instructions.
The sword of selfless insight will cut
the eight worldly dharmas[28] that contradict the Dharma.
May the demonic spy who adheres to dualism
attain the realization of the nondual Truth Body.
Realize that all mental fluctuations of happiness and suffering
are luminous and empty awareness.

One with the karmic connection of being a messenger of the *ḍākinīs*—
even though they don't want you to do it, benefit beings.
Like a precious jewel,
it is impossible for you to be stained by negative, inferior wrong views.
Like water bubbles up from hard earth,
you will naturally accomplish the two purposes.
Still, until none of your disciples remains in this world,
with your vows and aspirations as a witness,
skillfully establish in bliss those disciples
from various regions of the demonic land of eastern Tibet.

Until you are twenty, keep this secret.
Abandon the bliss of ordinary men.

Benefit beings, both formless and with form,
by means of auspicious connection substances.
You must not break the seal of secrecy of the profound Treasure.
From now on, if you rely on the essential point of auspicious connections,
you will definitely obtain the jewel of benefiting yourself and others.

Having said this, [Yeshé Tsogyel] gave me a full skull cup of beer and said, "Drink every drop of this. Because it is *ḍākinīs*' accomplishment substance, it is certain that you will effortlessly know everything there is to be known."[29]

Although this was not the moment for Sera Khandro to meet Gara Terchen, Yeshé Tsogyel's exhortation that she would need to rely on a specially prophesied consort was definitive, as was her confidence that she would accomplish her religious purpose. Even so, because Yakza prevented Sera Khandro from approaching Gara Terchen until he was at death's door, she did not have a chance to benefit him as the *ḍākinīs* had commanded. Instead, she met him in another dimension:

Then, seven days later, during a clear light dream I saw an expanse of swirling primordial wisdom rainbow light in the sky before me. Inside of this, surrounded by many heroes and heroines, was Dündül Wangchuk Lingpa dressed as a renunciate and smiling. With intense devotion, I prostrated to him and offered this prayer:

Display of the compassion of the buddhas of the three times,
Great Treasure revealer and Dharma King,
I pray with reverence to you:
until I attain enlightenment, may we not separate.

The retinue of heroes and heroines spoke the following in unison:

In the pure Place of the Boundless Ultimate Sphere of Reality Buddhafield
the pure Teacher is the personification of the four boundless Bodies.

> The pure Retinue is the boundless heroes and heroines.
> The pure Dharma is boundless inexpressible primordial wisdom.
> The pure Time is the boundless Wheel of Time.
> Fortunate one with a karmic connection [based on former] prayers,
> for you to arrive here at this abode endowed with these five excellences is wondrous!

Saying this, they arranged many offering feasts.

The Lama said,

> Fortunate woman, even though we did not meet in person in the world, our meeting here now is greatly wondrous! As the Protector Padmasambhava's aspirations are unwavering, it will be impossible for us not to always meet. Now the time has come to give you ripening [empowerments] and liberating [instructions].

In my Treasure scriptures, I elaborated on the several empowerments he conferred upon me, including the *Troma, Wrathful Lady*, empowerment from his own profound Treasures, among others; the way he placed me [on the path of] ripening and liberation; and the advice and prophecies he gave me.

I responded,

> Lama, sir, because I am an inferior woman (*lus dman*), it is difficult for me to benefit beings in the world. Hence, if I abandon this body and try to attain a man's body, I wonder if I will benefit beings?

The lama said,

> Don't think like this. This body you have is that of a great female bodhisattva, a mother who gives birth to all the buddhas. It is the chariot that traverses the grounds and paths, the foundation that gives rise to beings who uphold the Sūtras and Tantras. Like the source of a river is snow, the pure source of both *saṃsāra* and *nirvāṇa* is the expansive space of the greatly secret and empty ultimate sphere mother, the space (*mkha'*) of reality itself in which the energy of compassion goes (*'gro*). Hence, this body of yours is the superior way to benefit beings. If you wonder how it is that it is superior, before, during the time of the previous Buddha Kāśyapa, when you were the daughter of a Brahmin named Namkha

> Drönma, based on your pure aspiration to benefit others by attaining the supreme Awakening and by the power of your prayers to Lady Tsogyel, you dispelled all visible and invisible negative obstacles to the life forces of beings who upheld the teachings. You raised the victory banner of the teachings. Via skillful means and auspicious connections, you propagated beings' happiness and established them in bliss. In particular, be like a mother to exhausted sentient beings, and it is certain that inconceivable benefit will gradually arise.[30]

Instead of the old Buddhist scriptural associations of the womb with the cycle of birth and death, cradle and grave, Gara Terchen's presentation of the great female bodhisattva as the pure source of all recast Sera Khandro's womb as the mother's expansive space (*mkha' klong*). His etymology of "*khandro*" (*mkha' 'gro*) as the "the space (*mkha'*) of reality itself in which the energy of compassion goes (*'gro*)" enveloped both the expansive space of the insight of emptiness, gendered female, and the dynamism of compassion, also called method or skillful means and gendered male. He insisted that rather than being inferior on account of her female body, Sera Khandro, as a *khandro*, was able to "establish beings in bliss," and rendered her "the mother who gives birth to all the buddhas."

Gara Terchen's theological exoneration of the female body and its maternal capacity did not map smoothly onto Sera Khandro's social life at Benak Monastery, where her religious pursuits appear to have offended as many people as they enriched. Particularly troubling was her vexed relationship to Gyelsé. From the start of their relationship, Gyelsé doubted Sera Khandro's claim to be a Treasure revealer. She writes that during her twenty-first year, in 1913, she discovered some Treasures, and then,

> I arrived home and offered Gyelsé the [Treasure] chests.
>
> "What are these?" he said.
>
> Wondering if he would angrily slap me like Marpa [slapped Milarepa] if I answered him honestly, I replied with a mixture of truth and lies.
>
> He responded, "Before, during the time when there were one hundred great Treasure revealers, two of them manifested as female Treasure revealers. These days in this degenerate age, we don't see female Treasure revealers."
>
> Unsure of whether or not he would be pleased to hear about my Treasures, from that time forward I wrote down the Treasures that came to me secretly.[31]

Gyelsé refers here to Jamgön Kongtrül Lodrö Tayé's *One Hundred Treasure Revealers*, a nineteenth-century compilation of Treasure revealers' biographies that includes just two female Treasure revealers, Jomo Menmo and Künga Bumpa (or Buma, as Sera Khandro writes). Gyelsé seems to use these two as exceptions that prove the rule that only men could be Treasure revealers, but Sera Khandro's autobiography indicates that they were both former incarnations of hers as well as sources of inspiration. Künga Buma (b. fifteenth century) appeared to Sera Khandro several times in visions, exhorting her to practice the Dharma and reveal Treasures. Jomo Menmo (thirteenth century) is the source of one of the seven prophecies that introduce Sera Khandro's autobiography. Additionally, Jomo Menmo's life story as depicted in Jamgön Kongtrül's *One Hundred Treasure Revealers* shares several common features with that of Sera Khandro: both women lost their mothers when they were children, Vajravārāhī empowered both of them in Treasure teachings when they were twelve, and both acted as consorts who aided their partners in revealing Treasures and benefited from consort practices themselves.[32]

With or without precedents, acting as a female Treasure revealer embroiled Sera Khandro in some fiery disputes not only with Gyelsé but also with other members of the Benak religious community. She reports that during that same year she went to gather firewood on the peak of a nearby mountain called Solung Drakar, which was one of her Treasure sites as well as the abode of a local deity and a former location of Gara Terchen's revelations. In this instance, a demonic female apparition accosted her. After Sera Khandro subjugated her,

> Then, I collected firewood, but because I was very late coming back home, I was delayed in serving Gyelsé tea. He slapped me and threw me outside. I was devastated and sang a song of despair like this:
>
> In the forest of sorrow at Benak, "bad monk,"[33]
> this negative community circles around.
> When I sing this despairing song of sadness,
> a crow cries, "*aiiiii*."
> The face of my mean life partner
> is like the crooked shadow of a rocky mountain.
> Our residence is a dark cavity with a hollow interior,
> a foundation of contamination, coldness, and depression.

I, a beggar girl from a remote land,
have only the sky as my friend in sorrow.
Forget about accomplishing the completely pure Dharma—
I have difficulty putting an end to our daily quarreling.
Now, I will not be a servant and this is not my home.
I will abandon these negative acts
and go wander about the country.

Gyelsé said, "What are you talking about?" and he told me to come boil his tea. I returned to the house, and his anger subsided. He asked, "What was that song that you sang?"

I replied,

I sang a song like this:

In the pleasure grove of Benyak, "good monk,"
the man born in the horse year [Gyelsé]
has a complexion like the weather in the three summer months;
there is no end to its lightness and darkness.
Although the turquoise dragon[34] that came from the land to the south
has exuberant strength,
sometimes she will be unable to do anything.
When the damage to her karmic energy has subsided,
karma will determine what will happen.

I sang this song.

Then the local people hated me and said that I was a demoness. I took a low place and kept the Treasure texts that had come to me extremely secret.

During this time, one day Gyelsé went to visit his middle brother, Jikmé Könchok, who was a monk at Pelyül Monastery. I was alone and there wasn't anybody around. I had a final testament of Tsogyel from the Oral Transmission Dharma cycle of my Treasure together with a biography of her that came to me as a revelation. I had written it down earlier, but the end was unfinished. When I was writing the lines,

I have no purpose aside from [benefiting] sentient beings.
It is impossible for a jewel to be stained by mud.
Phenomena depend only on interdependent causation . . .

all of a sudden an old monk named Kyaga Künzang arrived. Saying he had an offering to give, he came with a full plate of *tsampa* bread (*thos ba*).

He saw the text that I was writing and asked, "What is this?"

"It is a Treasure scripture," I replied.

He said, "It is amazing that you are taking care of Gara Lama's Treasure scripture. It is not suitable for you to contaminate Lama Gyelsé."

I answered, "Your Gyelsé having a wife like me is like the proverb of a donkey having golden ornaments on his head. I am not inflicting any harm on your Gyelsé. Like the saying 'a nectar vase on top of a well-assembled *maṇḍala*,' aside from benefiting him with the inner meaning of primordial wisdom, I didn't harm him. If you think that I harmed Gyelsé, it wasn't me. It is certain that earlier your Gyelsé was already contaminated."

He too became angry and said whatever harmful things he could to hurt me. On account of this, I burned the Oral Transmission Instructions of Tsogyel in the fire and vowed not to write profound Treasures.[35]

Sera Khandro's autobiographical writings make no attempt to sugarcoat her deteriorating relationship with Gyelsé and his entourage, which Gara Terchen's previous visionary edification could do little to ameliorate. Her fury at these men's dismissal of her seeps through her account of their interactions, prompting readers to wonder: who better to record the biography of Yeshé Tsogyel than another female practitioner renowned as her emissary? From passages like this, it appears that Sera Khandro's recognition as Yeshé Tsogyel's *ḍākinī* emanation came about only gradually, and in her thousands of pages of collected revelations, there remains no biography of Yeshé Tsogyel.

Nevertheless, Sera Khandro's vow to stop revealing Treasures did not last long. The same year that her Tsogyel revelations met their fiery end (1913), Sera Khandro added fuel to Gyelsé's ire by giving birth to their daughter, Yangchen Drönma, and revealing more Treasures. From the beginning, motherhood as a metaphor for the Buddhist ideal of compassionate concern for others, as Gara Terchen portrayed it in his inspirational postmortem appearance, and motherhood in the flesh-and-blood sense of caring for one's own children do not appear to have mixed well for Sera Khandro. Just after the infant was born female, to Gyelsé's great regret,

At that time, I secretly taught a Treasure I had newly revealed that was a *Lapdrön Drupa*, [*Machik*] *Lapdrön Liturgy*, to some lamas and monks from the

Khangsar family. Having pleased them, I returned home. Afterward, Gyelsé heard about it and scolded me. On account of this, I felt intensely depressed and offered a prayer something like this to the heroes and *ḍākinīs* of the three realms:

I beseech the Omniscient Mother Yeshé Tsogyel
and the heroes and heroines
in the invisible sacred land of the Glorious Copper-Colored
  Mountain.

I, this messenger sent by the mother *ḍākinīs*—
my impure body is being born as a woman (*za ma mo lus*).
My impure karma is grasping on to *saṃsāra*.
My impure place is the demons' island of Golok.
My impure deed is always having a negative community.

From what causes and conditions did karma like this arise?
I am not one whose mind stream took on the afflictions of the five
  poisons
and became a householder out of craving.
I acted in accordance with the prophecies of the deities and lamas.
I thought that I would certainly benefit the teachings and beings.
Now, not to mention benefiting others,
even my own mind stream is on the verge of becoming spoiled.

Marshall the mighty forces of the *ḍākinīs* who course in the ultimate
  sphere of the mother!
I beseech you to repel these obstacles of negative conditions!
Bless this impure realm of *saṃsāra*'s ocean,
that it may become the Glorious Lotus Light [Buddhafield].
Bless this impure body made of flesh and blood,
that it may become the stainless rainbow body of the ultimate sphere.

Bless this delusional cycle of mind and mental events,
that it may be liberated into the state of great primordial wisdom.
Liberate grasping to the two types of erroneous ignorance that is
  Rudra

into the great unimpeded nonreferential state of the ultimate
    sphere.
In short, for me, the tramp of the unfabricated dimension,
experiences of the way things are arose like this—
I am beyond hatred or no hatred for my life partner.
I am beyond falling or not falling into *saṃsāra.*
I am beyond liberation or nonliberation from this illusory body.
I am beyond the delusions or nondelusions of sentient beings.
I am beyond seeing or not seeing buddhafields.
I am beyond attaining or not attaining buddhahood.
I am beyond knowing or not knowing the view.
I am beyond having or not having the meditative experience of
    realization.

The nature of mind that is without delusion
Does not enter into mental fabrications regarding delusory
    forms.
Like space, it is completely pure and impartial.
It is solely vital nuclei, without elaboration.
This is my short song about the way things are.

I heard a formless voice coming from the sky say something like this:

Oh my, oh my *yogi*—
Is the great self-emergent primordial wisdom
free from exertion?
Is the unborn self-emergent spontaneous presence
the basis of *saṃsāra* and *nirvāṇa*?
Are appearances of good and bad, happiness and suffering
the play of reality itself?
Is the poisonous water lily that is the eight worldly *dharma*s
to be abandoned quickly?
Will you retrieve your [Treasure] wealth, the *ḍākinī*'s heart
    nectar,
in time?
Will benefiting both the teachings and beings
come from the south?

> You don't need to feel frustrated and exhausted
> by what appears as an illusory emanation.
> Padmasambhava's testament does not change.
> It is certain that in time, your prayers will come together.[36]

Not long after this vision, Sera Khandro and the nun Chötreng went off to collect firewood. Just as they finished, Sera Khandro intuited that she had a Treasure to reveal at Solung Drakar, the mountain near Benak Monastery. When they were on their way there, all of a sudden:

> I said, "We need to go back quickly."
>
> Chötreng answered, "But don't we need to go to Drakar? It's not far—let's go."
>
> "Let's not go," I replied. "Now, if it takes a long time, Gyelsé will scold me. Not only that, but I gave Yangchen Drönma to Tupzang to look after and if Gyelsé hears her cry, he will definitely scold me."
>
> After I said this, we carried the firewood and returned home.[37]

Sera Khandro's family responsibilities with Gyelsé and her calling as a Treasure revealer seem to have been at loggerheads. But as negative as many interlocutors in her quotidian life were toward her religious ambitions, *ḍākinīs*' inspiration regularly counterbalanced them, as seen in the passages examined in this chapter so far. This back-and-forth between depressing worldly encounters and uplifing visions gives Sera Khandro's autobiography a tone sufficiently humble for an unusual nonmonastic female religious specialist but superlative enough to signal her extraordinary accomplishments.

Going to Visit Gotrül Rinpoché

Nowhere in Sera Khandro's autobiography is the careful attention she gave to wording and voice more apparent than in her description of her meetings with Jikdrel Chökyi Lodrö, the lama from Pelyül Dartang Monastery in Golok whom she called Gotrül Rinpoché.[38] From the very beginning of their acquaintance, *ḍākinīs* foreshadowed Gotrül Rinpoché's importance in Sera Khandro's life at the same time as she vociferously refused to approach the esteemed monastic hierarch, giving an ambiguous pitch to their relationship:

Then, when I was twenty-three years old, together with my disciple Tupten Zangpo I went to collect garlic on the mountainside. A pleasant chick landed on a thorn bush and said,

The call "*ting ting*" is the language of the gods.
The expression "*dem dem*" is my native tongue.
I come to convey to you, noble *yogi*,
the metric and melody of these secret *ḍākinī* words.[39]
Without distraction, hold the meaning of these in your heart.

Though the eastern sun is hot,
it will meet the karma of the western wind.
Though the southern cuckoo traverses a long road,
the call of the season will summon the cuckoo in time.

Since Padmasambhava's final testament is undeceiving,
act in accordance with the *ḍākinī*'s symbolic prophetic guide, and
in time you will certainly meet with your allotment of bodhisattvas.
If indications, auspicious connections, and empowerments from
the being who upholds the Dharma named Dharma Mati[40] appear,
it is crucially important that you carefully examine them.

Whatever appears—happiness and suffering— is child's play;
you don't need to believe it, becoming frustrated and exhausted.
The *ḍākinīs*' emissary who is like a wish-fulfilling jewel
will unwittingly accomplish the two benefits [of self and other].
Stop quarrelling with your partner [Gyelsé].
Practice assiduously in an unknown land
and you will meet those with the karma to be your consorts and
Dharma holders.
You will certainly attain your paternal inheritance of profound
Treasures.
Keep this hidden deep in your heart.
Did you understand? Did you understand, noble *yogi*?

I wondered, did this chick come from the Glorious [Copper-Colored] Mountain? If so, by engaging her in conversation, I would know for certain, so I said,

How wonderful, little miraculous chick!
From which land have you come?
Was your journey long or short?
Are you fatigued from flying here?
Is your land blissfully happy?
What is the name of the *ḍākinī* who has sent me
the secret words of this clear message?

I am a servant of another who has not accomplished her purpose,
so it is decided that benefiting others will not happen.
Now I, this inferior woman (*lus dman*), fervently desire
to go to the blissful, blissful *Ḍākinīs*' Land.
By the power of Shelkar Tsogyel's prayers,
I was empowered in extremely profound extraordinary Treasures.
Nevertheless, since I am an inferior woman (*lus dman*) with little courage,
I didn't find a way to summon consorts or Dharma holders.
Even though I treated local people, whether high or low,
without a hateful mindset,
they responded by displaying all sorts of negativity.
They are the basis for wrong views and criticism.
Now, in the region of this bad village of Benak,[41]
I will not disseminate one word of my profound Treasures.
Having reconcealed my chests and profound pages,
I will go wander through the country as an ordinary person.

The chick replied,

Listen, powerful noble woman—
this splendorous miraculous Garuda
comes from the direction of directionlessness possessing the five [certainties],[42]
the Glorious Mountain.
My flight did not fatigue me.
I came propelled by wind along a path in the sky.
This is the *ḍākinī*'s music of symbolic words,
the secret message of Lekyi Wangmo:

The time has still not come for you [to go]
to the *Ḍākinīs*' Land.
When the bull's horns appear,
the splendorous tiger will welcome
this companion from the directionless direction.
Continuously apply yourself to making numerous feast offerings
to the *maṇḍala* of the mother deities and *ḍākinīs*.
Performing good or bad actions
depends only on auspicious connections.
When you meet with consorts and Dharma holders,
don't be swayed by the hindrance of laziness.
Act in accord with the *ḍākkīs*' command, and
the lantern of the two Treasure teachings
will certainly illuminate the east and south.
In time, *ḍākkīs* will certainly give you
symbolic indications about the future.
In time, we will meet
in the invisible *Ḍākinīs*' Land.

Saying this, she disappeared into the sky in the form of a five-colored sphere of light.

I thought, Now when my karma is going downward, instead of *ḍākinī* prophecies, the prophecies of birds and chicks come forth. I wonder if there will be any truth to them?

A few days later, someone named Chönkhor Lama Jikmé arrived. I told him, "Gyelsé is not home. For what purpose did you come here?"

He replied, "I didn't come to see Gyelsé. Our lama Gotrül sent me to see you. He sent you this letter and said that he must certainly meet you, so that is why I came here." Saying this, he handed me a sealed letter.

Thinking that this was similar to the prophecy spoken by the chick earlier, I said, "I have heard of a high-ranking religious encampment member named Pelyül Gochen Trülku, but I have never met him or heard his voice. I don't know his real name—what is it?"

He responded, "The Trülku has many names, but he is commonly known as Jikdrel Chökyi Lodrö."

I thought that of the four pillars who were my [main] doctrine holders, he was the northern pillar called "Dharma Mati." However, since I had an inferior female body (*skye lus dman pa*), I thought that others would have wrong views about the *trülku*, so I told Jikchö,

> Your lama seems to be someone who doesn't know anything. He tells me to write a text about whatever this old lady remembers—best a prophecy, middling a liturgy, worst no less than just four words—and send it to him. Now in my twenty-three years, I have traveled in all directions from the upper regions of Dzachukha to the lower regions of Rongzhi and Khaksum.[43] I have met many lamas and *trülkus* in these places and received teachings from them. Not one of them has ever said that they needed this old lady to write down whatever she remembers. Nevertheless, if I were to write down what is in my mind about the primordially present ocean of phenomenal elements of *saṃsāra* and *nirvāṇa*, I would never reach the end.

He replied,

> Our *trülku's* mind is not oppressed by any hindrance or suffering; he is definitely an omniscient one. Whatever he does, he does in the manner of being a knowledgeable person. All of his outer, inner, and secret conduct is extremely disciplined, so much so that the lamas and *trülkus* of the monastery's abbey dare not approach him if they have not acted with the utmost morality. Hence, now this seems to be extremely crucial—you must send him a letter of the nature he requested. He was very close to the late Gara Lama and it is said that he is his main doctrine holder.

In accordance with the *ḍākinīs*' symbolic prophetic guide, I sent him a letter, and he considered it to be an indication of future occurrences. When he performed the rituals [my letter prophesied], his life span was freed from hindrances.[44]

Hesitant as this "old lady" who was nothing but a "lowly woman" was to approach Gotrül Rinpoché, her self-deprecation offsets a major claim she simultaneously makes: this Pelyül Dartang Monastery lama was one of the four pillars, or main doctrine holders, predestined to inherit and propagate her Treasure revelations. If it is shocking that a monastic hierarch would receive religious teachings from a young mother, Sera Khandro was, after all, only reiterating what the *ḍākinī*'s emissary had told her about Gotrül's true identity as Dharma Mati. The proof of this emerges in the outcome of their exchange, for according to Sera Khandro's report, her revelations enhanced Gotrül Rinpoché's longevity, which was a characteristic feature of *ḍākinīs*' power.

Given that Gotrül Rinpoché was a prominent monastic hierarch and she a noncelibate religious woman, Sera Khandro presents her relationship with him with the utmost delicacy. Still he figures prominently as one of her main supporters during the decade she lived at Benak Monastery. In fact, Gotrül Rinpoché was the first human figure in Sera Khandro's autobiography to publicly claim her identity as a *ḍākinī* emanation of Yeshé Tsogyel, soon after they met in 1915, when she was twenty-three, though others had given her secret indications of this:

> At that time, near the area where Gotrül Rinpoché lived, the head of a large household died, so Gotrül Rinpoché acted as the lead officiate of the funeral. Gyelsé went to see him. Since I had an inferior female body (*skye lus dman pa*), I didn't dare go to see him, fearing that others would see, hear, and be suspicious. Instead I went to circumambulate the pile of stones [with prayers carved in them] and the prayer wheel house. Again, Jikchö arrived and I asked, "Where are you going?"
>
> He replied, "Trülku sent me to summon you, so we need to go quickly," and we set off together.
>
> Then, as a greeting present, I offered Gotrül Rinpoché a high-quality turquoise wrapped in five-colored silk along with a stainless scarf, and I prostrated to him.
>
> "How are you?" I asked.
>
> In response, the Trülku got up from the middle of the assembly and offered me silver and a "good day" scarf. All the lamas, monks, laymen, and laywomen gathered there didn't know what was going on. Each one looking at the other, they didn't say anything. The Trülku said, "You all don't need to have doubt. I think this *ḍākinī* is certainly the speech incarnation of Yeshé Tsogyel. Abandon your wrong views and be faithful. This is not a deception; it is real."
>
> I thought, "He has never met or heard from anyone in my community, so how can he know if I am Tsogyel? Not only that, how is it possible for an inferior woman (*lus dman*) like me to be a *ḍākinī*? On the outside, I have little learning. On the inside, I am ignorant with regard to generation and perfection stage practice.[45] No matter what I begin doing, I cannot get beyond the activities of *saṃsāra*."

After I wondered this, he said, "Not needing to exert yourself in learning and training, you fully comprehend all the paths of generation and perfection. Not needing to learn how to read and write, [your literacy stems] from the awakening of residual karma from having learned before. Nevertheless, not letting your own Treasures go, you must write and propagate them, or the *ḍākinīs*' punishment will draw near."

I said, "Sir, I am not a Treasure revealer. I have never attained even one type of Dharma teaching, and I don't know about generation and perfection."[46]

Gotrül's recognition of Sera Khandro as a *ḍākinī* emanation of Yeshé Tsogyel drew dumbfounded stares from those who heard it; his reassurances that they should abandon doubt and wrong views and instead be faithful and accept her true identity seem to speak directly to both the audience written into Sera Khandro's autobiography and those who would later read it, providing proof, ventriloquized through Gotrül Rinpoché's voice, that she was authentic. Sera Khandro's first line of defense was to ask how it was possible for someone with an inferior female body to be a *ḍākinī*. Yet this only accentuates Gotrül's claim, for who better to be Yeshé Tsogyel's emanation than Üza Khandro, the "Central Tibetan Lady *Ḍākinī*"? The extent to which Sera Khandro deflected the praise that lamas such as Gotrül Rinpoché bestowed upon her suggests the atypical nature of her claim to be a Treasure revealer as a woman and a foreigner to Golok. Concerned that others would "see, hear, and be suspicious," she stressed her humility by portraying herself as nearly needing to be dragged in front of Gotrül Rinpoché. Nevertheless, after all the denial, she indicated that her revelations did indeed aid Gotrül Rinpoché and other powerful religious hierarchs with whom she interacted, thereby proving her credentials without needing to state them outright in her own voice.

Gyelsé Loses Power and *Ḍākinīs* Take Charge

Gotrül Rinpoché's public acknowledgment of Sera Khandro's extraordinary religious status as Yeshé Tsogyel's incarnation and as a Treasure revealer may have inspired some, but not Gyelsé, who still seemed underwhelmed. Sera Khandro narrates that a few years after this, in 1918, when she was twenty-six,

In the dragon month [the third month] a letter arrived from Gotrül, so Gyelsé and I along with some disciples went to the sacred land of [Nyenpo] Yutsé to see the *trülku*. His arthritis having improved, all of his disciples and attendants meditated on joy. While they exerted themselves in their respective practices, we met Gotrül, who was revived with happiness as if meeting a person who came alive from the dead. Then, during the fifteen days we stayed there, we spoke in detail with Gotrül about everything, both worldly and religious, leaving nothing out.

In particular, when Gotrül Rinpoché gave Gara Trülku [Gyelsé] much advice regarding my present and future, it didn't agree with him and he said the following:

> It seems as though you are a *ḍākinī* who appears to be Yeshé Tsogyel and who someone like me is not empowered to have as a consort. Gotrül always says, "It is not suitable to separate from your *ḍākinī* by any means." Even if a man must lose power to a woman, what is the meaning of my not having power over someone like you? If this were the case, old householder laymen would never have a way to get a wife!

I replied,

> Did Gotrül, thinking that I was of a high birth, give you advice? As you know and everyone can see, I am an old sinner from a polluted family who is inferior to Seldrön, so you don't need to say this. You have control [over me]. For one thing, it is easy to be reborn in a female body (*za ma mo lus*). For another, my paternal relatives are far away. Moreover, people who have a little sympathy [for me] are like the proverb "uncle rabbit's crown jewel." Of course Gotrül offered this advice to you because he feels sorry for me. You don't need to be upset and worried about this.[47]

Gotrül's attention to Sera Khandro seems to have rubbed Gyelsé the wrong way, in particular his unsolicited advice about how Gyelsé should respect her. She responded to his jealous outrage by performing a type of early twentieth-century Golok "damage control" in which she lowered herself by accentuating all the reasons she was inferior according to Golok social mores. She was not from the right type of Golok religious family, and her place as Gyelsé's spouse had been superseded by his new love interest, Seldrön. She was not only an inferior woman but also one whose "paternal relatives are far away," and therefore was defenseless.

Even so, if it is not possible for rabbits to have a crown jewel, as this Tibetan proverb seems to indicate, some must have had them despite all expectations, for it is clear to readers of Sera Khandro's autobiography that there *were* prominent people who pitied her, Gotrül Rinpoché for one.

Though Sera Khandro's stay in Benak as Gyelsé's spouse had been souring from almost the moment it began, finally word came from a *ḍākinī* that enough was enough. In 1921, when the twenty-nine-year-old Sera Khandro was returning to Gyelsé's encampment after her final visit to Drimé Özer before she joined him in Dartsang, she writes,

> When we were returning home, we arrived at a place called Rizap. That night, in my dream again the terrifying spontaneously born woman arrived and said,
>
>> Why are you going toward those with deteriorated commitment vows? It is as if you have mistaken brass for gold, water for wine. You cast away your destined *bodhisattva* as unnecessary. You turn away from upholding your profound Treasure. You are distracted, grasping onto *saṃsāra*. From the time you were young until now, I have given you honest advice. I have given you your paternal inheritance of profound Dharma Treasures. Although I have reared you like a mother who loves her child, repelling negative conditions, outer and inner obstacles, and so forth, still you are unable to be independent and you need only to be under others' power. What is the meaning of this?
>
> I explained,
>
>> It is not that I had too many thoughts and mistook who was or was not my consort. I didn't have the power to break the commands of gods and lamas, so I turned away from my own purpose and wondered if I could uphold [Gara Terchen] Dündül Wangchuk Lingpa's profound Treasures. Since I directed my intentions toward this, until now I have not accomplished my purpose. In particular, all my consorts and Dharma holders have fallen under others' sway. Because I am one with an inferior female body (*skye lus dman pa*), I did not have a way to meet them. Now, too, I am powerless not to go [back to Gyelsé]. That is my response.

She stated,

> Thinking that since you were of bad ancestry, you needed to do all kinds of work without retribution, until now you have remained with the Gara family. From this year forward, you belong to us. The time for you to live with the Gara family is finished. Still, if you are encouraged by a person with perverse aspirations, I don't know what will happen to your life, Dharma, and disciples. Like wind is to butter lamps, fire is to water, and iron is to rock, you need to be extremely careful.

As she said this, I awoke from sleep. Then we went on. The encampment base of [Gyelsé's] residence had merged into the Gar [kinsmen's] circle.[48] I told Tupzang, "There aren't any good prophecies about the encampment base joining the Gar circle this year; it isn't a good omen."

Tupzang said, "Yes, before when Gyelsé had no wealth or food, I never saw those who say they are 'the Gar kinsmen circle.' These days, when there is property and wealth thanks to your kindness, their identity as [part of] the Gara family is awakened and they say they need to take care of Gyelsé."

I said, "It is not acceptable for you to speak as if you are a young person with a child's intellect who doesn't know anything. If they hear you, they will say bad things."[49]

Ḍākinīs' encouragement came in peaceful and wrathful varieties to suit the circumstances; just as a *ḍākinī* had fiercely ended Sera Khandro's childhood suicide contemplation, the present *ḍākinī* did not mince words in expressing her dismay at Sera Khandro's return to Gyelsé, foreshadowing their imminent separation. Even so, the difficulty of extricating herself from Gyelsé sounds through her dialogues with human and celestial interlocutors. She felt powerless to leave him, as she told the *ḍākinī*, but she also had serious misgivings about living with him in his newly extended Gara family encampment. Sera Khandro ventriloquized Tupzang's voice to express resentment that she presumably also felt toward Gyelsé and his relatives' newfound interest in him, and in so doing implied that she played an unacknowledged role in enlarging his stature. Just as she artfully expressed her discontent with Gyelsé and his relatives through Tupzang's voice, she expressed her sense that she should be with Drimé Özer and not Gyelsé through her conversation with the *ḍākinī*, all the while refuting both.

PART II: COMPARING CONFIDENCE WITH SERA KHANDRO'S LAMAS

Tibetan autobiographies share a characteristic balance between self-deprecation and self-aggrandizement, but the way the autobiographers accentuate their lowliness or their realization varies. In comparison with Düjom Lingpa's and Gara Terchen's autobiographies, Sera Khandro's presents her as much more hesitant to claim an authoritative religious status. Sera Khandro provides much more detail in terms of word count and emotional intensity about the obstacles to accomplishing her religious ambitions, which necessitated extensive and recurrent divine intervention. Without this seesaw oscillation between dark days and luminous visions, Düjom Lingpa's and Gara Terchen's self-presentations take a more confident tone.

Düjom Lingpa's *A Clear Mirror*

Düjom Lingpa's autobiography, *A Clear Mirror*, is even more drenched in visionary encounters than Sera Khandro's auto/biographical writings. In his visions, enlightened *ḍākinīs* including Vajravārāhī, Yeshé Tsogyel, and Tārā; buddhas and bodhisattvas including Padmasambhava, Avalokiteśvara, and Mañjuśrī; and great masters of the past such as Longchen Rapjampa bestow blessings and teachings upon him. The cast of characters and the nature of the prophecies in Sera Khandro's visionary accounts resonate in many ways with Düjom Lingpa's spirit-infused vignettes. In both texts, *ḍākinīs* perform their characteristic functions of prophesying about future events, ways to overcome obstacles, and which teachings to practice and propagate. They appear as terrifyingly wrathful demonesses and as pleasing beauties, at times helping to decode revelations, escorting the authors to buddhafields, and acting as the main deity in their visions. Land deities manifest regularly in the forms of men on horseback, uncanny children, and animals before both Düjom Lingpa and Sera Khandro, displaying their powers and challenging their authority. Some of the same land deities residing at sacred mountains required propitiation from both Düjom Lingpa and Sera Khandro, such as Drong Mountain in Serta.

Amid these visions, however, an important difference between the autobiographies is that Düjom Lingpa's is much sparser on commentary about his mundane life and therefore lacks the back-and-forth between inspiring visions and depressing worldly events typical of Sera Khandro's writing. He begins *A Clear Mirror* with the statement:

> To write of the various activities and affairs
> of an ordinary being passing endlessly through *saṃsāra*
> is a cause of boredom and weariness.
> Knowing this, I had no interest in writing anything down,
> yet could not bear the insistent requests of my disciples.
> If I expound in detail about my various visionary experiences,
> which are like ripples on water, I will never reach the end,
> so here I will convey the gist of my pure visionary experiences.[50]

Though conventional, this précis may also offer some explanation why Düjom Lingpa's autobiographical reflections contain so little narrative about his daily affairs. After a more elaborate opening chapter in which he details his family genealogy down to his father, Abten, and his mother, Bodzok, he describes tending herds as a youth and then becoming a monk at the age of ten in 1845. Later we hear briefly of the birth of several of Düjom Lingpa's sons and their respective enthronements at monasteries in eastern Tibet, including Dodrupchen Monastery, Dzagyel Monastery, and Taktsé Samdrup Monastery. There were tensions in his communities, mostly concerning litigation over thievery, and in one instance Düjom Lingpa's own cattle herd was pilfered. He includes one line about becoming the head of Kelzang Monastery in Dartsang when he was fifty-five. Additionally, he expresses concerns about warfare with Mongols and Chinese. Aside from these snippets of nineteenth-century life on the Golok highlands, what little else he mentions about his earthly surroundings seems only to serve as the backdrop for his next visionary encounter.

Another difference between Düjom Lingpa and Sera Khandro's self-presentations is the degree to which they deny their interlocutors' praise. In only a handful of the nearly one hundred richly dialogical visions in Düjom Lingpa's *Clear Mirror* does he respond to *ḍākinī*s or others with self-deprecating rhetoric. One of these few instances is the following passage, in which a red *ḍākinī* wearing a white cotton lower garment appeared before him during his twenty-fourth year (ca. 1859) and predicted the locations of his prophetic guides hidden as Treasures in Drakmar or "Red

Cliff," located in the upper Mar valley of Golok. Düjom Lingpa reacted with self-doubt, inspiring the *ḍākinī*'s encouragement:

In response, I said:

Alas! Lady, queen with a beautiful face,
I, this beggar with no source of refuge,
On the outside, I have no insight from learning.
On the inside, I have no realization from meditating.
I have no wealth, riches, or fortune.
Above, I have no one to rely upon for protection;
below, I have no support to hold me up.
In between, I have no close relatives.
Aside from those who envy and humiliate me,
I have no helpful friends who honor and praise me.

Even if this humble, powerless beggar
has a share of Treasure,
I think it will not benefit beings.
I wonder whether in my future
I can become a fearless and pure mendicant monk.
Lama, consider me—may I accomplish my aspirations!

She replied,

Alas—son, don't let your mental confidence wane.
Your disciples will amass like a constellation of stars.
Even though at first you are humble without refuge,
later, you will rise above the others.
Everyone will praise you and regard you as an object of respect.
You will benefit disciples with a karmic connection to you,
bringing them on the path to liberation.
Carry out my commands accordingly.
This will commence your happiness.
Your wealth will increase like the waxing moon.
Deities and protectors will fulfill your desires.
Your consorts will be mother deities and *ḍākinīs*.
Keep this in mind, fortunate son.[51]

Düjom Lingpa responded to the *ḍākinīs'* bestowal of prophetic guides by expressing his insecurities—insufficient wealth, insight, family connections, and friends—not unlike Sera Khandro's response to Vajravārāhī, in which she complained about her inferior female body. Also resonant with Sera Khandro's writing is the sense of insecurity that manifests at times regarding his status as a Treasure revealer. At one point when he was twenty-three, a lama questioned the authenticity of his Treasure teachings, causing him to burn them just as Sera Khandro had done after the monk disparaged her Yeshé Tsogyel revelations.[52] Later an old man named Lekpé Lodrö accosted the thirty-nine-year-old Düjom Lingpa, provoking him by hinting that he was a fraud. In response, the lama proved his authenticity by promising that his disciples would gain realization from practicing his Treasures and that performing rituals from them would cause immediate death for those who harmed him or his livestock.[53] The difference between the two Treasure revealers' works is the relative frequency of such moments in which the protagonists expressed misgivings about their spiritual capacities and had to defend themselves from charges of being imposters. Not only did Sera Khandro not threaten immediate death for her enemies, but she vociferously decried her own abilities as a Treasure revealer in a way that Düjom Lingpa did not. She reiterated like a mantra her despair at not being able to bring together auspicious connections, including male consorts and doctrine holders necessary to reveal Treasures, always pinning the blame on her "inferior female body." Düjom Lingpa did face challenges—proving his authenticity as a Treasure revealer being central among them—but did not dwell on the down side in his autobiographical writings nearly as much as Sera Khandro did.

Gara Terchen's *Account of How This Yogi Traversed the Grounds and Paths*

Gara Terchen's autobiography seems not to have shied so far away from narrating the activities of someone "passing endlessly through *saṃsāra*," if commentary on his daily life, travels, and conversations with his companions counts as such. From his *Account*, we learn that he was born in the district of Chakmo Golok in the village near the monastic seat of Golok Pemayak (an alternate name for Benak) to a father who was a noncelibate Tantric religious specialist (a *ngakpa*) descending from a family line named Gara, and a mother named Dechen Drön. He writes of taking novice monastic ordination at age nine in 1866 with Kyabjé Drupwang Pema Drondül Dorjé, who founded Benak Monastery in the mid-nineteenth century. Then he lived for several years at Ngedön Tekchen Ling Monastery, located in what is today Chikdril County, Golok, which began as a Jonang sect tent encampment and developed into a nonsectarian monastery in 1865.[54] His autobiography details his extensive religious education from an early age that included studying Buddhist canonical scriptures, pure visions, and Treasure scriptures such as those of the Treasure revealer Pema Dupatsel, who gave him the name Pema Longyang Gyatso.[55] Additionally, he describes immersing himself in an extensive list of religious practices as a young man, including preliminary practices (*sngon 'gro*), channel and wind practices (*rtsa rlung*), Severance (*gcod*), Great Seal (*mahāmūdra*), Great Perfection (*rdzogs chen*), and various Treasure teachings, with a focus on those of Ratna Lingpa (1403–1479). Later he became a capable scribe, and he mentions copying several texts for his teachers, including the fourteenth-century Treasure revealer Karma Lingpa's *Bardo Tödröl, Liberation Through Hearing in the Intermediate States*, popularly known in English as *The Tibetan Book of the Dead.*

Gara Terchen wrote about his life's challenges as well as transformative religious experiences. He mentions being impoverished as a youth and traveling to perform village rituals many times, presumably as a means to finance his monastic studies. At one point he went to work for his aunt and uncle, herding livestock and gathering firewood, receiving only tattered clothes and poor food in return. In the midst of these hardships,

> One day when I was herding livestock near the *stūpa* at Mar Selé Kyilkhor Tang,[56] I felt depressed and wondered, "Who was the lama who originally built this *stūpa*? Is it true what they say about him being an incarnation of Master Mila? How happy I would be if I too could be a renunciate like Mila." Thinking this, I felt sad and cried.
>
> When I looked up at the expanse of the sky, I saw a white cloud that looked like a heap of fresh yogurt. The torso of a white man appeared, who said,
>
> Alas, you fortunate boy,
> in the village of ignorant cyclic existence

suffering is infinite!
You don't need to be depressed.
When the time comes for your karmic heritage to awaken as a great being,
If you request ripening [empowerments] and liberating [instructions]
from a lama who is an emanation of a supreme noble one,
accomplishments will come from this.

After he spoke, he transformed into a rainbow cloud and then disappeared in the ultimate sphere to the east.[57]

The white man in this vision consoled the eleven-year-old Gara Terchen much the same way that *ḍākinīs* repeatedly did Sera Khandro. Later in Gara Terchen's life as well, visions of Padmasambhava, Yeshé Tsogyel, and other *ḍākinīs* appeared on several occasions, succoring him after troubles with his family. But even in these instances when visionary forces came to his defense, Gara Terchen, like Düjom Lingpa, rarely responded to their encouragement by presenting himself in negative terms.

Gara Terchen recounts countless visions journeying to Padmasambhava's Copper-Colored Mountain and encountering *ḍākinīs*, most often Ekajaṭī and Yeshé Tsogyel but also Dorjé Yudrönma, Palden Lhamo, Machik Lapdrön, and Vajravārāhī, among others. But unlike Sera Khandro's visually and dialogically rich accounts of her visionary experiences, those of Gara Terchen are comparatively terse and devoid of self-humbling deference. For example, when he was thirteen, around the same age as Sera Khandro was when Vajravārāhī empowered her in her two main Treasure cycles, Gara Terchen experienced his first visionary encounter with Padmasambhava:

When I was thirteen, in the male iron horse year [1870], on the evening of the tenth day of a winter month I went to the naturally appearing pure buddhafield, the Glorious Mountain of Lotus Light, where I met the Refuge Master, the Great One from Oḍḍiyāna.[58] He introduced me to about forty volumes of profoundly secret Dharma instructions. After I saw these, he told me they were my share of Dharma. I prostrated and received the four empowerments. He touched the top of my head and made expansive prayers. From that time forward, vajra hymns about the profound essence burst forth from the expanse of awareness.[59]

We find the same matter-of-fact tone in other passages from Gara Terchen's autobiography:

When I was sixteen, in the female water bird year [1873], early in the middle month of the fall, I saw Machik Ekajaṭī and the Protectress Dorjé Yudrön in visions and dreams. They prophesied,

Behold! Great being Pema Dündül, listen—
now the time has come for your karmic heritage to awaken.
Heart emanation of the Great One from Oḍḍiyāna,
yogi practicing the Great Perfection,
if you meet the supreme awareness holder,
discuss the profoundly secret Great Perfection.
You have a karmic connection from before pertaining to this.[60]

In another instance, Gara Terchen narrates,

When I was eighteen years old, on the tenth day of the bird month [the eighth month] of the female wood pig year [1875], I actually saw the face of the Great One from Oḍḍiyāna. He conferred the royal vase empowerment on me and appointed me as his regent. The Ḍākinī Dawa Drönma gave me ink, a pen, and paper and taught me white, black, and variegated symbols like X, XX, and XXX.[61] On account of her instruction, the pure vision *Yeshé Khorlö Chö, Dharma of the Wheel of Primordial Wisdom*, burst forth from the expanse.[62]

Gara Terchen closes these visions without any sort of denial of Padmasambhava and the *ḍākinīs*' recognition. This is true for his accounts of receiving prophetic guides and for other types of visions. For example, when he was nineteen, in 1876:

A white man with a white horse who was a *tsen* spirit saying he was the land deity of Chakri came and said this:

[At] Bedrak Dorjé Rolwa,
self-arisen Treasure chests

have been entrusted to you by Vairotsana, [including]
the prophetic guide for your profound Dharma.
When the time comes, retrieve them.

After he spoke, he rose up higher and higher from the earth and then disappeared into the eastern direction of the sky.[63]

Chakri, or Chakri Ömbar, Iron Mountain of Blazing Light, is a sacred mountain along the Mar River across from Benak Monastery, where Sera Khandro also would discover Treasures several decades later. Gara Terchen received a prophetic guide from the *ḍākinī* Ekajaṭī when he was twenty-two, directing him to the same Treasure site, called Bedrak Dorjé Rolwa or "Hidden Cliff of Vajra Revelry":

I actually saw the face of the one mother Ekajaṭī, who said,

How wonderful! Listen, regent of the one from Oḍḍiyāna—
at Bedrak Dorjé Rolwa
a paper scroll containing the prophetic guide of the three cycles of
Nyingtik, Heart Essence,
is hidden in a woven chest.
Remove it on the tenth day of the dragon month [the third month] and
decode the meaning of the symbols on the tenth day of the monkey
month [the seventh month].
Keep mother's heart advice in mind.

In accordance with what she said, on the tenth day of the dragon month I discovered the Treasure's prophetic guide. [In return] I offered the *Ratna Lingpa Tukdrup kyi Tsokchö, Feast Offering of the Ratna Lingpa Heart Liturgy*, and kept it extremely secret.[64]

Gara Terchen writes of his visions in pithy and unapologetic prose—without the intense concern about inferiority and extensive reassurances from *ḍākinī*s and other divinities prevalent in Sera Khandro's writing. He never denies his ability to abide by *ḍākinī*s' prophecies or Padmasambhava's commands; their appearances seem only to confirm his religious insight. His writing appears comparatively unconcerned with allaying readers' suspicions, befitting someone like him, a Golok native from an esteemed family of religious specialists.

As men educated from their youths as monks, Gara Terchen and Düjom Lingpa expressed an unqualified confidence in the propriety of their claims to have direct access to buddhas and bodhisattvas, for both had other sources of religious authority beyond the visions that punctuated their life narratives. Neither one regularly bemoaned his inability to find suitable consorts or doctrine holders or to gather auspicious connections nearly as often as Sera Khandro did. The comparatively greater intensity, length, and frequency of her lamentations about the difficulties of survival and success as a Treasure revealer in Golok suggest that being female, not to mention being far from home, without wealth, lacking a monastic education, and later a single parent added layers of challenges to her life as a Treasure revealer. Defending herself from the charge of hubris required more finesse for a woman with fewer obvious claims to religious vocation, and detailing the circumstances through which she transcended her limitations as well as the many voices who supported her were important ways she calibrated the right autobiographical tone. But although Sera Khandro emphasized her feelings of inferiority and inadequacy more than her male teachers did, this was not the end of the story, for *ḍākinīs* always had the last word.

PART III: *ḌĀKINĪS*' ROLES IN FINDING A FEMALE VOICE IN WOMEN'S AUTOBIOGRAPHIES

That Sera Khandro's self-denigrating comments about her lowly female form occasioned *ḍākinīs*' and lamas' reassurances to a greater degree than in the autobiographical writings of two of her male teachers begs the question: is it because of Sera Khandro's femaleness that *ḍākinīs* appear to her with such frequency to encourage her? Lamenting the female body is a theme in female mystics' writings far from the Tibetan cultural sphere—medieval Christian mystic Hildegard of Bingen describes herself as "a weak and fragile rib"; Clare of Siena calls herself "a useless handmaid and unworthy servant"; and Julian of Norwich claims to be "a woman ignorant, weak, and frail."[65] Monica Furlong understands this "ritual obeisance" of gender-based self-denigration in medieval women mystics' writings as both a reflection of a socially imposed sense of inferiority and a literary device that helped their divine mystical visions to be heard, an interpretation I suggest applies to Sera Khandro's writings as well. But what about other Tibetan female-authored autobiographies? A look at two other examples, written by Jetsün Lochen Rinpoché and Orgyen Chökyi, suggests the difficulty of correlating gender with particular writing styles, for these female autobiographies portray a diversity of self-representations. Even so, in all three of these extraordinary women's life narratives, *ḍākinīs* provide positive feminine images of Buddhist divinity, which female autobiographers and their disciples incorporated in varying ways and with varying success in promoting their sanctity.

The Life of Jetsün Ani Lochen

The closest Tibetan female autobiographer to Sera Khandro in terms of temporality and geography was the famous nun and cofounder of Shuksep Nunnery, Jetsün Ani Lochen (Rindzin Chönyi Zangmo, 1865–1951). We might expect to read about more commonalities than divergences between Sera Khandro's and Ani Lochen's lives, given their proximity on many levels. Though Ani Lochen was twenty-seven years Sera Khandro's senior, the two could easily have met in central Tibet during Sera Khandro's childhood, though neither provides any evidence that they did. Some of the same lamas were important in both of their lives; in the early 1890s, both visited a Taklung Kagyü lama whom Sera Khandro called Mahā Rinpoché and Ani Lochen called Matrül Rinpoché. This lama was Matrül Tekchok Jikmé Pawo, the twenty-seventh abbot at Taklung Monastery in Jang, north of Lhasa.[66] Later in their religious careers, both women mentioned Katok Situ Chökyi Gyatso (1880–1925).[67] Additionally, both shared a spiritual lineage connected to Nyingma and Taklung Kagyü teachings; Sera Khandro's root guru, Drimé Özer, was Nyingma, but both her birth and death had associations with the Taklung Kagyü lineage—her parents brought her to Mahā Rinpoché as an infant to request a name for her, and she died at the Taklung Kagyü stronghold of Riwoché. Another connection between these two women recognized as *ḍākinīs* during their lifetimes is that both gave teachings to Jadrel Sangyé Dorjé Rinpoché.[68]

Despite their slight degree of separation, Sera Khandro's and Ani Lochen's autobiographies share little in terms of writing style, tone, and content. On the one hand, this is little surprise given the vast disparities between Sera Khandro's life in Golok as a Treasure revealer who had male consorts and children and Ani Lochen's life as a prominent nun and abbess in central Tibet. Ani Lochen's autobiography narrates that she was born at Tsopema (Rewalsar) in the northern Indian state of Himachal Pradesh in 1865, to a Nepali Sherpa mother named Tsentsar and a nobleman from central Tibet named Tonglek Tashi. Her parents' relationship was turbulent due to her often drunk, abusive, and unpredictable father, who even sold them on one occasion for money to pay for beer before abandoning the family completely when Lochen was eleven or twelve years old. Through this trauma, her savior was her kind mother, with whom she lived and traveled until her mother's death in circa 1909. Together with her parents, Ani Lochen spent her childhood traveling widely as a religious pilgrim to sacred Buddhist sites in northern India, Nepal, and central Tibet. As a young child she became well known even to local north Indian kings as a professional reciter, or *maṇipa*, who sang Avalokiteśvara's mantra *oṃ maṇi padmé hūṃ* as well as biographies of Buddhist saints, particularly that of the female revenant (*delok*) Nangsa Obum.

When Ani Lochen was thirteen years old (c. 1877), she met her root lama, Pema Gyatso (b. 1829), who was a disciple of Shabkar Tsokdruk Rangdröl from Amdo. Ani Lochen became his devoted disciple, completing a three-year meditation retreat in her teens and traveling with his entourage to sites sacred for their associations with Padmasambhava, Milarepa, and Shabkar throughout central Tibet and westward as far as Mount Kailash. She persevered through Pema Gyatso's harsh treatment—at one point he even branded Lochen with the word "dog" on her forehead with a hot iron as a way to break her pride. Having become one of his closest disciples, she was devastated by his death in 1889. Soon after, she took novice ordination from Ngawang Tenpé Nyima and received an array of teachings from famous lamas from Kham who had inherited the Nyingma master Patrül Rinpoché's teachings, as had Sera Khandro's lamas in Golok. Like Shabkar before her, Ani Lochen wore monastic robes but kept her hair long, as a sign of her maintenance of both the code of monastic discipline and Tantric vows. After Pema Gyatso's death, she became a disciple of Trulshik Rinpoché Künzang Tongdröl Dorjé (d. c. 1923), who was also in Shabkar's lineage and who became her root lama. She traveled with his entourage for several years and then in 1903–04 settled first in Zangyak Drak. Soon after, due to the disturbance of the

British Younghusband invasion, she relocated to Gangri Tökar, a site sacred for its association with the fourteenth-century Nyingma polymath Longchen Rapjampa. Together with her third root lama, Tokden Semnyi Rinpoché, she founded a dynamic religious institution there called Shuksep Nunnery. Semnyi Rinpoché was officially the main lama, but Ani Lochen was equally famous and highly respected among their disciples and sponsors.[69]

For about twenty years, Ani Lochen remained at Shuksep primarily in strict meditation retreat. By the time she had reached her mid-fifties in the 1920s, Semnyi Rinpoché asked Ani Lochen to end her retreats and begin teaching the many religious practices she had mastered. After Semnyi Rinpoché's death in 1922, she moved to the lama's residence and formally became the abbess of Shuksep. During the 1930s and '40s she steadily gained recognition in the form of a growing entourage of nun disciples and lay patrons from nearby Lhasa, as well as visits from some of the most famous religious hierarchs of her day, including the regent of Tibet, Reting Rinpoché; the King of Lingtsang in Degé; the Sixteenth Karmapa, Rangjung Rikpé Dorjé; and the father of the Fourteenth Dalai Lama. She died in 1951 not just a revered Tibetan female master, but a revered Tibetan master.

Ani Lochen's and Sera Khandro's life narratives share some elements, including extraordinary childhood occurrences (which they have in common with many male-authored autobiographies) such as miracles at birth, supernatural learning abilities, and proclivities to teach Avalokiteśvara's mantra. As young women, both experienced great hardship during their years of spiritual training. Both aspired from an early age to live a religious life and experienced major turning points in their early teens after the loss of one parent: in Ani Lochen's case, her father's abandonment and meeting her root guru Pema Gyatso; in Sera Khandro's case, her mother's death and Vajravārāhī's visionary conferral of prophetic guides. Both women describe traveling to the realm of the dead and returning as revenants or *delok*. Both record having very close relationships with their mothers and feeling suicidal when they passed away. Additionally, both narrate a gradual process, over hundreds of manuscript pages, of transforming into a sought-after religious teacher, which happened much later in their lives than it did for many male religious lamas; Jetsün Lochen did not begin teaching widely until Tokden Semnyi Rinpoché decreed that the fifty-odd-year-old woman should do so, and Sera Khandro did not teach widely until after Drimé Özer's death, when Sotrül Natsok Rangdröl Rinpoché urged her to do so while she was living with him at Sera Monastery.

Ani Lochen and Sera Khandro both write of special connections to *ḍākinīs* in the forms of enlightened Buddhist bodhisattvas and divinized female masters of the past. In particular, Ani Lochen's autobiography tells of her connection to Machik Lapdrön, though Yeshé Tsogyel also appears occasionally as her former incarnation. Several of Ani Lochen's teachers recognized her as Machik's incarnation, which seems to have helped Ani Lochen and others around her to carve out a social and religious space for her as a female religious exemplar. Toward the end of her life, she records, "I was uncertain (whether I was Machig or not), but Gangshar Rinpoche and other lamas said, "Real wisdom is residing (in Lochen Rinpoche)!" Thereby I gained confidence (that I was Machig)."[70]

The eleventh-twelfth century Tibetan *yoginī* Machik Lapdrön is remembered for her agility at reciting *Prajñāpāramitā* (*Perfection of Wisdom*) scriptures, as Ani Lochen did, and for being the founder of *Chö* or "Severance," which was one of Ani Lochen's main religious practices. *Chö* refers to a Tantric ritual in which the meditator symbolically offers her body parts as a way to cut ego attachment. *Chö* practitioners often performed the liturgical and visualization practice in charnel grounds and sky burial sites to enhance its effect. Under Jetsün Lochen's guidance, Shuksep Nunnery practiced *Chö* rituals in the forms of funerals for corpses brought to the nunnery as well as meditation retreats, feasts, and fire offerings.[71] Ani Lochen also had a special relationship to the place Machik Lapdrön resided in the latter part of her life, Zangri Kharmar, where she experienced visions and performed *Chö* practice.[72]

Although Sera Khandro primarily portrayed herself as an emanation of Yeshé Tsogyel, she also wrote of having a connection to Machik Lapdrön. One of the very few human female religious teachers mentioned in her autobiography is a nun named Ané Zangmo, whom she describes as a famous incarnation of Machik Lapdrön. Sera Khandro recollected her disappointment that she never got to meet the illustrious nun, who died when Sera Khandro was twenty years old. She wrote that she did meet two of the nun's disciples, who came to offer her a skull cup and seal that Ané Zangmo had bequeathed to her. After this, she had a vision of meeting Machik Lapdrön:

That night, after I prayed to the lama and the deities, while sleeping I dreamed about a beautiful *ḍākinī* who said she was Machik Lapdrön. She had an attractive body clothed in a sky blue skirt and a stainless white cotton upper shawl, and her hair hung loosely down her back. With her right hand she played a two-faced drum and with her left, she rang a white silver bell. In a melodious voice, she uttered something like this:

Pray to the unborn mother,
whose Truth Body is the Great Mother of the Buddhas.
Pray to the unimpeded mother,
whose Enjoyment Body is Vajrayoginī.
Pray to the all-pervading mother,
whose Emanation Body is Tsogyel Lapdrönma.
Eradicate the error of grasping to a self!

I bless you with the realization of selfless insight.
I bless you with unobstructed, nonreferential vision.
I bless you that negative conditions will dawn as favorable ones.
I bless you with the capacity to turn your body into food.
I bless you with the realization of the enlightened mind of the Great Mother.
I bless you that the connections you have with others will be meaningful.
I bless you that you will attain the permanent domain of the Truth Body!
Phaṭ, Phaṭ, Phaṭ!

As soon as she said this, my perception transformed. Together with two *ḍākinī* companions, the appearance of wandering in many buddhafields arose.[73]

That Sera Khandro represented Machik Lapdrön supplicating the divine in the form of the multifaceted Great Mother is especially fitting, given that Machik was one of the few female Tibetan Buddhist masters who actually was a mother, not only in the philosophical sense but also in the physiological sense of having several children.

Despite the many commonalities between the two *ḍākinī*s' lives, Ani Lochen's autobiography shares neither Sera Khandro's emphasis on interactive pep talks with *ḍākinīs* nor lamentations about her inferior female body. Lochen's autobiography includes about a dozen visions in its more than five hundred pages, the majority of which involve *ḍākinīs*, whereas Sera Khandro's autobiography, of a similar length, contains nearly eight times as many visions, the majority of which feature dialogues with *ḍākinīs*. *Ḍākinīs* appear at certain pivotal moments in Ani Lochen's life, such as the woman who materializes from the sky to save the young girl and her mother from drowning during a river crossing in Spiti after her father had tried to sell them to pay for beer. Later, Ani Lochen recounts,

> We stayed in Nagtshel Monastery in Henang, and while staying there in meditational retreat I had a vision of a woman (clad) in local costume who said, "Do not stay here, but come to my land!" When the vision arose, I achieved a sudden breakthrough in my understanding of religious texts (*bstan bcos*). As I had no paper, I thought that I needed bark from the birch tree, and immediately it seemed that I arrived in a land where there were many people. When I awoke from the vision, I was in the hermitage, but in front of me there was a big heap of birch bark. It must have been the local deity of that area (*gzhi bdag*). In my vision (*nyams snang*) many (ritual texts) appeared (such as) rTsa gsum bla sgrub, Ma cig srog sgrub, Ma 'ong lung bstan and others. I wrote many of them down as there were many heaps of birch bark. When Teacher Chosang saw this he said, "You are not allowed that kind of writing!" and then he burnt everything in the fire. He kicked me in the head and from then on these visions stopped forever.[74]

Ani Lochen's account of this vision resembles Sera Khandro's many revelation experiences, but unlike Sera Khandro, she records that her teacher permanently stymied her visionary revelations. In some of her visions, *ḍākinīs* usher her to Padmasambhava's buddhafield and in others, the *ḍākinī* Dorjé Yudrön and her *ḍākinī* sisters possess Ani Lochen and her nun disciples. But *ḍākinīs* do not consistently appear with support after difficulties arise in her mundane life, as they do in Sera Khandro's autobiography. Ani Lochen's interactions with them are less frequent, less verbose, and less focused on encouraging her. The counterbalance between *ḍākinī* inspiration and depressing earthly circumstances typical of Sera Khandro's autobiography is less pervasive.

Ani Lochen faced challenges such as poverty and abuse as a young person, rigorous meditation practices, depression, other mental problems, and difficulty securing continuous patronage, but she did not single out her female body as the source of her suffering as often as Sera Khandro did. Gender discrimination affected both women—signs of it include preferential treatment of male over female children, exclusion from visiting monasteries on account of being female, and very gradual recognition as authentic Buddhist masters only after decades of intensive meditation retreat. Even so, decrying her female body was not the primary way Ani Lochen presented herself with humility. Instead, she often deferred disciples' requests for teachings, claiming that she had insufficient knowledge. At one point she urged her would-be disciple Gangshar Rinpoché to request teachings from Semnyi Rinpoché, reflecting, "He hoped that I would give him (religious instructions), but because I knew nothing I made him ask for *sPyod 'jug* (*Bodhicaryāvatāra*) and instruction on mind (*sems khrid*) and so forth there (from Semnyi)."[75] In response to another group of disciples' request for teachings, Ani Lochen writes, "although I did not possess the knowledge to do welfare to others, I was unable to refuse their expectations."[76] Though conventional, this rhetoric presents Ani Lochen as hesitant to claim religious mastery for herself, a stance that "reflects the general Tibetan ambivalence towards female talent," as Hanna Havnevik interprets it.[77] The same can be said about Sera Khandro's writing, only she singled out her gender far more often and relied more strongly on *ḍākinīs*' reassurance to express this ambivalence.

Could the ways Sera Khandro and Ani Lochen thematize the female body (or don't) in their writings have to do with the fact that one was a noncelibate visionary and the other a nun? That one had to escape from her family to pursue her religious ambition and the other received support from childhood to pursue a religious life? That one knew a kind of suffering associated with being female through first-hand experience of the pain of childbirth and the death of two children, and the other did not? Or do their differences have to do with how they authored their texts—was Sera Khandro more involved with the actual writing of her autobiography than Ani Lochen was with hers? Ani Lochen was in her eighties by the time she dictated her recollections to the nun Gen Thinley. After Gen Thinley wrote them down, the male reincarnation of her root lama, Drupchen Dawa Dorjé Zangpo, edited the autobiography and inserted songs of his own composition into it.[78] According to the colophon of Sera Khandro's autobiography, she was half Ani Lochen's age when she wrote it. She specifies that her scribe Tsültrim Dorjé wrote down her words for the first segment of the text that recounts her life up to the age of thirty-four, and that she wrote the final segment of about seventy pages herself, narrating her life up to the age of forty-two. Though suggestive, these differences are difficult to draw conclusions from. Authorship in Tibet was rarely the enterprise of a single individual and more commonly involved a team of craftspeople including scribes, editors, printers, carvers, and others.[79] Therefore, while some amount of scribal and editorial influence cannot be ruled out for both narratives, the same holds true for all other Tibetan autobiographies. Alternately, the differences in tone between Ani Lochen and Sera Khandro's autobiography might be attributable to variations in life experience—did Sera Khandro write extensively about her inferior female body because she experienced a greater degree of gender discrimination than Jetsün Lochen did? The multiplicity of possible influences on the two women's writing styles serves to confirm the impossibility of sifting an autobiographer's gender out from other variables such as monastic status, education level, family support, wealth, geographic location, and religious lineage. That said, it does appear that Jetsün Lochen's community of nuns at Shuksep provided an environment conducive to women's spiritual practice, which is perhaps more than can be said of Sera Khandro's life in Golok religious encampments.

The Life of Orgyen Chökyi

Jetsün Lochen and Sera Khandro's autobiographies are from the same century, but Sera Khandro's treatment of gender and the female body shares more with the oldest extant female-authored autobiography written in the Tibetan language, that of Orgyen Chökyi. At first glance, Orgyen Chökyi's life story bears little resemblance to that of Sera Khandro. Instead of elaborate and lengthy prose replete with visionary interludes, the writing is terse and simple, grounded in her humble life experiences. She was born in 1675 in the mountainous Dolpo region of northwest Nepal to a father named Drangsong Püntsok and a mother named Künga Zangmo. Her parents named her Kyilo, "Happiness Dashed," because they had hoped for a boy. Her childhood was full of suffering after her father contracted leprosy and her mother descended into extreme poverty. According to Orgyen Chökyi, both parents hated her, and they beat her and fed her poorly. She struggled to learn how to work with wool before becoming a goatherd for a time. Anticipating a life of back-breaking corvée labor if she remained a laywoman, Orgyen Chökyi took nun's ordination as a teenager and became the disciple of Orgyen Tendzin (c. 1656–1737), a Nyingma lama from Dolpo. Under his direction Orgyen Chökyi spent long periods studying and meditating for several decades. This intensive practice was interrupted, however, by monastic duties keeping horses and working in the kitchen. Orgyen Chökyi's autobiography traces her struggle to avoid the drudgery of kitchen and pasture labor, eventually earning the opportunity to remain in meditation retreat accompanied only by her fellow nun retreatants. Having transcended her humble birth and manual labor responsibilities, she died a nun and hermitess in 1729 at the age of fifty-five when a wooden beam fell on her head, to be remembered for centuries to come as a *ḍākinī*.

Despite their temporal, cultural, and geographic distance, Orgyen Chökyi and Sera Khandro's autobiographies thematize suffering and the female body in similar ways. Orgyen Chökyi focuses on the suffering of female animals, likening it to her own. After a leopard snatches away a mare's young foal, Orgyen Chökyi laments,

> When I ponder our female bodies
> I am sorrowful; impermanence rings clear.
> When men and women couple—creating more life—
> Happiness is rare, but suffering is felt for a long time.
> May I not be born again in a female body.
> May the mare not be born as a mare.[80]

Again, after the death of a female yak crossbreed and her calf, she despairs:

> Humans, horses, dogs, all beings,
> Male and female all think alike,
> But the suffering of life comes to females as a matter of course.
> I could do without the misery of this female life.
> How I lament this broken chest, this female body.
>
> I could do without this female body with its misery.
> Ranting thoughts dwell in this woman's body.
> From within the body, spreading outward,
> From the center of the mind misery comes unchecked.

Like the yak protecting her calf,
They give up life for their children.

This female body is itself samsara—the round of existence.
May I attain a male body, and keep the vows,
May I never again be born in the body of a woman![81]

Both Orgyen Chökyi and Sera Khandro lament their female birth and pray to be reborn in a male body. Both explicitly compare their female body with *saṃsāra*, an analogy with ancient Buddhist roots: Orgyen Chökyi prays to be reborn as a man and never again as a woman because "This female body is itself samsara—the round of existence," while Sera Khandro describes her body as "the foundation of *saṃsāra*," a "contaminated, unclean, negative body."[82]

And yet, the very existence of Orgyen Chökyi's and Sera Khandro's autobiographies suggests their disavowal of the negative gender stereotypes they reiterate, for clearly they found their lives as female renunciates worthy of remembrance. Important sources of reinforcement were *ḍākinīs*, whose inspiration was central to both female autobiographers' ability to go against prevailing cultural norms that did not consider women's lives worth documenting. Orgyen Chökyi opens her autobiography not with a typical account of her past lives but with an explanation of how she came to write her life story. She records that at first she requested her teacher to do it, but he refused, saying, "There is no reason to write a liberation tale for you—a woman."[83] Despairing because she did not know how to write, Orgyen Chökyi explains that she was "struck with the spiritual instruction of the dakini" and "the impediment of not being able to write disappeared."[84] She also recollects that during her intensive meditation training, her teacher, Orgyen Tendzin, doubted her capacity, telling her, "Your woman's mind does not understand great philosophy," and "You are like an old woman who needs a lesson on how to get started," but Orgyen Chökyi refused to accept the insults. She wrote, "'I am not an old woman,' I thought. 'I have no burning desire, so he speaks falsely.'"[85] In the Tibetan Buddhist world, where disciples were taught to view their teacher as the Buddha himself, the degree of defiance Orgyen Chökyi expressed gives us an indication of the resolve necessary to become one of the first, if not the first Himalayan Buddhist woman to write an autobiography, even one peppered with prayers never to be reborn as a woman.

In her autobiography Orgyen Chökyi mentions other extraordinary women remembered as *ḍākinīs* often enough to suggest that they served as inspirations for her. In particular, she idealized Gelongma Palmo, the Indian royal nun so devoted to Avalokiteśvara that her practice of fasting (*smyung gnas*) cured her leprosy. She also mentions Machik Lapdrön as well as two famous *delok*s, Nangsa Obum and Lingza Chökyi. Nevertheless, at least as it has survived into the twenty-first century, Orgyen Chökyi's autobiography serves as a reminder that *ḍākinīs* were symbols that could be interpreted to divergent ends by those who invoked them. Her life story closes with a pithy editorial note: "If the *Life* of the dakini were written down from the beginning, it would be nothing more than a copy of the Life of Nangsa Obum, so it was not written."[86] This is a curious conclusion for a work that is unique in many respects, not to mention the nearly complete dissimilarity between Nangsa Obum's and Orgyen Chökyi's lives: Nangsa Obum is the protagonist of a popular Tibetan opera who is born to wealthy parents, married to a king, and becomes mother to the crown prince. Through a series of traumas, she dies and becomes a revenant who witnesses the sufferings of hell and returns to preach Buddhist virtue. Aside from their shared female sex and Buddhist vocation, Orgyen Chökyi was completely different. The very inspiration she seems to have drawn from her divine foremothers provided her editor with a means to silence her; whatever additional kernels of Orgyen Chökyi's life experience this zealous editor cut have been lost to history.

Fortunately, Sera Khandro's extensive writings found no such abbreviation. Yet her autobiography lacks one of the most positive elements in the otherwise unrelentingly difficult life of Orgyen Chökyi: female friendship. Both women found *ḍākinīs* to deflect the many who would discourage their religious aspirations, but Orgyen Chökyi also found a supportive community of like-minded nuns with whom to share her joys, as did Jetsün Lochen. Sera Khandro does not seem to have found such a group, beyond a few individual nuns and *yoginīs* she befriended. Like Orgyen Chökyi, Sera Khandro dreamed of independence and autonomy away from the drudgery of women's work, including milking animals, gathering firewood, preparing meals, sewing, and caring for her children. Life in Golok's religious encampments did not initially afford her respite from these obligations, as Orgyen Chökyi struggled to escape monastic physical labor and enter meditation retreat. Not until the latter part of Sera Khandro's life, when she traveled throughout Golok and Kham conferring empowerments, reading transmissions, and giving explanations of her own Treasure teachings as well as those of Drimé Özer and Düjom Lingpa, did she find relief from women's work and widespread respect for her spiritual realization—a victory she attained largely in spite of, not because of, her closest female community members.

CONCLUSION: *ḌĀKINĪ*S INSTIGATE SERA KHANDRO'S SELF WRITING

*Ḍākinī*s provided inspiration to write autobiography for many Tibetan Buddhist exemplars. The eighteenth-century male Treasure revealer Jikmé Lingpa even named one of his secret autobiographies *Ḍākki's Grand Secret-Talk* after her.[87] The final vision in Düjom Lingpa's *Clear Mirror* attributes his motivation to write the autobiography to the Tibetan *ḍākinī* par excellence:

> Then, in the last month of winter on the evening of the fifteenth day, in my dream the torso of Khandro Yeshé Tsogyel appeared amid an expanse of dense clouds and rainbows. She said,
>
> > Hey, son, listen to my few words of advice:
> > putting your biography in writing
> > is the tradition of the Buddhas of the past.
> > For the sake of your excellent and fortunate disciples,
> > don't delay; find a way to quickly finish it![88]

*Ḍākinī*s exhorted Sera Khandro similarly, though in her case they had to be loud enough to drown out her detractors. As in Ani Lochen and Orgyen Chökyi's autobiographies, *ḍākinī*s in the form of famous female Tibetan religious masters of the distant past provided powerful precedents for Sera Khandro, even though she mentions knowing no other female Treasure revealers or autobiographers in her own time. Yeshé Tsogyel was of particular importance in this regard, as were several other *ḍākinī*s, including Machik Lapdrön and the female Treasure revealers Jomo Menmo and Künga Buma mentioned in Jamgön Kongtrül's *One Hundred Treasure Revealers*.

The *ḍākinīs*' words that blended into Sera Khandro's self-narrative through visionary dialogical interchanges did more than provide her with encouragement; they formed the heart of her auto/biographical writing projects. The intersubjectivity of *ḍākinīs*' voices with her own suggests an ontological overlap in Tibetan conceptions of the self as both a coherent subject and an interdependent matrix of earthly and celestial presences that included not only *ḍākinīs* but also bodhisattvas, Tantric masters of the past, Treasure protectors, and other types of land deities. Beyond signaling the profoundly relational nature of Sera Khandro's self, these interactions reveal a growing confidence that manifested in a gradual transformation from writing that she attributed to *ḍākinī* prophecies and ventriloquized through others' voices to writing in the first person about herself. She reports that in 1925, when she was thirty-three and living at Sera Monastery just after Drimé Özer's tragic death, two *ḍākinīs* named Dewé Gocha and Rikpé Reltri appeared before her and told her the full story of Drimé Özer's life. They gave her symbolic scriptures to decode and transcribe, which later became his biography. In its colophon, she explains her authorship in the following manner:

> If the tongues of the buddhas didn't have the power to proclaim this eloquent liberation story in detail, which is a *ḍākinī* prophecy that dispels the heart's darkness, how would someone like me? For the sake of leading the chariot of disciples' faith a bit, this Dharma teaching emanated as self-emergent symbols, unpolluted by the stains of the conceptual mind's corrections. Relying on the compassion of the Awareness Holder Lama that is like the cool shade of a white parasol, I deciphered them.[89]

Whether she or the *ḍākinīs* authored it, the act of putting together Drimé Özer's biography with the help of her scribe Tsültrim Dorjé initiated her autobiographical impulse. Throughout the first 234 folios of his biography, she refers to herself regularly, but always in the third person using her "Treasure name," Dewé Dorjé, aside from direct speech quotations in which she uses the first person. This changes 15 folios before the end, in the midst of her description of Drimé Özer's funeral proceedings, when the voice of the narrator suddenly becomes "I."

During part of the next eight years, from 1926 to 1934, while she was writing her long autobiography, she also wrote a short autobiography in verse titled *The Excellent Path of Devotion: The Short Story of a Mendicant's Experiences in Response to Questions from My Vajra Kin*. Unlike in Drimé Özer's biography, the colophon explicitly claims her authorship of the text:

> So as not to disappoint them [my disciples], I, Künzang Dekyong Chönyi Wangmo, the lowest among all the group of disciples of the omniscient refuge master, wrote this when I was thirty-seven on the sixteenth day of the ninth month of the earth snake year (1929) at Sera Monastery's secluded retreat place. My attendant, the Buddhist monk Tsültrim Dorjé, gathered the resources necessary to produce this text.[90]

If her short verse autobiography is the condensed version of her life story, we might expect a summary of the major events interspersed with pivotal visionary experiences, following the style of her longer autobiographical work, in which roughly half recounts events that occurred in her everyday life while the other half details her elaborate visions. Instead, the short autobiography is suffused with *ḍākinī* prophecies and visionary encounters, with only brief allusions to her life in Lhasa and Golok. In this essentialized self-portrait, it appears that her esoteric visionary life was more fundamental than the exoteric linear backdrop of her quotidian affairs.

In her long autobiography, *ḍākinī* prophecies form the warp into which Sera Khandro threaded the woof of her life story. Evidence of this weaving process can be found in the more than 27 cross references she makes to parts of her Treasure scriptures, most often to her *Cycle of Prophecies*.[91] For example, Sera Khandro concluded the *ḍākinī* vision quoted earlier in this chapter, experienced after her daughter's birth when Gyelsé scolded her for teaching her revelation to monks, with the words, "I have described the prophecies about the future that she [the *ḍākinī*] spoke in my Treasure scriptures."[92] In other instances she notes, "I elaborated the few prophecies that appeared at that time in my Treasure scriptures."[93] These references demonstrate that many of the detailed visions and poetic songs included in her autobiography are elaborations of shorter visionary experiences she recorded after they occurred. Others are summaries of visions that she related in detail in her Treasure scriptures, such as the plethora of visions she had of Drimé Özer after his death, which she glosses in her autobiography; she then directs readers to her revelations for fuller treatment. Her *Cycle of Prophecies* includes 65 short entries totaling about 150 folios, depending on the manuscript edition. She signed and dated each individual prophecy, indicating that she wrote them throughout her life from the age of 18 through 46, 1910–1938. The *Cycle of Prophecies* reads like a journal, but instead of chronicling mundane daily occurrences, it documents her dreams and visions. The protagonist in these visions is not Sera Khandro, but *ḍākinī*s and deceased lamas including Düjom Lingpa, Gara Terchen, and Drimé Özer (after his death), who address her with advice, instructions, and reassurance.

Only in her final auto/biographical work, her long autobiography, did Sera Khandro fill in the spaces between the extraordinary visions she had been writing about elsewhere with new information about the comings, goings, conversations, frustrations, disappointments, and joys of her daily life. Her literary trajectory as an auto/biographer is thus a move from the esoteric to the exoteric, from words "unpolluted by the stains of the conceptual mind's corrections," as she refers to Drimé Özer's biography, to words more daring precisely because they were more personal, individual, and mired in the muck of cyclic existence that Düjom Lingpa had eschewed as "a cause of boredom and weariness." Perhaps what is most unusual about Sera Khandro as an author is not her record of her lucid visions but her choice to connect the dots between them with stylized accounts of her everyday affairs, a choice audacious enough for a Tibetan woman that it required a strong measure of humility to gain acceptance. The most audacious of all the myriad topics she wrote about with prolixity was arguably her portrayal of Tantric Buddhist consort practices, our next focus.

4

SACRED SEXUALITY

I am called "neither nun nor laywoman" (*jo min nag min*).
Though not a nun, I am disciplined like a nun—
my vows related to the three trainings of the path[1] are without deterioration.
Though faultless, I am called a laywoman.
As if I were a criminal, I am seen as someone to abandon and exile from the land,
[but] I don't recall even a hair's breadth of guilt.[2]

Sera Khandro described her status as neither nun nor laywoman to a beautiful *ḍākinī* who appeared in her dream when she was thirty-nine by punning on the many negative valences of the word *nak*, which include fault (*nag*), laywoman (*nag mo*), criminal (*nag can*), and guilt (*nag nyes*). That she positioned herself between the virtue of nunhood and the vice of lay life raises a number of questions: What do her auto/biographical writings reveal about the nature and purpose of religious practices involving sexuality in her religious communities? How did religious specialists such as Sera Khandro negotiate between the competing demands of maintaining celibacy and engaging in sexuality for religious purposes? How did this equation change when those soliciting her were monks? Were women like Sera Khandro who acted as consorts to male lamas objects to aid in their partners' enlightenment, agents concerned with their own, or something between?

The fact that Tibetan Buddhism preserves some elements of the sexual practices described in Vajrayāna scriptures has inspired both disgust and fascination among its European and American interpreters for more than a century.[3] Mirroring this, scholars have hailed women involved in consort practices within both Hindu and Buddhist Tantric contexts as either goddesses deserving of feminist valorization or prostitutes victimized by a misogynist religion, but rarely anything in between. For a few examples among the many in the positive cohort:

> Moreover, women as well as men are eligible not only to receive the highest initiation but also to confer it in the role of guru. "Initiation by a woman is efficacious; that by a mother is eightfold so," we read in the Yoginī Tantra.[4] (Heinrich Zimmer, *Philosophies of India*)

> We must never lose sight of this primacy of the Śakti—in the last analysis, of the Divine Woman and Mother—in tantrism and in all the movements deriving from it.[5] (Mircea Eliade, *Yoga: Immortality and Freedom*)

> In the place of Mahāyāna neutrality in regard to gender dualism, Tantra highlights gender polarities. In this gendered discourse, the female pole receives more emphasis than the male. Technically men are considered to be of equal metaphysical status and value, but in the empirical realms of image and ritual women receive more explicit affirmation.[6] (Miranda Shaw, *Passionate Enlightenment*)

Alternately, among a long a long list of negative appraisals of women's roles in Tantric practices are:

> The social inferiority of woman is even a necessary presupposition for the liberating antinomianism of Tantric *sādhanā*. The *sādhaka* is the bee, woman is the flower which is left behind when the nectar of siddhi has been gathered.[7] (Sanjukta Gupta et al., *Hindu Tantrism*)

> Thus despite the eulogies of woman in these tantras and her high symbolic status, the whole theory and practice is given for the benefit of males. While the relative neglect of woman's interest in pursuing a higher religious life is typical of Buddhism of all periods . . . this form of tantric Buddhism appears to offer her hope at last, but in the actual event seems to fail to do so.[8] (David Snellgrove, *Indo-Tibetan Buddhism*)

> Tantra is a practice in which men sexually utilize women for their own spiritual benefit. . . . The male practitioner requires a female, any female, to complete his spiritual training or to speed it up. He takes her bodily fluids and the powers attributed to them into himself, for his own benefit, not hers.[9] (Serinity Young, *Courtesans and Tantric Consorts*)

This diversity of interpretations can be explained in part by the broad scope and unclear boundaries of what constitutes Tantra.[10] Another reason is the highly esoteric nature of Tantric texts, whose symbolic language can only be interpreted as a historical resource with the greatest caution. But the main reason for the confusion about women's roles in Tibetan Tantric practices involving sexuality is that the vast majority of Tibetan texts describing consort practices were authored by and for men, leaving many questions about the nature of women's involvement unanswered. Lists of ideal *ḍākinī* consorts suitable for every type of male meditator feature regularly in Tibetan Tantric manuals, as do visions of sexual unions with ephemeral *ḍākinī*s in Tibetan biographies of male religious virtuosos. Far less visible is evidence of the historical roles human women played in Tibetan Buddhist religious communities.

Sera Khandro's writings are exceptional among Tibetan texts for presenting a female perspective on life as a Tibetan Buddhist religious specialist who engaged in Tantric consort practices. Taken as a whole, her auto/biographical works endorse neither the view that women in Vajrayāna Buddhism are deified nor the view that women are debased; they contain firsthand descriptions of both serving as a consort for male lamas and utilizing male consorts for her own spiritual benefit. In her autobiography Sera Khandro explicitly writes about attaining spiritual realization for herself through contemplative practices that included sexual liaisons with multiple male consorts. Her forthright accounts of sexual yoga from the standpoint of female physiology flip the familiar Buddhist paradigm of male subjectivity and female subordination on its head, suggesting that at least in some cases, women did gain religious realization from participation in sexual rituals, a claim prominent Vajrayāna Buddhist masters have made for centuries.[11] And yet, the picture Sera Khandro's writings paint of the social dynamics within her religious communities could hardly be considered gynocentric—for one thing, she reports being traded between male lamas for sexual services without her consent. For another, her relationships with fellow female religious devotees do not appear to have offered much consolation, given the vengeful jealousy she repeatedly describes among the women with whom she competed for the attentions of male religious leaders. The candor with which Sera Khandro writes about such matters takes consort practices out of the distant, abstract, and highly symbolic frameworks in which they often appear in prescriptive doctrinal and ritual Tantric texts and situates them within the specific context of early twentieth-century religious encampments in the nomadic highlands of eastern Tibet. Her writing is not necessarily representative of Tibetan women's consort experiences in general; nor can we be certain that it is entirely objective about the particular social world it presents, for Sera Khandro clearly had something to prove about her liaisons with religious men. But her very embeddedness in the relationships about which she wrote makes her words valuable correctives to prevailing polemics on the subject of women and sexuality in Tantric Buddhism.

This chapter will examine Sera Khandro's multifaceted portrayal of her consort relationships as well as the ways she carefully expresses these matters through others' voices, leaving the most significant of all her relationships, her union with Drimé Özer, for fuller treatment in the following chapter. The first part delineates three major purposes for engaging in consort practices that we can deduce from Sera Khandro's writings: the Buddhist soteriological goal of attaining enlightenment; the hermeneutical goals of revealing and decoding Treasures; and the pragmatic goals of curing illness and increasing longevity. In putting forth these three reasons, Sera Khandro follows normative presentations found within Nyingma Buddhist works, particularly those related to the Treasure tradition. Yet her take on the place of consort practices within the tradition also contains an unusually clear message that all three goals were accessible to female practitioners as well as male. Also significant is her emphasis on pragmatic purposes—more than their esoteric significance for liberation and revelation, the most common reason in Sera Khandro's auto/biographical writings for consort practices is curing illness and prolonging life, powers closely associated with *ḍākinīs*.

As we might expect, given their prominence in Sera Khandro's auto/biographical writings, *ḍākinīs*' voices sound strongly on the topic of consort practices. What they say with the greatest urgency is that Sera Khandro has to engage with the appropriate prophesied male consorts even if others fault her for doing so. *Ḍākinīs* appear to Sera Khandro in visions and dreams, teasing and taunting her to overcome her bashfulness and to differentiate between immoral sexual indulgence and pure spiritual union. At stake in many of these dialogues is the question of the ethics of sexuality as a part of Tibetan Buddhist religious practice. Sera Khandro depicts herself as constantly rejecting the *ḍākinīs*' hints and allegations, yet in the end she capitulates to their injunctions and reports benefiting from encounters with male consorts. By presenting the necessity of having a consort not in her own voice but ventriloquized through *ḍākinīs*' and prominent male lamas' words, Sera Khandro portrays herself as a legitimate participant in esoteric Tantric practices involving multiple male partners without appearing to be lustful, immoral, or arrogant. In this way, others give her the divine backing she needs to transform perceptions of her from a woman of ambiguous moral virtue to an emissary of the *ḍākinīs* entitled to occupy the in-between status of "neither nun nor laywoman." *Ḍākinīs*' injunctions are spliced throughout this chapter, underscoring everything Sera Khandro conveys about this sensitive subject.

The second part of the chapter will focus on one of the most delicate topics pertaining to consort practices in Tibetan Buddhism—what role, if any, they should have for celibate monastics. At least since the time of the eleventh-century Indian Buddhist master Atīśa, tensions have simmered within Tibetan Buddhist religious communities between the competing religious dictums of monastic celibacy and religiously motivated sexuality such as that called for in Tantric initiations and other contemplative exercises.[12] Atīśa argued for the preservation of monastic purity by forbidding celibates from receiving full Tantric initiation, whereas later Tibetan monastic scholars attempted to aestheticize explicit mention of sexuality in Tantric scriptures and initiations by metaphorically or symbolically interpreting their erotic content. Nevertheless, sexuality remains an esoteric part of specific Tibetan Buddhist teachings. Even so, only a small minority of Tibetan Buddhist practitioners ever practice with an actual human consort; the majority visualize such spiritual unions as a part of individual meditation practice.

In the context of Sera Khandro's writings, celibacy and religiously motivated sexuality share the spotlight as ideal Vajrayāna forms of conduct, though at times they were incompatible. This is clear in the many instances in which others question Sera Khandro's virtue, raising doubts about her choice not to become a nun, as well as the negative gossip she repeatedly mentions swirling around her near monasteries and monks. But if her intentions were suspect, so too were those of some of her monastic brethren—she records multiple instances of being solicited for sexual services by ostensibly celibate monks, whose advances she invariably rejected, though at times was compelled to reconsider by *ḍākinīs* and other authorities. Sera Khandro was not the only one whose consorting inspired tongues to wag, for Gyelsé's father Gara Terchen's autobiography depicts a scandal that he instigated by exchanging his monastic vows for a female consort. Both Sera Khandro's and Gara Terchen's accounts of breaching the divide between celibacy and sacred sexuality demonstrate that public opinion of consort practices did not always align with doctrinal justification. The second part of this chapter will listen to the traces of public opinion in both works that manifested in the forms of gossip and badmouthing, considering when this backtalk was broadcast the loudest and what the protagonists did to quell it, in an effort to contextualize consort practices in early twentieth-century eastern Tibet.

PART I: THE PURPOSES OF CONSORT PRACTICES

In her autobiography Sera Khandro writes that during her childhood, lamas prophesied that she should not become a nun. Beyond these early indications, she explains why she chose to heed this advice in a conversation she narrates between herself and a nun named Tsüldrön. When she was seventeen years old and trying to extricate herself from her stint working as a maidservant after being expelled from Drimé Özer's residence for the first time, her employers suggested she live with their relative:

> "[Her employer said] . . . At the religious encampment, since our nun Tsüldrön is there, go and live there and don't lose our horse."

I did what he said and went to Tsüldrön's place.

She stated, "Now you need to go before Trülku Mura and cut your hair and request vows. Otherwise, you certainly won't live at my place."

It occurred to me that perhaps Tsüldrön had become jealous thinking that I would live in the wealthy household owned by a man named Sotra, who didn't look down on me and who always gave me vegetarian food, such as rice and wild sweet potatoes, whenever they had them.

I replied: "It is okay if I don't cut my hair and take vows. It won't harm your purity. Even when I think of the conduct of you completely pure nuns, someone like me who is young and without wealth would surely not make it on my own as a nun."

She got mad and stood up. Grabbing my shoulder, she led me before Mura and said, "Sir, Trülku, please take a tuft of her hair [i.e., make her a nun]. She has gone astray from the middle [way] and although she has a pure mind, she doesn't listen to anybody, and I don't know what to do with her."

The attendant responded, "Wait here for a moment. Speak to him after he eats his food."

The lama said, "Pity, you seem to be someone from a big city with vast resources."[13] He gave me a piece of joint from the meat he was eating.

Tsüldrön said, "Sir, the central Tibetan girl doesn't eat meat."

He gave me some *tü*,[14] and I perceived that it was my accomplishment substance. He didn't even give her a bit of it. I alone ate it, and my ensuing understanding was that the lama's mind and my own mixed together inseparably. When I stayed there like that for a while, the attendant said, "Amazing, the eyes of this girl are like those of a meditator. What kind of lamas have you had in the past?"

Using the sky to illustrate intrinsic awareness, I pointed to the sky.

He replied, "She must be a heretic. She says that her lama is the sun."

Again he asked, "Do you know the Dharma?"

As the symbol of knowing the ocean of various phenomenal elements as the self-arising sense pleasures, I touched my eyes, nose, ears, tongue, and body with my hand.

He didn't understand and asked Tsüldrön, "What did she say?"

"Last year she requested some Dharma. Perhaps she is talking about the meaning of that. Otherwise, I don't understand." Having said this, she ran out of time and left.

I waited and after the lama had his food, I explained:

"Sir, from the time I was fourteen years old, I wondered if I could accomplish the genuine Dharma. Hence, don't overlook helping me traverse this path. Because I have a great purpose, it seems that it doesn't matter whether I cut or don't cut my hair. It was Tsüldrön's idea. If this body of mine doesn't fall under the strong influence of another, I will not have relationships with religious people or lay householders if I think there's no purpose. At all times, I will see if I can benefit myself and others. Not becoming attached to food, clothing, or wealth, I will try to accomplish the pure divine Dharma, sir. If, on account of being an inferior woman (*lus dman*) I do not follow the path I intend to, please understand that I am not in opposition to you."

In a loving manner, the lama replied, "Oh, yes, not getting attached to food, clothing, and wealth and wondering if you will accomplish the pure Dharma is the same as accomplishing the Dharma. Having great attachment to *saṃsāra* is the same as not accomplishing the Dharma. These days religious people don't banish *saṃsāra* from their minds; they beg for butter in the summer, barley in the winter, and at all times they shoulder the debt of the dead."[15]

He spoke about many religious topics such as this, and placing a golden statue on my head, he prayed. He gave me a set of seven pills made from power derived from Patrül Rinpoché's skull and also other religious medicinal pills, blessed juniper powder, protection cords, and so forth, and he gave me advice.

Then I came back and told Tsüldrön, "I promised not to have a physical relationship with laypeople or with religious people without a purpose. Aside from that, I am not going to be a nun."

She said, "Wow—it is as if you wear wild yak hide on your face.[16] Who would dare say such dirty words to a great lama like him?" and she pulled her cheeks.[17]

I replied, "Since I told him what I am able to do, there is no 'not daring.' I wouldn't dare let my vows and precepts secretly deteriorate."

She didn't say anything.[18]

In the course of this conversation, Sera Khandro gives multiple reasons conveying both pragmatic and esoteric dimensions of her choice not to become a nun. On the pragmatic level, she suggests that her youth and lack of wealth would make it difficult for her to survive. Given that Tsüldrön's initial dismay was a response to the prospect of competition between the two women over the patronage of a local lay household, we can deduce that choosing between a celibate and a noncelibate religious life had economic as well as moral ramifications. These may have been especially significant for someone like Sera Khandro, who had no family in Golok to support her; finding benefactors like the Sotra family was essential for her survival. On another level, that Sera Khandro gives herself the last word in the interaction above could indicate that in her opinion Tsüldrön was less morally superior than her shaved head and maroon robes signaled. On an esoteric level, Sera Khandro's promise not to have sexual relationships with lay or religious men that did not have a purpose implies that she would engage in relationships that did have a purpose, which for her always meant a religious purpose. What were these religious purposes for sexuality that Sera Khandro upheld as more important for her than the virtue of celibacy? The answers we will explore in the following sections become relevant right away in Sera Khandro's narrative after this dialogue with Tsüldrön, for the very next words of her autobiography describe Gara Terchen's summons for her to serve as his consort.

The Soteriological Goal: Attaining Enlightenment

To understand how sexuality could be a part of Vajrayāna Buddhist contemplative practice requires an introduction to the physiology of the subtle body akin to that Sera Khandro reports receiving from the Indian Tantric master Kukkuripa.[19] In her autobiography she wrote that while she was celebrating the New Year in 1906, which marked her fourteenth birthday, at her brother's house in Lhasa, she dreamed that she traveled to a place called Siddhi Ling, Place of Accomplishment, in southern India. Recalling that in a past life she had been Kukkuripa's "secret consort who generates bliss" (*bde bskyed kyi gsang ba'i grogs*), she saw a mountain at the junction of two rivers blanketed with trees and houses in which Sanskrit letters stood. Kukkuripa explained that this was not an outer location in the world, but an appearance of her inner subtle body. Versions of this subtle body, or "vajra body" (*rdo rje phung po* or *rdo rje lus*), as Sera Khandro often referred to it, are common features of Tantric traditions. Just as the coarse physical body contains the cardiovascular and lymphatic circulatory systems comprising networks of arteries, veins, capillaries, and vessels in which blood and lymph flow, the vajra body is comprised of channels (*rtsa*) in which wind (*rlung*) and vital nuclei (*thig le*) flow.[20]

Three main channels run vertically in the torso, the central channel along the axis of the body flanked by two subsidiary channels on either side. A series of wheels (Skt. *cakra*, Tib. *'khor lo*) run down the central channel at key locations including the crown of the head, throat, heart, navel, and genitals, as well as other points, depending on the tradition. In ordinary people, each wheel contains a cluster of channels that are constricted in knots obstructing the smooth circulation of wind and vital nuclei. The aim of the yogic practices Kukkuripa taught Sera Khandro, called by the general term "channel and wind" (*rtsa rlung*), is to loosen these channel knots so that the wind and vital nuclei can circulate freely, thereby enabling the meditator to draw them up into the central channel, resulting in both physical well-being and spiritual realization.

In particular, in Sera Khandro's dream Kukkuripa presented a detailed teaching called *Pith Instructions on Enjoying the Three Elements* (*Khams gsum rol ba'i man ngag*) containing three parts on purifying the channels, winds, and vital nuclei, respectively. First, purifying the channels involves sealing the impure channels with the wind of primordial wisdom. In order to do this, Kukkuripa instructed Sera Khandro to clearly visualize the channels and *cakra*s of her vajra body:

> Like this, from the three main channels there are five *cakra*s and channels that spread out everywhere throughout the body from head to toe. As for the five *cakra*s, the essence of the crown [*cakra*] is mirrorlike primordial wisdom, and it appears as thirty-two transparent white channel petals. The essence of the throat [*cakra*] is discriminating primordial wisdom that appears as sixteen vivid red channel petals. The essence of the heart [*cakra*] is the expanse of reality primordial wisdom that appears as eight light blue channel petals. The essence of the navel is the primordial wisdom of sameness that appears as sixty-four light yellow channel petals. The essence of the secret [*cakra*] is the quintessential accomplishment of action primordial wisdom that appears as seventy-two light green channel petals. Like this, you must meditate until these channels appear extremely clearly. Having thereby naturally purified the channel element, you will attain the seed of becoming a completely ripened awareness holder (*rnam smin rig 'dzin*).[21]

Without reference to any type of mind-body dualism, the subtle body maps both physiological processes and states of mental realization onto each other, in this case five types of buddha wisdom, which abide as potentials to be realized through purifying obstructions to the channel knots located at the five *cakras*.

Complex layers of analogies between external and internal domains characterize descriptions of the Tantric subtle body, which meditators envision as a microcosm of the universe in its pure, divine form, replete with hosts of buddhas and bodhisattvas residing within. These analogies are apparent in the second section of Kukkuripa's *Pith Instructions* called "Purifying the Winds," which aims to "purify the karmic winds into the expanse."[22] These include ten types of wind divided into two sets. The first set of five overlays physical processes related to each of the five *cakras* with the five wisdom buddhas: the wind at the throat *cakra* allows for taste and speech and is a manifestation of Amitabha; wind at the secret *cakra* (genitals) expels urine and excrement and is a manifestation of Amoghasiddhi. Wind at the navel digests food and is a manifestation of Ratnasambhava, and wind at the heart *cakra* enables memory and is a manifestation of Vajrasattva. A wind that enables motion is located throughout the joints of the body and is a manifestation of Vairocana. The second set of five karmic winds powers the five sense faculties, including the eye, ear, nose, tongue, and touch, which are connected respectively to the five elements (*khams*) comprised by the physical world, including fire, space, earth, water, and wind. Kukkuripa tells Sera Khandro:

> Arriving at training in the three [practices of] entering, abiding, and dissolution of the wind, if you exert yourself in inhaling, exhaling, abiding, and raising up [wind at] the three syllables,[23] ultimately the seed of becoming an awareness holder with the power of longevity (*tshe dbang rig 'dzin*) will be established. Your energetic mind having merged into your central channel, your karmic winds will be extinguished into the expanse.[24]

By rendering these ten types of karmic wind pliant, the practitioner aims to eventually extinguish them while drawing the energetic mind (*rlung sems*) into the central channel, a process that Sera Khandro associates with the ability to experience many visions.

The third section of Kukkuripa's *Pith Instructions*, titled "Purifying the Vital Nuclei," consists of three parts or "seals" (*phyag rgya*). The first is the "activity seal (Skt. *karma mudrā*; Tib. *las kyi phyag rgya*) meditation," which Kukkuripa explains as follows:

> Visualize the three channels and five *cakras*. Visualize [the letter] "*haṃ*" at the great bliss *cakra* on the crown [of the head], an "*a*" stroke at the manifestation *cakra* at the navel, and the letter appropriate for each of the [other] three [*cakra*] centers. By the "*a*" and "*haṃ*" meeting and touching, the nectar at the crown drips down like milk. The wind guides the vital nuclei and they pervade, spread, and get pulled upward throughout all of the channel wheels. For example, like sucking water into a bamboo shoot, it is important to gain the capacity to draw *bodhicitta*[25] everywhere by means of wind. To render the wind and vital nuclei pliant in this manner, fix the mind on the letter in the middle of the channel wheels. By doing this, the wind in the left and right [channels] will dissolve into the central [channel], causing the primordial wisdom of the four joys to manifest.[26]

The "*haṃ*" letter at the crown of the head is associated with male vital nuclei, which melt down like drops of milk when the fire associated with the digestive processes of the navel and with female vital nuclei in the form of the "*a*" stroke (*a shad*) blazes forth, appearing as a single vertical stroke that is part of the Sanskrit and Tibetan vowel "*a*." The rising heat allows the wind to circulate the vital nuclei throughout the body's channels. As the milklike nectar melts down from the crown *cakra* and drips into the *cakras* below, this movement produces four increasingly intense states of joy correlated to the *cakras* the vital nuclei have reached.

In the context of Tantric physiology, white vital nuclei associated with the male and red vital nuclei associated with the female have existed within a single person since they were conceived, which was the moment in which their mother's and father's vital nuclei initially joined. The coexistence of male and female vital nuclei within one person's body allows solitary meditators to perform the contemplative practices Kukkuripa taught up to this point by themselves while maintaining celibacy. Both male and female bodies therefore contain all elements of the subtle body; the main difference is that in female bodies the two channels on either side of the central channel are reversed. Tantric physiology operates according to a heterosexual model not only in the sense of male and female sexes being understood as reverse images of each other, but also in the sense that the opposite sex was presumed to arouse the meditator.[27] We see this in Kukkuripa's description of the second seal, "the body seal meditation" (*lus kyi phyag rgya bsgom pa*), in which he directed Sera

Khandro to visualize a four-petaled lotus, a red triangle symbolizing the female sexual organ, and a white five-pronged vajra symbolizing the male sexual organ. After this,

> Then, from the "*a*" stroke at the navel, the fire of primordial wisdom moves through the central channel to the "*haṃ*" at the crown of the head and touches it. This is the cause and the secondary condition is the [*bodhi*]*citta* from the male's sexual organ. Think that the *bodhicitta* continuously rains from each of the channel centers and merges into the central channel. Think that by sixteen drops of nectar falling from the "*haṃ*" on the crown of the head, the primordial wisdom of joy increases. When eight [nectar drops] fall to the throat, think that the primordial wisdom of supreme joy increases. When four [nectar drops] fall to the heart center, think that the primordial wisdom of special joy increases. When two drops fall to the navel, think that the primordial wisdom of innate joy increases. When one drop falls to the secret center, think that the primordial wisdom of transcendent joy increases. These are the downward-moving four joys. Again, by the power of wind and awareness, the vital nuclei [move] from the lower [*cakras*] and mix with the "*haṃ*" in the crown *cakra*; this is the upward-moving four joys.[28]

Mastery of this capacity to draw vital nuclei upward and push them downward produces grades of intense joy, resulting in attaining the level of a "seal awareness holder" (*phyag rgya'i rig 'dzin*).

The third and last section of Kukkuripa's instruction, titled the "Method Seal" (*thabs kyi phyag rgya*), calls for the practitioner to bring the heterosexual element of channel-and-wind teachings from an internal visualized level to an actual physical act of sexual union. The male participant is the method or skillful means (Skt. *upāya*, Tib. *thabs*) necessary to complement the female participant, who is insight (Skt. *prajñā*, Tib. *shes rab*). Earlier Mahāyāna traditions understood the realization of buddhahood to entail a perfect understanding of the skillful means of compassion and the insight realizing emptiness. Vajrayāna Buddhism applied new Tantric techniques to the Mahāyāna dyad that ritually enacted this gendered symbolism, at times literally through contemplative practices involving heterosexual union. Although both male and female bodies contain the potential for awakening via purifying the subtle body's channels, winds, and vital nuclei, the vast majority of Tantric manuals describe these practices from the perspective of a male meditator summoning and training female sexual partners to serve as aids for his contemplative objectives.[29] Kukkuripa's instructions to Sera Khandro on the final part of the third section of *Pith Instructions* stand as a rare example of a contemplative practice taught for a female meditator seeking a suitable male consort (*thabs grogs*) or hero (*dpa' bo*) with whom to cultivate her spiritual attainment:

> Thirdly, regarding the "method seal" [i.e., the male consort], excellently examine, summon, and train a fully qualified hero who is an emanation of the five buddha families. First, [the hero] should enter the door of ripening and liberation and should be made to manifest signs of his capability in outer, inner, and secret generation and perfection [stages]. Once you excellently confer commitment vows pertaining to body, speech, and mind upon him, anything that he does with his body, speech, and mind will not contradict the Dharma for even an instant. By the third essential empowerment, he is placed on [the path of] ripening and liberation.
>
> Then, visualize method [male] and insight [female] as a deity. In the middle of this body, visualize the three channels and the five wheels. At the five centers [*cakras*], method is the five heroes and insight is the five heroines. The four limbs are the gatekeeper male-female couples. All of the other channel centers appear as heroes and *ḍākinīs* like the five centers. In this manner, meditate on method and insight.
>
> In the middle of the wheel of primordial wisdom at the crown of the head, meditate on a "*haṃ*" on a moon disk. At the extremity of the central channel about four finger widths [below] the navel, in the middle of a channel knot of joy and bliss that is like the sun's rays, meditate on a red "*a*" stroke that is [as small] as the cut tip of a Chinese needle on which the flickering flame of primordial wisdom burns.
>
> Then, having begun uniting the eight limbs, including the four method causes and the four insight conditions, establishing these as one is the path of accumulation.[30] The dominant condition is the physical sense consciousness and the supporting condition is the wavering clouds of [*bodhi*]*citta* nectar at the crown of the head. Gradually experiencing the four joys is the path of joining.
>
> Then, the method's [the man's] cloud of [*bodhi*]*citta* rains into the insight lady's secret space (*mkha' gsang*) and the white and red meet.[31] Having dispelled the eighty types of discursive thoughts into the ultimate

sphere, the inexpressible primordial wisdom of equanimity manifests. This is called *Enjoying the Three Physical Elements of the Lower Door.*

The vital nuclei having arrived from the [woman's] secret space into the pollen bed of the lotus [the womb], the wind of the first time period dissolves and you attain the realization of the first ground.[32] By pulling [the vital nuclei] from the pollen bed up to the secret center, the wind of the second time period dissolves and you attain the second ground. By pulling [the vital nuclei] between the secret [center] and the navel, the wind of the third time period is purified and you attain the third ground. [The vital nuclei] having reached the navel, the wind of the fourth time period is purified and you attain the fourth ground. By pulling them between the navel and the heart, the wind of the fifth time period is purified and you attain the fifth ground. When they reach the heart center, the wind of the sixth time period is purified and you attain the sixth ground. By pulling them up between the heart center and the throat, the wind of the seventh time period is purified and you attain the seventh ground. When they reach the throat, the wind of the eighth time period is purified and you attain the eighth ground. When they reach between the throat and eyebrows, the wind of the ninth time period is purified and you attain the ninth ground. By pulling the [vital nuclei] between the eyebrows and the crown of the head, the wind of the tenth time period is purified. Having attained the tenth ground, you will manifest as a spontaneously arisen awareness holder.[33] When the vital nuclei again reach the crown of the head, this is the eleventh ground [called] pervasive light. When they reach between the crown of the head and the crown protrusion,[34] this is the twelfth ground [called] the one with the lotus of nonattachment. When [the vital nuclei] mix as one taste with the "*haṃ*" at the crown protuberance, you will be established on the thirteenth ground of the vajra holder.

Having relied on the essential instructions on union according to the above description, this is traversing the excellent quick path in which liberation is instantaneous, not depending on all the gradual causes, results, grounds, and paths. Practice according to this, and having ripened the vital nuclei in your body, you will manifest as an awareness body endowed with the seven aspects of union.[35] In this lifetime you will attain the unified level of Vajradhāra.

As he said this, [Kukkuripa] transformed into a white vital nucleus and dissolved into the crown of my head. Just then I awoke from sleep.[36]

Tantric Buddhist channel and wind instructions such as this aimed to manipulate the flow of vital energies within the body by reversing their natural downward and outward movement, which Tantric traditions associated with aging, losing vitality, and death. One reason for celibacy was to slow this shedding process and to preserve more physical vitality for use in yogic practices. But even more efficacious than abstinence, according to Tantric Buddhist theory, was the ability to turn back this downward flow through drawing vital nuclei up into successively higher energy centers of the body, ultimately resulting in the complete realization of buddhahood.

Typically, Tantric manuals describe this reversal of the downward flow of vital nuclei through descriptions centered on male physiology. For example, the more common male perspective appears in the fourteenth-century Nyingma master Longchenpa's commentary on the *Guhyagarbha Tantra* titled *Dispelling the Darkness of the Ten Directions* (*Phyogs bcu mun sel*). Longchenpa explains that initially vital nuclei (here called seminal fluid) move down from the crown of the male practitioner's head through the throat, heart, and navel along with the arising of successive stages of primordial wisdom. Once the seminal fluid reaches the man's secret center,

> Then the white and red seminal fluids are drawn in through the pathway of the vajra (penis), whence they fill the four centres and their petals from the navel as far as the crown. In this way they are visualized to be extended with unceasing bliss and pervaded with pristine cognition free from all conceptual elaborations.[37]

Instead of the male emission that culminates ordinary sex, Longchenpa's instruction involves the opposite: the male meditator not only retains his own semen but also draws in female vital nuclei in order to conceive spiritual insight. In light of this more standard portrayal of channel and wind practice, Kukkuripa's instructions in Sera Khandro's vision again invert the Tantric reversal of ordinary sex, for Sera Khandro describes the man's cloud of semen raining into the woman's secret center and pervading upward in a process that at least initially mirrors the flow of conventional heterosexual intercourse. Kukkuripa's words strongly suggest that if Buddhist sexual yoga is about arousing vital nuclei, retaining them, and "sucking them up like water in a bamboo shoot" along the energy centers of the body, then the cloud of *bodhicitta* raining into the wisdom lady's secret center in Sera Khandro's vision cannot be about her male partner's spiritual advancement. Rather, this instruction is oriented toward her liberation, despite the tomes of Tantric literature that leave women's subjectivity unexplored.

Sera Khandro's visionary encounter with Kukkuripa may have appeared from nowhere, but his words have identifiable resonances. Prominent among them is the hagiography of Yeshé Tsogyel, who was at times Sera Khandro's spiritual and literary inspiration. Kukkuripa's instruction on pulling *bodhicitta* upward and conceiving thirteen successive stages of realization culminating in buddhahood is extremely similar to a passage in Yeshé Tsogyel's biography revealed by Taksham Nüden Dorjé in the seventeenth century. In this work, Yeshé Tsogyel intones that "to allow the bodhichitta to be spilled outside is like slaying the Buddha Amitabha . . . but I was able to reverse the bodhichitta upward."[38] She proceeds to draw the *bodhicitta* upward progressively in twelve stages corresponding to sites on and between her channel wheels and to the twelve stages or "grounds" of realization, culminating in gaining "mastery of all the qualities of a Buddha."[39] As considered in chapter 2, this intertextuality between Sera Khandro and Yeshé Tsogyel's life stories at pivotal moments indicates mimesis not in the derisive sense of plagiarism but in the constructive sense of finding an effective language to describe a female perspective seldom put into written words. Like many other instances in Sera Khandro's narrative when *ḍākinīs* did the talking, referencing Yeshé Tsogyel's hagiography bolstered the credibility of Kukkuripa's unusually female-focused channel and wind teaching. In that hagiography, Padmasambhava cautions Yeshé Tsogyel just after her transformative meditative experience, "Mistress, without a valiant partner as a skillful means, there is in truth no way for you to undertake the practice of the Secret Mantra (Vajrayāna),"[40] thereby inspiring Yeshé Tsogyel to purchase a young Indian man, Atsara Salé, to aid her practice. Similarly, Kukkuripa's instruction foreshadows the watershed moment of Sera Khandro's youth that she introduces in the next folio: her initial meeting with Drimé Özer, the man who would become her most important guru and a "fully qualified hero" with whom she would practice Kukkuripa's teaching.

The Hermeneutical Goal: Sex and Text

Among the selective group of Tibetan Buddhist practitioners who engaged in contemplative practices with actual consorts were Treasure revealers, though their reasons for doing so went beyond those of general Tantric Buddhist soteriology. The Treasure tradition maintains a distinctly substantial connection between sex and text, more specifically between channel and wind practices involving sexuality and the revelation of scriptures and religious artifacts. Not all Treasure revealers had consorts—notably, the celibate monastic Treasure revealer Khenpo Jikmé Püntsok (1933–2004) of Larung Gar in Serta did not—but the tradition considers consorts of the opposite sex necessary for a revealer to discover his or her (usually his) full share of Treasures. The third Dodrupchen Jikmé Tenpé Nyima, Drimé Özer's older brother, explained the reason for this in *Wonder Ocean: An Explanation of the Dharma Treasure Tradition*:

> Furthermore, in order to arouse the accomplishment from their depths, the teachings which have been concealed in the natural sphere of the luminous state (*A'od gSal Gyi Khams*) [of their minds], it is also necessary to have the spontaneously arisen bliss (*Lhan sKyes Kyi dGa' Ba*) which can be produced by a special consort who has made the appropriate aspirations in the past, and who is to become the key to accomplishment. That is one of the reasons why all Tertons happen to have consorts.[41]

The "spontaneously arisen bliss" that Dodrupchen Rinpoché describes is the fourth joy that appears in Sera Khandro's vision of Kukkuripa, which I translate above as "innate joy." The Vajrayāna Buddhist tradition understands this intense joy or bliss generated by contemplative practices involving sexual union to be entirely unlike the lustful desire aroused in ordinary sexuality. Like an insect who is born from wood but then matures by eating that very same wood, Tantric practitioners aim to transform ordinary desire into bliss infused with the insight of realizing emptiness, which in turn consumes the desire that gave rise to it.[42] Additionally, in the Treasure tradition, a special by-product of generating bliss through releasing circulation blockages within the subtle body is the release of what we might call "writer's block." In other words, generating bliss enhances the Treasure revealer's ability to discover, decode, and write down revelations.

The flow of vital nuclei and the flow of words correspond on multiple levels in the Treasure tradition, all coalescing around the figure of the *ḍākinī*. As we have seen in previous chapters, the tradition remembers its first lady, the *ḍākinī* Yeshé Tsogyel, as the one who compiled, retained, and wrote Padmasambhava's teachings in a symbolic script called *ḍākinī* script. The final stage of Treasure transmission, called "entrustment to the *Ḍākinī*s," reflects their role in preserving and protecting Treasures in the interim between Padmasambhava's concealment and their future discovery. Additionally, *ḍākinī*s in the form of celestial goddesses appear regularly in Treasure revealers' visions with prophetic words of wisdom. Finally, for male Treasure revealers, *ḍākinī*s manifest as human female consorts to help them discover and decode their Treasures. The Third Dodrupchen encapsulates these connections between female consorts and language in the following words:

> The Discoverer must reach the identification of the true text, one word and one meaning, by achieving fully perfected power in decoding the symbolic script. This is accomplished through favorable conditions such as meeting with the Doctrine-holder of those Termas; being in the right place or being present at an important occasion; and most important, by encountering the miraculous skill of a Vajradūta [consort] whose mind has been purified by empowerments and precepts, who has practiced the path of two stages (*Rim gNyis*), who has been blessed by Guru Rinpoche himself in order to take the birth of an appropriate sacred support [consort] for the Terton in future to discover the Termas of the sphere of primordial wisdom (*Ye Shes dByings*) by means of the hook (*lChags Kyu*) of spontaneously arisen bliss, and who himself or herself has made the appropriate aspirations [in the past]. Because of those conditions the Terton will become certain about the real words and meanings of the texts, and other appearances will disappear.[43]

As one indispensable element of the five auspicious connections necessary for successful revelation, the special function of a Treasure revealer's consort is to ignite the bliss from which meaningful words flow.[44]

Yet one facet of this equation between sex and text, between having a *ḍākinī* consort and decoding symbolic script, is left unclear in Dodrupchen's explanation. Given that Vajradūta (Tib. *rdo rje pho nya mo*) is a feminine term for "consort" in both Sanskrit and Tibetan, literally meaning "vajra envoy," what happens when the Treasure revealer is female? Though the English editor or translator attempted to make Dodrupchen's words gender neutral by referring to the Treasure revealer as "himself or herself," in fact Dodrupchen's Tibetan can only refer to a male Treasure revealer (called "Discoverer" and "Terton" in quotation above), because the consort he describes is female. If we change the subject to a female Treasure revealer, does she then require a *ḍākinī*, whose very nature is tied to language, to decode her symbolic Treasures? Or does she require the bliss generated by contemplative practices involving heterosexual union with a male consort? Sera Khandro's writings definitively claim the latter, reversing the more typical paradigm of male subject and female support. Though Tibetan terms for "consort" often implicitly or explicitly refer to a female, this is not always the case. Tibetan terms for sexual partners in Tantric practices, whether real or imagined, include those that can only refer to a female, such as "awareness lady" (*rig ma*), "insight lady" (*shes rab ma*), "she who holds" (*gzungs ma*),[45] "sky-going lady" (*mkha' 'gro ma*), "female envoy" (*pho nya mo*), and "female seal" (*phyag rgya ma*), but also terms without gender markers such as "method consort" (*thabs grogs*), "consort" (*grogs*), "envoy" (*pho nya*), and "seal" (*phyag rgya*). Among these, the most common term Sera Khandro uses for the male consorts she needed to reveal her Treasures is "method consort" or simply "consort."

In accordance with the Third Dodrupchen's explanation above, Sera Khandro writes extensively about needing a male consort in addition to other auspicious connections (*rten 'brel*) in order to successfully reveal Treasures. For example,

> Then, when I was twenty-two years old, since there was a gathering of sacred land [deities] at the sacred site called Chakri Ömbar in the Mar [valley], I went there. While I spent some days circumambulating the mountain, the land deity (*gnas bdag*) appeared as a raven. Everybody gathered there actually saw him give me a six-cornered crystal chest with the profound pages of a *Drölkar Yishin Tsephel, Wish-fulfilling Life-extending White Tārā*, scripture. They said, "You are a Treasure revealer." At that sacred site there were also profound pages of the *Lama Gongpa Düpa, Embodiment of the Lama's Realization*, from the *Guru Zapdrup, Guru's Profound Liturgy*, Dharma cycle in three small chests made of turquoise, agate, and the semiprecious stone *chong*.[46] But because at that time the consort (*thabs grogs*) and doctrine holder had not gathered there, aside from just some Dharma medicine and saffron, the auspicious connections went away.[47]

In spite of her frequent lamentations that she could not manage to gather together auspicious connections and in particular, suitable consorts, visionary *ḍākinī*s and land deities insisted throughout her autobiography that engaging with prophesied consorts was mandatory. For example, Sera Khandro writes that when she was twenty-four she conversed with a *ḍākinī* emissary in the form of a blue bird who appeared before her:

> This servant always without leisure
> reaped the suffering of physical and verbal hardship.
> Sick with an uncertain illness, several years went by.
> On the outside, I was constantly afflicted with physical illness.
> On the inside, I quarreled with my kind life partner.
> In between, the people of the area criticized and insulted me,
> saying bad words to me as if they saw me as their archenemy.
> Good and bad things such as these have happened.
> Thinking about what has become of my disciples and enlightened activities
> is a basis for my sorrow to increase.
> Who has negative karma like me?
>
> Although I attained freedom, I am without power to go to the buddhafields.
> Although I want to help beings, I am unable to guide my disciples.
> Although I am empowered in Treasures, I did not rely on the essential point of auspicious connections.
> Because I have an inferior female body (*skye lus dman pas*), all the male householders hate me.
> Supreme consorts who enhance the practices of skillful means and liberation are as rare as stars in the daylight;
> there are more ordinary sinful consorts than trees in the forest.
> [With them] it would be difficult to practice according to the Dharma, and I would become the cause of ruin for myself and others.
> Having considered this, I maintained moral conduct.
>
> Nevertheless, mother deities and *ḍākinī*s always
> said that I needed to rely on the one commitment vow
> of never parting from one with the supreme form of a bliss-arousing hero bodhisattva
> whom I had skillfully examined, summoned, trained, and placed [on the path of] ripening and liberation.

Again and again they expressed in symbolic prophetic registries:

> Exhort the mind seal (*yid kyi phag rgya*) Vima Raśmi [Drimé Özer],
> the great hero bodhisattva who relies on commitment vows,
> with whom you are connected through prayers from many lifetimes.
> By this you will be empowered in a bit of Dharma endowed with auspicious connections
> and in a secret manner benefit for oneself and others will gradually arise.

Hence, I tell you, friendly turquoise blue bird,
this brief story about me.

[The bird] replied:

> *Ki ki yogi!*
> *Ki ki yogi!*
> A turquoise bird's habitat is a fruit-bearing tree;
> around the tree, the bird is carefree and happy.
> When the flock of birds with compatible voices gathers,
> thoughts that accord with the Dharma naturally arise.
>
> A Treasure revealer's home base (*gnas rten*) is his or her supreme consort.
> If you rely solely on this disciplined commitment vow,
> the auspicious connections of skillful means will naturally come together.
> Like a bevy of golden swans amassing,
> your good deeds and enlightened activity will expand to the utmost."[48]

Though this blue bird projected a dark road ahead for Sera Khandro, she insisted that it would be one that benefited beings as long as she relied on a consort.

In Drimé Özer's biography Sera Khandro also decried her difficulty finding appropriate male consorts for her revelations. She presented an interaction with Drimé Özer during the turbulent decade she lived with

Gara Gyelsé at Benak Monastery, referring to herself in the third person by her Treasure name, Dewé Dorjé:

> The Master said,
>
> > . . . In particular, don't forget to find a way to let the Dharma cycles that are earth Treasures come to you.
>
> Dewé Dorjé replied,
>
> > I am a beggar, as Master Milarepa said [about himself]. Aside from this, although I was empowered in many earth Treasures, because I didn't rely on a consort, I only retrieved three earth Treasures. Now, it will be okay for them to come.[49]

Implicit in this exchange is an equation between having a physical consort present at the moment of revelation and the physicality of earth Treasures that appeared in the forms of scriptures and artifacts (as opposed to mind Treasures that appeared in Treasure revealers' visions). Elsewhere Sera Khandro made a much more concrete connection between producing earth Treasures and the (potential) physical product of heterosexual sexuality. For example, in a conversation she narrates in her autobiography between herself and Gotrül Rinpoché during a visit when she was twenty-five:

> He said,
>
> > You are an actual wisdom *ḍākinī*, but because you belong to the leader from a bad lineage, it is difficult to understand whether you think positively or negatively. Not behaving like this, in accordance with the minds of beings in this degenerate age, you must endeavor to find a way to gradually benefit yourself and others. In particular, now, when you come back from pilgrimage, do whatever you can not to forget to find a way to take out one Treasure of whatever type—body, speech, mind, good qualities, or enlightened activities—as my paternal inheritance.
>
> Having said this, he gave me silver and a gleaming blessed silk scarf and made aspiration prayers.
>
> I answered,
>
> > Aside from being one who can take out the Treasure of boys and girls, I don't have a way to take out vast earth Treasures.

When I said this, again he replied,

> Even if you don't want to be a Treasure revealer, you are empowered with the karma of Treasures. You cannot keep this secret or it is certain that the auspicious connections will fall apart because of other circumstances. Hence, don't keep secrets and speak to me honestly. Because we are connected by the karma of prayers from our former lifetimes, if we rely upon each other, I think that benefit will arise for beings. Hence, we need to act accordingly.[50]

Although Sera Khandro is elusive about precisely what sense they relied upon each other, here Gotrül's main point was that she needed to reveal her Treasures, and she concluded the conversation with the promise that she would. A few pages later, Sera Khandro employs the very same analogy between procreation and revelation when narrating her pilgrimage to Anyé Machen Mountain, also during her twenty-fifth year, where she revealed a Treasure (see chapter 2 for the full translation of this passage):

> When all this happened, my companions wondered what it was and came back quickly, saying, "It is certain that you have taken out a Treasure. You need to show it to us."
>
> I replied, "This is my daughter that I have taken out as a Treasure—I wonder if I can take out a son?"
>
> When I said this, Chötreng said, "Your daughter has already seen the Treasure. We need to see this Treasure from which a fragrant aroma wafts!" and she repeated this again and again.[51]

In both of these episodes, Sera Khandro attempts to deflect her companions' interest in her discovery by playfully joking that the only revelations she can discover are children. Her quip builds on the Tantric correspondence between manipulating the flow of vital nuclei and engendering spiritual realization by analogizing their potential products, progeny and revelations. Bearing children and discovering Treasures are both generative processes that rely on the physiology of the human body, coarse or subtle, to produce something new. But these productions are not entirely new, for lineage ties both to their predecessors, whether in the biological sense or the religious sense of spiritual lineage. Just like the Tantric process of drawing up male and female vital nuclei into one's own body to catalyze spiritual realization aligns better with human physiology if the subject performing the meditation is female, the analogy Sera

Khandro drew between conceiving children and revealing Treasures makes the most sense if spoken by a woman. If there are female perspectives on Buddhist Tantra and the Tibetan Treasure tradition that remain largely unvoiced in Tibetan texts, Sera Khandro's analogy between sexual and textual (re-)production gives us an inkling of what they would sound like. As the feminist biblical scholar Elisabeth Schüssler Fiorenza wrote in reference to early Christian writings, perhaps we can surmise that Sera Khandro's female metaphors for subtle body processes are "like the tip of an iceberg, indicating a rich heritage now lost to us."[52]

The Pragmatic Goal: Curing Sickness and Prolonging Longevity

Indian and Tibetan Tantric Buddhist traditions link yogic mastery of channel and wind practices not only with the ultimate soteriological goal of spiritual realization but also with the more mundane physical goals of curing illness and increasing longevity.[53] Sera Khandro wrote much more about the curative effects than the enlightening effects of such practices, though the two cannot be entirely separated. Curing illness was not merely a subsidiary product of channel and wind practices, but often their main objective; Sera Khandro recounts being invited to serve as a consort to several lamas, *trülku*s, and Treasure revealers most often for the purpose of prolonging their life and curing their illnesses. As catalysts of bliss emptiness (Tib. *bde stong*) who aid the male meditator in achieving these goals, *ḍākinī*s and their curative powers are well attested in Tibetan texts. But could male consorts also cure the ailments of female meditators? In this regard, Sera Khandro's auto/biographical writings again turn around the familiar paradigm of male agent and female aide. Just as she presents Tantric subtle body physiology in reference to a female meditator and illustrates the reproductive link between having a consort and revealing Treasures in a way that only a female Treasure revealer could, with the help of her *ḍākinī* interlocutors Sera Khandro affirms that male consorts did more than demand her healing powers—they cured her as well.

One prominent instance among many in Sera Khandro's writing in which a male lama summoned her to serve as a consort to cure his illness was her interaction with Gara Terchen. As detailed in chapter 3, Gara Terchen invited her to Benak Monastery during her late teen years because he was gravely ill and intuited that she could potentially lengthen his life span. She attempted to visit the lama for a few years but was repelled by his jealous consort, Yakza. She writes that a lama named Kyilung Trülku observed Yakza's antics and interpreted her behavior in the following manner: "Now, Yakza has no need for the lama. She says, 'If the lama passes away right here in front of my eyes, I won't care.' Whatever happens, this is certainly creating an obstacle for the lama's longevity."[54] Interestingly, two other more recent Tibetan sources confirm the interpretation Sera Khandro put forth in her autobiography, that Yakza caused Gara Terchen's death by forbidding him the curative salvation Sera Khandro could have provided. The *Dartang Monastery Abbatial History* includes a short biography of Gara Terchen in which the author states that one reason for his death was that "The auspicious connection of [Gara Terchen] taking on the supreme consort (*gzungs ma'i mchog*) prophesied by the *ḍākinīs* named Üza Khandro Chönyi Dekyong Wangmo as a consort (*rig ma*) were confused."[55] Also mirroring this interpretation of Gara Terchen's death, the contemporary publication editor of Gara Terchen's autobiography describes Yakza as a bad person who did everything she could to harm Gara Terchen, causing him to "set his aspirations on [going to] the buddhafield" no matter what protective rituals his disciples performed. He adds,

> At that time there was an extraordinarily great need [based on] prayers they had made in the past for the auspicious connection of meeting with the fully qualified consort (*rig ma*) named Üza Khandro to come together in order to dispel obstacles to [Gara Terchen's] longevity, but it fell apart because of the inferior merit of beings in the degenerate age.[56]

Sera Khandro's autobiography appears to be the source for both more recent authors' narratives about these events, signaling that her version of Gara Terchen's death has become the official history remembered by prominent descendants of his lineage.

Another famous Treasure revealer expressed an interest in Sera Khandro's curative powers, namely Andzom Drondül Pawo Dorjé (1842–1924). His summons in 1923, when she was thirty-one years old, was a sign of her growing stature as a *ḍākinī* and a Treasure revealer. The head of a religious encampment south of Golok in Kham called Andzom Gar (see map 1), Andzom Rinpoché was one of the pre-eminent religious masters of his era. He received teachings from the most famous Nyingma lineage holders in the Tibetan Buddhist world at the time, including Khyentsé Wangpo, Patrül Rinpoché, Ju Mipham, and many others. He was a prolific writer, editor, and Treasure revealer, and he taught ecclesiastic hierarchs of the most important Nyingma monasteries in Kham, including Katok, Dzokchen, Zhechen, and Pelyül.[57] Receiving Andzom Rinpoché's seal of approval was a major recognition for Sera Khandro. Considering that they did not live in the same region of eastern Tibet, his request indicates that her renown as a Tantric consort had spread beyond Golok. The problem, according to Sera Khandro, was that when Andzom Rinpoché summoned her, she had only been reunited with Drimé Özer for two years and didn't wish to separate from him again even for a short journey of great importance. In her autobiography she described her dilemma in conversation with Drimé Özer:

> At that time, a messenger arrived from Andzom's religious encampment with a written order saying that I needed to go to there. I said the following to the Master:
>
>> I won't go to Andzom's religious encampment. For one thing, I don't have [good] legs and since my little son is so young, I cannot just leave him here. On top of that, in any case, I have never let my mind run wild and let myself fall under another person's sway. Although it seems like I have come to you of my own accord, as you know, I only came because Gartrül [Gara Gyelsé] didn't want me; it wasn't my idea. That's why, now, no matter how I think about things, I won't do anything that is misleading for myself and others. In particular, after your lifetime is finished, I wonder if I can practice assiduously on a secluded mountain. Aside from this, I have no thought of needing to live with a consort, nor do I want to go now. That is my answer.
>>
>> Even so, I am a helpless woman, so it is easy for just about anyone to lead me around like a stray dog. Because Lama Andzom is a holy master renowned in all of China and Tibet, if he sends a messenger with a written command summoning an inferior one like me, of course I must go. But since I am narrow-minded, I feel uncomfortable replying that I will go. In particular, because before you and I were under others' sway, we didn't live together until now. Now, negative circumstances have become favorable and we have the opportunity to live together in one residence. At this time, I cannot separate from you for even an instant. Like a child circles around her mother, my mind has become extremely attached to you. Hence, if I don't have to go, I would prefer not to.

The Master replied,

> I too will miss you—if I could never be apart from you for even one day, I would feel extremely happy, happier than if I had a house full of jewels. Yet, if you could be a consort endowed with auspicious connections to prolong Lama Andzom's life if not for one year then even for one month, if not for one month then even for one day, in general this would benefit the Buddhist teachings and sentient beings would be happy. In particular, it would be a resource for you and others to accumulate a vast store of merit. Specifically, as it was previously expressed in your vajra prophecy, if the essential point of an auspicious connection with Akṣara Vajra[58] occurs, benefit will certainly arise for the lives, Dharma, and disciples of all of us, here and there.

Hence, it was decided that I would go there.[59]

At first glance, this does not sound at all like the voice of an empowered woman. She writes of being sick, needing to care for her young child, being powerless to choose which man with whom to live, and being entirely uninterested in living with a male consort. Yet, what transpired during and after Andzom Rinpoché and Sera Khandro's meeting suggests something else. At their initial encounter, the eighty-two-year-old Andzom Rinpoché recognized Sera Khandro as an incarnation of the *ḍākinī* Künga Buma, one of the two female Treasure revealers from Jamgön Kongtrül's *One Hundred Treasure Revealers*. He interrogated her about how she came to reveal Treasures until he was fully satisfied with her responses. Then, the senior male and junior female Treasure revealers exchanged their revealed teachings and conversed. She writes, "In particular, the Lama [Andzom] Rinpoché took care of me with great love. He gave me advice about religious and worldly affairs and offered me blessings, thus dispelling faults pertaining to auspicious connections. He cured all of my sickness."[60]

When Sera Khandro returned to Drimé Özer's residence in Dartsang after her two-month sojourn, those who came to welcome her home were amazed because "my leg was not like it was before and I could move independently. They rejoiced and their faith was nourished."[61] Not only did Andzom Rinpoché temporarily cure Sera Khandro's debilitating arthritic leg pain, but unlike Yakza's antics, Andzom's family, even his wife (*yum*), treated her with great affection. Sera Khandro recounts that when she prepared to depart from their religious encampment, Andzom Rinpoché, his wife, and two of their children escorted her for a long time on the road and made her promise that she would return to give them more teachings in the future. If this is what it means to be a stray dog easy to lead around, Sera Khandro seems to have turned this injustice into a positive circumstance that benefited herself as well as served others.

Sera Khandro's descriptions of consort practices are euphemistic and metaphoric, avoiding salacious detail, but *ḍākinī*s' injunctions make up for any modesty on her part. If her readers did not already pick up on her point that she required male consorts for her own physical and spiritual needs, *ḍākinī*s repeatedly laid it out with aplomb. In one instance, Sera Khandro writes that after Drimé Özer's passing when she was thirty-five, in approximately 1927,

> Then, in the tenth month of that year, I was oppressed with a terrible illness and was nearing death. During the twelfth month on the night of the twenty-second, in my delusory perception an old wretched woman with an ugly body and great lustful desire but with faultless sense faculties like those of a young woman came and said the following:
>
> Ya, ya—girlfriend, what sickness do you have?
> Tell me the symptoms of your sickness.
> If you are sick with lustful desire (*'dod sred*) that is the cause of cyclic existence,
> I know a good cure.
>
> To that, I replied,
>
> Older sister who is neither an old woman nor a young girl,
> this one who is neither a nun nor a laywoman will describe my sickness.
> From the time I was young, lamas took care of me.
> They blessed my mind stream by means of both ripening [empowerments] and liberating [instructions].
> I am expert in the essential points of enhancement, skillful means, and liberation.
> I don't need to be bound by the noose of lustful desire.

By the kindness of my consort Wish-fulfilling Jewel [Drimé Özer],
the three types of karmic propensities are liberated from their basis;
the awareness and emptiness of *saṃsāra* and *nirvāṇa* are equal.
I have seen the unsurpassed meaning
of primordial wisdom without desire and freed from desire
in which bliss and emptiness are indivisible.

I am not sick with the cause of cyclic existence.
My lust has been purified into great bliss.
I have actualized habitual tendencies as coemergent primordial wisdom.
Grasping has ripened into the intrinsically empty Truth Body.
I am not afraid of this sickness of lustful desire.

I am tormented by a sickness that is a combination of illnesses:
my heart is uncomfortable, beating as if it were a large drum.
My lungs are uncomfortable like bellows being blown.
Both my gall bladder and spleen are working as if putting wild horses in order.
The nerves of my two eyeballs feel as if they are about to be cut.
I can't hold up my head—it is heavier than a diamond.
Blood and bile pervade all my channels like water.
My wind is not harmonious, as if quarreling with an enemy opponent.
Long and short sighs emerge from both my mouth and nose.
This collection of elements that is my body is like inanimate matter.
This collection of various illnesses has gathered together.
This mass of light that is the primordial wisdom of mind
is on the verge of going out via the path of the white silk channel.
This is the manner in which I am sick.
If you know how to diagnose, then diagnose this.

She said:

You, *yoginī* who is a doctor of channels and winds—
one with a beautiful face whose body liberates into light,

the origin of these various illnesses is
obscuration by the *sapta* [hindrance-causing demons] regarding the auspicious connection of method.

You abandoned the youth who sustains your body,[62]
brought on negative conditions involving deteriorated vows, and so forth.
Because of these things, many negative conditions afflict your body.

Although you see the meaning of not staying in cyclic existence,
you have not purified subtle karmic propensities.
On account of the mental illusions of hopes and fears,
you didn't act in accordance with the prophecies.
You forsook your bodhisattva Dharma holder.

Why are you attached to behaving in the manner of the doctrine of the lesser vehicle
with your body, speech, and mind?
You don't see attaining the superior result
of the quick path of Mantra?

I replied,

Listen, older sister of compatible heritage:
if one practices superior Secret Mantra,
I have no doubt
in the reality of the quick result one will attain.
I pray that in this and all my lives
I meet with this swift path.

Nevertheless, these days in the degenerate age,
peoples' lustful desire burns like fire.
Under the pretense of Mantra, they practice nonvirtue.
They assemble false Treasures, which are the ruin of both themselves and others.
They throw away their *bodhicitta* through fornication
like spit in the dust.

> Practicing in accordance with Mantra is next to impossible.
> Because of this, thinking that my inferior female body
> would become the cause of my own and others' ruin,
> I entered the path of monastic discipline.
> Thinking I would be able to abandon negative thoughts and negative rebirths,
> I cast wrongdoing and negative consorts far behind.
> How could it harm anyone if I delight in
> entering into the path of the two truths?[63]

The apparitional *ḍākinī* with whom Sera Khandro converses presents the need to engage with a suitable male consort, a bodhisattva, as a requirement of the quick path of Secret Mantra, also called Vajrayāna. In so doing she casts celibacy as an easier, if not also more straightforward, form of conduct associated with the "lesser vehicle" (Skt. Hīnayāna) of Buddhism. Despite Sera Khandro's explanations, the *ḍākinī* insists that her sickness is actually caused by her celibacy, and therefore curable by uniting with the proper consort. Sera Khandro's rhetorical denial rejects her prescription at the same time as it voices it from an authoritative source.

If the previous *ḍākinī*'s message was not explicit enough, the following vision leaves little room for doubt. Sera Khandro writes that when she was thirty-seven, she gave an expansive teaching on Düjom Lingpa's and Drimé Özer's Treasure revelations to a large gathering of lamas and monks at Sera Monastery. At that time,

> I got a strange illness that caused an extremely sharp pain in my lotus [i.e., female sexual organ]. On the tenth day of the twelfth month, during a practice session, a vision arose. An old woman came to me and asked: "What kind of sickness do you have?"
>
> "I cannot explain my sickness to you since it is in an embarrassing place," I replied.
>
> She said, "I know a medicine that will cure your sickness."
>
> "What kind of medicine is it? Do you have something to give me?" I asked.
>
> She responded, "I don't have it. Another person does, but you won't take it, right?"
>
> I said, "I haven't found anything to take. If I can find something that might help, it's okay if I take medicine."

She answered,

Ha ha, you won't take it! You won't take the medicine!
If you will take it, I will teach you the supreme medicine!

The ambrosia that conquers afflictions abides
in the moonlight at the top of the thirty-two [channels][64]
[in] a vajra body possessing the six elements and five [*cakras*].

From its abode it moves through the path of great emptiness [the central channel].
By falling down through the four centers,
it emerges at the city of the sixty-four [the navel *cakra*].

If your lotus receives and is nourished by this sprinkling [of ambrosia],
this auspicious connection will cure all your physical sickness.

The king of medicine who possesses this [ambrosia]
is the one named Vajra who is in the south.
You will meet him at the place where the three rivers gather.
By this, dangers to your life will temporarily be dispelled.

Again, I said,

Listen, old woman who talks like a monkey,
I, the woman Dewé Dorjé,
am not sick because I haven't found a husband.
The four elements of my illusory body are disturbed and
because I have not destroyed self-cherishing,
I am constantly tormented by sickness.
If there is any possible way to cure this,
I think I should rely on the protection of this supreme medicine.
Nevertheless, it is decided that I will not rely on
this perverse medicine of yours.
Don't speak these false words and
go away to whatever land you like.

She replied, "Girlfriend, don't get angry! My words are definitive and are not monkey talk! If you do not rely on a consort, even if you take other medicines for a lifetime, it seems that there will be no benefit and you won't find a way to cure your various illnesses."

I said, "If I am sick, I am the one who has to experience suffering. You do not need to experience it. Now I would like you to leave me alone. At the end of my life that is like a setting sun, aside from wondering if I can accomplish the completely pure Dharma, I don't think about needing to take on a consort."

Although our conversation was not finished, because of something else, I awoke from sleep.[65]

Sera Khandro's feisty responses to the old woman's prognosis that ambrosia sprinkled into her "lotus" by a "king of medicine" will cure her gynecological affliction strongly imply that the *ḍākinī* is advocating literal sexual union and not imagined Tantric visualization. Sera Khandro rejects her words as perverse, appearing to be shocked by the *ḍākinī*'s lascivious suggestion, but as in the previous passage, the message comes through loud and clear as ventriloquized through Sera Khandro's pen. In case even this was not convincing enough, shortly after the above vision the mountain deity Nyenchen Tanglha, whom Sera Khandro indicates elsewhere was her real father, appears before her and reiterates the *ḍākinī*'s words:

He said, "It is difficult for what you are thinking to happen—who has a way to contradict the prayers of Guru Padma? Moreover, in accordance with the prophecies of the mother deities and *ḍākinīs*, it is important to be skilled in the method of auspicious connections. When you don't act accordingly, forget about finishing out your life span. Your body will become completely exhausted. Because I say this with good intentions toward you, examine this viewpoint. You are not a nun maintaining Vinaya rules who needs to let auspicious connections fall under others' sway. You are also not a cheating woman who engages in sexual misconduct. When the circumstances of favorable conditions gather together, because there will be great benefit to yourself and others, you need to consider this."

Saying this, he gave me a Treasure chest.

"What is this?" I asked.

> As he answered, "It is a hidden registry that discloses a testament of Yeshé Tsogyel," he disappeared like a rainbow in the sky.[66]

As in the previous visions, Sera Khandro communicated her in-between status as neither chaste nun nor sinful laywoman by expressing this sensitive point through others' voices. By doing this, she presented herself as a participant in legitimate Vajrayāna consort practices that augmented her physical and spiritual strength as much as they aided others, all the while denying her abilities. Nevertheless, who could defy Padmasambhava's command, even if "practicing in accordance with Mantra is next to impossible"?

PART II: TALK ABOUT CELIBACY AND SEXUALITY

Can Monks Be Consorts?

The *ḍākinī* who aligned celibacy with the "lesser vehicle" of Buddhism and sexual yoga with Vajrayāna drew a hierarchical distinction between the two forms of conduct, but elsewhere in Sera Khandro's writings she indicates that the lines between the two were less clear-cut. Many conversations Sera Khandro narrates in her auto/biographical works suggest that celibate and noncelibate interpretations of ideal Vajrayāna conduct were at times competing religious dictums in her communities. We saw this tension in the nun Tsüldrön's offense at Sera Khandro's choice to pursue the noncelibate religious path and in Sera Khandro's vociferous refusals to heed the *ḍākinī*s' and land deity's directives that she engage with the proper male consorts. As a much sought-after Tantric consort, Sera Khandro found herself on the fault lines of alternative interpretations of Vajrayāna Buddhist sexual conduct, for the onus often fell upon her to determine who was and was not a suitable consort, and many of those who came calling were monks. Though she always portrays herself rejecting monks' advances, the celestial *ḍākinī*s whose voices saturate her auto/biographical works seem to have operated on an alternative moral compass in which celibacy was not always the highest virtue.

*Ḍākinī*s were not alone in claiming that under specialized circumstances, highly realized monastics could maintain their celibacy vows and engage in consort practices, though the capacity to accomplish this correctly was hardly the norm. Tibetan Buddhism maintains a long commentarial tradition about how to reconcile different religious protocols, including the celibacy required of those who maintain individual liberation vows (Skt. *prātimokṣa*) and the sexuality that is sometimes part of the religious path for those adhering to bodhisattva and Tantric vows. According to the twentieth-century commentary on Ngari Penchen Pema Wangki Gyelpo's (1487–1542) *Ascertaining the Three Vows* (*Sdom gsum rnam gnes*) written by Düjom Lingpa's reincarnation, Düjom Jikdrel Yeshé Dorjé Rinpoché, "in prātimokṣa, sexual intercourse must be abandoned, whereas the two higher vow categories view sexual intercourse as a method. However, as a method, intercourse must be unstained by desire so that it is performed as a practice."[67] Düjom Rinpoché elaborates that if a monk has sexual intercourse unstained by desire, in which he is able to perceive both subject and object as male and female wisdom deities, to transform his desire into the recognition of great bliss, and to transform his loss of seminal fluid and his attachment into primordial wisdom awareness, then his act is not a violation of any of his vows.[68] Tulku Thondup sums up the difficulty of effecting this in his introduction to the English translation of the above work: "Highly accomplished tantrics . . . can maintain the vow of celibacy even if they have consorts, but such claims of attainment are authentic only if they are also able to bring the dead back to life."[69] Even if one is capable of such a feat, Düjom Rinpoché cautions that "whenever one is in a gathering of others who are beginners on the path, one should refrain from activity that may appear to be negative. At such times, the code of prātimokṣa morality and behavior should be applied."[70] In other words, public opinion is important even if one possesses sufficient internal mastery to utilize sexuality as a method, for appearing to mix celibacy with sexuality could cause others to lose faith.

In Sera Khandro's auto/biographical writing, we hear the clash that sometimes rang out between social sanction and doctrinal precedence mostly in the form of gossip, badmouthing, criticizing, and disparaging talk that she reports both fearing and facing consistently when she was in close proximity to monks and monasteries. The term Sera Khandro uses for this gossip is *mo kha*, literally "female talk" or "female mouth," meaning in context something more like "gossip about having a relationship with a woman," since she writes of it mostly affecting ecclesiastic hierarchs with whom she interacted.[71] Other words she uses that relate to negative talk or badmouthing include being demoralized or disheartened (*sems bsad pa*), causing offense to others (*mig lam du gnod pa*), and being a foundation for wrong views (*log lta gzhi*). On the one hand, we can understand the gossip surrounding Sera Khandro as a sign that others perceived her as someone who was transgressing social norms. We can read the many instances in which Sera Khandro presents herself as the butt of others' gossip as a sort of public opinion barometer highlighting the moments when she least complied with others' expectations. This interpretation mirrors a prevalent theory of gossip as a form of social control that regulates behavior within a group.[72] But basing our interpretation of Sera Khandro's writing on the theory of gossip as a form of group boundary maintenance leaves an important question unanswered: why would Sera Khandro have mentioned negative talk about herself so often in her life narrative, even suggesting that she was "a contentious woman" (*gyod mo*) in danger of making monks "notorious" (*grags pa*) if they associated with her? How would repeating others' derisive comments serve her interests, contributing positively to her legacy? With this in mind, we will now listen to how Sera Khandro describes her interactions with monks, and how gossip and badmouthing factored into these dynamics.

Kyitrül and His Sister

In her autobiography Sera Khandro writes that when she was eighteen years old, after Gara Terchen's funeral in 1910, she went to see a lama named Kyilung Tukchok Dorjé, or Kyitrül for short. Kyitrül was a celibate monk, unlike Gara Terchen, without a consort the likes of Yakza for her to contend with. Even so, her visit ran into trouble:

> Then, I went to stay with Kyitrül for a few days. When I told him all about my happy and sad circumstances, he said, "Now don't go anywhere—live here at my place and you won't have to think about [finding] food and clothes."
>
> When I thought I would stay there for a while, the Trülku's sister had negative thoughts and said, "Your actions are unacceptable. I don't know what our Trülku will consider. In his last life, Kyilung Tukchok Dorjé was a Tantric adept."[73] Also saying other negative words to me, she demoralized me.
>
> I replied, "Why do you think like this? It is certain that the Trülku will not take me as a wife. He is old, and moreover, he is extremely strict re-

garding his monastic behavior. Since we know this, why do you have wrong views [about us]?"

Even though I said this, still she didn't believe me and constantly mentioned many unnecessary things to both the Trülku and me. Hence, one day, because an old woman had died in Rizap, the Trülku went there. I secretly left and went to Kharnang Gapma, where I stayed for a few months near Gara Lochö and Garwa So.

One day a vision arose in which I arrived at the feast assembly of the *ḍākinīs* of the Three Bodies. Although it seemed as if I had a vision like this, I didn't have the capacity to discern [what it was]. All the channels in my body were numb, and it was as if my mind had suddenly become dark. I asked someone who said she was Dorjé Zungma, "Although I have come to the *ḍākinīs*' feast assembly since I was young, I have never experienced anything like this before. My body is uncomfortable, and it is as if my mind is shrouded in darkness—what caused this?"

She answered, "Since you are of a Treasure lineage, the time has come that you need to rely on a method consort. It is important to place a noble man [on the path of] ripening and liberation and to rely on him as a consort. Because your channel elements are disturbed, likewise your perception is also disturbed."

Again I said,

> In this area of Golok, eastern Tibet, it seems that [men] are of poor ancestry with a ghostly pallor. They are ash-colored, without food or clothes, and have rude, thornlike personalities. Thinking that adhering to them would not bring the perfect realization of liberation via skillful means, I let it go. Although a man of good lineage is like a winter flower, some have already gone under others' sway, some hesitated because of the Vinaya precepts, and since some were rich, they seemed not to want me because I was poor. Now, whatever you say, the need for a consort does not arise in me. Although there are method consorts superior to those who possess the secret pith instructions of the quick path on whom I could rely to bring me to actually realize the true primordial wisdom in which lust is naturally liberated, I have no ability to understand [who they are] and to attain them. If I meet with a man who is an unsuitable receptacle, it will be seen as a perversion of the path of Mantra and will certainly be the cause for myself and others to go to the lower realms. Hence, I think I will make a pledge to live alone.

When I said this, she responded,

Enchanting woman who desires desirelessness—
associate with a method consort and
the primordial wisdom of great bliss will manifest.

Through your pure karma and prayers, you are empowered in
Treasures.
If auspicious connections do not arise, benefiting oneself and others
will be difficult.
If method, insight, prayers, and the right time come together,
abandon lazy people and those who save face.
You must be careful regarding finding a way for the auspicious con-
nections to arise.

Since you are not one who can live alone,
energize all men with bliss and
show those with desire the desireless clear light.
Find a way to lead them to the ground of union.
By this, the two benefits will arise, *yoginī*.

Although primordial wisdom free from desire manifests in you,
if you don't separate from a noble consort,
having excellently attained stability in progressing [on the path],
the knots at the wheels of the five centers will loosen.

All appearances will arise as the *cakra*s with letters.[74]
In this life you will attain the awareness body of union.
This is the Dharma of great *yogi*s of Mantra.
There is nothing more profound than this quick path.
Seal it deep in your heart.
Show this path to fortunate ones.
It is certain that they will attain the unified form of no more
learning.[75]
Keep it secret from those who are unsuitable receptacles.

Don't even show it to the wind—
this is the chariot [leading] to wandering in the lower realms.

Your domain is marvelous.
It is certain that whomever you connect with, it will be meaningful.

I have elucidated the other prophecies about consorts that she spoke in my Treasure scriptures.

Then Kyitrül came to beg for alms for a few days. On the way, he stopped to drink tea at the home of a mother named Taza Drönpo and her child. Because he sent a messenger to summon me there, I went along with the messenger to see him. When I asked him how he was, the Trülku said, "Why did you secretly run off when I wasn't there?"

I answered, "Sir, wherever I go, I offend everyone and become a basis for their wrong views. That is the reason I didn't stay."

He added, "If that is so, since I don't know if we two will meet again and again, wherever you go, you need to be careful about rivers, enemies, and dogs. In particular, if you want to go to [Anyé] Machen, it is not okay unless you go with a fortunate friend. Since I have heard that it is difficult to free oneself from the mouths of jackals and so forth, there is a risk that tragedies could happen." He gave me a protection cord and commitment substances along with five Chinese silver coins (*yan cha*) for provisions on the road, and then he returned home.[76]

Contention seems to have followed Sera Khandro everywhere—when she befriended noncelibate Treasure revealers like Drimé Özer and Gara Terchen, their consorts were nonplussed by her, and when she befriended celibate monks like Kyitrül, she fared little better. But the *ḍākinī* Dorjé Zungma's advice lent some degree of credence to Kyitrül's sister's concerns, for the *ḍākinī*'s diagnosis did not mince words about the antidote Sera Khandro needed—a good man with whom she could experience the primordial wisdom of great bliss. In response, Sera Khandro did not refute the *ḍākinī*'s advice, but rather bemoaned the difficulty of finding the right man in the rough terrain of Golok, one who would not reject her because of his celibacy vows or her poverty. She then complained to Kyitrül not of the impropriety of a young noncelibate woman living with a celibate monk, but of the public scorn such cohabitation attracted. Kyitrül's caring parting advice signals the many dangers Sera Khandro faced on her own in Golok. In addition to running afoul of social codes, she risked encountering bandits on the road, hazardous river crossings, and ferocious Tibetan mastiff dogs, which still lick their chops in wait for unsuspecting trespassers today.

Rejecting Gara Gyeltsen

Some good men, as rare as "winter flowers," were suitable to be Sera Khandro's consort, but that did not mean that any monk who styled himself as such could have access to her. She emphasizes in multiple passages that she was not in the habit of breaking monks' vows, no matter who accused her of that, and could not be convinced to do so by anyone. In one such passage she narrates that when she was twenty-five years old, unhappily living as Gyelsé's spouse and caring for their young daughter at the same time as she was revealing Treasures,

> One day a man named Gara Gyeltsen came and said again and again, "Since I have received permission from Gyelsé, we need to have a physical relationship."
>
> I thought that it seemed as if his mind had been possessed by demons. I said many times that from whichever of the two [religious or worldly] perspectives, according to completely pure morality one must amass the accumulations [of merit and wisdom] by means of the six perfections, including generosity and so forth, and that it was unacceptable to waste a human body endowed with the freedoms.[77] But because passionate attachment (*chags sred*) had arisen in his mind stream, he ignored the significance of my words. He said many things that undermined cause and effect and related to mistaken behavior.
>
> I felt extremely depressed and saddened about people's attitude in the degenerate era. I said the following:
>
> Padmaṣambhava, refuge and protector of the world,
> *Ḍākki* Tsogyel of the changeless dimension, think of me!
> Look upon this vagabond Dewé Dorjé with compassion!
> Bestow blessings that will dispel negative conditions and obstacles!
>
> Listen, you who are losing the Sūtric teachings on physical
> discipline,
> send this thought from your mind!
> Examine your body, speech, and mind:
>
> On the outside, your attire is that of a monk's three robes.
> On the inside, you have great lustful desire equal to that of a bird.[78]

The thoughts in your mind are like those of a petty thief or a bandit.
At all times, you consume negative offerings.[79]
I don't desire someone like you with a negative body.

Even though I am an ordinary person with an inferior female body (*skye lus dman pa*),
If you look at my face, I am of a beautiful *ḍākinī* heritage.
Although I appear like a woman (*bud med*) with childish intellect,
my mind sees the essence of the unborn Three Bodies.
Although I labor as a householder,
I do not need to separate from the primordial wisdom of equality.
As I have mastered the ten winds,
everything that appears is the nature of great bliss,
and is liberated in the expanse of evenly extensive primordial wisdom.

I don't need somebody with a body like yours.
I won't make myself miserable in both this and the next life.
You, imprudent one, consider this well:
don't exchange your body endowed with a purpose for one with little purpose.

When the fruits of karma undeceivingly ripen,
you will be one who has done worthless things like this.
Now, consider this meaning.

Having said this, I was freed from obstacles.

Then, that year in the tenth month the elements of my body were extremely disturbed and I became insufferably ill. On the basis of this and some other factors, I thought, if only I could separate from this body and mind! Just then the terrifying coemergent woman (*mi mo*) who had followed me since my childhood appeared, holding a knife in her right hand and a red noose radiating light in her left.

She said:

Ha ha he he,[80] from the time you were young until now, I have lovingly raised you as if you were my only child. Now, on the basis of one small

> situation, you abandon your altruistic intention to become enlightened in order to benefit others. What is the meaning of your putting forth this selfish mental confusion?[81]

Sera Khandro's response to the wayward monk is strong and uncompromising: she may be a householder, but behind her humble countenance lies the insight of a wisdom *ḍākinī*. She may be an inferior woman, but no permission from her partner Gyelsé trumps her power to decide for herself who is and is not a worthy consort. And yet, the uncompromising boundary Sera Khandro set between proper ethical behavior for celibate and noncelibate practitioners is not without ambiguity, for the consequence of clearing away this "obstacle" was illness and a terrifying *ḍākinī* apparition threatening to stab her. In the conversation that ensues, Sera Khandro responds to the *ḍākinī*'s attack with a lament about the difficulties of being a lowly woman tied to a husband in a world where disciples view women as inferior to men, leaving them with little prospect of actualizing the *ḍākinī*s' commands. In response, the terrifying woman gives Sera Khandro an elaborate vote of confidence through prophesying the many disciples, consorts, and Treasures that will come to her. We could read this encounter with the perverse monk and the illness that then befalls Sera Khandro as two proximate yet unrelated autobiographical vignettes. However, given the connection that appears repeatedly elsewhere in her autobiography between eschewing prophesied male consorts and becoming physically ill, we may also read her sudden malady as the *ḍākinī*s' reprimand for insisting on the supremacy of the monk's monastic vows over her own *ḍākinī* imperatives.

Gotrül Rinpoché and Tibir Tuktsa Trülku

Similar ambiguities regarding the relative virtue of celibacy and sexuality arise in the close relationship Sera Khandro had with Gotrül Rinpoché, the monastic hierarch from Pelyül Dartang Monastery in Golok. As seen in the previous chapter, Sera Khandro describes her meetings with Gotrül Rinpoché with the utmost care, emphasizing her reticence to approach the lama in every instance. She writes that when she met him for the first time at the age of twenty-three, "since I had an inferior female body, I thought that others would have wrong views about the *trülku*."[82] Later, she prefaces her description of a visit by explaining that "Since I had an inferior female body (*skye lus dman pa*), I didn't dare go to see him, fearing that others would see, hear, and be suspicious. Instead I went to circumambulate the pile of stones [with prayers carved in them] and the prayer wheel house."[83] Sera Khandro writes that she received a letter from Gotrül Rinpoché shortly after she turned twenty-five. Because she had grown increasingly ill, another lama intuited that she should go to Pelyül Monastery to visit Gotrül because he could dispel her obstacles. Here is her description of the ensuing visit:

> Then, gradually we arrived at Pelyül Monastery. I thought that I didn't know Gotrül well, so it would be okay if I didn't go to see him. We settled in a house above the monastery.
>
> My disciples Palden Gyatso and Jikmé Chömpel both arrived and said, "The Trülku has summoned you, so you better come quickly."
>
> I replied, "Aside from just meeting Gotrül in the past, I don't know him very well. Moreover, it is not appropriate for me to go, for he will become notorious for gossip about women (*mo kha grags yong*)."
>
> They replied, "No matter what others say, let them say it. We are going."
>
> I responded,
>
>> I won't go. Why should I? I won't wander around a monastery without a purpose like a dog or a beggar. If gossip about women affects him, since he is a sacred object, it will be the cause of a great fault. Otherwise, for me, the best would be uniting with him in the ultimate sphere. Mediocre would be if we form a relationship. The worst would be if just gossip about women affects him. Serving as a catalyst for attaining the result of supreme accomplishment is the capacity of the class of *ḍākinīs*. Nevertheless, don't tell even a hint of this to anyone. These are the secret words of a traveler about to depart.
>
> Saying this, I fell asleep. They couldn't do anything and returned home.[84]

Sera Khandro's words may have been secret, but she spoke and then wrote them to a community of her disciples, suggesting that indeed she did have business that was worthy of Gotrül's attention. She writes that a few days later,

> Again on the twelfth, an attendant of Gotrül's who was angry and had a foul mouth named Ösel came to me. I didn't utter a word. Saying, "I came to summon you, so let's go," he grabbed my shoulder. Like a small bird carried away by a hawk, I was helpless and had to go. Even though I was greatly disappointed, there was nothing to be done.

Then, gradually, when I met Gotrül Rinpoché I remembered karmic propensities from my previous lifetime and the residue of former prayers awakened. It was as if his mind and mine became of one taste. When this happened, I sat there without saying anything.

Gotrül Rinpoché said,

> What is the meaning of your not thinking expansively about benefiting teachings and beings, growing weary of the misconceptions of your disciples, and instead concentrating on going to the buddhafields? I am praying again and again that in general you will uphold the Buddha's teachings, in particular the profound Treasures of Gara Terchen Rinpoché, and specifically your remaining disciples in the eastern and southern parts of eastern Tibet—not weakening the armor of your aspirations and vows, may your lotus feet remain on the vajra throne for one hundred eons! You know my hope is without deceit. If you don't act accordingly, since we are vajra siblings in Guru Padma's lineage, then you are not paying attention to our Dharma commitment vows.

He gave me an auspicious silk scarf, a silver ring inlaid with an expensive, high-quality piece of coral, and in particular a vajra and bell as supports for secret commitment vows. On account of this, although various uncertain signs arose, such as all the large channels in my illusory body vibrating with fluttering and trembling movements and a tapping like the sound of a horse's tail swishing, I didn't pay attention to them. As if he knew [what was happening in my body], in the state of the divine pride of glorious Hayagrīva, he resided in the realization of the great bliss of awareness and emptiness.

Because of my sickness, for a long time I could clearly intuit what was in other people's mind streams. Based on this, as soon as he visualized something, I visualized [myself as] the insight body [i.e., the female consort] of that deity. Having invoked the sixteen goddesses of the five root bodhisattvas, I made offerings to the self-emergent and spontaneously present heroes and *ḍākinīs* in the palace of the completely pure five elements. Satisfied with the taste of bliss and emptiness, the minds of the teacher and disciple became inseparable, of one taste, and reveled in nondual space and primordial wisdom. As soon as that happened, all the previous visualizations disappeared into the ultimate sphere like a dream when one wakes from sleep.[85]

Sera Khandro defers culpability for approaching Gotrül Rinpoché at Pelyül Monastery, for she was powerless "like a small bird carried away by a hawk," and "greatly disappointed" by her eventual appearance in front of the great lama. After this reticent opening, which invites us to read it as hyperbole, her description of their pivotal meeting is highly visionary and symbolic, without concrete detail. Nevertheless, the implication is strong that Gotrül cured Sera Khandro's ailments by means that threatened to bring both gossip and notoriety upon him.

If the exact nature of the exchange between Gotrül and Sera Khandro is euphemistic, his command that she should "sustain the longevity" of another monastic hierarch was not. Soon after Sera Khandro's visit to Gotrül Rinpoché, he requested her to serve as a consort to a monk she didn't know named Tibir Tuktsa Trülku. Sera Khandro narrates that when she was twenty-six, during the turbulent decade that she was living with Gyelsé at Benak,

> At that time, Tibir Tuktsa Trülku along with a few of his attendants was doing a retreat in the area. Gotrül said to me, "Now since you have the auspicious connections to be able to dispel the obstacles to Titrül's longevity, please don't err in finding the best possible way to do this. He is dressed as a monk—last year he requested full ordination vows from Dodrup Rinpoché. The astrological signs were extremely disturbed. In particular, the prophecies of Dzokchen Rinpoché and many other great masters proclaim that for the sake of sustaining his longevity, he needs to have a secret liaison with one with the heritage of an insight lady. Not only that, even though he is also a Treasure revealer, since he is the abbot of a big monastery, he doesn't behave as a *ngakpa* but as a venerable monk engaged only in meditation practice. Because there is no one better than you to sustain his longevity, don't err in doing this."
>
> Again I said, "If he is an authentic Treasure revealer, why does he need to be a hypocrite? The abbot of Orgyen Minling Monastery is of course very famous for being a Treasure revealer. Hence, I'm not sure if it is certain that if one is not a monk, one cannot be the abbot of a monastery. I will not be his method for dispelling obstacles to his longevity. For one thing, I am committed to someone.[86] Additionally, because stealing the vows of a monastic is the cause for a great offense, I certainly will not do that."
>
> Gotrül replied, "Why do you have to be so narrow minded about your body? You have mastered the pith instructions on the channels, vital nuclei, and wind, and you do not engage in perverse behavior. Moreover, aside from acting for the benefit of another person, if you are without any selfishness and negative thoughts, how could it be an offense? Since I can

certainly decide on behalf of Gyelsé, from his point of view, you will not be affected by defilement. I will take responsibility for that. Now if you don't act skillfully, it is certain that Titrül will not live beyond thirty-eight or thirty-nine years old."

I responded, "Even if Gyelsé agrees, more important than him, I have an extraordinary root consort [Drimé Özer], and without his agreement I will not embark upon an important undertaking. Is it okay if I help him by just reciting a feast offering? Even if it isn't okay, I can't do anything about it—I will not abide by public and private commitment vows."

He said, "Now go together with one of my monks to see Titrül, and it will be meaningful for both of you."

Then I went according to his order.[87]

Through passages such as this one, Sera Khandro presents herself as both stridently opposed to "stealing the vows of a monk" and widely renowned as a virtuoso consort. The force of her refusal to engage with this hypocritical monastic abbot parading as celibate but secretly seeking a liaison is mitigated by her ultimate compliance with Gotrül's request. In passages such as this, Sera Khandro characteristically leaves ambiguous whether she perceived herself as an agent modestly deferring Gotrül's acknowledgment of her supremacy as an insight lady unparalleled in sustaining lamas' longevity or as an object of Gotrül's grand design, dispatched from one lama to the next.

Also ambiguous in Sera Khandro's writing is the line between meditative visualization and physical sexuality, as is evident in her description of becoming pregnant with her third child (second living child) in 1918:

Then on the tenth day of the twelfth month, Gyelsé and his brother, myself and my child, and some of our monk disciples such as Tupzang opened the *Rindzin Düpa Maṇḍala, The Embodiment of the Awareness Holders Maṇḍala*. When we were performing the feast offering and arrived at the invocation, my perception transformed and I resided in a state without conceptual elaboration or fixation [in which I saw] a hero who was white with a rosy complexion. His naked body was adorned with the six bone ornaments and a handsome head ornament made of five dry skulls. White, red, and blue silk ribbons hung down from it, and he wore a lower garment made of tiger skin. The experience of the primordial wisdom of great bliss blazed forth in

> him. His hair was in a topknot, with the remainder hanging loosely down his back. He had one face, and his two hands performed the seal of reveling in blissful union. He came before me and he acted as my hero who arouses the primordial wisdom of bliss and emptiness. He transformed into a "*haṃ*" letter and disappeared into the crown of my head. As soon as this happened, my body was uncomfortable as if I had conceived a child.[88]

A month later, the twenty-six-year-old Sera Khandro heard that Gotrül Rinpoché was becoming increasingly ill and returned to visit him at Pelyül Monastery. She writes that during their conversation, Gotrül told her, "As I have said before, I think the son that you have [conceived] is my consciousness (*rnam shes*). Otherwise, he is a noble exalted one."[89] Though not necessarily the same as a claim to biological fatherhood, Gotrül's recognition of Sera Khandro's fetus as his "before-death reincarnation" (*ma 'das sprul sku*) reinforces a somatic dimension of their relationship. After Sera Khandro returned home to Benak, Gotrül's illness worsened. His monastic disciples suggested that he summon her again to help cure him, but Gotrül replied to them,

> Because the *ḍākinī* is growing increasingly sick [i.e., pregnant], she cannot come here. Even if she could come, she is the one about whom you all had wrong views before. Like the proverb, "If a person is facing hardship, he will even prostrate to a dog," you don't need to tell her to come since the stain of broken commitment vows will harm her.[90]

Indeed, a beautiful young consort and religious visionary appearing at a monastery to visit a monastic hierarch while pregnant with a son who was his "consciousness" appears likely to inspire some talk. Sera Khandro did not return to see Gotrül, and he died the following month in the late winter of 1919, leaving her without his support in Gyelsé's household.

Suspicions Around Sotrül Rinpoché at Sera Monastery

As Sera Khandro aged, her reputation as a legitimate Dharma heir of Düjom Lingpa and Drimé Özer as well as a revealer of her own Treasures solidified, especially after Drimé Özer's death. Yet her enhanced stature did not stop her from being a controversial figure near monasteries and monks. The very first recollection Sera Khandro writes about her years at Sera Monastery after Drimé Özer's death is that in 1924, when Sotrül Natsok Rangdröl brought her to live at Sera,

> At that time even though Sotrül said that I needed to position my camping area a bit close to his, everyone from inside and out took this the wrong way, so I didn't do it quite like that. Because of this, I wondered if perhaps this was a place I wasn't meant to stay for very long.[91]

A few months later, while Sera Khandro and Sotrül Rinpoché were building a reliquary in honor of Drimé Özer and performing the requisite consecration rituals at Sera Monastery, again, she noted,

> At that time the local people were offended by me. Some said, "The central Tibetan woman is Sotrül's consort (*gzungs ma*)." Others said, "Because the Trülku is getting older, it seems she won't stay here." Still others said, "Since she is a contentious woman (*gyod mo*), she will harm all of us."[92]

Sotrül Rinpoché was one of the most important incarnate lamas of Sera Monastery and also a major sponsor and lineage holder of Düjom Lingpa's lineage, as well as a member of the ruling Washül family of Serta. His support provided Sera Khandro and her two children with food, shelter, and encouragement to teach the Dharma after Drimé Özer's other consort(s) expelled her from Dartsang. He figures prominently especially in the latter part of her autobiography, but she makes no clear indication that they had a consort relationship. Interestingly, the current incarnation of Sotrül Rinpoché, who was enthroned at Sera Monastery in 1983, Trülku Pema Lodoe (b. 1964), told me that old people who lived near Sera Monastery during the 1980s remembered her as Sotrül Rinpoché's "secret consort" (*gsang grogs*).[93] This oral history suggests that in the vicinity of Sera, over time Sera Khandro's contentious status as a potential Tantric consort of Sotrül Rinpoché transformed along with her increasing prominence into a positive aspect of her reputation.

Two Apparitional Monks Come Calling

When Sera Khandro was thirty-six years old and actively traveling around Golok and upper Kham giving teachings, she received signs that there was a Treasure she needed to reveal. However, she writes that because she didn't have a consort, she had to let it go. Immediately after this,

> That night in a dream, two monks[94] traveling as mendicants, one big and one small, arrived at my place after sunset.
>
> They said, "How are you, lady?"
>
> I answered, "I'm fine. Are you two tired?"
>
> The big monk replied, "Although we are not tired, for a long distance we didn't find much to eat on the road. Nevertheless, we have come before you because we need to receive a Dharma teaching. Hence, we both offer our bodies to you. We need you to please first give us food to fill us and later Dharma to liberate us."
>
> I said, "If you two stay only on a remote mountain practicing completely pure Dharma, I can give you as much food and clothing as possible. Otherwise, although you give me your bodies, you don't need to be my servants; you may practice assiduously on a remote mountain."
>
> The monk answered, "The meaning of our offering our bodies to you is not to find a way to be your servant or to reside like a sage in rock caverns and mountain slopes! Because you are a Treasure revealer, for the purpose of being your consorts, we thought we would stay with you."
>
> Feeling great fear, I said, "Precious Lama think of me! Kind One, think of me!"
>
> The big monk said over and over again, "Although you don't desire me, at the very least you need to take this small monk under your care."
>
> I responded by saying, "I am not even a Treasure revealer. I don't need a consort. In the past, I never had disciples with deteriorated vows like you two, and still now I won't look after you. You two, wherever you go, go away. Don't stay in this land. Even if I have to kill you both, I won't consider engaging with you."
>
> Again, he said, "I know whether or not you are a Treasure revealer. Look in your prophetic registry—among your five main method consorts, one is this small monk. If you don't rely on him as a consort, you won't be able to decipher your Treasures as well, so consider this."
>
> I became a bit confused and asked, "What land are you two from?"
>
> He replied, "We are from the Nyak Valley.[95] The small monk's name is X.[96] Since Guru Padma's prophecies are undeceiving, in time his prayers will come together."

I answered, "Although the Guru's prophecies are undeceiving, because I am of bad ancestry, I cannot find a way to act in accordance with the prophecies. For one thing, since I have an inferior female body (*skye lus dman pa*), even though I have met doctrine holders and method consorts, I don't dare recognize them as such. For another, the distinguishing features of a great bodhisattva who has attained an awareness body are that his physical body has entered into [the path of] Mantra, that he has exerted himself in the unsurpassed practice, and, not needing to depend upon gradually traversing the grounds and paths, that he relied upon the path of enhancement and the union of skillful means and liberation. So as not to displease him, I guard my commitment vows like the eyes in my forehead. Until I obtain permission from this consort [i.e., Drimé Özer], even if it accords with my Treasure prophecy, my mind is decided and I don't think about associating with a single consort. And despite the fact that I am not a Treasure revealer, I will certainly act without [maintaining separate] public and private commitment vows. So, by all means, you two go home."

Then the bigger mendicant dissolved into the smaller one and with both of their bodies invisible, their voices spoke the following:

Young ravishing beauty,
irresistible to look at, one with the body of supreme great bliss,
one who speaks the truth, whose mind has abandoned deception,
greatly loving, powerful *ḍākkī*, I praise you.`

[On] the excellent path that brings buddhahood in one lifetime
and simultaneously accomplishes the two benefits [of self and
    other], the vajradharahood,
may we assemble together without a moment's separation and
assist [each other] in generating bliss and emptiness together.

Having said this, they transformed into red light and disappeared in the direction of the sunset.

Then an old woman came and asked, "Did you know those two monks?"

I replied, "Although I don't know them, they spoke about various strange things. I wonder what that was about?"

She answered, "The small monk was sent to you by your method consort, [named] Akṣara. The big monk is known as Segyel. Hence, since there are some obstacles between method and insight [male and female consorts], you need to be careful." As soon as she said this, I awoke from sleep.[97]

Sera Khandro's adamant rejection may initially seem like the only moral response to the monks' provocative advance, but this is not the only way to interpret their actions. The monks' claim that one of them had been prophesied by Padmasambhava to be a consort necessary for Sera Khandro to decode her Treasure revelations, coupled with the old woman's validation of the monks' unsullied credentials, implies that the intentions behind the solicitation were genuine. Once again, Sera Khandro's refusal to engage with monks has the heuristic value of upholding the sacrality of monastic celibacy vows while defending her virtue. Yet the import of this dream is far from clear, for the ephemeral monks' parting verses and the *ḍākinī*'s warning of obscurations between male and female consorts suggest that Sera Khandro chose the safer, but less efficacious path when she rejected the monks.

Ḍākinīs Overrule the Court of Public Opinion

The path of a noncelibate Treasure revealer like Sera Khandro was also complicated by the fact that others in her social and religious milieu appear to have had difficulty distinguishing between religiously sanctioned consort relationships and the impure sexual relations of lay householders. Though Düjom Rinpoché's commentary on *Ascertaining the Three Vows* affirms that spiritually advanced monks can engage in consort practices, Sera Khandro's writings are as concerned with social sanction as they are with doctrinal precedent. We hear this through the nun Tsüldrön's horror at Sera Khandro's noncelibate status, Sera Khandro's repeated mentions of the gossip that swirled around her each time she got anywhere near a celibate monk, and her defiant refusals to engage in sexual interactions with monks regardless of their realization level. We might conclude from these elements of her writing that according to her perception, public opinion in early twentieth-century eastern Tibet mandated strictly separate spheres between celibate and noncelibate religious specialists. Her role, then, was to avoid celibate monastics and reject their advances.

Nevertheless, the authoritative voices in her auto/biographical writings consistently overruled this interpretation of Vajrayāna ethics, privileging the expedient means of sexuality over the virtue of celibacy. Sera Khandro never indicates anything but the strongest respect for celibate monastics of both sexes, some of whom were her teachers and disciples. But at times she also indicates that celibacy was not always the most efficacious choice. For example, toward the end of her autobiography she recounts being invited to perform rituals at the deathbed of the leader of Dzongda named Sogyé, when she was forty years old in 1932. While there performing transference of consciousness (*'pho ba*) rites, she encountered monks from the nearby Nyabgé Monastery as well as the abbot, who were also conducting rituals for the leader. She writes,

> All of them, headed by the incarnate lama himself, came to receive a blessing from me. A bit of good and bad delusory appearances arose at that time, and I thought I should recite a "life summoning" [liturgy for the incarnate lama]. But since he followed the Vinaya precepts and was a new school adherent, and since I was a nonsensical wild woman, out of concern that faults brought on by other circumstances and by people seeing, hearing, and becoming suspicious would arise, I didn't have a way to benefit his longevity.[98]

In this case, Sera Khandro seems to say, the incarnate lama's commitment to the monastic code of discipline as well as concerns about others' perceptions caused him to miss the opportunity she could have provided to lengthen his life span. This hint written in Sera Khandro's voice is reinforced exponentially by *ḍākinīs*' prophecies correcting her discretions. After all, a *ḍākinī* exhorted Sera Khandro that she was "not one who can live alone"; instead her path was to benefit both herself and others by acting to "Energize all men with bliss and / Show those with desire the desireless clear light."[99]

Returning to the question why Sera Khandro would have mentioned so many contemptuous comments about herself and her involvements with celibate monks, I suggest that we can read this as more than a barometer of public opinion reflecting the values of her community: it was also a form of reputation management.[100] By acknowledging and repeating aspects of the negative talk that surrounded her, Sera Khandro regained control of the storyline by presenting her own version of the scenarios that held the greatest potential to cause scandal. She rechanneled the gossip, suspicion, and negative talk that accompanied her around monks and monasteries primarily through ventriloquizing *ḍākinīs*' directives.

With backup fresh from the *ḍākinīs*' breath, she transformed the meaning of others' talk about her alleged infractions to affirmations of her spiritual attainment. Just as her many lamentations about being an inferior woman prompted others to extol her superiority, acknowledging her many detractors' worst interpretations of her behavior afforded her the space to refute them in writing. The success of her efforts to define the true version of her life story can be measured by the fact that some of Sera Khandro's and her supporters' perspectives have become part of the permanent record in Tibetan texts and in social memory retained by people in Golok generations after her death.

Not Alone: Gara Terchen's Disgrace

Certain aspects of the scandal that Sera Khandro reports verging upon regularly seem specific to being female: jealous female consorts expelled her, irate nuns chastised her, monks demanded sexual services from her, and the list goes on. However, she was not the only one who had to play defense in an autobiography for transgressing boundaries between celibate and noncelibate interpretations of ideal Vajrayāna conduct: there is some family history of such upsets, as demonstrated by Gara Terchen's autobiography. As noted in the previous chapter, the terse and confident style of Gara Terchen's autobiographical writing largely lacks the interactive dialogue and ready self-deprecation in Sera Khandro's writing. Yet there is one exception: his account of the birth of his first son, which parallels Sera Khandro's intense and dialogical expressiveness. This son was Gara Gyelsé Pema Namgyel, who would later become Sera Khandro's life partner. Apparently Gara Gyelsé was a source of contention for his father as well as for Sera Khandro, but for different reasons. Gara Terchen begins his account of Gyelsé's birth by describing this *ḍākinī* prophecy that appeared to him when he was twenty-three, in about 1880, and had lived as a celibate monk since childhood:

> At that time, a blue *ḍākinī* with a smiling face appeared. In order to clearly explain the symbols [associated with my Treasures], she gave me prophecies about good and bad things and told me that I needed to rely on the method of a "cipher consort" (*lde mig phyag rgya*). In accordance with this,

> in the village there was a nun named Garza who came from a family who worked for the Garwa family. She was the same age as I, and her [full] name was Ngak Chödrön. On account of relying on her as a consort, I found the prophetic guide that I needed to discover the *Khandro Sangdzö, Secret Treasury of the Ḍākinī*, at the supreme holy site Tashi Gomang, in which the *Rindzin Nyingtik, Heart Essence of the Awareness Holder*; *Wangchen Nyingtik, Heart Essence of the Mighty One*; *Khandro Nyingtik, Heart Essence of the Ḍākinī*; and the *Secret Treasury of the Ḍākinī* were also concealed.[101]

Initially Gara Terchen's comments focus on the fruitful revelation experiences that his union with Ngak Chödrön catalyzed. But hints that not everyone perceived his shift from celibate to noncelibate religious specialist in such a noble light seep into his narrative. He notes that a few years later, when he was twenty-five, he began building a new house, but villagers snickered about his conduct:

> Some old ladies and people from the village said, "Now Longyang [Gara Terchen] has a house up high. On the outside, he built a retreat house, but on the inside it is falling apart. Even though his house is high, since he is doing bad things with Ngak Chödrön, he will fall down to a low place. That family's monk lineage is bad, and the father, paternal uncle, and so forth do dirty jobs. *Ha ha*."[102]

The following year, things fell apart:

> My consort Ngak Chödrön had a son. The Peyak [alt. Benak] community had perverse views about this and slandered us. Negative talk buzzed around us, and it was as if we were expelled from the group of humans and thrown into the group of dogs. I wandered around performing village rites. Aside from Lama Tsampa Rinpoché and my nephew the holy lama Sonam Rabgyé, everyone high and low, famous and insignificant criticized me as much as they could. Some of my elder and younger brothers held a discussion about whether Ngak Chödrön and I should be separated, whether [she] should be killed, or whether Longyang [I] needed to be exiled to a distant land.[103]

Though Gara Terchen had been with Ngak Chödrön for two years when their first child was born, the fallout from his change in status seems to have caught up with him in earnest after their child was born. He records being ostracized by everyone:

> All the local people who had heard about it had perverse views [about us] and blamed us. Dissenting with my root lama Sangtrül Rinpoché, no one agreed with me and instead they all hated me as if I were an enemy, causing me to become exhausted and depressed. Praying steadfastly to the Great Venerable One from Oḍḍiyāna [Padmasambhava] and the *ḍākinīs* of the three realms diverted my mental consciousness, and for three days my perception of this world ceased. During this time, I arrived at the Unsurpassed Copper-Colored Glorious Mountain:
>
> *E ma ho*! How wonderful!
> Precious embodiment of the buddhas of the three times [past, present, future],
> Orgyen Dorjé Chang, I prostrate to you.
> A rain of people's perverse views and slander falls
> on me, this beggar monk of the degenerate era endowed with the eight worldly dharmas,
> named Pawo Lerap Dorjé.
> During my twenty-fifth year, in the male water horse year [1882],
> this beggar, despairing and exhausted,
> hides, lying alone in the crevasse of an isolated mountain.[104]

Padmasambhava consoled Gara Terchen, promising him that if he supplicated him earnestly, "You will always achieve your profound aspirations and will be reborn in your next life here in my presence."[105] Visionary and dream encounters with Padmasambhava, Yeshé Tsogyel, and other *ḍākinīs* reassured him many times over, predicting the ill consequences for his detractors, reinforcing his decision to heed their prophecies, and offering him Treasure teachings, just as they would do for Sera Khandro several decades later. Nevertheless, locals from the Benak area persisted in their hostility, insisting that the couple separate. On top of this, Gara Terchen indicates that Ngak Chödrön herself was not entirely committed to being his consort:

> At that time [in 1884 when he was twenty-seven], Ngak Chödrön also had befriended some young laymen and on account of obscurations to the lady

from the vajra [buddha] family, her son Pema Namgyel was also affected by the defilement of the seer Rāhu.[106]

Meanwhile, the Gara family's wrath persisted. Gara Terchen records,

> Soon after that time, Gara Rangdröl and Gara Rindzin visited [Sangtsang] Dradra Rinpoché, and Rangdröl said,
>
> > Longyang's behavior is extremely negative. It would be good if he and Ngak Chödrön separated. Otherwise, doesn't he need to be exiled to another land by himself? He doesn't perceive you as a lama. Doing and thinking all sorts of things, he pretends to be a Treasure revealer and an accomplished master, but in actuality he seems to have been possessed by King Dotsa.[107] He was expelled from the monastic community of the Peyak [alt. Benak] family. He then went to Trangnyibar to the Hor family's place and seems to have found a bit of wealth through speaking about his visions of gods and demons.
>
> After they said many things like this, he [Dradra Rinpoché] became enraged. Scolding them endlessly, he said, "I expel these commitment vow breakers from my land. They must be punished."
>
> That night, Gara Rangdröl died from planetary defilement.[108]

Though the entire community and even his own relatives were against him, Gara Terchen's lama maintained his support. Signs of the superiority of his view manifested in the form of the death of Gara Rangdröl as well as the affirmations of those enlightened beings who appeared to Gara Terchen in his visions. However, this did not signal a long and productive relationship between Gara Terchen and Ngak Chödrön, for one year later, when he was twenty-eight in 1885,

> I heard that my consort called Ngak Chödrön had befriended someone called Kyaka Chösung and that preparations for her to marry him had been made. I sent Ngak Seldrön[109] a message saying, "Why did you stray from your vajra words? I did not stray from them."
>
> I wrote her this in a letter:
>
> > Loved, loved, consort named Ngak,
> > relationship, relationship, for years and months we have had a
> > consort relationship.

> Attachment, attachment, having become attached to illusory
> appearances
> contrary, contrary, contrary to vajra commitment vows,
> seduced, seduced, a negative consort has seduced you.
> Experience, experience, you will certainly experience the suffering
> of hell.
> Spoken, spoken, these words have been spoken before.
> Yes, yes, [your] words are very deceptive, but
> certain, certain, for me, Padma's representative,
> harm, harm, even though you double-crossed me, I am unharmed.
> Profound, profound, the Great One from Oḍḍiyāna's prophecies,
> in time, time, the *ḍākinīs* will propagate them.

I wrote this in a letter and sent it.

At that time, the *ḍākinī* Dashelma said,

> Wonderful—great representative of the one from Oḍḍiyāna,
> you will benefit beings in five realms of disciples.
> Five consorts, eight doctrine holders, and
> a thousand disciples will gradually arise
> by means of your pure prayers.
> It is certain that you will bring good welfare and fortune
> to the teachings and sentient beings.
> Fortunate son, you don't need to be depressed.
> Saying this, she disappeared.[110]

The *ḍākinī* Dashelma's appearance the moment he received the news of Ngak Chödrön's betrayal, followed by additional sublime *ḍākinī* visions, all comforted and reassured him; some even acted as his consorts.

Gara Terchen's rendition of the Ngak Chödrön saga presages the pattern in Sera Khandro's autobiographical writing of suspicion of a licentious, rather than religious, affair between a monk and a Tantric consort, followed by social censure and visionary encouragement from *ḍākinīs* and bodhisattvas. His account demonstrates that the gossip and criticism that plagued Sera Khandro were not unique to women who were "neither nun nor laywoman," though they play a comparatively larger role in her autobiography. It appears that negative talk followed those who ventured into the interstices between celibate and noncelibate life, requiring them to provide incontrovertible evidence of authorization in order not to be viewed as guilty of breaking or causing others to break vows. The primary source of that evidence for Gara Terchen, as for Sera Khandro, was their root lamas and their direct visions of Padmasambhava and *ḍākinīs* in celestial buddhafields. Enlightened forces in Sera Khandro's and Gara Terchen's writings seem to have rooted consistently for auspicious connections over and above celibacy vows; this perhaps indicates that those who risked social censure out of religious motivations needed more backing than those who showed the external signs of virtue in the form of monastic robes and shaved heads. We see much the same pattern in Sera Khandro's biography of Drimé Özer, whose forays into celibate monasticism were met in short order with *ḍākinīs*' castigation.[111]

CONCLUSION: AGENT OR OBJECT?

Sera Khandro's portrayal of her life as a noncelibate religious specialist does not point to straightforward conclusions about the roles of women as objects or agents in Vajrayāna Buddhist practices involving sexuality. At times her word choices present harsh images of being dominated by others—like a stray dog being dispatched to Andzom Rinpoché, like a small bird carried away by a hawk when Gotrül sent her to Tibir Trülku. She presents what was perhaps the most important event in her life, her reunion with Drimé Özer and the spiritual realization it catalyzed, as a product of Gyelsé and Drimé Özer's decision to exchange rights over her entirely without her consent. Much of her resistance to powerful male lamas' plans to engage her sexual services ends in passive compliance; she loudly refuses monks' solicitations, but her bark has less bite when *ḍākinīs* imply that her rejections were mistaken. And her relationships with women were no less complicated. Being a Tantric consort, according to Sera Khandro's presentation, was less about communing with a circle of *yoginīs* than about avoiding their venom. From Akyongza's jealous refusal to allow her any access to Drimé Özer, to Yakza's wrath at Gara Terchen's summons, to her bitter rivalry for Gyelsé's favor with his mistress, Seldrön, other female consorts were more often sources of competition than camaraderie.

Even so, there is more to Sera Khandro's picture of life as a Tantric consort than exploitation. The vehemence with which she denied any intentional pursuit of consort relationships and the extent to which she insisted on refusing Gyelsé's decision to give her away to Drimé Özer suggest an alternative interpretation. Positioning herself as uninterested in consorting with men and dispassionate about whether she lived with her unpleasant spouse, Gyelsé, or the object of all her devotion, Drimé Özer, accentuated her virtue as a woman who made choices based on prophecy instead of passion. Obeying Padmasambhava and Yeshé Tsogyel's command was the highest good, not engaging in discursive decision making, which we might be tempted in the contemporary context to valorize as "agency," the ability to assert power and produce desired effects. Portraying herself as lacking this type of agency solidified the veracity of her claim to be a messenger of the *ḍākinīs*, serving as their mouthpiece without any creative additions or subtractions. With this in mind, Sera Khandro's writing about being hustled to consort with Andzom and Tibir is clearly meant to indicate more than her powerlessness, no matter how servile the metaphors she used for herself, for these prominent male lamas also promoted her reputation as a Treasure revealer and an "insight lady" unsurpassed in her capacity to sustain longevity. That she presented herself as forced against her will to visit these lamas needs to be interpreted in light of her concurrent claims to have benefited both physically and spiritually. Perhaps we can understand Sera Khandro's self-presentation as an abject victim as another way she emphasized her humility, not unlike the many instances in which she called attention to her lowly female body.

There is no reason to doubt that Sera Khandro really did experience discrimination, harassment, and suspicion in her career as a religious specialist for being a noncelibate female. Indeed, Tibetan lamas have told me that reading Sera Khandro's autobiography left them in tears over the many painful experiences, challenges, and sorrows she chronicled with such candor and intensity. But equally striking is her tale of transformation, the ways her narrative turns tough situations into affirmations of her potential. For just as Sera Khandro's critiques of her inferior female body invite others, primarily *ḍākinīs*, to extol her superiority, her revulsion against consort practices incites others to reiterate her authority to engage in them for her own gain. Her entire presentation of channel and wind practices maps them onto the female body, a bold but skillfully enacted change of subject endorsed by the mother *ḍākinī* herself, Yeshé Tsogyel. Never without a way to humble herself, Sera Khandro jests that the only revelations she can produce are children, but in so doing she reclaims the generative processes of sexual and textual production as special capacities of the female form. She may have "energized all men with bliss," but they returned the favor, curing her chronic arthritic illness and catalyzing her enlightenment. Sera Khandro's accounts of consort practices cast a pall on arguments that claim Buddhist Tantra is pro-woman or sex-positive, given the many indignities she suffered and the endless talk against her, but they simultaneously speak volumes about women's potential for liberation through Vajrayāna Buddhist methods.

5

LOVE BETWEEN METHOD AND INSIGHT

A haṃ. I am the supreme method, the great bliss Heruka.
You are the great mother of insight into the ultimate sphere of emptiness.
By the contemplation of engaging in nondual union,
in the immense buddhafield in which the three—appearances, sounds, and
    awareness—are purified,
the expanse of indivisible form and primordial wisdom,
may we attain the fully awakened youthful vase body of buddhahood
as Hayagrīva and Vajravārāhī in indestructible union.[1]

With his final breath, Drimé Özer spoke these words to Sera Khandro before he passed away into buddhahood, according to his biography. The image of Drimé Özer as the supreme method and Sera Khandro as the insight realizing emptiness, united inseparably in the form of the Tantric deities Hayagrīva and Vajravārāhī, embodies the Tantric Buddhist vision of complete buddhahood. The roots of this gendered two-in-one symbolism stem from Mahāyāna Buddhist conceptions of bodhisattva training involving a set of perfections, first six and later ten. Method (Skt. *upāya*, Tib. *thabs*) refers to the skillful means by which one seeks enlightenment for oneself and others, encapsulating the first five perfections:

FIG. 5.1 A Rendition of Hayagrīva and Vajravārāhī in union

RUBIN MUSEUM OF ART, NEW YORK F1996.10.1

generosity, morality, patience, discipline, and meditation. More generally, the supreme method is compassion (*karuṇā, snying rje*). The sixth perfection, insight (*prajñā, shes rab*), is the realization of emptiness (*śūnyatā, stong pa nyid*), or the realization that all people and phenomena do not exist as separate and permanent entities but rather are conditional, impermanent, and subject to change. Already in Mahāyāna scriptures such as the *Vimalakīrtinirdeśasūtra*, insight and method appear as a gendered dyad, mirroring their respective genders according to Sanskrit grammar: "Wisdom [i.e., insight] is the bodhisattva's mother, expedient means [i.e., method] his father."[2] Later Indian Tantric Buddhist scriptures that formed bedrocks of Tibetan Buddhism built upon this symbolism to depict the union of method and insight in the form of male and female deities in sexual union, called *yab yum*. Tibetan Buddhist scriptures are pervaded with this imagery that conveys wholeness as the conjoining of complementary

FIG. 5.2 Vajrasattva *yab yum*, with Samantabhadra and Samantabhadrī *yab yum* above

RUBIN MUSEUM OF ART, NEW YORK C2006.66.395

male and female principles. Beyond texts, sexual symbolism is impossible to miss in Buddhist temples throughout Tibet and the Himalayas, where temple walls and shrines are replete with scroll paintings and statues of deities in *yab yum* embrace, serving as visual insignia of the nondual union of male method and female insight.

Drimé Özer's final words as recalled by Sera Khandro invoke this rich symbolism to imagine their relationship as both the path to and the goal of complete buddhahood. We could read Sera Khandro's portrait of herself and Drimé Özer in his final moments as *yab* and *yum* in indestructible union as an impersonal modeling based on the Tantric principle of gender complementarity. But her six-hundred-plus folios of auto/biographical writings, including Drimé Özer's biography and her own autobiography, convey something far more intimate than formulaic applications of Vajrayāna Buddhist theology: her works are suffused with sentimental renditions of longing for, loving, and eventually losing Drimé Özer. Sera Khandro's depictions of her feelings are at once expressions of devotion typical of disciple-guru relationships and more than that, as compared to other such relationships represents in her works and those found in the writings of other Treasure revealers close to her, such as Düjom Lingpa and Gara Terchen. In particular, her portrayal of her intense affection for her guru, and his for her, manifests in the following forms: 1) the terms of endearment each uses for the other; 2) the heavy focus on both prophecy and personal affinity linking them; 3) a carefully emphasized opposition between lust and love; 4) exclusivity as *yab* and *yum* (male and female Tantric partners); 5) the mutuality and even equality (*mnyam pa*) that only they shared, according to Sera Khandro; 6) the power of their love to catalyze a joint spiritual enlightenment in which the basic unit was the *yab yum* couple instead of the individual; and 7) the power of their love to transcend death. The first part of this chapter presents a brief overview of the main languages of love in Tibet that exerted some degree of influence on Sera Khandro's writing; then the second part moves sequentially through all seven of the above points to listen to the ways she expressed the special nature of her relationship with Drimé Özer. Throughout, we will hear a specific locution she used for their connection: the two were bound by male and female Tantric commitment vows (*yab yum dam tshig*), sacred pledges preventing them from ever separating.

That Sera Khandro describes her primary *yab yum* relationship in strongly affective terms may not initially seem surprising given the pervasive symbolism of gender complementarity in Tantric Buddhism as well as the existence of Tantric practices involving sexuality. However, the truism that Tantra involves sex, literal or imagined, has not extended among its interpreters to suggest that it involves any sort of love between partners. Charlotte Vaudeville found Hindu and Buddhist Tantra utterly devoid of love symbolism: "Far from according any value to any human relationship, the Tantric *sādhaka* emphatically rejects all such forms of relationship, including human love in its psychological and social aspects."[3] Lee Siegel reiterated the point that "sacred sexuality is not necessarily 'sacred love.' Love plays no part in the *Tantras*."[4] The Austrian American Sanskritist cum Hindu monk Agehananda Bharati remarked to a community of American enthusiasts of Tantra, "most of you . . . believe that the sexual element in Tantra is somehow *nice* and *romantic* and lovely and full of nice, warm love-making. Nonsense. The sex of Tantra is hard-hitting, object-using, manipulative ritual without any consideration for the person involved."[5] In the context of Tibetan Buddhist Tantra, Janet Gyatso drew on extensive Tibetan materials to conclude that when couples engage in fulfillment yoga involving sexual union, "there is no talk of love, nor any celebration of the union of the sexes," for sexual union in this context is "not a sacralization of the love act."[6] As Gyatso rightly points out, unifying male and female elements was most often performed by a single person, not a couple, for both "male" and "female" elements reside within one individual, according to Tantric conceptions of the subtle body.

Love or no love between male and female sexual partners, the use of gender complementarity to symbolize transcendent wholeness is also not without critics. In particular, feminist theorists have demonstrated that theories of gender complementarity predicate hierarchy more readily than equality.[7] This is true whether the category of analysis is society, as in the case of the separate spheres ideology of the Victorian era, or an individual's psyche, as in Jung's theory of contrasexuality in which each person contains an other within of the opposite sex.[8] Scholars have also found evidence of hierarchical gender binarism within the symbolism of gender complementarity prevalent in Tantric Buddhism. José Cabezón has demonstrated that in some Tibetan works the gender-based symbolism of male method and female insight was not as egalitarian as it might seem, given that for Mahāyāna Buddhist identity the female pole, insight, was less important than the male pole, the skillful means of compassion.[9]

Adelheid Herrmann-Pfandt drew a similar conclusion through analyzing Tantric Buddhist iconography, suggesting that the prevalent posture of Tantric deities in sexual embrace privileges the masculine deity as dominant because he is larger and faces the viewer, while the female deity is smaller and gazes up toward the male in a subordinate position.[10] Likewise, Bernard Faure claims that "The gender equality of Tantric ritual works usually to the advantage of men," and that the female symbol insight is "utterly passive and inferior in status."[11]

If there is no love in Tantra, and if Tantric religious symbolism positing gender complementarity tends to reinforce women's subordination, what are we to make of Sera Khandro's highly sentimental rendition of her loving relationship with Drimé Özer, and of her claim that she found fulfillment in the form of spiritual liberation through their union? Must we interpret Sera Khandro as the exception that proves the rule of Tantric misogyny, an astute woman who may have gamed the system but didn't change its rules? Or do our categories of what constitute profane lust and sacred love, bondage and release, hierarchy and equality need further interrogation? What is the nature of the love (*brtse ba*) Sera Khandro charted between herself and Drimé Özer, and how did she position this sentiment vis-à-vis other shades of amorous attraction, such as lust (*'dod chags*), that the Buddhist path aims to eradicate? If her love-inflected vision of the sacred commitment between male and female Tantric partners (*yab yum dam tshig*) figures more prominently in her auto/biographical writings than in those of others, why, and from where did she derive this?

PART I: THE LANGUAGES OF LOVE IN TIBET

Before delving deeper into these questions, it is important to step back and consider the larger Tibetan literary context for Sera Khandro's sentimental rendition of her relationship with Drimé Özer. To begin with, there is no word in the Tibetan language that corresponds directly to the English word "emotion."[12] Given this, talk of love is readily lost in translation between the two languages. This is not to say that Sera Khandro and her contemporaries in early twentieth-century Tibet didn't feel things we might term emotions—love, sorrow, fear, joy, anger, and so forth—but that the meanings of these affective responses are culturally specific and contextually derived, not universal descriptions of internal states. In Catherine Lutz's words, "emotional experience is not precultural but pre-

eminently cultural."[13] Emotions do things in the world—they shape judgments, advance particular interests, and define situations in particular ways. Haiyan Lee asks of Chinese literature in the first half of the twentieth century "how the discourses of sentiment situated the individual in society, what kind of power relations they sought to undermine or reinforce, and what kind of community they endorsed and endeavored to realize."[14] We may explore similar ramifications of Sera Khandro's terms of endearment, considering the ways expressions of love positioned her within her communities, allowed her to participate in and resist intimate relationships with powerful men, and enabled her to represent herself for posterity. Although we cannot have unmediated access to Sera Khandro's most intimate feelings through the hundreds of folios of auto/biographical recollections she left behind, we can examine the semantic range of affection she expresses, the relative frequency of terms of endearment, the situations in which words expressing love arise, the metaphors and similes she uses to convey shades of love, and instances of physical reactions such as crying, trembling, fainting, smiling, hair standing on end, and so forth. Paying attention to these markers of sentiment and contextualizing them amid other relevant writings enables us to begin to envision what Barbara Rosenwein terms the "emotional community" in which Sera Khandro's auto/biographical works belong. By this Rosenwein means the "systems of feeling" in which historical persons operated, including what they defined as valuable or harmful to them, how they evaluated others' emotions, "the nature of the affective bonds between people that they recognize, and the modes of emotional expression that they expect, encourage, tolerate, and deplore."[15] She advocates starting the project of establishing the emotional community of an author by listing the emotion words, articulated by theoreticians, salient to that person's historical and temporal context as a way to avoid anachronism and provincialism.[16] With this in mind, three discourses on love that deserve mention before we delve into Sera Khandro's terms of endearment are Buddhist doctrinal conceptions of lust and love, Indian aesthetic theory, and secular eastern Tibetan love songs (*la gzhas, rogs 'then*).

Lust and Love in Buddhism

In Buddhist terms, lust is a poison in opposition to a universalized concept of compassionate love devoid of any hint of lust, which is the highest ideal. The three root poisons that entrap beings in an endless cycle of rebirth (*saṃsāra*) are delusion (*moha*, *gti mug*), hatred (*dveṣa*, *zhe sdang*), and lust (*rāga*, *'dod chags*).[17] By its definition, the Buddhist root poison of lust is closely related to craving (*tṛṣṇā*, *sred pa*), a term whose etymology suggests unquenchable thirst.[18] Thirst encapsulates the urge to quench three types of craving: for sensual pleasure; for possessions, power, and continued life; and to cease living and rid oneself of people and things. The three poisons form the root causes of entrapment in continual rebirth and are part of a longer list of negative mental factors or afflictions (Skt. *kleśa*, Tib. *nyon mongs*), which contains a series of what we might call "negative emotions," such as anger, pride, doubt, resentment, spite, jealousy, and so forth. Sera Khandro mentions these afflictions many times in her writing, exclusively casting all such things as worthless and to be abandoned by anyone on the Buddhist path. However, *kleśa* is not synonymous with contemporary English-language meanings of the term "emotion," for the list of afflictions also includes many things we would be unlikely to classify as an emotion, such as ignorance, forgetfulness, laziness, and distraction.[19]

There are other positive mental factors worthy of cultivation on the Buddhist path, some of which we might call positive emotions; primary among them is compassion (*karuṇā*, *snying rje*). The compassion heralded by Buddhist teachers and texts is an impartial love, a mental disposition wishing all beings to be freed from suffering. The paradigmatic Buddhist analogy for this is that one should love all beings as a child loves her mother, since all beings cycling through endless rebirths have been our mothers at one time or another. Compassionate love is idealized as a deep concern for others' well-being, but generalized to encompass all forms of life, unlike the more exclusive passionate attraction felt by lovers. That loving sexual relationships are an impediment to the pursuit of enlightenment is exemplified by the popular version of the Buddha's life story in which he abandons his royal wife, Yaśodharā, in favor of cultivating a universal love for all beings through celibate renunciation.

Buddhist practitioners cultivate four sublime attitudes (*brahmaviharās*), also called four immeasurables (*tshad med bzhi*), including immeasurable love (*byams*), compassion (*snying rje*), sympathetic joy (*dga' ba*), and impartiality (*btang snyoms*). These shades of love have a decidedly parental tone, in keeping with the injunction to love all beings as one's mother. A popular nineteenth-century Tibetan Buddhist practice guide that Sera Khandro knew well, *The Words of My Perfect Teacher* by Patrül Rinpoché, explains these four qualities using the following similes: one should cultivate *love* like that of a nurturing mother bird making a nest for her chicks, *compassion* like one would feel for a destitute mother with no arms whose children are being swept away by a river, *joy* like a camel finding her lost calf, and *impartiality* like a sage offering a feast to all beings regardless of their means.[20]

Perhaps the strongest loving sentiments in Tibetan Buddhist narrative literature can be found in descriptions of disciples' devotion to their gurus, though the theme of loving and missing one's mother crops up often as well.[21] The guru-disciple relationship is of paramount importance in Tibetan Buddhism; disciples develop intense devotion for their masters, aiming to perceive them as living buddhas. In the words of the famous eastern Tibetan Nyingma master Dilgo Khyentsé (1910–91), one should cultivate devotion for one's guru through perceiving him as

> a wish-fulfilling tree that bestows temporal happiness and ultimate bliss, a treasury of vast and deep instructions, a wish-fulfilling jewel granting all the qualities of realization, a father and a mother giving their love equally to all sentient beings, a great river of compassion. . . . In brief, he is the equal of all the Buddhas.[22]

Arousing devotion for one's guru is codified in a set of practices called guru yoga (*bla ma'i rnal 'byor*), one of the final preparatory practices for engaging in more advanced Tantric contemplation. In Patrül Rinpoché's practice guide *Words of My Perfect Teacher*, he instructs disciples to visualize themselves as Yeshé Tsogyel in the form of the *ḍākinī* Vajrayoginī, "gazing longingly at the heart of her teacher," who appears above her head seated on a bejeweled lotus in the form of Padmasambhava. Lest we mistake what type of longing Vajrayoginī harbors for Padmasambhava, Patrül Rinpoché clarifies that "'longingly' (*rings pa'i tshul gyis*) here [is] expressing a sense of impatience to be with the teacher, this being the only source of joy."[23] The impact of such intensive and detailed visualization practices on the visions and dreams that permeate Sera Khandro's auto/biographical writings and those of other Tibetan religious virtuosos cannot be underestimated. But within the Tibetan Buddhist purview, metaphors of parental love trump those between lover and beloved.

Reflections from India

Tibetan religious literature reflects Indic and indigenous Tibetan writing styles in addition to influences from other corners of Tibet's historical borders. In Tibet, monasteries were the sites of classical Buddhist learning, which included five major sciences: interior knowledge (i.e., Buddhism), logic, language, medicine, and arts and crafts. Added to these were five minor sciences including poetics, prosody, synonymy, dramaturgy, and astrology/divination. However, since the latter were predominantly secular in nature, their mastery was often the province of the lay aristocracy.[24] As a woman who had never had access to the Tibetan monastic curriculum, nor even the Tibetan literary education available to both boys and girls among the Lhasa nobility, Sera Khandro would have had little direct access to these sciences.[25] She reports learning how to read and write Tibetan in her late teens in Golok, where she immersed herself in religious communities centered around Treasure revealers and their prolific scriptural productions, particularly those of Düjom Lingpa and his sons.

Sera Khandro presumably received no formal instruction in poetics (*kāvya*, *snyan ngag*), one of the five minor Buddhist sciences. She would not have studied the *locus classicus* of Tibetan poetics, Daṇḍin's *Mirror of Poetry* (*Kāvyādarśa*, *Snyan ngag me long*), translated in full from Sanskrit to Tibetan by the thirteenth century. Daṇḍin's work remained the pinnacle of Tibetan *belles lettres* until the twentieth century because it was the only Sanskrit treatise on poetics (*alamkāraśāstra*) available in Tibetan, inspiring a series of Tibetan commentaries.[26] Even though Tibetan writers' degree of *kāvya* influence was a function of how steeped they were in classical monastic academics, elements drawn from the Sanskrit language sciences filtered into Sera Khandro's writing. These influences came perhaps through her familiarity with the works of some among the long list of religious elite from eastern Tibet who wrote *kāvya*, including Shabkar Tsokdruk Rangdröl, Patrül Rinpoché, and Mipham Rinpoché.[27] In particular, resonances of the literary science of synonymy (*mngon brjod*) appear in the *ḍākinīs*' words ventriloquized by Sera Khandro. She wrote those verses in a Tibetan style of hymn (*mgur*) but added many synonyms of Sanskrit origin:

summer drum (*dbyar rnga*) / one hundred sounds (*sgra brgya*) = thunder
illuminator (*gsal byed*) / jewel of the sky (*nam mkha'i nor bu*) = sun
water holder (*chu 'dzin*) = cloud
queen of spring (*dpyid kyi rgyal mo*) = cuckoo
faculty that ascertains sound (*sgra 'dzin dbang po*) = ear

king who suppresses (*zal gnon gyi rgyal po*) = lion
water born (*mtsho skyes*) = lotus

Perhaps it is no accident that these rhetorical ornaments appear only in Sera Khandro's *ḍākinī* prophecies, marking their elusive meaning as both foreign and familiar, fresh from the Buddhist motherland of India through the flight of the "sky-goers."

The science of poetics is the source of a major discourse on emotions in the Tibetan language distinct from that found in Buddhist philosophy. Sanskrit aesthetic theory centers on the cultivation of *rasa* (Tib. *nyams*), originally developed in the context of Indian dramaturgy and translated variously into English as "aesthetic experience," "sentiment," "emotion," or in its literal meaning, "taste."[28] What we may loosely term emotion is divided into two categories: *rasa* and *bhāva*, or aesthetic experience and the basic emotion that produces it. Many *rasa* theorists understood basic emotion (*bhāva*) as the direct experience of an emotion, whereas aesthetic experience (*rasa*) is a universalization of the basic emotion in which one tastes it without experiencing any of its painful aspects; it is an empathetic, distanced observation *as if* one felt such an emotion.[29] However, Tibetans seem to have followed Daṇḍin's interpretation that *rasa* is an intensification of *bhāva*.[30] For example, the twentieth-century Tibetan literary theorist and poet Döndrup Gyel presented the distinction between *rasa* (*nyams*) and *bhāva* (*'gyur*) as one of intensity and degree of outward expression, using the paradigmatically Buddhist tripartite division of the person into body, speech, and mind:

> Joy and anger and so forth are basic emotions (*'gyur*)[31] that do not manifest in one's body or speech. Generally when basic emotions cannot be felt by anyone except yourself, they are devoid of aesthetic experience (*nyams*). But if those grow in intensity—if when you feel joyous a smile arises on your face and your limbs dance, or when you are angry a frown knits on your brow and you stamp your feet and clap your hands—that basic emotion (*'gyur*) is an aesthetic experience (*nyams*) manifesting externally in your body and speech.[32]

The basic emotions whose flavor of aesthetic experience one can taste through dramatic and poetic arts are divided into eight main types, although other enumerations also exist:[33]

BASIC EMOTION (*BHĀVA*, *'GYUR*)	intensifies into the	AESTHETIC EXPERIENCE (*RASA*, *NYAMS*)
1. sexual love (*rati, dga' ba*)	⟶	erotic (*śṛṅgāra, sgeg pa*)
2. humor (*hāsa, dgod bro ba*)	⟶	comic (*hāsya, bzhad gad*)
3. grief (*śoka, mya ngan*)	⟶	compassionate (*karuṇa, snying rje*)
4. anger (*krodha, khro ba*)	⟶	furious (*raudra, drag shul*)
5. energy (*utsāha, spro ba*)	⟶	heroic (*vīra, dpa' ba*)
6. fear (*bhaya, 'jigs pa*)	⟶	apprehensive (*bhayānaka, 'jigs rung*)
7. disgust (*jugupsā, skyug bro ba*)	⟶	loathsome (*bībhatsa, mi sdug pa*)
8. astonishment (*vismaya, ngo mtshar ba*)	⟶	marvelous (*adbhuta, rmad byung*)

The skilled poet applies poetic figures based on semantic and phonological relationships within a verse to arouse one or a suitable combination of these aesthetic experiences in the reader/listener. The question of which mixtures of aesthetic experiences are harmonious and which discordant became a theme of reflection in Tibetan commentaries on poetics more frequently than Indian analyses of the differentiation between basic emotions and their aesthetic intensification.[34] But Tibetans did import ways to enhance aesthetic experience from India into their own literary works. For example, Jayadeva's twelfth-century *Gītagovinda* features Rādhā and Kṛṣṇa as lover and beloved, certain times like night and spring, places like the forest and a riverbank, and other romantic garnishes such as the moon, lotuses, sandalwood, ornaments, bees, cuckoos, breezes, and rainclouds.[35] That versions of these also figured into centuries of Tibetan literature is evident in Döndrup Gyel's enumeration of stimuli that inspire pleasure and awe, including: "village and forest, flowering trees, mountain and lake, clouds, green meadows, birds and herbivores, jewelry and raiments, spring winds and rains, summer lakes, the sun and moon."[36] For Vaiṣṇavas in Bengal, the aesthetic experience of *śṛṅgāra rasa* heightened by Jayadeva's *Gītagovinda* becomes a religious experience of union in which separation between lover and beloved, taster and tasted, dissolves.[37] Seven hundred years later and over the Himalayas, Sera Khandro attained liberation the moment when "The two, method and insight, actually merged as one taste

(Tib. *ro gcig*)." She was not formally educated in *rasa* theory, but a hint of its flavor lingered on.

Tibetan Love Songs

The languages of love did not always obey boundaries between monastery and village in Tibet, as elsewhere, even if their inhabitants (mostly) did. One Tibetan monastic ruler who seems to have found ample chance to stray during his ill-fated life was the Sixth Dalai Lama, Tsangyang Gyatso (1683–1706), whose escapades are memorialized in Tibet's most famous love lyrics, composed of quatrains of three trochaic feet typical of central Tibetan folk songs (*gzhas*).[38] Even those who hewed closer to the monastic life, such as Kelden Gyatso (1606–77), wrote less amorous songs of spiritual experience (*mgur*) that show significant influence from local Tibetan song styles.[39] Just as the religious love symbolism of the thirteenth-century Beguines converged with the secular rhetoric of courtly love, or the sixteenth-century Teresa of Avila's stages toward mystical union reflected novels of chivalry, we may imagine that even more than her monastic brethren Sera Khandro knew something of the local love songs (*la gzhas, rogs 'then*) in her eastern Tibetan region.[40] Pronounced "*layi*" (written *la gzhas*) in Amdo Tibetan, these "songs of the mountain pass" are distinctive of the Amdo region in which most of Golok is situated.[41] *Rokten* (*rogs 'then*), "love singing," is a longer type of local Amdo love song, usually about two young people pursuing each other in love against all odds with tragic consequences.[42] Below the mountain passes where young people could meet while herding their family's livestock, *layi* and *rokten* are regular features of celebrations and summer festivals, along with horse races, archery contests, and ample refreshment. Customarily, both *layi* and *rokten* may only be sung when elders, relatives, and monastics are out of earshot. They can also be written down to woo the object of one's affection; in the past few decades Tibetans have published a growing number of *layi* and *rokten* collections in Xining.[43] Though we cannot know precisely how different the current secular love songs are from those that circulated in eastern Tibet nearly a hundred years ago, when Sera Khandro could have heard them, there is evidence of secular love songs during her era.[44] *Layi* and *rokten* are always in verse, often in four-line stanzas made up of seven- or eight-syllable meter types characteristic of Tibetan folk songs (*glu*).[45] A good portion of the verse that appears in Sera Khandro's auto/biographical writing, especially *ḍākinī* prophecies, follows similar patterns. Printed collections of *layi* often divide the songs based on their main theme into categories, including: songs about beginning an affair (*'go rtsom pa*), loving each other (*'grog pa*), mutual harmony (*mthun pa*), missing each other (*dran pa*), separation (*'bral ba*), sorrow (*smre ba*), lovers' quarreling (*'gal ba*), and saying farewell (*bde mo*). Sera Khandro's auto/biographical writings contain many similar themes, with especially strong emphasis on beginnings, loving each other, mutual harmony, the yearning of love in separation, and the grief of parting.

PART II: SERA KHANDRO'S TERMS OF ENDEARMENT

Buddhist doctrine, elements of Indian aesthetics filtered through Tibetan literature, and oral forms of singing such as secular Amdo love songs were part of the larger Tibetan cultural context in which Sera Khandro's terms of endearment fit. In her own writing, the vocabulary ranges in tone from villainized terms for lust to valorized terms for love that garnish her verse and prose:

	PHONETIC TIBETAN	EXACT SPELLING
NEGATIVE AMOROUS EMOTION WORDS		
lust	*döchak*	*'dod chags*
passionate attachment	*chaksé*	*chags sred*
infatuation	*yi shorwa*	*yid shor ba*
liking a boy	*po gawa*	*pho dga' ba*
USUALLY NEGATIVE BUT VARYING DEPENDING ON CONTEXT		
to be attached to	*chakpa*	*chags pa*
NEUTRAL/POSITIVE		
wanting or desiring	*döpa*	*'dod pa*
aspiring	*dünpa*	*'dun pa*
longing	*dungwa*	*gdung ba*

POSITIVE

affection	*chetré*	*gces spras*
love	*tsewa*	*brtse ba*
great love	*tsewa chenpo*	*brtse ba chen po*
missing	*drenpa/ yi trengwa*	*dran pa/yid 'phreng ba*

AFFECTIONATE NAMES SERA KHANDRO AND DRIMÉ ÖZER USE ONLY IN REFERENCE TO EACH OTHER

jewel of my heart	*nyingi nor*	*snying gi nor*
root consort	*tsawé drok/tsawé rikma*	*rtsa ba'i grogs/rtsa ba'i rig ma*
heart consort	*nyingdrok*	*snying grogs*
dear child[46]	*chetruk*	*gces phrug*

Out of all of these words expressing shades of love that we will encounter in the following sections, the most frequent is *tsewa*; various compounds including it appear thirty-eight times in Drimé Özer's biography and forty-one times in Sera Khandro's autobiography. Although *tsewa* is a common Tibetan word for love, its semantic range differs from the English word in that it is not a love between peers but rather a compassionate concern for others below oneself in rank, age, or means. The *Great Tibetan-Chinese Dictionary* defines *tsewa* as "a. having affectionate concern or compassion for, for example concern for the sick, children, elderly, and the poor and b. a term for compassion, for example taking care of someone with great love, a merciful attitude, compassionate love."[47] Instances of *tsewa* in Sera Khandro's writing depict a top-down love for those below, such as a guru's love for her disciple at parting moments or a disciple's supplication to his guru (or a bodhisattva/*ḍākinī*) to look upon him with love. In Drimé Özer's biography, his brother Dodrupchen Jikmé Tenpé Nyima, who was sixteen years his senior and under whom he apprenticed as a young child, "treated him lovingly" (*thugs brtse brtse mdzad*) when he prepared to return home to study with their father, Düjom Lingpa. He reflected that Dodrupchen Rinpoché had "nurtured me affectionately, feeding and clothing me well. In particular, from a religious perspective, he cared for me lovingly (*thugs brtse bas rjes su bzung*) by giving me the profound cherished treasure of empowerments and explanations and so forth without keeping anything secret."[48] One of the primary "lovers" in

Drimé Özer's biography in this sense of bestowing compassionate love was his father. Sera Khandro indicates the closeness of the father-son and guru-disciple relationship they shared in the following departure scene just before Drimé Özer embarked on a pilgrimage:

> The Master [Drimé Özer] said, "Lama Rinpoché [Düjom Lingpa], don't withhold your kindness—please make aspiration prayers for us to be indivisible in this and all our future lifetimes." He clasped the Lama's hand and father and son wept, not bearing to part. The Lama too, because he felt intense love (*thugs la shin tu brtse bas*) for the Master, was saddened.[49]

Later Sera Khandro depicts the final farewell between father and son in strong terms. While living with his father at Dartsang, Drimé Özer felt compelled to stay with him all night, but Düjom Lingpa's consort (*yum*) demanded he leave so she could get some sleep. Acquiescing to this,

> The Lama said, "Come early tomorrow morning," and he treated him lovingly (*thugs brtse brtse mdzad*) by stroking the Master's head with his hand and kissing his face. The Master prostrated to the Lama and went to his sleeping area.[50]

The next day was the eighth day of the eleventh month of 1904, and when Drimé Özer returned to Düjom Lingpa's tent, he discovered that his father had already passed away.

Drimé Özer himself also dispensed a great deal of love for his disciples, in particular one very special "root" disciple, Sotrül Natsok Rangdröl Rinpoché of Sera Monastery, with whom Sera Khandro lived after Drimé Özer's death while writing his biography. She writes that on one occasion, when Drimé Özer and Sotrül parted ways, each heading out on separate pilgrimages,

> In particular [the Master] advised Sotrül Rinpoché on both [worldly and religious] affairs. Their minds having mixed, the Master treated him lovingly (*thugs brtse mdzad*). He promised not to delay returning to his own land, and Sotrül and his entourage left for central Tibet.[51]

Hearing that Sotrül cried upon leaving his presence, missing him (*dran pa*), Drimé Özer prayed to the lamas and gods for his safe travels and the success of his religious aspirations, referring to Sotrül as "The doctrine holder of my profound Treasures, possessor of awareness, my holy disciple who is my only heart son."[52]

As one would expect, given Sera Khandro's authorship of both works, her autobiography demonstrates much the same focus on guru-disciple, parent-child, elder-junior love in the form of *tsewa*. *Ḍākinīs* are among the main bestowers of love in Sera Khandro's life. Especially when perturbed by her behavior, they apply maternal guilt to goad her to comply with their injunctions, reminding her, "*Ha ha, he he*, from the time you were young until now I have lovingly raised you as if you were my only child."[53] Out of all the speakers in the two biographies, *ḍākinīs* make the most use of parental similes for their love. Ironically, as effusive as Sera Khandro's writing is in describing deities' love for humans or lamas' love for disciples using parental metaphors, there are very few references to actual instances of love between parents and children in her writing beyond the example of Düjom Lingpa and Drimé Özer, for whom religious and parental love blended. Sera Khandro notes that her parents raised her affectionately (*gces spras su bskyangs*) but not that they loved her (*brtse ba*). After the debacle of her firstborn child supposedly transforming from a boy to a girl in utero, a nun named Getso "consoled Gyelsé and told him that he must have affection (*gces spras*) for the baby."[54] She also records that after she gave birth to Gyelsé's stillborn child, he felt great regret for not performing more protective rituals for the fetus, prompting her to retort, "If you truly love this small boy (*bu chung la nges par brtse ba yin na*), what he needs is Dharma, so if you practice meritorious Dharma by abandoning as many possessions as you can, he will certainly receive [the merit]."[55] After all this, it may come as little surprise that Sera Khandro never describes any feeling of affection or love whatsoever for Gyelsé. More startling perhaps, she records the death of Drimé Özer's mother in his biography without any mention of love or sorrow in the following words: "Then when the Master was twenty-five, his mother passed into peace."[56] In contrast, in her own autobiography she recounts her devastation at her mother's passing when she was only twelve, lamenting that "although Father cared for me affectionately (*gces spras su bskyangs*), I missed (*dran pa*) Mother so much that I felt I could not bear it."[57] Even so, after describing her departure from Lhasa at fifteen, she never references her birth family again. Also sparse are descriptions of affection for her children. She never writes about feeling love or affection for her daughter Yangchen

(Chöying) Drönma, although she indicates that she traveled nearly everywhere with her. After her youngest son, Rindzin Gyurmé Dorjé, suddenly passed away at the age of five, only three days before Drimé Özer, Sera Khandro wrote extensively about her grief and mourning, mostly directed toward her guru, not her son, except for the following lament in the first-person voice at the end of Drimé Özer's biography:

> Whatever I think about becomes a cause of unnecessary hardship.
> My heart's beloved son (*snying brtse ba'i bu*) has gone to his next life.
> My consort, the Wish-fulfilling Jewel, has gone to the buddhafields,
> leaving me, Dekyong Wangmo, behind.[58]

The absence of love or even extensive mention of affection for parents and children in Sera Khandro's writing is not proof that she or others did not feel these emotions, but rather indicates that aside from her devastation at her mother's passing, love for her biological family did not figure prominently in the context of her story of spiritual realization.

In contrast, Sera Khandro recounts receiving a great deal of love from lamas in her autobiography, not just from Drimé Özer. For example, when the nun Tsüldrön dragged the seventeen-year-old Sera Khandro before Lama Murasang to request nun's vows and she refused to do so,

> In a loving manner (*thugs brtse ba'i tshul gyis*), the lama [Murasang] replied, "Oh yes, not getting attached to food, clothing, and wealth and wondering if you will accomplish the pure Dharma is the same as accomplishing the Dharma."[59]

At the close of her visit to Andzom Rinpoché in 1923 when she was thirty-one, she writes that, "the Lama [Andzom] Rinpoché took care of me with great love (*thugs brtse ba chen pos rjes su bzung*)," and also that his "consort (*yum*), son, and entourage escorted me with great love (*thugs brtse ba chen pos*)."[60] The lama who treated Sera Khandro lovingly most often, aside from Drimé Özer, was Gotrül Rinpoché. She wrote that after an intense visit with Gotrül when she was twenty-five, "He spoke much to me about the Dharma and practice instructions and cared for me with great love (*brtse ba chen po'i sgo nas rjes su gzung*)."[61] A few years later, in 1919 when she was twenty-seven, she received the news that Gotrül Rinpoché was growing increasingly ill. Describing her final visit to him, she writes,

When I was getting ready to go home, he said, "This is an auspicious connection so that in the three—this life, the next, and the intermediate state—and in all our lives we will be without separation," and he gave me a high-quality vajra and bell, many other substances, and various types of fruit and things made from the three sweets [sugar, molasses, and honey]. With this, he treated me lovingly (*thugs brtse brtse mdzad*).[62]

What sets Sera Khandro's writings apart from those of her compatriots regarding talk of love in the form of *tsewa* is not the top-down, master-disciple/deity-human directionality of the sentiment, but its relative abundance in her writings. In Gara Terchen's autobiography, *tsewa* appears about eight times. He writes that when he was twelve in 1869–70, his left his mother's house and went to study with a lama named Pema Gyurmé Sangngak Tendzin, who looked after him lovingly (*thugs brtse bas rjes su bzung*) and gave him teachings including preliminary, channel and wind, and Great Perfection practices.[63] A few years later, when he was sixteen and about to set out to meet another important lama, his "root lama," Tsampa Rinpoché, gave him advice and instructions, prayed that he would not encounter obstacles, and treated him lovingly (*thugs brtse mdzad*).[64] On another occasion the *ḍākinī* Drupgyelma embraced him, thus catalyzing his experience of the four joys, and then she "lovingly (*brtse brtse'i ngang nas*) said to me, 'Now I think I must go.'"[65] In another miraculous vision he encountered Padmasambhava himself, who assured him, "Noble son, I will care for you lovingly (*thugs brtse bas bskyang*)," before transforming into a spherical light ray and disappearing into the ultimate sphere.[66] Interestingly, the same word for love also appears in a letter Gara Terchen wrote when he was twenty-eight, in 1885, to Ngak Chödrön, his (ex-)consort, who spurned him to marry another man:

Loved, loved (*brtse brtse*), consort named Ngak,
Relationship, relationship, for years and months we have had a consort relationship.
Attachment, attachment, having become attached to illusory appearances
Contrary, contrary, contrary to vajra commitment vows,
seduced, seduced, a negative consort has seduced you.[67]

Gara Terchen's verse seems to be both warning Ngak Chödrön of the dangers of her attachment to her new beau and reaffirming the propriety of his own loving relationship with her. In any case, even if less often, Gara Terchen writes of love in parallel situations as Sera Khandro does: particularly during parting scenes in which a guru loves his disciple or a *ḍākinī* loves those to whom she appears, Padmasambhava loves his emissaries, and a male Tantric master loves his female consort.

Düjom Lingpa's autobiographical writings are comparatively light on love. On a few occasions love comes up in the midst of his stream of lucid visions. At the beginning of *The Clear Mirror*, his former incarnation Dündül Drakpo Tsel supplicates Padmasambhava in his buddhafield, beseeching him not to have to reincarnate again and return to the world:

> Alas, supreme embodiment of the buddhas of the three times,
> supreme permanent refuge Orgyen Rinpoché,
> by your great loving compassion (*thugs brtse thugs rje chen po*),
> listen to me and give me permission.[68]

In another instance, when Düjom Lingpa was thirty-one in about 1866, a blue *ḍākinī* appeared and escorted him to Padmasambhava's Copper-Colored Mountain, where he beheld an array of the heads of the eighty great Indian *siddha*s, some wearing scholar's hats and some with hair bound in topknots, all smiling at him with a loving demeanor (*brtse ba'i nyams kyis*).[69] In keeping with the heavily visionary tone of Düjom Lingpa's autobiographical writings and sparse detail about his mundane affairs, he says little about who he loved in this world.

Gara Terchen's and Düjom Lingpa's writings are not the models Sera Khandro drew from most directly for her abundance of talk of love, and we cannot find a direct model in Yeshé Tsogyel's hagiography either. Previous chapters have explored multiple layers of intertextuality between the two *ḍākinī*s' life stories, but concerning terms of endearment, there is little overlap. In Taksham's version of Yeshé Tsogyel's life story, Padmasambhava's affectionate sentiment toward her is always compassion (*thugs rje*), not love in the form of *tsewa*. Quoting the popular Padmakara Translation Group's rendering of the work, Tsogyel beseeches Padmasambhava as her "Loving (*thugs rje*) Master, swift to liberate."[70] When Padmasambhava departs for his southwestern buddhafield, Yeshé Tsogyel is rent with grief and begs him, "Sorrow! Alas! Look swiftly on me in your love (*thugs rje*)!"[71] Before departing to the buddhafield, Yeshé Tsogyel informs the people of Tibet, "The Guru's love (*thugs rje*) has never left me: /

His emanations fill the world, and here they are inviting me."[72] *Tsewa* appears at least once in Tsogyel's hagiography, and like Sera Khandro's usage of the word, it is a top-down feeling of mercy, as in the instance when a leper entreats Tsogyel to "look on me with loving (*brtse bas*) eyes!"[73] Yeshé Tsogyel's sentiments for her guru range from extreme devotion to angst-filled sorrow when he departs, but neither of them expresses how much they love each other (*brtse ba*), how much they will miss (*'phreng ba*) each other, or how attached (*chags pa*) they are to each other. Nor do they call each other by affectionate names such as "jewel of my heart" (*snying gi nor*) and "heart consort" (*snying grogs*), all of which Sera Khandro and Drimé Özer do repeatedly.

Prophecy and Personal Affinity

Sera Khandro describes a great deal of *tsewa* between Drimé Özer and herself, but this alone does not mark the distinctiveness of their *yab yum* relationship aside from underscoring her devotion to him and his compassion for her. Nevertheless, there are many other elements of Sera Khandro's relationship with Drimé Özer that set it apart from all others in her writing. One is the heavy foreshadowing in both his biography and her autobiography that prepares readers for their initial meeting in Lhasa in 1906. Just as Tibetan religious masters' biographies rarely begin with an account of their present incarnation, the sacred commitment of *yab* and *yum* that Sera Khandro and Drimé Özer shared stretches back through a series of previous lifetimes, according to her accounts. She portrays her interconnection with Drimé Özer as at once foretold by *ḍākinīs* and open to many possible futures. To get a sense of what this foreshadowing sounds like, we turn first to Drimé Özer's biography, because Sera Khandro wrote it before her autobiography. When he was eighteen, in 1899, the *ḍākinī* Künselma offered him an enigmatic prophecy along with a prophetic guide delineating the Treasures he would reveal. Unsure if he understood her meaning, he repeated her words to his father, with whom he was living and studying in Dartsang, Serta:

> When the Master told the Lama [his father] about the prophecy and the way he saw the *ḍākinī* without keeping anything secret, he replied, "If you have excellent auspicious connections, your consort of successive lifetimes (*tshe rabs kyi gzungs ma*), the site of your earth Treasures, and the domain of

your disciples will be in the upper regions of Ü Tsang [central Tibet]. Even so, by the power of former karma, these will benefit my teachings. Hence, if they are not lost to demonic forces, the auspicious connections will probably come together to a middling degree."

The Master asked, "Was this prophetess my consort of successive lifetimes?"

"You are empowered to have her only temporarily; besides this, it will be difficult to have the karma to be with her for successive lifetimes."

The Master thought, "Is it that I don't have the auspicious connections for this consort? If I have the auspicious connections, why wouldn't I have the power to have her?"

The Father Master Lama spoke, "You don't have to worry. If I invoke the Dharma protectors, you will have these auspicious connections. Like the proverb 'when the gods are mighty, the demons are mighty,' it is difficult."

Again the Master asked, "Precious Lama, I beseech you to tell me, what do I have to do to be able to retrieve my consort of successive lifetimes and my profound Dharma earth Treasures?"

The Lama replied, "If you go to Lhasa, all of this will probably come together," so the Master promised to go to central Tibet.[74]

If the *ḍākinī* prophecy compelling Drimé Özer westward to central Tibet to discover Treasures and reunite with his consort is a type of predestination, there is also a degree of hesitation mixed with it. Düjom Lingpa's words reinforce the tenuous nature of auspicious connections—making them come together was a joint venture between powers outside of Drimé Özer, such as deities and demons, as well as his own willpower and decisions. Prefigured here are both the strong connection between Drimé Özer and his "consort of successive lifetimes," Sera Khandro, as well as the difficulties they would encounter in joining their lives. Perhaps, Düjom Lingpa warns, Drimé Özer will only be able to have Sera Khandro temporarily, hinting at the obstacles (problems with other partners, differences in social rank and homeland, etc.) that could prevent their union from materializing.

Despite this forecast for Sera Khandro and Drimé Özer's future together, *ḍākinī*s left little room for doubt about what the two *yab* and *yum* partners should do. Many of their efforts to motivate Drimé Özer to follow their prescriptions sound like versions of the following reminder Dewé

Gocha offered him when he was twenty-four, just after he set out on pilgrimage to Lhasa. In an eight-syllable verse form typical of Tibetan folk songs and of Amdo love songs (*layi*), but here infused with religious meaning, Dewé Gocha intoned:

Eh, eh

In the changeless and radiantly luminous ultimate sphere,
the five-colored self-emergent primordial wisdom shines forth.
The gloom having effortlessly self-liberated,
you will soon obtain the turquoise dragon's jewel.

The snow lion's turquoise mane descends from the gods.
The tiger's brilliant stripes blaze.
The peacock's dexterity will show itself before long.

The meaning is that when you are empowered in your father's wealth of Treasures,
it is very important to be skillful regarding your actions and auspicious connections.
[Arising from] the display of the manifestation of the Protector Lake-Born Vajra [Padmasambhava]
is his secret *yogi*, the awareness holder
named Samanta Sukha Vajra.

She is the supreme holder of your profound Dharma teachings.
Not casting aside actions and auspicious connections due to laziness,
if you excellently gather together Treasure revealer and doctrine holder,
you will gradually encounter the keys to your secret Treasures,
and will open the doors to many Treasures in Lhodrak.[75]

Prophecies such as this one are meant to be enigmatic, written in code hard to crack without the *ḍākinīs*' favor. We might interpret Dewé Gocha's words to mean that the gloomy influence of Drimé Özer's stagnant life in Golok was about to be shattered into the brilliant luminosity of his arrival in Lhasa, literally the "city of the gods." Lhasa was the abode of the bejeweled turquoise dragon, a symbolic reference to Sera Khandro because she was born in the Tibetan calendric system's water dragon year, 1892. In case

Sera Khandro's readership was less astute than necessary to intuit this, Dewé Gocha laid it bare: Sukha Vajra, Sanskrit for Dewé Dorjé, was the emissary of Padmasambhava, empowered to be the supreme doctrine holder (*chos bdag*) of his Treasure teachings. Though auspicious connections had the potential to bind them together in ways that could electrify Drimé Özer's capacity to reveal Treasures, making this happen required his active effort. Laziness would cause their synergetic potential to fall apart.

Lust Versus Love

In Sera Khandro's autobiography as well, *ḍākinīs* augur the momentous occasion of her first encounter with Drimé Özer in the present lifetime. Unlike in Drimé Özer's biography, introspection about what kind of attraction she feels—lust (*'dod chags*) or a spiritual tone of love (*dad pa, gdung ba, brtse ba*)—take center stage in her own portents. The *ḍākinī* Dorjé Yudrönma had a special relationship with Sera Khandro because she was the "earth possessor" (*sa 'dzin*) or land deity associated with the Lumotil neighborhood west of the Jokhang Temple in Lhasa, where Sera Khandro was born. In 1905, the year prior to Drimé Özer's arrival, when Sera Khandro was thirteen, Dorjé Yudrönma did some matchmaking work of her own, appearing in Sera Khandro's dream and teasing her about the man to whom she was unwillingly betrothed:

> A young and beautiful bejeweled woman saying she was Dorjé Yudrönma asked the following: "Lady, what is your boyfriend's name? Do you know whose rebirth he is? What is his destiny?"
>
> I said, "I don't have a boyfriend I chose voluntarily. Even though I don't want (*'dod*) him, my parents and relatives say that I have been given to the junior leader from Kyidrong."
>
> She said, "The junior leader from Kyidrong is an attractive youth. It is no mistake that he is your husband."
>
> Unhappy, I sang this song:
>
> *He, he*, cunning girl—
> you are definitely not Dorjé Yudrön.
> This manner of becoming attached (*chags*) to a man's body
> makes you a prostitute.

Although the junior leader from Kyidrong has a great body,
it is impermanent like a summer flower;
when autumn frost comes, its luster will fade.
Like this example, his nature is transient.

I don't know about the merit from his rebirths.
In physical appearance, he is dressed in layman's clothes.
Although he is a handsome, splendid youth,
I have no need for him—I give him to you.

Again, she said, "Lady, don't be angry! I spoke honest words."

I replied, "If you don't talk about liking (*dga'*) the junior leader from Kyidrong, it is okay if I listen."

She said, "I am testing your mentality. Otherwise, I am not one who needs a husband. Nevertheless, I have honest words to tell you. Listen and you will accomplish your intention."

Cupping her hands to my ear so that others wouldn't hear, she said, "Next year it is certain that your Treasure consort from former lifetimes and your karmic lama from [former] lifetimes named Drima Mepé Özer Tayé, who is an incarnation of Namnying, Vairo, and Yudra[76] together and who is an unrivaled Treasure revealer, will come up from the lower regions of eastern Tibet. If you stay together with him in the moon fortress at Gangri Tökar,[77] it is certain that China and Tibet will remain peaceful and happy for the next fifty years. If you don't do this, it will be time for you to go eastward to eastern Tibet."

As soon as I heard the lama's name, the hair on my body stood on end, tears ran from my eyes, and like a thirsty person longing (*gdung ba*) for water, I felt an extremely strong aspiration (*'dun*) to meet the lama. Nevertheless, I thought that in my prophetic guide there was the name Sherap Özer, but I was unsure if the name Drima Mepé Özer Tayé was there.

She spoke, "You don't need to worry about that. Prajñā Raśmi[78] is the great Treasure revealer from Trango. He emanated from the same source as Vima Raśmi [Drimé Özer], so the meaning is the same. From the time of the Guru [Padmasambhava] you two have had an extremely profound connection based on your prayers; there is no possibility of mistake or delusion."[79]

The dream dialogue between Dorjé Yudrönma and Sera Khandro accentuates the strict separation between profane attachment and sacred connection; different words for desire divide lust (*'dod chags, dga' ba*) from spiritual longing (*gdung ba*). Becoming attached to the body of a handsome young man and liking him is incomparable to longing intensely to connect with one's guru.

And yet, the mutually intense somatic responses of lust and spiritual longing required further effort to parse when the much-predicted moment of Sera Khandro and Drimé Özer's initial encounter actually arrived. Shortly after the long dream sequence in which Kukkuripa taught her channel and wind practices (described in part I of chapter 4), Drimé Özer appeared:

> Then in the tenth month, some people from Kham came to visit central Tibet. Among those was the encampment headed toward central Tibet of one who was said to be the incarnation of Dzokchen Palgé[80] from Dzagyel Monastery. He asked my older brother to give him a place to stay, so he did and the guests arrived. I looked at the guests from the sun-viewing glass window. Among them there was one lama with hair on his head. As soon as I saw him, my perception transformed. As I thought that he was really the one called Künkhyen Longchen Rapjam, tears flowed from my eyes and the hair on my body stood on end. On account of this, I put my palms together and prayed, "Don't withhold your compassion—in all my lifetimes may I never separate from you."
>
> My brother's wife named Drönkar said:
>
>> *Ho ho*! It seems as if you are not one who has no thought of liking a man (*pho dga'*)! You do have a man whom you like—when you see that lama over there, lust (*'dod chags*) arises in you and you say, 'May we never part,' not thinking of (*yid mi 'phreng*) the young Kyidrong leader, who is [handsome] like the full moon. What is the meaning of your becoming infatuated (*yid shor*) with this man from Kham with a long black beard?
>
> I replied, singing the following words in a song:
>
>> "Listen, wife of my elder brother!
>> I am not one with an intense liking (*pho dga' che ba*) for a man.
>> [Since] it seems he is a holy and great *yogi*,
>> involuntarily faith arose in me.
>> I prayed that in this life and the next we will be inseparable.

I am not one in whom lust for "doing a man" (*khyo byed 'dod chags pa*) arises.
I am a nun who is without attachment (*chags med*).
I will not do negative acts with passionate attachment (*chags sred*).
I will not fall under the influence of that negative companion,
the young leader who is splendidly handsome [like] the moon.

I pray that my final action will be to practice the Dharma.
I am like a fall and winter flower;
although I am here today, I am gone tomorrow.
Sister, I don't know what will happen."

She said,

Ho, ho, listen Künga!

The inclination of a she-goat not to obey the shepherd
results in her killing herself.
The inclination of this girl not to obey her parents
is the basis for dispute.
Expel this thought from the depth of your mind.
There are many different songs;
there are several words that cause mental doubt—
don't say unnecessary things like this!

I thought that through her sharp intellect she had understood the meaning of my words, so I said, "Hey, I'm joking. If I have a husband like the Kyidrong leader, of course he will be my life partner. Like the proverb 'buying misery with happiness, fat with butter,' in my own land I'm royalty. If I wander in another land, I'll be a beggar woman."[81]

Dorjé Yudrönma's dream conversation and Drönkar's conversation in waking life highlight a range of affective possibilities that ironically were similar in outward expression. Yudrönma teased her about having a handsome boyfriend that she likes (*dga' ba*), but her intention was to test her resolve and predict the coming of the true partner with whom she had a profound connection. Just hearing Drimé Özer's name uttered for the first time elicited a strong physical response in Sera Khandro, but this appeared to Drönkar to be just what Sera Khandro insisted it was not, a manifestation of lust (*'dod chags*) and infatuation (*yid shor*). Both Dorjé Yudrönma's and Drönkar's taunts presented Sera Khandro with an opportunity to defend the purity of her sentiment, which she did in both cases by insisting on her lack of lustful attachment, the *sine qua non* of true Buddhist love. Thus Sera Khandro addressed the potential doubters among her readership, setting her sublime connection to Drimé Özer into relief by defining it starkly against profane forms of sexual love.

Sera Khandro's female interlocutors pushed her in opposite directions, pitting carnal lust against spiritual love—if she hesitated to follow Drimé Özer back to Golok, the auspicious connections that both needed to actualize their spiritual potential would dissipate. But if she did follow him, she would upend her family's plans to marry her off and would become a "basis for dispute." Her dilemma reflects a central tension that arises in many religious biographies about women, Buddhist and not: the struggle to escape arranged marriage in order to seek a religious life. That this tension between marriage and monastery (or in her case, religious encampment) was especially charged for female religious practitioners emerges in the contrast between Sera Khandro's depiction of her own turmoil and her presentation of Drimé Özer's thoughts in this crucial moment. In his biography, she narrates,

> Then, in accordance with the *ḍākinī* prophecy from before and the words of the Lama [Düjom Lingpa], there was a person born in the dragon year of a high class from a royal Mongolian leader's family who the Master thought was the one designated as the consort (*grogs*) for his profound Treasures.
>
> The Master said to his direct disciple named Gonla Sherap, who was clever in both [worldly and religious] affairs, "How can I find a way to obtain her as a consort for my profound Treasures?"
>
> Sherap replied, "Because we are from a negative, inferior land with poor merit, aside from a bit of temporary auspicious connection, it is certain that they won't give her to us as a long-term consort. If you invoke your Dharma protectors, because the prayers of the victoriously powerful Padmasambhava are not deceiving, it is sure that gradually you will find an excellent way [to attract her]." The Master acted accordingly.[82]

Here we find no teasing banter accentuating tensions between lust and love, but rather attention to practical aspects such as social status, wealth, and region of origin that Tibetans typically factored into choosing suitable marriage partners. Though theirs was not a prospective marriage but a prophesied consort relationship, Sera Khandro inserted some of the same concerns into Drimé Özer's words. He seems to have concluded, according to her account, that his best bet was to pray for the attentions of this high-class urban girl looking down on his group of dusty and tattered pilgrims from her estate's upper-story window. Sera Khandro followed suit:

> I wasn't able to go to him on account of my high status. Watching him from the sun-viewing glass window going in and out of his small tent, I prayed with my body, speech, and mind acting as one. Making him my main "body seal,"[83] our minds merged together.[84]

What is the nature of this profound sentiment that Sera Khandro felt for Drimé Özer (and he for her, as Sera Khandro portrays him in what follows)? Was it involuntary religious devotion signaling the reawakening of many previous lifetimes of karmic connection between guru and disciple, or something more mundane, as Drönkar hints? The intense physical responses Sera Khandro reports—trembling, tears, hair standing on end, etc.—are paradigmatic Tibetan expressions of religious faith. Minus the reference to heterosexual channel and wind practices in which Drimé Özer was Sera Khandro's "body seal," she describes his devotion to his root guru and father using some of the same affective responses. When Düjom Lingpa passed away, Drimé Özer sang a mourning prayer to him lamenting that, "When I hear your name, my body hair stands on end out of faith / and my attachment to *saṃsāra* is thoroughly cut."[85] But is there nothing to Drönkar's suspicions? After all, she was not the only one to poke fun at Sera Khandro's affections for her guru. One of the few members of Drimé Özer's group of traveling pilgrims to treat their newest young Lhasa recruit kindly was a nun named Tongpön Zangmo. She nourished the starving Sera Khandro with tea and encouragement from time to time on the rough road to Golok, and once there, helped her find a place to stay. In her autobiography Sera Khandro narrates what happened when they finally arrived in Golok:

At that time, Akhu Darlo came and asked, "Are you staying?"

Zangmo replied by telling him everything about my situation regarding finding a place to stay.

He responded, "The cherished *trülku* said that if you stay, there is a room in the lower part of the lama's residence."

"Which *trülku* said this?" I asked.

Zangmo replied, "*Your trülku* said it," and she teased me a lot.

I said, "This is a good auspicious connection. As you say, it is not certain that I won't become his consort (*grogs*) by the end of my life."

Then, Zangmo escorted me to the lower part of the lama's residence, and I stayed there for a few days.[86]

A few years later Zangmo teased her again when Sera Khandro asked her if she had a small piece of Drimé Özer's hair or clothing, which Sera Khandro wanted because these substances could serve as substitute auspicious connections necessary for her to reveal a Treasure in lieu of Drimé Özer's physical presence with her at the Treasure site. She writes,

Thinking that my Treasure site was just there and that it seemed I needed a material substance as an auspicious connection, I went to Zangmo's place and said, "Ané Zangmo, do you have any of Trülku Drimé's hair or clothing that you could give me?"

She replied, "I have a bit. Why do you need it?"

I said, "I have a need for it."

She said jokingly, "Isn't it that you have a need for the actual *trülku*? If it is sufficient to only have his hair, I'll give it to you."[87]

Zangmo found humor in Sera Khandro's affections, but others close to Drimé Özer who also noticed their closeness found fault. During those first few days of Sera Khandro's stay in the lower part of Trülku Drimé's residence, he made sure that no one was looking before dropping by to refill Sera Khandro's supply of provisions such as roasted barley flour, butter, and cheese. Even so, to her dismay the caretaker of his residence, Akyap Trülku, sent her away on account of Drimé Özer's consort, Akyongza. When Abten came to collect Sera Khandro to work as a maidservant in his household, Drimé Özer was not home and Akyap Trülku gave her no choice but to leave. She narrates,

> Together with Dongkor Abten, I put my bowl in the pocket [of my cloak] and my boots under my arms and set out on the small stone path. The Master was performing a prosperity ritual at Jiksam's house, and it was time for his tea break. When I saw him stand up, my mind was oppressed with suffering and my eyes filled with tears so that I couldn't see the path. I sat down for a little while as if to put on my boots.
>
> Abten said, "You take this road and go. I need to request a divination from the Trülku," and with that he whipped his horse and went off. Though it was my heart's desire (*snying 'dod*) to go [with him], I didn't dare.
>
> When Abten returned, I asked, "What did the Trülku say?"
>
> He replied, "He said you wouldn't be able to bear the hardship [working as a maidservant] and he scolded Ömbar."[88]

The intensity of Sera Khandro's desire to be near Drimé Özer conveys her great devotion to her guru. However, her nun friend's teasing, her repeated requests to know what Drimé Özer said about her, his attentiveness to her needs, and the secrecy with which he gave her provisions, in combination with his consort and her supporters' wrath, suggest they found a surplus of affection between disciple and guru.

The *Yab Yum* Couple

Another distinctive element of Sera Khandro's rendition of her relationship with Drimé Özer is the exclusivity with which she presents them as a *yab yum* dyad. We can be sure that both had other sexual partners during the years of their association, given that she mentions the birth of three children to her and one to him, none of whom appears to be a product of their union. Nevertheless, in her own voice Sera Khandro presents only Drimé Özer as her *yab*. The dyadic nature of their relationship is reflected not only in the content of Sera Khandro's auto/biographical writings but also in their form: two biographies, one about *yab* and the other *yum*, tracing the auspicious connections that bind them together in past, present, and future lifetimes. Emphasizing this two-in-one element of Sera Khandro's biographical writing projects, the Treasure revealer Namtrül Jikmé Püntsok (1944–2011) cautioned me not to focus only on Sera Khandro's autobiography but also to study Drimé Özer's biography; he stressed that the two works are meant to be read together since they embody male and female, method and insight, which he likened to the two hands of one body.[89]

Yab and *yum* are honorific Tibetan terms for mother and father. In Drimé Özer's biography, Sera Khandro called his parents, Düjom Lingpa and Keza Sangyetso, his *yab* and *yum*. Düjom Lingpa had several "*yums*" who were mothers of his many children, but Sera Khandro only mentions Drimé Özer's mother by name in his biography. Likewise, in her autobiography she refers to her father and mother as *yab yum*. As we have already seen, *yab yum* also refers to male and female deities in sexual union, symbolizing the nondual union of method and insight. In both biographies "*Guru yab yum*" or "*Guru Padmasambhava yab yum*" appears frequently, meaning the "Guru Couple" Padmasambhava and Yeshé Tsogyel. Other Buddhist deities arise in *yab yum* form in Sera Khandro's writing, such as Hayagrīva and Vajravārāhī. Additionally, Tibetans often refer to a lama's female partner as his *yum*. In the case of a female lama, more often called a *khandroma* (Skt. *ḍākinī*), her male partner can be referred to as her *yab*. Also, a few times Sera Khandro describes Drimé Özer's younger brother Dorjé Drandül and his consort using a condensed version of his name, "Dordra *yab yum*," perhaps something akin to "Mr. and Mrs. Dordra," though no formal marriage ceremony is necessarily implied by the designation.

Otherwise, when *yab yum* appears together as a compound in Drimé Özer's biography, it refers exclusively to Drimé Özer and Sera Khandro. This is not the case for the word *yum* alone: in one instance in Drimé Özer's biography, Sera Khandro mentions that when he was twenty-nine, his *yum* "gave birth to a son amid wondrous signs without any harm to the mother (*yum*),"[90] though she does not provide the name of either the mother or the son. One wonders how this other "*yum*" (was it Akyongza?) would have perceived Sera Khandro's hundreds of pages of descriptions of Drimé Özer and herself as an inseparable two-in-one *yab yum* pair. In her autobiography, there is also only one instance in which Sera Khandro calls another man besides Drimé Özer her *yab*, and importantly, she writes this not as the narrator but in a direct speech quotation from Gotrül Rinpoché, who addressed Gyelsé and Sera Khandro once as *yab yum*. Gotrül urged Gyelsé to perform a retreat at Mowatowa on the Anyé Machen circumambulation route in order to "dispel obstacles between *yab* and *yum*."[91] When Gyelsé failed to heed this advice, the rift between them deepened.

Sera Khandro draws on the *yab yum* paradigm of Padmasambhava and Yeshé Tsogyel as developed in the latter's hagiography while also rendering this relationship in more exclusive terms. In Tsogyel's hagiography, Taksham often refers to Padmasambhava and Yeshé Tsogyel together as "*yab yum*." For example, quoting Padmakara's English translation, after the king offers his queen, Yeshé Tsogyel, to Padmasambhava for the sake of Secret Mantra practice, "they (*yab yum*) went to Chimphu Geu, where they practiced in secret."[92] Later at Tidro "they (*yab yum*) engaged in secret practice"[93] and the king made an offering to "the Guru and his Consort (*yab yum*)," whereupon a palanquin of white light appeared and "The Guru and his Consort (*guru yab yum*) stepped into it. The palanquin rose into the air and they departed."[94] Many other references to the two leading figures in Yeshé Tsogyel's hagiography follow this pattern, but not all. Padmasambhava urges Yeshé Tsogyel to find a particular Indian slave boy named Atsara Salé with whom to perfect her practice. When she successfully buys him for herself with a sum of gold, according to the Padmakara translation, she "made her way to the temple of É in Nepal, taking Salé with her."[95] Here the Tibetan literally reads "again *yab yum* both went to the temple of É in Nepal," referring to Yeshé Tsogyel and Atsara Salé.[96] After Nepal, according to the Padmakara translation, "Then the Lady Tsogyal and Salé, her companion, made their way to Tibet."[97] Here the Tibetan reads "Then the lady *yab yum* (*jo mo yab yum*) arrived in the Tsang region," meaning the couple Yeshé Tsogyel and Atsara Salé.[98] Further adding to the flexibility of the designation *yab yum* in Yeshé Tsogyel's hagiography is a passage in which the term refers explicitly to three people, not two: "Yeshe Tsogyal was the main consort, while later Trashi Kyidren was the 'liberation' consort. The Guru and his two Consorts (*gu ru yab yum gsum*) opened the mandala of forty-two Étram."[99] Nowhere in Sera Khandro's auto/biographical writing do we find this variety of referents for *yab yum*.

Sera Khandro further accentuated the importance of Drimé Özer and her identity as an exclusive *yab yum* couple using a special term to describe the commitment that only they shared, *yab yum damtsik* (Skt. *samaya*). Translated literally, *damtsik* are the tripartite "commitment vows" necessary to attain the highest realization in the Tibetan Buddhist tradition: individual liberation vows (*prātimokṣa*), bodhisattva vows, and Tantric vows. In the words of Tulku Thondup, *damtsik* are the sacred obligations that Tantric practitioners must uphold; just as karma is the rope that forms the heart of causality in exoteric Buddhism, *damtsik* form the electric wire of connectivity between a Tantric practitioner, her guru, and her vajra siblings that she must keep intact. The expression "*yab yum* commitment vows" appears once in Yeshé Tsogyel's hagiography, when Tsogyel cautions her disciple Kalasiddhi to "Guard *samaya* with your partner (*yab yum dam tshig*) as you would your eyes."[100] In Sera Khandro's writing, it appears many times, always referring to the sacred bond between herself and Drimé Özer. The attribute of this electric current between them that appears most often is the promise that method and insight would never part.

Mutual Love in Separation

In spite of their commitment vows, remaining together proved to be a challenge. Obstacles such as Sera Khandro's high status, Akyongza's jealousy, the disapproval of others in Drimé Özer's religious community, and later Sera Khandro's involvement with Gyelsé rendered their union nearly impossible. This theme of love in separation permeates love stories both secular and religious, whether it be the "separation" (*'bral ba*) theme of Tibetan *layi* love songs, the tragic obstacles that rent lovers apart in the "Mandarin Duck and Butterfly School" literature (Ch. *yuanyang hudie pai*) popular in late Qing/early Republican era China during Sera Khandro's youth, or the "love in separation" (Skt. *vipralambha*) theme found in Indian *bhakti* traditions. Presumably Sera Khandro would not have had direct access to the latter two types of literature, nor for that matter the European romantic tradition's long history of idealizing love in separation. Nevertheless, a theme of love in separation suffuses her narrative, beginning in earnest when Sera Khandro was twenty-three and living with Gyelsé in 1915. That year, when Sera Khandro heard that Drimé Özer was nearby, "I wanted (*'dun*) to see him like a thirsty person longs (*gdung ba*) for water, but not daring to ask Gyelsé, I let it go."[101] Soon she got her wish when Drimé Özer, Gyelsé, and Sera Khandro met at a consecration ceremony for a new prayer wheel. Sera Khandro reports that shortly after this, Gyelsé gave her away to Drimé Özer. The six years between the men's initial agreement and the time that Sera Khandro actually left Gyelsé to live with Drimé Özer span 93 folios of her autobiography and 130 folios of Drimé Özer's biography. During this period Sera Khandro describes four visits to Drimé Özer in which their *yab yum* relationship took root and transformed from a hierarchical master-disciple relationship consisting of Drimé Özer offering love and Sera Khandro devotion to a mutual interaction in which both *yab* and *yum* consorted with each other (*phan tshun*) and nourished each other's health, revelations, and spiritual realization. The mutuality Sera Khandro inscribes between herself and Drimé Özer in the visits described below does not appear in any other relationship in her writings, for not only were the two bound by exclusive *yab yum* commitment vows, but they came to share what Sera Khandro renders as an equal partnership of the heart.

The first visit occurred in 1918, when the twenty-six-year-old Sera Khandro had just given birth to a stillborn son and endured her mother-in-law Yakza's accusations of infanticide. When the downtrodden Sera Khandro arrived at Drimé Özer's retreat cave called Naidro Dorjé Dzong, not far from Dartsang in Serta, the two offered each other explanations why they had not yet acted on the auspicious connections prophesied for their union. In her autobiography, Sera Khandro tells Drimé Özer,

> From the time I was young until now, although just a bit of the Guru Couple's aspirations pertained to me, I aspired to fulfill them and wondered if I could. However, prophesied consorts that were objects of my desire (*'dod rgyu*) didn't desire (*'dod*) me. Consorts that I didn't desire, of bad ancestry with small karmic connection to Secret Mantra, desired me and seduced me by means of various methods, including rare and difficult to come by material wealth. In this way, my actions became contradictory [to the Guru Couple's aspirations]. Perhaps the reason is that I did not rely on auspicious connections the way they were intended to be. . . . Please pay attention to me, protect me, and don't withhold your kindness toward me![102]

Drimé Özer responded to this apology with his own:

> Don't think like this. . . . As I have said before, in many of the prophetic guides for my Treasures, your vajra prophecies appear clearly. Despite this, from one perspective, you were with Gyelsé. From another perspective, because your conduct was extremely virtuous, I didn't dare say whatever I thought. In particular, it was extremely difficult to maintain the consorts in my entourage. Because I was very irritated, I didn't follow through on all my actions. Not relying on prophecies, I let them go.[103]

Sera Khandro and Drimé Özer's justifications for why they had not yet come together highlight the different challenges they faced as female and male religious specialists. Her explanation for becoming involved with the wrong consorts, implying Gyelsé without using his name, was that they seduced her by offering financial support. This underlines her comment to the nun Tsüldrön years before that "someone like me who is young and without wealth would surely not make it on my own as a nun."[104] In contrast, Drimé Özer faced the "very irritating" (*sems sun che ba*) problem of how to manage the competing demands of his consorts. After Sera Khandro offered Drimé Özer teachings she revealed as Treasures, she concludes her description of their first visit with the following: "Then, in mutual accord (*phan tshun thugs mthun*), he loved me attentively (*rjes brtse lhod med*), and we returned home."[105] Her rendition of the end of this first visit in his biography emphasizes their mutual affection to an even greater degree: "They both acted as each other's consort (*phan tshun gnyis ka nas gcig grogs gcig gis byas*). They prayed that method and insight would be indivisible, and they nurtured each other's devotion as if his mind and hers were one."[106]

Their second visit occurred the following year, in 1919, when the twenty-seven-year-old Sera Khandro was pregnant with the boy Gotrül Rinpoché claimed as his consciousness (*rnam shes*). In Drimé Özer's biography, she explains that he instigated the visit by sending Gyelsé a letter requesting Sera Khandro's presence for the sake of an auspicious connection that he needed to cure his illness. When Gyelsé arrived with Sera Khandro and their entourage, the two men closest to Sera Khandro reconferred with each other about her status:

> The Master said, "Even though deities' and lamas' prophecies are like this, if you are not in agreement, it is like I said before."[107]
>
> Gyelsé replied, "Since this year her astrological chart is extremely disturbed, if you two act as consorts for each other and benefit arises, that is good. I stand by my earlier words that you are her guardian (*bdag po*). Despite this, it is important that people in your residence are in agreement with this."
>
> The Master said, "In accordance with their wishes regarding *yab* and *yum* living together with everyone, as for me, I will look after everyone with actions that are long-lasting and harmonious from whichever of the two worldly and religious perspectives. In particular, thinking of my com-

mitment vows to my consorts (*rig ma'i dam tshig*), we are in harmony. Even though no one is saying anything bad at all about the suitability of the *khandro* living with me, since I am getting older [39 years old], I think that I will not engage in too much activity of any kind."[108]

Sera Khandro's rendition of Drimé Özer's description of the two of them as *yab* and *yum* is the first time in his biography that she uses this locution, suggesting an increasing intimacy. But the concern about the other women in the household loomed large. This is the one instance in either work that Drimé Özer refers to his "commitment vows to his consorts" (*rig ma'i dam tshig*) in a slightly different expression than the "*yab yum* commitment vows" that always refer to his relations with Sera Khandro. In this case, his "commitment vows to his consorts" appear connected to maintaining harmony among all of them. Even Gyelsé, who Sera Khandro always portrays as eager to get rid of her, checks and double-checks with Drimé Özer that his household will be amenable to Sera Khandro's entry, suggesting doubt about Drimé Özer's optimism.

After this reconfirmation between the two men, Sera Khandro writes that Drimé Özer asked her to show him the prophetic registry from her Treasure scriptures in which his name was clearly written as her prophesied consort, but at first she hesitated because she feared Gyelsé's reaction. She offered the registry despite Gyelsé, and then "both *yab* and *yum* each acted as each other's consort."[109] Drimé Özer gave her religious teachings and a new name, Künzang Dekyong Chönyi Wangmo, "The All-Good Bliss-Nurturing Queen of Reality," with which she signed many of her Treasure texts (others she signed Dewé Dorjé). As Gyelsé and Sera Khandro prepared to return home, "The Master treated me lovingly (*thugs brtse brtse mdzad*) as if I were his root consort (*rtsa ba'i rig ma*)."[110] This closing comment suggests a special affinity between *yab* and *yum* that set Sera Khandro apart from other women in Drimé Özer's life, yet it indicates that she was "as if" but not actually his main or root consort. Later, in her autobiography, she described this second visit in very similar terms:

> Each one of us having relied on the other, the obstacles to our life forces were dispelled. Then, the Master gave Gyelsé very expensive items and a rug adorned with images of auspicious things together with a nice offering scarf. Gyelsé was extremely pleased, and they strengthened their

long-lasting friendship with each other. The Master also took care of me with great love (*thugs brtse ba chen po*) as if I were his root consort (*rtsa ba'i gzungs ma*).[111]

Sera Khandro's accounts emphasize a relationship of mutual benefit between herself and Drimé Özer while acknowledging the continuing care with which the two men closest to her negotiated the terms of their exchange.

A year later, in 1920 after Sera Khandro had given birth to her son, Rindzin Gyurmé Dorjé, she returned with her young children and her disciple Tupzang to visit Drimé Özer for a third time. Her auto/biographical works account for this visit in similar terms, although each emphasizes a different reason for it: in Drimé Özer's biography she visits out of fear that he would soon depart for a journey to distant Gangri Tökar in central Tibet, whereas in her autobiography she elaborates more on her infant son's illness necessitating Drimé Özer's ritual protection. In his biography the dialogue she narrates during their third visit presents the strongest language in either work portraying *yab* and *yum* as two parts of a relationship defined on mutual, even equal, terms. Initially Sera Khandro attempted to dissuade Drimé Özer from leaving by reminding him of their commitment vows:

> "Specifically, for all the people of the lands of Washül Serta, the three districts of Akyong, the seven districts of Pema Bum, and so forth, you are the place the dead direct their consciousness. For the living, you are the source of refuge and the object of hope for this life and the next. The inner specific reason is that for this life, the next, and the intermediate state, I, this beggar woman, have no other refuge but you alone, Trülku Wish-fulfilling Jewel. Don't go to a faraway land! Stay here in comfort. Tell your disciples without hiding anything or keeping anything secret what you need to preserve your life. When you don't find a way to preserve your life, you don't care enough about our *yab yum* Dharma commitment vows and about all our aspirations." Saying this again and again, she sobbed.
>
> The Master couldn't bear it and said, "Don't do this! We can talk about this." Then both *yab* and *yum* abided by their mutual commitment vows and he didn't go far away.[112]

Sera Khandro and Drimé Özer were connected by "mutual commitment vows" (*phan tshun gyi dam tshig*) that required both to promise that they would not take long journeys apart. After Drimé Özer offered ritual protection for Sera Khandro's infant son, who was sick with worms (*ya ma*), she makes a significant claim about herself and her guru:

> Then, Dewé Dorjé handed a symbolic prophetic guide from the *ḍākinīs* to the Master and asked him, "Do you understand the meaning of this?"
>
> He looked at it and replied, "I have taken out a Treasure that belongs to you."
>
> Dewé Dorjé said, "Why is that?"
>
> The Master answered, "Our Treasures are principal and subsidiary. In particular, there is a prophecy that I will have four Treasure retinues and three consorts who will benefit the Treasures. Out of those, the prophecy clearly indicates that there will be one extraordinary consort who will benefit the Treasures who is equal (*mnyam pa*) to me—this is you. Hence, because of this, we can act as consorts for each other."
>
> Although Dewé Dorjé thought, "It is certain that an inferior one like me is not equal to Trülku Rinpoché," for the purpose of the auspicious connection, she didn't say anything but "Okay."
>
> The two *yab* and *yum* spoke in detail about worldly and religious affairs, exchanged advice, and then Dewé Dorjé returned home.[113]

This dialogue follows Sera Khandro's typical style of autobiographical ventriloquy in which she presents praise about herself through others' voices, only to then humbly deny their claims. When Drimé Özer calls Sera Khandro his equal, she hastens to qualify that it couldn't possibly be the case. But even with this partial denial, her act of inscribing his words recognizing her as "his extraordinary consort who is his equal" is striking. Drimé Özer was eleven years her senior and a highly regarded Treasure revealer who had inherited the mantle of his father's dynamic religious enterprise at Dartsang. Sera Khandro was widely recognized as a *ḍākinī* and a Treasure revealer by this point at the age of twenty-eight, but she was not Drimé Özer's equal in the sense of Golok social status or religious pedigree. She was an "inferior woman" as she reminded her readership at every turn, the mother of two, and she was Gyelsé's spurned spouse who lacked the social capital to maintain her position in his home. She alludes to this latter difficulty in her autobiographical rendition of this third visit, in which she presents herself refusing to visit Drimé Özer even though prophecies suggest she should because he could cure her infant son's illness:

I said, "I won't go. Yesterday Seldrön [Gyelsé's new spouse] told me that everybody is saying that I am preparing to go be the Treasure Revealer Trülku's [Drimé Özer's] consort. Because she told Gyelsé this, still now I experience domestic disputes like this. If I go there with my child, since various undesirable things such as not being permitted to come back and so forth are close at hand, I certainly won't go."

When I gave up on going, my little son's sickness became extremely serious. They couldn't handle it and without offending the household, they got a horse and food. After they gathered the necessities together, I, mother and two children, together with my disciple Tupzang, went to Naringma in the Ja Valley (*bya khog*) where the Master had settled the religious encampment.[114]

If Sera Khandro had so little standing in her own household with Gyelsé, what did she mean when she wrote that she was prophesied to be Drimé Özer's equal? The word she used for equality is *nyampa* (*mnyam pa*), meaning "compatible, equal, similar, same" but also "even, level, balanced."[115] The latter meanings indicate a proximity to the more specialized religious term *nyamnyi* (*mnyam nyid*), "The abiding nature which remains unaffected in its character by the dichotomies of *saṃsāra* and *nirvāṇa*, good and evil, acceptance and rejection, and so forth."[116] A contemporary lineage holder of Sera Khandro's Treasure teachings named Dzongsar Khyentse Rinpoche offers his own interpretation of equality that accords with the above:

> Western perspectives on sexual relationships emphasize "equality," yet this is very different from what is meant by equality in Vajrayāna Buddhism. Where equality in the West stands for two aspects reaching equal footing, in Vajrayāna Buddhism equality is going beyond "twoness" or duality altogether.[117]

Keeping this in mind, we may extrapolate that Sera Khandro was not proposing a social equality between herself and Drimé Özer in which they had equal rights or similar religious opportunities. But she was making a claim about their compatibility as consorts whose relationship embodied the two-in-one union of method and insight at the heart of Vajrayāna Buddhism. One outgrowth of this was that they could each benefit the other in terms of physical and spiritual well-being, at times even revealing each other's Treasures. In the dialogue about equality above from Drimé Özer's biography, he tells Sera Khandro, "I have taken out a Treasure that belongs to you." She elaborates on the meaning of this cryptic comment in her autobiographical account of this third visit:

> Then, to prevent demonic obstructions from affecting both *yab* and *yum*, I had a Treasure [to reveal called] *Trolö kyi Drupa Dülé Yülgyé, A Wrathful Guru Rinpoché Liturgy [Called] Conquering Demons*, that was hidden separately in a dark red scorpion chest in a place called Dongtrom. Although the Treasure entrance and [revelation] time was clear to me, for the sake of auspicious connections, the opportunity to reveal the Treasure came to the Master. The Master having ascertained this, he nurtured the auspicious connections of method and insight. The *yab* was empowered in the *yum*'s Treasure and the *yum* was able to reveal the *yab*'s Treasure, whereby their minds became one.[118]

This is one of several instances in which she and Drimé Özer revealed Treasures together as a *yab yum* couple. This is not social equality, nor is it necessarily religious equality as many might think of it, since Drimé Özer also predicted that their Treasures were "principle and subsidiary" (*ma dang bu*, literally "mother and child"), but it was a form of exclusive mutuality that sets their relationship apart from all others in her biographical writings. At the end of her description of the third visit in her autobiography, Sera Khandro writes that Drimé Özer "cared for me lovingly (*thugs brtse bas rjes su bzung*)" and gave her many precious items she would need for revealing and practicing her Treasures, such as a vajra, bell, paper, and ink. Then, they "made aspirations and prayers that *yab* and *yum* would be without separation for even an instant from now until they attained buddhahood."[119]

One year later, when Sera Khandro was twenty-nine in 1921, her situation had deteriorated: her recurring arthritis worsened, tensions with Gyelsé intensified, and the Golok region surrounding her was increasingly embroiled in fighting with the "northern Chinese," the troops of the Chinese Muslim Ma family warlords. Sera Khandro narrates in Drimé Özer's biography that their fourth and final visit during her partnership with Gyelsé at Benak began when "Dewé Dorjé suddenly came down with a serious illness. On the way back from circumambulating Drong [Mountain], she came before the Master. Both *yab* and *yum* were overjoyed as if meeting a person raised from the dead."[120] This is the only moment in Drimé Özer's biography that she uses this particular metaphor for any meeting, expressing the extremity of their mutual joy upon seeing each other again. I have translated Sera Khandro's full account of her journey to Drong Mountain in the section of chapter 2 titled "The Head of Washül Serta, Drong Mountain," but in his biography she summarized this journey in narrating the story of her fourth visit to Drimé Özer:

> "On the twenty-fifth I arrived in front of Drong [Mountain]. On that day, although I was on the verge of death and felt great suffering, a monk appeared and said, 'I have been sent by Trülku Lendrel [Drimé Özer]. You need to abide by your *yab yum* commitment vows.' As he said this, a red light pervaded my perception and I was revived from being [nearly] dead."
>
> The Master said, "Why did you do this? Earlier at Narangma,[121] didn't we promise not to let our lifespan be affected by negative circumstances?"
>
> "It is as if neither of us adhered to those earlier promises," Dewé Dorjé said, crying.[122]

Sera Khandro had also intuited that Drimé Özer was aspiring to depart from this life and go to the buddhafields. Once they had secured each other's promises that they would not travel far apart or prepare to die, Drimé Özer asked Sera Khandro if it was true that Gyelsé was mistreating her:

> Thinking that they would develop animosity toward each other, although Gartrül [Gyelsé] had taken up a Golok lady named Seldrön as his wife and was getting ready to expel Dewé Dorjé, she said, "It isn't like that," and kept it secret. She said, "I want to go to an unknown place—please direct your mind and do rituals for me."
>
> When she requested this, the Master said, "In my *ḍākinī* prophecies, you are my means to dispel obstacles to my life and Dharma. Hence, don't go far away. In particular, don't forget to find a way to spend just a few years here at this encampment. My household is definitely not opposed to this."
>
> Dewé Dorjé replied, "Although I pray that in this life and all my future incarnations I will be without separation from you, it is difficult to find a way to be with you. For one thing, there is Gartrül and for another, I'm not sure if those around you will stick to their word [about not opposing me]. I don't need this. We *yab* and *yum* get along really well, and from the time

I was fifteen years old I prayed to you and held you as my crown jewel. Since in this life, the next, and the intermediate state I have no other refuge but you, don't withhold your kindness—please do not expel me from your heart!"[123]

In her autobiographical account of this fourth visit, she reiterates the joy she felt upon seeing Drimé Özer using the same simile, "rejoicing as if I were meeting someone raised from the dead."[124] Pondering whether they would ever meet again, Sera Khandro said,

> "Your looking after me with great love (*brtse ba chen po*) takes me out of the assembly of humans and puts me in the assembly of deities. You are the pillar who upholds my life force, my secret consort for traversing the quick path, my hero with expansive profound Treasures and disciples. You are the holy origin of all worldly and religious deeds. Before, I never found someone like you. Later I can forget about finding someone like you. Because of this, I wonder if you won't remain as a manifestation of my merit. In particular, last year when you were staying at Naringma, even though my requests were truly without hypocrisy, I am not sure what outcome my words had. Since I am one with bad karma, if I die before you, Master, I wonder—what wouldn't be good about that?"
>
> Again as before, he replied, "Don't let your lifespan be affected by negative circumstances."
>
> We each acted as each other's consort, thus nurturing abundant auspicious connections.[125]

Their talk of love, mutual consorting, and relying on *yab yum* commitment vows orbited closer and closer to death—fear of the other's death, wishing to die first, and a foreboding sense on Sera Khandro's part that her days and even her moments with Drimé Özer were numbered.

As Sera Khandro was returning home from her fourth visit to her guru, a *ḍākinī* accosted her on the road, railing at her for "mistaking brass for gold, water for wine," Gyelsé for Drimé Özer. Shortly after she arrived back at Gyelsé's encampment,

> Then, one day I went to shepherd the livestock in a place with extremely thick forest and trees saturated with dew. Since I didn't have rain clothes, I was tormented by snow and rain from above and I got wet inside and

> outside as if I had been submerged in water. On account of this, the next morning, when I stretched the muscles of my legs, I couldn't walk.[126]

On top of that,

> Although I was nearing death, [Gyelsé] neglected to do a healing ritual for me. Tupzang and Jikmé Könchok both attended to me. When [Gyelsé] seemed to be unhappy with this, I told the two of them the following: "If I recover from this illness, I certainly won't live at the Gara household. From the time I was nineteen years old until twenty-eight, with my arms I have made fire and with my shoulders I have cleared ashes [from the stove]. My whole life has been spent working as a servant. Now, although I am on the verge of death, he neglects doing healing rituals. Everyone from outside and inside the encampment circle and in particular Gyelsé thinks that I am faking illness."[127]

As her health declined, a letter arrived from Drimé Özer informing her of the ominous prophesies he had received indicating that he was not long for this world. In his biography Sera Khandro quotes the letter, including these lines in the nine-syllable meter typical of classical Tibetan verse:

> My consort of many lifetimes who generates bliss,
> great joy Dewé Dorjé, jewel of my heart (*snying gi nor*),
> quickly bring together the excellent assembly of auspicious connections
> of joining with me inseparably without parting for an instant.
>
> Supreme key who opens the threshold of profound Treasures,
> if method and insight do not come together for this Treasure revealer,
> at the end of my life in the sixth month on the tenth day
> I will certainly go to the Copper-Colored Mountain;
> this is clarified in the Lama's undeceiving prophecy.
>
> Nevertheless, not thinking of going against
> the holy pledge I made to my heart consort (*snying grogs*),
> if I have the power, I will live until I'm sixty.
> But the demon's power is mighty; what will happen is not certain.[128]

When Sera Khandro received his letter and heard of his illness, she was devastated. Her problem, according to his biography, was that "From whatever perspective, she had no way to go quickly to the Master: on the outside, she was oppressed with illness, on the inside, she was oppressed with domestic disputes, and in between, the Master was going to the buddhafield. Thinking of this, she felt great suffering day and night."[129] She wrote Drimé Özer a letter in response begging him not to leave this world and promising him that if she didn't die, she would visit him in the first month of the year. She included the following supplication verses in the identical nine-syllable meter:

Embodiment of all the buddhas, Pema Tötrengtsel,
mother of the ultimate sphere, Khandro Yeshé Tsogyel,
I pray to you; please offer me your protection.

By the karmic residue of pure prayers from former lifetimes,
I have associated with this authentic consort for many lifetimes.
Now, by the influence of strong negative circumstances,
I must separate from my consort who is like my heart—
my mind is seized with misery and I cry.

When you reveal your delightful face and utter words,
the blissfully happy impression arises that I am transported to the land of the gods.
Heart consort (*snying grogs*), even though I have no intention to part from you,
I, this one with negative karma, have been reborn in a negative and inferior body (*lus ngan dman par skye*).
I have fallen under the sway of another and lost my freedom.
As in the realm of the Lord of Death, I am without any essential purpose.
In this and my future lives you are my only hope—
I constantly long to remain with you, not separating for even an instant.[130]

Drimé Özer called Sera Khandro "the jewel of my heart"; she told him that he was like her heart itself. Both referred to the other as their "heart consort," with whom they shared a deep connection developed over many lifetimes and without whom they could not live.

Enlightenment as a *Yab Yum* Couple

After all these exchanges reflecting their predestined roles as *yab* and *yum*, their growing intimacy, their deteriorating health without the support of the other, and Sera Khandro's imploding domestic life with Gyelsé, finally the tide turned. Only a few days after the exchange of letters excerpted above, the *yab yum* couple reunited in the winter of 1921, when Sera Khandro was twenty-nine. Their reunion marks the climax of her auto/biographical narratives and the moment of her spiritual liberation. But unlike standard Buddhist stories featuring the awakening of an individual renunciate, this is a story of the *mutual* enlightenment of a Tantric Buddhist couple.

Sera Khandro summarized this critical moment in Drimé Özer's biography and expanded upon it in her own life story, but in both accounts it is the *yab* and *yum* in union who gain liberation. In his biography Sera Khandro writes, "A few days later [after the letter exchange] both of Dewé Dorjé's legs became paralyzed. Gara treated her as if she was a corpse to be carried to the cemetery, so Gyelsé's brother Jikmé Könchok and others escorted her [to Drimé Özer]."[131] After a brief exchange between the two men,

> Then, the Master gave Dewé Dorjé medicine and performed all sorts of rituals. One of her legs was cured and the other wasn't cured but became painless. Then *yab* and *yum* gathered together at one residence. On the outside, they opened the thresholds of the three profound Treasures[132] and clearly wrote them down and disseminated them. On the inside, having relied on the quick path of method and insight, they bolstered their progress and the vessel knots at their five centers loosened. Secretly, they transformed into an awareness body in union. The way the realization of the path of fulfillment arose, [including] purification, perfection, and ripening,[133] is clarified in both of the Treasure scriptures. Hence, fearing too many words, I won't write about it here. At that time, during the day a rain of flowers fell and a sound came forth and at night the earth quaked, mountains bellowed, the sounds of drums and cymbals played, and so forth. Fortunate ones gathered there actually witnessed this.[134]

These dramatic outer, inner, and secret results of Sera Khandro and Drimé Özer's reunion as *yab* and *yum* living and practicing together document how they realized the "path of fulfillment" (*mthar phyin pa'i lam*), also called the "path of no more learning" (*mi slob lam*), which is the final stage of practice before realizing buddhahood. She alludes to the intertextuality of her biographical writings and her revelations by directing her readers to her and Drimé Özer's Treasure scriptures for more details, but summarizes the effects of their accomplishment including prolific Treasure revelation, the release of blockages in the circulatory system of the subtle body, and the actualization of their contemplative practices as male method and female insight.

In her longer autobiographical account of this pivotal moment, instead of expressing her yearning to reunite with Drimé Özer, she presents herself as resisting others' demands that she go to him, as if to emphasize that it was not her own volition but circumstances and prophecy that compelled her actions:

> When I was nearing death, Lhapel, Gyelsé, and his brothers had a discussion and said that they needed to escort my children and me to [the Master's] Treasure encampment.
>
> I said, "You don't need to make them a charnel ground where corpses are disposed. Why would you bring us, mother and children, to the Treasure revealer's household? In the early part of my life when I had [working] legs, you said I should be the servant of the Gara household. Now that I am about to die, there is no point in your telling me I need to go to someone else's place. If we mother and children offend you, it is okay if we go to Dzongné or Drongdün.[135] Otherwise, before when you took me to see the Treasure revealer Trülku, what did you, the Gara household, say to me? What speculations did you have? It is whatever one has in one's mind. You didn't pour water on top of me. You didn't burn fire under me. Other than that, from whatever perspective, in your mind of course you know what your household did to me."
>
> Lhapel and Gyelsé both said, "Because there is no way for the Gar encampment circle to go to Drongdün and Dzongné, we must go to the Treasure encampment."
>
> [Gyelsé] sent both Jikmé Könchok and his attendant to escort me. In the eighth month on the third day of the iron bird year [1921] the three of us, mother and children, together with Tupzang, set out on the road. At that time, Gyelsé acted sorrowful and escorted us up to the lower part of the valley. Many unusual signs arose, such as a vulture landing on the tent

> in which I was staying and a great gust of wind cutting the main rope that secured the tent. All those who escorted me grieved as if I had died. Then, Gara Lhapel escorted me up to the road for the interval of time it takes to drink tea. Gyelsé and the others in his group returned home.[136]

Thus ends the volatile chapter of Sera Khandro's life with Gyelsé at Benak Monastery.

By the time she arrived in Drimé Özer's presence, her energy was depleted and she could not speak. Drimé Özer nursed her back to health, providing medicine, healing rituals, and specially blessed food, including meat, which Sera Khandro notes that she ate in order to restore her health even though she was normally a vegetarian. Then,

> For three months together in one place, *yab* and *yum* practiced the conclusion of the esoteric instructions on *Dorjé Chutung, Drinking Vajra Water*, that I had previously given the Master. At that time, the signs in the outer environment were that day and night the mountains bellowed, the earth quaked, a roaring was heard, the sound of a flute and cymbals came forth, a fragrant aroma wafted, and so forth. All the group of fortunate disciples actually witnessed this.
>
> The inner signs of the domains of the channels, winds, and vital nuclei becoming purified were that the knots in my head and throat loosened. Not needing to train in and traverse the path, I understood all the Dharma vehicles without attachment or hindrance. From the hidden chest of profound Treasure, all the symbolic pith meanings of instructions appropriate for beings' dispositions and devotion came forth spontaneously. The ten winds became pliant, and our bodies had youthful flesh and were light like cotton wool. When hymns containing vajra words burst forth from my throat, the seeds of the first concentration were planted in the mind streams of those who heard them. By many small deeds such as this, benefit for sentient beings arose. In particular, we directly realized the inexpressible and inconceivable meaning of awareness and emptiness, the primordial wisdom of great bliss and emptiness endowed with the three liberations[137] and free from elaborations. The two, method and insight, actually merged as one taste.
>
> We entered the feast assembly of the *ḍākinīs* of the Three Bodies, and during a pure vision a special emanation of Shiwa Dorjetso arose. The Master really saw Dorjetso. I saw her in the form of Künzik Wangmo. There was

an inconceivable celebration feast for completing the greatly secret quick path.[138]

It would seem that Sera Khandro's account of spiritual realization has moved far away from the example of the Buddha's enlightenment as a solitary renunciate meditating under the bodhi tree. We see here instead Buddhist enlightenment transposed into Vajrayāna terms and realized in *yab yum* union. Even if Drimé Özer was always already enlightened in Sera Khandro's perception of him (as she states in his biography), she depicted a collective enlightenment in which the energetic knots at all five *cakras* within the subtle bodies of *yab* and *yum* were liberated together. The basic unit who awakened was not the solitary renunciate but the *yab yum* couple. Renouncing attachment to loved ones was still required, as in earlier forms of Buddhism, but her spiritual realization and the entire life story she framed around it took place in relationship to another.

This might seem a departure from the earlier Buddhist paradigm of solitary enlightenment but can also be an extension of it. The earth quaked in acknowledgment of Siddhārtha's enlightenment under the bodhi tree, as it did for Sera Khandro amid other miraculous occurrences. Not all versions of the Buddha's life story emphasize his status as a lone ascetic to the same degree. In the Mūlasarvāstivāda Vinaya, the Buddha does not abandon his wife, Yaśodharā, and newborn son on the night of his great departure from household life, but rather impregnates her before departing. This instigates a parallel experience of asceticism and gestation for separated husband and wife, resulting six years later in the Buddha's enlightenment and Yaśodharā's giving birth to their son Rāhula.[139] Sera Khandro's account brings this parallelism a step further, for the two *yab* and *yum* don't attain separate goals but rather the same highest goal of completing the Vajrayāna Buddhist path.

Although there is some Buddhist precedent for Sera Khandro's rendition of a joint awakening, the way the union of *yab* and *yum* takes center stage in her auto/biographical writings has few correlates in other biographies of Treasure revealers. Other works make ample mention of Tantric practices involving sexuality and of merging one's mind with that of the guru in a state of nondual unity, but little parallel to Sera Khandro's emphasis on enlightenment as a shared experience of the Tantric couple instead of the solitary renunciate. In Düjom Lingpa's autobiographical writings, for example, *ḍākinīs* appear in visionary and human form to confer prophecies and to serve as auspicious connections enabling him to discover and decode his Treasures, but only briefly as aids on his spiritual journey. Though he describes many ephemeral *ḍākinī*s by name who appear to him in visions, Düjom Lingpa presumably also had more permanent associations with the human women who bore him eight sons, but we find neither their names nor any information about them in his autobiographical writings. These works chart the miraculous path of one spiritual virtuoso, not the union of *yab* and *yum*.

Likewise, the autobiography written by Gyelsé's father, Gara Terchen Pema Dündül Wangchuk Lingpa, does not present a central *yab yum* relationship as his path to and realization of buddhahood. Gara Terchen's autobiography is incomplete, ending when he was thirty and lacking a colophon, but in the 148 extant codex pages he describes no parallel to Sera Khandro and Drimé Özer's *yab yum* and guru-disciple relationship. The level of gossip, controversy, and social approbation Gara Terchen experienced by heeding *ḍākinī* prophesies and nurturing auspicious connections with his consort Ngak Chödrön resonates with elements of Sera Khandro's accounts, as seen in the previous chapter, but Ngak Chödrön was a vehicle more to notoriety than to enlightenment. Gara Terchen also wrote about his visions of *ḍākinī*s who catalyzed his spiritual realizations. For example, during his twenty-seventh year in 1884–85, he had a vision of Vajravārāhī and other *ḍākinī*s, and "On account of their conferring the secret empowerment on me, the vessel knot at each of my *cakra*s loosened and the letters at the vessels appeared outwardly."[140] This dream takes up a few lines in his writing and is one of many similar dreams with different *ḍākinī*s. There is more to Gara Terchen's life story than this, as he indicates in another short autobiographical work of fourteen codex pages summarizing key events in his life up to the age of forty-eight, titled *Core Commentary on the Awakening of Karmic Propensities of Being a Yogi: A Personal Account in My Own Words About my Experience on the Path and Its Results.* In this short account, Gara Terchen mentions an extraordinary consort with whom he attained realization amid miraculous occurrences:

> When I was thirty-six I met a consort (*thabs grogs*) who, among the five families of *ḍākinī*s, was an incarnation of Yeshé Tsogyel. The realization of the illusory body of clear light endowed with bliss and emptiness manifested, and having conquered the wheel of birth and death, I attained confidence. At the supreme holy site Tashi Gomang, during a feast offering, rainbows

appeared and the sound of the earth quaking and cymbals playing came forth. I revealed a *vajrakīla* as a profound Treasure and it generated faith in my disciples, my consort, and others.[141]

Gara Terchen writes of mourning intensively when this unnamed "holy consort" (*thabs grogs dam pa*) passed away during his forty-fifth year. This would have been 1902, before Yakza became his *yum*, and before Sera Khandro had left her childhood in Lhasa. Despite this intriguing mention of another extraordinary Yeshé Tsogyel incarnation, the lead character in Gara Terchen's extant autobiographical writings, as in those of Düjom Lingpa, is himself alone. Many other famous Tibetan Treasure revealers such as Guru Chöwang (thirteenth century), Tangtong Gyelpo (fourteenth–fifteenth century), Pema Lingpa (fifteenth century), and Jikmé Lingpa (eighteenth century) included little to nothing about the human women with whom they consorted, despite the ubiquity of *ḍākinīs* and channel and wind practices involving sexuality in their autobiographical works.[142]

In contrast, Sera Khandro framed the ensuing phase of her life in residence with Drimé Özer as centered around the activities of the *yab yum* couple. This emphasis on liberation in relationship with another might seem disempowering from a feminist perspective.[143] Although one could interpret it as a sign of her disenfranchisement as an outsider woman who could only establish her identity in relation to powerful others, Sera Khandro's writings indicate that she found renewed strength and support from her relationship with Drimé Özer. In her words, their union mobilized an abundance of auspicious connections, allowing them to "decode each other's profound Treasures extremely quickly."[144] After the two *yab* and *yum* entered another retreat together, "The obstacles to the Master's forty-first year were dispelled and disciples clustered and expanded like a constellation of stars."[145] That year, 1922, Drimé Özer gave the whole group of his disciples expansive empowerments and reading transmissions for his entire collection of sixteen volumes of Treasures. At one point Sera Khandro writes that familiar fears gave her pause. She worried, "If we, mother and children, stay here, even though the Gara family thinks it's pointless, I'm not sure if the Master's relatives, such as the Dordra *yab yum* [Drimé Özer's younger brother Dorjé Drandül and his consort], approve."[146] She resolved to go on her own to a retreat at another place, but this met with strong opposition from Drimé Özer, who offered either to go with her himself or send his attendant to accompany her. In her autobiography she writes that he told her, "It's not acceptable for you to feel depressed. Since our commitment vows merge us together and since you are a lama, I won't do anything that displeases you by even a hair's breadth."[147] This is the language that a disciple would use toward his guru, and here instead it is Drimé Özer calling Sera Khandro a lama. In response, Sera Khandro called him "the jewel of my heart" (*snying gi nor bu*), and abandoned her plans to distance herself from him. Instead, the two grew closer, and in the following year they revealed more Treasures together. In his biography Sera Khandro recounts some details of the way they revealed Treasures jointly, referring to herself in the third person as "the *khandro*" at times and by her name Dewé Dorjé at others:

> Both *yab* and *yum* secretly went. They went slowly on account of the *khandro*'s bad leg. The Master said he was going to look for the Treasure entrance and went ahead. A little while later he came back.
>
> When the *khandro* asked, "Why did you go?" the Lord thought that it was unacceptable to mix up the auspicious connections, so he said, "I took out my Treasure and came to get you." Together, they went into a cave.
>
> Then the Master asked, "Why are so many fish and frogs gathered at the Treasure site?"
>
> Dewé Dorjé replied, "Since the Treasure protector in this life and beyond is a *lu tsen* spirit,[148] perhaps they are its miraculous emanations."
>
> As they neared the Treasure entrance, a fragrant aroma wafted and vultures swirled in the sky and sang melodiously. When the two *yab* and *yum* arrived at the Treasure entrance, the Master sat and recited the seven-line prayer. Dewé Dorjé opened the Treasure entrance and took out three Treasure chests.
>
> After she gave them to the Master, he said, "Amazing," and received empowerment from them. Feeling extremely joyous, he inserted a Treasure substitute and closed the Treasure entrance.[149]

Where Drimé Özer traveled, so did Sera Khandro, and when auspicious connections arose for them to reveal Treasures, they did so as a *yab yum* couple for the remainder of Drimé Özer's life. The degree of relationality with which Sera Khandro presented her life story exceeds that of her fellow male Treasure revealers, but her writings emphasize that rather than signaling her subordination, being part of a *yab yum* couple led to her liberation.

Love Medicine and (Im)permanence

Denis de Rougemont famously claimed, "Romance only comes into existence where love is fatal, frowned upon and doomed by life itself."[150] Tristan and Iseult as well as Romeo and Juliet epitomize the tragic consequences of romantic love in European literature. But the lethal effects of love also factor into Tibetan literature, such as the nineteenth-century Nyingma renunciate Patrül Rinpoché's *Holy Dharma Advice: A Drama in the Lotus Garden.*[151] *Holy Dharma Advice* tells the story of two tiny honeybees in love—golden-colored Wide Lotus Wings and turquoise-colored Sweet Lotus Voice. Following the classical Indian aesthetic association between honey, bees, and the erotic mood of *śṛṅgāra rasa*, Patrül Rinpoché's honeybees spend their days enamored with each other, frolicking together in a beautiful garden of lotus flowers, distracted from the Buddhist truth of impermanence by their love. The word that Patrül Rinpoché uses for their love is *tsewa* (*brtse ba*), the same word that pervades Sera Khandro's writing. The honeybees are loving companions (*brtse ba'i zla grogs*) who feel uninterrupted love for each other (*thugs brtse 'du 'bral med pa*).[152] Catastrophe strikes when suddenly dark clouds obscure the sun and the lotus flower in which Sweet Lotus Voice is sipping nectar clamps shut, trapping her inside. After a grief-stricken exchange between the two honeybees as she slowly smothers, the rains seal Sweet Lotus Voice's fate and she dies, leaving Wide Lotus Wings devastated and alone. Armed with an intense resolve to renounce worldly attachments, Wide Lotus Wings dedicates himself to practicing the true Dharma at the feet of his lama, Lotus Joy, and finds lasting happiness and peace through perfecting the Buddhist teachings. According to Tulku Thondup, *Holy Dharma Advice* is based on a true story of the devastation of one of Patrül Rinpoché's disciples named Tashi Delek, whose beautiful young bride abruptly died during an epidemic in the Degé region of eastern Tibet.[153] This poetic tale drives home the Buddhist message of impermanence:

> Whoever practices Dharma is joyful,
> whoever is attached to this life suffers.

Among the solitary mountains, it is always joyous.
The city of *saṃsāra* is suffering by all means.[154]

For Patrül Rinpoché, passionate love even between two virtuous and deeply committed partners is nothing but a distraction from the truth of impermanence that tempts the lovers to while away their precious human lives, bringing them closer to death and inevitable suffering.

Though Sera Khandro and Patrül Rinpoché both use the word *tsewa* for love, which goes hand in hand with grief, Patrül's story is a warning about the dangers of secular love and Sera Khandro's story is a tribute to love bound by the seal of Tantric commitment vows. Both types of love are punctuated by the inevitability of impermanence and the grief of separation, but unlike Patrül Rinpoché's honeybees, Drimé Özer and Sera Khandro's love leads them not closer to death but to its defiance. That Sera Khandro's affection helped preserve Drimé Özer's life follows the longstanding association between *ḍākinī*s and the power to increase longevity. But similar to other aspects of their consort relationship, this power to prolong life was mutual between Sera Khandro and Drimé Özer. In particular, Drimé Özer saved her from near death the year after their reunion. Not mentioned in his biography but prominent in hers, during her thirtieth year she revealed a Treasure scripture pertaining to the transference of consciousness at death while Drimé Özer was giving a large assembly of disciples empowerment in his Treasure teachings. When Drimé Özer saw her revelation, he immediately understood it as a sign that she was preparing for death and lamented,

> What is the meaning of your casting both your son and daughter and in particular me from your heart and not staying in this world? Whom will we rely on and for whom will we have affection (*sems 'khri*)? In particular, since you know that I have no other source of refuge and no other person who is both my consort and lama to rely on, how miserable that you would cast me from your heart![155]

Again Sera Khandro presents Drimé Özer addressing her as both his consort and his lama. In response, she promised not to make further preparations for her death, but later that month the *ḍākinī*s came to welcome her to their buddhafield anyway. As myriad *ḍākinī*s and offering goddesses invited her to their luminous realm, her vital signs began to fade:

The four elements of my body dissolved inwardly and it became as if empty. My mind was the same as the outer ultimate sphere. Discriminative insight became naturally purified. Although there was no difference between clarity and obscuration in my perception of *saṃsāra* and *nirvāṇa*, it became difficult to distinguish appearances. At that time, the weeping and wailing of the Master and Sotrül along with those close to them resounded. The others in the religious encampment gathered there were also filled with sadness. As when a hawk destroys a bird's nest, there was a commotion.

In particular, the Master sorrowfully put my head on his lap and said the following:

> Dear child, if you cast me from your heart and go to the buddhafield, very soon I will certainly direct my intention toward being there with you. I will forget about maintaining and propagating all of my Treasure Dharma and so forth until not even a trace of it remains. You are the object of my hopes in this life and the next. You are the great chariot for traversing the quick path. My consort, jewel of my heart, in all my successive lives may I be without separation from you!

When he was grieving, a teardrop fell into my ear. It was as if it hit my heart. Although my external breath was about to stop, I seemed to regain a bit of consciousness. Again, the Master himself touched his face to my ear and said again and again,

> Dear child, don't forget me. Direct your attention to three [letters] "*A Nṛī Hūṃ*" in your heart center and your consciousness will become clear.

After this, I remembered the words of the Wish-fulfilling Jewel and when I focused my attention on him, all of the previous appearances of light went further and further away and then disappeared. My perception of all the material things of this world became as if clear sometimes and unclear other times. My illusory body also became like a frozen rock. Like a person who was abruptly awakened from sleep, I forgot all of the things I had previously perceived. Unsure what anything was, since my eyes could see a little bit, I looked around. The entire house was filled with butter lamps. Sotrül and Tupzang were trying to warm my legs with fire. The Master still had my head on his lap and was performing [rituals] of consecrating my body *maṇḍala* and sense faculties as well as summoning my life force. Even so, I was unable to say anything, as if I had become mute. Early in the morning when all the other doctors and ritualists presumed that I would die, by the great blessing power of my secret consort the Wish-fulfilling Jewel and since the fruition of my negative karma had not been exhausted, he gradually resuscitated me from being in the state in which my external breath had stopped. All the group of disciples gathered there, especially the Master and Sotrül, were extremely joyous and rejoiced as if meeting someone raised from the dead.[156]

The mutual reliance and devotion both *yab* and *yum* expressed continued to deepen. One year after Drimé Özer's miraculous resuscitation, Andzom Drondül Pawo Dorjé's messenger arrived, summoning Sera Khandro to dispel his obstacles. As we have seen in the previous chapter, she despaired at having to part from Trülku Drimé, likening herself to a stray dog being banished. In her autobiography, she tells him,

> At this time, I cannot separate from you for even an instant. Like a child circles around her mother, my mind has become extremely attached (*sems shin tu chags*) to you. Hence, if I don't have to go, I would prefer not to.
>
> The Master replied, I too will miss (*yid 'phreng*) you—if I could never be apart from you for even one day, I would feel extremely happy, happier than if I had a house full of jewels.[157]

Sera Khandro's words followed the standard parental metaphor for love between a disciple and guru as she likened herself to a child circling around her mother, but the extreme mental attachment she professed as well as his declaration of how much he would miss her resonate more closely with the constellation of afflictions (Skt. *kleśa*) the Buddhist path aims to eliminate than the impartial compassionate love it heralds. In her autobiography Sera Khandro expressed how she felt at her departure for Andzom Gar in Kham:

> When the Master escorted me, I was unable to part with him and felt misery as if I was going to the realm of the dead. But there was nothing I could do, so I sang a song of sorrow like this:
>
> Lord of the dance of co-emergent awareness and great bliss,
> one who arises in a form body as the method aspect,
> jewel of my heart, Pema Lendreltsel—
> when I am together with you without an instant of separation,
> your joyous smile, soothing words,

and your mind's insight bring down a rain of whatever Dharma I desire (*'dod*).
When method and insight become one taste in bliss and emptiness,
I feel inconceivable blissful happiness like being in a god realm.
Hero, even though I don't wish to part from you,
I must go for a time to another unseen place,
invoked by the power of former auspicious connections.
Hence, my mind is tormented by misery as if I'm going to the realm of the Lord of Death.
Nevertheless, through the aspirations of the Padmasambhava Couple and
by the pure vows and love (*dam gtsang thugs brtse ba*) between us, method and insight,
I pray that I will quickly see your face.

When I sang this, the Master also made a similar aspiration. He gave me advice about the present and future and then he returned home. Other disciples escorted us and we set out on the road. At that time, I missed the Master so much my heart's desire was not to go.[158]

The comparison between leaving Drimé Özer and traveling to the realm of the dead that Sera Khandro made a few times when she described her visit to Andzom Rinpoché hints at the more serious departure the *yab yum* couple was about to face, as do a series of bad omens and inauspicious affairs that arose in 1923 and 1924, including a lawsuit Gyelsé pressed for custody of Sera Khandro's son (see chapter 1 for details). In 1924 the thirty-two-year-old Sera Khandro dreamed that she was riding a vulture, looking for parents to whom she should be born in her next incarnation, but she couldn't find any that suited her. She told Trülku Drimé about her dream, foretelling that

This year it is difficult to ascertain what will happen. If I go before you, I'll have no regret. Because of this, if you have a long life, I will take birth in your family and direct my aspirations toward serving your and your father's teachings. I wonder if I will have the capacity to maintain and protect the teachings?[159]

Drimé Özer reacted with predictable reprimand, demanding to know why she was "casting him from her heart" by aspiring to reincarnate into her next life. He continued,

> When I think about the misery I felt before in Nyimalung when you were preparing to go to the buddhafield, now that I am old and that our feelings are in harmony (*thugs snang mthun pa*), I cannot live without you for even the time it takes to drink a cup of tea. From now on it is unacceptable for you to direct your aspirations in this way.
>
> So saying, he commanded me strongly. I responded,
>
> I did not arrange my incarnation according to my own volition without being attached to you (*yid ma chags*). A vulture arrived and didn't permit me not to go. Aside from that, Wish-fulfilling Jewel, you can forget about me casting you from my mind.[160]

Until this point Sera Khandro and Drimé Özer's *yab yum* commitment vows preserved their lives and kept the many centrifugal forces working against their union at bay. However, like Patrül Rinpoché's honeybees, *yab* and *yum* would not escape the great divide of death.

In the spring of 1924, the moment of earthly separation came for Sera Khandro and Drimé Özer. She summarizes the most painful three days of her life in her autobiography:

> All of a sudden on account of a serious epidemic, everyone—*yab* and *yum*, children, and disciples—was on the verge of death. That year in the fourth month on the seventh day my young son Rindzin Gyurmé Dorjé suddenly became ill and departed from this life. *Yab*, *yum*, and everyone in the community were overcome with grief. Then, the Master said,
>
> > Now, on account of obstacles regarding place and time, it seems as if we two will only temporarily need to appear as if we are separated. Dear child, jewel of my heart, don't be wearied. We have never gone against our commitment vows by even a hair's breadth, and our mind streams are one. Hence, at all times and occasions we will meet in the assembly of the *ḍākinīs*' feast.
>
> That month on the tenth day when the sun rose, he put his hand on my head and staring into space, he prayed for method and insight to arise in the form of Vajradhāra in nondual union. His physical body departed into the ultimate sphere of reality.
>
> I elaborated the details of all the dialogue *yab* and *yum* exchanged at this time in the Master's great biography.[161]

In the more comprehensive account of Drimé Özer's death she wrote in his biography the year after these events occurred, the two bound by *yab yum* commitment vows contemplated the truth of impermanence in the wake of the young Rindzin Gyurmé Dorjé's death, only days before Drimé Özer would also depart:

He looked into space and said the following:

> Although this *maṇḍala* of the sun's clear light
> rises in the east, it sets in the direction of the western mountain.
> This is a display of impermanence.
>
> During the three summer months, plants flourish in the meadows;
> during the three autumn months, frost and hail vanquish their zeal.
> This too is a display of impermanence.
>
> The assembly of disciples is like a group of guests;
> although they were here earlier, they are gone later.
> This too is a display of impermanence.
>
> This illusory body is like a rainbow in the sky;
> without light and darkness, it disappears into the sky.
> This too is a display of impermanence.
>
> The Truth Body of Pema Lendrel
> manifests as a buddha in the Glorious Mountain Buddhafield.
> This too is a display of impermanence.
>
> You, Künzang Chönyi Wangmo,
> don't miss my body.
> Meditate on appearances as the lama's body.
> Recite sounds as great bliss mantra.
> Make your conceptual mind, in nature one with reality,
> nondual with my mind.
> I bless you to always be inseparable from me.
> Later I will come to welcome and guide you
> to the palace at the Glorious Mountain.

Until then, following your aspirations and pledges,
perform vast benefit for the teachings and sentient beings.

After saying this, he put his two hands on Dewé Dorjé's head and prayed. Although Dewé Dorjé felt extreme suffering, she endured it. Seizing the Master's hand, she spoke:

Father Omniscient Pema Lendreltsel—
think of me with great love (*thugs brtse ba chen pos*).
By the power of past prayers of Tsogyel and Shelkar
and now by the prayers' pure karmic residue,
I became a fortunate one who was near you, Protector.
From the time I was twenty-six,
you took me on as your heart's consort.
Since I was twenty-nine, our union has helped the teachings and beings,
and we have performed vast good deeds and enlightened activities.

At this time, because of the demonic influence of those with perverse aspirations,
your body's solar *maṇḍala* is setting into the ultimate sphere.
What will we blind people do?
If the *ḍākinīs* guide father Wish-fulfilling Jewel away,
who will increase mother sentient beings' happiness?
If our protector goes to the buddhafields of the buddhas of the three times,
who will guide sentient beings who grasp onto duality?
Father Pema Lendrel is departing for the Glorious Mountain—
who will protect fortunate disciples?
The consort Wish-fulfilling Jewel not staying here,
who will become the source of refuge and hope for
me, this inferior woman (*lus dman*) Dekyong Wangmo?
Actual manifestation of Protector Padmasambhava, if you depart into the ultimate sphere—
who will uphold and protect the two Treasures?

The Master himself not actually staying here,
now I will have to supplicate a statue of you.

The Master not uttering his profound oral instructions,
I will need to write down your pith instructions in scriptures.
If you will not look after me lovingly (*thugs brtse bas gces par*),
I will have to meditate in darkness on integrating our minds.
Not looking after the fortunate ones in our entourage of disciples,
I will need to go to the pleasant land where you are.
Now, no matter how I think about it, please don't withhold your kindness—
may I be inseparable from you, Protector.[162]

Drimé Özer was departing, but not into another round of the endless cycle of birth and death that is *saṃsāra*. He was none other than Pema Lendreltsel, literally "One with the Dynamism of Karmic Connection to Padma[sambhava]." Padmasambhava departed from Tibet riding a burst of flashing light rays, heading toward the southwest, where he resides in his Glorious Copper-Colored Mountain Buddhafield. He with a powerful karmic connection to Padmasambhava was soon to join him there.

Coming full circle to the passage with which this chapter began, at sunrise on the tenth day Drimé Özer put both hands on Sera Khandro's head and prayed, "I am the supreme method, the great bliss Heruka. You are the great mother of insight into the expanse of emptiness." As soon as Drimé Özer finished his prayer, "May we attain the fully awakened youthful vase body of buddhahood as Hayagrīva and Vajravārāhī in indestructible union," Sera Khandro reports that his physical body dissolved into the ultimate sphere and he passed into complete buddhahood. She writes that the instant this occurred and for three days afterward, everyone present witnessed a sound booming and roaring, the earth quaking, a fragrant aroma wafting, rainbows filling the sky, and music with drums and cymbals playing.[163]

All of Drimé Özer's disciples gathered there at his deathbed "were tormented with grief as if they could not breathe in, [their feet] could not touch the ground, and they lacked a heart."[164] More than the others, Sera Khandro was devastated by both of her losses within only a few days. On top of that, even before Drimé Özer's funeral concluded, others from his household demanded that she and her daughter leave. She writes,

Thinking that, "What the Master said before is certainly true. Even though I am alone, they won't let me stay here. Now surely there is nobody who has negative karma like I do," she went toward the cairn on the rear mountain. She threw her body down on the ground and wailed in a loud voice, crying out in despair to the Master. A strong wind made her feel as if she was about to faint. Because of the wind, when she opened her eyes a bit, her eyesight was blurry. After wiping her eyes a little, she saw that the Master himself had actually come and was blowing on her face. Dewé Dorjé was extremely overjoyed and hugged the Master's neck.

She said, "Because you had passed away, I felt extreme suffering." She explained all the good and bad things that had happened in full and said, "Now I will be inseparable from you."

The Master said, "I wander from land to land, but I have never gone anywhere. Why are you feeling this much suffering about what appears in this world that is like an illusory dream? Aside from your having the perception that we, *yab* and *yum*, have separated, why would we separate by even a hair's breadth? Having gained confidence that all phenomena are illusions and dreams, conclude that all is the great nondual primordial wisdom. Then it will not be difficult to realize the ultimate sphere in which the Three Bodies are equal, as it is. Now you come later. I have to go earlier." Having treated me lovingly (*thugs brtse byas*), he left.[165]

The inseparability of *yab* and *yum*, Drimé Özer and Sera Khandro, was not a promise that the two human embodiments of method and insight could remain together forever, for nothing stays the same in the world of phenomenal appearances. Instead the symbolism of gender complementarity that they embodied in life gave way to the deeper truth that their separateness was only ever an illusion from the perspective of primordial wisdom. Ultimately Sera Khandro had to find wholeness beyond that which she embodied in physical union with Drimé Özer. But her writings indicate the difficulty of taking this wisdom to heart amid her intensive grieving:

I trained in [perceiving] suffering as illusory, but it was like putting a bridle on a wild horse. At times it was as if my suffering was stronger; at times its antidote was stronger; I focused my intention on aspiring to experience everything with the great equality of taste (*ro snyoms chen po*). When I was supplicating the Master, wind caused my consciousness to fade. Right in front of me, inside of a vital nucleus made of five colors of light, two *ḍākinī*s saying they were Dewé Gocha and Rikpé Reltri appeared together with the Wish-fulfilling Jewel. As soon as I saw that, I became extremely depressed, which caused my senses to become dull. At that time, a *ḍākinī* saying she was Künselma called me three times and said:

> Alas! Noble *ḍākinī*—
> Not letting your hearing be distracted, listen!
> All phenomena of *saṃsāra* and *nirvāṇa* are illusory emanations;
> abandon attachment to objects of perception.
> Adhere to the fortress of changeless awareness.
> Don't reject or accept, negate or affirm whatever appears.
> All phenomena have the one nature of reality itself.
> Whatever arises and whatever appears is the ornament of awareness.
> Unceasing appearances are the display of the heroes.
> Inexpressible emptiness is the insight mother.
> The seal of their union is indivisible.
> As an interdependent arising of illusory conventional truth,
> We will be separated for just a moment; this is its nature.
> In the ultimate sphere of great bliss, method and insight are
> indivisible.
> Stay and we will go to see the hero.

Having said this, she touched her thumb to my *cakra* of collected memory [at my heart] and my circumstances appeared as a buddhafield. When I looked around, the Wish-fulfilling Jewel approached me and asked,

> How are you? You are not fatigued? In general, the phenomena of *saṃsāra* and *nirvāṇa* are amazing. In particular, isn't it amazing that we illusory apparitions seem to have dissolved into the ultimate sphere?

Although he spoke about many reasons for impermanence, I believed [in permanence]. Sobbing relentlessly, I spoke many sad words, including,

> Why did you leave us behind and go to the buddhafield? Specifically, as you know, everyone from the outside and inside mistreats me and does whatever they can do to harm me. You know this. Now without a protector and refuge, what will I do?

He replied,

> Don't do this. We two are not separated for even an instant. In general, [we appear as if separated because of] the characteristics of compounded phenomena and specifically, because we both have nurtured the teachings. By

> the power of outer and inner negative circumstances and the weak merit of beings who are affected by the greatly changing times, the appearance that we have separated arises. However, this is just an illusion of conventional truth. The [ultimate] truth is that because of the great profundity of our connection from past aspirations and currently because of our strong connection based on mutually pure conduct, we lack any separation even for an instant. In the expanse of clear light, we two will always meet.[166]

At the conclusion of his biography, Sera Khandro's nostalgic laments to Drimé Özer and his loving responses continue for many folios of nine-syllable lyric typical of classical Tibetan verse. The tenor in which Sera Khandro grieved and the way multiple visionary apparitions of Drimé Özer responded as he receded to the southwestern buddhafield hark directly back to the two whose previous aspirations their union actualized, Padmasambhava and Yeshé Tsogyel. In her seventeenth-century hagiography revealed by Taksham Nüden Dorjé, Yeshé Tsogyel despaired at Padmasambhava's departure, imploring him with verse after verse of seven-syllable supplications choked with her tears, lamenting

> Sorrow and sadness! O my Lord of Orgyen!
> Until this moment we were so inseparable,
> And shall we in an instant now be parted?
> Is this not the meaning of "to join and to divide"?
> How might I be with you, never separate?[167]

Padmasambhava reappeared in apparitional form, reassuring his Tibetan *ḍākinī* consort again in nine-syllable verse,

> *Kyema!*
> Hear me, Lady, virtuous and faithful!
> I, the Lotus-born, now leave for others' benefit.
> My compassion is impartial, all-regarding;
> I cannot be compared to beings blinded by delusion.
> Practice Guru yoga if you would be with me constantly.
> With pure perception, all arises as the Teacher:
> There is no other teaching for inseparability.[168]

As Padmasambhava instructed Yeshé Tsogyel to perceive that "all arises as the Teacher," Drimé Özer told Sera Khandro to "meditate on appearances as the lama's body." Even though both *ḍākinīs*' gurus stressed their ultimate inseparability, Yeshé Tsogyel could not immediately accept Padmasambhava's display of impermanence any more than Sera Khandro could:

Kyema!
Revered and Precious One of Orgyen
Only father who protects Tibet,
You have gone away to realms of dakinis,
Tibet has now become an empty land.
Quintessential jewel, where have you gone?
For you, in truth, there is no "going" or "remaining,"
Yet on this day, away you go to Orgyen.
For all the dwellers in Tibet, both gods and men,
Behind each head the sun has set.
Who will warm them, naked and unclothed?
The eyes have fallen from the people's brow,
Who will lead them now, the staring blind?
From the people's breasts their hearts are torn,
Who will lead them, the living dead?
You came here for the good of beings,
How then that you do not stay forever?[169]

At the end of Drimé Özer's biography Sera Khandro too grieves over and over, crying out:

When I remember the sun *maṇḍala* of your face,
tears fall ceaselessly from my eyes.
When I remember the way your benevolent speech affectionately cared
for me,
I wonder, why should I preserve my life and limb?
When I remember the loving (*thugs brtse ba'i*) instructional teachings you
gave me,
my suffering is endless and I have no wish to spare my life.
No matter what I think about, I miss the lama.
Whatever region I live in, I miss the lama.
No matter which consort I associate with, I miss the lama.
When I think about instructional teachings on Dharma, I miss the lama.
By the vajra aspirations of the Protector Namnying and

the compassion of the divine Padmasambhava Couple,
I pray that not long from now I will actually meet you,
my secret consort of all my lifetimes.[170]

Despite their mourning, neither Yeshé Tsogyel's hagiography nor Sera Khandro's auto/biographical works end tragically, for both transcend their destitution as nondual realization dawns. Through Padmasambhava's blessings, Yeshé Tsogyel discovers that "the torment of defiled emotions was cleared away. I experienced directly that the Teacher was inseparable from myself."[171] In response to Sera Khandro's sorrowful verses translated above, the two *ḍākinīs* Rikpé Reltri and Dewé Gocha instructed her:

Aha, listen, noble and beloved woman (*mdza' na mo*),
train in viewing all phenomenal appearances as illusory.
This everlasting, thoroughly established adamantine awareness
is not different than the mind of Pema Lendrel.[172]

So saying, the *ḍākinīs* relay the story of Drimé Özer's life as a prophecy for her to write down as his biography. But the end of that story brings a new beginning to her life; after her biographical account of his funeral ushers the autobiographical "I" into her writing, her long autobiography details her life story, continuing beyond his death for another one hundred-plus folios. Within her account of more than ten post-Drimé Özer years, she writes of returning to Dartsang for the purpose of compiling Düjom Lingpa's and Drimé Özer's complete works when she was thirty-seven in 1929, her first visit since the community had exiled her five years earlier. After meeting her old friends and foes, she reflected on her joyous and painful years there, concluding with an expression of her newfound confidence:

Even without worldly ways, my mind is carefree.
Even having been expelled from the community, I accomplished my purpose.
Even though everyone criticized me, I am victorious over all.
Even though they exiled me to a distant land, my mind is resolved.
I have seen the original face of the changeless innate nature.
I have realized self-awareness inseparable from the lama.
No prejudice is possible in my compassion.

> The vase of my body, speech, and mind is filled with blessings.
> Perhaps I will go soon
> to the victorious place of the all-good Truth Body.[173]

The loving relationship between Drimé Özer and Sera Khandro did not cushion her from the truth of impermanence any more than the love between Patrül Rinpoché's honeybees did. But even though her love corresponded in word and feeling to that of the honeybees, it was embedded in Dharma and not contrary to it, for it provided a vehicle for transcending the suffering caused by believing in the realness of the divide between self and other, lover and beloved. Their love did not end with the inevitability of death, but lived on with the internal realization that they were never really separate. Sera Khandro and Drimé Özer's mutual vow as *yab* and *yum* committed them to each other as inseparable and complementary parts of a whole, but ultimately Sera Khandro realized that wholeness within herself.

Sera Khandro's account of her spiritual liberation in tandem with Drimé Özer depicts the path to buddhahood not as a distant, detached, and solitary venture but one characterized by a great love between male and female Tantric partners. This intense, exclusive, and mutual love appears where least expected—embedded in a Tantric Buddhist metaphysic purportedly devoid of passionate love, removed from Euro-American literary influences, and in a nomadic Tibetan cultural context noted more often for its banditry and backwardness than for its own forms of modernity.[174] We need not scour Sera Khandro's writing for foreign influences from Euro-American conceptions of romantic love, the Chinese cult of *qing*, or other cultural expressions of love beyond those available to late nineteenth- and early twentieth-century Goloks, the majority of whom spoke and read only Tibetan. Nor must we presuppose the universality of love in the human psyche to explain Sera Khandro's particular formulation of it, for we cannot easily separate human experience from its linguistic expression, biochemistry from social behavior.[175] Sera Khandro found ample precedent for her vision of Drimé Özer and herself in a mutually fulfilling and loving relationship primarily from the model of the Tibetan Treasure tradition's progenitors, Padmasambhava and Yeshé Tsogyel. As the chapters of this book have explored, she creatively superimposed her life and her story about it onto that of Yeshé Tsogyel in myriad ways. Just as Taksham Nüden Dorjé's seventeenth-century hagiography of Tsogyel presented her as Padmasambhava's consort who gained enlightenment from their union, so did Sera Khandro from her union with Drimé Özer. As Yeshé Tsogyel pined for her departing guru, so did Sera Khandro. And just as Padmasambhava's passing from this world was less a death than a departure to the southwestern buddhafield where he is eternally available to those with devotion, Drimé Özer's death did not ultimately separate him from Sera Khandro, for their powerful connection lives on forever, to be embodied by their reincarnations.

But forever is a long time for love to last, or at least for the same cultural, literary, and historical understanding of love to last. Indeed, a closer comparison between Taksham Nüden Dorjé's description of Yeshé Tsogyel and Padmasambhava's relationship in her hagiography and of the relationship between Sera Khandro and Drimé Özer also reveals significant differences. Taksham's work places less emphasis on the exclusivity of Yeshé Tsogyel and Padmasambhava's consort relationship: the locution *yab yum* does not only refer to the two of them. Also much less pronounced in Yeshé Tsogyel's hagiography is the great love (*brtse ba chen po*) that suffuses Sera Khandro's writing about Drimé Özer. Both Sera Khandro and Yeshé Tsogyel feel impassioned devotion to their gurus and receive their gurus' transformative compassion, but Sera Khandro and Drimé Özer's sentiments for each other are more mutual than those of Yeshé Tsogyel and Padmasambhava. Though Taksham portrays Padmasambhava as requiring a woman to practice Vajrayāna, he underscores the guru's status as already enlightened and Yeshé Tsogyel as in need of his liberating instruction. In contrast, Sera Khandro portrays herself and Drimé Özer each consorting with the other for the physical and spiritual benefit of both.

Can these differences be explained in large part by the temporal distance between the two biographies, suggesting that Sera Khandro's writings present a distinctively modern early twentieth-century Tibetan vision of love between Tantric partners?[176] Alternately, does the abundance of Sera Khandro's sentimental prolixity, apparently unmatched by any other Tibetan female writer prior to Tibet's incorporation into the PRC, stem from her privileged urban upper-class childhood as a part-Mongolian, part-Tibetan noblewoman? Or does the unusual prominence of the rhetoric of mutual *yab yum* affection in her life story have more to do with the fact that she was a female Treasure revealer whose associations with powerful male religious hierarchs helped establish her own identity? When more Tibetan women's writings come to light, and when more studies on love and other sentiments in Tibetan literature and social life emerge, the place of Sera Khandro's works in her emotional community and within the broader genealogy of love in Tibet will continue to be illuminated.

Sera Khandro's writings do not prove that Tantra was (or is) necessarily about love between sexual partners, nor do they prove that the symbolism of gender complementarity in Vajrayāna Buddhism predicated equality between men and women in Buddhist societies or valorized positions of women in religious contexts. Nevertheless, as Caroline Walker Bynum and others have demonstrated, gendered religious symbols don't necessarily mean the same thing for male and female practitioners who modeled their lives in relation to them.[177] The female pole of the method and insight two-in-one Vajrayāna Buddhist theology may be represented iconographically as smaller than her male counterpart, and insight may or may not be less crucial than compassion for Mahāyāna and Vajrayāna identity, but Sera Khandro's auto/biographical writings announce with lucidity that she found a meaningful place for herself through invoking the Vajrayāna symbolism of gender complementarity. That she defined herself so ardently in relation to Drimé Özer as well as other important male lamas, such as Andzom Drondül Pawo Dorjé and Gochen Trülku Jikdrel Chökyi Lodrö, may strike some as indicative of her subordination to male ecclesiastic authority in early twentieth-century Tibet. The frequency of her self-descriptions as an inferior woman alone in Golok "with no paternal relatives to back me up" as well as the fact that male Treasure revealers in her milieu did not define themselves in relation to their consorts to the degree that she did could reinforce this interpretation. Nonetheless, Sera Khandro's portrayal of herself and Drimé Özer as inseparable method and insight gave her a platform from which to be more than a *ḍākinī* consort endowed with the capacity to dispel others' obstacles; it gave her incontrovertible precedent to be a religious authority in her own right. Her emphasis on her genealogical link to Yeshé Tsogyel justified her unusually forthright claim (through Drimé Özer's words) to be his equal. After all, Padmasambhava told Yeshé Tsogyel in Taksham's account of her life, "Your Body, Speech, and Mind will be the equal of my own."[178] Not all among the handful of Tibetan women who wrote autobiographies employed the gendered symbolism of method and insight to the degree Sera Khandro did—for example, the nuns Orgyen Chökyi and Jetsün Lochen found other ways to tell the story of their lives. But Sera Khandro effectively wrote herself into the annals of the Treasure tradition and Tibetan literary history through presenting herself as Drimé Özer's *yum* and him as her *yab*. The very existence and survival of her tandem auto/biographical tomes is testimony to the success of her story of love and liberation.

EPILOGUE

Love After Death

LOVE PREVAILED OVER DEATH in Sera Khandro's auto/biographical writings, in the sense that separation by death was not the end of her *yab yum* relationship with Drimé Özer. After his passing, a *ḍākinī* consoled Sera Khandro, telling her that their parting was only an illusion of conventional truth, and "In the ultimate sphere of great bliss, method and insight are indivisible."[1] Two other *ḍākinī*s reminded her that *yab* and *yum* could never really be separated because her "adamantine awareness is not different than the mind of Pema Lendrel."[2] Beyond pointing toward a transcendent nonduality between method and insight, Sera Khandro's auto/biographical works also planted seeds for their sequels here on earth. Her vision of her relationship with Drimé Özer stretched back to a distant past born from the aspirations of Padmasambhava and Yeshé Tsogyel and looked forward to reiterating their mutual commitment in successive rebirths. She prayed in the midst of one of her visits to Drimé Özer during her years with Gyelsé "that in this life and all my future incarnations I will be without separation from you."[3] When at last they lived together and Sera Khandro seemed near death, Drimé Özer put her head in his lap and lamented, "My consort, jewel of my heart, in all my successive lives may I be without separation from you!"[4] On his deathbed, Drimé

FIG. 6.1 Namtrül Jikmé Püntsok and Tāré Lhamo

PHOTOGRAPHER UNKNOWN

Özer reassured her, "As we have never gone against each other by even a hair's breadth, in all our rebirths and lifetimes—this, the next, and the intermediate state—it is certain that we will be without separation."[5]

The implications of these words have not been lost on succeeding generations in eastern Tibet who have inherited the mantle of Sera Khandro's and Drimé Özer's religious lineages. For instance, their memory as inseparable *yab* and *yum* lived on until the early twenty-first century in the form of the Treasure revealer couple Namtrül Jikmé Püntsok (1944–2011) and Tāré Lhamo (1938–2002). Namtrül Rinpoché of Nyenlung Monastery in Serta described himself to me as the incarnation of Drimé Özer, among others. Tāré Lhamo was the daughter of a famous Treasure revealer, Apang Tertön Pawo Chöying Dorjé (1895–1945), of Tsinda Monastery in Pema County, Golok, and was widely recognized as an incarnation of Sera Khandro. Namtrül Jikmé Püntsok explained his Treasure revelation process to me as a mutual act with Tāré Lhamo: "We wrote the Treasure texts together and we both gave empowerment and reading transmissions of them together."[6] Even when they were separated, he claims, they wrote identical revelations. One of the ways he presented the special character of his partnership with Tāré Lhamo was through referencing Drimé Özer and Sera Khandro's union. In his estimation, both Treasure revelation couples came together not out of lustful desire, but through the power of previous karmic propensities. Just as Sera Khandro had a strong urge to be near Drimé Özer, Namtrül Rinpoché told me that Tāré Lhamo had an inner calling to go to him that inspired her to leave her home in Pema County to live with him at Nyenlung Monastery. He reflected, "In the case of Drimé Özer and Sera Khandro, they write about each other in their biographies; they are not two separate beings. They are Namkhai Nyingpo and Shelkar Dorjetso. Since these two united in Lhodrak Karsha, they have been in union. They will function in union even in death; they are together in a sacred bond."[7]

Pema Ösel Tayé (b. 1957) further cemented the connection between the early and late twentieth-century Treasure revealer couples in the joint biography he wrote, *The Biography of Namtrül Jikmé Püntsok and Khandro Tāré Lhamo*, published in 1997.[8] Pema Ösel himself, a monk and writer living in Serta but originally from Drimé Özer's home area of Dartsang, serves as an additional link between the two generations of Treasure revealer couples. Not only has he written biographies of all four, but also he called my attention to his identity as the reincarnation of Tsültrim Dorjé, who was Sera Khandro's main scribe, personal attendant, and one of her doctrine holders (*chos bdag*).[9] As Drimé Özer and Sera Khandro were inseparable *yab* and *yum*, Pema Ösel emphasizes Namtrül Rinpoché and Tāré Lhamo's status as a Treasure revealing couple in his joint biography of them. In the longer part that comprises Namtrül Rinpoché's life, Pema Ösel often refers to him in the plural as "male and female partners" (*yab yum*) or as "the master male and female partners" (*rje yab yum*). His rendition of Tāré Lhamo's life in the latter part of the joint biography is modeled directly on the life of Sera Khandro; nearly half of it is a word-for-word reproduction of Sera Khandro's short autobiography titled *The Excellent Path of Devotion: The Short Story of a Mendicant's Experiences in Response to Questions from my Vajra Kin*.[10]

Another woman from Darlak County, Golok, named Khandro Rinpoché (b. 1954) has become increasingly renowned in Golok and farther east in Gyalrong as an incarnation of Sera Khandro. She too recently became the subject of one of Pema Ösel's biographical writing projects.[11] At birth she was given the name Khandrokyi or "Happy *Ḍākinī*," a popular girl's name in eastern Tibet; her life story charts her transformation from a

FIG. 6.2 Khandro Rinpoché and Choktrül Rangrik Dorjé

PHOTOGRAPH BY SARAH JACOBY, AUGUST 2007

childhood under the repressive economic and religious policies enforced during China's Cultural Revolution to an efflorescence as a religious specialist recognized by her community as a *khandroma*. Khandro Rinpoché's apotheosis into a living *ḍākinī* was circuitous, hindered not only by limitations imposed by the restrictive political climate during her youth but also by her arranged marriage at the age of nineteen to a Tibetan man she describes as a "Chinese official" (*rgya mi las byed pa*) working in a senior position within the Darlak County government. Five children soon followed, and this in addition to the arduous work of caring for large numbers of livestock made life as a householder, or in her words, "one who adheres to *saṃsāra*" (*'khor ba bzung mkhan*), extremely taxing. The turning point came when she met the lama who would become her root guru, Khenpo Münsel (1916–93), a Nyingma lama from the Wangchen Tö region of Golok educated at Katok Monastery, who was especially renowned as a Great Perfection master. When they met in about 1978, he was an impoverished political prisoner on parole for a brief period while serving a twenty-year prison sentence, and she was suffering from an acute illness that left her unable to speak. The Dharma teachings he bestowed upon the ailing Khandro cured her affliction and turned her mind toward intensive contemplative practice. In return, when Khenpo Münsel was released from prison a few years later in the early 1980s, Khandro Rinpoché's connections through her husband to local government officials were instrumental in helping him secure permission to rebuild his monastery in Darlak County, called Pönkor Tupten Shedrup Tashi Chönkhor Ling. As her devotion to practicing Khenpo Münsel's contemplative instructions deepened, she tried to maintain her household obligations caring for her family. After several years of balancing her growing religious commitments with householder life, she left Darlak to receive a religious empowerment from Khenpo Jikmé Püntsok of Larung Gar in Serta. What she initially intended to be a brief sojourn transformed into a decade-long tenure in Serta County when she entered into a consort relationship with an incarnate lama from Sera Monastery named Trülku Jikga (Jikmé Gawé Dorjé). During her time at Sera, her connection to Sera Khandro emerged in earnest. In particular, Khandro Rinpoché understands their connection to be based on shared life experiences prolonging the longevity of lamas (*bla ma'i sku tshe brten pa*), and shared suffering related to this. In Khandro Rinpoche's words: "The way we suffered was that we went before lamas, and again we were not able to preserve the longevity of the lamas (*bla ma sku tshe brten du ma bcug*). Then we wandered, then wandered, and so on. That is what is similar."[12]

Khandro Rinpoché also finds a close parallel between Sera Khandro's life and her own concerning the events that occurred when each turned forty-eight (forty-nine in Tibetan years). This is the age that Sera Khandro reached when she died. Khandro Rinpoché did not die, but Trülku Jikga took on another consort when she reached that age, causing her abrupt departure from Sera Monastery. She understands this traumatic change also in relation to Sera Khandro's life experience: "First I prolonged the life of Khenpo Münsel. Then I prolonged the life of Jikga. Then Jikga got another wife, just like Gyelsé. And like Sera Khandro, I left. Whatever he likes, that's fine, but she left and so did I."[13] Khandro Rinpoché now spends much of her time at a Vairotsana Cave in Gyalrong. Not only has she restored the cave complex, but in 2007 Khandro Rinpoché also completed a new monastery next to the cave called Siddhi Dechen Ling. Aiding her building project was her companion Choktrül Rangrik Dorjé (b. 1966), a *trülku* and Treasure revealer from Dungkar Monastery in Serta. Though Khandro Rinpoché does not claim to be a Treasure revealer, according to

Choktrül Rinpoché, she is his "method consort." He considers the revelations he has discovered in reliance upon Khandro Rinpoché to be theirs together: "Her Treasures are the same as mine. They are one. Whatever appears to her appears to me."[14] The two can sometimes be found in residence at the Vairotsana Cave, where Khandro Rinpoché's story as a contemporary *khandroma* increasingly renowned as Sera Khandro's incarnation continues to unfold.

Sera Khandro's disciple Jadrel Sangyé Dorjé Rinpoché told me that before she died, Sera Khandro predicted that multiple Tibetan women and men, some heirs to illustrious religious lineages and some born to ordinary laity, would be recognized as her incarnations.[15] Among others, in Golok the daughter of Dzongtrül Rinpoché, Lhacham Chökyi Drönma (mid-twentieth century), and Drimé Özer's great-grandson, Trinlé Tendzin (b. ca. 1990), have been recognized as incarnations of Sera Khandro.[16] Outside of Golok in the Tibetan diaspora, Jadrel Rinpoché's oldest daughter, Semo Saraswati (b. 1965), is widely recognized as her incarnation. These extraordinary Tibetan women and men suggest that even though Sera Khandro's and Drimé Özer's lives are complete and bound in biographies, more is yet to come, for their intentions to return together again and again predicted an open future.

SPELLING OF KEY TIBETAN NAMES AND TERMS

PHONETICS	WYLIE TRANSLITERATION
Abten	a bstan
Aché Riktong Gyelmo	a lce rig stong rgyal mo
Ado	a do
Akhu Darlo	a khu dar lo
Akyap Lama Karma Döndrup	a skyabs bla ma kar+ma don 'grub
Akyong Bum	a skyong 'bum
Akyong Khangen	a skyong khang rgan
Akyongza	a skyong bza'
Andzom Drondül Pawo Dorjé	a 'dzom 'gro 'dul dpa' bo rdo rje
Ané Zangmo	a ne bzang mo
Apang Tertön Pawo Chöying Dorjé	a pang gter ston dpa' bo chos byings rdo rje
Anyé Machen	a mye rma chen
Asé Khenpo Norbu Wangyel	a bswe mkhan po nor bu dbang rgyal
Bedrak Dorjé Rolwa	sbas brag rdo rje rol ba

Benak	ban nag (alt. ban yag, pad nag, pad+ma yag)
Benshül	ban shul
Bodzok	bo rdzogs
Chakmo Golok	lcags mo mgo log
Chakri Ömbar	lcags ri 'od 'bar
Chaktar	phyag thar
Chaktsa Trülku Pema Trinlé Gyatso (Chaktrül Rinpoché)	phyag tsha sprul sku pad+ma phrin las rgya mtsho (phyag sprul rin po che)
Changdrong Druptop Rinpoché	lcang grong grub thob rin po che
Chi Wangchentang	lci'i dbang chen thang
Chikdril	gcig sgril
Chödrön	chos sgron
Choktrül Rangrik Dorjé	mchog sprul rang rig rdo rje
Chökyi	chos skyid
Chölhün	chos lhun
Chönkhor Lama Jikmé	chos skor bla ma 'jigs med
Chönyi Khandro Sangdzö	chos nyid mkha' 'gro gsang mdzod
Chötreng	chos phreng
Chöying Drönma	chos dbyings sgron ma
Chushül County	chu shul rdzong
Damé	zla smad
Dartsang	gdar tshang (alt. zlar tshang, brda tshang, brdar tshang)
Dashelma	zla zhal ma
Dawa Cave	zla ba phug
Dayül	zla yul
Dechen Drön	bde chen sgron
Degé	sde dge
delok	'das log
Dodrup Rinpoché Jikmé Tenpé Nyima	rdo grub rin po che 'jigs med bstan pa'i nyi ma
Dodrupchen Monastery	rdo grub chen dgon

Dongkor Abten	gdong skor a bstan
Dongtrom	sdong phrom
Dordra	rdo dgra
Dorjé Drandül (Sangdak Mingyur Dorjé)	rdo rje dgra 'dul (gsang bdag mi 'gyur rdo rje)
Dorjé Dechen Pematso	rdo rje bde chen pad+ma tsho
Dorjé Yudrönma	rdo rje g.yu sgron ma
Dorjé Zungma	rdo rje gzungs ma
Drak Yerpa	brag yer pa
Drakar Dreldzong	brag dkar sprel rdzong
Drakargo	brag dkar mgo
Drakgo	brag 'go
Drandül Wangchuk	dgra 'dul dbang phyug
Drepung Monastery	'bras spungs dgon
Drimé Namdak	dri med rnam dag
Drimé Özer (Drima Mepé Özer Tayé)	dri med 'od zer (dri ma med pa'i 'od zer mtha' yas)
Drogön	'gro mgon
Drokchen Khobü Valley	'brog chen kho 'bud lung
Drongwasang	'brong ba sang
Drugu Tingkar Cliff	gru gu rting dkar brag
Düjom Jikdrel Yeshé Dorjé	bdud 'joms 'jigs bral ye shes rdo rje
Dungra Drakar	dung ra brag dkar
Dza Mura Trülku	rdza mu ra sprul sku
Dzagyel/Dzagya Monastery	rdza rgyal/rdza rgya dgon
Dzakhok	rdza khog
Dzamtang Monastery	dzam thang dgon
Dzatö	rdza stod
Dzokchen Palgé	rdzogs chen dpal dge
Dzongda	rdzong mda'
Gangri Tökar	gangs ri thod dkar
Gar Lama Gelek Gyatso	'gar bla ma dge legs rgya mtsho
Gara	mgar ra

Gara Gyeltsen	mgar ra rgyal mtshan
Gara Lochö	mgar ra blo chos
Gara Rangdröl	mgar ra rang grol
Gara Rindzin	mgar ra rig 'dzin
Gara Terchen Pema Dündül Wangchuk Lingpa	mgar ra gter chen pad+ma bdud 'dul dbang phyug gling pa
Garwa	mgar ba
Garwa So/Gar Sö	mgar ba bso/mgar bsod
Garza	mgar bza'
Gelek Pema Namgyel	dge legs pad+ma rnam rgyal
Geluk	dge lugs
Geshé Lodrö	dge bshes blo gros
Getsé Datö	dge rtse zla stod
Getso	dge mtsho
Gochen Trülku Jikdrel Chökyi Lodrö	sgo chen sprul sku 'jigs bral chos skyid blo gros
Gogentang	rgod rgan thang
Golok	mgo log
Gonla Sherap	mgon bla shes rab
Gönpa Kyap	dgon pa skyabs
Gyarong Ternyön	rgya rong gter smyon
Gyelsé Pema Namgyel	rgyal sras pad+ma rnam rgyal
Gyerza Hermitage	gyer za ri khrod
Hashül Lama Chödrak	ha shul bla ma chos grags
Hor Öchung	hor 'od chung
Jadrel Sangyé Dorjé	bya bral sangs rgyas rdo rje
Jamgön Kongtrül Lodrö Tayé	'jam mgon kong sprul blo gros mtha' yas
Jang	byang
Jangchup Chödrön	byang chub chos sgron
Jampa Gönpo	byams pa mgon po
Jamyang Zhepa	'jam dbyangs bzhad pa
Jedrung	rje drung
Jetsün Lochen	rje btsun lo chen

Jikdrön	'jigs sgron
Jikga Trülku Rindzin Chönyi Döntok	'jigs dga' sprul sku rig 'dzin chos nyid don rtogs
Jikmé Chömpel	'jigs med chos 'phel
Jikmé Gawé Dorjé	'jigs med dga' ba'i rdo rje
Jikmé Könchok	'jigs med dkon mchog
Jiksam	'jigs bsam
jikten	'jig rten
Jomo Menmo	jo mo sman mo
Jonang	jo nang
Jyekundo	skye dgu mdo
Kagyü	bka' rgyud
Kandzé	dkar mdzes
Kardon Hermitage	kar don ri khrod
Karlung Hermitage	dkar lung ri khrod
Katok Monastery	kaḥ thog dgon
Katok Situ Chökyi Gyatso	kaḥ thog si tu chos kyi rgya mtsho
Kelzang Monastery	bskal bzang dgon
Keza Sangyetso	ske gza' sangs rgyas mtsho
Kham	khams
Kham Sengé Namchong	khams seng ge gnam 'phyong
Khandro Tuktik	mkha' 'gro thugs thig
Khandro Yangdzong	mkha' 'gro yang rdzong
Khangdong Wönpo Gönwang	khang gdong dbon po mgon dbang
Khangsar family	khang sar sang
Kharnang gapma/gongma	mkhar nang 'gab ma/gong ma
Khenpo Ngawang Pelzang/Ngakchung	mkhan po ngag dbang dpal bzang/ngag chung
Khenpo Sangyé/Tupten Lodrö Tayé	mkhan po sangs rgyas/thub bstan blo gros mtha' yas
Khyentrül	mkhyen sprul
Kyala	kya la
Kyangö	rkyang rgod

Kyidrong	skyid grong
Kyitrül/Kyilung Tukchok Dorjé	skyid sprul/skyid lung thugs mchog rdo rje
Kuchok Khyentsé	sku phyogs mkhyen brtse
Künga Buma	kun dga' 'bum ma
Künkhyap Wangmo	kun khyab dbang mo
Künzang Chimé	kun bzang chi med
Künzang Dekyong Chönyi Wangmo	kun bzang bde skyong chos nyid dbang mo
Kyabjé Drupwang Pema Drondül Dorjé	skyabs rje grub dbang pad+ma 'gro 'dul rdo rje
Kyaga Künzang	skya ga kun bzang
Kyaka Chösung	skya ka chos srung
Lama Ngawang Demchok	bla ma ngag dbang bde mchog
Lama Tsechok	bla ma tshe mchog
Lekyi Wangmo	las kyi dbang mo
Lerap Lingpa	las rab gling pa
Lhachen Topgyel	lha chen stobs rgyal
Lharigo	lha ri mgo
Lhasé Sonam Dorjé	lha sras bsod nams rdo rje
Lhasé Sonam Norbu	lha sras bsod nams nor bu
Lhaten	lha rten
Lhokha	lho kha
Lingkar	gling dkar
Longchen Rapjampa	klong chen rab 'byams pa
Longyang	klong yangs
Lungshar Gar	rlung shar sgar
Machik Lapdrön	ma gcig lab sgron
Mar (Valley)	smar
Mar River	smar chu
Mar Selé Kyilkhor Tang	smar se le dkyil 'khor thang
Mardringpo	smar 'bring po
Marong	rmar rong
Matrül Tekchok Jikmé Pawo	ma sprul theg mchog 'jigs med dpa' bo
Mön	mon

Mowatowa	mo ba gto ba
Naidro Dorjé Dzong	nai gro rdo rje rdzong
Naktar	nag thar
Namkha Drönma	nam mkha' sgron ma
Namkha Jikmé	nam mkha' 'jigs med
Namkhai Nyingpo	nam mkha'i snying po
Namtrül Jikmé Püntsok	rnam sprul 'jigs med phun tshogs
Nechung Dharma Protector	gnas chung chos skyong
Ngak Chödrön	ngag chos sgron
ngakpa	sngags pa
Ngawa Prefecture	rnga ba khul
Ngawang Tenpé Nyima	ngag dbang bstan pa'i nyi ma
Ngedön Tekchen Ling Monastery	nge don theg chen gling dgon
Ngedön Wangpo	nge don dbang po
Nup	gnubs
Nyabgé Monastery	nyab dge dgon
Nyaktrül Guru Özer	nyag sprul gu ru 'od zer
Nyangrel Nyima Özer	nyang ral nyi ma 'od zer
Nyarong	nyag rong
Nyenchen Tanglha/ Genyen Tanglha	gnyan chen thang lha/ dge bsyen thang lha
Nyenchen Yusé	gnyan chen g.yu bswe
Nyenpo Yutsé	gnyan po g.yu rtse
Nyi Valley	snyi lung
Nyitö	snyi stod
Ömbar	'od 'bar
Önphu Taktsang	'on phu stag tshang
Orgyen Dzong	o rgyan rdzong
Orgyen Lingpa	o rgyan gling pa
Orgyen Minling	o rgyan smin gling
Ösel	'od gsal
Palden Gyatso	dpal ldan rgya mtsho
Patrül Orgyen Jikmé Chökyi Wangpo	dpal sprul o rgyan 'jigs med chos kyi dbang po

Pelyül Dartang Monastery	dpal yul dar thang dgon
Pema Bum	pad+ma 'bum
Pema County	pad+ma rdzong
Pema Drondül Dorjé	pad+ma 'gro 'dul rdo rje
Pema Drondül Sangngak Lingpa	pad+ma 'gro 'dul gsang sngags gling pa
Pema Dupatsel	pad+ma 'dus pa rtsal
Pema Gyurmé Sangngak Tendzin	pad+ma 'gyur med gsang sngags bstan 'dzin
Pema Longyang Gyatso	pad+ma klong yangs rgya mtsho
Pema Tötrengtsel	pad+ma thod phreng rtsal
Penchen	paṇ chen
Penpo	'phan po
Pom	spom
powa	'pho ba
Pünsumtsok Chömpel	phun sum tshogs chos 'phel
Üri	dbus ri
Rangjung Rikpé Dorjé	rang byung rig pa'i rdo rje
Ratna Lingpa Tukdrup	rat+na gling pa thugs sgrub
Remda	re mda'
Reting Rinpoché	rwa sgreng rin po che
Rikzang	rig bzang
Rindzin Chönyi Zangmo	rig 'dzin chos nyid bzang mo
Rindzin Gyurmé Dorjé	rig 'dzin 'gyur med rdo rje
Rindzin Jikmé Lingpa	rig 'dzin 'jigs med gling pa
Rindzin Künzang Nyima/ Nüden Dorjé	rig 'dzin kun bzang nyi ma/ nus ldan rdo rje
Riwoché	ri bo che
Rongtsa	rong tsha
Śākya Tar	sha'+kya thar
Samdo Tashikyil	sa mdo bkra shis 'khyil
Samkar Drön	bsam dkar sgron
Sanglung Monastery	gsang lung dgon pa
Sangtsang Dradra/ Sangtrül Rinpoché	sangs tshang grwa grwa/ sangs sprul rin po che

Sechok Norbu Ömbar	sras mchog nor bu 'od 'bar
Segyel	bswe rgyal
Seldrön	gsal sgron
Sengcham Trukmo	seng lcam khrug mo
Sera Khandro Dewé Dorjé	se ra mkha' 'gro bde ba'i rdo rje
Sera Tekchen Chönkhor Ling	se ra theg chen chos 'khor gling
Serta [alt. Sertar]	gser rta [gser thar]
Shabkar Tsokdruk Rangdröl	zhabs dkar tshogs drug rang sgrol
Shardzapa Tashi Gyatso	shar rdza pa bkra shis rgya mtsho
Shartra family	shar khra sang
Sherap Özer	shes rab 'od zer
Shiwa Dorjetso	zhi ba rdo rje mtsho
Shuksep	shug gseb
Sogyé	bso rgyas
Solung Drakar	bswo lung brag dkar
Sotra	bsod bkra
Sonam Khyap	bsod nams skyabs
Sonam Rabgyé	bsod nams rab rgyas
Sonam Tendar	bsod nams bstan dar
Songtsen Gampo	srong btsan sgam po
Sotrül Natsok Rangdröl	bsod sprul sna tshogs rang grol
Tachok	rta mchog
Tagé Sumdo	rta sga'i sum mdo
Taklung Monastery	stag lung dgon
Taksham Nüden Dorjé	stag sham nus ldan rdo rje
Taktsé Samdrup Monastery	stag rtse bsam grub dgon
Tangtong Gyelpo	thang stong rgyal po
Tāré Lhamo	tā' re lha mo
Tashi Chidren	bkra shis spyi 'dren
Tashi Gomang Monastery	bkra shis sgo mang dgon
Tashi Lhünpo	bkra shis lhun po
Tashül	rta shul
Tashül Tsedrupkyap	rta shul tshe sgrub skyabs

Taza Drönpo	rta bza' sgron po
Tengchen Monastery	steng chen dgon
Tersar	gter gsar
Tibir Tuktsa Trülku	rti bir rtug rtsa sprul sku
Tonglek Tashi	mthong legs bkra shis
Tongpön Zangmo	stong dpon bzang mo
Trakor Monastery	bkra skor dgon
Traktung Düjom Lingpa	khrag 'thung bdud 'joms gling pa
Tralek/Dralek/Dralak Monastery	bkra legs/dra legs/grwa lag dgon
Tranglayun	krang la yun
Trangnyibar	'phrang gnyis bar
Trango	'phrang 'go
Tromgé Khandro Dawa Drönma	khrom dge'i mkha' 'gro zla ba sgron ma
Trulshik Rinpoché Künzang Tongdröl Dorjé	'khrul zhig rin po che kun bzang mthong grol rdo rje
Tsampa Rinpoché	mtshams pa rin po che
Tsang Gar	rtsang sgar
Tsangchen Monastery	tsang chen dgon
Tsentsar	mtshan mtshar
Tsering Chöndzom	tshe ring chos 'dzom
Tsering Tashi	tshe ring bkra shis
Tsinda Monastery	rtsis mda' dgon
Tsüldrön	tshul sgron
Tsültrim Dorjé	tshul khrims rdo rje
Tsültrim Norbu	tshul khrims nor bu
Tsurpu	mtshur phu
Tupten Zangpo/Tupzang	thub bstan bzang po/thub bzang
Wangchen Bum	dbang chen 'bum
Washül Serta	dbal shul/wa shul gser rta
Yakshülza	yag shul bza'
Yaktsé	g.yag tshe
Yangchen Drönma/ Chöying Drönma	dbyangs can sgron ma/ chos dbyings sgron ma

Yeru religious encampment	gyas ru'i chos sgar
yeshé	ye shes
Yeshé Drön	ye shes sgron
Yeshé Tsogyel	ye shes mtsho rgyal
yidam	yi dam
yülkyong	yul skyong
Yungdrung Chaktsé	g.yung drung lcags rtse
Yungshül Sungchok Dorjé	g.yung shul gsung mchog rdo rje
Yusé	gyu bswe
Yutsi	gyu rtsi
Zhapdrung Tsewang Drakpa	zhabs drung tshe dbang grags pa
Zurkhang family	zur khang sang

NOTES

INTRODUCTION

1. See, for example, Ronald Davidson's critique in *Indian Esoteric Buddhism* (New York: Columbia University Press, 2002, 92 n. 62) of some feminist Buddhist studies scholars' methodology.
2. Significant studies of women in Tibet include Janice Willis, *Feminine Ground: Essays on Women and Tibet* (Ithaca: Snow Lion, 1987); Kim Gutschow, *Being a Buddhist Nun* (Cambridge, Mass.: Harvard University Press, 2004); Janet Gyatso and Hanna Havnevik, eds., *Women in Tibet* (New York: Columbia University Press, 2005); and Charlene Makley, *The Violence of Liberation: Gender and Tibetan Buddhist Revival in Post-Mao China* (Berkeley: University of California Press, 2007). See below for references to studies on Tibetan women's biographies and autobiographies.
3. For collections of her revelations, see Bde ba'i rdo rje, *Mtsho rgyal dngos snang bde skyong dbang mo yi zab gter gsang ba'i chos mdzod rin po che*, 4 vols. (Kalimpong: Dupjung Lama, 1978) and Dbus bza' mkha' 'gro, *Dbus bza' mkha' 'gro'i gsung 'bum*, vols. 2–5 (Chengdu: Si khron mi rigs dpe skrun khang, 2009). Her commentary on *Buddhahood Without Meditation* has been published as Dbus bza' mkha' 'gro, *Rang bzhin rdzogs pa chen po ma bsgom sangs rgyas kyi zin bris dpal ldan bla ma'i zhal rgyun nag 'gros su bkod pa tshig don rab gsal skal ldan dgyes pa'i mgul rgyan* (Beijing: Mi rigs dpe skrun khang, 2002). See the

introduction section on sources for references to her biographical and autobiographical works.

4. Others include Aché Riktong Gyelmo (15th century), Trinlé Wangmo (1585–1668?), Orgyen Chökyi (1675–1729), and Jetsün Lochen Rinpoché (Rindzin Chönyi Zangmo, 1865–1951). Michael Sheehy is preparing a study of Trinlé Wangmo's autobiography. For full English translations of the latter two, see Kurtis R. Schaeffer, *Himalayan Hermitess* (New York: Oxford University Press, 2004); and Hanna Havnevik, "The Life of Jetsun Lochen Rinpoche (1865–1951) as Told in Her Autobiography" (University of Oslo, 1999). Biographies of women that may contain autobiographical elements include the biography of Sonam Peldren (14th century) and the Bönpo woman Dechen Chökyi Wangmo (1868–1927?). See Suzanne Bessenger, "Echoes of Enlightenment: The Life and Legacy of Sonam Peldren" (The University of Virginia, 2010); Donatella Rossi, "mKha' 'gro dBang mo'i rNam thar, The Biography of the gTer ston ma bDe chen Chos kyi dBang mo (1868–1927?)," *Révue d'Études Tibétaines* 15, Tibetan Studies in Honour of Samten Karmay no. 2 (2008).
5. Dbus bza' mkha' 'gro, "Ku su lu'i nyams byung gi gnas tshul mdor bsdus rdo rje'i spun gyis dris lan mos pa'i lam bzang." In *Dbus bza' mkha' 'gro'i gsung 'bum*, vol. 5 (Chengdu: Si khron mi rigs dpe skrun khang, 2009), 83. Henceforth I refer to this work, which is a short autobiography Sera Khandro wrote in verse, by the abbreviation KSL. For an English translation, see Sarah H. Jacoby, "The Excellent Path of Devotion: An Annotated Translation of Sera Khandro's Short Autobiography," in *Himalayan Passages: Tibetan and Newar Studies in Honor of Hubert Decleer*, ed. Benjamin Bogin and Andrew Quintman (Boston: Wisdom, 2014).
6. Sera Khandro recorded her age according to the Tibetan system of tabulating age from conception, which I have modified to accord with the international convention of tabulating age from birth. Hence, when Sera Khandro writes that her mother died when she was thirteen, I give the age as twelve.
7. KSL, 87.
8. KSL, 94.
9. KSL, 97.
10. Mkha' 'gro bde skyong dbang mo, *Skyabs rje thams cad mkhyen pa grub pa'i dbang phyug zab gter rgya mtsho'i mnga' bdag rin po che pad+ma 'gro 'dul gsang sngags gling pa'i rnam par thar pa snying gi mun sel dad pa'i shing rta ra tna'i chun 'phyang ut+pala'i 'phreng ba* (Dalhousie: Damchoe Sangpo, 1981). Henceforth this work is abbreviated as SLNT.
11. SLNT, fol. 244b.4–6.
12. Bde ba'i rdo rje, *Dbus mo bde ba'i rdo rje'i rnam par thar pa nges 'byung 'dren pa'i shing rta skal ldan dad pa'i mchod sdong* (Unpublished manuscript, ca. 1934). Henceforth this work is abbreviated as DDNT.
13. Dbus bza' mkha' 'gro, *Dbus bza' mkha' 'gro'i gsung 'bum*, ed. Mgo log khul gna' rtsom bya ba'i gzhung las khang, vols. 1–6 (Chengdu: Si khron mi rigs dpe skrun khang, 2009) (henceforth DDP). Whenever I quote from Sera Khandro's auto-

biography in this book, I cite page numbers from both the manuscript edition lent to me by Jadrel Rinpoché (abbv. DDNT) and this published version (the autobiography is vol. 1 of the above). The three versions of the autobiography available to me vary only slightly; the differences in page numbers reflect handwriting size/publication font and not substantial differences in content.

14. Dbus bza' mkha' 'gro, "Rtsom pa po ngo sprod mdor bsdus," in *Dbus bza' mkha' 'gro'i gsung 'bum* vol. 1: 3, 5.
15. Ibid., 4.
16. DDNT, fol. 7b.1–2; DDP, 9.
17. DDNT, fol. 406a.2–6; DDP, 536.
18. DDNT, fol. 406b.5–407a.4; DDP, 537. *Sarva mangalaṃ* means "May all be auspicious" in Sanskrit.
19. Janet Gyatso, *Apparitions of the Self: The Secret Autobiographies of a Tibetan Visionary* (Princeton, N.J.: Princeton University Press, 1998), 116–22.
20. Ibid., 103.
21. Sidonie Smith and Julia Watson, *Reading Autobiography: A Guide for Interpreting Life Narratives* (Minneapolis: University of Minnesota Press, 2001), 14.
22. Philippe Lejeune, "The Autobiographical Pact," in *On Autobiography*, ed. Philippe Lejeune (Minneapolis: University of Minnesota Press, 1989), 4.
23. Georges Gusdorf, "Conditions and Limits of Autobiography," in *Autobiography: Essays Theoretical and Critical*, ed. James Olney (Princeton, N.J.: Princeton University Press, 1980), 29.
24. Ibid., 30–31.
25. Karl Joachim Weintraub, *The Value of the Individual: Self and Circumstance in Autobiography* (Chicago: University of Chicago Press, 1978), xvii.
26. Paul John Eakin, *How Our Lives Become Stories: Making Selves* (Ithaca, N.Y.: Cornell University Press, 1999), 48.
27. Mary Mason, "The Other Voice: Autobiographies of Women Writers," in *Autobiography, Essays Theoretical and Critical* (Princeton, N.J.: Princeton University Press, 1980); Estelle Jelinek, ed., *Women's Autobiography: Essays in Criticism* (Bloomington: Indiana University Press, 1980).
28. Studies of women's autobiography are too numerous to cite exhaustively here, but for a selection of important works, see Sidonie Smith, *A Poetics of Women's Autobiography: Marginality and the Fictions of Self-Representation* (Bloomington: Indiana University Press, 1987); Shari Benstock, ed., *The Private Self: Theory and Practice of Women's Autobiographical Writings* (Chapel Hill: University of North Carolina Press, 1988); Bella Brodzki and Celeste Schenck, eds., *Life Lines: Theorizing Women's Autobiography* (Ithaca, N.Y.: Cornell University Press, 1988); Personal Narratives Group, ed., *Interpreting Women's Lives: Feminist Theory and Personal Narratives* (Bloomington: Indiana University Press, 1989); Françoise Lionnet, *Autobiographical Voices: Race, Gender, Self-Portraiture* (Ithaca, N.Y.: Cornell University Press, 1989); Sidonie Smith and Julia Watson, *De/Colonizing the Subject: The Politics of Gender in Women's Autobiography* (Minneapolis: University of Minnesota Press, 1992); Liz Stanley, *The*

Auto/biographical I: The Theory and Practices of Feminist Auto/biography (Manchester: Manchester University Press, 1992); Leigh Gilmore, *Autobiographics: A Feminist Theory of Women's Self-Representation* (Minneapolis: University of Minnesota Press, 1994); Sidonie Smith and Julia Watson, eds., *Women, Autobiography, Theory: A Reader* (Madison: University of Wisconsin Press, 1998); Tess Cosslett, Celia Lury, and Penny Summerfield, eds., *Feminism and Autobiography: Texts, Theories, Methods* (London: Routledge, 2000); and Adalgisa Giorgio and Julia Waters, eds., *Women's Writing in Western Europe: Gender, Generation and Legacy* (Newcastle: Cambridge Scholars Publishing, 2007).

29. Nancy K. Miller, "Representing Others: Gender and the Subjects of Autobiography," *Differences* 6, no. 1 (1994); Eakin, *How Our Lives Become Stories.*
30. Two recent examples are Natalie Edwards and Christopher Hogarth, eds., *This "Self" Which Is Not One: Women's Life Writing in French* (Newcastle: Cambridge Scholars Publishing, 2010); Natalie Edwards, *Shifting Subjects: Plural Subjectivity in Contemporary Francophone Women's Autobiography* (Newark: University of Delaware Press, 2011).
31. An early exception is the autobiography of the lay Tibetan statesman Dokarwa Tsering Wangyel (1697–1793). See Mdo mkhar ba tshe ring dbang rgyal, *Bka' blong rtogs brjod* (Chengdu: Si khron mi rigs dpe skrun khang, 1981).
32. Historical Tibetan women prior to the 1950s who were the subjects of spiritual biographies include Sonam Peldren (14th century), Lhadzin Yangchen Drölma (17th century), Minling Jetsün Mingyur Peldrön (1699–1769), Minling Jetsün Gyurmé Trinlé Chödrön (early 19th century), and Dechen Chökyi Wangmo (1868–1927?). Additionally, there are biographies of the women who were part of the Samding Dorjé Pakmo lineage, including Chökyi Drönma (1422–1455/6), Samding Dorjé Pakmo Chöying Dechen Tsomo (19th century), and Gyakari Dorjé Pakmo Dekyong Yeshé Wangmo (1886–1909). There are also biographies of some of the women in the Gungri Khandro female incarnation line from Amdo including that of Rindzin Palmo (19th century). Recently a fifteen-volume compilation of Indian and Tibetan women's biographies was published in Tibet; see *'Phags bod kyi skyes chen ma dag gi rnam par thar ba pad+ma dkar po'i phreng ba* (Lhasa: bod ljongs bod yig dpe rnying dpe skrun khang, 2013). For an English language account of select Tibetan women's biographies, see Tsultrim Allione, *Women of Wisdom* (London: Routledge & Kegan Paul, 1984). For a study of the Samding Dorjé Pakmo lineage and a translation of Chökyi Drönma's biography, see Hildegard Diemberger, *When a Woman Becomes a Religious Dynasty* (New York: Columbia University Press, 2007).
33. Jérôme Edou, *Machig Labdrön and the Foundations of Chöd* (Ithaca, N.Y.: Snow Lion, 1995); Sarah Harding, *Machik's Complete Explanation: Clarifying the Meaning of Chöd* (Ithaca, N.Y.: Snow Lion, 2003).
34. Lawrence Epstein, "On the History and Psychology of the 'Das-log'," *Tibet Journal* 7, no. 4 (1982); Françoise Pommaret, *Les Revenants de L'au-Delà Dans*

le Monde Tibétain (Paris: Center National de la Recherche Scientifique, 1989); Brian Cuevas, *Travels in the Netherworld: Buddhist Popular Narratives of Death and the Afterlife in Tibet* (New York: Columbia University Press, 2008).

35. Hayden White, *The Content of the Form* (Baltimore: Johns Hopkins University Press, 1987), 24.
36. Louis O. Mink, *Historical Understanding* (Ithaca, N.Y.: Cornell University Press, 1987), 60.
37. Paul de Man implied this when he asked, "can we not suggest . . . that whatever the writer [of autobiography] does is in fact governed by the technical demands of self-portraiture and thus determined, in all its aspects, by the resources of his medium?" See Paul de Man, "Autobiography as De-facement," in *The Rhetoric of Romanticism*, ed. Paul de Man (New York: Columbia University Press, 1984), 69. In *Roland Barthes by Roland Barthes* (New York: Farrar, Straus and Giroux, 1977), 56, Barthes also problematized the idea that text can relate to the world in his "autobiographical" text, in which he denied the referentiality of the "I": "I do not say: 'I am going to describe myself' but: 'I am writing a text, and I call it R.B.' I shift from imitation (from description) and entrust myself to nomination. Do I know that, *in the field of the subject, there is no referent*?"
38. Kali Israel makes a similar assertion in her study of the writings by and about the Victorian woman Emily Dilke; see Kali Israel, "Changing the Place of Narrative in Biography: From Form to Method," *Life Writing* 7, no. 1 (2010): 10. However, I am more inclined than Israel to assert a degree of referentiality, however imperfect, between texts and the individuals in the world to whom they refer.
39. Joan Scott, "The Evidence of Experience," *Critical Inquiry* 17 (summer 1991): 797.
40. Jerome Bruner, "Life as Narrative," *Social Research* 71, no. 3 (2004 [1987]): 708. See also Stephen Crites, "The Narrative Quality of Experience," *Journal of the American Academy of Religion* 3 (1971): 291; David Carr, "Narrative and the Real World: An Argument for Continuity," *History and Theory* 25, no. 2 (1986): 117.
41. Oliver Sacks, *The Man Who Mistook his Wife for a Hat* (New York: Harper & Row, 1987), 110. For critiques of the narrative identity thesis, see Galen Strawson, "Against Narrativity," *Ratio* XVII, no. 4 (2004); and Pekka Tammi, "Against Narrative ('A Boring Story')," *Partial Answers: Journal of Literature and the History of Ideas* 4, no. 2 (2006).
42. Jerome Bruner, "The Narrative Construction of Reality," *Critical Inquiry* 18, no. 1 (1991): 13.
43. Ann Swidler, *Talk of Love* (Chicago: University of Chicago Press, 2001), 25.
44. A. I. Vostrikov, *Tibetan Historical Literature* (Richmond: Curzon Press, 1994 [1962]), 188–89.
45. Giuseppe Tucci, *Tibet: Land of Snows*, trans. J. E. Stapleton Driver (New York: Stein and Day, 1967), 174.

46. I borrow the terms "reliable real-life testimony" and "pure literary invention" from Aviad M. Kleinberg, *Prophets in Their Own Country: Living Saints and the Making of Sainthood in the Later Middle Ages* (Chicago: University of Chicago Press, 1992), 62.
47. Jaber F. Gubrium and James A. Holstein, *Analyzing Narrative Reality* (Thousand Oaks, Calif.: Sage Publications, 2009), 10, 31.
48. Patrick Geary, "Saints, Scholars, and Society: The Elusive Goal," in *Living with the Dead in the Middle Ages* (Ithaca, N.Y.: Cornell University Press, 1994), 12.
49. Robert Ford Campany, *Making Transcendents: Ascetics and Social Memory in Early Medieval China* (Honolulu: University of Hawai'i Press, 2009), 10.
50. Roland Barthes and Lionel Duisit, "An Introduction to the Structural Analysis of Narrative," *New Literary History* 6, no. 2 (1975): 245.
51. Mikhail Bakhtin, "Discourse in the Novel," in *The Dialogic Imagination*, ed. Michael Holquist (Austin: University of Texas Press, 1981), 280.
52. Barbara H. Rosenwein, "Worrying About Emotions in History," *The American Historical Review* 107, no. 3 (2002): 842.

1. THE LIFE AND TIMES OF SERA KHANDRO

1. The demons' island (Skt. *cāmara dvīpa*, Tib. *srin po'i gling*) is a subcontinent in Buddhist cosmology known as the island inhabited by the Rākṣasa demons, a group of humanoid cannibals found in many traditions of South Asian mythology.
2. DDNT, fol. 98a.5–b.3; DDP, 136–37.
3. KSL.
4. L. A. Waddell, *Lhasa and Its Mysteries: A Record of the Expedition of 1903–1904* (New York: E. P. Dutton, 1905), 343.
5. Sarat Chandra Das, *Journey to Lhasa and Central Tibet* (London: J. Murray, 1902), 146.
6. G. Ts. Tsybikoff, "Lhasa and Central Tibet," *Smithsonian's Annual Report for 1903, Government Printing Office* (1903): 734.
7. Edmund Candler, *The Unveiling of Lhasa* (Berkeley, Calif.: Snow Lion Graphics, 1987), 266.
8. Waddell, *Lhasa and Its Mysteries*, 340.
9. Tsybikoff, "Lhasa and Central Tibet," 731.
10. Candler, *The Unveiling of Lhasa*, 267; Waddell, *Lhasa and Its Mysteries*, 341.
11. Waddell, *Lhasa and Its Mysteries*, 344.
12. Tsybikoff, "Lhasa and Central Tibet," 735; Waddell, *Lhasa and Its Mysteries*, 345.
13. Waddell, *Lhasa and Its Mysteries*, 340.
14. Ibid., 352–53; Das, *Journey to Lhasa and Central Tibet*, 193.
15. Tsybikoff, "Lhasa and Central Tibet," 745.
16. Waddell, *Lhasa and Its Mysteries*, 340.

17. Tsybikoff, "Lhasa and Central Tibet," 745.
18. Waddell, *Lhasa and Its Mysteries*, 353–54.
19. Rongtsa was a relative of the mythic hero Gesar.
20. A *ngakpa* (Skt. *mantrin*) is a noncelibate Tantric Buddhist ritual specialist often with expertise in incantations to ward off obstacles, demons, bad weather, and so forth.
21. This probably refers to the baby being born "in the caul," or inside the intact amniotic sac as if born in an egg. It is considered to be an auspicious birth sign.
22. Awareness woman (*rig ma*) is another word for female Tantric consort.
23. Tulku Thondup explains this analogy in the following manner: as a white silk knot is both tight and soft, so too should religious law be upheld with strictness and gentleness.
24. DDNT, fols. 7b.2–9b.5; DDP, 9–12.
25. Waddell, *Lhasa and Its Mysteries*, 358.
26. Tsybikoff, "Lhasa and Central Tibet," 728.
27. DDNT, fol. 17b.3; DDP, 24. For a description of Chögyel Ngakyi Wangpo's ancestry, see Appendix 3 of Shabkar Tsogdruk Rangdrol, *The Life of Shabkar: The Autobiography of a Tibetan Yogin*, trans. Matthieu Ricard et al. (Ithaca, N.Y.: Snow Lion, 2001), 565–68.
28. Josef Kolmaš, "The Ambans and Assistant Ambans of Tibet (1727–1912)," in *The History of Tibet*, ed. Alex McKay (London: RoutledgeCurzon, 2003), 604.
29. Waddell, *Lhasa and Its Mysteries*, 335.
30. For an early twentieth-century map of Lhasa showing the Dokhar (*Mdo mkhar*) estate called Rakhashak (*Rag kha shag*), also spelled Rakhashar (*Rag kha shar*), see building no. 76 of L. Austine Waddell's "Plan of Lhasa" map from 1905 reproduced in Knud Larsen and Amund Sinding-Larsen, *The Lhasa Atlas* (Boston: Shambhala, 2001), 25. For a description of the Dokhar family, see Luciano Petech, *Aristocracy and Government in Tibet, 1728-1959*, Rome Oriental series, 45 (Roma: Istituto italiano per il Medio ed Estremo Oriente, 1973), 70–87. An intriguing connection between Sera Khandro's account and the Rakhashar family is that both were affiliated with the Kagyü Taklung Monastery (Stag lung dgon) and its abbots, including Ma Rinpoché, the first lama mentioned in Sera Khandro's autobiography (she calls him Mahā Rinpoché; see DDNT, fol. 9a.3; DDP, 12).
31. Rinchen Dolma Taring, *Daughter of Tibet* (London: Camelot Press, 1970), 30.
32. Peter Richardus, *Tibetan Lives: Three Himalayan Autobiographies* (Richmond: Curzon Press, 1998), 165–69.
33. DDNT, fols. 9b.6–10a.1; DDP, 13.
34. DDNT, fols. 11b.5–12a.3; DDP, 15–16.
35. DDNT, fol. 12b; DDP, 16–17.
36. Réne de Nebesky-Wojkowitz, *Oracles and Demons of Tibet: The Cult and Iconography of the Tibetan Protective Deities* (The Netherlands: Mouton, 1956), 205–8. Nyenchen Tanglha is also said to be the father of Dokhyentsé Yeshé Dorjé

(1800–1866), a Nyingma lama from Golok. See Tulku Thondup, *Masters of Meditation and Miracles: Lives of the Great Buddhist Masters of India and Tibet* (Boston: Shambhala, 1999), 180.

37. DDNT, fol. 20a.4–5; DDP, 28.
38. Translated literally as "Happy Valley City," Kyilung Drongchen or Kyidrong is a region southwest of Lhasa located in what is now Zhikatsé Prefecture, Tibetan Autonomous Region.
39. Daloyi (Tib. *da lo yi'i*, Ch. *da lao ye*) is a Chinese honorific title meaning "great old gentleman" or "grandfather." It was a minor title meaning "your honor" that was given to local leaders as a polite way to refer to a prefect, department, or district magistrate. Elliot Sperling translates it as "his honor" in the context of the title of a translator of the Qianlong Emperor in the late eighteenth century. See Elliot Sperling, "Awe and Submission: a Tibetan Aristocrat at the Court of Qianlong," *The International History Review* 20, no. 2 (1998): 331.
40. DDNT, fol. 28a.6 includes the line "*thob gnyis non byed na chog*," which I translate as "it is acceptable if they take control over both." However in the printed edition of her autobiography (DDP, 40), it is written as "*thob nyes non byed na chog*," which appears to be a misprint. If we read this passage as "take control over both," it could refer to Sera Khandro and her betrothed taking control of both of their inherited jurisdictions.
41. DDNT, fols. 27b.4–28b.1; DDP, 38–40.
42. Tsybikoff, "Lhasa and Central Tibet," 730.
43. Waddell, *Lhasa and Its Mysteries*, 379.
44. According to Tulku Thondup, "Jipa Treasure revealer" (Byis pa'i gter ston) refers to the thirteenth-century Treasure revealer Kalden Jipa (Skal ldan byis pa).
45. DDNT, fols. 31a.2–31b.2; DDP, 43–44.
46. *The Secret Treasury of Reality Ḍākinīs* (*Chos nyid mkha' 'gro gsang mdzod*) and *The Ḍākinīs' Heart Essence* (*Mkha' 'gro thugs thig*).
47. DDNT, fol. 52a.1–3; DDP, 73.
48. DDNT, fols. 66b.6–67a.1; DDP, 94.
49. DDNT, fol. 73a.3; DDP, 102.
50. DDNT, fol. 74b; DDP, 104.
51. DDNT, fols. 76a.5–77b.1; DDP, 106.
52. Don grub dbang rgyal and Nor sde, *Yul mgo log gi lo rgyus deb ther pad+ma dkar po'i chun po* (Xining: Mtsho sngon mi rigs dpe skrun khang, 1992), 6.
53. For a brief essay on Golok's history, politics, social structure, and religion, see Sarah Jacoby, "An Overview of Golok," The Tibetan & Himalayan Library, http://places.thlib.org/features/15434/descriptions/1209.
54. There is a vigorous debate among people from Serta about whether or not Serta was ever a part of Golok. For an analysis of this question that argues strongly against Serta having been part of Golok, see chapters 2 and 3 of Gser

rta tshul khrims, *Dbal shul gser rta'i lo rgyus dang 'brel ba'i gtam* (Dharamsala: Gser rta tshul khrims, 2006). However, here I follow Sera Khandro's lead in making no strong division between Serta and Golok.

55. Don grub dbang rgyal and Nor sde, *Mgo log lo rgyus deb ther*, 11.
56. DDNT, fol. 73a.4–6; DDP, 102.
57. Joseph Francis Charles Rock, *The Amnye Ma-chhen Range and Adjacent Regions: A Monographic Study*, vol. 12, Serie orientale Roma (Rome: Is. M.E.O., 1956), 126–27. Other similar perceptions of Golok from Europeans who traveled there in the early twentieth century include Ernst Schäfer, *Dach der Erde: Durch das Wunderland Hochtibet* (Berlin: Paul Parey, 1938), 61, and André Guibaut, *Tibetan Venture in the Country of the Ngolo-Setas: Second Guibaut-Liotard Expedition* (London: John Murray, 1948), 97–98.
58. G. A. Combe and Paul Sherap, *A Tibetan on Tibet: Being the Travels and Observations of Paul Sherap (Dorje Zödba) of Tachienlu: With an Introductory Chapter on Buddhism and a Concluding Chapter on the Devil Dance* (London: Fisher Unwin, 1926), 107. See also Leonard Clark, *The Marching Wind* (New York: Funk & Wagnalls, 1954), 141, for Ma Bufang's secretary Chutsu Tsereng's perceptions of Golok aggression as recorded by Leonard Clark on his expedition to Golok in 1949.
59. Rinzin Thargyal, *Nomads of Eastern Tibet: Social Organization and Economy of a Pastoral Estate in the Kingdom of Dege*, vol. 15, Brill's Tibetan Studies Library (Leiden: Brill, 2007), 185–86.
60. Bianca Horlemann, "The Goloks Through Western eyes: Fascination and Horror," in *Tibet in 1938–1939: Photographs from the Ernst Schäfer Expedition to Tibet*, ed. Isrun Engelhardt (Chicago: Serindia, 2007), 96–97.
61. P. K. Kozloff, "Through Eastern Tibet and Kam (Continued)," *The Geographical Journal* 31, no. 5 (1908): 526.
62. Don grub dbang rgyal and Nor sde, *Mgo log lo rgyus deb ther*, 1–2.
63. "Black Chinese" (*rgya nag po*) is a pun on the Tibetan word for "Chinese" (*rgya nag*), in which *nag* means black and is meant to accord with the color metaphor in the earlier part of the sentence, "the golden-headed ones" (*dbus ser po*), which refers to the yellow hats worn by Geluk monastic hierarchs, who held authority in the central Tibetan government.
64. Krung go mi dmangs srid gros gser thar rdzong u yon lhan khang gi rig gnas lo rgyus dpyad yig tsho chung, ed., *Dbal shul gser thar gyi lo rgyus gsar bsgrigs blo ldan mig gi bdud rtsi* (Dartsedo: Gan zi bao she yin shua chang, 1989), 76–77. For a paraphrase of this passage, see "Mdo khams sbas yul gser rta ru yod pa'i shar khra mo gling gi rjes shul rags tsam ngo sprod gnang ba" in Pad+ma 'od gsal mtha' yas, *Deb chung a ru ra'i dga' tshal* (Chengdu: Si khron mi rigs dpe skrun khang, 2003), 221–22.
65. Don grub dbang rgyal and Nor sde, *Mgo log lo rgyus deb ther*, 274–75.
66. Gelek, "The Washu Sertar: A Nomadic Community of Eastern Tibet," in *Development, Society, and Environment in Tibet*, ed. Graham E. Clarke, *Proceedings*

of the 7th Seminar of the International Association for Tibetan Studies, Graz 1995 (Wien: Verlag der Österreichischen Akademie der Wissenschaften, 1998), 47, 49.

67. For a description of two Golok leaders' submission to the Tibetan government, namely Golok Arkyong Trülku (chief of the Rimang) and Rinchen Wangkyi Gyelpo (chief of the Sishu), see Lodey Lhawang, "The Conferring of Tibetan Government Ranks on the Chieftains of Golok," *Lungta* 8 (1994). For a succinct account of Golok history up to the modern period, see Bianca Horlemann, "Modernization Efforts in Mgo log: A Chronicle, 1970–2000," in *Amdo Tibetans in Transition: Society and Culture in the Post-Mao Era*, ed. Toni Huber (Leiden: Brill, 2002).
68. Don grub dbang rgyal and Nor sde, *Mgo log lo rgyus deb ther*, 294.
69. DDNT, fol. 73b.2–3; DDP, 103.
70. DDNT, fol. 75a.3; DDP, 105.
71. DDNT, fol. 75a.5–6; DDP, 105.
72. I.e., one who will not return to be reborn in cyclic existence (*saṃsāra*).
73. DDNT, fol. 75a.6–76a.2; DDP, 105–6.
74. DDNT, 76a.3–4; DDP, 106.
75. DDNT, 81b.6–82a.1; DDP, 114.
76. Patrül Rinpoché is best known outside of Tibet as the author of *The Words of My Perfect Teacher* (*Kun bzang bla ma'i zhal lung*). For a brief biography of him, see Thondup, *Masters of Meditation and Miracles*, 201–10.
77. Khrag 'thung bdud 'joms gling pa, "Chos nyid sgyu mar rol pa'i snang lam gsang ba nyams byung gi rtogs brjod gsal ba'i me long," in A bu dkar lo, ed., *Khrag 'thung bdud 'joms gling pa'i rnam thar* (Xining: Zi ling mi rigs par khang, 2002), 188. Henceforth this work is abbreviated as DLNT.
78. 'Jigs med bsam grub et al., ed., *Khams phyogs dkar mdzes khul gyi dgon sde so so'i rgyus gsal bar bshad pa*, vol. 2 (Beijing: Krung go'i bod kyi shes rig dpe skrun khang, 1995), 367–69.
79. DDNT, fol. 87a.1–2; DDP, 121.
80. The preliminary practices (*sngon 'gro*) include five practices to be repeated 100,000 times or more each: 1) reciting the refuge prayer; 2) reciting the *bodhicitta* prayer; 3) performing the Vajrasattva recitation and visualization; 4) performing the *maṇḍala* offering; and 5) performing *guru yoga*, which for many Nyingma traditions involves reciting the *vajra guru* prayer more than 10 million times.
81. DDNT, fol. 87a.5–6; DDP, 121.
82. Düjom Lingpa's *Refining One's Perception* has been translated into English; see Bdud-'joms-gliṅ-pa and Richard Barron, *Buddhahood Without Meditation: A Visionary Account Known as Refining One's Perception (Nang-jang)*, rev. ed. (Junction City: Padma Publishing, 2002).
83. Sera Khandro's commentary on *Refining One's Perception* has recently been published in the PRC as Dbus bza' mkha' 'gro, *Rang bzhin rdzogs pa chen po ma bsgom sangs rgyas kyi zin bris dpal ldan bla ma'i zhal rgyun nag 'gros su bkod*

pa tshig don rab gsal skal ldan dgyes pa'i mgul rgyan (Beijing: Mi rigs dpe skrun khang, 2002).

84. In early twentieth-century Golok, people put grass or straw inside their leather boots to act as a type of sock.
85. DDNT, fols. 87b.6–88a.3: DDP, 122.
86. DDNT, fol. 89b.1–2; DDP, 124–25.
87. Tongpön (Stong dpon) is the name of a subdivision (*tsho skor*) of Kharnang Gongma, which could indicate that Mönlam Gyatso was a lama from this community.
88. Andreas Gruschke, *The Cultural Monuments of Tibet's Outer Provinces: Amdo* (Bangkok: White Lotus Press, 2001), 85.
89. 'Phrin las, ed., *Mgo log bod rigs rang skyong khul gyi bod brgyud nang bstan dgon sde khag gi lo rgyus snying bsdus* (Xining: Mtsho sngon mi rigs dpe skrun khang, 2008), 466. On p. 156 of the *Mgo log lo rgyus deb ther*, Don grub dbang rgyal and Nor sde cite its founding date as 1860.
90. DDNT, fol. 107a.1; DDP, 148.
91. Sera Khandro never mentions Gara Gyelsé's full name in her auto/biographical writings, only that he was Gara Terchen's oldest son, who according to Gara Terchen's autobiography was Pema Namgyel (1882/3–?). For references to him, see Mgar gter chen pad ma bdud 'dul dbang phyug gling pa, *Mgar gter chen pad+ma bdud 'dul dbang phyug gling pa'i rang rnam* (Chengdu: Si khron zhing chen khron lin par 'debs bzo grwa, 2005), 77, 103. Henceforth this work is abbreviated as GTNT.
92. DDNT, fol. 113a.6–b.4; DDP, 157.
93. DDNT, 113b.5–6; DDP, 157.
94. Sera Khandro was never formally educated in Tibetan, but she did become literate in Tibetan on her own as a young adult. In the biography she wrote of Drimé Özer, she writes, "When I was eighteen years old I had an illusory dream, and when I awoke I effortlessly knew how to read and write." SLNT, fols. 163b.6–164a.1.
95. DDNT, 121a.5. The page on which this information came is missing in the published version of Sera Khandro's autobiography; DDP, 168 mentions this missing page.
96. DDNT, fol. 138b.3–4; DDP, 190.
97. DDNT, 146a.5–146b.2; DDP, 201.
98. DDNT, 147b.3; DDP, 202.
99. "Guardian" is a translation of *bdag po*, which can mean "owner, lord, master, boss, husband, and guardian." The word implies that she was now Drimé Özer's responsibility.
100. DDNT, fol. 164a.5–b.3; DDP, 225.
101. DDNT, fol. 215a. 4–b.2; DDP, 295.
102. DDNT, fol. 225a.3; DDP, 308.
103. DDNT, fols. 233b.5–234a.1; DDP, 319–20.

104. Robert Ekvall, "Mi sTong: The Tibetan Custom of Life Indemnity," *Sociologus* 4, no. 2 (1954): 139.
105. DDNT, fol. 266a.1; DDP, 361.
106. DDNT, fol. 286b.2–3; DDP, 388.
107. One dotsé (*rdo tshad*) of silver is a Tibetan measure equal to fifty sang (*srang*) of silver according to the *Bod rgya tshig mdzod chen mo* vol. 2, ed. Krang dbyi sun (Beijing: The Nationalities Publishing House, 1993), 1445.
108. DDNT, fol. 287b.5; DDP, 390.
109. DDNT, fol. 294a.2–4; DDP, 397.
110. DDNT, fol. 295a.4–5; DDP, 399.
111. *Khams phyogs dkar mdzes khul gyi dgon sde so so'i lo rgyus*, vol. 2, 356. Information also drawn from the unpublished autobiography of the Sixth Sogen Rinpoché of Sera Monastery, Tulku Pema Lodoe (b. 1964).
112. Sera Khandro refers to the location of Sanglung Monastery as 'Dzi ska'i na mda' sang.
113. In his summary of the end of Sera Khandro's life, Jadrel Rinpoché mentions that Sherap Özer was a renunciate lama from the Nyarong Trakya (Nyag rong khra skya) region of Kham who was a prophesied doctrine holder (*chos bdag*) of Sera Khandro's Treasure teachings.
114. It is noteworthy that Sera Khandro mentions Drimé Özer's eighteen Treasure volumes (in DDNT, fol. 337b.3; DDP, 452), given that to date these texts are no longer available in either Golok or the Tibetan diaspora communities.
115. Pelyül was a Nyingma lineage like her own, but Sera Khandro was probably drawing a distinction between it and her own Katok-affiliated Nyingma lineage. DDNT, fols. 351b.5–352a.1; DDP, 470.
116. The King of Lingkar (Gling dkar rgyal po) probably refers to the King of Lingtsang (Gling tshang) named Wangchen Tendzin (?–1942), although Sera Khandro does not mention the king's full name. Lingtsang was an independent kingdom near Degé in Kham whose rulers were thought to be incarnations of the Tibetan mythic hero Gesar of Ling. See Tashi Tsering, "History of the Gling-tshang Principality of Khams: A Preliminary Study," in *Tibetan Studies: Proceedings of the 5th Seminar of the International Association for Tibetan Studies Narita 1989*, ed. Shōren Ihara and Zuihō Yamaguchi (Narita: Naritasan Shinshoji, 1992), 793–821.
117. DDNT, fol. 362a.3; DDP, 483.
118. *Tam* was a form of Tibetan currency, also called *tangka*.
119. DDNT, fol. 362b.5; DDP, 484.
120. Tshul khrims rdo rje, *Rgyal yum ye shes mtsho rgyal mi mngon rnam thar bzhengs pa mkha' 'gro rin po che bde ba'i rdo rje'i 'das rjes kyi rnam thar don bsdus su bkod pa* (unpublished manuscript, 1948). Recently, this text has been published in Dbus bza' mkha' 'gro, *Dbus bza' mkha' 'gro'i gsung 'bum*, vol. 1, 538–47. Here I reference the page numbers of the published version.
121. Bya bral sangs rgyas rdo rje, *Dbus bza' mkha' 'gro bde ba'i rdo rje'i rnam thar chen mo'i mjug gi kha skong nyung du g.yu yi phra tshom* (unpublished manuscript, 1976).

122. Bya bral sangs rgyas rdo rje, *Dbus bza' mkha' 'gro bde ba'i rdo rje'i rnam thar kha skong*, fols. 5b.3–6a.2; Tshul khrims rdo rje, *Mkha' 'gro rin po che bde ba'i rdo rje'i 'das rjes kyi rnam thar*, 538–39.
123. Tshul khrims rdo rje, *Mkha' 'gro rin po che bde ba'i rdo rje'i 'das rjes kyi rnam thar*, 539.
124. Tshul khrims rdo rje, *Mkha' 'gro rin po che bde ba'i rdo rje'i 'das rjes kyi rnam thar*, 539.
125. Bya bral sangs rgyas rdo rje, *Dbus bza' mkha' 'gro bde ba'i rdo rje'i rnam thar kha skong*, fol. 6a.5. The Tibetan reads that she was his "*gsang ba'i las rgya*."
126. Ibid., fol. 7a.5–6.
127. Taking the rainbow body (*'ja' lus*) is a sign of a practitioner having attained an extremely high level of realization during his or her lifetime, after which the corporeal body disappears, leaving only the hair and nails behind.
128. The *Katang Sheldrakma* (*Bka' thang shel brag ma*) is a revelation discovered by the fourteenth-century Treasure revealer Orgyen Lingpa.
129. For a biography of Tsewang Drakpa written by his son that largely covers politics between Chamdo and the central Tibetan government, see Ha rten dpal rnam, "Ha rten tshe grags kyi lo rgyus mdor bsdus dang 'brel yod zi bod sa mtshams 'khrugs 'dum skor gyi gnas tshul 'ga' zhig," in *Bod kyi lo rgyus rig gnas dpyad gzhi'i rgyu cha bdams bsgrigs*, vol. 23 (Beijing: Mi rigs dpe skrun khang, 2003), 206–63.
130. Tshul khrims rdo rje, *Mkha' 'gro rin po che bde ba'i rdo rje'i 'das rjes kyi rnam thar*, 544.
131. Ibid., 545.
132. Ibid., 546. "*Hik*" and "*phaṭ*" are sounds that one shouts during *powa* practice in order to transfer the deceased person's consciousness into the buddhafield.
133. Ibid.
134. Bya bral sangs rgyas rdo rje, *Dbus bza' mkha' 'gro bde ba'i rdo rje'i rnam thar kha skong*, fol. 14b.5. He actually wrote "eight-year-old child," but as with other Tibetan ages in this book, I have adjusted them to reflect the international standard.

2. A GUEST IN THE SACRED LAND OF GOLOK

1. *Sukha* (bliss) is the Sanskrit translation of the first word of Sera Khandro's name, Dewé. Sera Khandro signed many of her texts as Dewé Dorjé (Blissful Vajra), which she explained was her Treasure name (*gter ming*), the name she received in connection with her identity as a Treasure revealer.
2. DDNT, fols. 6b.5–7a.2; DDP, 8–9.
3. Paul John Eakin, "Relational Selves, Relational Lives: The Story of the Story," in *True Relations: Essays on Autobiography and the Postmodern*, ed. G. Thomas Couser and Joseph Fichtelberg (Westport, Conn.: Greenwood Press, 1998).

4. *The Connected Discourses of the Buddha*, trans. Bhikkhu Bodhi (Boston: Wisdom, 2000), 552.
5. For a discussion of Yeshé Tsogyel's historicity, see Janet Gyatso, "A Partial Genealogy of the Lifestory of Ye shes mtsho rgyal," *Journal of the International Association of Tibetan Studies*, no. 2 (2006).
6. Tulku Thondup, *Hidden Teachings of Tibet: An Explanation of the Terma Tradition of Tibetan Buddhism* (Boston: Wisdom, 1986), chapter 3; Janet Gyatso, *Apparitions of the Self: The Secret Autobiographies of a Tibetan Visionary* (Princeton, N.J.: Princeton University Press, 1998), chapter 6.
7. For a selection of notable studies on Tibetan land deities, see Anne-Marie Blondeau and Ernst Steinkellner, *Reflections of the Mountain: Essays on the History and Social Meaning of the Mountain Cult in Tibet and the Himalaya* (Wein: Verlag de Österreichischen Akademie der Wissenschaft, 1996); Anne-Marie Blondeau, ed., *Tibetan Mountain Deities, Their Cults and Representations: Papers Presented at a Panel of the Seventh Seminar of the International Association for Tibetan Studies, Graz, 1995* (Graz: Verlag der Osterreichischen Akademie der Wissenschaften, 1998); Samten G. Karmay, *The Arrow and the Spindle: Studies in History, Myths, Rituals and Beliefs in Tibet* (Kathmandu: Mandala Book Point, 1998); Toni Huber, *The Cult of Pure Crystal Mountain: Popular Pilgrimage and Visionary Landscape in Southeast Tibet* (New York: Oxford University Press, 1999); and Katia Buffetrille and Hildegard Diemberger, eds., *Territory and Identity in Tibet and the Himalayas: PIATS 2000: Tibetan Studies: Proceedings of the Ninth Seminar of the International Association for Tibetan Studies, Leiden 2000* (Leiden: Brill, 2002).
8. The three times are past, present, and future.
9. The Unsurpassed Realm (Skt. Akaniṣṭha, Tib. 'Og min) refers to the highest of all the buddhafields.
10. The Three Bodies (Skt. *trikāya*, Tib. *sku gsum*) refers to three dimensions of buddhahood, including the Truth Body (*dharmakāya*, *chos sku*), the Enjoyment Body (*sambhogakāya*, *longs sku*), and the Emanation Body (*nirmāṇakāya*, *sprul sku*). In KSL, 86, Sera Khandro follows a standard mode of explaining this trinity according to Great Perfection thought in which the Truth Body is "the essence of emptiness" (*ngo bo stong pa*), "free from conceptual elaboration"; the Enjoyment Body is "clarity" (*gsal ba*), "unobstructed natural radiance"; and the Emanation Body is "the projection and re-absorption of manifestations" (*'phro 'du'i rtsal snang*).
11. Mön refers to an eastern Himalayan region southeast of Tibet.
12. Above the earth, on the earth, and below the earth.
13. The six times include three segments of time during the day and three at night; hence "during the six times" means all day and all night.
14. DDNT, fols. 3a.1–5b.1; DDP, 3–6.
15. Dudjom Jikdrel Yeshe Dorje Rinpoche, *The Nyingma School of Tibetan Buddhism: Its Fundamentals and History*, trans. Gyurme Dorje and Matthew Kapstein, 2 vols. (Boston: Wisdom, 1991), vol. 1, 746–47.

16. DDNT, fol. 79b.3–4; DDP, 111.
17. DLNT, 2.
18. GTNT. Locals around Benak say that the remainder of his life story was written in a different book, which was either lost, destroyed, or hidden during the Cultural Revolution and has not (yet) come to light (personal communication with Gelek Pema Namgyel from Pema County, Golok, July 2010). The work is therefore not dated, as the colophon is part of the missing section.
19. GTNT, 6.
20. Gara Terchen explains the etymology of his family name, Gara (Mgar ra), by linking his paternal ancestors to the important imperial Tibetan minister Gar (Mgar) and also by the livelihood of more recent generations who worked as blacksmiths (*mgar*). GTNT, 6–12.
21. SLNT, fols. 3a–4b.
22. Stag sham nus ldan rdo rje, *Bod kyi jo mo ye shes mtsho rgyal gyi mdzad tshul rnam par thar pa gab pa mngon byung rgyud mangs dri za'i glu phreng* (Kalimpong: Zang mdgog dpal ri Monastery, 1972). Henceforth, I abbreviate this work as YSNT. For English, see Gyalwa Changchub and Namkhai Nyingpo, *Lady of the Lotus-Born: The Life and Enlightenment of Yeshe Tsogyal* (Boston: Shambhala, 1999).
23. Changchub and Nyingpo, *Lady of the Lotus-Born*, 3; YSNT, fol. 4a.1–2.
24. DDNT, fol. 3a.1–3; DDP, 3.
25. Changchub and Nyingpo, *Lady of the Lotus-Born*, 6; YSNT, fols. 4–a.6–5a.2.
26. DDNT, fols. 3a.4–3b.1; DDP, 3.
27. Changchub and Nyingpo, *Lady of the Lotus-Born*, 197–98; YSNT, fol. 128b.4–6.
28. DDNT, fols. 4a.5–4b.1; DDP, 4.
29. John Sturrock, "Theory Versus Autobiography," in *The Culture of Autobiography: Constructions of Self-Representation*, ed. Robert Folkenflik (Stanford: Stanford University Press, 1993), 27.
30. The Treasure tradition is not uniquely Buddhist but also appears in Tibet's Bön religion. The same Treasure revealer sometimes even revealed both Buddhist and Bön Treasures; Sera Khandro writes that Drimé Özer revealed both (SLNT, fol. 108b.2–5). For other examples of this, see Ramon Prats, "Some Preliminary Considerations Arising from a Biographical Study of the Early gter ston," in *Tibetan Studies in Honour of Hugh Richardson, Proceedings of the International Seminar on Tibetan Studies Oxford 1979*, ed. Michael Aris and Aung San Suu Kyi (Warminster: Aris & Phillips, 1980), 256; and Anne-Marie Blondeau, "Le 'Decouvreur' du Mani Bka'-'bum etait-il Bon-po?" in *Tibetan and Buddhist Studies Commemorating the 200th Anniversary of the Birth of Alexander Csoma de Koros*, ed. Louis Ligeti (Budapest: Akademiai Kiado, 1984).
31. For more information about Treasure transmission in Nyingma Tantra, see the explanation written by the Third Dodrupchen Jikmé Tenpé Nyima (1865–1926), which Tulku Thondup has translated in his *Hidden Teachings of Tibet* (Boston: Wisdom, 1986). Jikmé Tenpé Nyima's explanation of the Treasure

tradition is particularly apropos for the study of Sera Khandro because he was one of Drimé Özer's older brothers.

32. The eight sublime qualities of water are that it is cool, refreshing, pleasant tasting, smooth, clear, odorless, soothing on the throat to drink, and easily digestable.
33. DDNT, fol. 321a.4–b.4; DDP, 431–32.
34. DDNT, fol. 323a.3–4; DDP, 434.
35. Mahāyoga teachings contain two sections: the means of accomplishment or Sadhana section (*sgrub sde*) mentioned here and the Tantra section (*rgyud sde*).
36. "Placed me [on the path of] ripening and liberation" is a translation of "*smin grol la bkod.*" This expression appears many times in Sera Khandro's writing and refers to the lama's ability to ripen her disciple's mind stream via empowerments and guide her on the path to liberation by means of instructions.
37. DDNT, fols. 324a.2–327b.2; DDP, 437–39.
38. DDNT, fols. 333b.6–334a.6; DDP, 448.
39. DDNT, fol. 209a.6–209b.3; DDP, 287.
40. DDNT, fols. 309b.5–310b.1; DDP, 417–18.
41. DDNT, fol. 370b.3; DDP, 494.
42. DDNT, fol. 380a.2–3; DDP, 504–5.
43. DDNT, fol. 383a.2–6; DDP, 507.
44. Notable historical studies of the Treasure tradition include Janet Gyatso, "The Logic of Legitimation in the Tibetan Treasure Tradition," *History of Religions* 33, no. 1 (1993); Gyatso, *Apparitions of the Self*; and David Germano, "Remembering the Dismembered Body of Tibet: Contemporary Tibetan Visionary Movements in the People's Republic of China," in *Buddhism in Contemporary Tibet: Religious Revival and Cultural Identity*, ed. Melvyn C. Goldstein and Matthew T. Kapstein (Berkeley: University of California Press, 1998).
45. DDNT, fols. 199a.5–200a.3; DDP, 273.
46. Here spelled Lha rig gnyen rtse, but in the passage translated above in "The Interdependent Process of Revelation" section of this chapter, the same land protector (*yul skyong*) is spelled Lha reg gnyan rtse (DDNT, fol. 310a.5; DDP, 418). In both cases, this deity is associated with the territory near Dodrupchen Monastery's branch named Sanglung Monastery.
47. DDNT, fols. 342b.1–343a.2; DDP, 458–59.
48. Samten G. Karmay, "Mountain Cult and National Identity in Tibet," in *The Arrow and the Spindle: Studies in History, Myths, Rituals and Beliefs in Tibet*, ed. Samten G. Karmay (Kathmandu: Mandala Book Point, 1998), 426–27. Regarding the assertion that many Tibetan territorial deities predate the arrival of Buddhism, see Ibid., 427; Réne de Nebesky-Wojkowitz, *Oracles and Demons of Tibet: The Cult and Iconography of the Tibetan Protective Deities* (The Netherlands: Mouton, 1956), 3; and Katia Buffetrille, "Reflections on Pilgrimages to Sacred Mountains, Lakes and Caves," in *Pilgrimage in Tibet*, ed. Alex McKay (Richmond, UK: Curzon Press, 1998), 20.

49. Samten G. Karmay explains that, "The arrow is man's symbol and the ritual gesture of planting it in the cairn places each man who does so under the mountain deity's protection; in the same way, by ritually scattering the 'wind-horses'—itself a symbol of fortune—into the air each man calls upon the mountain deity to increase his fortune." See Karmay, "Mountain Cult and National Identity in Tibet," 429.
50. Samten G. Karmay, "The Cult of Mount dMu-rdo in rGyal-rong," in *The Arrow and the Spindle: Studies in History, Myths, Rituals and Beliefs in Tibet*, ed. Samten G. Karmay (Kathmandu: Mandala Book Point, 1998), 461.
51. My thoughts on Treasure substitutes have benefited greatly from conversation with Antonio Terrone, who first called my attention to their significance for Tibetan conceptions of the environment. For further treatment of this topic, see Antonio Terrone, "The Earth as a Treasure: Visionary Revelation in Tibetan Buddhism and Its Interaction with the Environment," *Journal for the Study of Religion, Nature, and Culture*, forthcoming.
52. Buffetrille, "Reflections on Pilgrimages to Sacred Mountains, Lakes and Caves," 24.
53. Personal communication with Gelek Pema Wangyel Rinpoché, Pema County, Golok TAP, June 2005. See also Samten G. Karmay, "The Cult of Mountain Deities and Its Political Significance," in *The Arrow and the Spindle*, ed. Samten G. Karmay (Kathmandu: Mandala Book Point, 1998), 443.
54. A different story of the genesis of Golok with similar themes can be found at the beginning of Do Khyentsé Yeshé Dorjé's autobiography. For Tibetan, see the opening sections of Mdo mkhyen brtse ye shes rdo rje, *Mdo mkhyen brtse ye shes rdo rje'i rnam thar* (Chengdu: Si khron mi rigs dpe skrun khang, 1997). For English, see Robin Kornman, "A Tribal History," in *Religions of Tibet in Practice*, ed. Donald S. Lopez Jr. (Princeton, N.J.: Princeton University Press, 1997).
55. Don grub dbang rgyal and Nor sde, *Yul mgo log gi lo rgyus deb ther pad+ma dkar po'i chun po* (Xining: Mtsho sngon mi rigs dpe skrun khang, 1992), 11–33.
56. Don grub dbang rgyal and Nor sde, *Mgo log lo rgyus deb ther*, 51.
57. Gelek, "The Washu Serthar: A Nomadic Community of Eastern Tibet," in *Development, Society, and Environment in Tibet*, ed. Graham E. Clarke (Wien: Verlag der Österreichischen Akademie der Wissenschaften, 1998), 47–58.
58. Ibid., 91.
59. Don grub dbang rgyal, "Mgo log gi lo rgyus deb ther pad+ma dkar po'i ge sar," in In *Mgo log rig gnas lo rgyus*, vol. 1 (Xining: Mtsho sngon zhin hwa dpar khang, 1991), 101–4.
60. Don grub dbang rgyal and Nor sde, *Mgo log lo rgyus deb ther*, 107–8.
61. Don grub dbang rgyal, "Mgo log gi lo rgyus deb ther pad+ma dkar po'i ge sar," 104.
62. *Gnyan*, *mkhar*, and *ba* refer to the three groups (Gnyan rtse, Mkhar re, and Ba le) who lived in the Rdo, Smar, and parts of the Rma valleys before these regions were taken over by the descendants of Dri Lha Gyelbum.

63. Don grub dbang rgyal, "Mgo log gi lo rgyus deb ther pad+ma dkar po'i ge sar," 97–98.
64. Don grub dbang rgyal and Nor sde, *Mgo log lo rgyus deb ther*, 112. For more detail on *Bön*, *sgrung*, and *lde'u*, see Namkhai Norbu, *Drung, Deu and Bön: Narrations, Symbolic Languages and the Bön Tradition in Ancient Tibet*, trans. Adriano Clemente (Dharamsala: Library of Tibetan Works and Archives, 1995).
65. Tachok (Rta mchog) is the uppermost pass of the circumambulation route around Anyé Machen. For more on this route, see Kun dga' mkhas dbang dpal bzang po's pilgrimage guide as translated in Katia Buffetrille, "The Great Pilgrimage of A-myes rma-chen," in *Maṇḍala and Landscape*, ed. A. W. Macdonald (New Delhi: D.K. Printworld [P] Ltd., 1997), 100.
66. "Our sacred relationship as land [deity] and guest became unified" is a translation of *gnas mgron dam tshig gcig par song*.
67. DDNT, fols. 118b.5–120a.4; DDP, 164–66.
68. Nebesky-Wojkowitz, *Oracles and Demons of Tibet*, 212. For reference to Drandül Wangchuk as Magyel's younger brother, see Buffetrille, "The Great Pilgrimage of A-myes rma-chen," 76.
69. Serving as the commitment vow substance (*dam tshig rdzas kyi rten du*) means that Jikmé Könchok's presence provided the requisite material/substance (*rdzas*) that served as an auspicious connection necessary for Sera Khandro's Treasure revelation. Garter Rinpoché is another name for Gara Terchen.
70. Vimala Raśmi is the Sanskrit translation of Drimé Özer, meaning "Stainless Ray of Light."
71. The *Yabzhi* (*Ya bzhi*) refers to the fourteenth-century Longchen Rapjampa's systematization of Great Perfection (*rdzogs chen*) teachings in a collection called the *Snying thig ya bzhi*, *Heart Essence in Four Parts*.
72. "Semiprecious stone" is a translation of *mchong*, which is also sometimes translated as "agate" or "quartz."
73. DDNT, fols. 203a.4–205b.4; DDP, 278–82. I have also translated this passage in Sarah Jacoby, "A Treasure Revealer: Sera Khandro," in *Sources of Tibetan Tradition*, ed. Kurtis R. Schaeffer, Matthew T. Kapstein, and Gray Tuttle (New York: Columbia University Press, 2013), 696–99.
74. Mowatowa (Mo ba gto ba) is a site along the Anyé Machen pilgrimage circuit known for being the location of the meditation cave of Shabkar Natsok Rangdröl (1781–1851). See reference to it in Rangdrol, *The Life of Shabkar*, 177 n. 10.
75. A ground-attaining bodhisattva (*sa 'dzin sems pa*) is one who has attained one of the ten grounds or levels of bodhisattvahood, in this case referring to Machen Pomra.
76. DDNT, fols. 206b.4–207b.3; DDP, 283–84.
77. Krung go mi dmangs srid gros gser thar rdzong u yon lhan khang gi rig gnas lo rgyus dpyad yig tsho chung, ed., *Dbal shul gser thar gyi lo rgyus gsar bsgrigs blo ldan mig gi bdud rtsi* (Dartsedo: Gan zi bao she yinshua chang, 1989), 68–69.
78. Ibid., 74. In 1940, André Guibaut and Louis Victor Liotard's expedition passed through Serta and observed the Gogentang Stūpa, which they called "Chor-

taintong." Guibaut, the only one of the two who made it out of Golok alive, wrote, "We see to our astonishment, in this apparently waste expanse, a gigantic edifice, a chortain bulbed like a muscovite steeple and high as a cathedral. Its presence in these solitudes is as unlikely as the presence of a ship in the desert" (92). Also, "In this lonely spot, more than 13,000 feet above sea-level, it is really an astounding construction. Bedded in a square socket, each side forty-five feet long, the bulbed tower with its gilded copper shafts rises a hundred feet above the ground" (93). Guibaut mentions that at the site there was also a little chapel and three or four stone houses in what is today the bustling town of Serta. See Guibaut, *Tibetan Venture in the Country of the Ngolo-Setas: Second Guibaut-Liotard Expedition* (London: John Murray, 1948).

79. Interview with current Washül Serta leader in Serta, May 14, 2005.
80. *Dbal shul gser thar gyi lo rgyus*, 81.
81. *Dbal shul gser thar gyi lo rgyus*, 85. Gelek quotes different figures for the population of Serta; according to Gelek, prior to 1960 Serta included 48 encampment groups or tribes (*tsho ba*), as he calls them, consisting of 5,340 households with a total population of 21,900. See Gelek, "The Washu Serthar," 50.
82. *Dbal shul gser thar gyi lo rgyus*, 151.
83. A long list of local Buddhist Treasure revealers have discovered Treasures at Drong Mountain, including Düjom Lingpa, Drimé Özer, Sera Khandro, Sotrül Natsok Rangdröl, Khenpo Jikmé Püntsok, Namtrül Jikmé Püntsok, Tāré Lhamo, and Rindzin Nyima, to name just a few.
84. SLNT, fols. 28a.5–30a.1.
85. DLNT, 204–5. Yu Chama (G.yu lcam ma) means "Turquoise Lady," a fitting name for the daughter of Nyenpo Yutsé, meaning "Powerful Turquoise Peak." Venerable Tro Nyerma ('Phags ma khro g.nyer ma) or "Frowning Lady" is one of the twenty-one Tārās.
86. Ibid., 205.
87. Thondup, *Hidden Teachings of Tibet*, 114.
88. Karmay, "Mountain Cult and National Identity in Tibet," 429.
89. This description of the annual Washül Serta propitiation ritual at Drong Mountain comes from my personal observation of the ritual in June 2005.
90. DDNT, fol. 250b.3–4; DDP, 342.
91. The Glorious Mountain (*dpal ri*) refers to Padmasambhava's Glorious Copper-Colored Mountain Buddhafield.
92. The secret center (*gsang gnas*) is the lowest of the five *cakras*, located at the genitalia.
93. DDNT, fols. 251b.2–253a.1; DDP, 343–45.
94. Thondup, *Masters of Meditation and Miracles*, 121.
95. "Going out to tame disciples" (*gdul byar byon*) means that he went out to seek alms by performing rituals and giving religious instruction.
96. SLNT, fol. 197a.2–197b.3.
97. Robert Ekvall, "Mi sTong: The Tibetan Custom of Life Indemnity," *Sociologus* 4, no. 2 (1954): 136–45; Robert B. Ekvall, "Peace and War Among the Tibetan

Nomads," *American Anthropologist* 66, no. 5 (1964): 1125; Fernanda Pirie, "Legal Complexity on the Tibetan Plateau," *Journal of Legal Pluralism* 53–54 (2006).

98. Interview with current Washül Serta leader in Serta, May 14, 2005.
99. Germano, "Remembering the Dismembered Body of Tibet," 64.
100. DLNT, 152. For English, see Traktung Dudjom Lingpa, *A Clear Mirror: The Visionary Autobiography of a Tibetan Master*, trans. Chönyi Drolma (Anne Holland) (Hong Kong: Rangjung Yeshe Publications, 2011), 141. Regarding Shabkar's brushes with Golok bandits, see Shabkar Tsogdruk Rangdrol, *The Life of Shabkar: The Autobiography of a Tibetan Yogin*, trans. Matthieu Ricard et al. (Ithaca, N.Y.: Snow Lion, 2001), 166–68; 486–88.
101. SLNT, fol. 107a.2–5.
102. Ibid., 181a.3–6.
103. Samten G. Karmay, "Gesar: the Epic Tradition of the Tibetan People," in *The Arrow and the Spindle* (Kathmandu: Mandala Book Point, 1998), 465–71.
104. Don grub dbang rgyal and Nor sde, *Mgo log lo rgyus deb ther*, 260–65.
105. *Zi khron gyi dus rabs rim byung gi lo rgyus* as quoted in Don grub dbang rgyal and Nor sde, *Mgo log lo rgyus deb ther*, 29–31.
106. DLNT, 207.
107. Ibid., 208.
108. Merrill Ruth Hunsberger, "Ma Pu-fang in Chinghai Province, 1931–1949" (Ph.D. diss., Temple University, 1978), 8–32.
109. Don grub dbang rgyal and Nor sde, *Mgo log lo rgyus deb ther*, 272–92.
110. "Awo Sera Monastery" description written by Ven. Sogan Rinpoché (Tulku Pema Lodoe, b. 1964), contemporary reincarnation of Sotrül Natsok Rangdröl, http://www.tuptenoselcholing.org/awo_sera.html (accessed December 9, 2011).
111 SLNT, fol. 192a.3–4.
112. SLNT, fol. 195a.4–6. In Sera Khandro's autobiography (DDNT, fol. 254a.1–2; DDP, 346) she describes this move with the following words: "Then, on account of the agitation caused by the northern Chinese, the inner retinue held a discussion and decided to move the Master's residence to Yusé."
113. DDNT, fol. 250a.3-b.1; DDP, 341.
114. Tib. *rgan mo*, "the old lady," referring to his consort.
115. SLNT, fols. 48b.6–49a.6.
116. SLNT, fol. 80a.4–80b.1.
117. For reference to Ann Swidler's discussion of cultural repertoires, see Swidler, *Talk of Love* (Chicago: University of Chicago Press, 2001), 24–25, 89.

3. *ḌĀKINĪ* DIALOGUES

1. DDNT, fols. 174b.6–175a.4; DDP, 240.
2. Janet Gyatso, *Apparitions of the Self: The Secret Autobiographies of a Tibetan Visionary* (Princeton, N.J.: Princeton University Press, 1998), 105.

3. For discussions of the term *skye dman*, see Barbara Nimri Aziz, "Moving Towards A Sociology of Tibet," in *Feminine Ground: Essays on Women and Tibet*, ed. Janice D. Willis (Ithaca: Snow Lion, 1987), 77; and Janet Gyatso and Hanna Havnevik, *Women in Tibet* (New York: Columbia University Press, 2005), 9.
4. Hildegard Diemberger has found a similar contrast in the fifteenth-century Chökyi Drönma's biography between *skye dman* as a derogatory term for woman and *bud med* as a more honorific and positive term. See Diemberger, *When a Woman Becomes a Religious Dynasty: The Samding Dorje Phagmo of Tibet* (New York: Columbia University Press, 2007), 10–13. For analysis of Sera Khandro's repeated mentions of her lowly female form, see also Sarah H. Jacoby, "'This inferior female body': Reflections on Life as a Tibetan Visionary Through the Autobiographical Eyes of Se ra mkha' 'gro (Bde ba'i rdo rje, 1892–1940)," *Journal of the International Association of Buddhist Studies* 32, no. 1–2 (2010).
5. Rinchen Lhamo, *We Tibetans* (1926; reprint, New Delhi: Srishti Publishers & Distributors, 1997), 125; Beatrice Miller, "Views of Women's Roles in Buddhist Tibet," in *Studies in the History of Buddhism*, ed. A. K. Narain (Delhi: B. R. Publishing, 1980); and Pema Dechen, "The Oppression and Resistance of Tibetan Women," in *The Anguish of Tibet*, ed. Gert Bastian, Petra K. Kelly, and Pat Aiello (Berkeley: Parallax Press, 1991).
6. For references to misogyny in Indian Buddhism, see Nancy Auer Falk, "The Case of the Vanishing Nuns: The Fruits of Ambivalence in Ancient Indian Buddhism," in *Unspoken Worlds: Women's Religious Lives in Non-Western Cultures*, ed. Nancy Auer Falk and Rita M. Gross (San Francisco: Harper & Row, 1980); Alan Sponberg, "Attitudes Toward Women and the Feminine in Early Buddhism," in *Buddhism, Sexuality, and Gender*, ed. José Ignacio Cabezón (Albany: State University of New York Press, 1992); and Liz Wilson, *Charming Cadavers: Horrific Figurations of the Feminine in Indian Buddhist Hagiographic Literature* (Chicago: University of Chicago Press, 1996).
7. Kim Gutschow, *Being a Buddhist Nun* (Cambridge, Mass.: Harvard University Press, 2004), ch. 1, 3.
8. Hanna Havnevik, *Tibetan Buddhist Nuns: History, Cultural Norms, and Social Reality* (Oslo: Norwegian University Press, 1989), 147–48; Charlene E. Makley, "The Body of a Nun: Nunhood and Gender in Contemporary Amdo," in *Women in Tibet*, ed. Janet Gyatso and Hanna Havnevik (New York: Columbia University Press, 2005).
9. Peter Skilling, "Nuns, Laywomen, Donors, Goddesses: Female Roles in Early Indian Budhism," *Journal of the International Association of Buddhist Studies* 24, no. 2 (2001); Jinah Kim, "Unheard Voices: Women's Roles in Medieval Buddhist Artistic Production and Religious Practices in South Asia," *Journal of the American Academy of Religion* 80, no. 1 (2012).
10. One among the many examples of such Tantric valorizations of women is the following verse in chapter 8 of the *Caṇḍamahāroṣaṇa Tantra*: "Women are heaven; women are Dharma; and women are the highest penance. Women

are Buddha; women are the Saṃgha; and women are the Perfection of Wisdom," as translated in Christopher S. George, *The Caṇḍamahāroṣaṇa Tantra, Chapters I–VIII*, American Oriental Series Vol. 56 (New Haven: American Oriental Society, 1974), 82.

11. David Gordon White, *Kiss of the Yoginī* (Chicago: University of Chicago Press, 2003), chapter 2.
12. Adelheid Herrmann-Pfandt, "Ḍākinīs in Indo-Tibetan Tantric Buddhism: Some Results of Recent Research," *Studies in Central and East Asian Religions*, no. 5/6 (1992–93): 46–49. For the most comprehensive study to date on the South Asian history of *ḍākinīs* in both Hindu and Buddhist texts, see Adelheid Herrmann-Pfandt, *Ḍākinīs: Zur Stellung und Symbolik des Weiblichen im Tantrischen Buddhismus* (Bonn: Indica et Tibetica Verlag, 1992).
13. For an overview of the ways scholars have defined and understood *khandroma* in the context of Tibetan Buddhism, see Janice Willis, "Ḍākinī; Some Comments on Its Nature and Meaning," in *Feminine Ground: Essays on Women and Tibet*, ed. Janice Willis (Ithaca: Snow Lion, 1987).
14. Anne Carolyn Klein, *Meeting the Great Bliss Queen: Buddhists, Feminists, and the Art of the Self* (Boston: Beacon, 1995), 172. The quoted phrase is drawn from Klein's translation of Ngakwang Tendzin Dorjé's commentary on Jikmé Lingpa's liturgy dedicated to the "Great Bliss Queen" Yeshé Tsogyel. See chapter 7 of *Meeting the Great Bliss Queen* for fuller treatment of this ritual and its implications for Buddhist practitioners' encounters with the *ḍākinī* as the primordial nature of one's own mind.
15. Sponberg, "Attitudes Toward Women and the Feminine in Early Buddhism," 28. Additionally, in *Traveller in Space: In Search of Female Identity in Tibetan Buddhism* (London: Athlone, 1996), June Campbell argues that "the *ḍākinī*, par excellence, came to represent the secret, hidden and mystical quality of absolute insight required by men" (128), and that the gendered symbolism *ḍākinīs* represented was damaging for human women's subjectivity.
16. Sera Khandro's autobiography thus exemplifies Judith Simmer-Brown's claim that in Tibetan biographies of female religious figures "the ḍākinī appears not as an oppositional figure but as an ally, mirror, or companion of the yoginī focused primarily on empowering and encouraging her." See Judith Simmer-Brown, *Dakini's Warm Breath: The Feminine Principle in Tibetan Buddhism* (Boston: Shambhala, 2001), 259.
17. Gyatso, *Apparitions of the Self*, 254.
18. The one other Tibetan female teacher Sera Khandro mentions briefly in her auto/biographical works was a nun incarnation of Machik Lapdrön named Ané Zangmo, who died before Sera Khandro had the opportunity to meet her.
19. DDNT, fol. 13b.1–5; DDP, 18.
20. The manuscript edition (DDNT) of Sera Khandro's autobiography reads Önpu Taktsang ('On phu stag tshang) but the published version (DDP) reads Paro Taktsang (Spa gro stag tshang).

21. The Dharma King Ngaki Wangpo (Chos rgyal ngag kyi dbang po, 1736–1807) was a descendant of Gushri Khan (1582–1655). Ngaki Wangpo lived in the Kokonor region of Amdo and renounced his claim to Gushri Khan's kingdom to become a prominent Nyingmapa master. He was the teacher of Shabkar Tsokdruk Rangdröl (1781–1851).
22. DDNT, fols. 17b.1–18a.1; DDP, 23–24.
23. The measure is *gru gang*, the length from the elbow up to the tips of the fingers.
24. DDNT, fols. 48b.2–50b.2; DDP, 68–71.
25. Tulku Thondup, *Hidden Teachings of Tibet: An Explanation of the Terma Tradition of Tibetan Buddhism* (Boston: Wisdom, 1986), 137–38. For a semiotic history of *byang* (guide/certificate) that outlines its pre-Treasure tradition connotations, see Janet Gyatso, "The Relic Text as Prophecy: The Semantic Drift of Byang-bu and Its Appropriation in the Treasure Tradition."
26. DDNT, fol. 96.1–3; DDP, 133.
27. Jadrel Rinpoché explains Sapta (*sab+ta*) as a type of negative force that causes hindrances.
28. The eight worldly Dharmas refer to being caught up in gain and loss, fame and infamy, praise and blame, pleasure and sorrow.
29. DDNT, fols. 98a.2–99b.6; DDP, 136–38.
30. DDNT, fols. 104b.2–106a.2; DDP, 145–47.
31. DDNT, fol. 141a.1–5; DDP, 193–94.
32. 'Jam mgon kong sprul blo gros mtha' yas, *Dpal snga 'gyur rnying ma'i gter ston brgya rtsa'i rnam thar bai d'u+rya'i phreng ba* (Odiyan: Dharma Publishing, 2004), 378–84.
33. Sera Khandro is punning on the name of Gyelsé's residence, which she normally spells Benak (Ban nag). It can be etymologized to mean "bad or negative monk," though this certainly was not its intended meaning. When she rephrases her song below in front of Gyelsé, she changes the spelling to Benyak (Ban yag), which could be etymologized to mean "good or virtuous monk." Contemporary publications call this monastery Peyak (Pad yag); see *Mgo log khul gyi dgon sde khag gi lo rgyus*, 442.
34. The turquoise dragon is a metaphor for Sera Khandro, who was born in the water dragon year (1892).
35. DDNT, fols. 143a.6–145a.3; DDP, 196–99.
36. DDNT, fols. 147b.3–149a.3; DDP, 202–4.
37. DDNT, fol. 153a.4–b.1; DDP, 210.
38. For a brief biography of him, see O rgyan brtson 'grus, *Dar thang dgon pa'i gdan rabs* (Chengdu: Si khron mi rigs dpe skrun khang, 1999), 392–93.
39. The metric of these particular *ḍākinī* verses is eight-syllable lines following a 2+2+2+2 pattern until "The chick replied," where the verses become hexasyllabic, divided into three equal feet (2+2+2), which is a common meter for central Tibetan folk songs. See Victoria Sujata, *Tibetan Songs of Realization* (Leiden: Brill, 2005), 122.

40. Dharma Mati is the Sanskrit translation of Chökyi Lodrö, Gotrül Rinpoché's name.
41. Here again Sera Khandro is punning on the monastery name Benak (Ban nag), which can be etymologized to mean "bad monk," by situating it in a *trong nak* (*khrong nag*), or "bad village."
42. The five certainties (*nges pa lnga*) are the five defining features of a *sambhogakāya* buddha, including 1) the certainty of place (that they always reside in a buddhafield), 2) the certainty of body (that they are endowed with the 32 major and 80 minor marks of buddhahood), 3) certainty of time (they will live for as long as beings remain in *saṃsāra*), 4) the certainty of teachings (always the Great Vehicle), and 5) the certainty of disciples (they will always teach advanced bodhisattvas).
43. Dzachukha (Rdza chu kha, Clay River Mouth) is a wide grasslands region just west of Golok and Serta. Rongzhi (Rong bzhi, Four Valleys) is unclear; it could possibly refer to the lower parts of the Mar (Smar) Valley in Golok that are known by this name or to a geographic region in the kingdom of Lingtsang near Degé. Khaksum (Khag gsum, Three Parts) refers to the three parts of Golok: Akyong Bum, Wangchen Bum, and Pema Bum.
44. DDNT, 156a.4–159b.3; DDP, 214–18.
45. Tantric meditation includes two stages of practice: the generation stage (*bskyed rim*), in which the meditator engages in complex visualizations of deities whereby she purifies ordinary appearances of forms, sounds, and perceptions into deities, mantras, and primordial wisdom, respectively; and the perfection stage (*rdzogs rim*), involving contemplative practices focused on the channels, winds, and vital nuclei of the subtle body as well as on the direct contemplation of emptiness.
46. DDNT, fols. 162a.1–163a.4; DDP, 222–23.
47. DDNT, fols. 221a.6–222a.6; DDP, 303–4.
48. Gelek explains what I refer to as the Gar kinsmen's "circle" (*skor/ru skor*) as a pastoral economic unit smaller than an encampment group (*tsho ba*) but larger than a family, consisting of five to ten households mostly from the same patrilineage, but not exclusively so. They were called "circles" because the nomads would arrange their tents in a circular shape for protection. See Gelek, "The Washu Sertar: A Nomadic Community of Eastern Tibet," in *Development, Society, and Environment in Tibet*, ed. Graham E. Clarke (Wien: Verlag der Österreichischen Akademie der Wissenschaften, 1998), 50.
49. DDNT, fols. 254b.2–255b.5; DDP, 347–48.
50. DLNT, 1.
51. DLNT, 72–73.
52. DLNT, 70–71.
53. DLNT, 151–52.
54. *Mgo log khul gyi dgon sde khag gi lo rgyus*, 351.
55. For a discussion of pure visions (*dag snang*) and their differences from Treasure revelations, see Thondup, *Hidden Teachings of Tibet*, 90–91.

56. This name means the Maṇḍala Field at Mar Selé (Smar se le) and is a version of the name Selitang, the capital of Pema County.
57. GTNT, 22.
58. Oḍḍiyāna (Tib. O rgyan) is the name of Padmasambhava's land of origin.
59. GTNT, 26–27.
60. GTNT, 30.
61. The "X" marks here refer to undecipherable *ḍākinī* script symbols that Gara Terchen wrote in his autobiography.
62. GTNT, 37–38.
63. GTNT, 45.
64. GTNT, 60.
65. Monica Furlong, *Visions and Longings: Medieval Women Mystics* (London: Mowbray, 1996), 14.
66. Hanna Havnevik, "The Life of Jetsun Lochen Rinpoche (1865–1951) as Told in Her Autobiography" (University of Oslo, 1999), 79. See this work for an excellent study and translation of Jetsün Ani Lochen's autobiography from which this précis is drawn.
67. This Katok Situ may not have had the most positive estimation of female religious practitioners; Havnevik cites Katok Situ's expression of dissatisfaction with the Padmasambhava cave Zangyak Drak where Ani Lochen did meditation retreats because of impurity accruing from the nuns staying there. See ibid., 81. Additionally, Sera Khandro includes the following cryptic comment about not being able to receive teachings from Katok Situ on account of being female in her autobiography: "Then, that year [c. 1915] in the beginning of the tenth month, Katok Situ Rinpoché was giving the complete empowerments and reading transmissions for the *Lama Gongpa Düpa, Embodiment of the Lama's Realization* at Pelyül Monastery. When Gyelsé, the disciple Tupten Zangpo, and my daughter and I were getting ready to go there, because my daughter and I had the negative karma of having inferior female bodies (*lus dman*), there was no way for us to go." See DDNT, fol. 165b; DDP, p. 227.
68. Personal communication with Jetsün Ani Lochen's disciple Rindzin Yudrön (b. 1923-?), Pharping, Nepal, spring 1995.
69. Havnevik, "The Life of Jetsun Lochen Rinpoche (1865–1951) as Told in Her Autobiography," 88–90.
70. Ibid., 613.
71. Ibid., 101.
72. Ibid., 114.
73. DDNT, fols. 122b.3–123a.5; DDP, 169–70.
74. Havnevik, "The Life of Jetsun Lochen Rinpoche (1865–1951) as Told in Her Autobiography," 284–85.
75. Ibid., 513.
76. Ibid., 625.
77. Ibid., 103.
78. Ibid., 19–20.

79. José Ignacio Cabezón, "On Authorship and Literary Production in Classical Buddhist Tibet," in *Changing Minds: Contributions to the Study of Buddhism and Tibet in Honor of Jeffrey Hopkins*, ed. Guy Newland (Ithaca: Snow Lion, 2001).
80. Kurtis R. Schaeffer, *Himalayan Hermitess* (New York: Oxford University Press, 2004), 142.
81. Ibid., 143.
82. DDNT, fol. 13b.2; DDP, 18.
83. Schaeffer, *Himalayan Hermitess*, 131.
84. Ibid., 132.
85. Ibid., 149–50.
86. Ibid., 180.
87. Gyatso, *Apparitions of the Self*, 243.
88. DLNT, 208.
89. SLNT, fol. 241b.6–242a.2.
90. KSL, 101–102; Sarah H. Jacoby, "The Excellent Path of Devotion: An Annotated Translation of Sera Khandro's Short Autobiography," in *Himalayan Passages: Tibetan and Newar Studies in Honor of Hubert Decleer*, ed. Benjamin Bogin and Andrew Quintman (Boston: Wisdom, 2014), 198.
91. Sera Khandro's *Cycle of Prophecies* (*Lung bstan skor*) is part of her Treasure revelation volumes, specifically *The Secret Treasury of Reality Ḍākinīs Explanatory Manual* (*Chos nyid mkha' 'gro gsang mdzod khrid yig*). I have found two handwritten manuscript versions of it in Tibet, one near Tralek Monastery in Kandzé and one in Serta.
92. DDNT, fol. 149a.3; DDP, 204.
93. DDNT, fol. 348b.6; DDP, 466.

4. SACRED SEXUALITY

1. The three trainings on the path (*bslab gsum*) are moral discipline, concentration, and insight.
2. DDNT, fol. 376b.1–3; DDP, 500.
3. For more on the play of opposites in European and American appraisals of Tibetan Buddhism, see Donald S. Lopez, *Prisoners of Shangri-la: Tibetan Buddhism and the West* (Chicago: University of Chicago Press, 1998), 4.
4. Heinrich Robert Zimmer, *Philosophies of India*, Bollingen Series XXVI (New York: Pantheon, 1951), 572–73.
5. Mircea Eliade, *Yoga: Immortality and Freedom*, Bollingen Series, 56 (New York: Pantheon, 1958), 202–3.
6. Miranda Shaw, *Passionate Enlightenment: Women in Tantric Buddhism* (Princeton, N.J.: Princeton University Press, 1994), 69.
7. Sanjukta Gupta, Dirk Jan Hoens, and Teun Goudriaan, *Hindu Tantrism* (Leiden: Brill, 1979), 34.

8. David Snellgrove, *Indo-Tibetan Buddhism* (1987; reprint, Boston: Shambhala, 2002), 287–88.
9. Serinity Young, *Courtesans and Tantric Consorts: Sexualities in Buddhist Narrative, Iconography, and Ritual* (New York: Routledge, 2004), 168.
10. Though there is no scholarly consensus on the definition of Tantra, many suggest a polythetic definition in which traditions are deemed Tantric if they contain some among a set of features often including *mantras* (incantations); *yantras/maṇḍalas* (symbolic diagrams); *mudrās* (gestures); secrecy; initiation; dyadic symbolism of male and female divinities; yogic practices; ritual use of forbidden substances including meat, alcohol, and sexual fluids; and deity yoga (visualizing oneself as a deity). Precisely which features characterize Tantra or how many a tradition must contain are open to debate. For more, see Douglas Renfrew Brooks, *The Secret of the Three Cities* (Chicago: University of Chicago Press, 1990), 55–72; Ronald M. Davidson, *Indian Esoteric Buddhism: A Social History of the Tantric Movement* (New York: Columbia University Press, 2002), 118–21; and Hugh Urban, *Tantra: Sex, Secrecy, Politics, and Power in the Study of Religion* (Berkeley: University of California Press, 2003), 6–7.
11. For example, from Candrakīrti's *Pradīpoddyotana*: "It is not only men who bring about the accomplishment of awakening born from passion, but women as well who accomplish this." From Bhavabhadra's *Vajraḍāka-vivṛti*: "The *yoginīs* will bestow *siddhis* of ultimate truth pristine wisdom on the male practitioners. . . . And the male practitioners will bestow the ultimate truth pristine wisdom on the *yoginīs* as well. . . . Thus, by means of this path, both men and women will attain [awakening] without difficulty." From Tsongkhapa's commentary on the Guhyasamāja Tantra, the *Mtha' gcod rin chen myu gu*: "Though it seems the majority of the Tantras and the Indian *sādhanas* teach mostly from the point of view of a man, it is not impossible [to attain enlightenment, the stage of Vajradhara] in a body of a woman." These passages are quoted in Yael Bentor, "Can Women Attain Enlightenment Through Vajrayāna Practices?" in *Karmic Passages: Israeli Scholarship on India*, ed. David Shulman and Shalva Weil (New Delhi: Oxford University Press, 2008), 130–31.
12. Ronald M. Davidson, "Atiśa's 'A Lamp for the Path to Awakening,'" in *Buddhism in Practice*, ed. Donald S. Lopez, Jr. (Princeton, N.J.: Princeton University Press, 1995).
13. What I have translated as "resources" is unclear in the Tibetan: *so gnam lto yangs pa*, fol 94a.1–2; 130–31; DDP, 130–31.
14. *Tü* (Tib. *thud*) is a combination of butter, cheese, and sometimes roasted barley flour pressed together into a block.
15. "Shouldering the debt of the dead" (*gshin po'i ro dom khur*) refers to ritual specialists who receive offerings to pray for the dead but lack the capacity to help them in their transmigration process, thus accruing financial gain tinged with karmic debt, which must be repaid in the future by experiencing suffering.
16. In other words, you have thick skin; you are not easily ashamed.

17. Pulling one's cheeks (*'gram sha 'then*) is a Tibetan gesture expressing shock.
18. DDNT, fols. 93a.4–95b.4; DDP, 129–33.
19. Kukkuripa (spelled ku ku ras pa by Sera Khandro) was one of the eighty-four Great Siddhas or "Accomplished Ones" heralded in the Indian Buddhist hagiographical tradition. He is known for his love of his dog, who later revealed herself as a *ḍākinī*. See James Robinson, *Buddha's Lions: The Lives of the Eighty-Four Siddhas* (Berkeley: Dharma Publishing, 1979), 128–30.
20. *Thig le* (Skt. *bindu*) in this context refers to the regenerative fluids that course through the subtle body channels, conveyed by the force of wind. Common alternative translations include "sphere," "circle," "creative essence," and "seminal nuclei." I have chosen to translate *thig le* as "vital nuclei" throughout this book because it is gender neutral (*thig le* exist in both male and female bodies) and because it conveys the spherical nature of *thig le*. For a cogent explanation of *thig le*, see Janet Gyatso, *Apparitions of the Self: The Secret Autobiographies of a Tibetan Visionary* (Princeton, N.J.: Princeton University Press, 1998), 193–94.
21. DDNT, fol. 61a.2-b.1; DDP, 85–86.
22. DDNT, fol. 61b.1; DDP, 86.
23. The three Sanskrit syllables are *oṃ ah hūṃ* and are associated respectively with the wheels at the crown of the head, the throat, and the heart.
24. DDNT, fol. 62a.6-b.1; DDP, 87.
25. *Bodhicitta* (Tib. *byang chub sems*) is a Sanskrit term meaning literally "mind of enlightenment." In Mahāyāna contexts it refers to generating the altruistic intention to benefit others, but in Tantric Buddhism it also refers to the physical substrate of this intention, which is vital nuclei.
26. DDNT, fol. 62b.2–6; DDP, 87–88.
27. There do not appear to be any traditional Tantric sources in South Asian languages describing channel and wind practices involving homosexual union.
28. DDNT, fol. 63a.6–b.6; DDP, 89.
29. For a few examples among the ubiquitous male perspectives of Tantric sexual yoga, replete with lists of ideal female consorts, found in Vajrayāna Buddhist Tantras, see chapter 11 of the *Guhyagarbha Tantra* or chapters 16–19 of the *Cakrasamvara Tantra*.
30. The path of accumulation (*tshogs lam*) is the first of five paths, traversal of which results in buddhahood. The other four (respectively) are the path of joining (*sbyor lam*), seeing (*mthong lam*), cultivation (*yongs byang lam*), and no more learning (*mi slob pa'i lam*).
31. That is, semen rains into the vagina and the white male and red female vital nuclei meet.
32. There are thirteen grounds on the bodhisattva path, each referring to an additional level of realization. Here, the gradual drawing up of the vital nuclei into the woman's body is linked to successive stages of attaining the bodhisattva grounds.

33. A spontaneously arisen awareness holder (*lhun gyis grub pa'i rig 'dzin*) is the final stage of four successive stages of spiritual realization that the practitioner attains through traversing the five paths that lead to buddhahood.
34. The crown protrusion (*gtsug tor*) is the protuberance at the top of a buddha's head, one of the thirty-two major marks of a buddha.
35. The seven aspects of union (*kha sbyor yan lag bdun*): 1) complete enjoyment (*longs spyod rdzogs pa*); 2) union (*kha sbyor*); 3) great bliss (*bde ba chen po*); 4) no self-nature (*rang bzhin med pa*); 5) completely filled with compassion (*snying rjes yongs su gang ba*); 6) uninterrupted (*rgyun mi chad pa*); and 7) unceasing (*'gog pa med pa*).
36. DDNT, fols. 64a.4–65b.6; DDP, 90–92.
37. Gyurme Dorje, "The Guhyagarbhatantra and Its XIVth Century Tibetan Commentary, *phogs bcu mun sel*" (Ph.D. diss., School of Oriental and Africal Studies, University of London, 1987), 909.
38. YSNT, fol. 28b.4–6; Gyalwa Changchub and Namkhai Nyingpo, *Lady of the Lotus-Born: The Life and Enlightenment of Yeshe Tsogyal* (Boston: Shambhala, 1999), 42.
39. YSNT, fols. 28b.4–30a.3; Changchub and Nyingpo, *Lady of the Lotus-Born*, 42–44.
40. Changchub and Nyingpo, *Lady of the Lotus-Born*, 45.
41. Tulku Thondup, *Hidden Teachings of Tibet: An Explanation of the Terma Tradition of Tibetan Buddhism* (Boston: Wisdom, 1986), 107.
42. Lama Yeshe, *Introduction to Tantra* (Boston: Wisdom, 1987), 37.
43. Thondup, *Hidden Teachings of Tibet*, 130.
44. See also the erudite exploration of the connections between *ḍākinīs*, talk, and bliss in Gyatso, *Apparitions of the Self*, 254–56.
45. The etymology of *gzungs ma* is another example of the overlap between female consorts and language, as *gzungs* is the Tibetan translation of the Sanskrit *dhāraṇī*, a magical formula or mantra associated with remembering the meaning of religious teachings.
46. *Mchong* is a semiprecious mineral in Tibet, translated in some instances as quartz or agate.
47. DDNT, fol. 149a.4–149b.2; DDP, 204–5.
48. DDNT, fols. 179a.4–180a.6; DDP, 245–47.
49. SLNT, fol. 174b.3–6.
50. DDNT, fols. 198a.3-b.4; DDP, 272.
51. DDNT, fols. 204b.2–4; DDP, 280.
52. Elisabeth Schüssler Fiorenza, *Bread Not Stone: The Challenge of Feminist Biblical Interpretation* (Boston: Beacon, 1984), 111.
53. Connections between reversing the downward flow of sexual fluids and physical health/longevity are by no means unique to Buddhist Tantra. For a broader discussion of the phenomenon in Indian Tantric traditions, see chapter 1 of David Gordon White, *The Alchemical Body: Siddha Traditions in*

Medieval India (Chicago: University of Chicago Press, 1996). Parallels can also be found in other Asian contexts, including Taoist immortality practices.

54. DDNT, fols. 96b.6–97a.1; DDP, 134–35.
55. O rgyan brtson 'grus, *Dar thang dgon pa'i gdan rabs*, 378–79.
56. GTNT, 161.
57. Thondup, *Masters of Meditation and Miracles*, 228–29.
58. Akṣara Vajra is the Sanskrit translation of Gyurmé Dorjé, who was Andzom Drondül Pawo Dorjé's son.
59. DDNT, fols. 277b.3–279a.2; DDP, 377–78.
60. DDNT, fols. 283b.1–2; DDP, 384.
61. DDNT, fols. 284b.5–6; DDP, 386.
62. "The youth who sustains your body" (*lus 'tsho byed gzhon nu*) is a literal translation of a term, *'tsho byed gzhon nu*, which can also refer to a specific doctor at the time of the Buddha or to doctors more generally.
63. DDNT, fols. 335a.1–337a.1; DDP, 449–51.
64. This refers to the *cakra* at the crown of the head.
65. DDNT, fols. 367a.3–368b.2; DDP, 489–91.
66. DDNT, fol. 369a.5–b.5; DDP, 492–93.
67. Ngari Panchen Pema Wangyi Gyalpo, *Perfect Conduct: Ascertaining the Three Vows*, trans. Khenpo Gyurme Samdrub and Sangye Khandro (Boston: Wisdom, 1996), 142.
68. Gyalpo, *Perfect Conduct*, 144.
69. Gyalpo, *Perfect Conduct*, xi.
70. Gyalpo, *Perfect Conduct*, 145.
71. The more common Tibetan term for gossip is *mi kha*, literally "person's talk" or "person's mouth"; see Krang dbyi sun, ed., *Bod rgya tshig mdzod chen mo*, 2 vols. (Beijing: Mi rigs dpe skrun khang, 1993), 2064, which defines *mi kha* as "badmouthing or negative talk."
72. Max Gluckman, "Gossip and Scandal," *Current Anthropology* 4 (1963).
73. The point Kyitrül's sister was making is that in his last life he was a non-celibate Tantric adept (*sngags 'chang*), and therefore he might revert to that status if tempted by Sera Khandro to abandon his celibacy vows.
74. The wheels or *cakras* of the body each have letters (*yi ge*), or Sanskrit syllables, associated with them.
75. "No more learning" (*mi slob*) is the fifth and final path of a bodhisattva.
76. DDNT, fols. 107b.4–110b.5; DDP, 149–53.
77. The eight freedoms include freedom from 1) being born in the hells, 2) being born as a hungry ghost, 3) being born as an animal, 4) being born as a long-lived god, 5) being born as a barbarian, 6) having wrong views, 7) being born where there is no buddha, and 8) being born deaf and mute.
78. The association between lust and a bird relates to a common depiction of the three poisons (hatred, ignorance, and lust) in the central part of the Wheel of Existence (*srid pa'i 'khor lo*), in which the bird (in particular the rooster) symbolizes lust, the pig symbolizes ignorance, and the snake symbolizes hatred.

79. Negative offerings (*dkor nag*) are alms donated to religious specialists by the faithful that become negative (*nag*) when their recipients consume them with self-interest and without the proper intention and ability to benefit others.
80. *Ha ha he he* is an onomatopoeia indicating laughter, but here according to the relevant *Tshig mdzod chen mo* definitions, *ha ha* can be "a scoffing laughter" (3062) and *he he* can be "a laughter which induces fear" (3069); hence this chuckling is more like a cackle.
81. DDNT, fols. 172b.6–74a.5; DDP, 237–39.
82. DDNT, fols. 158b.4–5; DDP, 217.
83. DDNT, fols. 162a.2–4; DDP, 222.
84. DDNT, fols. 190b.5–191b.2; DDP, 261–62.
85. DDNT, fols. 192b.1–193b.6; DDP, 264–66.
86. "I am committed to someone" is a translation of *nga rang bdag po can red*, which could also mean I am one who has a partner or spouse. In its most literal sense, it means "I am one with an owner."
87. DDNT, fols. 222b.2–24a.2; DDP, 305–6.
88. DDNT, fols. 224b.2–225a.3; DDP, 307–8.
89. DDNT, fol. 228a.3–4; DDP, 312.
90. DDNT, fol. 231a.1–2; DDP, 316.
91. DDNT, fol. 301b.2–4; DDP, 407.
92. DDNT, fol. 305b.4–6; DDP, 412.
93. Personal communication with Tulku Pema Lodoe, Berkeley, California, November 2011.
94. The term I am translating as "monk" is *dge sbyong*, which usually refers to monks or nuns but also can refer to a wider category of ascetics or mendicants. I have chosen to translate it as "monk" here because Sera Khandro implies that their offering themselves to her as potential consorts was a deterioration of their celibacy vows.
95. The Nyak Valley (Nyag khog) probably refers to Nyarong (Nyag rong), a large valley in Kham located in Kandzé Tibetan Autonomous Prefecture, Sichuan.
96. The small monk's name is written as a symbol in DDNT, fol. 353b.1; the symbol is missing in the published version, DDP, 472.
97. DDNT, fols. 352a.4–54b.4; DDP, 470–74.
98. DDNT, fol. 384b.1–4; DDP, 509.
99. DDNT, fols. 109b.4–5; DDP, 152.
100. In claiming this, I am influenced by the theory of gossip as a form of information management. Robert Paine wrote, "there is always some information that he [the gossiper] wishes certain people to possess—e.g. as a reassurance to them about his activities—in order that his, and not their, definition of the situation prevails." See Robert Paine, "What is Gossip About? An Alternative Hypothesis," *Man* 2, no. 2 (1967): 283. Erving Goffman wrote, "The object of a performer is to sustain a particular definition of the situation, this representing, as it were, his claim as to what reality is." See Erving Goffman, *The*

Presentation of Self in Everyday Life (Garden City, N.Y.: Doubleday, 1959), 85. Paine's and Goffmans' theories are focused on the motivations of gossipers, and although I would not label Sera Khandro "a gossiper" because of her repeated mentions of gossip affecting others with whom she interacted, she nonetheless understood the power of such talk and was able to recast it in a way that presented herself more favorably.

101. GTNT, 61.
102. GTNT, 72–73.
103. GTNT, 77.
104. GTNT, 78.
105. GTNT, 79.
106. GTNT, 103. Rāhu is a deity associated with heavenly bodies who causes solar and lunar eclipses as well as illnesses such as paralysis and strokes.
107. "King Dotsa" (*do tsha rgyal po*) is a harmful local spirit that took birth in the potentially malevolent "king" (*rgyal po*) class of spirits.
108. GTNT, 104. "Planetary defilement" (*gza' grib*) often refers to epilepsy, which Tibetans understood to be caused by astrological imbalances.
109. This appears to be a textual error; the name should read Ngak Chödrön.
110. GTNT, 115–16.
111. For more on Drimé Özer's dilemma about whether or not to become a monk, see Sarah Jacoby, "To Be or Not to Be Celibate: Morality and Consort Practices According to the Treasure Revealer Se ra mkha' 'gro's (1892–1940) Auto/biographical Writings," in *Buddhism Beyond the Monastery: Tantric Practices and Their Performers in Tibet and the Himalayas*, ed. Sarah Jacoby and Antonio Terrone (Leiden: Brill, 2009), 49–52.

5. LOVE BETWEEN METHOD AND INSIGHT

1. SLNT, fol. 230a.1–3.
2. *The Vimalakirti Sutra*, trans. Burton Watson (New York: Columbia University Press, 1997), 96. For a discussion of the significance of the Sanskrit grammatical genders of the terms Mahāyāna Buddhists chose for method and insight, see José Ignacio Cabezón, "Mother Wisdom, Father Love," in *Buddhism, Sexuality, and Gender*, ed. José Ignacio Cabezón (Albany: State University of New York Press, 1992), 183–84.
3. Charlotte Vaudeville, "Evolution of Love-Symbolism in Bhagavatism," *Journal of the American Oriental Society* 82, no. 1 (1962).
4. Lee Siegel, *Sacred and Profane Dimensions of Love in Indian Traditions as Exemplified in the Gītagovinda of Jayadeva* (Delhi: Oxford University Press, 1978), 17.
5. Agehananda Bharati, "The Future (if Any) of Tantrism," *Loka* 1 (1975): 130.
6. Janet Gyatso, *Apparitions of the Self: The Secret Autobiographies of a Tibetan Visionary* (Princeton, N.J.: Princeton University Press, 1998), 195.

7. For one of the most important of many such feminist works critiquing the notion of gender as a binary consisting of masculine and feminine poles, see Judith Butler, *Gender Trouble: Feminism and the Subversion of Identity* (New York: Routledge, 1990).
8. For an analysis and critique of Jung's theory of contrasexuality, see Polly Young-Eisendrath, "Gender and Contrasexuality: Jung's Contribution and Beyond," in *The Cambridge Companion to Jung*, ed. Polly Young-Eisendrath and Terence Dawson (New York: Cambridge University Press, 1997).
9. Cabezón, "Mother Wisdom, Father Love," 190.
10. Adelheid Herrmann-Pfandt, "Yab Yum Iconography and the Role of Women in Tibetan Tantric Buddhism," *The Tibet Journal* XXII, no. 1 (1997): 19.
11. Bernard Faure, *The Power of Denial: Buddhism, Purity, and Gender* (Princeton, N.J.: Princeton University Press, 2003), 124.
12. Georges Dreyfus, "Is Compassion an Emotion? A Cross-Cultural Exploration of Mental Typologies," in *Visions of Compassion: Western Scientists and Tibetan Buddhists Examine Human Nature*, ed. Richard J. Davidson and Anne Harrington (Oxford, New York: Oxford University Press, 2002).
13. Catherine Lutz, *Unnatural Emotions: Everyday Sentiments on a Micronesian Atoll and Their Challenge to Western Theory* (Chicago: University of Chicago Press, 1988), 5.
14. Haiyan Lee, *Revolution of the Heart: A Genealogy of Love in China, 1900–1950* (Stanford, Calif.: Stanford University Press, 2007), 8–9.
15. Barbara H. Rosenwein, "Worrying About Emotions in History," *The American Historical Review* 107, no. 3 (2002): 842.
16. Barbara H. Rosenwein, "Emotion Words," in *Le Sujet des Émotions au Moyen Âge*, ed. Piroska Nagy and Damien Boquet (Paris: Beauchesne, 2008).
17. Regarding the latter poison that I translate as "lust," the Sanskrit *rāga* has more of a general meaning of "passion." In Tibetan, *'dod chags* can be translated as "desire," "attachment," or "passion" as well as "lust," but I have chosen the latter because it aligns most closely with the way Sera Khandro uses the word in her writings, as we will see in several passages translated in this chapter.
18. Padmasiri de Silva, "Theoretical Perspectives on Emotions in Early Buddhism," in *Emotions in Asian Thought: A Dialogue in Comparative Philosophy*, ed. Joel Marks and Rodger T. Ames (Delhi: Sri Satguru Publications, 1997), 113–14.
19. Dreyfus, "Is Compassion an Emotion?" 41–42.
20. Patrul Rinpoche, *The Words of My Perfect Teacher* (San Francisco: HarperCollins, 1994), 196–217.
21. Take, for example, the devastation Shabkar Tsokdruk Rangdröl recorded in his autobiography when his mother passed away before he returned home to visit her as promised, or the anguished departure scene between Milarepa and his mother in Tsangnyön Heruka's fifteenth-century biography.

22. Dilgo Khyentse and Rabsel Dawa, *The Wish-fulfilling Jewel* (Boston: Shambhala, 1988), 11.
23. Dpal sprul rin po che o rgyan 'jigs med chos kyi dbang po, *Rdzogs pa chen po klong chen snying thig gi sngon 'gro'i khrid yig kun bzang bla ma'i zhal lung* (Delhi: Konchhog Lhadrepa, n.d.) fol. 240a.4–5; Patrul Rinpoche, *The Words of My Perfect Teacher*, 313.
24. Matthew T. Kapstein, "The Indian Literary Identity in Tibet," in *Literary Cultures in History*, ed. Sheldon Pollock (Berkeley: University of California Press, 2003), 785.
25. For reference to girls' and boys' education among the nobility in early twentieth-century Lhasa, see Rinchen Dolma Taring, *Daughter of Tibet* (London: The Camelot Press, 1970), 30–32.
26. E. Gene Smith, *Among Tibetan Texts* (Boston: Wisdom, 2001), 205; Leonard van der Kuijp, "Tibetan Belles-Lettres: The Influence of Daṇḍin and Kṣemendra," in *Tibetan Literature: Studies in Genre*, ed. José Ignacio Cabezón and Roger R. Jackson (Ithaca: Snow Lion, 1996).
27. For a more comprehensive list, see Kapstein, "The Indian Literary Identity in Tibet," 782–83, n. 102.
28. A. K. Warder, *Indian Kāvya Literature*, vol. 1 (Delhi: Motilal Banarsidass, 1972), 21.
29. June McDaniel, "Emotion in Bengali Religious Thought: Substance and Metaphor," in *Emotions in Asian Thought*, ed. Joel Marks and Roger T. Ames (Delhi: Sri Satguru Publications, 1995), 46–48. For more on the historical development of meanings of *rasa*, see Sheldon Pollock, "Rasa After Abhinava," in *Goodness of Sanskrit: Studies in Honour of Professor Ashok Aklujkar*, ed. Chikafumi Watanabe, Michele Desmarais, and Yoshichika Honda (New Delhi: D. K. Printworld, 2012), 429–445.
30. Warder, *Indian Kāvya Literature*, 1:35; Lauran Hartley, "Contextually Speaking: Tibetan Literary Discourse and Social Change in the People's Republic of China (1980–2000)" (Ph.D. diss., Indiana University, 2003), 21.
31. The Tibetan translation of *bhāva* is *bsam blo'i 'gyur ba*, which would more literally be translated into English as "transformation of thought," or *'gyur*, "transformation."
32. Don grub rgyal, *Bod kyi mgur glu byung 'phel gyi lo rgyus dang khyad chos bsdus par ston pa rig pa'i khye'i rnam par rtsen pa'i skyed tshal* (Beijing: Mi rigs dpe skrun khang, 1985), 271. Tshe tan zhabs drung draws a similar distinction in his *Snyan ngag me long gi spyi don sdeb legs rig pa'i 'char sgo* (Lanzhou: Kan su'u mi rigs dpe skrun khang, 2005), 15.
33. See Warder, *Indian Kāvya Literature*, 1:23; Hartley, "Contextually Speaking," 20. For twentieth-century Tibetan presentations of these eight, see Don grub rgyal, *Bod kyi mgur glu byung 'phel gyi lo rgyus*, 271; and Tshe tan zhabs drung, *Snyan ngag me long gi spyi don*, 15–16.
34. Kapstein, "The Indian Literary Identity in Tibet," 781.
35. Siegel, *Sacred and Profane Dimensions of Love in Indian Traditions*, 48.

36. Don grub rgyal, *Bod kyi mgur glu byung 'phel gyi lo rgyus*, 275.
37. Siegel, *Sacred and Profane Dimensions of Love in Indian Traditions*, 54.
38. Per K. Sørensen, *Divinity Secularized: An Inquiry Into the Nature and Form of the Songs Ascribed to the Sixth Dalai Lama*, Wiener Studien zur Tibetologie und Buddhismuskunde Heft 25 (Wien: Arbeitskreis für Tibetische und Buddhistische Studien Universität Wien, 1990), 19.
39. Victoria Sujata, *Tibetan Songs of Realization* (Leiden: Brill, 2005).
40. Barbara Newman, "La mystique courtoise: Thirteenth-Century Beguines and the Art of Love," in *From Virile Woman to WomanChrist*, ed. Barbara Newman (Philadelphia: University of Pennsylvania Press, 1993); Carole A. Slade, "'Este Gran Dios de las Cavallerías' [This Great God of Chivalric Deeds]: St. Teresa's Performances of the Novels of Chivalry," in *The Vernacular Spirit: Essays on Medieval Religious Literature*, ed. Renate Blumenfeld-Kosinski, Duncan Robertson, and Nancy Bradley Warren (New York: Palgrave, 2002).
41. For English-language research on *layi*, see Donatella Rossi, "Some Notes on the Tibetan Amdo Love Songs," in *Tibetan Studies: Proceedings of the 5th Seminar of the International Association for Tibetan Studies Narita 1989*, ed. Shōren Ihara and Zuihō Yamaguchi (Narita: Naritasan Shinshoji, 1992); Alexandru Anton-Luca, "Glu and La ye in A mdo: An Introduction to Contemporary Tibetan Folk Songs," in *Amdo Tibetans in Transition: Society and Culture in the Post-Mao Era*, ed. Toni Huber (Leiden: Brill, 2002).
42. For recent examples of the genre, see G.yung drung, *A mdo'i rogs 'then 'dem bsgrigs* (Xining: Mtsho sngon mi rigs dpe skrun khang, 1988); Bkra shis rgyal mtshan, *Rogs 'then rdo rje'i tshe mdud* (Xining: Mtsho sngon mi rigs dpe skrun khang, 1997).
43. For *rokten*, see note 41. For *layi*, see Bkra shis rgyal mtshan and Ra rdza dkon mchog, *La gzhas mthun pa drug skor* (Xining: Mtsho sngon mi rigs dpe skrun khang, 1997); Kun dga' rgyal mtshan, *Bod kyi la gzhas gzhon nu 'gugs pa'i lcags kyu* (Lanzhou: Kan su'u mi rigs dpe skrun khang, 2000); Stag 'bum thar and skal bzang, *La gzhas bung ba gzhon nu'i mgrin dbyangs* (Xining: Mtsho sngon mi rigs dpe skrun khang, 2002).
44. Marion H. Duncan collected eastern Tibetan love songs from 1921 to 1936, during which time he was stationed at a mission in Batang, Kham, now part of Kandzé Tibetan Autonomous Prefecture, Sichuan. His collection unfortunately does not include the Tibetan originals, only his English translations, so it is difficult to ascertain the precise terms of endearment the songs used. See Marion H. Duncan, *Love Songs and Proverbs of Tibet* (London: The Mitre Press, 1961).
45. Specifically, the seven-syllable lines typical of Tibetan folk songs are subdivided into feet following a 1+2+2+2 pattern; eight-syllable lines are subdivided into a 1+2+2+3 pattern. See Sujata, *Tibetan Songs of Realization*, 132–33; Sørensen, *Divinity Secularized*, 18–19.
46. Only Drimé Özer calls Sera Khandro this in her writings; Drimé Özer and Sera Khandro both refer to each other using the other affectionate names listed here, according to her writings.

47. *Bod rgya tshig mdzod chen mo*, 2239.
48. SLNT, fol. 9a.2–3.
49. SLNT, fol. 53a.6–b.3.
50. SLNT, fol. 89a.6–b.1.
51. SLNT, fol. 106a.2–4.
52. SLNT, fol. 106b.4–5.
53. DDNT, fol. 174a.3–4; DDP, 239.
54. DDNT, fol. 146b.3; DDP, 201.
55. DDNT, fol. 214b.4–5; DDP, 294.
56. SLNT, fol.107b.5.
57. DDNT, fol. 45b.3; DDP, 64.
58. SLNT, fol. 245a.5–6.
59. DDNT, fol. 95a.2–3; DDP, 132.
60. DDNT, fol. 283b.1 and 5–6; DDP, 384–35.
61. DDNT, fol. 196b.5–6; DDP, 270.
62. DDNT, fol. 229a.1–3; DDP, 313.
63. GTNT, 24.
64. GTNT, 34.
65. GTNT, 86.
66. GTNT, 112.
67. GTNT, 115–16. The eight-syllable verse form in which Gara Terchen wrote this letter includes phonemic repetition (*yamaka*) in three syllables of each verse line, characteristic of ornamentation found in Daṇḍin's treatise on Indian poetics (*kāvya*), although this poetic figure also appears in Tibetan songs of realization (*mgur*).
68. DLNT, 10.
69. DLNT, 108.
70. Gyalwa Changchub and Namkhai Nyingpo, *Lady of the Lotus-Born: The Life and Enlightenment of Yeshe Tsogyal* (Boston: Shambhala, 1999), 159; YSNT, fol. 107b.1: "*myur grol thugs rje can.*"
71. Changchub and Nyingpo, *Lady of the Lotus-Born*, 144; YSNT, fol. 97a.4: "*kye ma kye hud thugs rjes myur bar gzigs.*"
72. Changchub and Nyingpo, *Lady of the Lotus-Born*, 199; YSNT, fol 129b.4–5: "*gu ru'i thugs rjes nam yang ma btang bas.*"
73. Changchub and Nyingpo, *Lady of the Lotus-Born*, 150; YSNT, fol. 101b.1: "*khyed bdag la brtse bas gzigs dgongs nas.*"
74. SLNT, fol. 43a.1–b.4.
75. SLNT, fols. 101b.4–102a.3. Lhodrak (*lho brag*) is a site in south-central Tibet famous for being the birthplace of Marpa, founder of the Kagyü School of Tibetan Buddhism and master of the renowned yogi Milarepa.
76. Namkhai Nyingpo (Nam mkha'i snying po), Vairotsana (Bai ro tsa na), and Yudra Nyingpo (G.yu sgra snying po) were all members of Padmasambhava's original twenty-five disciples, and thus validate Drimé Özer's pedigree as an authentic Treasure revealer. See chapter 2 for more detail on this.

77. Gangs ri thod dkar (White Summit of the Snow Mountain) near Shuksep Nunnery in Chushül County, central Tibet, is a mountain famous for being the site of Longchen Rapjampa's hermitage.
78. The Sanskrit translation of Sherap Özer.
79. DDNT, fols. 53b.1–54b.6; DDP, 75–77.
80. Dzokchen Palgé is another name for Patrül Jikmé Chöki Wangpo (1808–87), author of *The Words of My Perfect Teacher*. Drimé Özer's brother Namka Jikmé was recognized as his incarnation.
81. DDNT, fols. 66b.2–68a.1; DDP, 93–95.
82. SLNT, fol. 110a.4–b.3.
83. Body seal, "*lus kyi phyag rgya*," refers to one part of the channel and wind practices that Kukkuripa taught Sera Khandro in her dream just before Drimé Özer appeared. See chapter 4, part I for more detail on this.
84. DDNT, fol. 68a.5–b.1; DDP, 95–96.
85. SLNT, fol. 92a.5.
86. DDNT, fol. 85b.1–5; DDP, 119.
87. DDNT, fol. 112a.5–b.2; DDP, 155–56.
88. DDNT, fol. 86b.1–6; DDP, 120–21. Ömbar was Drimé Özer's disciple who initiated the plan for Sera Khandro to work for Dongkor Abten's household as a maidservant.
89. Interviews with Namtrül Jikmé Püntsok in August 2004 in Pema County, Golok , and spring 2005 in Nyenlung, Serta County, Kandzé.
90. SLNT, fol. 133b.3–4.
91. DDNT, fol. 197b.6; DDP, 271.
92. Changchub and Nyingpo, *Lady of the Lotus-Born*, 22; YSNT 15a.4: "*yab yum gnyis thog mar mchims phu dge'u ru gsang spyod la gshegs so*."
93. Changchub and Nyingpo, *Lady of the Lotus-Born*, 34; YSNT, fol. 23b.4: "*yab yum gnyis gsang spyod la gshegs so*."
94. Changchub and Nyingpo, *Lady of the Lotus-Born*, 35; YSNT, fols. 23b.6–24a.1: "*gu ru yab yum gnyis bzhugs te nam mkha' la btegs nas gshegs bas*."
95. Changchub and Nyingpo, *Lady of the Lotus-Born*, 54.
96. YSNT, fol. 37a.1: "*slar bal yul e yi gtsug lag khang du yab yum gnyis byon nas*."
97. Changchub and Nyingpo, *Lady of the Lotus-Born*, 57.
98. YSNT, fol. 38b.2: "*de nas gtsang phyogs su jo mo yab yum brtol nas*."
99. Changchub and Nyingpo, *Lady of the Lotus-Born*, 96; YSNT, fol. 65a.2–3: "thog mar rtsa ba'i gzungs ma mtsho rgyal rang mdzad nas/de nas sgrol ba'i gzungs ma bkra shis khyi 'dren mdzad de/gu ru yab yum gsum gyis . . . dkyil 'khor e khram bzhi bcu rtsa gnyis . . . zhal phyes nas."
100. Changchub and Nyingpo, *Lady of the Lotus-Born*, 173; YSNT, fol. 115a.4: "*yab yum dam tshig mig ltar bsrung*."
101. DDNT, fol. 155b.3–4; DDP, 213.
102. DDNT, fol. 217a.4–b.3; DDP, 297–98.
103. DDNT, fols. 217b.3–218a.2; DDP, 298.
104. DDNT, fol. 93b.4; DDP, 130.

105. DDNT, fol. 219b.4; DDP, 301.
106. SLNT, fol. 165b.1–3.
107. Just prior to this exchange, Drimé Özer said to Gyelsé, "Just out of need for an auspicious connection, if you agree, let's do that [i.e., send Sera Khandro to me]. If you don't agree, even though you previously gave her to me, it would become a basis for discomfort between us, so the *khandro* doesn't need to come to me." SLNT, fol. 172a.3–5.
108. SLNT, fols. 172b.4–173a.3.
109. SLNT, fol. 174a.3.
110. SLNT, fol. 175a.3.
111. DDNT, fols. 235b.4–236a.1; DDP, 322.
112. SLNT, fols. 182b.1–183a.1.
113. SLNT, 184a.4–b. 4.
114. DDNT, fols. 242b.4–243a.3; DDP, 331–32.
115. Gyurme Dorje and Tudeng Nima, *An Encyclopaedic Tibetan-English Dictionary* (Bejing and London: The Nationalities Publishing House and The School of Oriental and African Studies, 2001), 1336.
116. Ibid., 1334.
117. Dzongsar Khyentse Rinpoche, "The Distortions We Bring to the Study of Buddhism," *Shambhala Sun* 6, no. 1 (1997): 28.
118. DDNT, fols. 244b.5–245a.3; DDP, 334.
119. DDNT, fol. 245a.6–b.1; DDP, 335.
120. SLNT, fol. 193b.2–3.
121. Elsewhere Narangma is written Naringma (Sna ring ma).
122. SLNT, fol. 194a.2–6.
123. SLNT, fols. 196a.4–197a.1.
124. DDNT, fol. 253a.3; DDP, 345.
125. DDNT, fol. 253b.1–254a.1; DDP, 345–46.
126. DDNT, fol. 257a.3–6; DDP, 350.
127. DDNT, fols. 257b.6–258a.5; DDP, 351–52.
128. SLNT, fols. 199b.6–200a.5.
129. SLNT, fol. 201a.1–2.
130. SLNT, fol. 201a.4–b.4.
131. SLNT, fol. 202b.4–5.
132. The three Treasures were those of Düjom Lingpa, Drimé Özer, and Sera Khandro.
133. Tulku Thondup explains that "purification, perfection, and ripening (*dag rdzogs smin*)" refers to purifying sounds as the mantra of great bliss, perfecting appearances as the signs of the deities' form, and ripening thoughts and recollections as the clear light of the dharmakāya.
134. SLNT, fol. 203a.4–b.3.
135. Dzongné (Rdzong gnas) is a sacred mountain in Serta between the Ser (Gser) and Do (Rdo) valleys. Drongdün ('Brong mdun) means "in front of Drong," i.e., in front of the sacred mountain Drongri.

136. DDNT, fols. 259a.6–260a.6; DDP, 353–54.
137. The three liberations are emptiness, signlessness, and wishlessness.
138. DDNT, fols. 262b.3–263b.2; DDP, 357–58.
139. For a summary and analysis of this Vinaya passage, see John S. Strong, "A Family Quest: The Buddha, Yásodharā and Rāhula in the Mūlasarvāstivāda Vinaya," in *Sacred Biography in the Buddhist Traditions of South and Southeast Asia*, ed. Juliane Schober (Honolulu: University of Hawai'i Press, 1997).
140. GTNT, 108.
141. The title of this short autobiography is *Rnal 'byor las 'phro sad pa'i gtam gzhi lam 'bras bu'i nyams myong rtogs pa'i rang skad mngon sum du ston pa*, found in GTNT, 189.
142. For references to the brief mentions in the autobiography of Pema Lingpa about his consorts and the children he produced with them, see Michael Aris, *Hidden Treasures and Secret Lives* (Delhi: Motilal Banarsidass, 1988), 79–82. Although Guru Chöwang is affiliated with Jomo Menmo in later sources, this connection does not appear in his autobiography according to Janet Gyatso, "Guru Cos-dbang's gTer 'byung chen mo: An Early Survey of the Treasure Tradition and Its Strategies in Discussing Bon Treasure," in *Tibetan Studies*, ed. Per Kvaerne (Oslo: Institute for Comparative Research in Human Culture, 1994), 283–84 n. 8. Tangtong Gyelpo's biographies do not mention any of his human wives, although several of his sons appear; see Janet Gyatso, "A Literary Transmission of the Traditions of Thang-stong rGyal-po: A Study of Visionary Buddhism in Tibet" (Ph.D. diss., University of California, 1981), 58 n. 84. For reference to Jikmé Lingpa's reticence on the subject of the identity of his consort(s) including his lack of mention of the name of the mother of his son, see Gyatso, *Apparitions of the Self*, 140.
143. For the classic feminist critique of the position of women in romantic couples, see Chapter 23, "The Woman in Love," in Simone de Beauvoir, *The Second Sex* (New York: Vintage, 1989). For more recent feminist critiques of romantic love, see Wendy Langford, *Revolutions of the Heart: Gender, Power, and the Delusions of Love* (London, New York: Routledge, 1999); Mary Evans, *Love, an Unromantic Discussion* (Cambridge: Blackwell, 2003).
144. DDNT, fol. 264a.2; DDP, 359.
145. DDNT, fols. 265b.6–266a.1; DDP, 361.
146. DDNT, fols. 266a.2–3; DDP, 362.
147. DDNT, fols. 266b.6–267a.1; DDP, 363.
148. *Lu tsen* (*klu btsan*) appears to be a combination of two types of spirits: serpentine water spirits (Skt. *nāga*) and fierce Tibetan mountain spirits called *btsan*.
149. SLNT, fol. 211a.2–b.4.
150. Denis de Rougemont, *Love in the Western World*, rev. and augmented ed. (New York: Pantheon, 1956), 15.
151. For Tibetan, see Dpal sprul rin po che, *Gtam pad+ma'i tshal gyi zlos gar* (Chengdu: Si khron mi rigs dpe skrun khang, 1986 and 2000) and for an

English translation, see *Enlightened Living: Teachings of Tibetan Buddhist Masters*, trans. Tulku Thondup (Boston: Shambhala, 1990).

152. Dpal sprul rin po che, *Gtam pad+ma'i tshal gyi zlos gar*, 22, 28.
153. Thondup, *Enlightened Living*, 10.
154. Thondup, *Enlightened Living*, 10, 77.
155. DDNT, fols. 268b.4–269a.3; DDP, 365.
156. DDNT, fols. 271b.4–273a.6; DDP, 369–71.
157. DDNT, fol. 278b.1–4; DDP, 378.
158. DDNT, fol. 279a.5–280a.2; DDP, 379–80.
159. DDNT, fol. 291a.5–b2; DDP, 394.
160. DDNT, fol. 292a.2–6; DDP, 395.
161. DDNT, fols. 294b.2–295a.4; DDP, 398–99.
162. SLNT, fols. 226b.3–228a.5.
163. SLNT, fol. 230a–b.
164. SLNT, fols. 230b.6–231a.1.
165. SLNT, fols. 232a.3–233a.2.
166. SLNT, fols. 233b.1–235a.2.
167. Changchub and Nyingpo, *Lady of the Lotus-Born*, 137; YSNT, fol. 93a.3–5.
168. Changchub and Nyingpo, *Lady of the Lotus-Born*, 138; YSNT, fol. 94a.1–3.
169. Changchub and Nyingpo, *Lady of the Lotus-Born*, 145; YSNT, fol. 97b.3–98a.1.
170. SLNT, fol. 246a.2–6.
171. Changchub and Nyingpo, *Lady of the Lotus-Born*, 146; YSNT, 98a.5–6.
172. SLNT, fol. 246b.1–3.
173. DDNT, fol. 364b.1–3; DDP, 486.
174. For a selection of scholarship arguing that the idealization of passionate love bears exclusively European roots, see Denis de Rougemont, *Love in the Western World*; Alan Macfarlane, *Marriage and Love in England 1300–1840: Modes of Reproduction 1300–1840* (Oxford: Basil Blackwell, 1986); Robert Endleman, *Love and Sex in Twelve Cultures* (New York: Psyche Press, 1989); Robert C. Solomon, *Love: Emotion, Myth and Metaphor* (Buffalo, N.Y.: Prometheus Books, 1990); and Anthony Giddens, *The Transformation of Intimacy: Sexuality, Love, and Eroticism in Modern Societies* (Stanford, Calif: Stanford University Press, 1992). For a more nuanced argument about the distinctive features of European conceptions of romantic love compared to two Asian contexts, see William M. Reddy, *The Making of Romantic Love: Longing and Sexuality in Europe, South Asia, and Japan, 900–1200 CE* (Chicago: University of Chicago Press, 2012). However, Reddy's claim that distinctions of "desire, conceived of as an appetite, from love, conceived of as selfless care and devotion to another" (3) are of uniquely European province would seem to be contradicted by many Buddhist contexts. For scholarship connecting love and modernity, see note 176.
175. For a selection of scholarship arguing that the idealization of passionate love is a human universal, see William R. Jankowiak, *Romantic Passion: A Universal Experience?* (New York: Columbia University Press, 1995); Victor C. de

Munck, *Romantic Love and Sexual Behavior: Perspectives from the Social Sciences* (Westport, Conn.: Praeger, 1998); Helen E. Fisher, *Why We Love: The Nature and Chemistry of Romantic Love* (New York: Henry Holt, 2004); Robert J. Sternberg and Karin Weis, *The New Psychology of Love* (New Haven: Yale University Press, 2006); and William R. Jankowiak, *Intimacies: Love and Sex Across Cultures* (New York: Columbia University Press, 2008).

176. For a selection of the large body of scholarship articulating links between the rise of romantic love and modernity in European contexts, see Philippe Ariès, *Centuries of Childhood: A Social History of Family Life* (New York: Knopf, 1962); Lawrence Stone, *The Family, Sex and Marriage in England, 1500–1800* (New York: Harper & Row, 1977); Lawrence Stone, "Passionate Attachments in the West in Historical Perspective," in *Passionate Attachments: Thinking About Love*, ed. Willard Gaylin and Ethel Spector Person (New York: Free Press, 1988); Charles Taylor, *Sources of the Self: The Making of the Modern Identity* (Cambridge, Mass.: Harvard University Press, 1989), ch. 17; Anthony Giddens, *The Transformation of Intimacy*, ch. 3; Anthony Giddens and Christopher Pierson, *Conversations with Anthony Giddens: Making Sense of Modernity* (Stanford, Calif.: Stanford University Press, 1998), 137–39. For an instructive study of love and modernity closer in time and space to Sera Khandro, focusing on early to mid-twentieth-century China, see Lee, *Revolution of the Heart*.
177. Caroline Walker Bynum, Stevan Harrell, and Paula Richman, eds., *Gender and Religion: On the Complexity of Symbols* (Boston: Beacon, 1986), 2–3.
178. Changchub and Nyingpo, *Lady of the Lotus-Born*, 142; YSNT, fol. 96a.1: "*ji srid bdag dang sku gsung thugs mnyam ste*."

EPILOGUE: LOVE AFTER DEATH

1. SLNT, fol. 234a.3.
2. SLNT, fol. 246b.2–3.
3. SLNT, fol. 196b.2–3.
4. DDNT, fol. 272a.5–6; DDP, 370.
5. SLNT, fol. 223a.5–6.
6. Interview with Namtrül Rinpoché, August 2004.
7. Ibid.
8. Padma 'od gsal mtha' yas, *Nam sprul 'jigs med phun tshogs dang mkha' 'gro tā' re lha mo'i rnam thar* (Chengdu: Si khron mi rigs dpe skrun khang, 1997).
9. He provides prophetic documentation of this claim in his collection of essays, *Deb chung a ru ra'i dga' tshal* (Chengdu: Si khron mi rigs dpe skrun khang, 2003), 1.
10. KSL, 82–103; Sarah H. Jacoby, "The Excellent Path of Devotion: An Annotated Translation of Sera Khandro's Short Autobiography," in *Himalayan Passages: Tibetan and Newar Studies in Honor of Hubert Decleer*, ed. Benjamin Bogin and Andrew Quintman (Boston: Wisdom, 2014). For more on Namtrül Jikmé Pünt-

sok and Tāré Lhamo, see Holly Gayley's forthcoming research and her dissertation, "Agency and the Rhetoric of Destiny: Narrating the Buddhist Revival in the Lives and Letters of Khandro Tare Lhamo (1938–2002) and Namtrul Jigme Phuntsok (1944–)" (Harvard University, 2009).

11. He wrote an unpublished pamphlet about the cave in which she resides and about her life titled *Mdo khams rgyal mo tsha ba rong gi bai ro'i sgrub phug ngo sprod mdor bsdus, A Brief Introduction to the Vairotsana Cave in Gyalmo Tsawarong, Eastern Tibet*. The information in this paragraph about Khandro Rinpoché comes from this biography as well as extensive interviews I conducted with Khandro Rinpoché and members of her community in Serta and Gyalrong.
12. Interview with Khandro Rinpoché at Vairotsana Cave in Gyalrong, August 2007.
13. Ibid.
14. Interview with Choktrül Rangrik Dorjé at Vairotsana Cave in Gyalrong, August 2007.
15. Personal communication with Jadrel Rinpoché in Pharping, Nepal, Oct. 2004.
16. For reference to Chökyi Drönma, see Pad ma 'od gsal mtha' yas, *Deb chung a ru ra'i dga' tshal* (Chengdu: Si khron mi rigs dpe skrun khang, 2003), 73. According to Tulku Thondup, Lhacham Chökyi Drönma died during the tumultuous years of the Cultural Revolution; information about Trinlé Tendzin comes from a personal communication with Trinlé Tendzin, Dartsang, Serta 2004.

BIBLIOGRAPHY

TIBETAN SOURCES

Works Written by Sera Khandro

Mkha' 'gro bde skyong dbang mo. *Skyabs rje thams cad mkhyen pa grub pa'i dbang phyug zab gter rgya mtsho'i mnga' bdag rin po che pad+ma 'gro 'dul gsang sngags gling pa'i rnam par thar pa snying gi mun sel dad pa'i shing rta ra tna'i chun 'phyang ut+pala'i 'phreng ba*. Dalhousie: Damchoe Sangpo, 1981.

Bde ba'i rdo rje. "Dbus mo bde ba'i rdo rje'i rnam par thar pa nges 'byung 'dren pa'i shing rta skal ldan dad pa'i mchod sdong." Unpublished manuscript, ca. 1934.

——. *Mtsho rgyal dngos snang bde skyong dbang mo yi zab gter gsang ba'i chos mdzod rin po che*. Kalimpong: Dupjung Lama, 1978, vols. 1–4.

——. *Rare Rñin-ma-pa texts from Bir: including writings of the Se-ra Mkha'-'gro Bde-ba'i-rdo-rje and the A tsā ra snags yig*. Bir, Dist. Kangra, H.P.: Pema Gyaltsen, 1979.

Dbus bza' mkha' 'gro. "Ku su lu'i nyams byung gi gnas tshul mdor bsdus rdo rje'i spun gyis dris lan mos pa'i lam bzang." In *Dbus bza' mkha' 'gro'i gsung 'bum*. Chengdu: Si khron mi rigs dpe skrun khang, 2009, 5:82–103.

——. *Dbus bza' mkha' 'gro'i gsung 'bum*. Ed. Mgo log khul gna' rtsom bya ba'i gzhung las khang. Chengdu: Si khron mi rigs dpe skrun khang, 2009, vols. 1–6.

——. *Rang bzhin rdzogs pa chen po ma bsgom sangs rgyas kyi zin bris dpal ldan bla ma'i zhal rgyun nag 'gros su bkod pa tshig don rab gsal skal ldan dgyes pa'i mgul rgyan*. Beijing: Mi rigs dpe skrun khang, 2002.

WORKS FROM DGE RTSE BKRA LEGS DGON PRIVATE COLLECTION OF HANDWRITTEN MANUSCRIPTS

Bde ba'i rdo rje. *Chos nyid mkha' 'gro'i thugs thig.*
——. *Chos nyid mkha' 'gro'i gsang mdzod.* Vols. 1–2.
——. *Chos nyid mkha' 'gro'i gsang mdzod skor gyi khrid yig.*
——. *Zhus lan dang mgur tshogs.*
——. *Rang bzhin rdzogs pa chen po ma bsgom sangs rgyas kyi zin bris dpal ldan bla ma'i zhal rgyun nag 'gros su bkod pa tshig don rab gsal skal ldan dgyes pa'i mgul rgyan.*

WORKS FROM GSER RTA PRIVATE COLLECTION OF HANDWRITTEN MANUSCRIPTS

Bde ba'i rdo rje. *Chos nyid mkha' 'gro'i thugs thig.*
——. *Chos nyid mkha' 'gro'i gsang mdzod.* Vols. 1–2.
——. *Chos nyid mkha' 'gro'i gsang mdzod skor gyi khrid yig.*
——. *Dbus mo bde ba'i rdo rje'i rnam par thar pa nges 'byung 'dren pa'i shing rta skal ldan dad pa'i mchod sdong.*

Other Tibetan Works

Kun dga' rgyal mtshan. *Bod kyi la gzhas gzhon nu 'gugs pa'i lcags kyu.* Lanzhou: Kan su'u mi rigs dpe skrun khang, 2000.

Krang dbyi sun, ed. *Bod rgya tshig mdzod chen mo.* 2 vols. Beijing: Mi rigs dpe skrun khang, 1993.

Krung go mi dmangs srid gros gser thar rdzong u yon lhan khang gi rig gnas lo rgyus dpyad yig tsho chung, ed. *Dbal shul gser thar gyi lo rgyus gsar bsgrigs blo ldan mig gi bdud rtsi.* Dartsedo: Gan zi bao she yin shua chang, 1989.

Bkra shis rgyal mtshan. *Rogs 'then rdo rje'i tshe mdud.* Xining: Mtsho sngon mi rigs dpe skrun khang, 1997.

Bkra shis rgyal mtshan and Ra rdza dkon mchog. *La gzhas mthun pa drug skor.* Xining: Mtsho sngon mi rigs dpe skrun khang, 1997.

Khrag 'thung bdud 'joms gling pa. "Chos nyid sgyu mar rol pa'i snang lam gsang ba nyams byung gi rtogs brjod gsal ba'i me long." In *Khrag 'thung bdud 'joms gling pa'i rnam thar,* ed. A bu dkar lo. Xining: Zi ling mi rigs par khang, 2002.

Mkha' 'gro bde chen dbang mo. *Mkha' 'gro rgya mtsho'i rnam thar.* Dolanji: Tibetan Bonpo Monastic Community, 1985.

Mgar gter chen pad+ma bdud 'dul dbang phyug gling pa. "Rnal 'byor bdag gis sa lam bsgrod pa'i rang bzhin gyi rtogs brjod zol zog med pa'i drang gtam brjod pa." In *Mgar gter chen pad+ma bdud 'dul dbang phyug gling pa'i rang rnam.* Chengdu: Si khron zhing chen khron lin par 'debs bzo grwa, 2005, 3–179.

———. "Rnal 'byor las 'phro sad pa'i gtam gzhi lam 'bras bu'i nyams myong rtogs pa'i rang skad mngon sum du ston pa." In *Mgar gter chen pad+ma bdud 'dul dbang phyug gling pa'i rang rnam*. Chengdu: Si khron zhing chen khron lin par 'debs bzo grwa, 2005, 180-94.

'Gu log dam chos dpal bzang. *'Gu log gi lo rgyus gnyan po g.yu rtse'i bsang dud*. Dharamsala: Bod kyi dpe mdzod khang, 2000, vols. 1–2.

'Jam mgon kong sprul blo gros mtha' yas. *Dpal snga 'gyur rnying ma'i gter ston brgya rtsa'i rnam thar bai d'u+rya'i phreng ba*. Berkeley, Calif.: Dharma Publishing, 2004.

'Jigs med bsam grub et al., ed. *Khams phyogs dkar mdzes khul gyi dgon sde so so'i lo rgyus gsal bar bshad pa nang bstan gsal ba'i me long*. Beijing: Krung go'i bod kyi shes rig dpe skrun khang, 1995, vols. 1-3.

Rjes dkar o rgyan brtson 'grus. *G.yu rtse'i dmangs khrod rig gnas*. Beijing: Mi rigs dpe skrun khang, 2007.

Stag 'bum thar and Skal bzang. *La gzhas bung ba gzhon nu'i mgrin dbyangs*. Xining: Mtsho sngon mi rigs dpe skrun khang, 2002.

Stag sham nus ldan rdo rje. *Bod kyi jo mo ye shes mtsho rgyal gyi mdzad tshul rnam par thar pa gab pa mngon byung rgyud mangs dri za'i glu phreng*. Kalimpong: Zang mdog dpal ri Monastery, 1972.

Don grub rgyal. *Bod kyi mgur glu byung 'phel gyi lo rgyus dang khyad chos bsdus par ston pa rig pa'i khye'i rnam par rtsen pa'i skyed tshal*. Beijing: Mi rigs dpe skrun khang, 1985.

Don grub dbang rgyal. "Mgo log gi lo rgyus deb ther pad+ma dkar po'i ge sar." In *Mgo log rig gnas lo rgyus*. Xining: Mtsho sngon zhin hwa dpar khang, 1991, vol. 1.

Don grub dbang rgyal and Nor sde. *Yul mgo log gi lo rgyus deb ther pad+ma dkar po'i chun po*. Xining: Mtsho sngon mi rigs dpe skrun khang, 1992.

Mdo mkhar ba tshe ring dbang rgyal. *Bka' blon rtogs brjod*. Chengdu: Si khron mi rigs dpe skrun khang, 1981.

Mdo mkhyen brtse ye shes rdo rje. *Mdo mkhyen brtse ye shes rdo rje'i rnam thar*. Chengdu: Si khron mi rigs dpe skrun khang, 1997.

Pad+ma 'od gsal mtha' yas. *Nam sprul 'jigs med phun tshogs dang mkha' 'gro tā' re lha mo'i rnam thar*. Chengdu: Si khron mi rigs dpe skrun khang, 1997.

———. *Deb chung a ru ra'i dga' tshal*. Chengdu: Si khron mi rigs dpe skrun khang, 2003.

———. "Mdo khams rgyal mo tsha ba rong gi bai ro'i sgrub phug ngo sprod mdor bsdus." Unpublished pamphlet.

Dpal sprul rin po che o rgyan 'jigs med chos kyi dbang po. *Gtam pad+ma'i tshal gyi zlos gar*. Chengdu: Si khron mi rigs dpe skrun khang, 2000.

———. *Rdzogs pa chen po klong chen snying thig gi sngon 'gro'i khrid yig kun bzang bla ma'i zhal lung*. Delhi: Konchhog Lhadrepa, n.d.

'Phags bod kyi skyes chen ma dag gi rnam par thar ba pad+ma dkar po'i phreng ba. Lhasa: bod ljongs bod yig dper rnying dpe skrun khang, 2013, vols. 1–15.

’Phrin las, ed. *Mgo log bod rigs rang skyong khul gyi bod brgyud nang bstan dgon sde khag gi lo rgyus snying bsdus*. Xining: Mtsho sngon mi rigs dpe skrun khang, 2008.

Bya bral sangs rgyas rdo rje. “Dbus bza’ mkha’ ’gro bde ba’i rdo rje’i rnam thar chen mo’i mjug gi kha skong nyung du g.yu yi phra tshom.” Unpublished manuscript, 1976.

Tshe tan zhabs drung. *Snyan ngag me long gi spyi don sdeb legs rig pa’i ’char sgo*. Lanzhou: Kan su’u mi rigs dpe skrun khang, 2005.

Tshul khrims rdo rje. “Rgyal yum ye shes mtsho rgyal mi mngon rnam thar bzhengs pa mkha’ ’gro rin po che bde ba’i rdo rje’i ’das rjes kyi rnam thar don bsdus su bkod pa.” In Dbus bza’ mkha’ ’gro, *Dbus bza’ mkha’ ’gro’i gsung ’bum*, ed. Mgo log khul gna’ rtsom bya ba’i gzhung las khang. Chengdu: Si khron mi rigs dpe skrun khang, 2009, 1: 538–47.

Shekarlingpa, H. E. *Dpal gyi chos ’khor lha sa dran glu nor bu’i do shal*. Kalimpong: The Tibet Mirror Press, 1965.

G.yung drung. *A mdo’i rogs ’then ’dem bsgrigs*. Xining: Mtsho sngon mi rigs dpe skrun khang, 1988.

Rig stong rgal mo. *A lce rig stong rgyal mo’i rnam thar*. Unpublished manuscript, n.d. (TBRC W1CZ505).

Srid gros mgo log khul u rig gnas lo rgyus rgyu cha zhib ’jug u yon lhan khang, ed. *Mgo log rig gnas lo rgyus*, vol. 1. Xining: Mtsho sngon zhin hwa dpar khang, 1991.

——. *Mgo log rig gnas lo rgyus*, vol. 2. Xining: Zi ling la’o lan dpar las tshad yod kun zis dpar, 1991.

——. *Mgo log rig gnas lo rgyus*, vol. 3. Xining: Zi ling la’o lan dpar las tshad yod kun zis dpar, 1999.

——. *Mgo log rig gnas lo rgyus*, vol. 4. Xining: Zi ling la’o lan dpar las tshad yod kun zis dpar, 2004.

Gser rta tshul khrims. *Dbal shul gser rta’i lo rgyus dang ’brel ba’i gtam*. Dharamsala: Gser rta tshul khrims, 2006.

Ha rten dpal rnam. “Ha rten tshe grags kyi lo rgyus mdor bsdus dang ’brel yod zi bod sa mtshams ’khrugs ’dum skor gyi gnas tshul ’ga’ zhig.” In *Bod kyi lo rgyus rig gnas dpyad gzhi’i rgyu cha bdams bsgrigs*. Beijing: Mi rigs dpe skrun khang, 2003, 23: 206–63.

Hor gtsang ’jigs med. *Mdo smad lo rgyus chen mo*. 6 vols. Dharamsala: Bod kyi dpe mdzod khang, 2009.

O rgyan brtson ’grus. *Dar thang dgon pa’i gdan rabs*. Chengdu: Si khron mi rigs dpe skrun khang, 1999.

SOURCES IN EUROPEAN LANGUAGES

Allione, Tsultrim. *Women of Wisdom*. London: Routledge and Kegan Paul, 1984.

Anton-Luca, Alexandru. “Glu and La ye in A mdo: An Introduction to Contemporary Tibetan Folk Songs.” In *Amdo Tibetans in Transition: Society and Culture in the Post-Mao Era*, ed. Toni Huber. Leiden: Brill, 2002, 173–96.

Ariès, Philippe. *Centuries of Childhood: A Social History of Family Life*. New York: Knopf, 1962.
Aris, Michael. *Hidden Treasures and Secret Lives: A Study of Pema Lingpa (1420–1521) and the Sixth Dalai Lama (1683–1706)*. Delhi: Motilal Banarsidass, 1988.
Aziz, Barbara Nimri. "Moving Towards a Sociology of Tibet." In *Feminine Ground: Essays on Women and Tibet*, ed. Janice D. Willis. Ithaca: Snow Lion, 1987.
Bakhtin, Mikhail. "Discourse in the Novel." In *The Dialogic Imagination: Four Essays*, ed. Michael Holquist. Austin: University of Texas Press, 1981.
Barthes, Roland. *Roland Barthes by Roland Barthes*. Trans. Richard Howard. New York: Farrar, Straus & Giroux, 1977.
Barthes, Roland, and Lionel Duisit. "An Introduction to the Structural Analysis of Narrative." *New Literary History* 6, no. 2 (1975): 237–72.
Bdud-'joms-gliṅ-pa and Richard Barron. *Buddhahood Without Meditation: A Visionary Account Known as Refining One's Perception (Nang-jang)*. Rev. ed. Junction City, Calif.: Padma Publishing, 2002.
Beauvoir, Simone de. *The Second Sex*. New York: Vintage, 1989.
Benstock, Shari, ed. *The Private Self: Theory and Practice of Women's Autobiographical Writings*. Chapel Hill: University of North Carolina Press, 1988.
Bentor, Yael. "Can Women Attain Enlightenment Through Vajrayāna Practices?" In *Karmic Passages: Israeli Scholarship on India*, ed. David Shulman and Shalva Weil. New Delhi: Oxford University Press, 2008.
Bessenger, Suzanne. "Echoes of Enlightenment: The Life and Legacy of Sonam Peldren." Ph.D. diss., University of Virginia, 2010.
Bharati, Agehananda. "The Future (if Any) of Tantrism." *Loka* 1 (1975): 126–30.
Blondeau, Anne-Marie. "Le 'Decouvreur' du Mani Bka'-'bum etait-il Bon-po?" In *Tibetan and Buddhist Studies Commemorating the 200th Anniversary of the Birth of Alexander Csoma de Koros*, ed. Louis Ligeti. Budapest: Akademiai Kiado, 1984, 77–123.
——, ed. *Tibetan Mountain Deities, Their Cults and Representations: Papers Presented at a Panel of the 7th Seminar of the International Association for Tibetan Studies, Graz, 1995*. Graz: Verlag der Osterreichischen Akademie der Wissenschaf-ten, 1998.
Blondeau, Anne-Marie, and Ernst Steinkellner. *Reflections of the Mountain: Essays on the History and Social Meaning of the Mountain Cult in Tibet and the Himalaya*. Wein: Verlag de Österreichischen Akademie der Wissenschaft, 1996.
Bodhi, Bhikku, trans. *The Connected Discourses of the Buddha: A Translation of the* Saṃyutta Nikāya. Boston: Wisdom, 2000.
Brodzki, Bella, and Celeste Schenck, eds. *Life Lines: Theorizing Women's Autobiography*. Ithaca: Cornell University Press, 1988.
Brooks, Douglas Renfrew. *The Secret of the Three Cities: An Introduction to Hindu Śākta Tantrism*. Chicago: University of Chicago Press, 1990.
Bruner, Jerome. "The Narrative Construction of Reality." *Critical Inquiry* 18, no. 1 (1991): 1–21.
——. "Life as Narrative." *Social Research* 71, no. 3 (2004): 691–710.
Buffetrille, Katia. "The Great Pilgrimage of A-myes rma-chen." In *Maṇḍala and Landscape*, ed. A. W. Macdonald. New Delhi: D. K. Printworld (P) Ltd., 1997, 75–121.

———. "Reflections on Pilgrimages to Sacred Mountains, Lakes and Caves." In *Pilgrimage in Tibet*, ed. Alex McKay. Richmond, UK: Curzon Press, 1998, 18–34.

Buffetrille, Katia, and Hildegard Diemberger, eds. *Territory and Identity in Tibet and the Himalayas: PIATS 2000: Tibetan Studies: Proceedings of the Ninth Seminar of the International Association for Tibetan Studies, Leiden 2000*. Leiden: Brill, 2002.

Butler, Judith. *Gender Trouble: Feminism and the Subversion of Identity*. New York: Routledge, 1990.

Bynum, Caroline Walker, Stevan Harrell, and Paula Richman, eds. *Gender and Religion: On the Complexity of Symbols*. Boston: Beacon, 1986.

Cabezón, José Ignacio. "Mother Wisdom, Father Love." In *Buddhism, Sexuality, and Gender*, ed. José Ignacio Cabezón. Albany: State University of New York Press, 1992.

———. "On Authorship and Literary Production in Classical Buddhist Tibet." In *Changing Minds: Contributions to the Study of Buddhism and Tibet in Honor of Jeffrey Hopkins*, ed. Guy Newland. Ithaca: Snow Lion, 2001.

Campany, Robert Ford. *Making Transcendents: Ascetics and Social Memory in Early Medieval China*. Honolulu: University of Hawai'i Press, 2009.

Candler, Edmund. *The Unveiling of Lhasa*. Berkeley: Snow Lion Graphics, 1987.

Carr, David. "Narrative and the Real World: An Argument for Continuity." *History and Theory* 25, no. 2 (1986): 117–31.

Changchub, Gyalwa, and Namkhai Nyingpo. *Lady of the Lotus-Born: The Life and Enlightenment of Yeshe Tsogyal*. Boston: Shambhala, 1999.

Combe, G. A., and Paul Sherap. *A Tibetan on Tibet: Being the Travels and Observations of Paul Sherap (Dorje Zödba) of Tachienlu: with an Introductory Chapter on Buddhism and a Concluding Chapter on the Devil Dance*. London: Fisher Unwin, 1926.

Cosslett, Tess, Celia Lury, and Penny Summerfield, eds. *Feminism and Autobiography: Texts, Theories, Methods*. London: Routledge, 2000.

Crites, Stephen. "The Narrative Quality of Experience." *Journal of the American Academy of Religion* 3 (1971): 292–311.

Cuevas, Brian. *Travels in the Netherworld: Buddhist Popular Narratives of Death and the Afterlife in Tibet*. New York: Columbia University Press, 2008.

Das, Sarat Chandra. *Journey to Lhasa and Central Tibet*. London: J. Murray, 1902.

Davidson, Ronald M. "Atiśa's 'A Lamp for the Path to Awakening.'" In *Buddhism in Practice*, ed. Donald S. Lopez, Jr. Princeton, N.J.: Princeton University Press, 1995, 290–301.

———. *Indian Esoteric Buddhism: A Social History of the Tantric Movement*. New York: Columbia University Press, 2002.

Dechen, Pema. "The Oppression and Resistance of Tibetan Women." In *The Anguish of Tibet*, ed. Gert Bastian, Petra K. Kelly, and Pat Aiello. Berkeley, Calif.: Parallax Press, 1991.

Diemberger, Hildegard. *When a Woman Becomes a Religious Dynasty: The Samding Dorje Phagmo of Tibet*. New York: Columbia University Press, 2007.

Dilgo Khyentse Rinpoche and Rabsel Dawa. *The Wish-fulfilling Jewel: The Practice of Guru Yoga According to the Longchen Nyingthig Tradition.* Boston: Shambhala, 1988.

Dorje, Gyurme. "The Guhyagarbhatantra and Its XIVth Century Tibetan Commentary, *phogs bcu mun sel*." Ph.D. diss., School of Oriental and Africal Studies, University of London, 1987.

Dorje, Gyurme and Tudeng Nima. *An Encyclopaedic Tibetan-English Dictionary.* Beijing and London: The Nationalities Publishing House and The School of Oriental and African Studies, 2001.

Dreyfus, Georges. "Is Compassion an Emotion? A Cross-Cultural Exploration of Mental Typologies." In *Visions of Compassion: Western Scientists and Tibetan Buddhists Examine Human Nature*, ed. Richard J. Davidson and Anne Harrington. Oxford; New York: Oxford University Press, 2002, 31–45.

Dudjom Jikdrel Yeshe Dorje. *The Nyingma School of Tibetan Buddhism: Its Fundamentals and History.* Trans. Gyurme Dorje and Matthew Kapstein. 2 vols. Boston: Wisdom, 1991.

Duncan, Marion H. *Love Songs and Proverbs of Tibet.* London: The Mitre Press, 1961.

Dzongsar Jamyang Khyentse. "The Distortions We Bring to the Study of Buddhism." *Shambhala Sun* 6, no. 1 (1997): 24–29.

Eakin, Paul John. "Relational Selves, Relational Lives: The Story of the Story." In *True Relations: Essays on Autobiography and the Postmodern*, ed. G. Thomas Couser and Joseph Fichtelberg. Westport, Conn.: Greenwood Press, 1998.

——. *How Our Lives Become Stories: Making Selves.* Ithaca: Cornell University Press, 1999.

Edou, Jérôme. *Machig Labdrön and the Foundations of Chöd.* Ithaca: Snow Lion, 1995.

Edwards, Natalie. *Shifting Subjects: Plural Subjectivity in Contemporary Francophone Women's Autobiography.* Newark: University of Delaware Press, 2011.

Edwards, Natalie, and Christopher Hogarth, eds. *This "Self" Which Is Not One: Women's Life Writing in French.* Newcastle: Cambridge Scholars Publishing, 2010.

Ekvall, Robert. "Mi sTong: the Tibetan Custom of Life Indemnity." *Sociologus* 4, no. 2 (1954): 136–45.

——. "Peace and War Among the Tibetan Nomads." *American Anthropologist* 66, no. 5 (1964): 1119–48.

Eliade, Mircea. *Yoga: Immortality and Freedom*, Bollingen Series, 56. New York: Pantheon, 1958.

Endleman, Robert. *Love and Sex in Twelve Cultures.* New York: Psyche Press, 1989.

Epstein, Lawrence. "On the History and Psychology of the 'das-log'." *Tibet Journal* 7, no. 4 (1982): 20–85.

Evans, Mary. *Love, an Unromantic Discussion.* Cambridge: Blackwell, 2003.

Falk, Nancy Auer. "The Case of the Vanishing Nuns: The Fruits of Ambivalence in Ancient Indian Buddhism." In *Unspoken Worlds: Women's Religious Lives in Non-Western Cultures*, ed. Nancy Auer Falk and Rita M. Gross. San Francisco: Harper & Row, 1980, 207–24.

Faure, Bernard. *The Power of Denial: Buddhism, Purity, and Gender*. Princeton, N.J.: Princeton University Press, 2003.

Fiorenza, Elisabeth Schüssler. *Bread Not Stone: The Challenge of Feminist Biblical Interpretation*. Boston: Beacon, 1984.

Fisher, Helen E. *Why We Love: The Nature and Chemistry of Romantic Love*. New York: Henry Holt, 2004.

Furlong, Monica. *Visions and Longings: Medieval Women Mystics*. London: Mowbray, 1996.

Geary, Patrick. "Saints, Scholars, and Society: The Elusive Goal." In *Living with the Dead in the Middle Ages*. Ithaca: Cornell University Press, 1994.

Gelek. "The Washu Sertar: A Nomadic Community of Eastern Tibet." In *Development, Society, and Environment in Tibet*, ed. Graham E. Clarke. Wien: Verlag der Österreichischen Akademie der Wissenschaften, 1998, 47–58.

George, Christopher S. *The Caṇḍamahāroṣaṇa Tantra, Chapters I-VIII*. American Oriental Series Vol. 56. New Haven: American Oriental Society, 1974.

Germano, David. "Remembering the Dismembered Body of Tibet: Contemporary Tibetan Visionary Movements in the People's Republic of China." In *Buddhism in Contemporary Tibet: Religious Revival and Cultural Identity*, ed. Melvyn C. Goldstein and Matthew T. Kapstein. Berkeley: University of California Press, 1998.

Giddens, Anthony. *The Transformation of Intimacy: Sexuality, Love, and Eroticism in Modern Societies*. Stanford, Calif.: Stanford University Press, 1992.

Giddens, Anthony, and Christopher Pierson. *Conversations with Anthony Giddens: Making Sense of Modernity*. Stanford, Calif.: Stanford University Press, 1998.

Gilmore, Leigh. *Autobiographics: A Feminist Theory of Women's Self-Representation*. Minneapolis: University of Minnesota Press, 1994.

Giorgio, Adalgisa, and Julia Waters, eds. *Women's Writing in Western Europe: Gender, Generation and Legacy*. Newcastle: Cambridge Scholars Publishing, 2007.

Gluckman, Max. "Gossip and Scandal." *Current Anthropology* 4 (1963): 307–15.

Goffman, Erving. *The Presentation of Self in Everyday Life*. Garden City, N.Y.: Doubleday, 1959.

Gruschke, Andreas. *The Cultural Monuments of Tibet's Outer Provinces: Amdo*. Bangkok: White Lotus Press, 2001.

Gubrium, Jaber F. and James A. Holstein. *Analyzing Narrative Reality*. Thousand Oaks, Calif.: Sage Publications, 2009.

Guibaut, André. *Tibetan Venture in the Country of the Ngolo-Setas: Second Guibaut-Liotard Expedition*. London: John Murray, 1948.

Gupta, Sanjukta, Dirk Jan Hoens, and Teun Goudriaan. *Hindu Tantrism*. Leiden: Brill, 1979.

Gusdorf, Georges. "Conditions and Limits of Autobiography." In *Autobiography: Essays Theoretical and Critical*, ed. James Olney. Princeton, N.J.: Princeton University Press, 1980.

Gutschow, Kim. *Being a Buddhist Nun: The Struggle for Enlightenment in the Himalayas*. Cambridge, Mass.: Harvard University Press, 2004.

Gyalpo, Ngari Panchen Pema Wangyi. *Perfect Conduct: Ascertaining the Three Vows.* Trans. Khenpo Gyurme Samdrub and Sangye Khandro. Boston: Wisdom, 1996.

Gyatso, Janet. "A Literary Transmission of the Traditions of Thang-stong rGyal-po: A Study of Visionary Buddhism in Tibet." Ph.D. diss., University of California, 1981.

———. "The Logic of Legitimation in the Tibetan Treasure Tradition." *History of Religions* 33, no. 1 (1993): 97–134.

———. "Guru Chos-dbang's gTer 'byung chen mo: An Early Survey of the Treasure Tradition and Its Strategies in Discussing Bon Treasure." In *Tibetan Studies*, ed. Per Kvaerne. Oslo: Institute for Comparative Research in Human Culture, 1994, 275–87.

———. *Apparitions of the Self: The Secret Autobiographies of a Tibetan Visionary.* Princeton, N.J.: Princeton University Press, 1998.

———. "A Partial Genealogy of the Lifestory of Ye shes mtsho rgyal." *Journal of the International Association of Tibetan Studies*, no. 2 (2006): 1–27.

———. "The Relic Text as Prophecy: The Semantic Drift of Byang-bu and Its Appropriation in the Treasure Tradition." Unpublished paper.

Gyatso, Janet, and Hanna Havnevik. *Women in Tibet.* New York: Columbia University Press, 2005.

Harding, Sarah. *Machik's Complete Explanation: Clarifying the Meaning of Chöd.* Ithaca: Snow Lion, 2003.

Hartley, Lauran. "Con*text*ually Speaking: Tibetan Literary Discourse and Social Change in the People's Republic of China (1980–2000)." Ph.D. diss., Indiana University, 2003.

Havnevik, Hanna. *Tibetan Buddhist Nuns: History, Cultural Norms, and Social Reality.* Oslo: Norwegian University Press, 1989.

———. "The Life of Jetsun Lochen Rinpoche (1865–1951) as Told in Her Autobiography." Ph.D. diss., University of Oslo, 1999.

Herrmann-Pfandt, Adelheid. *Ḍākinīs: Zur Stellung und Symbolik des Weiblichen im Tantrischen Buddhismus.* Bonn: Indica et Tibetica Verlag, 1992.

———. "Ḍākinīs in Indo-Tibetan Tantric Buddhism: Some Results of Recent Research." *Studies in Central and East Asian Religions*, no. 5/6 (1992–93): 45–63.

———. "Yab Yum Iconography and the Role of Women in Tibetan Tantric Buddhism." *The Tibet Journal* XXII, no. 1 (1997): 12–34.

Horlemann, Bianca. "Modernization Efforts in Mgo log: A Chronicle, 1970–2000." In *Amdo Tibetans in Transition: Society and Culture in the Post-Mao Era*, ed. Toni Huber. Leiden: Brill, 2002, 241–68.

———. "The Goloks Through Western Eyes: Fascination and Horror." In *Tibet in 1938–1939: Photographs from the Ernst Schäfer Expedition to Tibet*, ed. Isrun Engelhardt. Chicago: Serindia Publications, 2007, 91–102.

Huber, Toni. *The Cult of Pure Crystal Mountain: Popular Pilgrimage and Visionary Landscape in Southeast Tibet.* New York: Oxford University Press, 1999.

Hunsberger, Merrill Ruth. "Ma Pu-fang in Chinghai Province, 1931–1949." Ph.D. diss., Temple University, 1978.

Israel, Kali. "Changing the Place of Narrative in Biography: From Form to Method." *Life Writing* 7, no. 1 (2010): 5–15.

Jacoby, Sarah H. "To Be or Not to Be Celibate: Morality and Consort Practices According to the Treasure Revealer Se ra mkha' 'gro's (1892–1940) Auto/biographical Writings." In *Buddhism Beyond the Monastery: Tantric Practices and Their Performers in Tibet and the Himalayas*, ed. Sarah Jacoby and Antonio Terrone. Leiden: Brill, 2009, 37–71.

——. "An Overview of Golok." The Tibetan & Himalayan Library, http://places.thlib.org/features/15434/descriptions/1209, 2010.

——. "'This inferior female body': Reflections on Life as a Tibetan Visionary Through the Autobiographical Eyes of Se ra mkha' 'gro (Bde ba'i rdo rje, 1892–1940)." *Journal of the International Association of Buddhist Studies* 32, no. 1–2 (2010): 115–50.

——. "A Treasure Revealer: Sera Khandro." In *Sources of Tibetan Tradition*, ed. Kurtis R. Schaeffer, Matthew T. Kapstein, and Gray Tuttle. New York: Columbia University Press, 2013, 696–99.

——. "The Excellent Path of Devotion: An Annotated Translation of Sera Khandro's Short Autobiography." In *Himalayan Passages: Tibetan and Newar Studies in Honor of Hubert Decleer*, ed. Benjamin Bogin and Andrew Quintman. Boston: Wisdom, 2014.

Jankowiak, William R. *Romantic Passion: A Universal Experience?* New York: Columbia University Press, 1995.

——. *Intimacies: Love and Sex Across Cultures*. New York: Columbia University Press, 2008.

Jelinek, Estelle, ed. *Women's Autobiography: Essays in Criticism*. Bloomington: Indiana University Press, 1980.

Kapstein, Matthew T. "The Indian Literary Identity in Tibet." In *Literary Cultures in History: Reconstructions from South Asia*, ed. Sheldon Pollock. Berkeley: University of California Press, 2003.

Karmay, Samten G., ed. *The Arrow and the Spindle: Studies in History, Myths, Rituals and Beliefs in Tibet*. Kathmandu: Mandala Book Point, 1998.

Kim, Jinah. "Unheard Voices: Women's Roles in Medieval Buddhist Artistic Production and Religious Practices in South Asia." *Journal of the American Academy of Religion* 80, no. 1 (2012): 200–32.

Klein, Anne Carolyn. *Meeting the Great Bliss Queen: Buddhists, Feminists, and the Art of the Self*. Boston: Beacon, 1995.

Kleinberg, Aviad M. *Prophets in Their Own Country: Living Saints and the Making of Sainthood in the Later Middle Ages*. Chicago: University of Chicago Press, 1992.

Kolmaš, Josef. "The Ambans and Assistant Ambans of Tibet (1727–1912)." In *The History of Tibet*, ed. Alex McKay. London: RoutledgeCurzon, 2003, 602–14.

Kornman, Robin. "A Tribal History." In *Religions of Tibet in Practice*, ed. Donald S. Lopez, Jr. Princeton, N.J.: Princeton University Press, 1997, 77–97.

Kozloff, P. K. "Through Eastern Tibet and Kam (Continued)." *The Geographical Journal* 31, no. 5 (1908): 522–34.

Langford, Wendy. *Revolutions of the Heart: Gender, Power and the Delusions of Love*. London, New York: Routledge, 1999.
Larsen, Knud, and Amund Sinding-Larsen. *The Lhasa Atlas: Traditional Tibetan Architecture and Townscape*. Boston: Shambhala, 2001.
Lee, Haiyan. *Revolution of the Heart: A Genealogy of Love in China, 1900–1950*. Stanford, Calif.: Stanford University Press, 2007.
Lejeune, Philippe. "The Autobiographical Pact." In *On Autobiography*, ed. Philippe Lejeune. Minneapolis: University of Minnesota Press, 1989.
Lhamo, Rinchen. *We Tibetans*. 1926; reprint, New Delhi: Srishti Publishers & Distributors, 1997.
Lhawang, Lodey. "The Conferring of Tibetan Government Ranks on the Chieftains of Golok." *Lungta* 8 (1994): 13–17.
Lionnet, Françoise. *Autobiographical Voices: Race, Gender, Self-Portraiture*. Ithaca: Cornell University Press, 1989.
Lopez, Donald S., Jr. *Prisoners of Shangri-la: Tibetan Buddhism and the West*. Chicago: University of Chicago Press, 1998.
Lutz, Catherine. *Unnatural Emotions: Everyday Sentiments on a Micronesian Atoll and Their Challenge to Western Theory*. Chicago: University of Chicago Press, 1988.
Macfarlane, Alan. *Marriage and Love in England 1300–1840: Modes of Reproduction 1300–1840*. Oxford: Basil Blackwell, 1986.
Makley, Charlene. *The Violence of Liberation: Gender and Tibetan Buddhist Revival in Post-Mao China*. Berkeley: University of California Press, 2007.
——. "The Body of a Nun: Nunhood and Gender in Contemporary Amdo." In *Women in Tibet*, ed. Janet Gyatso and Hanna Havnevik. New York: Columbia University Press, 2005, 259–84.
de Man, Paul. "Autobiography as De-facement." In *The Rhetoric of Romanticism*, ed. Paul de Man. New York: Columbia University Press, 1984.
Mason, Mary. "The Other Voice: Autobiographies of Women Writers." In *Autobiography, Essays Theoretical and Critical*. Princeton, N.J.: Princeton University Press, 1980.
McDaniel, June. "Emotion in Bengali Religious Thought: Substance and Metaphor." In *Emotions in Asian Thought: A Dialogue in Comparative Philosophy*, ed. Joel Marks and Roger T. Ames. Delhi: Sri Satguru Publications, 1995.
Miller, Beatrice. "Views of Women's Roles in Buddhist Tibet." In *Studies in the History of Buddhism*, ed. A. K. Narain. Delhi: B. R. Publishing, 1980, 155–66.
Miller, Nancy K. "Representing Others: Gender and the Subjects of Autobiography." *Differences* 6, no. 1 (1994): 1–27.
Mink, Louis O. *Historical Understanding*. Ithaca: Cornell University Press, 1987.
de Munck, Victor C. *Romantic Love and Sexual Behavior: Perspectives from the Social Sciences*. Westport, Conn: Praeger, 1998.
Nebesky-Wojkowitz, Réne de. *Oracles and Demons of Tibet: The Cult and Iconography of the Tibetan Protective Deities*. The Netherlands: Mouton, 1956.
Newman, Barbara. "La mystique courtoise: Thirteenth-Century Beguines and the

Art of Love." In *From Virile Woman to WomanChrist*, ed. Barbara Newman. Philadelphia: University of Philadelphia Press, 1993.

Norbu, Namkhai. *Drung, Deu and Bön: Narrations, Symbolic Languages and the Bön Tradition in Ancient Tibet*. Trans. Adriano Clemente. Dharamsala: Library of Tibetan Works and Archives, 1995.

Paine, Robert. "What Is Gossip About? An Alternative Hypothesis." *Man* 2, no. 2 (1967): 278–85.

Patrul Rinpoche. *The Words of My Perfect Teacher*. San Francisco: Harper-Collins, 1994.

Personal Narratives Group, ed. *Interpreting Women's Lives: Feminist Theory and Personal Narratives*. Bloomington: Indiana University Press, 1989.

Petech, Luciano. *Aristocracy and Government in Tibet, 1728–1959*. Rome Oriental series, 45. Roma: Istituto italiano per il Medio ed Estremo Oriente, 1973.

Pirie, Fernanda. "Legal Complexity on the Tibetan Plateau." *Journal of Legal Pluralism* 53–54 (2006): 77–99.

Pollock, Sheldon. "Rasa After Abhinava." In *Goodness of Sanskrit: Studies in Honour of Professor Ashok Aklujkar*, ed. Chikafumi Watanabe, Michele Desmarais, and Yoshichika Honda. New Delhi: D. K. Printworld, 2012, 429–45.

Pommaret, Françoise. *Les Revenants de L'au-Delà Dans le Monde Tibétain*. Paris: Center National de la Recherche Scientifique, 1989.

Prats, Ramon. "Some Preliminary Considerations Arising from a Biographical Study of the Early gter ston." In *Tibetan Studies in Honour of Hugh Richardson, Proceedings of the International Seminar on Tibetan Studies Oxford 1979*, ed. Michael Aris and Aung San Suu Kyi. Warminster: Aris & Phillips, 1980.

Reddy, William M. *The Making of Romantic Love: Longing and Sexuality in Europe, South Asia, and Japan, 900–1200 CE*. Chicago: University of Chicago Press, 2012.

Richardus, Peter. *Tibetan Lives: Three Himalayan Autobiographies*. Richmond: Curzon Press, 1998.

Robinson, James. *Buddha's Lions: The Lives of the Eighty-Four Siddhas*. Berkeley: Dharma Publishing, 1979.

Rock, Joseph Francis Charles. *The Amnye Ma-chhen Range and Adjacent Regions: A Monographic Study*. Vol. 12, Serie orientale Roma,. Rome: Is. M.E.O., 1956.

Rosenwein, Barbara H. "Worrying About Emotions in History." *The American Historical Review* 107, no. 3 (2002): 821–45.

——. "Emotion Words." In *Le Sujet des Émotions au Moyen Âge*, ed. Piroska Nagy and Damien Boquet. Paris: Beauchesne, 2008.

Rossi, Donatella. "Some Notes on the Tibetan Amdo Love Songs." In *Tibetan Studies: Proceedings of the 5th Seminar of the International Association for Tibetan Studies Narita 1989*, ed. Shōren Ihara and Zuihō Yamaguchi. Narita: Naritasan Shinshoji, 1992, 705–09.

——. "mKha' 'gro dBang mo'i rNam thar, The Biography of the gTer ston ma bDe chen Chos kyi dBang mo (1868–1927?)." *Révue d'Études Tibétaines* 15, Tibetan Studies in Honour of Samten Karmay no. 2 (2008): 371–78.

de Rougemont, Denis. *Love in the Western World*. Rev. and augmented ed. New York: Pantheon, 1956.

Sacks, Oliver. *The Man Who Mistook His Wife for a Hat and Other Clinical Tales*. New York: Harper & Row, 1987.
Schaeffer, Kurtis R. *Himalayan Hermitess: The Life of a Tibetan Buddhist Nun*. New York: Oxford University Press, 2004.
Scott, Joan. "The Evidence of Experience." *Critical Inquiry* 17 (summer 1991): 773–97.
Shabkar Tsogdruk Rangdrol. *The Life of Shabkar: The Autobiography of a Tibetan Yogin*. Trans. Matthieu Ricard et al. Ithaca: Snow Lion, 2001.
Shaw, Miranda. *Passionate Enlightenment: Women in Tantric Buddhism*. Princeton, N.J.: Princeton University Press, 1994.
Siegel, Lee. *Sacred and Profane Dimensions of Love in Indian Traditions, as Exemplified in the Gītagovinda of Jayadeva*. Delhi: Oxford University Press, 1978.
de Silva, Padmasiri. "Theoretical Perspectives on Emotions in Early Buddhism." In *Emotions in Asian Thought: A Dialogue in Comparative Philosophy*, ed. Joel Marks and Rodger T. Ames. Delhi: Sri Satguru Publications, 1997.
Simmer-Brown, Judith. *Dakini's Warm Breath: the Feminine Principle in Tibetan Buddhism*. Boston: Shambhala, 2001.
Skilling, Peter. "Nuns, Laywomen, Donors, Goddesses: Female Roles in Early Indian Budhism." *Journal of the International Association of Buddhist Studies* 24, no. 2 (2001): 242–74.
Slade, Carole A. "'Este Gran Dios de las Cavallerías' [This Great God of Chivalric Deeds]: St. Teresa's Performances of the Novels of Chivalry." In *The Vernacular Spirit: Essays on Medieval Religious Literature*, ed. Renate Blumenfeld-Kosinski, Duncan Robertson, and Nancy Bradley Warren. New York: Palgrave, 2002.
Smith, E. Gene. *Among Tibetan Texts: History and Literature of the Himalayan Plateau*. Boston: Wisdom, 2001.
Smith, Sidonie. *A Poetics of Women's Autobiography: Marginality and the Fictions of Self-Representation*. Bloomington: Indiana University Press, 1987.
Smith, Sidonie, and Julia Watson. *De/Colonizing the Subject: The Politics of Gender in Women's Autobiography*. Minneapolis: University of Minnesota Press, 1992.
——, eds. *Women, Autobiography, Theory: A Reader*. Madison: University of Wisconsin Press, 1998.
——. *Reading Autobiography: A Guide for Interpreting Life Narratives*. Minneapolis: University of Minnesota Press, 2001.
Snellgrove, David. *Indo-Tibetan Buddhism: Indian Buddhists and Their Tibetan Successors*. 1987; reprint, Boston: Shambhala, 2002.
Solomon, Robert C. *Love: Emotion, Myth and Metaphor*. Buffalo, N.Y.: Prometheus Books, 1990.
Sørensen, Per K. *Divinity Secularized: An Inquiry Into the Nature and Form of the Songs Sscribed to the Sixth Dalai Lama*. Wiener Studien zur Tibetologie und Buddhismuskunde Heft 25. Wien: Arbeitskreis für Tibetische und Buddhistische Studien Universität Wien, 1990.
Sperling, Elliot. "Awe and Submission: A Tibetan Aristocrat at the Court of Qianlong." *The International History Review* XX, no. 2 (1998): 32–35.

Sponberg, Alan. "Attitudes Toward Women and the Feminine in Early Buddhism." In *Buddhism, Sexuality, and Gender*, ed. José Ignacio Cabezón. Albany: State University of New York Press, 1992, 3–36.

Stanley, Liz. *The Auto/biographical I: The Theory and Practices of Feminist Auto/biography*. Manchester: Manchester University Press, 1992.

Sternberg, Robert J., and Karin Weis. *The New Psychology of Love*. New Haven: Yale University Press, 2006.

Stone, Lawrence. *The Family, Sex and Marriage in England, 1500–1800*. New York: Harper & Row, 1977.

——. "Passionate Attachments in the West in Historical Perspective." In *Passionate Attachments: Thinking About Love*, ed. Willard Gaylin and Ethel Spector Person. New York: Free Press, 1988, 15–26.

Strawson, Galen. "Against Narrativity." *Ratio* XVII, no. 4 (2004): 428–52.

Strong, John S. "A Family Quest: The Buddha, Yaśodharā and Rāhula in the Mūlasarvāstivāda Vinaya." In *Sacred Biography in the Buddhist Traditions of South and Southeast Asia*, ed. Juliane Schober. Honolulu: University of Hawai'i Press, 1997.

Sturrock, John. "Theory Versus Autobiography." In *The Culture of Autobiography: Constructions of Self-Representation*, ed. Robert Folkenflik. Stanford, Calif.: Stanford University Press, 1993.

Sujata, Victoria. *Tibetan Songs of Realization: Echoes from a Seventeenth-Century Scholar and Siddha in Amdo*. Leiden: Brill, 2005.

Swidler, Ann. *Talk of Love: How Culture Matters*. Chicago: University of Chicago Press, 2001.

Tammi, Pekka. "Against Narrative ('A Boring Story')." *Partial Answers: Journal of Literature and the History of Ideas* 4, no. 2 (2006): 19–40.

Taring, Rinchen Dolma. *Daughter of Tibet: The Autobiography of Rinchen Dolma Taring*. London: The Camelot Press, 1970.

Taylor, Charles. *Sources of the Self: The Making of the Modern Identity*. Cambridge, Mass.: Harvard University Press, 1989.

Terrone, Antonio. "Bya rog prog zhu, The Raven Crest: The Life and Teachings of bDe chen 'od gsal rdo rje, Treasure Revealer of Contemporary Tibet." Ph.D. diss., Leiden University, 2010.

Thargyal, Rinzin. *Nomads of Eastern Tibet: Social Organization and Economy of a Pastoral Estate in the Kingdom of Dege*. Vol. 15, Brill's Tibetan Studies Library. Leiden: Brill, 2007.

Thondup, Tulku. *Hidden Teachings of Tibet: An Explanation of the Terma Tradition of Tibetan Buddhism*. Boston: Wisdom, 1986.

——. *Enlightened Living: Teachings of Tibetan Buddhist Masters*. Boston: Shambhala, 1990.

——. *Masters of Meditation and Miracles: Lives of the Great Buddhist Masters of India and Tibet*. Boston: Shambhala, 1999.

Traktung Dudjom Lingpa. *A Clear Mirror, The Visionary Autobiography of a Tibetan Master*. Trans. Chönyi Drolma (Anne Holland). Hong Kong: Rangjung Yeshe Publications, 2011.

Tsering, Tashi. "History of the Gling-tshang Principality of Khams: A Preliminary Study." In *Tibetan Studies: Proceedings of the 5th Seminar of the International Association for Tibetan Studies Narita 1989*, ed. Shōren Ihara and Zuihō Yamaguchi. Narita: Naritasan Shinshoji, 1992.
Tsybikoff, G. Ts. "Lhasa and Central Tibet." *Smithsonian's Annual Report for 1903.* Washington, D.C.: Government Printing Office, 1903, 727–56.
Tucci, Giuseppe. *Tibet: Land of Snows*. Trans. J. E. Stapleton Driver. New York: Stein and Day, 1967.
Urban, Hugh. *Tantra: Sex, Secrecy, Politics, and Power in the Study of Religion*. Berkeley: University of California Press, 2003.
van der Kuijp, Leonard. "Tibetan Belles-Lettres: The Influence of Daṇḍin and Kṣemendra." In *Tibetan Literature: Studies in Genre*, ed. José Ignacio Cabezón and Roger R. Jackson. Ithaca: Snow Lion, 1996.
Vaudeville, Charlotte. "Evolution of Love-Symbolism in Bhagavatism." *Journal of the American Oriental Society* 82, no. 1 (1962): 31–40.
The Vimalakirti Sutra. Trans. Burton Watson. New York: Columbia University Press, 1997.
Vostrikov, A. I. *Tibetan Historical Literature*. 1962; reprint, Richmond: Curzon Press, 1994.
Waddell, L. A. *Lhasa and Its Mysteries: A Record of the Expedition of 1903–1904*. New York: E. P. Dutton, 1905.
Warder, A. K. *Indian Kāvya Literature*. Vol. 1. Delhi: Motilal Banarsidass, 1972.
Weintraub, Karl Joachim. *The Value of the Individual: Self and Circumstance in Autobiography*. Chicago: University of Chicago Press, 1978.
White, David Gordon. *The Alchemical Body: Siddha Traditions in Medieval India*. Chicago: University of Chicago Press, 1996.
——. *Kiss of the Yoginī: "Tantric Sex" in Its South Asian Contexts*. Chicago: University of Chicago Press, 2003.
White, Hayden. *The Content of the Form: Narrative Discourse and Historical Representation*. Baltimore: Johns Hopkins University Press, 1987.
Willis, Janice. "Ḍākinī; Some Comments on Its Nature and Meaning." In *Feminine Ground: Essays on Women and Tibet*, ed. Janice Willis. Ithaca: Snow Lion, 1987.
Wilson, Liz. *Charming Cadavers: Horrific Figurations of the Feminine in Indian Buddhist Hagiographic Literature*. Chicago: University of Chicago Press, 1996.
Yeshe, Lama. *Introduction to Tantra: The Transformation of Desire*. Boston: Wisdom, 1987.
Young, Serinity. *Courtesans and Tantric Consorts: Sexualities in Buddhist Narrative, Iconography, and Ritual*. New York: Routledge, 2004.
Young-Eisendrath, Polly. "Gender and Contrasexuality: Jung's Contribution and Beyond." In *The Cambridge Companion to Jung*, ed. Polly Young-Eisendrath and Terence Dawson. New York: Cambridge University Press, 1997, 223–39.
Zimmer, Heinrich Robert. *Philosophies of India*, Bollingen Series XXVI. New York: Pantheon, 1951.

INDEX

An Account of How This Yogi Traversed the Ground and Paths Spoken Truthfully Without Deception (autobiography of Gara Terchen), 17, 91; and auspicious connections, 86; compared to autobiography of Sera Khandro, 167–72, 298–99; contents of, 167–72, 241–46, 298–99 (*see also* Gara Terchen Pema Dündül Wangchuk Lingpa); *ḍākinīs* in, 137, 169–72, 241–45, 298–99; influence on autobiography of Sera Khandro, 86–87; loving relationships depicted in, 267–68
age, Tibetan convention for, 338n6
Akyap Lama Karma Döndrup, 68, 325
Akyong Bum, 106, 117, 325
Akyongza: antagonism toward Sera Khandro, 65–66, 246, 278; as consort to Drimé Özer, 5, 47–48; expulsion of Sera Khandro following death of Drimé Özer, 66, 69; high-status background, 48; refusal to admit Sera Khandro to Drimé Özer's household, 5, 50, 246, 278; Wylie transliteration, 325
Ambans, 31, 32, 33
Andzom Dröndül Pawo Dorjé, 213–14, 317, 325; family's support for Sera Khandro, 215–16, 266; recognition of Sera Khandro as incarnation of Künga Buma, 215; summons to Sera Khandro (1923), xxiv, 64, 213–15, 247, 304–5
Andzom Gar, xxiv, 64, 68, 213
Ané Zangmo, 176, 325, 358n18
animals: horse Kyangö, 101; suffering of female animals, 181–82; visionary encounters with birds and chicks, 155–57, 208–9
Annals of Golok History (Döndrup Wangyel and Nordé), 44–45, 105–8
Anyé Machen (sacred mountain), 42, 55, 59, 101, 105–13, 105(photo),

Anyé Machen (sacred mountain) (*continued*) 325, 354n65; as both Buddhist holy mountain and site associated with Tibetan mountain cult, 103; land deities and Treasure revealing associated with, 105–13; and Ma family warlords, 125; propitiation of, 124; Sera Khandro and, 110–13, 211, 227
Atsara Salé, 88, 204, 281
auspicious connections (*tendrel*), 11, 77–78, 207; and Andzom Rinpoché, 64; consequences of failure to gather auspicious connections as instructed, 97–99, 221; and difficulties of Treasure revealing, 207–10, 226–27 (*see also* Sera Khandro, as Treasure revealer: difficulties of Treasure revelation); fivefold auspicious connections required for successful Treasure discoveries, 11–12, 78, 95, 96, 97, 206; and Gara Terchen, 86; and partnership of Sera Khandro and Drimé Özer, 59, 270, 278, 283–84, 299–300
auto/biographical writings of Sera Khandro: contrast to other biographies, 297–99; as resource for social history, 14–19, 23–75 (*see also* Sera Khandro); reunion of Sera Khandro and Drimé Özer as climax of, 294–95; social world revealed through conversations, 17–19; and Tibetan literary genres/folk songs, 9–12, 30, 83–84, 261–62. See also *The Biography of the Central Tibetan Woman Dewé Dorjé*; *The Biography of the Omniscient Refuge Master, Lord of Accomplished Ones, the Precious Sovereign of the Ocean of Profound Treasures Pema Drondül Sangngak Lingpa*; *The Excellent Path of Devotion*
autobiography: "autobiographical pact" (Lejeune's concept), 12; auto/biographical writings of Sera Khandro (*see* auto/biographical writings of Sera Khandro; *The Biography of the Central Tibetan Woman Dewé Dorjé*; *The Excellent Path of Devotion*); *ḍākinīs* as common element in, 137; *delok* accounts, 14, 38, 175, 326; of Düjom Lingpa (see *A Clear Mirror*); of Gara Terchen (see *An Account of How This Yogi Traversed the Ground and Paths Spoken Truthfully Without Deception*); of Jetsün Ani Lochen, 173–80; *namtar* (spiritual biography), 9–11, 13, 19, 74; of Orgyen Chökyi, 180–84; *rangnam* genre, 10–11; scholarship on relational selfhood and women's autobiographies, 12–14
avadāna genre, 10
Avalokiteśvara, 28, 33, 68, 115–17, 164, 183
awareness holder, 112, 170, 185, 234, 271, 365n33; Pema Tötrengtsel as, 80, 89; Saraha as, 23, 144; and spiritual liberation, 197, 198, 200, 202, 365n33

Bakhtin, Mikhail, 18
banditry, 121–23, 227
Bardo Tödrol, Liberation through Hearing in the Intermediate States, 168
Barthes, Roland, 18, 341n37
Bedrak Dorjé Rolwa, 171, 325
Benak Monastery, xxvii(map), 53(photo), 325; alternate names, 53, 359n33; founder, 168; history of, 52–53; and religious encampment, 107; Sera Khandro at, xxiv, 53–63, 148–54, 156, 160–63; Sera Khandro's puns on name, 150, 359n33; Sera Khandro's summons to from Gara Terchen, xxiv, 5, 53–55, 143–48. *See also* Gara Terchen Pema Döndül Wangchuk Lingpa

Bentor, Yael, 363n11
bhāva (Tib. *'gyur*; emotions), 259–61
Bharati, Agehananda, 253
The Biography of the Central Tibetan Woman Dewé Dorjé (Sera Khandro), xxv, 6–9, 21, 23–27; and auspicious connections, 11; change in tone following move to Sera Monastery, 67; compared to autobiographies of male religious figures, 8, 85–87, 164–72; compared to biography of Drimé Özer, 8; compared to other women's autobiographies, 172–84; compared to Taksham's hagiography of Yeshé Tsogyel, 316–17; composition of, 8–9, 69; conclusion, 8–9; contents of (*see* Sera Khandro, life narrative); *ḍākinīs*' instigation of writing, 184–87; and "emotional community" (Rosenwein's term), 255; emphasis on connection to Yeshé Tsogyel, 83–84, 129, 160 (*see also* Yeshé Tsogyel: Sera Khandro as emanation of); female religious figures mentioned in, 176–77, 358n18; frame narrative, 80–92, 129; literary precedents and paradigmatic elements, 30, 83–91, 261–62; loving relationships depicted in, 265–68; manuscript and published versions, 7–8; and relationality of the self, 11, 185; relation between autobiography and biography of Drimé Özer, 279–80; reunion of Sera Khandro and Drimé Özer as climax of, 294–95; self-deprecating statements as narrative device, 20–21, 131–33, 137–38, 159–60, 229, 287; short version of autobiography, xxv, 24, 185, 186; and spiritual biography tradition (*namtar*), 9–11; and synonymy, 258–59; and Treasure revealing, 77; Tsültrim Dorjé as scribe, 8, 24, 179, 185–86; ventriloquy as narrative device, 21, 132, 160, 163, 192, 221, 258–59, 287–89
The Biography of Namtrül Jikmé Püntsok and Khandro Tāré Lhamo (Pema Ösel Tayé), 321
The Biography of the Omniscient Refuge Master, Lord of Accomplished Ones, the Precious Sovereign of the Ocean of Profound Treasures Pema Drondül Sangngak Lingpa (biography of Drimé Özer; Sera Khandro), 2, 6–7, 187; and banditry, 122–23; beginning of, 87; compared to autobiography of Sera Khandro, 8; composition of, xxv, 6–7, 69, 185, 314; contents of (*see* Drimé Özer); and loving relationships with family members and disciples, 263–65; and Ma family warlords, 126–27; prophecies about *yab yum* partnership of Sera Khandro and Drimé Özer, 269–72; relation to Sera Khandro's autobiography, 279–80; reunion of Sera Khandro and Drimé Özer as climax of, 294–95; writing style, 8
biography of Yeshé Tsogyel. *See* hagiography
birds and chicks, Sera Khandro's visions of, 155–57, 208–9
bliss, and Treasure revealing, 205, 206
bodhicitta, 199–201, 203–4, 218, 364n25
bodhisattvas, 77, 78, 185; and gendered dyad of method and insight, 249–52; and Tantric subtle body, 198; thirteen grounds on the bodhisattva path, 202, 364n32. *See also* Avalokiteśvara; Drongri Mukpo; Tārā
Bön religion, 6, 69, 72, 107–8, 351n30
Bruner, Jerome, 15
Buddha, the, 33, 40, 256; birth account, 30; and disciple-guru relationships, 182; enlightenment of, 297; *jātaka* stories, 10

buddhafields: *ḍākinīs* as messengers from, 137; and death of Drimé Özer, 266, 290, 293, 308, 311; and death of Gara Terchen, 213; and death of Sera Khandro, 74; and frame narrative of Sera Khandro's autobiography, 80, 84; as home of buddhas and bodhisattvas, 77; and illness of Sera Khandro, 232, 303, 306; and transfer of consciousness, 349n132; Unsurpassed Realm, 80, 81, 83, 90, 350n9; Yeshé Tsogyel and, 268. *See also* Glorious Copper-Colored Mountain Buddhafield

buddhas, 78, 94; buddhas of the three times, 80, 89, 142, 146, 243, 268, 308, 350n8; contrast to land deities, 100; crown protrusion as mark of a buddha, 202, 365n34; *ḍākinīs* as, 78, 135; and disciple-guru relationships, 257; Drimé Özer's passage into buddhahood, 249; in Düjom Lingpa and Gara Terchen's autobiographies, 164, 172; five types of buddha wisdom, 197–98; and frame narrative of Sera Khandro's autobiography, 80; and Tantric subtle body, 198; Tantric vision of buddhahood, 21, 22; and Treasure revelation, 74, 77, 129; women's wombs as the source of all buddhas, 135, 144, 147, 148, 177. *See also* buddhafields; Hayagrīva; Vajravārāhī

Buddhism: confluence with pre-Buddhist Tibetan deities and systems of governance, 107–8, 117 (*see also* land deities); and disciple-guru relationships, 252, 257 (*see also* Dharma holders; doctrine holders; *specific gurus*); eight worldly Dharmas, 145, 153, 243, 359n28; and emotions, 256; gender hierarchies in Tibetan Buddhism, 133–35; and impermanence, 301–15; and Indian aesthetic theory, 257–61; literary genres, 9–12; love and lust in, 255–57 (*see also* love); monasteries and religious encampments, 107 (*see also specific monasteries*); and sacred mountains, 102–20; schools of Tibetan Buddhism, 100, 107; the Three Bodies, 145, 177, 350n10; the Three Jewels (Buddha, Dharma, Saṅgha), 47, 102, 111, 136; the three poisons, 255–56, 366n78; three trainings of the path, 362n1. *See also* bodhisattvas; buddhas; channel and wind practices; Great Perfection teachings; Mahāyāna Buddhism; Nyingma school of Tibetan Buddhism; preliminary practices; "Severance" practice; Tantra; Tantric consort practices; Vajrayāna Buddhism

bud med (*bumé*; positive/neutral term for woman), 133, 139–40, 142, 229, 357n4

Bynum, Caroline Walker, 317

Cabezón, José, 253

cakras, 29, 197–98, 201, 297, 311

Campany, Robert, 17

Campbell, June, 358n15

Candler, Edmund, 25

Candrakirti, 363n11

Canzhi Zhen, 33

celibacy, 21; Düjom Lingpa on celibacy and consort practices, 223, 239; and flow of vital energies, 202–3; illness caused by, 216–22; scandal over Gara Terchen's shift from celibate to noncelibate religious specialist, 241–46; Tantric practices achieved through individual meditation, 193, 199, 234–35, 253; tensions between monastic celibacy and religiously motivated sexuality, 189, 192–93, 222–46

Chakri Ömbar (sacred mountain), xxvii(map), 103, 170–71, 207, 326
Chaktsa Trülku Rinpoché Pema Trinlé Gyatso (Chaktrül Rinpoché), 71, 72, 326
Changdrong Druptop Rinpoché, 33–34, 39, 326
channel and wind practices (*rtsa rlung*), 168, 196–204, 247, 360n45; and curing illness/increasing longevity, 212; described, 196–204; teachings given to Gara Terchen, 168; teachings given to Sera Khandro, 38, 51, 196–202, 373n80; and Treasure revealing, 205; and *yab yum* partnership of Sera Khandro and Drimé Özer, 296. *See also* Tantric consort practices
China, Chinese, 46, 106; agitation in Tibet, 123–28; and education of Sera Khandro, 32–33; Han Chinese, 26, 31, 123, 165; Ma family warlords, xxiv, 62, 124–26, 289; Manchus, 26, 31, 123; Mongols, 28, 30, 31, 123, 127, 165; Qing dynasty, 25, 27, 32, 123–25; Sera Khandro's father described as Chinese leader, 31–32; texts lost in Cultural Revolution, 6
Chögyel Ngakyi Wangpo, 31
Choktrül Rangrik Dorjé, 322(photo), 323–24, 326
Chökyi Drönma, 357n4
Chönkhor Lama Jikmé (Jikchö), 157–60, 326
Chönyi Khandro Sangdzö, 141–42, 326. See also *The Secret Treasure of Reality Ḍākinīs*
Chö practice. *See* "Severance" practice
Chötreng, 110–11, 154, 326
Chöying Drönma. *See* Yangchen Drönma/Chöying Drönma
chronology of events of Sera Khandro's life, xxiii–xxv, 3–6
A Clear Mirror: The Biography of My Secret Visionary Experiences of the Illusory Display of Reality (autobiography of Düjom Lingpa), 17, 85–86, 91, 116–17, 164–67; contents of, 164–67; and *ḍākinīs*, buddhas, bodhisattvas, and land deities, 137, 164–67, 184, 297–98; and Drong Mountain, 116–17, 124, 164, 355n83; Düjom Lingpa's motivation to write, 184; influence on autobiography of Sera Khandro, 85–86; loving relationships depicted in, 268
commitment vows, 252, 281–82, 286–87, 300, 306, 354n69
compassion, 256–57; Padmasambhava's compassionate love for Yeshé Tsogyel, 268–69; and spiritual liberation, 64, 200
compassionate love/affection, 256–57, 267–68
consort practices. *See* Sera Khandro, consort relationships of; Tantric consort practices
Core Commentary on the Awakening of Karmic Propensities of Being a Yogi (Gara Terchen Pema Dündül Wangchuk Lingpa), 298–99
Courtesans and Tantric Consorts (Young), 190
Cultural Revolution, texts lost in, 6
Cycle of Prophecies (Sera Khandro), 186–87

ḍākinīs, 23, 35–36, 59, 74–75, 131–87; and birth of Sera Khandro, 29, 30; Campbell on, 358n15; and composition of Drimé Özer's biography, 7, 314; and composition of Sera Khandro's autobiography, 184–87; as consorts, 206–8; and death of Drimé Özer, 310–11, 314, 319; defined/described, 1, 78–79; directives on consort practices, 216–22,

ḍākinīs (*continued*)
225–27, 229–30, 238–41; Drimé Özer and, 269–72; Düjom Lingpa and, 137, 164–67, 184, 297–98; Gara Terchen and, 137, 169–72, 241–46, 298–99; history in South Asia, 135–36, 358n15; and illness caused by desire, 216–22; intersubjectivity of *ḍākinīs*' voices and voice of Sera Khandro, 185; Jetsün Ani Lochen and, 176–78; Khandro Rinpoché as, 322; love expressed by, 97, 162, 265–68; Orgyen Chögyi and, 182–83; and prophecy, 79, 141–42, 269–75 (*see also* prophecy; prophetic guides); roles in Treasure tradition, 77–80, 92, 137, 142, 205–8; Sera Khandro as a *ḍākinī*, xxiv, 18, 54, 66–70, 132, 159–60 (*see also* Yeshé Tsogyel: Sera Khandro as emanation of); and Sera Khandro's anticipation of death, 302–3; Sera Khandro's first visions of, 138–43; and Sera Khandro's frame narrative, 80–91; and Sera Khandro's interactions with Gotrül Rinpoché, 154–60; and Sera Khandro's life with Gara family at Benak, 143–54; and Sera Khandro's move away from Gyelsé, 162–63; and social world revealed through conversations, 17–19; support and encouragement from, 137–38, 143–46, 155, 157, 163, 177–78; as symbols of insight, 137, 358n15; and synonymy, 258–59; and Tantric consort practices, 190, 192, 205–8, 216–22; teasing from, 272–75; threats and warnings from, 97, 163, 229–30, 238–39, 291; and Tibetan biographies, 137; and ventriloquy as narrative device, 163, 192 (*see also* ventriloquy, autobiographical); and *yab yum* partnership of Sera Khandro and Drimé Özer, 269–73, 296. See also *khandroma*; land deities; *specific ḍākinīs*

The Ḍākinīs' Heart Essence (Treasure teachings cycle), 38, 141–42

Dalai Lama, 13th (Gyelwa Tupten Gyatso), 25, 37

Dalai Lama, 6th (Tsangyang Gyatso), 261

Daloyi, 36, 344n39

Daṇḍin, 258

Dartsang, xxvii(map), 48–49, 326; manuscripts housed at, 69; Sera Khandro expelled from, 66, 69, 309–10, 314; Sera Khandro's work as maidservant near, xxiii, 5, 50–52. *See also* Drimé Özer; Kelzang Monastery

Dawa Drönma (*ḍākinī*), 170

death: of Drimé Özer (1924), xxiv, 66, 249, 306–15, 319–20; Drimé Özer's premonitions of, 292–93; of Düjom Lingpa, 264, 277; of Gara Terchen, xxiv, 54; of Gotrül Rinpoché, 235; and romantic love and impermanence, 301–15; of Sera Khandro (1940), xxv, 24, 73–74; Sera Khandro's anticipation of, 302–3; of Sera Khandro's mother (1904), xxiii, 4, 38, 140, 265; of Sera Khandro's son, xxiv, 65, 66, 266, 306–7; "shouldering the debt of the dead," 195, 363n15; "transference of consciousness" practice, 52, 69, 240, 302, 349n132. *See also* buddhafields; reincarnation

deities. See *ḍākinīs*; *khandroma*; land deities

delok accounts, 14, 38, 175, 326

de Man, Paul, 341n37

demonic forces, 101, 144, 149, 218, 289, 308, 342n1. *See also* land deities

"dependent arising," 77–78

de Rougement, Denis, 301

desire. *See* lust/desire

Dewé Dorjé, as Treasure name of Sera Khandro, 210, 285, 300, 349n1
Dewé Gocha (*ḍākinī*), 185, 270–71, 310, 314
dgra lha (war gods), 100, 105. *See also* land deities
Dharma holders, 141, 145, 155, 156, 157, 162, 218
Dharma Mati, 157–58, 360n40. *See also* Gotrül Rinpoché
Diemberger, Hildegard, 357n4
Dilgo Khyentsé, 257
Dipam Tāré (*ḍākinī*), 140–41
Direct Transcendence, 51, 72
doctrine holders: and auspicious connections, 11, 96, 206, 207; difficulties in revealing Treasures due to lack of appropriate consorts and doctrine holders, 97, 109, 110, 144, 167, 172; of Drimé Özer, 122–23, 265, 271–72 (*see also* Drimé Özer: disciples and attendants); role in Treasure tradition, 11, 95, 96, 97, 120, 206; of Sera Khandro, 157–59, 321, 348n113 (*see also* Sera Khandro: disciples and attendants); term meaning, 11, 158
Dodrup Rinpoché Jikmé Tenpé Nyima (Third Dodrupchen), 50, 117, 121, 205–7, 263, 326
Dodrupchen Monastery, 68, 97, 165, 326
Döndrup Gyel, 260
Döndrup Wangyel, 44
Dongkor Abten, 278–79, 326, 373n88
Dorjé Dechen Pematso, 83, 327
Dorjé Drandül (Sangdak Mingyur Dorjé), 50, 71, 280, 299, 327
Dorjetso. *See* Shiwa Dorjetso
Dorjé Yudrönma (*ḍākinī*), 38, 59, 169–70, 178, 272–73, 327
Dorjé Zungma (*ḍākinī*), 225–27, 327
Drakar Dreldzong (sacred mountain), 103, 327
Drakargo Monastery, 106, 327
Drakgyelma, Queen, 109, 112–13, 128
Drak Yerpa caves, 35, 327
Drandül Wangchuk, 108, 109, 327
Drepung Monastery, 38, 327
Dri Lha Gyelbum, 105–7
Drimé Namdak, 67, 327
Drimé Özer (Drima Mepé Özer Tayé), 348n113; agreement with Gyelsé on exchanging Sera Khandro (1915), xxiv, 59, 246–47, 282, 284–85, 374n107; and Andzom Rinpoché's summons to Sera Khandro, 214–15; arrival at Sera Khandro's brother's house (1906), xxiii, 39–40, 274–76; attempt to dissuade Sera Khandro from joining pilgrims, 46–47; and banditry, 122–23; biography of (see *The Biography of the Omniscient Refuge Master, Lord of Accomplished Ones, the Precious Sovereign of the Ocean of Profound Treasures Pema Drondül Sangngak Lingpa*); brothers, 49–50 (*see also* Dodrup Rinpoché Jikmé Tenpé Nyima; Dorjé Drandül; Lhachen Topgyel; Namkha Jikmé); consort Akyongza (*see* Akyongza); *ḍākinī*s and, 269–72; death of (1924), xxiv, 66, 249, 306–15, 319–20; death of father, 264, 277; death of mother, 265; disciples and attendants, 64, 66–67, 264–65 (*see also* Akyap Lama Karma Döndrup; Drimé Namdak; Gonla Sherap; Künzang Nyima; Ömbar; Sotrül Natsok Rangdröl Rinpoché); and Drong Mountain, 115–16, 119, 121–24, 126, 355n83; father of (*see* Düjom Lingpa); future and present incarnations, 72, 319–24; healing of Sera Khandro, 63, 296, 302–4; healing of Sera Khandro's son, 62, 286–88; and Ma family warlords, 126–27; as mediator in land disputes, 122; and Nyingma lineage, 173; premonitions of

Drimé Özer (Drima Mepé Özer Tayé) (*continued*)
death, 292–93; previous incarnations, 273; and prophecy given by Düjom Lingpa on Chinese agitation (1899), 127; provisions given to Sera Khandro in secret, 47–48, 278–79; and religious encampment, 107, 126; residence in Dartsang, 48–49, 278–79; Sera Khandro as *yab yum* partner (see *yab yum* partnership of Sera Khandro and Drimé Özer); and Sera Khandro's *Cycle of Prophecies*, 186–87; Sera Khandro sent to live with (1921), xxiv, 5–6, 63–67, 162–63, 294–96 (see also *yab yum* partnership of Sera Khandro and Drimé Özer); Sera Khandro's request to Tongpön Zangmo for hair or clothing of, 278; as Sera Khandro's root guru, 173; Sera Khandro's teaching of Drimé Özer's eighteen volumes of Treasures (1927), xxv, 348n114; and Sera Khandro's vision of Glorious Copper-Colored Mountain Buddhafield, 94, 96; Sera Khandro's visions of, 186–87, 310–12; Sera Khandro's visits to, 62, 63, 209–10, 283–93; teachings given to Sera Khandro, 51; as Treasure revealer, 122–24, 372n76; works compiled by Sera Khandro, 314

Drogön, 69, 327
Drokchen Khobü Valley, 71–72, 327
Drong Mountain/Drongri, xxvii(map), 62, 79, 103, 104(fig.), 113–20, 113(photo), 164; Avalokiteśvara and, 115–17; Drimé Özer and, 115–16, 119, 121–24, 126, 355n83; Düjom Lingpa and, 116–17, 124, 164, 355n83; propitiation of, 118, 124, 164; Sera Khandro and, 62, 119–20, 289–90, 355n83; Treasure revealers listed, 355n83
Drongri Mukpo (land deity, war god, and bodhisattva), 104(fig.), 114–17, 124
Drönkar (sister-in-law of Sera Khandro), 39, 274–75, 277
Drugu Tingkar Cliff, 73, 327
Drupchen Dawa Dorjé Zangpo, 179
Drupgyelma (*ḍākinī*), 267
Druptop Rinpoché. *See* Changdrong Druptop Rinpoché
Düjom Jikdrel Yeshé Dorjé, 49, 84–85, 327
Düjom Lingpa (Traktung Düjom Lingpa): as abbot of Kelzang Monastery, 49; authenticity and credibility issues, 167; autobiography (see *A Clear Mirror*); *Refining One's Perception*, 2, 51, 68, 72; on celibacy and consort practices, 223, 239; complete works compiled by Sera Khandro, xxv, 69, 314; consorts of, 298; and *ḍākinīs*, buddhas, bodhisattvas, and land deities, 137, 164–67, 184, 297–98; death of, 264, 277; disciples (*see* Gar Lama Gelek Gyatso); and Drong Mountain, 116–17, 124, 164, 355n83; Düjom Jikdrel Yeshé Dorjé as reincarnation of, 49, 84; as mediator in land disputes, 122; response to prophecy about Drimé Özer's Treasure revealing and *yab yum* relationship, 269–70; and Sera Khandro's *Cycle of Prophecies*, 187; sons of, 49–50 (*see also* Dodrup Rinpoché Jikmé Tenpé Nyima; Dorjé Drandül; Drimé Özer; Lhachen Topgyel; Namkha Jikmé); Wylie transliteration, 334
Duncan, Marion H., 371n44
Dündül Drapko Tsel, 268
Dzagyel/Dzagya Monastery, xxvi(map), 48, 165, 327
Dzakhok, 68, 71, 72, 327

Dzamtang Monastery, xxvii(map), 69, 327
Dza Mura Trülku, 52, 327
Dzirong Sanglung Monastery, 102
Dzokchen Monastery, 106–7
Dzokchen Palgé, 327, 373n80. *See also* Patrül Rinpoché
Dzongda, xxvii(map), 68, 69, 240, 327
Dzongné (sacred mountain), 63
Dzongsar Khyentse Rinpoché, 288
Dzongtrül Rinpoché, 324

Eakin, Paul John, 12–13
earth Treasures, 34–35, 59, 77, 110–13, 120, 207, 210–11. *See also* Treasure tradition
education: of Gara Terchen, 168; and monasteries, 13, 258; of Sera Khandro, 32–33, 138–39, 258, 347n94
Ekajaṭī (*ḍākinī*), 169–71
Ekvall, Robert, 62
Eliade, Mircea, 189
Emanation Body, 80, 90, 177, 350n10
emotion: Buddhism and negative and positive emotions, 256; and love languages of Tibet, 254–62; and Sanskrit aesthetic theory, 259–60; and Tibetan literature, 260. *See also* love
Enjoyment Body, 177, 350n10
enlightenment. *See* spiritual liberation
equality in *yab yum* partnership of Sera Khandro and Drimé Özer, 287–89, 300
The Excellent Path of Devotion: The Short Story of a Mendicant's Experiences in Response to Questions from My Varja Kin (short autobiography of Sera Khandro), xxv, 24, 185, 186

father of Sera Khandro. *See* Jampa Gönpo
Faure, Bernard, 254
female body, inferior status of, 19; as common theme in female mystics' writings, 172–73; and *ḍākinīs*' reassurances, 142–43; and difficulties in revealing Treasures, 167, 207–11; and Gara Terchen's reassurances, 147–48; and Gotrül Rinpoché's reassurances, 159–60; self-deprecating statements as narrative device, 20–21, 131–33, 147–48, 159–60, 229; and Sera Khandro's reluctance to meet with Gotrül Rinpoché, 159, 230; and social difficulties in Benak community, 208; suffering of female animals, 181–82; Tibetan terms for inferior birth/body, 133, 357n4. *See also* women
Fiorenza, Elisabeth Schüssler, 212
folk songs, 261–62, 282, 359n39, 371nn 44,45
frame narrative, 20, 80–92, 129
funerary practices, 176
Furlong, Monica, 172

Gara (family name), 327, 351n20
Gara Gyelsé Pema Namgyel, 347n91; agreement with Drimé Özer on transferring Sera Khandro (1915), xxiv, 59, 246–47, 282, 284–85, 374n107; brothers (*see* Jikmé Könchok); consort Seldrön, 5, 60, 161, 290; disapproval of Sera Khandro's Treasure revelations, xxiv, 5, 148, 152; father (*see* Gara Terchen Pema Dündül Wangchuk Lingpa); lack of affectionate references to, in Sera Khandro's autobiography, 265; land dispute in religious community, 122, 126–27; lawsuit over custody of son (1924), xxiv, 64–65, 305; low opinion of Sera Khandro, 55–56, 58, 148–49, 160–61; and Ma family warlords, 126–27; neglect of healing rituals for Sera Khandro, 292; pilgrimages to Anyé Machen Mountain, 101, 108–12; prophecies

Gara Gyelsé Pema Namgyel (*continued*) ignored by, 111–12; as prophesied "life partner" of Sera Khandro, 54–56; religious encampment, 107, 126–27; scandal over birth of, 241–46; Sera Khandro's departure from, xxiv, 5–6, 62–63, 162–63, 294–96; and Sera Khandro's second visit to Drimé Özer, 284–86; Sera Khandro's troubled life as "life partner" of, xxiv, 5–6, 54–63, 148–54, 160–63, 208, 292; and Treasure scriptures and objects of Gara Terchen, 56; Wylie transliteration, 328

Gara Gyeltsen, 228–30, 327

Gara Terchen Pema Dündül Wangchuk Lingpa: as abbot of Benak Monastery, 52; autobiography of (see *An Account of How This Yogi Traversed the Ground and Paths Spoken Truthfully Without Deception*); consort Ngak Chödrön, 242–45, 265–66, 298; consort Yakza (*see* Yakshülza); and *ḍākinīs*, buddhas, bodhisattvas, and land deities, 86, 169–72, 241–46, 298–99; daughter of Sera Khandro as possible incarnation of, 58; death of, xxiv, 54; death of unnamed consort, 299; disciples (*see* Ngakpa Lhakpa); education of, 168; etymology of family name, 351n20; and prophetic guidance, 171, 242; and scandal and gossip, 241–46, 298; and Sera Khandro's *Cycle of Prophecies*, 187; Sera Khandro's visions

of, 54, 146–48; son Gyelsé (*see* Gara Gyelsé Pema Namgyel); summons to Sera Khandro (1910), xxiii–xxiv, 5, 53–55, 143–48, 212–13; and Tantric consort practices, 168, 193, 241–46; as Treasure revealer, 54–55, 242; Treasure scriptures and objects taken by Gyelsé and Sera Khandro, 56; Wylie transliteration, 328

Gar Lama Gelek Gyatso, 72, 327

Garter Rinpoché. *See* Gara Terchen Pema Dündül Wangchuk Lingpa

Geary, Patrick, 16–17

Gelek, 45, 355n81, 360n48

Gelek Pema Namgyel, xiv, 328, 351n18

Gelongma Palmo (*ḍākinī*), 183

Geluk school of Tibetan Buddhism, 30, 35, 66, 107, 345n63

gender: gender complementarity in Tantric Buddhism, 249–54, 317 (*see also* method of compassion and insight of realizing emptiness; *yab yum* partnership of Sera Khandro and Drimé Özer; *yab yum* union); gender hierarchies in Tibetan Buddhism, 133–35, 253–54; suffering of female animals, 181–82; and Tantric physiology, 196–204. *See also* female body, inferior status of; women

Gesar of Ling (Tibetan epic), 123, 348n116

Geshé Lodrö (brother of Sera Khandro), 38, 328

Getso, 87, 265, 328

Gītagovinda (Jayadeva), 260

Glorious Copper-Colored Mountain Buddhafield, 88(fig.), 90, 93(fig.), 119, 155, 292, 306, 309, 355n91; Düjom Lingpa's visions of, 268; Gara Terchen's visions of, 169, 243; Sera Khandro's visions of, 92–97

Gochen Trülku Jikdrel Chökyi Lodrö. *See* Gotrül Rinpoché

Goffman, Erving, 367–68n100

Gogentang Stūpa, 114, 328, 354–55n77

Golok, xxvii(map), 277–78; climate and physical geography, 4, 42; dangers in, 122–23, 227; Guibaut and Liotard expedition in (1940), 354–55n77;

history of region, 42, 44–46, 105–8, 124–26; as independent confederation, 24; invasions by Ma family warlords, xxiv, 62, 124–26, 289; land deities in, 79 (see also *ḍākinīs*; land deities); location, xxvi(map), 41–42; monasteries in, 106–7; nomadism in, 40–43, 45, 107 (*see also* nomadism); people, 42–44, 106, 225; and People's Republic of China, 106; sacred mountains, 103, 105–13 (*see also specific mountains*); Sera Khandro's escape from Lhasa and difficult entry into Golok, xxvi(map), 40–52, 277–78; warfare, 123–24
Golok Tibetan Autonomous Prefecture, 42
Gonla Sherap, 276, 328
gossip: Gara Terchen and, 241–46, 298; Goffman on, 367–68n100; Paine on, 367–68n100; Sera Khandro and (*see* social dynamics in religious communities); Tibetan terms for, 223–24, 366n71. *See also* public opinion
Gotrül Rinpoché (Gochen Trülku Jikdrel Chökyi Lodrö), 132, 154–63, 317, 328, 335; death of, 235; loving treatment of Sera Khandro, 266–67; as main doctrine holder for Sera Khandro, 157–58; recognition of Sera Khandro as a *khandroma* (1915), xxiv, 58, 159–60; and request for Sera Khandro to serve as consort to Tibir Tuktsa Trülku, 233–35; Rindzin Gyurmé Dorjé as consciousness of, xxiv, 65, 235, 284; Sera Khandro's interactions with, 61, 154–61, 210–11, 230–35, 266–67; support for Sera Khandro during troubled times at Benak, 60–61, 159–62; and Tantric consort practices, 230–35. *See also* Dharma Mati
Great Perfection teachings, 4, 35–36, 43, 55, 68, 69, 72, 168, 170, 267, 322, 350n10, 354n71
Great Seal practice, 168
grief, 66, 301–15
Gubrium, Jaber, 16
Guibaut, André, 354–55n77
Gupta, Sanjukta, 189
Guru Chöwang, 299
guru-disciple relationship, 252, 257, 263–65, 304. *See also* Dharma holders; doctrine holders; *specific gurus*
Gusdorf, Georges, 12
Gushri Khan, 30, 31, 359n21
Gyanak Maṇi (religious site), xxvi(map), 48
Gyaragashar (family estate), 28, 32
Gyatso, Janet, 253
Gyelsé Pema Namgyel. *See* Gara Gyelsé Pema Namgyel
Gyelwa Tupten Gyatso, 13th Dalai Lama, 25, 37
'gyur (emotions). See *bhāva*
gzhi bdag ("masters of the territory"), 3, 79, 100, 105. *See also* land deities

hagiography: and Tibetan literary genres, 10–11, 16–17, 137; of Yeshé Tsogyel, 87–91, 143, 204, 268, 269, 281, 282, 312–14, 316–17
Han Chinese, 26, 31, 123, 165
Havnevik, Hanna, 179
Hayagrīva, 64, 249, 250(fig.), 280
Herrmann-Pfandt, Adelheid, 254
Hildegard of Bingen, 172
Hindu Tantrism (Sanjukta Gupta et al.), 189
Holstein, James, 16
Holy Dharma Advice: A Drama in the Lotus Garden (Patrül Rinpoché), 301–2

illness: caused by celibacy, 216–22; caused by disobeying *ḍākinīs*,

illness (*continued*)
229–30; caused by neglecting auspicious connections, 98–99, 221; illness of Sera Khandro's son healed by Drimé Özer, 62, 286–88; livestock disease, 121, 123; plague of 1924, 66, 306–7; of Sera Khandro, xxiv, 5–6, 38, 62–63, 208, 216–22, 229–33, 289–93; Sera Khandro's healing abilities, 37, 55, 212–16; Sera Khandro's illness cured by consort relationships, 63, 215, 231–33, 248, 296, 302–4; and Sera Khandro's second visit to Drimé Özer, 284; and Tantric consort practices, 191–92, 198, 212–22, 231–33, 248
Immortality and Freedom (Eliade), 189
impermanence, and love, 301–15
Indian aesthetic theory, 257–61
Indo-Tibetan Buddhism (Snellgrove), 190
insight (realization of emptiness), 205; *ḍākinīs* as symbols of, 137; description of bodhisattva training, 249–52; Drimé Özer as method and Sera Khandro as insight realizing emptiness, 249, 295–96, 309, 317; gendered dyad of method and insight, 63–64, 200, 249–53, 260–61, 317; and hierarchical gender binarism, 253–54
Israel, Kali, 341n38

Jadrel Sangyé Dorjé Rinpoché, 24, 71, 73, 173, 324, 328, 348n113, 359n27
Jamgön Kongtrül Lodrö Tayé, 73, 148–49, 184, 328
Jampa Gönpo (father of Sera Khandro), 28, 30–32, 215, 328; marriage plans for Sera Khandro, 36–38; premonitions about Sera Khandro's departure to Golok, 39; remarriage, xxiii, 4, 39; and Sera Khandro's early religious experiences, 35; and Sera Khandro's healing abilities, 37
jātaka stories, 10
Jayadeva, 260
Jelinek, Estelle, 13
Jetsün Ani Lochen (Rindzin Chönyi Zangmo), 68, 173–80, 317, 328
Jikchö. *See* Chönkhor Lama Jikmé
Jikdrel Chökyi Lodrö. *See* Gotrül Rinpoché
Jikga, 68, 70, 323
Jikmé Chömpel, 231, 328
Jikmé Könchok, xxiv, 62–63, 110, 294–95, 329, 354n69
Jikmé Lingpa. *See* Rindzin Jikmé Lingpa
Jomo Menmo, 149, 184, 329
Jonang school of Tibetan Buddhism, 6, 68, 107, 168, 329
Jowo Śākyamuni (statue), 28
Ju Kelzang, 8
Julian of Norwich, 172–73
Jung, Carl, 253

Kagyü school of Tibetan Buddhism, 6, 68, 100, 107, 173, 329, 372n75
Kalasiddhi, 81, 82, 84, 90
Kalden Jipa, 344n44
Kandzé Tibetan Autonomous Prefecture, 42, 114, 329, 371n44. *See also* Serta
Kardon Hermitage, 98, 329
karma: and consorts and Dharma holders, 155, 232; and death of Drimé Özer, 309; and death of Rindzin Gyurmé Dorjé, 65; and inferior female body, 361n67; karmic winds, 198; and past lives, 84; and prophecies about *yab yum* partnership of Sera Khandro and Drimé Özer, 269–73; and recent incarnations of Sera Khandro and Drimé Özer, 321; and Sera Khandro as a Treasure revealer, 211; and Sera Khandro's literacy, 160; and Sera Khandro's troubled life with Gyelsé, 154; and Sera Khandro's visions,

144–45; "shouldering the debt of the dead," 195, 363n15
Karma Lingpa, 168
Karmay, Samten, 102, 103, 353n49
Katang Sheldrakma revelation, 72, 349n128
Katok Monastery, 49, 71, 106, 329
Katok Situ Chökyi Gyatso, 173, 329, 361n67
Kelden Gyatso, 261
Kelzang Drönma (name given to Sera Khandro by Taklung Mahā Rinpoché), 29
Kelzang Monastery, 49, 49(photo), 71, 107, 114, 165, 329
Kham, xxv, 64, 105, 174, 329, 371n44
khandroma, 135–37, 148, 280; Khandro Rinpoché recognized as, 322; Sera Khandro recognized as, xxiv, 48, 54, 58, 148. *See also* Sera Khandro, as Treasure revealer
Khandro Rinpoché, 321–24, 322(photo)
Khandro Yangdzong Cave, 68, 71, 72, 329
Khangdong Wönpo Gönwang, 54–55, 56, 329
Kharnang Gapma/Gongma, xxvii(map), 52, 329
Khenpo Jikmé Püntsok, 122, 205, 323, 355n83
Khenpo Münsel, 322–23
klu (water spirits), 108–9. *See also* serpentine water spirits
Kozloff, P. K., 44
Kukkuripa, 196–202, 363–64n19, 373n83
Künga Buma, 141, 149, 184, 215, 329
Künga Wangmo (nickname of Sera Khandro), 29, 36
Künkhyap Wangmo (*ḍākinī*), 121, 330
Künselma (*ḍākinī*), 128, 269–70, 310–11
Künzang Dekyong Chönyi Wangmo (alternative name for Sera Khandro), 8, 330
Künzang Nyima, 67
Künzik Wangmo (*ḍākinī*), 296
Kyabjé Drupwang Pema Drondül Dorjé, 168, 330
Kyangö (horse), 101, 330
kyemen (*skye dman*; "inferior birth"), 133. *See also* female body, inferior status of
Kyidrong, junior leader from (betrothed of Sera Khandro), 36–38, 140, 272–76, 330
Kyitrül/Kyilung Tukchok Dorjé, 224–27, 330, 366n73

Lama Murasang, 266
Lama Ngawang Demchok, 126, 330
Lama Tsechok, 71, 330
land deities, 3, 20, 77–80, 98, 100–130, 185, 375n148; benevolent vs. malevolent, 101; described, 100–102; Düjom Lingpa and, 164; Gara Terchen and, 170–71; mountain deity Nyenchen Tanglha/Genyen Tanglha as real father of Sera Khandro, 35, 128; non-Buddhist origins, 79, 102, 107–8, 117; propitiation of, 100, 106, 107, 118, 118(photo), 164, 353n49; role in guarding Treasures, 92; sacred land deity and guest commitment vows, 20, 80, 112; and sacred mountains, 102–20; Sera Khandro and, 100–130, 207, 221–22, 272–73; Treasure revealers as mediators between land deities, political leaders, and local population, 79–80, 103; types of, 100–101, 105. See also *ḍākinīs*; *specific deities*
layi (love songs), 261–62, 282
laywomen, status in religious hierarchy, 133–34
Lee, Haiyan, 255
Lejeune, Philippe, 12
Lendreltsel, 120
Lerap Lingpa, 71, 330
Lhachen Chökyi Drönma, 324
Lhachen Topgyel, 50, 51, 330

Lharek Nyentsé (land deity), 98
Lharigo (site of Sera Khandro's first Treasure revelation), 34–35, 330
Lhasa, 23–27, 26(photo); described, 25–27; Drimé Özer in, xxiii, 39–40, 271; and land deity Dorjé Yudrönma, 272–73; Sera Khandro's birth and childhood in, 28–40; Sera Khandro's escape from Lhasa to Golok, xxiii, xxvi(map), 4, 39–46; smallpox epidemic (1900), 37
Lhasé Sonam Dorjé, 114, 124
Lhodrak, 271, 321, 372n75
The Life of Milarepa (Tsangnyön Heruka), 19, 56
The Life of Shabkar (Shabkar Tsokdruk Rangdröl), 19
Lingkar/Lingtsang, King of, xxv, 73, 330, 348n116
Lingza Chökyi, 183
Liotard, Louis Victor, 354–55n77
literacy, 13, 52, 55, 133, 160, 347n94
literary genres, Tibetan, 9–14, 19, 74; and social history of religious communities, 14–17
Longchen Rapjampa, 164, 330, 373n77
longevity, 323; and Gotrül Rinpoché, 159; and Tantric consort practices, 191–92, 198, 212–22, 233–34, 240, 365n53; and Tibir Tuktsa Trülku, 233–34
love, 21–22, 249–318; and commitment vows, 22, 252 (*see also* commitment vows); compassion, sympathetic joy, and impartiality as shades of, 256–57; compassionate love described, 256–57; and disciple-guru relationships, 252, 257, 304; disconnect between love and sacred sexuality, 253; in Drimé Özer's biography, 263; in Düjom Lingpa's autobiography, 268; elder-junior love, 263, 265; expressed by *ḍākinīs*, 97, 162, 265–68; in Gara Terchen's autobiography, 267–68; and guru-disciple relationships, 263–65; and Indian aesthetic theory, 257–61; love languages of Tibet, 22, 254–62; Padmasambhava's compassionate love for Yeshé Tsogyel, 268–69; parent-child love, 256, 264, 265–66; Patrül Rinpoché on, 256–57, 301–2; and prophecy and personal affinity, 252, 269–72; romantic love and (im)permanence, 301–15; and separation, 282–93; and Sera Khandro's relationships with lamas, 266–67; and spiritual liberation, 249–52 (*see also* method of compassion and insight of realizing emptiness); and terms of endearment, 262–69, 293; *thugs rje* term, 267–68; Tibetan love songs, 261–62, 282; *tsewa* term, 263–69, 301–2. *See also* lust/desire; *yab yum* partnership of Sera Khandro and Drimé Özer; *yab yum* union
Lungshar Gar (religious community), 50, 330
lus dman (inferior body), 133. *See also* female body, inferior status of
lust/desire, 205, 216–23, 228, 369n17; Buddhist view of, 228, 255–57, 366n78; and relationship of Drimé Özer and Sera Khandro, 272–79; and Sera Khandro's betrothal to Kyidrong leader, 272–76
Lutz, Catherine, 254–55

Machen Pomra (land deity), 105, 106, 109, 354n75
Machik Lapdrön, 13–14, 169, 176–77, 184, 330, 358n18
Ma family warlords, xxiv, 46, 62, 124–26, 289
Mahā Rinpoché. *See* Matrül Tekchok Jikmé Pawo
Mahāyāna Buddhism, 134–35; and method of compassion and insight

of realizing emptiness, 64, 200, 249–52 (*see also* method of compassion and insight of realizing emptiness)
Manchus, 26, 31, 123
maps, xxvi–xxvii
Māratika cave, 73
Mardringpo, xxvii(map), 59, 330
Marong, 73, 330
Mar River, 57, 143, 171, 330
Mar Valley, 101, 166, 207, 330
Mason, Mary, 13
"masters of the ground." See *sa bdag*
"masters of the territory." See *gzhi bdag*
Matrül Tekchok Jikmé Pawo (Mahā Rinpoché), 29, 173, 330
men (*sman*; demonic forces), 101. *See also* demonic forces; land deities
method of compassion and insight of realizing emptiness, 64, 200; description of bodhisattva training, 249–52; Drimé Özer as method and Sera Khandro as insight realizing emptiness, 249, 295–96, 309, 317 (*see also yab yum* partnership of Sera Khandro and Drimé Özer); gendered dyad of method and insight, 63–64, 200, 249–53, 260–61, 317; and hierarchical gender binarism, 253–54
Milarepa, 19, 56, 148, 174, 210, 369n21, 372n75
mind-mandate Treasure transmission, 92, 94, 94–96, 123, 124
mind Treasures, 34, 48, 55, 77, 120, 123, 124, 205, 210
Mink, Louis, 15
Mirror of Poetry (Daṇḍin), 258
monasteries: and classical Buddhist learning, 258; Golok monasteries, 107; religious encampments, 107; role in education, 13, 258. *See also* social dynamics in religious communities; *specific monasteries*
Mongols, 28, 30, 31, 123, 127, 165
monks: dilemmas concerning celibate monastics and Tantric consort practices, 19, 189, 222–46; status in religious hierarchy, 133–34; Tibetan term for, 367n94. *See also specific monks*
Mönlam Gyatso, 347n91
motherhood, 151–52, 211–12; child-mother love, 256, 265–66; conflicting roles of Treasure revealer and mother, 151, 154; maternal guilt deployed by *ḍākinīs*, 162, 229, 265; Treasure revealing as analogous to conceiving children, 211–12, 247–48. *See also* Sera Khandro, life narrative
mother of Sera Khandro. *See* Tsering Chöndzom
mountain deities. *See* land deities
mountains, sacred, 78, 102–20, 105(photo), 113(photo), 118(photo); as Buddhist holy mountains, 102–3, 108–13, 117–19 (*see also specific mountains*); list of, 103; and local networks of authority, 20, 108, 114; mountain cult worshippers, 102–3, 117–18, 353n49; and practical purposes of Treasure revelation (protection from warfare, disease, etc.), 120–30; as residences of local deities, 79, 102–20 (*see also* land deities); and Treasure revealers, 20, 105–20 (*see also* Treasure tradition). *See also* Anyé Machen; Drong Mountain/Drongri; Nyenpo Yutsé
Mount Murdo, 103
Mowatowa, 111, 330, 354n74

Naidro Dorjé Dzong, 283, 330
Namkha Drönma, 147, 330
Namkhai Nyingpo, 321, 331, 372n76
Namkha Jikmé (brother of Drimé Özer), 48, 331, 373n80

namtar (spiritual biography), 9–11, 13, 19, 74
Namtrül Jikmé Püntsok, 279, 320–21, 320(photo), 331, 355n83
Nangsa Obum, 14, 174, 183
narrative identity thesis, 15
Nechung Dharma Protector, 28, 331
Ngak Chödrön, 242–45, 265–66, 298, 331, 368n109
Ngaki Wangpo, Dharma King, 358–59n21
ngakpa (Tantric religious specialist), 28, 35, 168, 233, 331, 343n20
Ngakpa Lhakpa, 109
Ngawa Prefecture, 69, 331
Ngedön Tekchen Ling Monastery, 168, 331
nöjin (*gnod sbyin*; nature spirits), 100. *See also* land deities
nomadism, 40–43, 41(photo), 45, 50, 107, 114, 122, 360n48. *See also* religious encampments
Nordé, 44
nuns, 52, 173–84; and economic concerns, 195–96, 284; Sera Khandro's decision not to become a nun, 193–96, 284; status in religious hierarchy, 133–34. *See also* Ané Zangmo; Jetsün Ani Lochen; Ngak Chödrön; Orgyen Chökyi; Tongpön Zangmo; Tsüldrön
Nyaktrül Guru Özer, 73, 331
nyampa (equality), 288–89
nyams. See *rasa*
nyen (*gnyan*; local spirits), 100. *See also* land deities
Nyenchen Tanglha/Genyen Tanglha (mountain deity), 221–22, 331; as true father of Sera Khandro, 35, 128
Nyenchen Yusé (sacred mountain), 126, 331
Nyenlung Monastery, 320–21
Nyenpo Yutsé (mountain god/sacred mountain), xxvii(map), 59, 106, 117, 163, 331
Nyimalung Cave, xxvii(map), 63
Nyingma school of Tibetan Buddhism, 52, 92, 100, 106, 107, 173
Nyingtik Yabzhi, Heart Essence in Four Parts (Longchenpa), 68

Oḍḍiyāna, 170–71, 243. *See also* Padmasambhava
Ömbar, 50, 331, 373n88
One Hundred Treasure Revealers (Jamgön Kongtrül Lodrö Tayé), 149, 184, 215
"One with a Conch Top Knot" (war god), 108
Önpu Taktsang (sacred site), 35, 139, 331, 358n20
opera, 14
Orgyen Chökyi, 180–84, 317
Orgyen Dzong, 73, 331
Orgyen Lingpa, 331, 349n128
Orgyen Minling Monastery, 233, 331
Orgyen Tendzin, 181–83

Padmasambhava: and benevolent land deities, 101; compassionate love for Yeshé Tsogyel (*thugs rje*), 268–69; concealment of Treasures, 34, 79, 84, 92, 206; and disciple-guru relationships, 257; disciples of, 372n76; Drimé Özer and, 308–9; Düjom Lingpa and, 164; Gara Terchen and, 86, 169–70, 243; Jetsün Ani Lochen and, 178; as progenitor of Treasure tradition, 2–3, 34, 78, 85; reassurances to Yeshé Tsogyel about worthiness, 141–43; sacred sites associated with, 35; and Sera Khandro's frame narrative, 80–81, 85; Sera Khandro's visions of, 92–97; and stages of Treasure transmis-

sion, 92; and *yab yum* union, 280, 281, 315; Yeshé Tsogyel as consort of, 79, 88, 268–69; Yeshé Tsogyel's grieving at departure of, 312–14. *See also* Glorious Copper-Colored Mountain Buddhafield; Oḍḍiyāna; Pema Tötrengtsel
Paine, Robert, 367–68n100
Palden Gyatso, 231
Palden Lhamo (*ḍākinī*), 169
Passionate Enlightenment (Shaw), 189
path of accumulation, 201, 364n30
Patrül Rinpoché (Patrül Orgyen Jikmé Chökyi Wangpo), 48, 214, 315, 331, 373n80; *Holy Dharma Advice: A Drama in the Lotus Garden*, 301–2; *The Words of My Perfect Teacher*, 55, 256–57, 346n76, 373n80. *See also* Dzokchen Palgé
Pelyül Dartang Monastery, xxvii(map), 54, 65, 106, 132, 158, 231, 235, 331. *See also* Gotrül Rinpoché
Pelyül lineage, 68, 348n114
Pema Bum, 52, 69, 106, 331
Pema County, 52–54, 143, 331
Pema Drondül Dorjé, 52, 331
Pema Dupatsel, 168, 332
Pema Gyatso, 159, 174, 175
Pema Gyurmé Sangngak Tendzin, 267, 332
Pema Lendreltsel, 76, 77, 307–9
Pema Lingpa, 299
Pema Longyang Gyatso, 168, 332. *See also* Gara Terchen Pema Dündül Wangchuk Lingpa
Pema Ösel Tayé, 321
Pema Tötrengtsel, 80, 81, 293, 332. *See also* Padmasambhava
Peyak, Penak. *See* Benak Monastery
Philosophies of India (Zimmer), 189
Pith Instructions on Enjoying the Three Elements (Kukkuripa's instructions to Sera Khandro), 197–202
poetics, 258–61
Pönkor Tupten Shedrup Tashi Chönkhor Ling, 323
Posthumous Biography of Khandro Rinpoché Dewé Dorjé Who Arose as a Manifestation of the Mother of the Buddhas Yeshé Tsogyel (Tsültrim Dorjé), 70–71
powa (transfer-of-consciousness ritual), 69. *See also* "transference of consciousness" practice
Pradīpoddyotana (Candrakīrti), 363n11
preliminary practices, 51, 55, 72, 168, 346n80
prophecy, xxiv; and *ḍākinīs*, 79, 269–75 (see also *ḍākinīs*); about death of Drimé Özer, 292–93; Gyelsé as prophesied "life partner" of Sera Khandro, 54–56; influence of Tibetan love songs in style, 162; prophetic authorization and Treasure transmission, 92; Sera Khandro's *Cycle of Prophecies*, 186–87; and Sera Khandro's interactions with Gotrül Rinpoché, 154–60; and Sera Khandro's summons to Gara Terchen, 53, 55; and *yab yum* partnership of Sera Khandro and Drimé Özer, 62–63, 252, 269–73, 276. *See also* prophetic guides
prophetic guides: Drimé Özer and, 269–70; Düjom Lingpa and, 166–67; Gara Terchen and, 171, 242; Sera Khandro and, xxiii, 23, 38–39, 138–43, 145–46
public opinion: and Gara Terchen's consort relationships, 193, 241–46; and Sera Khandro's consort relationships, 223–24, 227, 239–41; Tantric consort practices and tension between doctrinal precedence and public opinion, 193, 223, 239–41,

public opinion (*continued*)
246–47. *See also* gossip; social dynamics in religious communities
Pünsumtsok Chömpel (brother of Sera Khandro), 39–40, 332

Qing dynasty, 25, 27, 32, 123–25
Qinghai Province, 42, 43. *See also* Golok

Rāhu, 244, 368n106
Rāhula, 297
rainbow body, 72, 349n127
Rangjung Rikpé Dorjé, 175, 332
rangnam genre, 10–11
rasa (Tib. *nyams*; aesthetic experience), 259–61
Ratna Lingpa Tukdrup, 168, 332
Ratnasambhava, 198
Refining One's Perception (Düjom Lingpa), xxv, 2, 51, 68, 72
reincarnation, 373n80; Ané Zangmo as incarnation of Machik Lapdrön, 176; Chaktsa Trülku Rinpoché Pema Trinlé Gyatso (Chaktrül Rinpoché) as reincarnation of Ngedön Wangpo, 71; Changdrong Druptop Rinpoché as reincarnation of Tangtong Gyelpo, 33; Düjom Jikdrel Yeshé Dorjé as reincarnation of Düjom Lingpa, 49; Düjom Lingpa as reincarnation of Dündül Drakpo Tsel, 268; and the eight freedoms, 228, 366n77; future and present incarnations of Sera Khandro, 83, 305, 319–24; interconnected relationships across multiple lifetimes, 18; and karma, 84 (*see also* karma); and lust as root poison, 255–56; Namkha Jikmé as incarnation of Patrül Orgyen Jikmé Chökyi Wangmo, 48, 373n80; and paradigmatic elements of Tibetan biography, 83–84; previous incarnations of Drimé Özer, 273; previous incarnations of Sera Khandro, 33, 34, 81, 82, 84, 149, 215 (*see also* Yeshé Tsogyel: Sera Khandro as emanation of); "transference of consciousness" practice, 52, 69, 240, 302, 349n132; Yangchen Drönma/Chöying Drönma as possible incarnation of Gara Terchen, 58. See also *saṃsāra*
relational selfhood, 12–14, 20, 76–130, 185. *See also* Sera Khandro, as Treasure revealer
religious encampments, xxiv, xxvii(map), 61, 64, 65, 107, 122, 125–27, 168, 213, 276. *See also* social dynamics in religious communities
reliquary of Sera Khandro, 74
Reting Rinpoché, 175, 332
Rikpé Reltri (*ḍākinī*), 185, 310, 314
Rindzin Chönyi Zangmo, 68, 332. *See also* Jetsün Ani Lochen
Rindzin Gyurmé Dorjé, 332; birth of, xxiv, 62; conception of, 234–35; as consciousness of Gotrül Rinpoché, xxiv, 65, 235, 284; death of, xxiv, 65, 66, 266, 306–7; illness healed by Drimé Özer, 62, 286–88; lawsuit over custody of, xxiv, 64–65, 305; and Sera Khandro's visit to Drimé Özer (1919), 284
Rindzin Jikmé Lingpa, 55–56, 184, 299, 332
Rindzin Künzang Nyima/Nüden Dorjé, 68, 332
Rindzin Nyima, 355n83
Riwoché, 332; Sera Khandro's death in, xxv, 6, 74, 173; Sera Khandro's invitation to teach at, xxv; and Taklung Kagyü lineage, 173
Rock, Joseph, 43
rokten (love singing), 261–62
Rosenwein, Barbara, 22, 255
rtsa rlung. *See* channel and wind practices

sa bdag ("masters of the ground"), 79, 100, 105. *See also* land deities
Sacks, Oliver, 15
Śākyamuni Buddha, 85, 92
Sakya school of Tibetan Buddhism, 100
Sakya Tamdrin Wangmo, 34
saṃsāra: and death of Drimé Özer, 309, 311; and inferior female body, 139, 182; and lust, 256; and purposes of Treasure revelation, 129; and Sera Khandro's decision not to become a nun, 195
Samantabhadra, 250(fig.)
Saṃyutta-nikāya, 77
Sanglung Monastery, xxvii(map), 68, 97, 332
Sangtsang Dradra/Sangtrül Rinpoché, 243, 332
Sangyé Lama, 100
Sanskrit, and aesthetic theory/synonymy, 258–60
sapta (demonic force), 144, 218, 359n27. *See also* demonic forces
Saraha, 23, 38, 144
Scott, Joan, 15
Sechok Norbu Ömbar, 115–16, 332
Secret Mantra teachings, 81, 85, 204, 218, 219, 281. *See also* Tantric consort practices; Vajrayāna Buddhism
The Secret Treasury of Reality Ḍākinīs (Treasure teachings cycle), 38, 57–58, 141–42
Seldrön, 5, 60, 63, 161, 246, 290, 332
Semnyi Rinpoché, 179
Semo Saraswati, xi, 324
Sengcham Trukmo, 123, 332
Sera Khandro, xxiii–xxv, 3–6, 23–75; auto/biographical works (*see* auto/biographical writings of Sera Khandro; *The Biography of the Central Tibetan Woman Dewé Dorjé*; *The Biography of the Omniscient Refuge Master, Lord of Accomplished Ones, the Precious Sovereign of the Ocean of Profound Treasures Pema Drondül Sangngak Lingpa*; *The Excellent Path of Devotion*); birth (1892), xxiii, 3, 28–30, 343n21; birth of daughter Yangchen Drönma (1913), xxiv, 5, 151–52, 265; birth of son Rindzin Gyurmé Dorjé (1919), xxiv, 62, 234–35; birth of stillborn son (1918), xxiv, 60, 265, 283; brothers (*see* Geshé Lodrö; Pünsumtsok Chömpel); childhood, xxiii, 3–4, 23–24, 28–40; chronologies/summaries of events, xxiii–xxv, 3–6, 24; commentary on *Refining One's Perception*, 51; compiling complete works of Düjom Lingpa, xxv, 69, 314; on composing Drimé Özer's biography, 6; composition of autobiography (long; 1926–1934), xxv, 6, 7–9, 69, 184–87; composition of autobiography (short), xxv, 185; composition of biography of Drimé Özer (1925), xxv, 6–7, 69, 185, 314; consort relationships (*see* Sera Khandro, consort relationships of); *ḍākinī* marks at birth, 29, 30, 34; death of (1940), xxv, 24, 73–74; death of Drimé Özer (1924), xxiv, 66, 249, 252, 306–15, 319–20; death of Gotrül Rinpoché (1919), 235; death of mother (1904), xxiii, 4, 38, 140, 265; death of son (1924), xxiv, 65, 66, 266, 306–7; decision not to become a nun, 193–96, 222; departure from Gyelsé's household and reunion with Drimé Özer (1921), xxiv, 5–6, 62–67, 162–63, 294–301; difficult entry into Golok, 40–52, 277–78; disciples and attendants, 6, 24, 231 (*see also* Jadrel Sangyé Dorjé Rinpoché; Sherap Özer; Tsültrim Dorjé; Tupten Zangpo/Tupzang; Zhapdrung Tsewang Drakpa); early religious aspirations and

Sera Khandro (*continued*)
experiences, 3–4, 33–40, 138–43; education, 32–33, 138–39, 258, 347n94; as emanation of Yeshé Tsogyel, 18, 20, 54, 76, 84, 91, 130–32, 143, 159, 317; enemies and rivals (*see* Akyongza; Seldrön; social dynamics in religious communities; Yakshülza); escape from Lhasa to follow Drimé Özer and entourage (1907), xxiii, xxvi(map), 4, 39–46; exile from Dartsang community following death of Drimé Özer, 66, 69, 309–10, 314; family background, 28, 31–33; father's remarriage (1904), xxiii, 4, 39; final years, 70–75; first Treasure revealing (1899), 34–35; future and present incarnations, 83, 305, 319–24; Gyelsé's agreement with Drimé Özer on exchanging Sera Khandro (1915), xxiv, 59, 246–47, 282, 284–85, 374n107; healing abilities, 37, 55, 212–16; illness, xxiv, 5–6, 62–63, 208, 212, 229, 231–33, 289–93, 302–4; interactions with *ḍākinīs* and lamas, 23, 79, 138–63 (see also *ḍākinīs*); language difficulties in Golok, 42–43, 50; lawsuit over custody of son (1924), xxiv, 64–65, 305; as "life partner" of Gyelsé (*see* troubled life with Gyelsé *under this heading*); as lineage holder of Düjom Lingpa and Drimé Özer's teachings, 68; low status in Golok society, 62, 287 (*see also* social dynamics in religious communities); marriage arranged by father (1902–1903), xxiii, 4, 36–38, 140–41, 272–76; and motherhood, 151–52, 211–12; mountain deity Nyenchen Tanglha/Genyen Tanglha as true father, 35, 128; move to Sera Monastery at invitation of Sotrül Natsok Rangdröl Rinpoché (1924), xxiv, 66–70; move to Yeru religious community (1918), xxiv; names and nicknames, 8, 29, 185, 210, 285, 300, 349n1; naming of, 29, 173; and Nyingma lineage, 173 (*see also* Drimé Özer); parents (*see* Jampa Gönpo; Tsering Chöndzom); posthumous sources for biographical information, 70–71; preliminary practices and teachings, and teasing received thereof, 50–52; previous incarnations, 33, 34, 81, 82, 84, 149, 215 (*see also* Yeshé Tsogyel); prophetic guides bestowed by Vajravārāhī (1904), xxiii, 23, 38–39, 138–43; reliquary of, 74; return to Benak Monastery on account of prophecy (1911), xxiv; return to Dartsang to compile works of Düjom Lingpa and Drimé Özer (1929), 314; and sacred mountains (*see under* Sera Khandro, as Treasure revealer); social difficulties (*see* social dynamics in religious communities); and sorcery, 56; spiritual liberation in union with Drimé Özer (1921), xxiv, 63–64, 260–61, 294–301; statue of, 136(photo); status as neither nun nor laywoman, 22, 188, 192, 239; suicide attempt (1903) and near-death experience, xxiii, 4, 38; summons from Andzom Drondül Pawo Dorjé (1923), xxiv, 64, 213–15, 304–5; summons from Gara Terchen of Benak Monastery (1910), xxiv, 5, 143–48, 212–13; supporters and allies (*see* Andzom Dröndül Pawo Dorjé; Drimé Özer; Gotrül Rinpoché; Jikmé Könchok; Sotrül Natsok Rangdröl Rinpoché; *and* disciples and attendants *under this heading*); and Taklung Kagyü lineage, 173; teachings throughout eastern Tibet (1925–1939), xxiv–xxv, 6,

68–75; teachings to King of Lingkar (1932), xxv, 73; tensions over life as worldly political leader vs. life as religious renunciate, 33–36, 276; as Treasure revealer (*see* Sera Khandro, as Treasure revealer); troubled life with Gyelsé (1911–1921), xxiv, 5–6, 54–63, 148–54, 160–63, 208, 292; vision of Glorious Copper-Colored Mountain Buddhafield (1926), 92–97; visits with Drimé Özer, 5, 209–10, 283–93; visits with Gotrül Rinpoché, 154–61, 210–11; work as maidservant near Dartsang (1907–1908), xxiii, 5, 50–52, 193, 278–79; works listed, 2; Wylie transliteration, 333; *yab yum* partnership with Drimé Özer (see *yab yum* partnership of Sera Khandro and Drimé Özer). *See also* Sera Khandro, as Treasure revealer; Sera Khandro, consort relationships of; *yab yum* partnership of Sera Khandro and Drimé Özer

Sera Khandro, consort relationships of, 2–3; and Andzom Drondül Pawo Dorjé, xxiv, 64, 213–15, 247; and authenticity and credibility issues, 247 (*see also under* Sera Khandro, as Treasure revealer); and curing illness/increasing longevity, 212–22, 240, 248; dilemmas concerning authority over choice of partners, 19, 191, 214–15, 228–30, 233–34, 246–47; dilemmas concerning celibate monastics, 19, 21, 224–40; dilemmas concerning other female consorts, 19, 191, 246 (*see also* Akyongza; Seldrön; Yakshülza); and directives from *ḍākinīs*, 222, 225–27; and Dorjé Drandül as secret consort, 71; and Drimé Özer (see *yab yum* partnership of Sera Khandro and Drimé Özer); and Gotrül Rinpoché, 230–35; Gyelsé's agreement with Drimé Özer on exchanging Sera Khandro (1915), xxiv, 59, 246–47, 282, 284–85, 374n107; Kukkuripa as secret consort in past life, 196–202; and Kyitrül and his sister, 224–27, 366n73; and negative gossip/social difficulties, 191, 193, 208, 223–27, 235–36 (*see also* social dynamics in religious communities); and practical purposes of consort practices, 191, 193–222; and prophetic guidance from Yeshé Tsogyel, 145–46; rejection of apparitional monks, 236–39; rejection of Gara Gyeltsen, 228–30; and reputation management, 240–41; self-portrayal as victim, 191, 214–15, 231–34, 246, 247; and Sotrül Rinpoché, 235–36; and teachings given to Sera Khandro in childhood, 38, 196–202; and Tibir Tuktsa Trülku, 233–35, 247; and Treasure revealing and decoding, 204–12; Vimala Raśmi as secret consort, 110

Sera Khandro, as Treasure revealer, 2, 20, 76–130; authenticity and credibility issues, 20, 91, 99, 129–30, 132–34, 143, 148, 160, 317; conflicting roles as Treasure revealer and mother, 151, 154; consequences of failure to gather auspicious connections as instructed, 97–99; and consorts rejected, 208, 236–39; *Cycle of Prophecies*, 186–87; difficulties in revealing Treasures, 97–99, 144, 156, 167, 172, 207–11; difficulty of assuming religious authority, 133–34, 160, 172, 188; early recognition of abilities, 48, 58; empowerment in revealing *The Secret Treasury of Reality Ḍākinīs* and *The Ḍākinīs' Heart Essence* (1904), 38, 141–42; first Treasure revealing

Sera Khandro, as Treasure revealer (*continued*)
(1899), 34–35; and frame narrative, 80–92; and Gotrül Rinpoché's advice, 210–11; Gyelsé's disapproval, xxiv, 58, 148, 152; and interdependent process of revelation, 92–100; and local networks of authority, 20, 78, 100; prophetic guides bestowed by Vajravārāhī (1904), xxiii, 23, 38–39, 138–42; and "relational selfhood," 77; sacred land deity and guest commitment vows, 20, 80; and sacred mountains/Treasure sites, 34–35, 48, 62, 73, 105–20, 149, 154, 207, 211, 330, 355n83 (*see also specific mountains and Treasure sites*); *The Secret Treasury of Reality Ḍākinīs*, 38, 57–58, 141–42; and social difficulties (*see* social dynamics in religious communities); Treasure names, 8, 185, 210, 285, 300, 349n1; Treasure revealing as analogous to conceiving children, 211–12, 247–48; Treasure revealing in final years, 73; Treasure revealing repudiated, 151, 156; Treasure scripture on transference of consciousness at death, 302; Treasures retrieved, 34–35, 48, 55, 59, 110–13, 120, 207, 210; Treasures revealed jointly by Sera Khandro and Drimé Özer, 289, 300; Treasure substitutes, 110, 112–13, 120; and visionary interactions with *ḍākinīs*, land deities, and lamas, 17–19, 77, 79–80, 100–130, 141–42, 147, 149 (see also *ḍākinīs*); and *yab yum* relationship with Drimé Özer, 64, 289, 300
Sera Monastery (Sera Tekchen Chönkhor Ling), xxvii(map), 67(photo), 323, 333; history of, 66; Sera Khandro's move to, following death of son and Drimé Özer (1924), xxiv, 66–70, 235–36. *See also* Sotrül Natsok Rangdröl Rinpoché
serpentine water spirits (*klu*), 100, 107, 375n148
Serta, xxvii(map), 113–20, 333, 344n54; as independent confederation, 24, 42, 114; monasteries, 114–15 (*see also* Kelzang Monastery; Sera Monastery); people, 44–45, 114–15; sacred mountains (*see* Drong Mountain/Drongri). *See also* Dartsang
"Severance" practice (*gcod*), 14, 168, 176
sexuality, 21, 207, 253. *See also* celibacy; love; lust/desire; method of compassion and insight of realizing emptiness; Sera Khandro, consort relationships of; Tantric consort practices; *yab yum* partnership of Sera Khandro and Drimé Özer
Shabkar Tsokdruk Rangdröl, 19, 31, 122, 174, 333, 354n74, 359n21, 369n21
Shardzapa Tashi Gyatso, 72, 333
Shaw, Miranda, 189
Sherap Özer, 68, 71, 73, 333, 348n113
Shiwa Dorjetso (*ḍākinī*), 81, 82, 84, 94, 95, 128, 296, 321, 333
Shuksep Nunnery, 175, 176, 333
Sichuan Province, 114, 124. *See also* Serta
Siegel, Lee, 253
skye dman, skye lus dmanpa (derogatory terms for women), 133, 357n4. *See also* female body, inferior status of
"sky-going woman," 135. See also *ḍākinīs*; *khandroma*
Smith, Sidonie, 11, 12
Snellgrove, David, 190
social dynamics in religious communities: and Gara Terchen's consort relationships, 193, 241–46, 298; gossip, 223–24, 241–46, 298, 366n71,

367–68n100; and Sera Khandro's consort relationships, 223–24, 227, 239–41; Sera Khandro's lack of acceptance at Sera, 235–36; Sera Khandro's lack of acceptance in Drimé Özer's community (Dartsang), 5, 46–48, 52, 65–66, 246, 309–10; Sera Khandro's lack of acceptance/low status in Gyelsé's community (Benak), 5, 56, 62, 149–51, 156, 208 (*see also* Yakshülza); tension between Tantric doctrinal precedence and public opinion, 21, 193, 223, 239–41, 246–47
Solung Drakar (Treasure site), 149, 154, 333
Sonam Khyap, 106, 107, 333
Sonam Rabgyé, 242, 333
Sonam Tendar, 37, 333
Songtsen Gampo, 30, 38, 333
Sotrül Natsok Rangdröl Rinpoché, 121; as beloved disciple of Drimé Özer, 264–65; controversy over relationship with Sera Khandro, 235–36; death of, 71; and Drong Mountain, 114, 125, 355n83; and illness of Sera Khandro, 303; invitation to Sera Khandro to move to Sera Monastery, xxiv, 66, 235–36; and Ma family warlords, 125; as mediator in land disputes, 122; support and encouragement for Sera Khandro, 65–67, 176, 236; Wylie transliteration, 333
Sperling, Elliot, 344n39
spiritual liberation, 363n11; and awareness holder, 197, 198, 200, 202, 365n33; and insight and method dyad, 63–64, 200, 249–52, 260–61, 317; path of accumulation, 201, 364n30; and Sera Khandro's Tantric consort practices, 190, 191; Siddhārtha's enlightenment, 297; as soteriological goal of Tantric consort practices, 196–204; thirteen grounds on the bodhisattva path, 202, 365n33; and *yab yum* partnership of Sera Khandro and Drimé Özer, 249, 260–61, 294–301, 309
Sturrock, John, 91
subtle body (varja body), 196–202, 205, 220, 253, 295, 360n45, 364n20
Sukhasiddhi (*ḍākinī*), 140–41
supernatural beings. *See* bodhisattvas; buddhas; *ḍākinīs*; land deities
Swidler, Ann, 16, 129
synonymy, 258–59

Tārā, 33, 78, 81, 164
Tāranātha, 38
Tāré Lhamo, 320–21, 320(photo), 355n83
Tachok, 108, 333, 354n65
Taklung Kagyü school of Tibetan Buddhism, 173
Taklung Mahā Rinpoché, 29
Taklung Monastery, 173, 333
Taksham Nüden Dorjé, 87–91, 204, 312–13, 316–17, 333. *See also* hagiography
Taktsé Samdrup Monastery, 49, 165, 333
Tangtong Gyelpo, 33, 299, 333
Tantra: consort practices (*see* Tantric consort practices); dearth of texts by women, 1; defined/described, 363n10; stages of Tantric meditation, 360n45; Tantric masters/*ngakpa*, 28, 35, 168, 185, 233, 331, 343n20; Tantric texts, 1, 189, 190, 201; and valorization of women, 357n10
Tantric consort practices, 19, 21, 188–248, 363n11; and auspicious connections required for successful Treasure discoveries, 11–12 (*see also under* Treasure tradition);

Tantric consort practices (*continued*)
and commitment vows, 22, 208, 209, 232, 252, 281–82; and curing illness/increasing longevity, 19, 64, 191–92, 198, 212–22, 231–34, 240, 248, 365n53; and *ḍākinīs*, 190, 192; and desire, 205, 216–23; disconnect between love and sacred sexuality, 253; Gara Terchen and, 193, 241–46; and hierarchical gender binarism, 253–54; homosexual union not practiced, 199, 364n27; and love, 21–22, 252–54 (*see also* love; *yab yum* partnership of Sera Khandro and Drimé Özer; *yab yum* union); misconceptions/oversimplifications of issues, 1, 21, 189–90; and path of accumulation, 201, 364n30; performed by single person, 193, 199, 234–35, 253; positive and negative views of, 189–90; purposes of, 21, 191, 193–222; scholarship on, 253–54; and social dynamics within religious communities, 191–93, 240–41, 246–47; and spiritual liberation, 196–204 (*see also* method of compassion and insight of realizing emptiness); and spiritual liberation of women, 190–91, 201, 203, 363n11; Tantric physiology, 196–204, 364nn 20,25,31,32; tension between doctrinal precedence and public opinion, 21, 193, 239–41, 246–47; tension between monastic celibacy and religiously motivated sexuality, 19, 192–93, 222–46; texts mostly authored by and for men, 190, 201; Tibetan terms for sexual partners, 207; and Treasure revealing/decoding, 191, 204–12, 242. *See also* channel and wind practices; Sera Khandro, consort relationships of; *yab yum* partnership of Sera Khandro and Drimé Özer; *yab yum* union
Tashi Chidren, 81, 82, 84, 90, 333
Tashi Gomang (sacred mountain), 103
Tashi Gomang Monastery, xxvii(map), 57–58, 57(photo), 333
tendrel, 11, 77–78. *See also* auspicious connections
Tengchen Monastery, 69, 72, 333
Teresa of Avila, 261
Third Dodrupchen. *See* Dodrup Rinpoché Jikmé Tenpé Nyima
Thondup, Tulku, 223, 281, 343n23, 374n133
Three Jewels (Buddha, Dharma, Saṅgha), 47, 102, 111, 136
three poisons (delusion, hatred, lust), 255–56, 366n78
Tibet: folk songs/love songs, 261–62, 282, 359n39, 371nn 44,45; history of governance, 30–31; Lhasa described, 25–27; and Mongol tribes, 30–31; and Qing dynasty, 25; religious literature of, 258–61 (*see also specific works*); warfare, 121, 123–28, 165; Younghusband expedition (1904), 25, 31, 175
The Tibetan Book of the Dead. See Bardo Tödrol
Tibir Tuktsa Trülku, 233–35, 247, 333
Tokden Semnyi Rinpoché, 175–76
tokjö genre, 10
Tongpön Mönlam Gyatso, 53
Tongpön Zangmo, 277–78, 334
Trakor Monastery, 68, 334
Traktung Düjom Lingpa. *See* Düjom Lingpa
Tralek/Dralek/Dralak Monastery, xxvii(map), 72, 334; Sera Khandro statue, 136(photo)
"transference of consciousness" practice, 52, 69, 240, 302, 349n132

Treasure tradition: auspicious connections required for successful Treasure discoveries, 11–12, 78, 95, 96, 97, 206; and Bön religion, 351n30; credibility of Treasure revealers, 91–92, 167 (*see also* Sera Khandro, as Treasure revealer: authenticity and credibility issues); and *ḍākinīs* and other supermundane forces, 77–80, 92, 100–130, 137, 142, 205–8; defined/described, 2, 77–78; earth Treasures, 34, 59, 77, 110, 112–13, 120, 207, 210–11; female Treasure revealers, 148–49; history of Treasure tradition, 34, 100; interdependent process of revelation, 92–100; and land deities, 100–130; link to epic *Gesar of Ling*, 123; list of Treasure revealers, 299; and local networks of authority, 20, 78–80, 103, 121–22; mind-mandate Treasure transmission, 92, 94, 94–96, 124; mind Treasures, 34, 48, 55, 77, 120, 123, 124, 205, 210; *One Hundred Treasure Revealers*, 149, 184, 215; practical purposes of Treasure revelation (protection from warfare, disease, etc.), 120–30; and present and recent incarnations of Sera Khandro and Drimé Özer, 320–24; progenitors of, 2–3, 34, 78, 85 (*see also* Padmasambhava; Yeshé Tsogyel); and "relational selfhood," 77; and religious encampments, 107; sacred land deity and guest commitment vows, 20, 80; sacred mountains/Treasure sites, 20, 48, 62, 73, 102–20, 149, 154, 207, 211, 355n83 (*see also specific mountains and Treasure sites*); stages of Treasure transmission, 92, 205–6; and Tantric consort practices, 191, 204–12, 242 (*see also* Tantric consort practices); Treasures revealed jointly by Sera Khandro and Drimé Özer, 289, 300; Treasure substitutes, 20, 103–4, 108, 110, 112–13, 120–24, 142. *See also* Andzom Drondül Pawo Dorjé; Drimé Özer; Gara Terchen Pema Dündül Wangchuk Lingpa; Jamgön Kongtrül Lodrö Tayé; Jomo Menmo; Karma Lingpa; Künga Buma; land deities; Pema Dupatsel; Rindzin Jikmé Lingpa; Sangyé Lama; Sera Khandro, as Treasure revealer
Trinlé Tendzin, 324
Tri Songdetsen, King of Tibet, 87
Tröma (deity), 101, 147
Trülku Mura, 194, 195
Trülku Pema Lodoe, 236
Trulshik Rinpoché Künzang Tongdröl Dorjé, 174–75, 334
Truth Body, 145, 177, 217, 307, 315, 350n10
Tsampa Rinpoché, 242, 267, 334
Tsangchen Monastery, 68, 334. *See also* Dodrupchen Monastery
Tsang Gar, 68, 72, 334
Tsangnyön Heruka, 369n21
Tsangyang Gyatso, 6th Dalai Lama, 261
tsen (*btsan*; local spirits), 100, 170. *See also* land deities
Tsering Chöndzom (mother of Sera Khandro), 28, 334; death of, xxiii, 4, 38, 140, 265; and Sera Khandro's early religious experiences, 35, 139–40
tsewa (love), 263–69, 301–2
Tsüldrön, 50, 193–96, 222, 239, 284, 334
Tsültrim Dorjé, 71, 102, 334; on death of Sera Khandro, 73, 74; *Posthumous Biography of Khandro Rinpoché Dewé Dorjé Who Arose as a Manifestation of the Mother of the Buddhas Yeshé Tsogyel*, 70–71; reincarnation of, 321; and reliquary for Sera Khandro, 74; as scribe, 8, 24, 179, 185–86

Tsültrim Norbu, 72, 334
Tsybikoff, G., 25
Tucci, Giuseppe, 16
Tupten Zangpo/Tupzang, 60, 62, 63, 67, 70, 154, 155, 163, 295, 303, 334, 361n67
Turquoise Inlay: A Short Supplement to the End of the Great Biography of the Central Tibetan Ḍākinī Dewé Dorjé (Jadrel Sangyé Dorjé Rinpoché), 71

Üri (Central Mountain), 139, 334
Üza Khandro (Golok name for Sera Khandro), 84

Vairocana, 198
Vairotsana, 171, 273, 372n76
Vairotsana Cave, 68, 323, 324
Vajradūta (consort), 206
Vajrasattva, 198, 250(fig.)
Vajravārāhī, 78, 134(fig.), 250(fig.), 280; Düjom Lingpa and, 164; and female Treasure revealers, 149; Gara Terchen and, 169; prophetic guides bestowed on Sera Khandro (1904), xxiii, 23, 38–39, 138–43; sacred sites associated with, 73; Sera Khandro's visions of, 38, 52, 64, 81, 83; and *yab yum* partnership of Sera Khandro and Drimé Özer, 249
Vajrayāna Buddhism: and consort practices, 189, 200, 205, 219, 222, 239, 246–48 (*see also* Tantric consort practices); and *khandroma*, 136–37; and *yab yum* partnership of Sera Khandro and Drimé Özer, 297 (see also *yab yum* partnership of Sera Khandro and Drimé Özer). *See also* method of compassion and insight of realizing emptiness; Secret Mantra teachings
Vajrayoginī (*ḍākinī*), 38, 257
varja body. *See* subtle body
Vaudeville, Charlotte, 253
ventriloquy, autobiographical, 21, 132, 160, 163, 192, 221; and equality with Drimé Özer, 287; and synonymy, 258–59
Vimala Raśmi, 110, 273. *See also* Drimé Özer
visionary revelations. See *ḍākinīs*; mind Treasures; Sera Khandro, as Treasure revealer; Treasure tradition
vital nuclei, and Tantric physiology, 198–99, 202–3, 205, 296, 360n45, 364nn 20,25,31,32
Vostrikov, A. I., 16
vows. *See* commitment vows

Waddell, L. Austine, 25–27, 31–32
warfare, 121, 123–28, 165
Washül Serta, 42, 45, 113–20, 236, 334
water, sublime qualities of, 94, 352n32
Watson, Julia, 11
Weintraub, Karl, 12
White, Hayden, 14–15
women: autobiography of Jetsün Ani Lochen, 173–80; autobiography of Orgyen Chökyi, 180–84; difficulties in revealing Treasures due to inferior status, 97, 144, 156, 172; female deities, 135–37 (see also *ḍākinīs*); female friendships, 183–84; gender discrimination in Tibetan society, 179; gender hierarchies in Tibetan Buddhism, 133–35; inferior status and Sera Khandro's self-deprecating statements, 144, 147–48, 156, 317; inferior status as common theme in female mystics' writings, 172–73; inferior status of women and birth of Yangchen Drönma, 58; low literacy rates in Tibet, 13, 133; roles in Tantric practices, 189–91, 246–48 (*see also* Tantric consort practices); scarcity of women in Tibetan historical

records and Buddhist hagiography, 137; Sera Khandro's birth story and inferior status of women, 30; spiritual liberation through Tantric practices, 190–91, 201, 203, 363n11; Tibetan terms for, 133, 139–40, 229, 357n4; valorization of, 135, 189, 317, 357n10. *See also* female body, inferior status of; gender

Wonder Ocean: An Exploration of the Dharma Treasure Tradition (Dodrup Rinpoché Jikmé Tenpé Nyima), 117, 121, 205

The Words of My Perfect Teacher (Patrül Rinpoché), 55, 256–57, 346n76, 373n80

yab yum partnership of Sera Khandro and Drimé Özer, 3, 6, 21–22, 63–64, 249–324; and auspicious connections, 270, 283–84, 299–300; and commitment vows, 252, 281–82, 286–87, 300, 306; and death of Drimé Özer, 306–15; Drimé Özer as method and Sera Khandro as insight realizing emptiness, 249, 295–96, 309, 317; Drimé Özer's final words to Sera Khandro, 249, 252; and equality, 252, 287–89, 300, 317; exclusivity as *yab* and *yum*, 252, 279–82; and future incarnations, 319–24; healing of physical ailments, 64, 296, 302–4; and impermanence, illness, and death, 301–15; and love transcending death, 252, 311–16, 319; and lust vs. love, 272–79; mutual love in separation, 282–93; obstacles to union, 282–84; and other consorts, 283–85; and prophecy and personal affinity, 252, 269–73, 276; reasons for delayed union, 283–84; and Sera Khandro's auto/biographical writing, 279–80, 294–301; Sera Khandro's first contact with Drimé Özer, xxiii, 39–40, 274–76; and spiritual liberation, xxiv, 63–64, 252, 260–61, 294–301, 309, 317; and terms of endearment, 252, 262–69, 293; and threats from Ma family warlords, 126; and Treasure names and teachings given by Drimé Özer to Sera Khandro, 285; Treasures revealed jointly, 289, 300

yab yum union, 250(fig.), 251–52, 251(fig.); and Buddhist deities, 280, 281. *See also* commitment vows; Padmasambhava; Yeshé Tsogyel

Yakshülza (Yakza): antagonism toward Sera Khandro, 54, 56, 60, 143, 246, 283; as consort to Gara Terchen, 5, 54, 143; prevention of Sera Khandro's intervention in death of Gara Terchen, xxiv, 54, 143, 146; Wylie transliteration, 334

Yangchen Drönma/Chöying Drönma (daughter of Sera Khandro), xxiv, 58, 65, 102, 326, 334, 361n67; at Anyé Machen, 110–11; birth of, xxiv, 5, 58, 151–52; lack of affectionate references to, in Sera Khandro's autobiography, 265–66; as possible incarnation of Gara Terchen, 58; reliquary for Sera Khandro, 74; transformation of gender *in utero*, 58, 265

Yaśodharā, 256, 297

Yeru religious encampment, xxiv, xxvii(map), 61, 64, 334

Yeshé Tsogyel, 88(fig.); and consort Atsara Salé, 88, 204, 281; as consort of Padmasambhava, 79, 88; as *ḍākinī*, 79; Düjom Lingpa and, 164; Gara Terchen and, 169, 243, 298–99; hagiography of, 87–91, 143, 204, 268, 269, 281, 282, 312–14, 316–17; and impermanence and grieving at departure of Padmasambhava,

Yeshé Tsogyel (*continued*)
312–14; and inspiration for writing autobiographies, 184; intersubjectivity between Yeshé Tsogyel and Sera Khandro, 20, 316; as maternal source of all the buddhas, 143; Padmasambhava's compassionate love for, 268–69; Padmasambhava's reassurances to, 141–43; and Patrül Rinpoché's *Words of My Perfect Teacher*, 257; as progenitor of Treasure tradition, 2–3, 34, 78, 85; sacred sites associated with, 35; and Secret Mantra teachings, 81, 85; Sera Khandro as emanation of, 18, 20, 54, 76, 84, 91, 130–32, 143, 159, 317; Sera Khandro's biography of (destroyed), 150–51; and Sera Khandro's frame narrative, 80–83, 85; Sera Khandro's visions of, 94–97, 143–46; suitors, 37–38; and Tantric practices, 204, 247; and Treasure transmission, 205–6; Wylie transliteration, 334; and *yab yum* union, 280, 281, 315
Young, Serinity, 190
Younghusband, Francis, 25, 31, 175
Yudra Nyingpo, 273, 372n76
yul lha (local deities), 79, 100. *See also* land deities
yul skyong (local protectors), 100. *See also* land deities
Yungdrung Chaktsé (land deity), 106, 334
Yungshül Sungchok Dorjé, 49, 335
Yusé Naringma nomadic encampment, xxvii(map)

Zangyak Drak, 174, 361n67
Zhapdrung Tsewang Drakpa, xxv, 6, 72–73, 335
Zimmer, Heinrich, 189
Zurkhang family, 36, 335